Nagios

Wolfgang Barth

Nagios

System and Network Monitoring

2nd Edition

open
source

PRESS

Munich

**no starch
press**

San Francisco

Publisher: William Pollock
Cover Design: Octopod Studios
Translation: Steve Tomlin
U.S. edition published by No Starch Press, Inc.
555 De Haro Street, Suite 250, San Francisco, CA 94107
phone: 415.863.9900; fax: 415.863.9950; info@nostarch.com; http://www.nostarch.com

Original edition © 2008 Open Source Press GmbH
Published by Open Source Press GmbH, Munich, Germany
Publisher: Dr. Markus Wirtz
Original ISBN 978-3-937514-46-8
For information on translations, please contact
Open Source Press GmbH, Amalienstr. 45 Rg, 80799 München, Germany
phone +49.89.28755562; fax +49.89.28755563; info@opensourcepress.de; http://www.opensourcepress.de

Library of Congress Cataloging-in-Publication Data

```
Barth, Wolfgang
  Nagios :  system and network monitoring / Wolfgang Barth.- 2nd ed.
       p. cm.
  Includes index.
  ISBN-13 978-1-59327-179-4
  ISBN-10 1-59327-179-4
1. Computer networks-Management-Automation.  I. Title.
TK5105.5.B374 2009
  004.6-dc22
                               2008038558
```

Contents

V Development 551

Foreword to the second edition

As soon as the stable Nagios version 3.0 appeared, as can be expected after going to press, the question was raised: Nagios 2 or Nagios 3? For those just starting out with Nagios, Nagios 3.0 is a safe bet. Even the release candidate 3.0rc1 was sufficiently stable for production environments, and you can benefit directly from the new features, rather than having to get used to them later on.

If you are already using Nagios 2 in a sizable environment, then you'll surely be thinking, *Never touch a running system.* Why change if your existing system is running smoothly? But there has been further development on Nagios 2 since the first edition of this book appeared, and various bugs have been fixed.[1] So it is perhaps advisable to change to the current Nagios 2 version, and then wait and see how things develop.

On the other hand, Nagios 3.0 does contain a number of improvements. In particular where there are performance problems in large environments, this major version provides some adjusting screws that can help the system to achieve a higher performance through its greatly improved hostcheck logic, thanks to the caching of check results and a series of optimization parameters. Otherwise, it is smaller changes, ones that are not so obvious, that distinguish Nagios 3.0 from Nagios 2. Many things, often hardly noticable, combine to make your work with Nagios 3.0 easier, and sometimes more pleasant as well. You can get to know and appreciate all these small details best if, as a Nagios 2 administrator, you just try out Nagios 3. Newcomers will probably take all these small improvements for granted, and not even notice them.

Fortunately, converting from Nagios 2 to Nagios 3.0, as described in Section H.13 from page 693, is relatively simple, and you can continue using your existing configuration unchanged in most cases.

What's New in the Second Edition?

The second edition deals with Nagios in both version 2.x and version 3.0, since there is no difference in the basic principles. At first glance the struc-

---

[1] Nagios 2.10 was the current version at the time of going to press.

ture of the book looks the same, as do the contents of many chapters. Nevertheless, much has changed, even in the chapters that existed in the first edition. Nearly all the chapters were revised and updated to do justice to the current state of development of the tools introduced, but also to take into account the differences between Nagios 2.x and Nagios 3.0.

The *Monitoring Servers* chapter was completely revised and expanded, in particular where the NSClient++ tool is concerned. The chapter on the processing of performance data was also extended. A new tool was added, in the shape of PNP, and the description of the NagiosGrapher was brought right up to date. Of the newly introduced plugins, `check_logfiles` by Gerhard Lauβer and `check_multi` by Matthias Flacke in particular deserve special mention, and the author considers these to have great potential. But caution is advised: both are for the advanced user.

There is a new chapter on NagVis, with which you can define a Web interface based on your own images or graphics, with complete freedom in its design. NagVis requires the database interface NDOUtils, to which a separate chapter is devoted.

The EventDB reveals a database-supported approach to processing events as an alternative to the classic log file check. A separate chapter is also devoted to this. The chapters *Writing Your Own Plugins* and *Determining File and Directory Sizes* are also new, and describe step by step how to write your own Perl plugin, introducing the Perl module `Nagios::Plugin` in so doing. To optimize the performance of Perl scripts, Nagios provides its own interpreter, which is also given its own chapter.

A chapter called *What's New in Nagios 3.0?* can't be missing, of course, which compactly summarizes all the changes made compared to Nagios 2.x. For the sake of completeness, there is a new chapter on macros in the Appendix. This compares the various macro types and explains their intended use.

A chapter on performance optimization was also included. It certainly doesn't contain any patent remedies, since this is just not possible, given the wide range of monitored environments and scenarios for use. But it does take a look at the problem zones of Nagios, and provides some tips on where to look for support.

The fact that authentification on the Nagios Web interface does not have to be restricted to the simple `basis` authentification described in the installation chapter is demonstrated by another new chapter about Single-Sign-On in Microsoft Active Directory environments.

Information Sources on the Internet

Despite an increase of over 200 pages, the book cannot describe all the existing tools and possibilities for use. The Internet provides a wealth of information that is useful while, or after, studying this book. The most important sources are listed here.

- The Nagios homepage at `http://www.nagios.org/`

- The homepage of Nagios plugins at `http://www.nagiosplugins.org/`

- The Nagios community at `http://www.nagioscommunity.org/`

- `http://www.nagiosexchange.org/` as an exchange platform for plugins

- The original mailing lists at
  `http://www.nagios.org/support/mailinglists.php`

Introduction

It's ten o'clock on Monday morning. The boss of the branch office is in a rage. He's been waiting for hours for an important e-mail, and it still hasn't arrived. It can only be the fault of the mail server; it's probably misbehaving yet again. But a quick check of the computer shows that no mails have got stuck in the queue there, and there's no mention either in the log file that a mail from the sender in question has arrived. So where's the problem?

The central mail server of the company doesn't respond to a `ping`. That's probably the root of the problem. But the IT department at the company head office absolutely insists that it is not to blame. It also cannot ping the mail node of the branch office, but it maintains that the network at the head office is running smoothly, so the problem must lie with the network at the branch office. The search for the error continues. . .

The humiliating result: the VPN connection to head office was down, and although the ISDN backup connection was working, no route to the head office (and thus to the central mail server) was defined in the backup router. A globally operating IT service provider was responsible for the network connections (VPN and ISDN) between branch and head office, for whom something like this "just doesn't happen." The end result: many hours spent searching for the error, an irritated boss (the meeting for which the e-mail was urgently required has long since finished), and a sweating admin.

With a properly configured Nagios system, the adminstrator would already have noticed the problem at eight in the morning and been able to isolate its cause within a few minutes. Instead of losing valuable time, the IT service provider would have been informed directly. The time then required to eliminate the error (in this case, half an hour) would have been sufficient to deliver the e-mail in time.

A second example: somewhere in Germany, the hard drive on which the central Oracle database for a hospital stores its log files reaches full capacity. Although this does not cause the "lights to go out" in the operating room, the database stops working and there is considerable disruption to work procedures: patients cannot be admitted, examination results cannot be saved, and reports cannot be documented until the problem has been fixed.

If the critical hard drive had been monitored with Nagios, the IT department would have been warned at an early stage. The problem would not even have occurred.

With personnel resources becoming more and more scarce, no IT department can really afford to regularly check all systems manually. Networks that are growing more and more complex especially demand the need to be informed early on of disruptions that have occurred or of problems that are about to happen. Nagios, the Open Source tool for system and network monitoring, helps the administrator to detect problems before the phone rings off the hook.

The aim of the software is to inform administrators quickly about questionable (WARNING) or critical conditions (CRITICAL). What is regarded as "questionable" or "critical" is defined by the administrator in the configuration. A Web page summary then informs the administrator of normally working systems and services, which Nagios displays in green, of questionable conditions (yellow), and of critical situations (red). There is also the possibility of informing the administrators in charge—depending on specific services or systems—selectively by e-mail but also by paging services such as SMS.

By concentrating on stop light states (green, yellow, red), Nagios is distinct from network tools that display elapsed time graphically (for example in the load of a WAN interface or a CPU throughout an entire day) or that record and measure network traffic (how high was the proportion of HTTP on a particular interface?). Nagios is involved plainly and simply with the issue of whether everything is on a green light. The software does an excellent job in looking after this, not just in terms of the current status but also over long periods of time.

The tests

When checking critical hosts and services, Nagios distinguishes between host and service checks. A *host check* tests a computer, called a *host* in Nagios slang, for reachability—as a rule, a simple `ping` is used. A *service check* selectively tests individual network services such as HTTP, SMTP, DNS, etc., but also running processes, CPU load, or log files. Host checks are performed by Nagios irregularly and only where required, for example if none of the services to be monitored can be reached on the host being monitored. As long as one service can be addressed there, then this is basically valid for the entire computer, so this test can be dropped.

The simplest test for network services consists of looking to see whether the relevant target port is open, and whether a service is listening there. But this does not necessarily mean that, for example, the SSH daemon really is running on TCP port 22. Nagios therefore uses tests for many services that go several steps further. With SMTP, for example, the software also tests whether the mail server announces itself with a "220" output, the so-called *SMTP greeting*; and for a PostgreSQL database, it checks whether this will accept an SQL query.

Nagios becomes especially interesting through the fact that it takes into account dependencies in the network topology (if it is configured to do so). If the target system can only be reached through a particular router that has just gone down, then Nagios reports that the target system is "unreachable" and does not bother to bombard it with further host and service checks. The software puts administrators in a position where they can more quickly detect the actual cause and rectify the situation.

The suppliers of information

The great strength of Nagios—even in comparison with other network monitoring tools—lies in its modular structure. The Nagios core does not contain one single test. Instead it uses external programs for service and host checks, which are known as *plugins*. The basic equipment already contains a number of standard plugins for the most important application cases. Special requests that go beyond these are answered—provided that you have basic programming knowledge—by plugins that you can write yourself. Before investing time in developing these, however, it is first worth taking a look on the Internet and browsing through the relevant mailing lists,[2] as there is lively activity in this area. Ready-to-use plugins are available, especially in The Nagios Exchange platform, `http://www.nagiosexchange.org/`.

A plugin is a simple program—often just a shell script (Bash, Perl, etc.)—that gives out one of the four possible conditions: OK, WARNING, CRITICAL, or (with operating errors, for example) UNKNOWN.

This means that in principle Nagios can test everything that can be measured or counted electronically: the temperature and humidity in the server room, the amount of rainfall, the presence of persons in a certain room at a time when nobody should enter it. There are no limits to this, provided that you can find a way of providing measurement data or events as information that can be evaluated by computer (for example, with a temperature and humidity sensor, an infrared sensor, etc.). Apart from the standard plugins, this book accordingly introduces further freely available plugins, such as the use of a plugin to query a temperature and humidity sensor in Chapter 21 from page 505.

---

[2] `http://www.nagios.org/support/mailinglists.php`

Keeping admins up-to-date

Nagios possesses a sophisticated notification system. On the sender side (that is, with the host or service check) you can configure when each group of persons—the so-called *contact groups*—are informed about which conditions or events (failure, recovery, warnings, etc.). On the receiver side you can also define on multiple levels what is to be done with a corresponding message—for example whether the system should forward it, depending on the time of day, or discard the message.

If a specific service is to be monitored seven days a week round the clock, this does not mean that the administrator in charge will never be able to take a break. For example, you can instruct Nagios to notify the person only from Monday to Friday between 8am and 5pm, every two hours at the most. If the administrator in charge is not able to solve the problem within a specified period of time, eight hours for example, then the head of department responsible should receive a message. This process is known as *escalation management.* The corresponding configuration is explained in Chapter 12.5 from page 282.

Nagios can also make use of freely configurable, external programs for notifications, so that you can integrate any system you like, from e-mail to SMS, to a voice server that the administrator calls up and receives a voice message concerning the error.

With its Web interface (Chapter 16 from page 327, Nagios provides the administrator with a wide range of information, clearly arranged according to the issues involved. Whether the admin needs a summary of the overall situation, a display of problematic services and hosts and the causes of network outages, or the status of entire groups of hosts or services, Nagios provides an individually structured information page for nearly every purpose.

Through the Web front end, an administrator can inform colleagues upon accepting a particular problem so that they can concentrate on other issues that have not yet been addressed. Information already obtained can be stored as comments on hosts and services.

By reviewing past events, the Web interface can reveal problems that occurred in a selected time interval, who was informed of the problems, and which hosts and/or services were affected. Nagios can be configured to recognize scheduled downtimes and to prevent false alarms from going off during these periods.

Taking in information from outside

For tests, notifications, and so on, Nagios makes use of external programs, but the reverse is also possible: through a separate interface (see 13.1 from page 292), independent programs can send status information and commands to Nagios. The Web interface makes widespread use of this possibility, which allows the administrator to send interactive commands to Nagios. But a backup program unknown to Nagios can also transmit a success or failure to Nagios, as well as to a syslog daemon. The possibilities are limitless. Thanks to this interface, Nagios allows distributed monitoring. This involves several decentralized Nagios installations sending their test results to a central instance, which then helps to maintain an overview of the situation from a central location.

Other tools for network monitoring

Nagios is not the only tool for monitoring systems and networks. The most well-known "competitor," perhaps on an equal footing, is *Big Brother* (BB). Despite a number of differences, its Web interface serves the same purpose as that of Nagios: displaying to the administrator what is in the "green area" and what is not.

The reason why the author uses Nagios instead of Big Brother lies in the license for Big Brother, on the BB homepage[3] called *Better Than Free License*: the product continues to be commercially developed and distributed. If you use BB and earn money with it, you must buy the software. The fact that the software, including the source code, may not be passed on or modified, except with the explicit permission of the vendor, means that it cannot be reconciled with the criteria for Open Source licenses. This means that Linux distributors have their hands tied.

For the graphical display of certain measured values over a period of time, such as the load on a network interface, CPU load, or the number of mails per minute, there are other tools that perform this task better than Nagios. The original tool is certainly the *Multi Router Traffic Grapher* MRTG,[4] which, despite growing competition, still enjoys great popularity. A relatively young, but very powerful alternative is called Cacti[5]: this has a larger range of applications, can be configured via Web interface, and avoids the restrictions in MRTG, which can only display two measured values at the same time and cannot display any negative values. Another interesting new alternative is Munin.[6]

Nagios itself can also display performance data graphically, using extensions (Chapter 19 from page 403). In many cases this is sufficient, but for very dedicated requirements, the use of Nagios in tandem with a graphic representation tool such as MRTG or Cacti is recommended.

---

[3] http://www.bb4.org/
[4] http://www.mrtg.org/
[5] http://www.cacti.net/
[6] http://munin.projects.linpro.no/

About This Book

This book is directed at network administrators who want to find out about the condition of their systems and networks using an Open Source tool. It describes the Nagios versions 2.x and 3.0. The plugins, on the other hand, lead their own lives, are to a great extent independent of Nagios, and are therefore not restricted to a particular version.

Even though this book is based upon using Linux as the operating system for the Nagios computer, this is not a requirement. Most descriptions also apply to other Unix systems,[7] only system-specific details such as start scripts need to be adjusted accordingly. Nagios currently does not officially work under Windows, however.[8]

The first part of this book deals with getting Nagios up and running with a simple configuration, albeit one that is sufficient for many uses, as quickly as possible. This is why Chapters 1 through 3 do not have detailed descriptions and treatments of all options and features. These are examined in the second part of the book.

Chapter 4 looks at the details of service and host checks, and in particular introduces their dependency on network topologies.

The options available to Nagios for implementing service checks and obtaining their results is described in Chapter 5.

This is followed by the presentation of individual standard plugins and a number of additional, freely obtainable plugins. Chapter 6 takes a look at the plugins that inspect the services of a network protocol directly from the Nagios host, while Chapter 7 summarizes plugins that need to be installed on the machine that is being monitored, and for which Nagios needs additional utilities to get them running. Several auxiliary plugins, which do not perform any tests themselves, but manipulate already established results, are introduced in Chapter 8.

Two utilities that Nagios requires to run local plugins on remote hosts are introduced in the two subsequent chapters. Chapter 9 describes SSH, while Chapter 10 introduces a daemon developed specifically for Nagios.

Wherever networks are being monitored, SNMP also needs to be implemented. Chapter 11 not only describes SNMP-capable plugins but also examines the protocol and the SNMP world itself in detail, providing the background knowledge needed for this.

The Nagios notification system is introduced Chapter 12, which also deals with notification using SMS, escalation management, and taking account of dependencies.

---

[7] For example, *BSD, HP-UX, AIX, and Solaris; the author does not know of any Nagios versions running under MacOS X.

[8] There are, however, rumors about Nagios running in Cygwin environments.

The interface for external commands is discussed in Chapter 13. This forms the basis of other Nagios mechanisms, such as the Nagios Service Check Acceptor (NSCA), a client-server mechanism for transmitting passive test results, covered in Chapter 14. The use of this is shown in two concrete examples—integrating `syslog-ng` and processing SNMP traps. NSCA is also a requirement for distributed monitoring, discussed in Chapter 15.

The third part of the book is devoted to how the extracted information can be represented graphically. Chapter 16 explains how this works and how it is set up in detail, supported by some useful screenshots. It also explains a series of parameters, for which there are otherwise no documentation at all, except in the source code.

Nagios can be expanded by adding external applications. The NDOUtils enable database-driven storage of all Nagios objects and are described in Chapter 17. Connection to a database, using the addon described in Chapter 18, enables you to build a Web interface that can be configured far beyond the basic range of Nagios.

Although in its operation, Nagios concentrates primarily on stoplight signals (red-yellow-green), there are ways of evaluating and representing the performance data provided by plugins, which are described in detail in Chapter 19.

The fourth part of this book is dedicated to special applications. Networks are rarely homogeneous—that is, equipped only with Linux and other Unix-based operating systems. For this reason, Chapter 20 demonstrates what utilities can be used to integrate and monitor Windows systems.

Chapter 21 uses the example of a low-cost hardware sensor to show how room temperature and humidity can be monitored simply, yet effectively.

Nagios can also monitor proprietary commercial software, as long as mechanisms are available which can query states of the system integrated into a plugin. In Chapter 22, this is described using an SAP-R/3 system.

Whereas event processing is only briefly outlined in Chapter 14, Chapter 23 presents a database-supported approach that provides more options for selecting and processing events, including interlinking with Nagios.

Building your own plugins is the subject of the fifth part of this book. Chapter 24 looks at the general requirements for a standard plugin, while Chapter 25 uses a step-by-step example of how to write your own plugins that are fit for publishing. Chapter 26 takes an example of the Instant Client of Oracle to demonstrate how to build your own plugins based on programs not really intended for this purpose.

Appendix A introduces all the parameters of the two central configuration files `nagios.cfg` and `cgi.cfg`, while appendices B and C are devoted to some useful but somewhat exotic features.

A separate appendix (Appendix D) is devoted to *macros*, which allow flexibility in configuration.

Appendix E wanders slightly away from the core topic of Nagios and demonstrates how single sign-on scenarios can also be used for authentication in the Nagios Web interface.

The larger the environment, the more important it is to have a powerful and quick-reacting Nagios system. Appendix F offers a series suggestions on this, while Appendix G is dedicated to a specific tool, the Perl interpreter integrated into Nagios.

Finally, Appendix H briefly summarizes all the changes made since Nagios 2.x.

Further notes on the book

At the time of going to press, Nagios 3.0 is close to completion. By the time this book reaches the market, there could well be some modifications. Relevant notes, as well as corrections, in case some errors have slipped into the book, can be found at `http://linux.swobspace.net/books/nagios/`.

Note of Thanks

Many people have contributed to the success of this book. My thanks go first of all to Dr. Markus Wirtz, who initiated this book with his comment, "Why don't you write a Nagios book, then?!", when he refused to accept my Nagios activities as an excuse for delays in writing another book. A very special thanks goes to Patricia Jung, who, as the technical editor for the German language version, overhauled the manuscript and pestered me with thousands of questions—which was a good thing for the completeness of the book, and which has ultimately made it easier for the reader to understand.

The book would not be possible, of course, without all the tools it describes. Very special thanks go to Ethan Galstad, who as author, developer and maintainer has made Nagios what it is today: an awesome, incredibly useful and helpful tool that also fulfills high-level requirements, and one that can rely on a very large—and above all very active— community. Also many thanks to Ton Voon, representing all members of the *Nagios Plugins Development Team*, who, together with his colleagues, manages the development of Nagios plugins.

My thanks also go to those who have not only developed the Nagios-related software introduced in this book, but have also helped to polish and improve the book with their proofreading and feedback: Matthias Flacke (of check_multi fame), Jörg Linge (PNP), and Steffen Waitz, who proofread the first edition, Hendrik Bäcker (npcd), Lars Michelsen, Michael Luebben (NagVis), Gerhard Laußer (check_logfiles), and the employees of NET-WAYS GmbH (NagiosGrapher, EventDB, the exchange platform, NagiosExchange).

It is not possible for me to name all the individuals who have contributed in one way or another to the success of Nagios. I would therefore like to thank everybody who actively supports the Nagios community, whether this is through free software or through involvement in forums and mailing lists. Where would Nagios be without its users?

Part I

From Source Code to a Running Installation

Installation

The simplest method of installation is for you to install the Nagios packages that are supplied with the distribution you are using. Nagios 2.x is by now extremely mature and is therefore a component of most distributions. The paths of individual directories in those packages maintained by Linux distributors are usually different from the default specified in the source package, and thus from the paths used in this book.

Nagios 3.0 is relatively new; it is recommended here that you "get your hands dirty" by compiling and installing the software yourself. The following installation guide also applies to Nagios 2.x, and any differences between versions 2.x and 3.0 are mentioned explicitly in the text.

If you compile your own software, you have control over the directory structures and a number of other parameters. A Nagios system compiled in this way also provides an almost complete main configuration file, in which, initially, nothing has to be changed. But it should be mentioned here that compiling Nagios yourself might involve a laborious search for the necessary development packages, depending on what is already installed on the computer.

1.1 Preparations

For compiling Nagios itself you require gcc, make, autoconf, and automake. Required libraries are libgd[1] and openssl[2]. The development packages for these must also be installed (depending on the distribution, with either the ending -dev or -devel): libssl-dev, libgd-dev, libc6-dev.

With Debian and Ubuntu you prepare by using apt-get install to install the packages apache2, build-essential, and libgd2-dev. In OpenSUSE you install apache2 via YAST2, along with all C/C++ development libraries, as well as the package gd. In Fedora you run the command yum install on the command line and enter the packages httpd, gcc, glibc, glibc-common, gd, and gd-devel as arguments.

For the plugins it is recommended that you also install the following packages: ntpdate[3] (possibly contained in the package ntp or xntp), snmp,[4] smbclient[5] (possibly a component of the package samba-client), the libldap2 library, and the relevant development package libldap2-dev[6] (depending on the distribution, the appropriate packages are also called openldap2-client and openldap2-devel). You will also need to install the client and developer packages for the database used (e.g., postgresql-client and postgresql-dev(el)).

1.1.1 Determining and setting up the required users

Prior to compiling and installing, use the command groupadd to set up the groups necessary for operation. Groups nagios and nagcmd are set up with groupadd, and the user nagios, who is assigned to these groups and with whose permissions the Nagios server runs is set up with useradd:

```
linux:~ # groupadd -g 9000 nagios
linux:~ # groupadd -g 9001 nagcmd
```

[1] http://www.boutell.com/gd/
[2] http://www.openssl.org/ Depending on the distribution, the required RPM and Debian packages are sometimes named differently. Here you need to refer to the search help in the corresponding distribution. For Debian, the homepage will be of help. For example, if a configure instruction complains of a missing gd.h file, you can search specifically at http://www.debian.org/distrib/packages for the contents of packages. The search will then come up with all packages that contain the file gd.h.
[3] http://ntp.isc.org/bin/view/Main/SoftwareDownloads
[4] http://net-snmp.sourceforge.net/
[5] http://samba.org/samba/
[6] http://www.openldap.org/

```
linux:~ # useradd -u 9000 -g nagios -G nagcmd -d /usr/local/nagios \
    -c "Nagios Admin" nagios
```

Instead of the user (9000) and group IDs (9000 or 9001) used here, any other available IDs may be used. The primary group `nagios` of the user `nagios` should remain reserved exclusively for this user.

The CGI scripts are run by Nagios under the user ID of the user with whose permissions the Apache Web server runs. In order for this user to access certain protected areas of Nagios, an additional group is required, the so-called *Nagios Command Group* `nagcmd`. Only the Web user and the user `nagios` should belong to this group. The Web user can be determined from the Apache configuration file. In Debian/Ubuntu this is located at `/etc/apache2/apache2.conf`; in Fedora it is at `/etc/httpd/httpd.conf`:

```
linux:~ # grep "^User" /etc/apache2/apache2.conf
User www-data
```

The user determined in this way (in Debian/Ubuntu `www-data`, in Open-SUSE `www-run`, and in Fedora `httpd`) is additionally assigned to the group `nagcmd`, shown here using the example for Debian/Ubuntu:

```
linux:~ # usermod -G nagcmd www-data
```

In the example, the Web user is called `www-data`. The command `usermod` (this changes the data for an existing user account) also includes the Web user in the `nagcmd` group thanks to the `-G` option, by manipulating the corresponding entry in the file `/etc/group`.

In addition, the directory specified as the home directory of the user `nagios`, `/usr/local/nagios`, the configuration directory `/etc/nagios`, and the directory `/var/nagios`, which records variable data while Nagios is running, are set up manually and are assigned to the user `nagios` and to the group of the same name:

```
linux:~ # mkdir /usr/local/nagios /etc/nagios /var/nagios
linux:~ # chown nagios.nagios /usr/local/nagios /etc/nagios /var/nagios
```

1.2 Compiling Source Code

The Nagios source code is available for download on the project page.[7] The installation description below is for version 3.0, which is provided by the developers as a tarball. A Nagios 2.x installation runs in an almost identical manner:

[7] http://www.nagios.org/

```
linux:~ # mkdir /usr/local/src
linux:~ # cd /usr/local/src
linux:local/src # tar xvzf path/to/nagios-3.0.tar.gz
...
```

The three commands unpack the source code into the directory created for this purpose, /usr/local/src. A subdirectory called nagios-3.0 is also created, containing the Nagios sources. To prepare these for compilation, enter the parameter deviating from the default value when running the configure command. Table 1.1 lists the most important parameters:

```
linux:~ # cd /usr/local/src/nagios-3.0
linux:src/nagios-3.0 # ./configure \
    --sysconfdir=/etc/nagios \
    --localstatedir=/var/nagios \
    --with-command-group=nagcmd
...
```

The values chosen here ensure that the installation routine selects the directories used in the book and sets all parameters correctly when generating the main configuration file. This simplifies fine tuning of the configuration considerably. If you want to use the Embedded Perl Interpreter to accelerate the execution of Perl scripts, then you also need the two switches --with-perlcache and --enable-embedded-perl.

In Nagios 3.0 you can leave out --with-perlcache, as it is enabled automatically by --enable-embedded-perl. You can find more on the Embedded Perl Interpreter in Appendix G, page 669.

Property	Value	configure **Option**
Root directory	/usr/local/nagios	--prefix
Configuration directory	/etc/nagios	--sysconfdir
Directory for variable data	/var/nagios	--localstatedir
Nagios user (UserID)	nagios (9000)	--with-nagios-user
Nagios group (GroupID)	nagios (9000)	--with-nagios-group
Nagios Command Group (GroupID)	nagcmd (9001)	--with-command-group

Table 1.1: Installation parameters for Nagios

If --prefix is not specified, Nagios installs itself in the /usr/local/na-gios directory. We recommend that you stick to this directory.[8]

The system normally stores its configuration files in the directory etc beneath its root directory. In general it is better to store these in the /etc hierarchy, however. Here we use /etc/nagios.[9]

Variable data such as the log file and the status file are by default stored in the directory /usr/local/nagios/var. This is in the /usr hierarchy, which should only contain programs and other read-only files, not writable ones. In order to ensure that this is the case, we use /var/nagios.[10]

Irrespective of these changes, in most cases configure does not run through faultlessly the very first time, since one package or another is missing. For required libraries such as libgd, Nagios almost always demands the relevant developer package with the header files (here, libgd-dev or libgd-devel). Depending on the distribution, their names will end in -devel or -dev.

After all the tests have been run through, configure presents a summary of all the important configuration parameters:

```
*** Configuration summary for nagios 3.0 ***:

General Options:
------------------------
         Nagios executable:  nagios
         Nagios user/group:  nagios,nagios
        Command user/group:  nagios,nagcmd
             Embedded Perl:  yes, with caching
              Event Broker:  yes
            Install $prefix:  /usr/local/nagios
                 Lock file:  /var/nagios/nagios.lock
     Check result directory:  /var/nagios/spool/checkresults
            Init directory:  /etc/init.d
    Apache conf.d directory:  /etc/apache2/conf.d
              Mail program:  /usr/bin/mail
                   Host OS:  linux-gnu

Web Interface Options:
------------------------
                  HTML URL:  http://localhost/nagios/
                   CGI URL:  http://localhost/nagios/cgi-bin/
    Traceroute (used by WAP):  /usr/sbin/traceroute
```

[8] In accordance with the *Filesystem Hierarchy Standard* FHS, version 2.3, or local programs loaded by the administrator should be installed in **/usr/local**.

[9] This is not entirely compatible with FHS 2.3, which would prefer to have the configuration files in **/etc/local/nagios**.

[10] This also does not quite match the requirements of the FHS 2.3. But since Nagios makes no differentiation between spool, cache, and status information, an FHS-true reproduction is not possible to achieve in a simple manner.

In Nagios 2.x the lines Check result directory, Apache conf.d directory, and Mail program are missing.

If a yes is written after the item Embedded Perl, the Embedded Perl Interpreter is enabled. The *Event Broker* provides an interface for extensions that can be loaded as additional modules while the system is running.[11]

If you are satisfied with the result, make starts the actual compilation and then installs the software:[12]

```
linux:src/nagios-3.0 # make all
...
linux:src/nagios-3.0 # make install
...
linux:src/nagios-3.0 # make install-init
...
linux:src/nagios-3.0 # make install-commandmode
...
linux:src/nagios-3.0 # make install-config
...
```

The command make all compiles all the relevant programs, which are then copied to the appropriate directories, together with CGI scripts and documentation, by make install. Apart from /etc/nagios and /var/nagios, further directories are created under /usr/local/nagios, which are summarized in Table 1.2.

Table 1.2:
Nagios directories
under
/usr/local/nagios

Directory	Contents
./bin	Executable Nagios main program
./libexec	Plugins
./sbin	CGI scripts
./share	Documentation, HTML files for the Web interface

The command make install-commandmode generates the directory that is required for later usage of the *command file mechanism* (see Section 13.1, page 292) onwards. This step is optional, depending on the intended use, but since it is easy to forget later on, it is better to take precautions now. The final make install-config creates the example configuration, which will be used in Chapter 2, page 53.

---

[11] At the time of going to press there were not yet any external extensions, which is why the Event Broker is currently only of interest to developers.

[12] Caution is needed when updating from Nagios 2.x to Nagios 3.0: Here you should first back up the existing configuration, initially run only make all, and carefully read Section H.13 on page 693 In Nagios 3.0 a make install-config command overwrites existing files!

1.3 Starting Nagios Automatically

The command `make install-init` installs a suitable init script for the system start. Here `make` automatically tries to detect the correct path, which for most Linux distributions is `/etc/init.d`. Depending on your system, this may not be correct, which is why you should check it. In order for Nagios to start automatically when the system is booted, symbolic links are created in the `/etc/rc?.d` directories. With Debian and Ubuntu using System-V-Init, the included system script `update-rc.d` performs this task:

```
linux:~ # update-rc.d nagios defaults 99
```

This command creates symlinks beginning with the prefix S99 to the directories `rc2.d` to `rc5.d`, so that Nagios starts automatically when changing to runlevels 2 to 5. In addition it ensures that K99 symlinks in the directories `rc0.d`, `rc1.d`, and `rc6.d` are responsible for stopping Nagios when the system is shut down and rebooted, as well as when it changes to maintenance mode. This corresponds to the following command-line commands:

```
linux:~ # ln -s /etc/init.d/nagios /etc/rc2.d/S99nagios
linux:~ # ln -s /etc/init.d/nagios /etc/rc3.d/S99nagios
linux:~ # ln -s /etc/init.d/nagios /etc/rc4.d/S99nagios
linux:~ # ln -s /etc/init.d/nagios /etc/rc5.d/S99nagios
linux:~ # ln -s /etc/init.d/nagios /etc/rc0.d/K99nagios
linux:~ # ln -s /etc/init.d/nagios /etc/rc1.d/K99nagios
linux:~ # ln -s /etc/init.d/nagios /etc/rc6.d/K99nagios
```

For OpenSUSE the required symlinks are created using the script `insserv`:

```
linux:~ # insserv nagios
```

Fedora users perform this task with `chkconfig`:

```
linux:~ # chkconfig --add nagios
linux:~ # nagios on
```

1.4 Installing and Testing Plugins

What is now still missing are the plugins. They must be downloaded separately from `http://www.nagios.org/` and installed. As independent programs, they are subject to a different versioning system than Nagios. The current version at the time of going to press was version 1.4.11, but you can, for example, also use plugins from earlier version if you don't mind doing without the most recent features. Although the plugins are distributed in a common source distribution, they are independent of one another, so that you can replace one version of an individual plugin with another one at any time, or with one you have written yourself.

1.4.1 Installation

The installation of the plugin sources takes place, like the Nagios ones, in the directory /usr/local:

```
linux:~ # cd /usr/local/src
linux:local/src # tar xvzf path /to/nagios-plugins-1.4.tar.gz
linux:src/nagios-plugins-1.4.11 # ./configure \
    --sysconfdir=/etc/nagios \
    --localstatedir=/var/nagios \
        --enable-perl-modules
...
```

When running the configure command you should specify the same non-default values as for the server, which here are the configuration directory (/etc/nagios) and the directory intended for the data saved by Nagios (/var/nagios). Since the Nagios plugins are not maintained by the same people as Nagios itself, you should always check in advance, with ./configure --help, whether the configure options for Nagios and the plugins really match or deviate from one another.

The switch --enable-perl-modules is only needed if you intend to install the Perl module Nagios::Plugin—for example, if you are using it to program your own plugins in Perl. You can read more on this in Section 24.2, page 560.

It is possible that a series of WARNINGs may appear in the output of the configure command, something like this:

```
...
configure: WARNING: Skipping radius plugin
configure: WARNING: install radius libs to compile this plugin (see
            REQUIREMENTS).
...
configure: WARNING: Tried /usr/bin/perl - install Net::SNMP perl
            module if you want to use the perl snmp plugins
...
```

If you are not using Radius, you need not have qualms about ignoring the corresponding error messages. Otherwise you should install the missing packages and repeat the configure procedure. The quite frequently required SNMP functionality is missing a Perl module in this example. This may be installed either in the form of the distribution package or via the online CPAN archive:[13]

```
linux:~ # perl -MCPAN -e 'install Net::SNMP'
...
```

If you are running the CPAN procedure for the first time, it will guide you interactively through a self-explanatory setup, and you can answer nearly all of the questions with the default option.

Running `make` in the directory `nagios-plugins-1.4.11` will compile all plugins. Afterwards you have the opportunity to perform tests, with `make check`. Because these tests have not been particularly carefully programmed, you will often see many error messages that have more to do with the test itself than with the plugin. If you still want to try it, then the Cache Perl module must also be installed. Regardless of whether you use `make check`, you should manually check the most important plugins after the installation.

The command `make install` finally anchors the plugins in the subdirectory `libexec` (which in our case is `/usr/local/nagios/libexec`). However, not all of them are installed through this command. The source directory `contrib` contains a number of plugins that `make install` does not install automatically.

Most plugins in this directory are shell or Perl scripts. Where needed, these are simply copied to the plugin directory `/usr/local/nagios/libexec`. The few C programs first must be compiled, which in some cases may be no laughing matter, since a corresponding makefile, and often even a description of the required libraries, can be missing. If a simple `make` is not sufficient, as in the case of

```
linux:nagios-plugins-1.4.11/contrib # make check_cluster2[14]
cc      check_cluster2.c   -o check_cluster2
```

then it is best to look for help in the mailing list `nagiosplug-help`.[15] The compiled program must also be copied to the plugin directory.

1.4.2 Plugin test

Because plugins are independent programs, they can already be used manually for test purposes right now—before the installation of Nagios has been

---

[13] The *Comprehensive Perl Archive Network* at `http://www.cpan.org/`

[14] With `check_cluster`, hosts and services of a cluster can be monitored. Here you usually want to be notified if all nodes or redundant services provided fail at the same time. If one specific service fails on the other hand, this is not critical, as long as other hosts in the cluster provide this service.

[15] `http://lists.sourceforge.net/lists/listinfo/nagiosplug-help`

completed. In any case you should check the `check_icmp` plugin, which plays an essential role. It checks whether another computer can be reached via `ping`, and it is the only plugin to be used both as a service check and a host check. If it is not working correctly, Nagios will not work correctly either, since the system cannot perform any service checks as long as it categorizes a host as "down." Section 6.2, 108, describes `check_icmp` in detail, which is why there is only short introduction here describing its manual use.

In order for the plugin to function correctly it must, like the /bin/ping program, be run as the user root. This is done by providing it with the *SUID bit*. With current plugin versions, `make install` sets this automatically. One way this can be seen is in the fact that the sources contain an additional directory, `plugins-root`. With older plugin versions you have to do this manually:

```
linux:~ # chown root.nagios /usr/local/nagios/libexec/check_icmp
linux:~ # chmod 4711 /usr/local/nagios/libexec/check_icmp
linux:~ # ls -l /usr/local/nagios/libexec/check_icmp
-rwsr-x--x  1 root nagios 61326 2005-02-08 19:49 check_icmp
```

Brief instructions for the plugin are given with the –h option:[16]

```
nagios@linux:~$ /usr/local/nagios/libexec/check_icmp -h
Usage: check_icmp [options] [-H] host1 host2 hostn

Where options are any combination of:
  * -H | --host        specify a target
  * -w | --warn        warning threshold (currently 200.000ms,40%)
  * -c | --crit        critical threshold (currently 500.000ms,80%)
  * -n | --packets     number of packets to send (currently 5)
  * -i | --interval    max packet interval (currently 80.000ms)
  * -I | --hostint     max target interval (currently 0.000ms)
  * -l | --ttl         TTL on outgoing packets (currently 0)
  * -t | --timeout     timeout value (seconds, currently  10)
  * -b | --bytes       icmp packet size (currenly ignored)
    -v | --verbose     verbosity++
    -h | --help        this cruft

The -H switch is optional. Naming a host (or several) to check is not.
```

For a simple test it is sufficient to specify an IP address (it is immaterial whether you prefix the –H flag or not):

```
user@linux:~$ cd /usr/local/nagios/libexec
user@linux:nagios/libexec$ ./check_icmp -H 192.168.1.13
OK - 192.168.1.13: rta 0.261ms, lost 0%|rta=0.261ms;200.000;500.000;0;
pl=0%;40;80;;
```

---

[16] The listed options are explained in detail in Section 6.2 from page 108.

The output appears as a single line, which has been line-wrapped here for the printed version: with zero percent package loss (lost 0%), the test has been passed. Nagios uses only the first 300 bytes of the output line. If the plugin provides more information, this is cut off.

If you would like to test other plugins, we refer you to Chapters 6 and 7, which describe the most important plugins in detail. All (reasonably well-programmed) plugins provide somewhat more detailed instructions with the --help option.

1.5   Configuration of the Web Interface

In order for the Web front end of Nagios to function, the Web server must know the CGI directory and the main Web directory. The following description applies to both Apache 1.3, Apache 2.0, and 2.2.

1.5.1   Setting up Apache

As long as you have not added a different address for the front end, through the configure script with -with-cgiurl, Nagios expects the CGI programs at the URL /nagios/cgi-bin (actual directory: /usr/local/nagios/sbin) as well as the remaining HTML files below /nagios (actual directory: /usr/local/nagios/share). Nagios 3.0 includes its own make target for the Web interface, which configures the directories and sets corresponding aliases for the two URLs:

```
linux:~ # make install-webconf
...
```

This command installs the file nagios.conf in the configuration directory of Apache. In Debian/Ubuntu and OpenSUSE it is named /etc/apache2/conf.d, or in Fedora /etc/httpd/conf.d. It looks like this:

```
ScriptAlias /nagios/cgi-bin "/usr/local/nagios/sbin"
<Directory "/usr/local/nagios/sbin">
    Options ExecCGI
    AllowOverride None
    Order allow,deny
    Allow from  all
#   Order deny,allow
#   Deny from all
#   Allow from 127.0.0.1
    AuthName "Nagios Access"
    AuthType Basic
    AuthUserFile /etc/nagios/htpasswd.users
```

```
        Require valid-user
</Directory>
```

In Nagios 2.x you have to set up the file by hand.

The directive `ScriptAlias` ensures that Apache accesses the Nagios CGI directory when calling a URL such as `http://nagios-server/nagios/cgi-bin`, irrespective of where the Apache CGI directories may be located. `Options ExcecCGI` ensures that the Web server accepts all the scripts located there as CGI. `Order` and `Allow` initially allow unrestricted access here to the Web server. If you want to restrict access, the sequence of the `Order` arguments is altered:

```
Order deny,allow
Deny from all
Allow from 127.0.0.1
Allow from 192.0.2.0/24
```

This example ensures that only clients from the network `192.0.2.0/24` (`/24` stands for the subnet mask `255.255.255.0`) and `localhost` gain access to the directory specified. The three `Auth*-` and the `Require` directives ensure authenticated access; more on user authentication in Section 1.5.3 on page 49.

The section for the Nagios documents directory `/usr/local/nagios/share` is constructed in a similar fashion: the directive `Alias` allows the directory beneath the URL `http://nagios-server/nagios` to be addressed, independently of where the Apache-`DocumentRoot` is located.

The directives `Order` and `Allow` (and also `Deny`, if needed) are set in identical manner to the CGI section. Authentication is not absolutely essential in the documentation sphere, but it is certainly useful if you want to install extensions such as PNP there (see Section 19.6, page 446).

The command

```
linux:~ # /etc/init.d/apache reload
```

loads the new configuration. If everything has worked out correctly, the Nagios main page appears in the Web browser under `http://nagios-server/nagios`.

1.5.2 SELinux

Just a few distributions—in particular, Fedora—enable the *Security Enhanced Linux* (SELinux) by default. When enabled and appropriately configured, this allows services such as the Apache Web server access only to files and

directories explicitly mentioned. The directories /usr/local/nagios/bin
and /usr/local/nagios/share used by Nagios are not among these. The
consequence: SELinux first refuses Apache access until this is allowed via
the configuration. The command getenforce shows whether the *Enforcing Mode*, in which SELinux enforces the strict observance of the configured
access rights, is switched on. This can be switched off with the command

```
linux:~ # setenforce 0
```

To retain this status at the next system start, the settings in /etc/selinux/
config are changed. Rather than switching off the Enforcing Mode, though,
it is better to configure the required accesses specifically. This does require
some understanding of how SELinux works, and some general Linux experience –knowledge that would go beyond the scope of this book. For those
who want to get to grips more intensively with the subject, further information can be found in the Wiki of the Nagios community,[17] including a
link to a concrete guide.[18]

1.5.3 User authentication

In the state in which it is delivered, Nagios allows only authenticated users
access to the CGI directory. This means that users not "logged in" have
no way to see anything other than the homepage and the documentation.
They are blocked off from access to other functions.

There is a good reason for this: apart from status queries and other display
functions, Nagios has the ability to send commands via the Web interface.
The interface for external commands is used for this purpose (Section 13.1,
page 292). If this is active, checks can be switched on and off via the Web
browser, for example, and Nagios can even be restarted. Only authorized
users should be in a position to do this. Besides, general security consid-
erations would indicate that the huge volume of information provided by
Nagios should only be made available to trustworthy persons.

First of all, the parameter use_authentication in the CGI configuration
file cgi.cfg[19] of Nagios must be set to 1:

```
use_authentication=1
```

This is the default during installation. The simplest authentication form
provided by Apache is the file-based Basic authentication, which is already
enabled in the configuration file:

---

[17] Search http://www.nagioscommunity.org/wiki/ for the keyword SELinux.
[18] http://www.rickwargo.com/2006/10/29/fc6-selinux-and-nagios/
[19] More on this in Section 2.13 from page 77.

```
AuthName "Nagios Access"
AuthType Basic
AuthUserFile /etc/nagios/htpasswd.users
Require valid-user
```

AuthName is an information field that the browser displays if the Web server requests authentication. AuthType Basic stands for simple authentication, in which the password is transmitted without encryption, as long as no SSL connection is used. It is best to save the password file—here htpasswd.users—in the Nagios configuration directory /etc/nagios. The final parameter, require valid-user, means that all authenticated users have access (there are no restrictions for specific groups; only the user-password pair must be valid).

The (freely selectable) name of the password file will be specified here so that it displays what type of password file is involved. It is generated with the htpasswd2 program, included in Apache. (In Apache 1.3 and some other distributions, the program is called htpasswd.) Running

```
linux:/etc/nagios # htpasswd2 -c htpasswd.users nagios
New password: passwort
Re-type new password: passwort
Adding password for user nagios
```

generates a new password file with a password for the user nagios. Its format is relatively simple:

```
nagios:7NlyfpdI2UZEs
```

Each line contains a user-password pair, separated by a colon.[20] If you want to add other users, you should ensure that you omit the -c (*create*) option. Otherwise htpasswd(2) will recreate the file and delete the old contents:

```
linux:/etc/nagios # htpasswd2 htpasswd.users another_user
```

The user name cannot be chosen freely but must match the name of a contact person (see Section 2.7, page 70). Only the Web user (depending on your distro, www-data, www-run oder httpd, see page 39) can access the generated htpasswd.users file, and it should be protected from access by anyone else:

```
linux:/etc/nagios # chown www-data htpasswd.users
linux:/etc/nagios # chmod 600 htpasswd
```

---

[20] To be precise, the second position does not contain the password itself, but rather its hash value.

In combination with its own modules and those of third parties, Apache allows a series of other authentication methods. These include authentication via an LDAP directory, via Pluggable Authentication Modules (PAM),[21] or using SMB via a Windows server. Here we refer you to the relevant literature and the highly detailed documentation on the Apache homepage.[22] A quite advanced example, in which a user already authenticated by Kerberos does not have to authenticate himself again, is described in Appendix E on page 637.

Even though configuration of the Web interface is now finished, at the moment only the documentation is properly displayed: Nagios itself must first be correspondingly adjusted—as described in detail in the following chapter—before it can be used for monitoring data made available in this way.

---

[21] The "Pluggable Authentication Modules" now control authentication in all Linux distributions, so that you can also use existing user accounts here.

[22] http://httpd.apache.org/

Nagios Configuration

Although the Nagios configuration can become quite large, you only need to handle a small part of this to get a system up and running. Luckily many parameters in Nagios are already set to sensible default settings. So this chapter will be concerned primarily with the most basic and frequently used parameters, which is quite sufficient for an initial configuration.

Further details on the configuration are provided by the chapters on individual Nagios features: in Chapter 6 on network plugins (page 105), there are many examples on the configuration of services. All parameters of the Nagios messaging system are explained in detail in Chapter 12, page 265, and the parameters for controlling the Web interface are described in Chapter 16, page 327. In addition to this, Nagios includes its own extensive documentation (/usr/local/nagios/share/docs), which can also be reached from the Web interface. This can always be recommended as a useful source for further information, which is why each of the sections below refer to the corresponding location in the original documentation.

The installation routine in make install-config (see Section 1.2 on page 39) stores examples of individual configuration files in the directory /etc/nagios. But be careful: whereas the names of the example files in Nagios 2.0 ended in -sample (so that a possible update does not overwrite the files required for production), this is no longer the case in the current Nagios 2.x versions and in Nagios 3.0. Existing files are overwritten here. Admittedly, make install does rename existing files: thus nagios.cfg is turned into nagios.cfg~. But this only happens once. After running make install one more time, the original contents of the file are deleted once and for all. For this reason it is essential that you back up the existing configuration *prior to* running make install-config.

After this command, the directory /etc/nagios of Nagios 3.0 contains the three main configuration files: nagios.cfg, cgi.cfg, and resource.cfg. Object definitions end up in other files in the subdirectory objects:

```
user@linux:/etc/nagios$ tree[1]
.
|-- nagios.cfg
|-- cgi.cfg
|-- resource.cfg
'-- objects
    |-- templates.cfg
    |-- commands.cfg
    |-- contacts.cfg
    |-- timeperiods.cfg
    |-- localhost.cfg
    |-- windows.cfg
    |-- printer.cfg
    '-- switch.cfg
```

Nagios 2.10 uses fewer files; objects are defined only in the files localhost.cfg and commands.cfg:

```
user@linux:/etc/nagios$ tree
.
|-- nagios.cfg
|-- cgi.cfg
|-- resource.cfg
|-- localhost.cfg
'-- commands.cfg
```

All subsequent work should be carried out as the user nagios. If you are editing files as the superuser, you must ensure yourself that the contents of directory /etc/nagios afterwards belong to the user nagios again. With the exception of the file resource.cfg—this may contain passwords, which is why only the owner nagios should have the read permission set—all other files may be readable for all.

---

[1] http://mama.indstate.edu/users/ice/tree/

2.1   The Main Configuration File `nagios.cfg`

The central configuration takes place in `nagios.cfg`. Instead of storing all configuration options there, it makes links to other configuration files (with the exception of the CGI configuration).

Those who compile and install Nagios themselves have the advantage that at first they do not even need to adjust `nagios.cfg`, since all paths are already correctly set.[2] And that's as much as you need to do. Nevertheless one small modification is recommended, which helps to maintain a clear picture and considerably simplifies configuration where larger networks are involved.

The parameter concerned is `cfg_file`, which integrates files with object definitions (see Sections 2.2 through 2.10 on page 59). The file `nagios.cfg`, included in the Nagios 3.0 package, contains the following entries:

```
nagios@linux:/etc/nagios$ fgrep cfg_file nagios.cfg
...
cfg_file=/etc/nagios/objects/commands.cfg
cfg_file=/etc/nagios/objects/contacts.cfg
cfg_file=/etc/nagios/objects/timeperiods.cfg
cfg_file=/etc/nagios/objects/templates.cfg
cfg_file=/etc/nagios/objects/localhost.cfg
...
```

Nagios 2.x gathers all example object files into just two configuration files:

```
nagios@linux:/etc/nagios$ fgrep cfg_file nagios.cfg
...
cfg_file=/etc/nagios/commands.cfg
cfg_file=/etc/nagios/localhost.cfg
...
```

As an alternative to `cfg_file`, you can also use the parameter `cfg_dir`: this requests that you specify the name of a directory from which Nagios should integrate all configuration files ending in `.cfg` (files with other extensions are simply ignored). This also works recursively; Nagios thus evaluates all `*.cfg` files from all subdirectories. With the parameter `cfg_dir` you therefore only need to specify a signal directory, instead of calling all configuration files, with `cfg_file`, individually. The only restriction: these must be configuration files that describe objects. The configuration files `cgi.cfg` and `resource.cfg` are excluded from this, which is why, like the main configuration file `nagios.cfg`, they remain in the main directory `/etc/nagios`.

---

[2]   If Nagios is from a distribution package, it is worth checking at least the path details. In a well-maintained distribution these will also be matched to the Nagios directories used there.

Simple structure

For the object-specific configuration, it is best to create a directory called /etc/nagios/mysite, then remove all cfg_file directives in nagios.cfg (or comment them out with a # at the beginning of the line) and replace them with the following:

```
...
cfg_dir=/etc/nagios/mysite
...
```

The contents of the directory /etc/nagios will be version-independent and look like this:

```
nagios@linux:/etc/nagios$ tree
.
|-- nagios.cfg
|-- cgi.cfg
|-- resource.cfg
|-- htpasswd
'-- mysite
    |-- contactgroups.cfg
    |-- misccommands.cfg
    |-- contacts.cfg
    |-- timeperiods.cfg
    |-- checkcommands.cfg
    |-- hosts.cfg
    |-- services.cfg
    '-- hostgroups.cfg
```

The main directory /etc/nagios contains only three configuration files and the password file for protected Web access. Whether you collect all objects of the same type in one separate file, that is all host definitions in hosts.cfg, all services in services.cfg, and so on, or divide these into separate files, is left to the individual.

In this example, only the top directory mysite needs to be integrated with cfg_dir in nagios.cfg. This forms the basis for our initial configuration.

A larger location

For larger installations, you should divide the object definitions into individual files (creating a separate file with the host definition for each host, for instance) and group these in subdirectories according to sensible criteria, as in the following example:

```
...
'-- mysite
    |-- linux
    |   |-- services
    |   '-- hosts
    |       |-- linux01.cfg
    |       |-- linux02.cfg
    |       '-- linux03.cfg
    |-- windows
    |   |-- services
    |   '-- hosts
    |       |-- win03.cfg
    |       '-- win09.cfg
    '-- router
        |-- services
        '-- hosts
            |-- edge01.cfg
            |-- edge02.cfg
            '-- backbone.cfg
```

This example arranges the objects according to the operating system (`li-nux`, `windows`, and `router`). Each of these system directories has two further subdirectories: `hosts` and `services`.

Each of the individual host objects are described in a separate file (for example `linux01.cfg`). These can easily be copied if you want to create other host objects with similar properties. You can copy services in a similar manner.

The other object definitions are placed either directly in the directory `my-site`, as in the simple structure on page 56, or you can create subdirectories, as described in more detail in the next section.

In `nagios.cfg` the object definitions are again bound with a single directive:

```
cfg_dir=/etc/nagios/mysite
```

Large installations with several different locations

For large installations, it is better to split up host and service objects according to location. Even for the remaining objects, we recommend that you split them up into individual files and group these into subdirectories:

```
|-- global
|   |-- commands
|   |   |-- check-host-alive.cfg
|   |   |-- check_http.cfg
|   |   |-- check_icmp.cfg
... ... ...
```

```
|   |-- contacts
|   |   |-- nagios.cfg
... ... ...
|   |-- templates
|   |   |-- host_generic_t.cfg
|   |   |-- service_generic_t.cfg
|   |   |-- service_perfdata_t.cfg
... ... ...
|   '-- timeperiods
'-- sites
    |-- foreignsite
    |   |-- hosts
    |   '-- services
    |-- mysite
    |   |-- hosts
    |   '-- services
    '-- othersite
        |-- hosts
        '-- services
```

In this example, the directory global gathers together all the objects that that do not themselves define a check (that is, everything that is not a host or service object). This is where the subdirectories commands, contacts, templates, and timeperiods are located, each of which contain the files for the object categories of the same name. For many command objects, individual files are easier to handle than one huge text file.

If the contact objects are also stored in individual files, it is easy to disable a contact: the file extension is simply changed from .cfg to .cfx and then a reload is performed. Nagios ignores all files in object directories that do not end in .cfg. The overlying directories global and sites are bound into nagios.cfg:

```
cfg_dir=/etc/nagios/global
cfg_dir=/etc/nagios/sites
```

Setting the European date format

The date specifications in Nagios appear by default in the American format $MM-DD-YYYY$:

```
date_format=us
```

If you prefer something else, e.g., the European date format, it is recommended that you change the parameter date_format in nagios.cfg right from the start. The value iso8601 ensures that Nagios date specifications are displayed in the ISO or DIN format $YYYY-MM-DD\ HH:MM:SS$. Table 2.1 lists the possible values for date_format.

The other parameters in `nagios.cfg` are described in Appendix A.1; in the original documentation these can be found at `http://localhost/nagios/docs/configmain.html` or `/usr/local/nagios/share/docs/config-main.html`.

Value	Representation
us	*MM-DD-YYYY HH:MM:SS*
euro	*DD-MM-YYYY HH:MM:SS*
iso8601	*YYYY-MM-DD HH:MM:SS*
strict-iso8601	*YYYY-MM-DD*T*HH:MM:SS*

Table 2.1:
Possible date format

2.2 Objects—an Overview

A Nagios object describes a specific unit: a host, a service, a contact, or the groups to which each belongs. Even commands are defined as objects. This definition has not come about by chance. Nagios is also able to inherit characteristics (Section 2.11 from page 75).

Object definitions follow the following pattern:

```
define object-type {
    parameter   value
    parameter   value
    ...
}
```

Nagios has the following values for the `object-type`:

host

> The host object describes one of the network nodes that are to be monitored. Nagios expects the IP address as a parameter here (or the *Fully Qualified Domain Name*) and the command that should define whether the host is alive (see Section 2.3, page 62). The host definition is re-referenced in the service definition.

hostgroup

> Several hosts can be combined into a group (see Section 2.4 on page 65). This simplifies configuration, since entire host groups instead of single hosts can be specified when defining services (the service will then exist for each member of the group). In addition, Nagios represents the hosts of a host group together in a table in the Web front end, which helps to increase clarity.

service

> The individual services to be monitored are defined as service objects (Chapter 2.5, page 66). A service never exists independently of a host. So it is quite possible to have several services with the same name, as long as they belong to different hosts. The following code,

```
define service {
    name PING
    host_name linux01
    ...
}
define service {
    name PING
    host_name linux03
}
```

> describes two services that both have the same service name but belong to different hosts. So in the language of Nagios, a service is always a host-service pair.

servicegroup

> As it does with host groups, Nagios combines several services and represents these in the Web front end as a unit with its own table (see Section 2.6, page 69). Service groups are not absolutely essential, but help to improve clarity, and are also used in reporting.

contact

> A person who is to be informed by Nagios of specific events (see Section 2.7, page 70). Nagios uses contact objects to show to a user via the Web front end only those things for which the user is listed as a contact person. In the basic setting users do not get to see hosts and services for which they are not responsible.

contactgroup

> Notification of events in hosts and services takes place via the contact group (Section 2.8, page 72). A direct link between the host/service and a contact person is not possible.

timeperiod

> Describes a time period within which Nagios should inform contact groups (Section 2.10, page 74). Outside such a time slot, the system will not send any messages. The messaging chain can be fine-tuned via various *time periods*, depending on the host/service and contact/contact groups. More on this will be presented in Section 12.3, page 267.

command
>   Nagios always calls external programs via command objects (Section 2.9, page 72). Apart from plugins, messaging programs also include e-mail or SMS messaging applications.

servicedependency
>   This object type describes dependences between services. If, for example, an application does not function without a database, a corresponding dependency object will ensure that Nagios will represent the failed database as the primary problem instead of just announcing the nonfunctioning of the application (see Section 12.6, page 285).

serviceescalation
>   Used to define proper escalation management: if a service is not available after a specific time period, Nagios informs a further or different circle of people. This can also be configured on multiple levels in any way you want (see Section 12.5).

hostdependency
>   Like servicedependency, but for hosts.

hostescalation
>   Like serviceescalation, but for hosts.

hostextinfo (Nagios 2.x)
>   *Extended Host Information* objects are optional and define a specific graphic and/or URL, which Nagios additionally integrates into its graphic output. The URL can refer to a Web page that provides additional information on the host (see Section 16.4, page 362).
>
>   hostextinfo This object is deprecated in Nagios 3.0, but it is still available. Nagios 3.0 integrated the object parameters into the host definition.

serviceextinfo (Nagios 2.x)
>   *Extended Service Information*, like *Extended Host Information*.

Not all object types are absolutely essential; especially at the beginning. You easily can do without the *dependency, *escalation, and *extinfo objects, as well as the servicegroup. Chapter 12 looks at escalation and dependencies in detail. hostextinfo and serviceextinfo are used to provide a "more colorful" graphical representation, but they are not at all necessary for running Nagios. Section 16.4 from page 362 looks at this in more detail. The original documentation also provides more information.[3]

---

[3] http://localhost/nagios/docs/objectdefinitions.html#hostextinfo or #serviceextinfo (Nagios 3.0)
http://localhost/nagios/docs/xodtemplate.html#hostextinfo or #serviceextinfo (Nagios 2.x); the files can be found locally in /usr/local/nagios/share/docs/.

Notes on the object examples below

Although the following chapters describe individual object types in detail, only the mandatory parameters and those that are absolutely essential for meaningful operation are described there. Mandatory parameters here are always printed in **bold** type. The first (comment) line in each example lists the file in which the recorded object definition is to be stored. For the parameters marked with [*], there are some differences between Nagios 2.x and Nagios 3.0, each of which will be explained in more depth in the text.

When you first start using Nagios, it is recommended that you restrict yourself to a minimal configuration with only one or two objects per object type, in order to keep potential sources of error to a minimum and to obtain a running system as quickly as possible. Afterwards extensions can be implemented very simply and quickly, especially if you incorporate the tips mentioned in Section 2.11 on templates (page 75).

Time details in general refer to time units. A time unit consists of 60 seconds by default. It can be set to a different value in the configuration file `nagios.cfg`, using the parameter `interval_length`. You should really change this parameter only if you know exactly what you are doing.

2.3   Defining the Machines to Be Monitored, with `host`

The host object is the central command post on which all host and service checks are based. It defines the machine to be monitored. The parameters printed in bold must be specified in all cases:

```
# -- /etc/nagios/mysite/hosts.cfg
define host{
    host_name               linux01
    hostgroups              linux-servers
    alias(*)                Linux File Server
    address                 192.168.1.9
    check_command           check-host-alive
    max_check_attempts      3
    check_period            24x7
    contact_groups          localadmins
    notification_interval   120
    notification_period     24x7
    notification_options    d,u,r,f,s(*)
    parents                 router01
}
```

host_name

>   This parameter specifies the host name with which Nagios addresses
>   the machine in services, host groups, and other objects. Only the
>   special characters - and _ are allowed.

hostgroups

>   This parameter allocates the host to a host group object, which must
>   already be defined (Section 2.4, page 65). A host group in the Web
>   interface combines several hosts into a group (see Figure 16.10 on
>   page 334). The second possibility of assigning a host to a host group,
>   compatible with version 1.x, uses the members parameter in defining
>   the host group itself. The two methods can also be combined.

alias

>   This parameter contains a short description of the host, which Nagios
>   displays at various locations as additional information. Ordinary text
>   is allowed here. The parameter is no longer obligatory from Nagios
>   3.0. If it is missing, the value from host_name is used.

address

>   This specifies the IP address or the *Fully Qualified Domain Name*
>   (FQDN) of the computer. If it is possible (i.e., for static IP addresses),
>   you should use an IP address, since the resolution of a name to an IP
>   address is always dependent on DNS working, which is not infallible.

check_command

>   This specifies the command with which Nagios checks, if necessary,
>   to see whether the host is reachable. The parameter is optional. If
>   it is omitted, Nagios will never carry out a host check! This can be
>   useful for network components that are frequently switched off (for
>   example, print servers).

>   The command usually used for check_command is called check-host
>   -alive, which is already predefined in the supplied file, checkcom-
>   mands.cfg (see Section 2.9, page 72). This makes use of either the
>   plugin check_ping or the more modern check_icmp. Both plugins
>   check the reachability of the host via the ICMP packets *ICMP Echo
>   Request* and *Echo Reply*.

max_check_attempts

>   This parameter determines how often Nagios should try to reach the
>   computer if the first test has gone wrong. The value 3 in the example
>   means that the test is repeated up to three times if it returns anything
>   other than OK in the first test. As long as there are still repeat tests
>   to be made, Nagios refers to this as a *soft state*. If the final test has
>   been made, the system categorizes the state as *hard*. Nagios notifies

the system administrator exclusively of hard states, and in the example, sends messages only if the third test also ends with an error or warning.

check_period

This specifies the time period in which the host should be monitored. Really, only "round the clock" makes sense—that is, 24x7. A timeperiod object is involved here, the definition of which is described in more detail in Section 2.10 on page 74. It only makes sense to use a specification other than 24x7 if you want to explicitly suppress the host check at certain times.

contact_groups

This specifies the receiver of messages which Nagios sends with respect to the hosts defined here, that is localadmin. Section 2.8 explains this more fully on page 72.

notification_interval

This specifies at what intervals Nagios should repeat notification of the continued existence of the state. 120 time units normally mean one message every 120 minutes, provided the error state continues.

notification_period

This specifies at what time interval a message should be sent. A time period different from 24x7 could certainly be useful here. It is important to understand the difference here with check_period: if check_period excludes time periods, Nagios cannot even determine whether there is an error or not. But if the host is monitored round-the-clock and only the notification period is restricted by the parameter notification_period, Nagios will certainly log errors and also display them in the Web front end and in log evaluations. Outside the notification_period the system does not send any messages. A more detailed description of the notification system is given in Section 12.3, page 267.

notification_options

This parameter describes the states about which Nagios should provide notification when they occur. Nagios knows the following states for computers:

d   down

u   unreachable (host is not reachable because a network node between Nagios and a host has failed and the actual state of the host cannot be determined)

r   recovery (OK state after an error)

f   flapping (state changes very quickly; more on this in Appendix B from page 611).

s   scheduled downtime (Nagios 3.0 provides information here on
      the start and end of a planned maintenance period, or in case
      a planned maintenance period is canceled. This option is not
      available for Nagios 2.x.)

By specifying d,u, the system will send messages if the host is not on
the network or not reachable over the network, but not if it can be
reached again after an error state (recovery). If n (none) is used as
the value, Nagios will normally not give any notification.

The form in which Nagios sends out a message depends on how the
contact is defined. Irrespective of when you want to be notified, the
Web interface always shows the current state, even if Nagios does
not send a message, because the time period does not match or the
system is still repeating the tests (the so-called soft state).

parents
      This allows the physical topology of the network to be taken into ac-
      count. Here the router or the network component is given by which
      the host is reachable if it is not in direct contact in the same network
      segment. This can also be a switch between the Nagios server and the
      host. If Nagios does not reach the host because all parents (separated
      by commas) are down, then Nagios categorizes it as UNREACHABLE,
      but not as DOWN.

Further information is provided by the Nagios 3.0 online help under `http:
//localhost/nagios/docs//objectdefinitions.html#host`.[4] In Na-
gios 2.x the file is called `xodtemplate.html` and can be found in the same
directory. The differences between Nagios 2.x and Nagios 3.0 are described
in Section H.1.1, page 678.

2.4 Grouping Computers Together with `hostgroup`

A host group contains one or more computers so that they can be represented in the Web interface together (see Figure 16.10 on page 334)—in
addition, certain objects (e.g., services) can be applied to an entire group
of computers instead of having to define them individually for each host.

The `hostgroup_name` parameter specifies a unique name for the group,
`alias` accepts a short description. The `members` parameter lists all hosts
names belonging to the group, separated by commas:

```
# -- /etc/nagios/mysite/hostgroups.cfg
define hostgroup{
```

_____

[4] Locally in `/usr/local/nagios/share/docs/objectdefinitions.html`.

```
    hostgroup_name        linux-servers
    alias                 Linux Servers
    members               linux01,linux02
    hostgroup_members(*)  hostgroup1,hostgroup2
}
```

If you specify to which group they belong in the host definition for individual member computers, with the parameter hostgroups (page 63), the members entry may be omitted from version 2.0. This means that you no longer have two search through all group definitions if you just want to delete a single host. The combined use—of members in the hostgroup object and at the same time, of hostgroups in the host object—is equally possible. A new host group in Nagios 3.0 is hostgroup_members, with which you can specify other host groups as members, and thus form hierarchies of host groups. This option is not available in Nagios 2.0.

2.5 Defining Services to Be Monitored with service

A service in Nagios always consists of the combination of a host and a service name. This combination must be unique. Service names, on the other hand, may occur many times, as long as they are combined with different hosts.

The simplest service consists of a simple ping, which tests whether the relevant host is reachable, and which registers the response time and any packet loss that may occur:

```
# -- /etc/nagios/mysite/services.cfg
define service{
    host_name                  linux01
    service_description        PING
    check_command              check_ping!100.0,20%!500.0,60%
    max_check_attempts         3
    normal_check_interval(*)   5
    retry_check_interval(*)    1
    check_period               24x7
    notification_interval      120
    notification_period(*)     24x7
    notification_options       w,u,c,r,f,s(*)
    contact_groups(*)          localadmins
}
```

In contrast to a host check, which Nagios carries out only if it cannot reach any other service of the host, a ping service is carried out at regular intervals. Problems in the network can be detected relatively simply through response times and packet loss rates. The host check is less suitable for this purpose.

host_name

This refers to the name defined in the host object. Nagios also obtains the IP address of the computer via this. Instead of a single host name, you can also enter a comma-separated list of multiple hosts. As an alternative to `host_name`, it is also possible to use the parameter `hostgroup_name` to specify an entire host group instead of individual hosts. The service is then considered to be defined for each of the individual computers groups together in this way. Whether you make use of this optimization, or allocate your own service definitions to each computer individually, makes no difference to Nagios.

service_description

This parameter defines the actual name of the service. Spaces, colons, and dashes may be included in the name. Nagios always addresses a service as a combination of host name (here: `linux01`) and service description (`PING`). This must be unique.

servicegroups

assigns the service to a service group object that must already be defined (section 2.6, page 69).

check_command

This defines the command with which Nagios tests the service for functionality. Arguments are passed on to the actual command, ie. `check_ping`, separated by exclamation marks. The definition of the `check_ping` command, predefined in the example files, is explained in Section 2.9 on page 72.

In the example, the values for the warning limit (100 `ms`, 20%) and for the CRITICAL status (500 `ms`, 60%) are determined. You could compare this to a traffic light: the state OK (green) occurs if the response time remains under the warning limit of 100 milliseconds, and if none or less than 20 percent of packets have been lost. The WARNING state (yellow) occurs if the packet loss or response time lies above the defined warning limit, but still beneath the critical limit. Above the critical limit, Nagios issues a CRITICAL state (red). The return value of the plugin is described at the beginning of Chapter 6 (page 6), the underlying plugin `check_icmp` is introduced in detail in Section 6.2 from page 108.

max_check_attempts

This specifies how often Nagios should repeat a test in order to verify and definitively accept an error state which has been discovered (or also the recovered functionality), that is, to recognize it as a *hard state.* In the transitional phase (for example from OK to CRITICAL) we speak of a *soft state.* Basic distinctions between soft and hard are only made by the Nagios notification system, which is why the two states are described in more detail in the context of this system (Chapter 12, page 265). The difference has no influence in the representation in the Web interface.

normal_check_interval

This specifies at what interval Nagios should test the service when the system is in a stable condition—this can equally be an OK or an error state. In the example this is five time units, which is normally five minutes. In Nagios 3.0 the parameter may also be written as check_interval; as for the host definition, both forms are equivalent.

retry_check_interval

This describes the time interval between two tests when the state is in the process of changing (for example, from OK to WARNING), that is, when there is a soft state. In Nagios 3.0 the parameter may also be written as retry_interval; both forms are equivalent.

As soon as Nagios has performed the number of tests specified in max_check_attempts, it checks the service again at intervals of normal_check_interval.

check_period

This describes the time period in which the service is to be monitored. The entry represents a timeperiod object, the definition of which is described in more detail in Section 2.10 from page 74. Here you should enter 24x7 for "round the clock" unless you want to explicitly stop the test from running at specific times (perhaps because of a scheduled maintenance slot). If the notification is to be prevented only at specific times, it is better to use the option notification_period or other filters of the Nagios notification system (see Section 12, page 265).

notification_interval

This determines at what regular intervals Nagios repeats reports on error states. In the example, the system does this every 120 time units (normally minutes), as long as the error state continues. A value of 0 causes Nagios to announce the current state only once. Beginning with Nagios 3.0, notification_interval is no longer an obligatory parameter. If it is missing, the value is taken from the accompanying host definition.

notification_period

This describes the time period within which a notification should take place. This again involves a timeperiod object (see Section

2.10). Here in the example, 24x7 is used, so notification is sent round the clock. A more detailed discussion of the `notification_period` parameter can be found in Section 12.3 from page 267. Beginning with Nagios 3.0 this parameter is optional. If it is missing, the value is taken from the accompanying host definition.

`notification_options`
> This determines which error states Nagios should report. Possible values which can be used here are the same states already described for host objects, i.e., `c` (critical), `w` (warning), `u` (unknown), `r` (recovered), `f` (flapping), and (from Nagios 3.0) `s` (planned maintenance interval). Specifying `c,r` only informs the system when a service is in a CRITICAL state and if it subsequently recovers (RECOVERY).
>
> If you use `n` (none) as the value, Nagios will normally not send any notification. The Web interface nevertheless shows the current states.

`contact_groups`
> Finally, this parameter defines the recipient group whose members should receive the notifications. Several groups can be entered as a comma-separated list. Beginning with Nagios 3.0 this parameter can be omitted. Then the value is taken from the accompanying host definition.

Further information can be found in the Nagios 3.0 online help at `http://localhost/nagios/docs/objectdefinitions.html#service`.[5] For version 2.x the file is called `xodtemplate.html`. The differences between Nagios 2.x and Nagios 3.0 are described in Section H.1.2 from page 680.

2.6 Grouping Services Together with `servicegroup`

Service groups, like host groups, combine several services into a group, so that they can be represented together in the Web front end. This increases clarity and simplifies certain evaluations, but it is optional, and is not recommended at the beginning, in order to keep configuration simple.

```
# -- /etc/nagios/mysite/servicegroups.cfg
define servicegroup{
    servicegroup_name       all-ping
    alias                   All Pings
    members                 linux01,PING,linux02,PING
    servicegroup_members(*) servicegroup1,servicegroup2
}
```

[5] The corresponding file is located after installation in the directory `/usr/local/nagios/share/docs/`.

`servicegroup_name` and `alias` have the same meanings as for the host group. It should be noted that the syntax is the same as for the `members` entry. Because a service in Nagios always consists of the combination of host and service names, both must always be listed in pairs. The computer comes first, and then the service:

```
members host1,service1,host2,service2, ...
```

The `members` details can be omitted if the `servicegroups` parameter is used in the service definition (page 67). If you want, you can use the two possibilities in combination. As for the host groups, hierarchies can be formed from service groups from Nagios 3.0, using the parameter `service-group_members`.

2.7   Defining Addressees for Error Messages: `contact`

A contact is basically a person to whom a message addressed via a contact group is sent:

```
# -- /etc/nagios/mysite/contacts.cfg
define contact{
    contact_name                       nagios
    alias                              Nagios Admin
    host_notification_period          24x7
    service_notification_period       24x7
    service_notification_options      w,u,c,r
    host_notification_options         d,u,r
    service_notification_commands     notify-by-email
    host_notification_commands        host-notify-by-email
    email                             nagios-admin@localhost
    can_submit_commands(*)            1
}
```

The contact also plays a role during authentication: a user who logs in at the Web front end only gets to see the hosts and services for which that user is entered as the contact. The user for logging in to the Web interface must therefore be identical with the value of `contact_name` specified here. The first time it is used, the user `nagios` is sufficient.

`contact_name`
> This parameter defines the user name. It must match the corresponding user name in the password file `htpasswd`.

`alias`
> This parameter describes the contact briefly. Spaces are allowed here.

host_notification_period
> This defines the time period during which messages on the reachability of a computer can be sent. Section 12.3 (page 267) shows how the time period details can be sensibly combined in the different object types. At the beginning, the value 24x7 (that is: always) is certainly not a bad option.

service_notification_period
> This defines the time period in which Nagios sends notifications to the relevant user service. The entry takes effect as a filter: the generated message is simply discarded here if it is sent outside the specified time period. If no further message follows, the contact remains uninformed. You must therefore think about combining individual time periods in various different definitions. Dependencies are described extensively in Section 12.3.

host_notification_options
> This defines what types of host messages the user should receive. The same options are used here as for the host parameter notification_options (page 64).

service_notification_options
> This parameter describes what types of service messages are received by the contact. The same five values are involved as for the notification_options parameter for service and host objects.

service_notification_commands
> This parameter defines which commands (one or more) take charge of notification. They must be defined as the command object type (see Section 2.9); basically any external programs can be integrated.

host_notification_commands
> Like the service_notification_commands this parameter specifies which commands are to be carried out to send the notification, although here it concerns the reachability of computers.

email
> This specifies one or more e-mail addresses (separated by commas) to which a message should be sent. The notification command can evaluate this value (one example of this is the command notify-by-email[6]).

can_submit_commands (Nagios 3.0)
> This controls whether the contact may execute commands via the Web interface. The value 0 forbids him from doing this. For Nagios

---

[6]   see table 12.1 on page 277

2.x, in general any contact may run commands via the Web interface (see Section 16.2.3, page 343). Beginning with Nagios 3.0, this parameter now also allows the definition of contacts with read-only permission.

Further information can be found in the Nagios 3.0 online help at `http://localhost/nagios/docs/objectdefinitions.html#contact`. In Nagios 2.x the file is called `xodtemplate.html`. The differences between Nagios 2.x and Nagios 3.0 are described in Section H.1.4, page 681.

2.8 The Message Recipient: `contactgroup`

The `contactgroup` serves as the interface between the notification system and the individual contacts. Nagios never addresses individual contacts directly in various object definitions, but always goes through the contact group.

Here Nagios also expects a name (`contactgroup_name`) and a comment (`alias`), which reveals to visitors of the Web site what the purpose of the group is. For members (`members`) of the group, you can enter an individual contact or a comma-separated list of several contacts:

```
# -- /etc/nagios/mysite/contactgroups.cfg
define contactgroup{
    contactgroup_name   localadmins
    alias               Local Site Administrators
    members             nagios
    contactgroup_members(*) contactgroup1,contactgroup2

}
```

The additional parameter `contactgroup_members` allows Nagios 3.0 to include further contact groups as members. In Nagios 2.x this parameter is not available.

2.9 When Nagios Needs to Do Something: The `command` Object

Everything that Nagios does is defined in `command` objects. In the example file supplied, `checkcommands.cfg` defines a broad range of commands which only need to be included. To do this, you just copy the file to the subdirectory `mysite`:[7]

---

[7] In Nagios 2.0 the example file lies directly in the directory `/etc/nagios`.

```
nagios@linux:/etc/nagios$  cp objects/checkcommands.cfg \
   mysite/checkcommands.cfg
```

The existing command `check_ping` illustrates the definition of this object type:

```
# -- /etc/nagios/mysite/checkcommands.cfg
...
define command{
   command_name check_ping
   command_line $USER1$/check_icmp -H $HOSTADDRESS$ -w $ARG1$ -c $ARG2$
-p 5
}
...
```

`check_ping` is the name by which the command will later be called when defining a service. `command_line` describes the command to be executed. Not only is the old plugin `check_ping` used here, but so is the more efficient `check_icmp`. The differences between the two are explained in more detail in Section 6.2 from page 108, but they use the same parameters to a large extent.

The identifiers used here, surrounded by dollar signs, are macros. Nagios recognizes three different types of macros: $USER*x*$ macros (*x* may take on values between 1 and 32) define the file `resource.cfg`. The macro $USER1$, which contains the path to the plugin directory, belongs to this.

The second group of macros are arguments which can be passed on when a command is called. These include $ARG1$ and $ARG2$.

The third group defined by Nagios includes the macro $HOSTADDRESS$, which references the IP address of the host in the host definition (that is, the parameter `address`). This type of macro is documented in the online help at `http://localhost/nagios/docs/macros.html`.

If you call the service `linux01,PING`, defined on page 66, as a `check_command`

```
check_ping!100.0,20%!500.0,60%
```

then `100.0,20%` will appear in $ARG1$, and `500.0,60%` in $ARG2$. To separate the command and the arguments to be passed on, the exclamation mark is used.

In theory, any programs at all can be started via the `command_line`, but Nagios expects a certain type of behavior here, particularly where the return value is concerned. For this reason, only Nagios plugins should be used (see Chapters 6 to 9).

2.10   Defining a Time Period with `timeperiod`

`timeperiod` objects describe time periods in which Nagios generates and/
or sends notifications. The included example files (Nagios 3.0: `objects/`
`timeperiods.cfg`; Nagios 2.x: `localhost.cfg`) contain a number of definitions that can simply be copied to your own `timeperiods.cfg` file.

In this, the definition of 24x7 is stated as "Sundays to Saturdays, from 0 to
24 hours in each case:"

```
# -- /etc/nagios/mysite/timeperiods.cfg
define timeperiod{
    timeperiod_name 24x7
    alias           24 Hours A Day, 7 Days A Week
    sunday          00:00-24:00
    monday          00:00-24:00
    tuesday         00:00-24:00
    wednesday       00:00-24:00
    thursday        00:00-24:00
    friday          00:00-24:00
    saturday        00:00-24:00
}
```

The times of day on individual weekdays can also be "cobbled together"
from time periods, separated by a comma:

```
define timeperiod{
    ...
    monday          00:00-09:00,12:00-13:00,17:00-24:00
    ...
}
```

If a day specification is omitted completely, the defined time period will not
include this day in its entirety.

Nagios 3.0 allows periods for individual calendar days to be defined:

```
2007-12-24    08:00-12:00
may 1         00:00-24:00
monday 2 may  00:00-24:00
monday 3      00:00-24:00
...
2007-12-24 - 2008-01-08 / 2  00:00-24:00
```

The first line names a fixed calendar day in the ISO format, the second line
describes every 1st May. The details in the third line refer to the second
Monday in May, and those of the fourth line, to the third Monday of each
month. The details can also be combined, in the form *from* - *to*. A subsequent / acts as a separator: the sixth line describes every second day
(/ 2) in the period from 24. 12. 2007 to 8. 1. 2008.

Section H.1.5, page 682 is also devoted to the extended format of Nagios 3.0. The complete documentation can be found in the Nagios 3.0 online help at `http://localhost/nagios/docs/objectdefinitions.html#contact`. In Nagios 2.x the corresponding file is called `xodtemplate.html`.

2.11 Templates

Nagios categorizes definitions as objects for a very good reason: their features can namely be inherited by other objects—a feature that can save a lot of time otherwise spent typing. You can define a so-called *template* and pass this on to other objects as a basis from which you only need to describe those details that are different.

This is best illustrated by an example (the parameters that are required for the use of templates are printed in bold):

```
# -- /etc/nagios/mysite/hosts.cfg
define host{
    name                    Generic-Host
    register                0

    check_command           check-host-alive
    max_check_attempts      3
    check_period            24x7
    contact_groups          localadmins
    notification_interval   120
    notification_period     24x7
    notification_options    d,u,r,f
}
```

With `name`, the template is first given a name so that it can be referenced later on. The following entry, `register 0`, prevents Nagios from trying to treat this template as a real host. In the example, the entries for the genuine host object are not sufficient; consequently Nagios would break off when reading the configuration file, with the error message that parameters are missing that are obligatory for such a definition, for example:

```
Error: Host name is NULL
```

All the other parameters involve settings that are to apply to all definitions dependent on `Generic-Host`.

In the actual host definition—in the following example for `linux03` and `linux04`—the parameter use references the template and thus takes over the preset values:

```
# -- /etc/nagios/mysite/hosts.cfg
define host{
```

```
   host_name                linux03
   use                      Generic-Host
   alias                    Linux File Server
   address                  192.168.0.1
}

define host{
   host_name                linux04
   use                      Generic-Host
   alias                    Linux Print Server
   address                  192.168.0.2
}
```

In this way you only need to complete those entries that vary in any way between the two hosts.

But parameters may also appear in host definitions that have already been defined by the template. In this case the definition at the host has priority, it overwrites the value from the template.

Templates created in this way can generally be used for all object types. Further information on their use can be found in the Nagios 3.0 online help at `http://localhost/nagios/docs//objectinheritance.html`.[8] In Nagios 2.x the file is called `templaterecursion.html`. The extended possibilities of Nagios 3.0, which only begin to play a role in more complex setups, are described by H.1.8 from page 684.

2.12 Configuration Aids for Those Too Lazy to Type

2.12.1 Defining services for several computers

You can simplify things a lot in the service definition by defining a service for several hosts, or even host groups, at the same time:

```
# -- /etc/nagios/mysite/services.cfg
define service{
   host_name            linux01,linux02,linux04,...
   service_description  PING
   ...
}
```

Specifying several hosts, separated by commas, ensures that Nagios defines multiple services in parallel. You can go one step further by specifying the * character instead of individual computer aliases. This will assign this service to all hosts.

---

[8] Locally in `/usr/local/nagios/share/docs//objectinheritance.html`.

A third possibility is an allocation in parallel via host groups:

```
# -- /etc/nagios/mysite/services.cfg
define service{
    hostgroup_name          linux-servers,windows-servers
    service_description     PING
    ...
}
```

In this case the parameter `hostgroup_name` is used instead of the parameter `host_name`.

2.12.2 One host group for all computers

The quickest way to describe a host group containing all defined computers is with the wild card *:

```
# -- /etc/nagios/mysite/hostgroups.cfg
define hostgroup{
    hostgroup_name    all-hosts
    members           *
    ...
}
```

2.12.3 Other configuration aids

In practice, the definition of services covering multiple hosts, described on page 76, is by far the most important. But there are other configuration aids based on the escalation and dependency objects, introduced on page 275 (see Sections 12.5 on page 282 and 12.6 on 285). There you can also use `hostgroup_name` instead of `host_name` (a list of host groups) or `servicegroup_name` instead of `service_description`. In addition you may set the value * for `host_name` and `service_description`, which covers all hosts or services.

2.13 CGI Configuration in `cgi.cfg`

In order for the Web front end to work correctly, Nagios needs the configuration file `cgi.cfg`. Nagios' example file can initially be taken over one-to-one, since the paths contained in it were set correctly during installation:

```
nagios@linux:/etc/nagios$ cp sample/cgi.cfg-sample ./cgi.cfg
```

Important: the file `cgi.cfg` must be located in the same directory as the file `nagios.cfg`, because the CGI programs have been compiled in this path permanently. If `cgi.cfg` is located in a different directory, the Web server must also be given an environment variable with the correct path, called `NAGIOS_CGI_CONFIG`. How this is set in the case of Apache is described in the corresponding online documentation.[9]

Out of the box, several parameters are enabled in the CGI configuration file. What these are is revealed by the following `egrep` command, which excludes comments and empty lines:

```
nagios@linux:/etc/nagios$ egrep -v '^$|^#' cgi.cfg-sample | less
main_config_file=/etc/nagios/nagios.cfg
physical_html_path=/usr/local/nagios/share
url_html_path=/nagios
show_context_help=0
use_authentication=1
...
```

main_config_file
> This parameter specifies the main configuration file.

physical_html_path
> This specifies the absolute path in the file tree to the directory in which the HTML documents—including online documentation, images, and CSS stylesheets—are located.

url_html_path
> This also describes the path to the Nagios HTML documents, but from the perspective of the Web server, not of the operating system.

show_context_help
> This option provides—as long as it is switched on (value 1)—a context-dependent help if you move the mouse in the Web interface over individual links or buttons.

use_authentication
> This option should always be switched on (value 1). Nagios will then only allow access to authenticated users. The authentication itself is configured in a `.htaccess` file in the CGI directory (see Section 1.5 on page 47). If this file is missing, and if `use_authentication=1`, then the CGI programs will refuse to work.

default_statusmap_layout and default_statuswrl_layout
> These two layout parameters describe forms of representation in the graphical illustration of network dependencies. Possible values are described in Appendix A.2 on page 608.

---

[9] http://httpd.apache.org/docs-2.0/env.html

`refresh_rate`
> This specifies the timespan in seconds after which the browser is instructed to reload data from the Web server. In this way the display in the browser is always up-to-date.

`authorized_for_all_services` and `authorized_for_all_hosts`
> In order for a specific user to be able to see all computers and services in the Web interface right from the beginning, without taking account of the allocation of hosts and services to the correct contact group, you should also activate the following two parameters in the file `cgi.cfg`:

```
authorized_for_all_services=nagios
authorized_for_all_hosts=nagios
```

> The Web user (and contact) `nagios` is now able to see all hosts and all services in the Web interface, even if he is not entered as the contact responsible for all hosts or services.

A complete list of all parameters can be found in Appendix A.2 on page 606.

2.14 The Resources File `resource.cfg`

Nagios expects to find the definition of macros, concerning how they are used to create command objects (Chapter 2.9 from page 72), in the resources file `resource.cfg`. This can also be use as supplied.

The location where Nagios should search for this file is defined by the `resource.cfg` parameter in the main configuration file `nagios.cfg`. It makes sense here to use the same directory in which `nagios.cfg` is also located.

In its "factory settings", `resource.cfg` defines only the $USER1$ macro, which contains the path to the plugins:

```
$USER1$=/usr/local/nagios/libexec
```

In total, Nagios has provisions for 32 freely definable $USER$x$ macros, where x can be from 1 to 32. These can be very useful in combination with passwords, for example: a password is defined via such a macro in the file `resource.cfg`, which may be read only by the user `nagios`. The defined macro is used in the actual service definitions, thus hiding the password from view of curious onlookers.

3 chapter

Startup

Once Nagios and the plugins are installed, Apache is set up for the Web interface, and a minimal configuration is created as previously described, operation of the system can get under way. If you have not already done so, it is recommended that you first spend a bit of time on the test for the check_icmp plugin, described in Section 1.4 (page 43), to check the initial configuration.

3.1 Checking the Configuration

The nagios program, which normally runs as a daemon and continually collects data, can also be used to test the configuration:

```
nagios@linux:~$ /usr/local/nagios/bin/nagios -v /etc/nagios/nagios.cfg
Nagios 3.0rc1
```

Copyright (c) 1999-2007 Ethan Galstad (http://www.nagios.org)
Last Modified: 12-17-2007
License: GPL

Reading configuration data...

Running pre-flight check on configuration data...

Checking services...
        Checked 2092 services.
Checking hosts...
Warning: Host 'eli-sw01' has no services associated with it!
        Checked 183 hosts.
Checking host groups...
        Checked 55 host groups.
Checking service groups...
        Checked 34 service groups.
Checking contacts...
        Checked 59 contacts.
Checking contact groups...
        Checked 7 contact groups.
Checking service escalations...
        Checked 0 service escalations.
Checking service dependencies...
        Checked 24 service dependencies.
Checking host escalations...
        Checked 0 host escalations.
Checking host dependencies...
        Checked 0 host dependencies.
Checking service groups...
        Checked 34 service groups.
Checking contacts...
        Checked 59 contacts.
Checking contact groups...
        Checked 7 contact groups.
Checking service escalations...
        Checked 0 service escalations.
Checking service dependencies...
        Checked 24 service dependencies.
Checking host escalations...
        Checked 0 host escalations.
Checking host dependencies...
        Checked 0 host dependencies.
Checking commands...
        Checked 105 commands.
Checking time periods...
        Checked 6 time periods.
Checking for circular paths between hosts...
Checking for circular host and service dependencies...
Checking global event handlers...
Checking obsessive compulsive processor commands...
Checking misc settings...

```
Total Warnings: 1
Total Errors:   0

Things look okay - No serious problems were detected during the pre-flig
ht check
```

Although warnings displayed here can in principle be ignored, this is not always what the inventor had in mind: perhaps you made a mistake in the configuration, and Nagios is ignoring a specific object, which you would actually like to use.

If you have not defined any service for a host, for instance, Nagios will issue a warning, as in the example above for eli-sw01. It is therefore recommended to define a "PING" service for every host, although this is not absolutely essential. Even if the same plugin, check_icmp, is used here as with the host check, this is not the same thing. The host check is satisfied with a single response packet—after all, it only wants to find out if the host "is alive". As a service check, check_icmp registers packet run times and loss rates, which can be used to draw conclusions, if necessary, concerning existing problems with a network card.

In contrast to warnings, genuine errors must be eliminated, because Nagios will usually not start if the parser finds an error, as in the following example:

```
Error: Could not find any host matching 'linux03'
Error: Could not expand hostgroups and/or hosts specified in service
(config file '/etc/nagios/mysite/services.cfg', starting on line 0)

***> One or more problems was encountered while processing the config
files...
```

Here the configuration mistakenly contains a host called linux03, for which there is no definition. If you read through the error message carefully, you will quickly realize that the error can be found in the file /etc/nagios/my-site/services.cfg.

In the definition of independencies (*host* and *service dependencies*; see Section 12.6, page 285) there is a fundamental risk that circular dependencies could be specified by mistake. Because Nagios cannot automatically resolve such dependencies, this is also checked before the start, and if necessary, an error is displayed.

When using the parents parameter, it is also possible that two hosts may inadvertently serve mutually as "parents;" Nagios also tests this.

3.2 Getting Monitoring Started

During the Nagios installation, the command

```
linux:src/nagios # make install-init
...
```

saves a startup script in the directory containing the boot-up scripts, usually /etc/init.d.

3.2.1 Manual start

If the configuration test ran without error, Nagios on Debian, Ubuntu, and OpenSuSE is first started manually with this script:

```
linux:~ # /etc/init.d/nagios start
```

Fedora provides its own startup mechanism:

```
linux:~ # service nagios start
```

If everything runs smoothly here (which can be checked by running the Web interface—see Chapter 3.3 on page 85), you only need to make sure that the script is executed at system start. The required steps, depending on the distribution, are described in Section 1.3 on page 43.

3.2.2 Making configuration changes come into effect

If configuration changes are made, it is not required, and not even recommended, that you restart Nagios each time. Instead, you just perform a reload:

```
linux:~ # /etc/init.d/nagios reload
```

This causes Nagios to reread the configuration, end tests for hosts and services that no longer exist, and integrate new computers and services into the test. However, with each reload there is a renewed *scheduling* of checks, meaning that Nagios plans to carry out all tests afresh.

To prevent all tests from being started simultaneously at bootup, Nagios performs a so-called *spreading*. Here the server spreads the start times of the tests over a configurable period.[1] Therefore, for a large number of

---

[1] The relevant configuration parameters are called `max_host_check_spread` and `max_service_check_spread`, see Appendix A.1, page 599.

services, it can take a while before Nagios continues the test for a specific service. For this reason you should never run reloads at short intervals: in the worst case, Nagios will not manage to perform some checks in the intervening period and will perform them only some time after the most recent reload.

Before being reloaded, the configuration is tested to eliminate any existing errors, as shown in Section 3.1.

3.3 Overview of the Web Interface

If you call the URL `http://nagios-server/nagios` in the browser when the Nagios daemon is running, you will be taken to the welcome screen shown in Figure 3.1.

Figure 3.1:
The start screen

The so-called "tactical overview" (Tactical Overview), which can be reached via the first `monitoring` link in the left menu bar, is shown in Figure 3.2. It summarizes the status of all tested systems.

Considerably more interesting in practice, however, is the display of the menu item Service Problems (Figure 3.3). It documents the services that are currently causing problems, those that are not in the OK status, in the very sense for which Nagios was conceived: to inform the administrator precisely of any problems.

Figure 3.2:
"Tactical" overview
of all systems and
services to be
monitored

Figure 3.3:
Nagios: summary of
all service problems

Current Network Status
Last Updated: Sun Jan 6 18:36:18 CET 2008
Updated every 90 seconds
Nagios® 3.0rc1 - www.nagios.org
Logged in as barthw@ELI.ST-ELISABETH.DE

View History For all hosts
View Notifications For All Hosts
View Host Status Detail For All Hosts

Host Status Totals

Up	Down	Unreachable	Pending
182	0	0	0

All Problems	All Types
0	182

Service Status Totals

Ok	Warning	Unknown	Critical	Pending
2018	44	6	15	0

All Problems	All Types
65	2083

Display Filters:

Host Status Types:	Pending	Up
Host Properties:	Any
Service Status Types:	All Problems
Service Properties:	Not In Scheduled Downtime & Has Not Been Acknowledged & Active Checks Enabled

Service Status Details For All Hosts
Entries sorted by service status (descending)

Host	Service	Status	Last Check	Duration	Attempt	Status Information
eligate2	VPN-Tunnel	CRITICAL	2008-01-06 18:33:07	0d 17h 28m 11s	3/3	Tunnels failed (2): wbb-eli vs-saar-eli
sap-57	SAPDialogNetworkTime	CRITICAL	2008-01-06 18:35:35	0d 0h 4m 43s	1/1	P10 p10ap057_P10_04 Dialog FrontEndNetTime 6846 msec
	SAPDialogResponseTime	CRITICAL	2008-01-06 18:35:37	0d 0h 4m 41s	1/1	P10 p10ap057_P10_04 Dialog ResponseTime 2285 msec
ELISAN01	DISK_D	WARNING	2008-01-06 18:34:29	0d 12h 18m 49s	3/3	D:\ - total: 2214,41 Gb - used: 1741,52 Gb (79%) - free 472,89 Gb (21%)
baaproxy	GATE-hspfire-Version	WARNING	2008-01-06 16:43:41	39d 10h 52m 38s	1/1	CRITICAL: hspfire is very old - 2007-07-06 (184d)/Build: 01101/V: 2.00/Kernel: 2.4/
	hspfire-Version	WARNING	2008-01-06 18:30:02	2d 17h 6m 16s	1/1	CRITICAL: hspfire is very old - 2007-07-06 (184d)/Build: 02096/V: 2.00/Kernel: 2.6/
bitproxy	GATE-Config-Version	WARNING	2008-01-06 16:43:41	1d 22h 52m 37s	1/1	WARNING: boot (2007-12-17_16:07) older than config (2008-01-04_18:13) / root@elix01 2008-01-04 18:13h
	hspfire-Config-Version	WARNING	2008-01-06 18:11:17	1d 23h 55m 1s	1/1	WARNING: boot (2007-12-17_08:00) older than config (2008-01-05_14:03) / root@elix01 2008-01-05 14:03h
dliproxy	GATE-hspfire-Version	WARNING	2008-01-06 18:24:07	47d 9h 12m 11s	1/1	CRITICAL: hspfire is very old - 2007-07-06 (184d)/Build: 01101/V: 2.00/Kernel: 2.4/
	hspfire-Version	WARNING	2008-01-06 18:32:25	0d 17h 3m 53s	1/1	CRITICAL: hspfire is very old - 2007-07-06 (184d)/Build: 02096/V: 2.00/Kernel: 2.6/

The first column names the host involved. If this has a gray background, Nagios can reach the computer in principle. If the host is "down" this can be seen by the red background. For services, red stands for CRITICAL and yellow for WARNING.

The second column provides the service name, the third column the status again, in plain text. Column four specifies the time of the last check. Column five is interesting—it shows how long the current status has been going on.

The sixth column with the heading **Attempt** reveals how often Nagios has already performed the test (unsuccessfully): 3/3 means that the error status has been confirmed for the third time in succession, but that the test is only performed three times if there is an error (parameter `max_check_attempts`, see Section 2.3).

Finally, the last column passes on the information from the plugin to the administrator, to whom it describes the current status in more detail. The above line in Figure 3.3 warns that only 21 percent of disk space is still available on drive D (service `DISK_D`) of the Windows server ELISAN01.

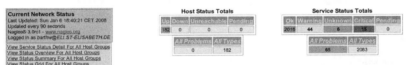

Figure 3.4:
An overview of all hosts (extract)

The `Host Detail` (Figure 3.4) and `Service Detail` overviews provide an overview of all hosts and services. In practice you will be looking more precisely for information, either via a single host or on a host group or service group. The name in question is entered in the **Show Host** search field. Figure 3.5 shows this using the example of the `elix01` host.

Alternatively you can search for the names of host and service groups. An interesting variation here is to have a *status grid* output shown via the link **Hostgroup Grid**, which displays an overview of all hosts and their corresponding services, together with the status of these (Figure 3.6). Through the color of the service (green/yellow/red), you can quickly see at a glance whether there are problems in the service group or host group that you are viewing.

Figure 3.5:
Services to the host
elix01 (extract)

Current Network Status
Last Updated: Sun Jan 6 18:42:33 CET 2008
Updated every 90 seconds
Nagios® 3.0rc1 - www.nagios.org
Logged in as barthw@ELI.ST-ELISABETH.DE

View History For This Host
View Notifications For This Host
View Service Status Detail For All Hosts

Host Status Totals

Up	Down	Unreachable	Pending
1	0	0	0

All Problems	All Types
0	1

Service Status Totals

Ok	Warning	Unknown	Critical	Pending
28	0	0	0	0

All Problems	All Types
0	28

Service Status Details For Host 'elix01'

Host	Service	Status	Last Check	Duration	Attempt	Status Information
elix01	HTTP	OK	2008-01-06 18:41:42	3d 9h 25m 55s	1/3	HTTP OK HTTP/1.1 200 OK - 1008 bytes in 0.005 seconds
	Mount_data_amdump	OK	2008-01-06 18:37:46	203d 10h 20m 59s	1/3	FILE_AGE OK: /data/amdump/.is_mounted is 77194208 seconds old and 1 bytes
	MySQL	OK	2008-01-06 18:38:04	22d 2h 9m 40s	1/3	Uptime: 1906559 Threads: 10 Questions: 66157673 Slow queries: 2 Opens: 206 Flush tables: 1 Open tables: 64 Queries per second avg: 34.663
	NRPE	OK	2008-01-06 18:40:37	238d 1h 44m 58s	1/3	NRPE v2.6
	NTP	OK	2008-01-06 18:39:27	238d 1h 32m 15s	1/3	NTP OK: Offset 1.277733827e-05 secs
	PING	OK	2008-01-06 18:41:57	328d 21h 6m 6s	1/3	OK - 172.17.129.2: rta 0.249ms, lost 0%
	PostgreSQL	OK	2008-01-06 18:38:33	3d 9h 24m 0s	1/3	OK - database nagdb (0 sec.)
	SMTP	OK	2008-01-06 18:38:47	3d 9h 23m 48s	1/3	SMTP OK - 0.049 sec. response time
	SSH	OK	2008-01-06 18:42:12	206d 22h 29m 15s	1/3	SSH OK - OpenSSH_4.3p2 Debian-9 (protocol 1.99)
	Service Latency	OK	2008-01-06 18:42:01	48d 9h 48m 32s	1/3	OK Service Latency = 199ms
	Users	OK	2008-01-06 18:37:48	214d 6h 55m 40s	1/3	USERS OK - 53 users currently logged in
	argus_logfile	OK	2008-01-06 18:37:46	94d 0h 53m 13s	1/3	FILE_AGE OK: /var/log/argus/argus.log is 0 seconds old and 138953516 bytes
	fs_a	OK	2008-01-06 18:38:07	203d 1h 43m 7s	1/3	DISK OK - free space: /net/elix01/a 25740 MB (26% inode=99%):
	fs_b	OK	2008-01-06 18:40:36	143d 10h 16m 28s	1/3	DISK OK - free space: /net/elix01/b 79784 MB (61% inode=99%):
	fs_root	OK	2008-01-06 18:41:42	238d 1h 47m 7s	1/3	DISK OK - free space: / 503 MB (55% inode=83%):
	fs_tmp	OK	2008-01-06 18:42:13	238d 1h 46m 27s	1/3	DISK OK - free space: /tmp 877 MB (96% inode=99%):
	fs_usr	OK	2008-01-06 18:39:06	238d 1h 44m 58s	1/3	DISK OK - free space: /usr 2596 MB (35% inode=79%):
	fs_var	OK	2008-01-06 18:38:33	35d 12h 12m 56s	1/3	DISK OK - free space: /var 7008 MB (36% inode=96%):

Figure 3.6:
The host group
eliLINUX in the grid
representation

Current Network Status
Last Updated: Sun Jan 6 18:56:03 CET 2008
Updated every 90 seconds
Nagios® 3.0rc1 - www.nagios.org
Logged in as barthw@ELI.ST-ELISABETH.DE

View Status Grid For All Host Groups
View Service Status Detail For This Host Group
View Host Status Detail For This Host Group
View Status Overview For This Host Group
View Status Summary For This Host Group

Host Status Totals

Up	Down	Unreachable	Pending
9	0	0	0

All Problems	All Types
0	9

Service Status Totals

Ok	Warning	Unknown	Critical	Pending
103	0	0	1	0

All Problems	All Types
1	104

Status Grid For Host Group 'eliLINUX'

Marienhaus GmbH/GF (eliLINUX)

Host	Services	Actions
ELIESX01	PING SSH	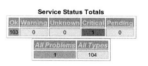
ELIESX02	PING SSH	
elibridge	NRPE PING SSH hspfire-Version proc_argus	
eligate1	DNS DSL-Link NRPE PING SSH hspfire-Version proc_argus proc_pppd proc_pppoe	
eligate2	DNS DSL-Link DynDNS-Registrierung GATE-x509cert NRPE OpenVPN Clients PING SSH VPN-Tunnel hspfire-Version proc_argus proc_openvpn proc_pppd proc_pppoe	
eligate3	DNS DSL-Link GATE-x509cert IPPP6-MOR NRPE OpenVPN Clients PING SSH VPN-Tunnel hspfire-Version proc_argus proc_otenvpn proc_pppd proc_pppoe	
eliproxy	DNS HTTP-mintra HTTP-mrelay NRPE NTP PING SSH clamav_database disk_var hspfire-Version proc_named proc_ntpd proc_squid unionfs_hidden www.hsp2000.de www.marienhaus-waldbreitbach.de www.st-elisabeth.de	
elix01	HTTP Mount_data_amdump MySQL NRPE NTP PING PostgreSQL SMTP SSH Service Latency Users argus_logfile fs_a fs_b fs_root fs_tmp fs_usr fs_var homedOffice tx-Load proc_apache2 proc_nidium procs proc_ndo2db-3x procs_nmbd procs_nipd procs_smbd procs_zombies	
mintra	HTTP HTTP_URL MySQL NRPE NTP PING SSH Users disks fs_root tx-Load procs procs_zombies	

Part II

In More Detail...

4

Nagios Basics

The fact that a host can be reached, in itself, has little meaning if no service is running on it on which somebody or something relies. Accordingly, everything in Nagios revolves around service checks. After all, no service can run without a host. If the host computer fails, it cannot provide the desired service. Things get slightly more complicated if, for example, a router that lies between users and the system providing services is brought into play. If this fails, the desired service may still be running on the target host, but it is nevertheless no longer reachable for the user.

Nagios is in a position to reproduce such dependencies and to precisely inform the administrator of the failure of an important network component, instead of flooding the administrator with irrelevant error messages concerning services that cannot be reached. An understanding of such dependencies is essential for the smooth operation of Nagios, which is why Section 4.1 will examine these dependencies and the way Nagios works in more detail.

Another important item is the *state* of a host or service. On the one hand Nagios allows a much finer distinction than just OK or "not OK;" on the other hand the distinction between *soft state* and *hard state* means that the administrator does not have to deal with short-term disruptions that have long since disappeared by the time the administrator has received the information. These states also influence the intensity of the service checks. How this functions is described in detail in Section 4.3.

4.1 Taking into Account the Network Topology

How Nagios handles dependencies of hosts and services can be best illustrated with an example. Figure 4.1 represents a small network in which the Domain Name Service on proxy is to be monitored.

Figure 4.1:
Topology of an
example network

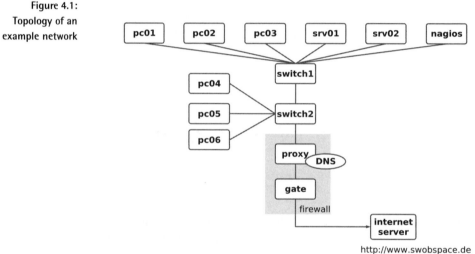

http://www.swobspace.de

The service check always serves as the starting point for monitoring that is regularly performed by the system. As long as the service can be reached, Nagios takes no further steps; that is, it does not perform any host checks.[1]

For switch1, switch2, and proxy, such a check would be pointless anyway, because if the DNS service responds to proxy, then the hosts mentioned are automatically accessible.

If the name service fails, however, Nagios tests the computer involved with a host check, to see whether the service or the host is causing the problem.

---

[1] Section 4.2 from page 95 deals with these *on-demand checks.*

If `proxy` cannot be reached, Nagios might test the *parent* hosts entered in the configuration (Figure 4.2). With the `parents` host parameter, the administrator has a means available to provide Nagios with information on the network topology.

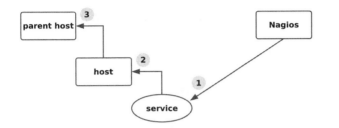

Figure 4.2:
The order of tests performed after a service failure

When doing this, the administrator only enters the direct neighbor computer for each host on the same path to the Nagios server as the parent.[2] Hosts that are allocated in the same network segment as the Nagios server itself are defined without a parent. For the network topology from Figure 4.1, the corresponding configuration (reduced to the host name and parent) appears as follows:

```
define host{
    host_name       proxy
    ...
    parents         switch2
}

define host{
    host_name       switch2
    ...
    parents         switch1
}

define host{
    host_name       switch1
    ...
}
```

`switch1` is located in the same network segment as the Nagios server, so it is therefore not allocated a parent computer. What belongs to a network segment is a matter of opinion. If you interpret the switches as the segment limit, as is the case here, this has the advantage of being able to more closely isolate a disruption. But you can also take a different view and interpret an IP subnetwork as a segment. Then a router would form

---

[2] The parameter name `parents` can be explained by the fact that there are scenarios—such as in high availability environments—in which a host has two upstream routers that guarantee the Internet connection, for example.

the segment limit; in our example, proxy would then count in the same network as the Nagios server. However, it would no longer be possible to distinguish between a failure of proxy and a failure of switch1 or switch2.

Figure 4.3:
Classification of
individual network
nodes by Nagios

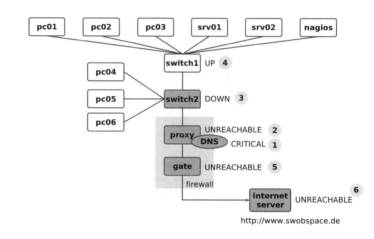

Figure 4.3:
Classification of
individual network
nodes by Nagios

If switch1 in the example fails, Figure 4.3 shows the sequence in which Nagios proceeds. First the system checks the DNS service on proxy and determines that this service is no longer reachable (1). To differentiate, it now performs a host check to determine the state of the proxy computer (2). Since proxy cannot be reached, but it has switch2 as a parent, Nagios performs a host check on switch2 (3). If this switch also cannot be reached, the system checks its parent, switch1 (4).

If Nagios can establish contact with switch1, the cause for the failure of the DNS service on proxy can be isolated to switch2. The system accordingly specifies the states of the host: switch1 is UP, switch2 DOWN; proxy, on the other hand, is UNREACHABLE. Through a suitable configuration of the Nagios messaging system (see Section 12.3 on page 267) you can use this distinction to determine, for example, that the administrator is informed only about the host that is in the DOWN state and represents the actual problem, but not about the hosts that are dependent on the down host.

In a further step, Nagios can determine other topology-specific failures in the network (so-called *network outages*). proxy is the parent of gate, so gate is also represented as UNREACHABLE (5). gate in turn functions as a parent; the Internet server dependent on this is also classified as "UNREACHABLE."

This "intelligence," which distinguishes Nagios, helps the administrator all the more when more hosts and services are dependent on a failed component. For a router in the backbone, on which hundreds of hosts and services are dependent, the system informs administrators of the specific disruption, instead of sending them hundreds of error messages that are not wrong in principle, but are not really of any help in trying to eliminate the disruption.

4.2 On-Demand Host Checks vs. Periodic Reachability Tests

As a matter of principle, Nagios performs service checks at regular intervals, with the exception of passive service checks. (See Section 13.2 on page 293.) Some slightly different rules apply for host checks, which play the main role. Nagios executes host checks when it needs them—that is, *on demand*—and uses them to monitor hosts where a service installed on them changes to an error state or hosts that lie in topological dependency to a failed host. A third way is via host dependencies, as described in Section 12.6.2 on page 289. On-demand host checks are a core function of Nagios, as this is the only way the system can precisely inform the administrator about a failed central switch, instead of bombarding him with thousands of error messages about unreachable services.

Planned host checks at regular intervals—*active host checks* in Nagios terminology —play only a minor role. Although Nagios 2.0 does provide a way to do this, Nagios 2.x only performs active host checks serially, which is considered to be a real performance killer.

In Nagios 3.0, checks are executed simultaneously, eliminating the drop in performance of earlier versions. If a Nagios version prior to 3.0 is used, you would be well advised not to use active host checks. However, in Nagios 3.0 regular host checks like these can help to improve performance, because this version caches the check results, if required, for a time that can be specified. Instead of running an on-demand check, Nagios then reverts to the cached result, saving considerable time—provided that this is still sufficiently up-to-date. The new logic for host checks in Nagios 3.0 is dealt with in Section H.7 on page 689.

The reachability of a host can also be regularly be checked in Nagios 2.x by using a trick in the shape of a ping-based service check (see Section 6.2 on page 108). Nagios performs service checks in parallel, so the serial brake in performance under Nagios 2.x is released. At the same time you will obtain further information such as the response times or possible packet losses, which provides indirect clues about the network load or possible network problems. A host check, on the other hand, also issues an OK even if many packets go missing and the network performance is catastrophic. What is involved here, as the name "host check" implies, is only reachability in principle and not the quality of the connection.

4.3 States of Hosts and Services

Nagios uses plugins for the host and service checks. They provide four different return values (see Table 6.1 on page 105): 0 (OK), 1 (WARNING), 2 (CRITICAL), and 3 (UNKNOWN).

The return value UNKNOWN means that the running of the plugin generally went wrong, perhaps because of wrong parameters. You can normally specify the situations in which the plugin issues a warning or a critical state when it is started.

Nagios determines the states of services and hosts from the return values of the plugin. The states for services are the same as the return values OK, WARNING, CRITICAL, and UNKNOWN. For the hosts the picture is slightly different: the UP state describes a reachable host, DOWN means that the computer is down, and UNREACHABLE refers to the state of nonreachability, where Nagios cannot test whether the host is available or not, because a parent is down (see Section 4.1, page 92).

In addition to this, Nagios makes a distinction between two types of state: soft state and hard state. If a problem occurs for the first time (that is, if there was nothing wrong with the state of a service until now), then the program categorizes the new state initially as a soft state and repeats the test several times. It may be the case that the error state was just a one-off event that was eliminated a short while later. Only if the error continues to exist after multiple tests is it then categorized by Nagios as a hard state. Administrators are informed only of hard states, because messages involving short-term disruptions that disappear again immediately afterwards only add to an unnecessary flood of information.

In our example the chronological sequence of states of a service can be illustrated quite simply. A service with the following parameters is used for this purpose:

```
define service{
    host_name               proxy
    service_description     DNS
    ...
    normal_check_interval³  5
    retry_check_interval⁴   1
    max_check_attempts      5
    ...
}
```

normal_check_interval specifies at what interval Nagios should check the corresponding service as long as the state is OK or if a hard state exists—

---

[3] As an alternative, Nagios 3.0 allows the notation known from the host definition, check_interval.

[4] For Nagios 3.0 you can alternatively use retry_interval.

in this case, every five minutes. `retry_check_interval` defines the interval between two service checks during a soft state—one minute in the example. If a new error occurs, then Nagios will take a closer look at the service at shorter intervals.

`max_check_attempts` determines how often the service check is to be repeated after an error has first occurred. If `max_check_attempts` has been reached and if the error state continues, Nagios inspects the service again at the intervals specified in `normal_check_interval`.

Figure 4.4 represents the chronological progression in graphic form. The illustration begins with an OK state (which is always a hard state). Normally Nagios will repeat the service check at five-minute intervals. After ten minutes an error occurs; the state changes to CRITICAL, but this is initially a soft state. At this point in time, Nagios has not yet issued any message.

Now the system checks the service at intervals specified in `retry_check_interval`. Here this is every minute. After a total of five checks (as specified in `max_check_attempts`) with the same result, the state changes from soft to hard. Only now does Nagios inform the relevant people. The tests are now repeated at the intervals specified in `normal_check_interval`.

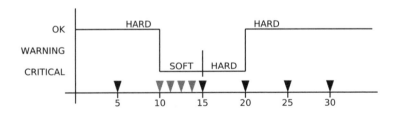

Figure 4.4:
Example of the chronological progression of states in a monitored service

In the next test the service is again available; thus its state changes from CRITICAL to OK. Since an OK state is always a hard state, this change is not subject to any tests by Nagios at shorter intervals.

The transition of the service to the OK state after an error in the hard state is referred to as a *hard recovery*. The system informs the administrators of this (if it is configured to do so) as well as of the change between various error-connected hard states (such as from WARNING to UNKNOWN). If the service recovers from an error soft state to the normal state (OK)—also called a *soft recovery*—the administrators will not be notified.

Even if the messaging system leaves out soft states and switches back to soft states, it will still record such states in the Web interface and in the log files. In the Web front end, soft states can be identified by the fact that the value 2/5 is listed in the column **Attempts**, for example. This means that `max_check_attempts` expects `five` attempts, but only two have been carried out until now. With a hard state, `max_check_attempts` is listed twice at the corresponding position, which in the example is 5/5.

More important for the administrator in the Web interface than the distinction of whether the state is still "soft" or already "hard," is the duration of the error state in the column **Duration**. From this a better judgment can be made of how large the overall problem may be.

For services that are not available because the host is down, the entry 1/5 in the column **Attempts** would appear, since Nagios does not repeat service checks until the entire host is reachable again. The failure of a computer can be more easily recognized by its color in the Web interface: the service overview figure on page 86 marks the failed host in red; if the computer is reachable, the background remains gray.

Service Checks and How They Are Performed

To test services, Nagios makes use of external programs called *plugins*. In the simplest case this involves testing an Internet service, for example, SMTP. Here the service can be addressed directly over the network, so it is sufficient to call a program locally on the Nagios server that tests the mail server on the remote host.

Not everything you might want to test can be reached so easily over the network, however; there is no network protocol for checking free capacity on a hard drive, for example. Then you must either start a plugin on the remote host via a remote shell (but first this has to be installed on the remote computer), or you use other methods, such as the *Simple Network Management Protocol (SNMP)*, to test the hard drive capacity.

The fact that different methods are available here does not make it any easier to get started with Nagios. For this reason, this chapter provides an overview of the common methods and attempts to develop an under-standing of the underlying concepts involved. Later chapters then provide detailed configuration examples.

Figure 5.1:
Nagios allows
different testing
methods.

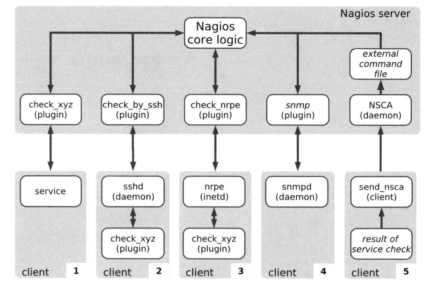

Figure 5.1 shows an overview of the various test methods supported by Nagios. The upper box with a gray background marks all the components that run directly on the Nagios server machine: this includes the server itself, as well as plugins and other auxiliary tools. This unit is in contact with five clients, which are tested in various ways. The following sections will go into somewhat more detail regarding the individual methods.

In order to monitor the network service on the first client (starting from the left) marked as `service`, the Nagios server runs its "own" plugin, `check_xyz` (Section 5.1, page 101). For the second client it starts the "middle plugin" `check_by_ssh`, in order to execute the plugin it really wants remotely on the client (Section 5.2, page 102).

In the third case the plugin is also executed directly on the client machine, but now Nagios uses the NRPE service, created specifically for this purpose. The query is made on the Nagios side with `check_nrpe` (Section 5.3, page 102).

The fourth method performs a query via SNMP. For this, the client must have an SNMP agent available (Section 11.1, page 228). Various plugins are available for querying data via SNMP (Section 5.4, page 103).

These four methods represent "active" checks, because Nagios takes the initiative and triggers the test itself. The fifth method, in contrast, is passive. Here Nagios does nothing actively, but waits for incoming information that the client sends to the Nagios server with the program send_nsca. On the Nagios server itself the *Nagios Service Check Acceptor*, NSCA, is running as a daemon that accepts the transmitted results and forwards them to the interface for external commands (see Section 5.5, page 104).

There are other ways of performing checks in addition to these. Usually a separate service is installed on the client, which is then queried by the Nagios server via a specialized plugin. A typical example here is NSClient/NC_Net, which can be used to monitor Windows servers (Section 20.2.1, page 464).

5.1 Testing Network Services Directly

Mail or Web servers can be tested very simply over the network, since the underlying protocols, SMTP and HTTP, are by definition network-capable (Figure 5.1, page 100, Client 1). Nagios can call here on a wide range of plugins, each specialized for a particular service.

Such a specific program has advantages over a generic one. A generic plugin tests only whether the corresponding TCP or UDP port is open and whether the service is waiting there, but it does not determine whether the correct service is on the port, or whether it is active.

Specific plugins adopt the network protocol and test whether the service on the port in question behaves as it is expected to. A mail server, for example, normally responds with a so-called *Greeting* after a connection has been established:

```
220 swobspace.de ESMTP
```

The important thing here is the number 220. A number in the 200 range means OK, 220 stands for the greeting. The check_smtp plugin evaluates this reply. It can also simulate the initial dialog when sending mail (in addition to the greeting), as shown in Section 6.3 on page 113.

It behaves in a similar way with other specific plugins, such as check_http, which not only can handle a simple HTTP dialog, but also manipulates HTTP headers where required, checks SSL capabilities and certificates of the Web server, and even sends data to the server with the POST command (more on this in Section 6.4 from page 118).

The package with the Nagios plugins, which is installed separately (see Section 1.4 from page 43), includes specific plugins for the most important network services. If one is missing for a specific service, it is worth taking a look at the Nagios homepage[1] or the Exchange for Nagios Add-ons.[2]

If no suitable plugin can be found in these locations, you can use the generic plugins `check_tcp` or `check_udp`, which apart from performing a pure port test, also send data to the target port and evaluate the response. (In most cases, this only makes sense if an ASCII-based protocol is involved.) More on generic plugins in Section 6.7.1 on page 132.

5.2 Running Plugins via Secure Shell on the Remote Computer

To test local resources such as hard drive capacity, the load on the swap area, the current CPU load, or whether a specific process is running, various *local plugins* are available. They are called "local" because they have to be installed on the computer that is to be checked.

The Nagios server has no way to directly access such information over the network, without taking further measures. However, it can start local plugins on the remote host via a remote shell (Figure 5.1, page 100, Client 2). Only the *Secure Shell*, SSH, should be considered for use here; the *Remote Shell*, RSH, simply has too many security holes.

To do this, the Nagios server runs the program `check_by_ssh`, which is given the command, as an argument, to run the local plugin on the target host. For this, `check_by_ssh` needs a way of logging into the target host without a password, which can be set up with *Public Key Authentication*.

From the viewpoint of the Nagios server, `check_by_ssh` is the plugin whose results are processed. It does not notice anything concerning the start of the secure shell connection and of the remote plugin—the main thing is that the reply corresponds to the Nagios standard and contains the status plus a line of comment text for the administrator. (See the introduction to Chapter 6 on page 105.)

Further information on the *Remote Execution* of plugins via Secure Shell is provided in Chapter 9 on page 205.

5.3 The Nagios Remote Plugin Executor

An alternative method of running plugins installed on the target computer via the secure shell is represented by the *Nagios Remote Plugin Executor* (NRPE). Figure 5.1 (page 100) illustrates this with the middle client.

[1] http://www.nagios.org/
[2] http://www.nagiosexchange.org/

The NRPE is installed on the target host and started via the inet daemon, which must be configured accordingly. If NRPE receives a query from the Nagios server via the (selectable) TCP port 5666, it will run the matching query for this. As with the method using the Secure Shell, the plugin that is to perform the test must be installed on the target host.

So all of this is somewhat more work than using the Secure Shell, especially as SSH should be installed on almost every Unix machine, and when it is used, enables monitoring to be configured centrally on the Nagios server. The Secure Shell method requires an account with a local shell, however, thus enabling any command to be run on the target host.[3] The Remote Plugin Executor, on the other hand, is restricted to the commands configured.

If you don't want the user `nagios` to be able to do anything more than run plugins on the target host without a password, than you are better off sticking with NRPE. The installation configuration for this is described in Chapter 10 on page 213.

5.4 Monitoring via SNMP

With the *Simple Network Management Protocol*, SNMP, local resources can be queried over the network (see also Client 4 in Figure 5.1, page 100). If an SNMP daemon is installed (NET-SNMPD is used extensively and is described in Section 11.2.2 on page 238), Nagios can use it to query local resources such as processes, hard drive, and interface load.

The advantage of SNMP lies in the fact that it is widely used. There are corresponding services for both UNIX and Windows systems, and almost all modern network components such as routers and switches can be queried via SNMP. Even uninterruptable power supplies (UPSs) and other equipment sometimes have a network connection and can provide current status information via SNMP.

Apart from the standard plugin `check_snmp`, a generic SNMP plugin, there are various specialized plugins that concentrate on specific SNMP queries but are sometimes more simple to use. `check_ifstatus` and `check_if-operstatus`, for example, focus on the status of network interfaces.

If you are grappling with SNMP for the first time, you will soon come to realize that the phrase "human-readable" did not seem to be high on the list of priorities when the protocol was defined. SNMP queries are optimized for machine processing, such as for a network monitoring tool.

If you use the tool available from the vendor for its network components, SNMP will basically remain hidden to the user. But to use it with Nagios,

---

[3] The Secure Shell does allow a single command to be executed without opening a separate shell. Usually, however, you will want to test several resources, so you'll need to run more than one command.

you have to get your hands dirty and get involved with the protocol and its underlying syntax. It takes some getting used to, but it's not really as difficult as it seems at first sight.

The use of SNMP is the subject of Chapter 11 (page 227); there you can learn how to configure and use an SNMP daemon for Linux and other UNIX systems.

5.5 The Nagios Service Check Acceptor

The fifth method of processing the results of service checks leads to the use of the *Nagios Service Check Acceptor*, NSCA. This runs as a daemon on the Nagios server and waits for incoming test results (see Figure 5.1 on the right on page 100). This method is referred to as *passive*, because Nagios itself does not take the initiative.

NSCA uses the interface for external commands used by CGI scripts, among others, to send commands to Nagios. It consists of a *named pipe*[4] from which Nagios reads the external commands. With the command PROCESS_ SERVICE_CHECK_RESULT Nagios processes test results that were determined elsewhere. The interface itself is described in more detail in Section 13.1 on page 292.

The main use for NSCA is *Distributed Monitoring*. By this we mean having several different Nagios installations that send their results to a central Nagios server. The distributed Nagios servers, perhaps in different branches of a company, work as autonomous and independent Nagios instances, except that they also send the results to a head office. This does not check the decentralized networks actively, but processes the information sent from the branches in a purely passive manner.

NSCA is not just restricted to distributed monitoring, however. With the program send_nsca, test results can be sent which were not obtained from a Nagios instance, but rather from a cron job, for example, which executes the desired service check.

Before you use NSCA, you should consider the security aspects. Because it can be used by external programs to send information and commands to Nagios, there is a danger that it could be misused. This should not stop you from using NSCA, but rather should motivate you into paying attention to security aspects during the NSCA configuration.

Further information on using NSCA, distributed monitoring and on security in general is provided in Chapter 14 on page 299.

---

[4] A named pipe is a buffer to which a process writes something and from which another process reads out the data. This buffer is given a name in the file system so that it can be specifically addressed, which is why it is called *named* pipe.

6

Plugins for Network Services

Every plugin that is used for host and service checks is a separate and independent program that can also be used independently of Nagios. The other way round, it is not so easy: in order for Nagios to use an external program, it must obey certain rules. The most important of these concerns the return status that is returned by the program. Using this, Nagios precisely evaluates the status. Table 6.1 displays the possible values.

Status	Name	Description
0	OK	Everything in order
1	WARNING	Warning limit has been exceeded, but critical limit not yet reached
2	CRITICAL	Critical limit exceeded or the plugin has broken off the test after a timeout

Table 6.1:
Return values for
Nagios plugins

continued:

Status	Name	Description
3	UNKNOWN	Error has occurred inside the plugin (the wrong parameter has been used, for example)

A plugin therefore does not distinguish by using the pattern "OK—Not OK," but instead is more highly differentiated. In order for it to be able to categorize a status as WARNING, it requires details of up to what measured value a certain event is regarded as OK, when it is seen as a WARNING, and when it is CRITICAL.

For example, apart from the response time, a ping also returns the rate of packet loss. For a slow network connection (ISDN, DSL), a response time of 1000 milliseconds could be seen as a warning limit and 5000 milliseconds as critical, because that would mean that interactive working is no longer possible. If there is a high load on the network connection, occasional packet loss could also occur,[1] so that 20 percent packet loss can be specified as a warning limit and 60 percent as the critical limit.

In all cases, the administrator decides what values shall serve as warning signs or be regarded as critical. Since all services can be individually configured, the values for each host may vary, even in the same plugin.

Plugins always have a *timeout*, which is usually ten seconds. This prevents the program from waiting endlessly, thus stopping a large number of plugin processes from accumulating at the Nagios host. In other ways too, a response time above 10 seconds makes little sense for many applications, since these interrupt connection attempts themselves after a certain time span, which has the same effect as the total failure of the corresponding service. Here the administrator can step in and explicitly specify a different timeout.

A further characteristic of all plugins is a text output, which Nagios shows in its overview. It is principally intended for the administrator, so it needs to be "human-readable." Nagios 2.x processes only the first line, and here the output may not exceed 300 characters. Nagios since version 3.0 no longer has this restriction. The output may have multiple lines and can be up to 8 KB in length (see Section 8.5.1, page 193). In the Web interface, however, Nagios 3.0 also displays only the first line. Simple plugins should therefore restrict their output to a single line, the multiple-line output is recommended only for special applications such as the plugin `check_multi` (Section 8.5 from page 191). The following form has become established for the text output:

```
TYPE_OF_CHECK STATUS - informational text
```

---

[1] ICMP packets are not re-sent; a lost packet remains lost.

In practice, the text output looks like this:

```
SMTP OK - 0.186 sec. response time
DISK WARNING - free space: /net/eli02/a 3905 MB (7%);
```

The above examples are from the plugin check_smtp and check_disk, respectively. In both cases, the type of check (here SMTP or DISK) is followed by the status in text form and then the actual information. Not all plugins adhere to this recommendation in their output. Sometimes the detail of the test type is missing, and sometimes even the status is missing.

Various plugins also provide performance information, which can be evaluated and graphically represented with external programs (see Chapter 19, page 403):

```
OK - 172.17.129.2: rta 97.751ms, lost 0%| rta=97.751ms;200.000;500.000;0
;pl=0%;40;80;;
```

As can be seen here from the example of the check_icmp plugin, the performance data follows the text output, separated by the pipe character |. These data do not appear in the Web interface.

check_icmp here provides two values: the medium reply time, rta (*Real Time Answer*), in milliseconds and the packet loss rate, pl.[2] For each variable, the plugin first displays the measured value (97.751 ms and 0%), followed by the warning limit (200 milliseconds or 40 percent) and the critical limit (500 milliseconds or 80 percent). The fact that only the first value in the rta or pl list is provided with a scale unit is specified by the Developer Guidelines—since the unit of a variable does not change, it only needs to be given once.

To keep the installation (Section 1.4 from page 43) as simple as possible, there are no manual pages for the plugins. Each of these programs must maintain an online help, which is displayed with the option -h or --help. Some plugins distinguish here between a short help (-h) and a long one (--help); it is therefore recommended that you always try --help as well.

This chapter introduces the most important plugins from the basic distribution of the nagios-plugins package, version 1.4.11,[3] which test network services. With their help, the Nagios server queries services on other servers. The description is restricted to the functionality that is important for normal operation. If you are interested in all the options, we refer you to the integrated online help.

---

[2] Short for *packet loss.*

[3] Versions prior to 1.4 should no longer be used. Some parameters have changed, and often performance data output is missing. In addition, plugin developers make great efforts to clean up existing errors and to continually improve the plugins.

6.1   Standard Options

Table 6.2 lists the options that are common to all plugins. The options in bold type must be known to all plugins. The key words not in bold type can be omitted by the programs, but if they are supported at all, they must be used in the sense specified.

If an option demands an argument, it is usually separated by spaces in the short form, but by equals signs in the long form. But for Perl or shell scripts in particular, not all authors adhere to these, so you have no option here but to take a look at the corresponding description.

Table 6.2:
Standard options of
plugins

Short form	Long form	Description
-h	--help	Output of the online help
-V	--version	Output of the plugin version
-v	--verbose	Output of additional information–this option may be given multiple times[4]
-H	--hostname	Host name or IP address of the target
-t	--timeout	Timeout in seconds after which the plugin will interrupt the operation and return the CRITICAL status
-w	--warning	Specificies the warning limit value
-c	--critical	Specifies the critical limit value
-4	--use-ipv4	Force IPv4 to be used
-6	--use-ipv6	Force IPv6 to be used

Thus it is not allowed to use -c, for example, for anything other than specifying a critical limit. How exactly -c and -w are used may, on the other hand, vary from plugin to plugin, because sometimes an individual value may be required, at other times, multiple values (see also the explanations on the plugin check_icmp), described below.

Most plugins also have the options -4 and -6, which was not necessarily the case prior to version 1.4.

6.2   Reachability Test with Ping

The classic reachability test in UNIX systems has always been a ping, which sends an ICMP echo request packet and waits for an ICMP echo response packet. The Nagios plugin package includes two programs that carry out

---

[4]   Whether this leads to more information depends on the individual plugin ...

this ping check: check_icmp and check_ping. Even though check_ping is used in the standard configuration, you should replace it with the more efficient check_icmp, which has been included since plugin version 1.4.

Whereas check_ping calls the UNIX program /bin/ping, which is why there are always compatibility problems with the existing ping version, check_icmp sends ICMP without any external help programs. check_icmp basically works more efficiently, since it does not wait for one second between individual packets, as ping does. In addition it evaluates ICMP error messages such as ICMP host unreachable, while check_ping discards these. check_icmp is backward-compatible to check_ping; this makes it easy to do without check_ping entirely and to replace it with check_icmp.

check_icmp measures the reply time of the ICMP packets and determines the proportion of packets that have been lost. If an error message arrives instead of the expected ICMP echo reply, this is evaluated immediately. Thus Nagios breaks off the test if an ICMP host unreachable message arrives.

check_icmp has the following options:[5]

-H address
: Without the host name or the IP address of the computer to be tested, check_icmp cannot work. With -H, multiple *host* entries can be separated, using spaces.

-w response_time,packet_loss_percent%
: This switch sets the warning limit for a warning. *response time* stands here for the desired response time in milliseconds, *packet loss percent* stands for the corresponding packet loss as a percentage. If you specify -w 500.0,20% the plugin will give a warning either if the response time is at least 500.0 milliseconds or if 20 percent or more of ICMP packets are lost.

-c response_time,packet_loss_percent%
: This switch specifies the critical limit in the same way as -w defines the warning value. The critical limit should always be larger than the warning limit.

-n packets
: With *packets* you can set the number of packets that check_icmp should use for each test. The default is 5 packets.

-i packet_interval
: This switch sets the time interval between two single packets that are going to the same host. The default is 80 milliseconds. It is specified as a floating point (e.g., -i 80.000).

---

[5] The online help check_icmp -h says that it knows some of the options in the long form as well, but these have not been implemented as of today.

-I *target_interval*

> This switch sets the time interval in which packets are sent to different hosts (provided that -H contains more than one host). The default is 0 milliseconds, meaning that packets to multiple hosts are sent simultaneously.

-m *number_of_reachable_hosts*

> This switch specifies the number of hosts that must be reachable for the plugin to return OK. This option allows a simple cluster check:

```
nagios@linux:local/libexec$ ./check_icmp -m 2 -H 192.168.1.9
\
192.168.1.11 192.168.1.13
OK - 192.168.1.9: rta 0.098ms, lost 0% :: 192.168.1.11: rta nan, l
ost 100% :: 192.168.1.13: rta 0.744ms, lost 0%|192.168.1.9rta=0.09
8ms;200.000;500.000;0; 192.168.1.9pl=0%;40;80;; 192.168.1.11rta=0.
000ms;200.000;500.000;0; 192.168.1.11pl=100%;40;80;; 192.168.1.13r
ta=0.744ms;200.000 ;500.000;0; 192.168.1.13pl=0%;40;80;;
```

> Of the three hosts specified, 192.168.1.11 (printed in bold) is not reachable. -m 2 requests only two reachable hosts; therefore, the result is OK. Without this detail, the result would be CRITICAL, because one host is not reachable.

-l *ttl*

> A value larger than 0 sets the TTL (*Time to Live*) of the IP packet. The default is the value 0, which means that the plugin leaves the choice of the TTL to the operating system.

-t *timeout*

> After *timeout* seconds have passed, the plugin interrupts the test and returns the CRITICAL status. The default is 10 seconds.

Like the program /bin/ping, check_icmp must also run with root permissions, which is why the SUID bit is set:

```
linux:~ #  chown root.nagios /usr/local/nagios/libexec/check_icmp
linux:~ #  chmod 4711 /usr/local/nagios/libexec/check_icmp
linux:~ #  ls -l /usr/local/nagios/libexec/check_icmp
-rwsr-x--x  1 root nagios 61326 2005-02-08 19:49 check_icmp
```

As a test, you should execute the plugin on the command line as the user nagios, since Nagios will later execute it under this account:

```
nagios@linux:~$  cd /usr/local/nagios/libexec
nagios@linux:nagios/libexec$  ./check_icmp -H 192.168.1.13 \
   -w 100.0,20% -c 200.0,40%

OK - 192.168.1.13: rta 0.253ms, lost 0%| rta=0.253ms;100.000;200.000;0;
pl=0%;20;40;;
```

check_icmp then sends the standard number of five ICMP packets on their way. Instead of an OK, it issues a WARNING as soon as the response time, averaged over all the packets, is at least 100.0 milliseconds or if 20 percent or more are lost—that is, at least one packet in five. For a CRITICAL status, the average response time must be at least 200.0 milliseconds, or at least two packets (40 percent of five) must remain unanswered.

6.2.1 check_icmp as a Service Check

In order for check_icmp to be used as a service check, you need to have a suitable command object. The file checkcommands.cfg, with check_ping, already has one for the ping service. We will just replace the check_ping plugin in it with check_icmp:

```
define command{
    command_name   check_ping
    command_line   $USER1$/check_icmp -H $HOSTADDRESS$ -w $ARG1$ -c $ARG2$
}
```

The macro $HOSTADDRESS$ provides the IP address of the address parameter from the host definition, and with the two freely defined macros $ARG1$ and $ARG2$, parameters can be taken over from the service definition, so that warning and critical limits can be set with these.

In the service definition (an extract of it is shown here)[6] for the PING service, the check_command entry, in addition to the name of the command object to be executed, now needs two arguments, which are entered after the command and separated by an exclamation mark:

```
define service{
    service_description   PING
    host_name             linux01
    check_command         check_ping!100.0,20%!500.0,60%
    ...
}
```

From the definition of the command object, you can see that the first parameter (100.0,20%) defines the warning limit, and the second one (500.0, 60%) defines the critical value.

6.2.2 check_icmp as a Host Check

To be able to use the plugin under the name check_host for host checks, a corresponding symbolic link to check_icmp is set:

---

[6] Like any other object, service definitions can also be defined in a file of your choice, from which Nagios loads object definitions. For the sake of clarity it is best to choose a descriptive name for the file, such as services.cfg, as in our example on page 56.

```
linux:~ #  cd /usr/local/nagios/libexec
linux:nagios/libexec #  ln -s check_icmp check_host
```

If it is called under its new name, check_host, the plugin modifies its behavior somewhat: it interrupts the test after receiving the first ICMP echo reply, because a single reply packet is enough to prove that the host "is alive." The same applies if the first response to be returned is an error message such as ICMP network unreachable or host unreachable—the host is then considered to be unreachable.

Host checks are defined like every other check. The only difference is that this test is specified during the definition of the host object (and not of a service object):

```
define host{
    host_name       linux01
    alias           Linux File Server
    address         192.168.1.21
    check_command   check-host-alive
...
}
```

The name used here, check-host-alive, can be freely defined and can be specified separately for each host. The definition of the command itself is made in checkcommands.cfg:

```
define command{
    command_name check-host-alive
    command_line $USER1$/check_host -H $HOSTADDRESS$
}
```

Host checks do not always need to be executed with check_icmp. You could just as well measure the refrigerator temperature or test, with the generic plugins for TCP or UDP (check_tcp and check_udp; see Section 6.7.1 from page 132), whether a specific port is open or not. The port scanner nmap, for example, uses TCP port 80 (HTTP).

The disadvantage of such a method lies in the fact that, apart from the host itself, another application also needs to run—that is, the Web server. In addition, the test of a specific application by no means proves that the computer is no longer reachable. A ping has the great advantage that the kernel replies to ICMP echo request messages itself, so that no application needs to be running for this. You should therefore change from ping to other host check methods only if there is a good reason to do so. One example might be a firewall that filters ICMP messages, and over which the administrator has no influence, but that does let through HTTP queries on TCP port 80.

6.3 Monitoring Mail Servers

A number of plugins are also available to monitor mail servers. The mail server itself (*Mail Transport Agent* (MTA)) is monitored by check_smtp, and the mail queue on the mail server can be checked with check_mailq. Since the latter test takes place locally, the plugin is described in the next chapter in Section 7.8 (page 180).

To monitor the *Mail User Agent* (MUA) protocols POP3 and IMAP —including the SSL variants, POP3S and IMAPS—the plugin check_tcp is used. check_pop and so forth are symbolic links to check_tcp, which determines which protocol it should test by means of the name by which it is called, and makes the relevant presettings.

6.3.1 Monitoring SMTP with check_smtp

The SMTP monitoring plugin check_smtp has the following options:

-H *address* / --host=*address*
> Details the computer on which the SMTP service should be checked.

-p *port* / --port=*port*
> *port* determines the ports, in case the mail service is not listening on the standard port 25. In this way the mail virus scanner Amavis (usually port 10024) can be monitored, for example. But this can normally be reached only from localhost.

-e *string* / --expect=*string*
> *string* defines the text which the mail server must provide in the very first reply line. The default setting for *string* is 220, with which the normal SMTP greeting begins, but there may be servers that have different settings. A wrong reply from the service monitored will generate a WARNING.

-f *address* / --from=*address*
> With *address* you specify a mail address that check_smtp then sends to the server with the "MAIL FROM:" command. This option is required to test a Microsoft Exchange 2000 Server.

-C "*mail command*" / --command="*mail command*"
> With -C you can send individual mail commands to the server, to extend the test slightly (see example below).

-R "*string*" / --response="*string*"
> If you send an SMTP command to the server with -C, you can specify the expected reply here instead of *string* (for example, 250). A "wrong" reply triggers a WARNING.

-S / --starttls
> The connection setup during the test uses STARTTLS.

-D *duration* / --certificate=*duration*
> The minimum duration in days for which the certificate used for STARTTLS must still be valid.

-A / --authtype=*authentication type*
> The authentication type for the SMTP-Auth procedure. The default is none (no authentication). The only procedure supported until now is LOGIN, which is based on user-password pairs.

-U / --authuser=*user*
> The user name for the SMTP authentication, if -A LOGIN is used.

-P / --authpass=*password*
> The accompanying password if -A LOGIN is specified.

-w *floating_point_dec* / --warning=*floating_point_dec*
> If the server takes longer than *floating_point_dec* seconds for the answer, check_smtp issues a WARNING.

-c *floating_point_dec* / --critical=*floating_point_dec*
> Like -w, except that check_smtp issues a CRITICAL after *floating_point_dec* seconds.

In the simplest case, you just enter the name or the IP address of the mail server:

```
nagios@linux:nagios/libexec$  ./check_smtp -H smtp01
SMTP OK - 0,008 sec. response time|time=0,008157s;;;0,000000
```

The plugin check_smtp sends back a HELO *hostname* after receiving the SMTP greeting, which should contain the reply 250.

The definition of the corresponding command object in this case appears as follows:

```
define command{
    command_name    check_smtp
    command_line    $USER1$/check_smtp -H $HOSTADDRESS$
}
```

To check the host object linux01 with this, it requires the following service definition:

```
define service{
    service_description    SMTP
```

```
    host_name              linux01
    check_command          check_smtp
    ...
}
```

Using the –C option, the SMTP dialog can be extended even further, roughly until RCPT TO:

```
nagios@linux:nagios/libexec$  ./check_smtp -H localhost \
   -C "MAIL FROM: <bla@gna.dot>" -R "250" \
   -C "RCPT TO: <bla@gna.dot>" -R "554"
SMTP OK - 0,019 sec. response time|time=0,018553s;;;0,000000
```

Such a test could be used, for example, to check the configuration of the restrictions built into the mail server (invalid domains, spam defenses, and more). The example checks whether the mail server refuses to accept a mail containing the invalid domain gna.dot (that is, in the RCPT TO:). The test runs successfully, therefore, if the server rejects the mail with 554. What check_smtp does here corresponds to the following mail dialog reproduced by telnet:

```
user@linux:~$  telnet localhost 25
Trying 127.0.0.1...
Connected to localhost.
Escape character is '^]'.
220 swobspace.de ESMTP
helo swobspace
250 swobspace.de
MAIL FROM: <bla@gna.dot>
250 Ok
RCPT TO: <bla@gna.dot>
554 <bla@gna.dot>: Recipient address rejected: test not existing top lev
el domain
...
```

If the mail server did not reject the recipient domain because of the configuration error, the reply would no longer contain 554 and the plugin would issue a WARNING.

In general you should remember, when checking restrictions, that the server rejects mails only after a RCPT TO:, depending on the configuration, even if the reason for this (a certain client IP address, the server name in HELO or the sender address in MAIL FROM:) has already occurred before this.

6.3.2 POP and IMAP

Four pseudo plugins are available for testing the POP and IMAP protocols: check_pop, check_spop, check_imap, and check_simap. They are called pseudo plugins because they are just symbolic links to the plugin `check_tcp`. By means of the name with which the plugin is called, this determines its intended use and correspondingly sets the required parameters, such as the standard port, whether something should be sent to the server, the expected response, and how the connection should be terminated. The options are the same for all plugins, which is why we shall introduce them all together:

`-H address / --host=address`
> This specifies the computer on which POP or IMAP is to be checked.

`-p port / --port=port`
> *port* specifies an alternative port if the plugin is intended to monitor a different port from the standard one: 110 for `check_pop`, 995 for `check_spop`, 143 for `check_imap`, and 993 for `check_simap` (see also `/etc/services`).

`-w floating_point_dec / --warning=floating_point_dec`
> The placeholder *floating_point_dec* is replaced by the warning limit for the response time in seconds, specified as a floating point decimal.

`-c floating_point_dec / --critical=floating_point_dec`
> This sets the critical limit for the response time in seconds (see `-w`).

`-s "string" / --send="string"`
> This string is to be sent to the server. In the default setting, none of the four plugins uses this option.

`-e "string" / --expect="string"`
> *string* specifies a text string, which must be contained in the response of the server. The default is +OK for (S)POP and * OK for (S)IMAP. This option may be given multiple times to search for different partial strings in the answer.

`-E / --escape`
> This switch allows the use of the escape sequences \n, \r, \t, or simply \ in the details for `-s` and `-e`. In all cases `-E` must be placed in front of the options `-s` and `-e` on which it is to have an influence.

`-A / --all`
> If you specify several reply strings with `-e`, the plugin with `-A` will only return OK if all required reply strings were found. Without this option, one string out of several sought is enough to trigger a positive acknowledgment.

`-M return value / -mismatch=return value`
> How should the plugin react if a returned string does not match the

statement in -e? The default is warn, which means there is a WARN-ING. With crit a false return can be assigned as CRITICAL, with ok as OK.

-q "string" / --quit="string"

This is the string with which the service is requested to end the connection. For (S)POP this is QUIT\r\n, for (S)IMAP, a1 LOGOUT\r\n.

-S / --ssl

The connection set up during the test uses SSL/TLS for the connection. If you call the plugins check_simap and check_spop, this option is set automatically. In order for a connection to be established, the server must support SSL/TLS directly on the addressed port.

STARTTLS[7] on its own does not support the plugin. With

```
./check_imap -H computer -s "a1 CAPABILITY" -e "STARTTLS"
```

you can at least check whether the server provides this method: the plugin returns OK if the reply string contains STARTTLS, or WARNING if it doesn't. But this is not really a genuine test of whether STARTTLS really does work properly.

-D duration / --certificate=duration

This switch specifies the number of days the certificate used for STARTTLS will remain valid.

-r return_value / -refuse=return_value

This switch specifies which value the plugin returns if the server rejects the TCP connection. The default is crit (CRITICAL). The value ok can be set in case no POP or IMAP service is available. The third possible value, warn, triggers a WARNING.

-m bytes / --maxbytes=bytes

This switch advices the plugin to close the TCP connection when the specified data amount (in bytes) has been received.

-d seconds / --delay=seconds

This switch waits for the specified time after a string has been sent to the server before the answer is searched for the string specified with -e.

---

[7] STARTTLS refers to the capacity of a service to set up an SSL/TLS-secured connection after a normal connection has been established—for example, for POP3, via TCP port 110. Every service that implements STARTTLS must have a suitable command available to do this. With POP3 this is called STLS (see RFC 2595). STARTTLS is used with SMTP, LDAP, IMAP, and POP3, among others, but not every server supports this method automatically.

Of course, all the other options of the generic plugin check_tcp (described in Section 6.7.1 on page 132) can be used with check_pop, check_spop, check_imap, and check_simap.

In the simplest case you just need to give the name of the computer to be tested (here: mailsrv) or the IP address:

```
nagios@linux:nagios/libexec$  ./check_pop -H mailsrv
POP OK - 0.064 second response time on port 110 [+OK eli11 Cyrus POP3
v2.1.16 server ready <1481963980.1118597146@eli11>]
|time=0.064228s;0.000000;0.000000;0.000000;10.000000
```

In each case the plugin provides just one line of output, which has been line-wrapped here for layout reasons. The details after the pipe character | in turn involve performance data not shown by the Web interface. The structure of performance data and how they are processed are described in more detail in Section 19.1 on page 404.

Implemented as a command object, the above check_pop command looks like this:

```
define command{
    command_name    check_pop
    command_line    $USER1$/check_pop -H $HOSTADDRESS$
}
```

As a service for the machine linux01, it is integrated like this:

```
define service{
    service_description    POP
    host_name              linux01
    check_command          check_pop
    ...
}
```

6.4 Monitoring FTP and Web Servers

The Nagios plugin package provides two plugins to monitor the classic Internet services FTP and HTTP (including HTTPS): check_ftp and check_http. When many users from a network are using Web services, a proxy is usually used in addition. To monitor this, you could also use check_http, but with the check_squid.pl plugin, The Nagios Exchange has a better tool available.

6.4.1 FTP services

The plugin `check_ftp` is, like the plugins for POP and IMAP, a symbolic link to the generic plugin `check_tcp`, so that it also has the same options. They are described in detail in Section 6.7.1 on page 132.

The generic plugin sets the following parameters if it is called with the name `check_ftp`:

```
--port=21 --expect="220" --quit="QUIT\r\n"
```

It does not send a string to the server, but it expects a reply containing the text 220, and it ends the connection to the standard port 21 cleanly with QUIT\r\n.

On the command line there is, as usual, a one-line reply (with line breaks for the printed version) with performance data after the | character that is not shown by the Web interface, (see Section 19.1 from page 404) for an explanation of this:

```
nagios@linux:nagios/libexec$  ./check_ftp -H ftp.gwdg.de
FTP OK - 0,130 second response time on port 21 [220-Gesellschaft fuer wi
ssenschaftliche Datenverarbeitung mbH Goettingen] |time=0,130300s;0,0000
00;0,000000;0,000000;10,000000
```

As a command object, this call appears as follows:

```
define command{
    command_name   check_ftp
    command_line   $USER1$/check_ftp -H $HOSTADDRESS$
}
```

A corresponding service definition looks like this:

```
define service{
   service_description   FTP
   host_name             linux01
   check_command         check_ftp
   ...
}
```

6.4.2 Web server control via HTTP

The `check_http` plugin for HTTP and HTTPS checks contains a large number of very useful options, depending on the intended use:

-H *virtual_host* / --hostname=*virtual_host*

This switch specifies the virtual host name that the plugin transmits in the HTTP header in the host: field:

```
nagios@linux:nagios/libexec$  ./check_http -H www.swobspace.de
HTTP OK HTTP/1.1 200 OK - 2553 bytes in 0.154 seconds
```

If you don't want check_http to send this, you can use -I instead.

-I *ip-address* / --IP-address=*ip-address*

Instead of *ip*, the host name or IP address of the target computer is given. For systems with several virtual environments, you will land in the default environment, and for most Web hosting providers you will then receive an error message:

```
nagios@linux:nagios/libexec$  ./check_http -I www.swobspace.de
HTTP WARNING: HTTP/1.1 404 Not Found
```

-u *url_or_path* / --url=*url_or_path*

The argument is the URL to be sent to the Web server. If the design document lies on the server to be tested, it is sufficient to enter the directory path, starting from the *document root* of the server:

```
nagios@linux:nagios/libexec$  ./check_http -H linux.swobspace.net \
    -u /mailinglisten/index.html
HTTP OK HTTP/1.1 200 OK - 5858 bytes in 3.461 seconds
```

If this option is not specified, the plugin asks for the document root /.

-p *port* / --port=*port*

This is an alternative port specification for HTTP.

-w *floating_point_dec* / --warning=*floating_point_dec*

This is the warning limit for the response time of the Web server in seconds.

-c *floating_point_dec* / --critical=*floating_point_dec*

This is the critical limit for the response time of the Web server in seconds.

-t *timeout* / --timeout=*timeout*

After *timeout* seconds have expired, the plugin interrupts the test and returns the CRITICAL status. The default is 10 seconds.

-L / --link-url

This option ensures that the virtual host in the text output appears on the Web interface as a link.

```
nagios@linux:nagios/libexec$  ./check_http -H www.swobspace.de -L
<A HREF="http://www.swobspace.de:80/" target="_blank"> HTTP OK HTT
P/1.1 200 OK - 2553 bytes in 0.156 seconds </A>
```

-a *username*:*password* / --authorization=*username*:*password*

If the Web server requires authentication, this option can be used to specify a user-password pair. The plugin can only handle *basic authentication*, however; *digest authentication* is currently not yet possible.

-f *behavior* / --onredirect=*behavior*

If the Web server sends a redirect as a reply to the requested Web page, the *behavior* parameter influences the behavior of the plugin. The values ok, warning, critical and follow are allowed. The default is ok, so the plugin will simply return an OK, without following the redirect. The plugin can be made to follow the redirect with follow. warning and critical with a redirect return the WARNING or CRITICAL status.

-e "*string*" / --expect="*string*"

This is the text that the server response should contain in its first status line. If this option is not specified, the plugin expects HTTP/1. as a *string*.

-s "*string*" / --string="*string*"

This is the search text that the plugin looks for in the contents of the page returned, not in the header.

-r "*regexp*" / --regex="*regexp*"

This is a regular expression[8] for which the plugin should search in the page returned.

-R "*regexp*" / --eregi="*regexp*"

This switch works like -r, except that the plugin now makes no distinction between upper and lower case.

--invert-regex

This inverts the search with -r or -R. The plugin now returns CRITICAL instead of OK if there is a match.

-l / --linespan

Normally the search for regular expressions is restricted to one line with -r and -R. If -l precedes these options, the search pattern can refer to text covering multiple lines.

---

[8] Posix regular expressions, see man 7 regex.

-P *string* / --post=*string*

Use this switch for data that you would like to send via a POST command to the Web server. The characters in *string* must be encoded in accordance with RFC 1738:[9] only the letters A to Z (upper and lower case), the special characters `$-_.+!*'()`, and the numbers 0 to 9 are allowed.

To send the text Übung für Anfänger ("Exercise For Beginners" in German) as a *string*, umlauts and spaces must be encoded before they are sent: `%DCbung%20f%FCr%20Anf%E4nger`.

-T *string* / -content-type=*string*

This specifies the content type of the header, if you are sending something with --post, for example, to the server. The default is `application/x-www-form-urlencoded`. A list of all content types is given in the file `/etc/mime.types`, and a description of the format can be found in RFC 2045.[10]

-m *min_bytes*:*max_bytes* / --pagesize=*min_bytes*:*max_bytes*

This parameter defines that the page returned must be at least *min_bytes* in size, otherwise the plugin will issue a WARNING. You can optionally use an upper limit as well—separated by a colon—to specify the size of the Web page. Now check_http will also give a warning if the page returned is larger than *max_bytes*. In the following example, everything is in order if the page returned is at least 500 bytes and at most 2000 bytes in size:

```
nagios@linux:nagios/libexec$  ./check_http -H www.swobspace.de \
    -m 500:2000
HTTP WARNING: page size 2802 too large|size=2802B;500;0;0
```

-N / --no-body

With this option the plugin does not wait for the server to return the complete page contents, but just reads in the header data. To do this it uses the HTTP commands GET or POST, and not HEAD.

-M *seconds* / --max-age=*seconds*

If the returned document is older than the date specified in the header (HTTP header field Date:), the plugin will generate a WARNING. Instead of seconds (without additional details) you can also use explicit units such as 5m (five minutes), 12h (twelve hours), or 3d (three days); combinations are not allowed.

-A "*string*" / --useragent="*string*"

This parameter explicitly specifies a user agent in the HTTP header,

___

[9] http://www.faqs.org/rfcs/rfc1738.html, paragraph 2.2
[10] http://tools.ietf.org/html/rfc2045#section-5

such as `-A "Lynx/1.12"` for Lynx version 1.12. Normally the plugin does not send this field.

`-k "string"` / `--header="string"`
: This specifies any HTTP header tags. If several tags are to be specified, they must be separated by a semicolon, as in the following example:

```
-k "Accept-Charset: iso-8859-1; Accept-Encoding: compress, gzip;"
```

`-S` / `--ssl`
: This forces an SSL connection to be used:

```
nagios@linux:nagios/libexec$ ./check_http --ssl -H \
    www.verisign.com
HTTP OK HTTP/1.1 200 OK - 33836 bytes in 1.911 seconds
```

The host `www.verisign.com` allows an SSL connection. If this is not the case, the server returns an error and the plugin returns the value CRITICAL:[11]

```
nagios@linux:nagios/libexec$ ./check_http --ssl -H www.swobspace.de
Connection refused
Unable to open TCP socket
```

`-C days` / `--certificate=days`
: Tests whether the certificate is at least valid for the given number of days. Otherwise a WARNING is issued.

`-4` / `--use-ipv4`
: The test is made explicitly over an IPv4 connection.

`-6` / `--use-ipv6`
: The test is made explicitly over an IPv6 connection.

The definition of a corresponding command object and its use as a service is no different from that based on other plugins; page 124 shows an example.

6.4.3 Monitoring Web proxies

Proxy test with `check_http`

A proxy such as Squid can also be tested with `check_http`, but this assumes that you have some knowledge of how a browser makes contact with the proxy. It does this in the form of an HTTP header:

---

[11] This can be checked in the shell with `echo $?`.

```
GET http://www.swobspace.de/ HTTP/1.1
Host: www.swobspace.de
User-Agent: Mozilla/5.0 (X11; U; Linux i686; de-DE; rv:1.7.5)
Gecko/20041108 Firefox/1.0
Accept: text/xml,application/xml,application/xhtml+xml,...
Accept-Language: de-de,de;q=0.8,en-us;q=0.5,en;q=0.3
Accept-Encoding: gzip,deflate
Accept-Charset: ISO-8859-15,utf-8;q=0.7,*;q=0.7
Keep-Alive: 300
Proxy-Connection: keep-alive
Pragma: no-cache
Cache-Control: no-cache
```

The decisive entries are printed in bold type. In contrast to normal Web server queries, the browser requests the document from the server via a GET command, not by specifying the directory path, but by using the complete URL, including the protocol type. In the `Host:` field it specifies the host name of the Web server that it actually wants to reach. With normal HTTP queries that go directly to a Web server (and not via a proxy), the host name of the Web server would be written there. This behavior can be reproduced with `check_http`:

```
nagios@linux:nagios/libexec$ ./check_http -H www.swobspace.de \
    -I 192.168.1.13 -p 3128 -u http://www.swobspace.de
HTTP OK HTTP/1.0 200 OK - 2553 bytes in 0.002 seconds
```

In order to set the `Host:` field in the header, you specify the name of a Web server with -H. The nonlocal URL is forced by a -u, and specifying -I at the same time ensures that the proxy is addressed, and not the Web server itself. Finally you need to select the proxy port, and the proxy test is then complete. Then `check_http` will send the following HTTP header to the proxy:

```
GET http://www.swobspace.de HTTP/1.0
User-Agent: check_http/v1861 (nagios-plugins 1.4.11)
Connection: close
Host: www.swobspace.de
```

This test does not use any implementation-specific information of the proxy, so it should work with every Web proxy.

The command object is defined as follows:

```
define command{
    command_name    check_proxy
    command_line    $USER1$/check_http -H www.googl
e.de -u http://www.google.de -I $HOSTADDRESS$ -p $ARG1$
}
```

The proxy computer `linux01` is then tested with the following service:

```
define service{
   service_description    Webproxy
   host_name              linux01
   check_command          check_proxy!3128
   ...
}
```

The parameter 3128 ensures that the command object `check_proxy` can read out the port from $ARG1$.

Proxy test with `check_squid`

The proxy check with `check_http`, introduced in the last section, works only if the desired Web page is available or is already in the cache. If neither is the case, this test will produce an error, even if the proxy is working in principle.

The plugin `check_squid.pl` uses a different method, but it is not part of the standard installation, and is to be found in the **Check Plugins** category, under **Software | HTTP & FTP | Squid Proxy**.[12]

It makes use of the *cache manager* of the Squid proxy, which is queried by a pseudo protocol. A command is sent in the form

```
GET cache_object://ip_address/command HTTP/1.1\n\n
```

to Squid and obtains the desired information. The plugin `check_squid.pl` uses the `info` command, which queries a range of statistical usage information:

```
user@linux:~$ echo "GET cache_object://192.168.1.13/info HTTP/1.1\n\n" \
    | netcat 192.168.1.13 3128
...
File descriptor usage for squid:
        Maximum number of file descriptors:   1024
        Largest file desc currently in use:     18
        Number of file desc currently in use:   15
        Files queued for open:                   0
        Available number of file descriptors: 1009
        Reserved number of file descriptors:   100
        Store Disk files open:                   0
...
```

It is targeted at the number of still-free file descriptors (the third line from the end); you can set a warning or critical limit for this value. The number of file descriptors plays a role when access is made to objects in the

---

[12] http://www.nagiosexchange.org/cgi-bin/pages/Detailed/1764.html

Squid cache at the same time. In environments with a high number of parallel accesses to the proxy, it is quite possible that 1024 file descriptors are insufficient. In smaller networks with just a few hundred users, not all of whom are surfing at the same time, the compiled-in value of 1024 will be sufficient.

Squid configuration   Normally Squid allows access to the cache manager only from `localhost`. So that Nagios can query it over the network, the proxy must be reconfigured accordingly:

```
...
acl manager proto cache_object
acl nagiosserver 192.168.1.9
http_access allow manager nagiosserver
http_access deny manager
cachemgr_passwd none info menu
...
```

The necessary changes to the configuration file `squid.conf` are printed in bold type, and the other relevant lines are already contained in the default file. The first line to be printed defines an access control list (*Access Control List*, `acl`) called `manager` by means of the internal protocol `cache_object`, so it refers to everything that accesses the proxy using the `cache_object` protocol. This is followed by an access control list for the Nagios server, based on its IP address, here `192.168.1.9`. The list name `nagiosserver` may be freely chosen here (as can `manager` in the first line). With `http_access allow`, `nagiosserver` obtains access to the cache manager (`manager`), before the line

```
http_access deny manager
```

prohibits access to all others through the `cache_object` protocol. Finally, `cachemgr_passwd` provides a password for the cache manager access. If you omit this, with `none`, then only selected commands should be allowed that have no potential to change things, such as `info` and `menu`, which shows all the things that the cache manager can do. After the configuration file has been modified, Squid needs to read it in again:

```
linux:~ #  /etc/init.d/squid reload
```

Applying the plugin   The test plugin `check_squid.pl` itself has the following options:

-H *address* / --hostname=*address*
>   This is the server on which Squid is to be tested, specified by IP address or FQDN.

-P *port* / --port=*port*
> This specifies the port on which Squid is listening. The default is the standard port 3128.

-p *password* / --password=*password*
> This is the password for access to the cache manager.

-w *free_descriptors* / --warning=*free_descriptors*
> This is the number of free file descriptors, where the plugin will issue a warning if the number drops below this. The default is 200.

-c *free_descriptors* / --critical=*free_descriptors*
> This is the critical limit for free file descriptors. If the number falls below this, check_squid returns CRITICAL. The default is 50.

When check_squid is run, it is usually very unspectacular:

```
nagios@linux:nagios/libexec$  ./check_squid.pl -H 192.168.1.13
Squid cache OK (1009 FreeFileDesc)
```

The matching command also presents no problems . . .

```
define command{
    command_name  check_squid.pl
    command_line  $USER1$/check_squid.pl -H $HOSTADDRESS$
}
```

. . . and the same goes for service definitions:

```
define service{
    service_description   Squid
    host_name             linux01
    check_command         check_squid.pl
    ...
}
```

6.5   Domain Name Server Under Control

Two plugins are also available for testing the *Domain Name Service (DNS)*: check_dns and check_dig. While check_dns tests whether a host name can be resolved, using the external nslookup program, check_dig allows any records at all to be queried. Both plugins are part of the standard distribution.

The situations in which they are used overlap somewhat. With check_dns, you can also explicitly query a specific DNS server, although this plugin is really for checking whether the name service is available generally.

6.5.1 DNS check with `nslookup`

The `check_dns` plugin checks whether a specified host name can be resolved to an IP address. Used locally, the plugin tests the DNS configuration of the computer on which it is run. For the name resolution, it uses the name server configured in `/etc/resolv.conf`.

The possible options are just as unspectacular.

-H *host* / --hostname=*host*
> This is the host name to be resolved to an IP address.

-s *dns-server* / --server=*dns-server*
> This switch explicitly specifies the name server to be used. If this option is missing, `check_dns` uses the name server from `/etc/resolv.conf`.

-a *ip_address* / --expected-address=*ip_address*
> The *ip_address* is the IP address that *host* should have. If the name service returns a different address, the plugin will raise the alarm with CRITICAL. This option makes sense only if it is necessary for the name server to provide a fixed IP address. Without this option, the plugin will accept every IP address as a reply.

-A / --expect-authority
> The name server specified with -s should answer the given query authoritatively, so the corresponding domain must act as a primary or secondary name server. If this is not the case, the plugin returns CRITICAL.

-w *floating point* / -warning=*floating point*
> This switch specifies the warning limit for the response time of the name server in seconds (specified as a floating point).

-c *floating point* / -critical=*floating point*
> This switch gives the critical response time of name server in seconds, specified as a floating point.

-t *timeout* / --timeout=*timeout*
> After *timeout* seconds have expired, the plugin interrupts the test and returns the CRITICAL state. The default is 10 seconds.

For the local test of the DNS configuration (not that for a name server) you just require a host name that is highly unlikely to disappear from the DNS, such as `www.google.com`:

```
nagios@linux:nagios/libexec$ /check_dns -H www.google.com
DNS OK: 0,009 seconds response time www.google.com returns 216.239.59.99
```

The corresponding command definition appears as follows in this case:

```
define command{
    command_name   check_dns
    command_line   $USER1$/check_dns -H www.google.de
}
```

The following service tests whether the name server configuration for the computer linux01 is functioning:

```
define service{
    service_description   DNS/nslookup
    host_name             linux01
    check_command         check_dns
    ...
}
```

6.5.2   Monitoring the name server with dig

The plugin check_dig provides more options for monitoring a name server than check_dns. As the name implies, it is based on the external utility dig, intended for precisely this purpose.

-H *address* / --hostname=*address*
> The *address* is the IP address for the DNS server to be tested. It is also possible to specify a host name (instead of an IP address), but in most cases this makes little sense, because this would first have to be resolved before it can reach the name server.

-p *port* / --port=*port*
> This switch specifies the UDP port to be used. The default is 53.

-l *hostname* / --lookup=*hostname*
> The *hostname* is the host name to be tested. If no particular computer is looked up, but only the functionality of the DNS server is to be tested, you should specify an address here easily reachable from the Internet, such as www.google.com.

-T *record_type* / --record_type=*record_type*
> This switch specifies the record type to be queried. The default is A (IPv4 address), but often NS (relevant name server), MX (relevant *Mail Exchange*), PTR (*Pointer*; IP address for reverse lookup), or SOA (*Source of Authority*, the administration details of the domain) are also used.

-w *floating_point_dec* / --warning=*floating_point_dec*
This switch sets the warning limit for the response time of the name server in seconds (floating point decimal).

-c *floating_point_dec* / --critical=*floating_point_dec*
This switch sets the critical response time of the name server in seconds (floating point decimal).

-a *address* / --expected_address=*address*
This is the address that dig should return in the *ANSWER SECTION*. In contrast to check_dns, check_dig delivers a WARNING only if the IP address does not match, but the reply itself has arrived within the given time limit.

-t *timeout* / --timeout=*timeout*
After *timeout* seconds have expired, the plugin breaks off the test and returns the CRITICAL state. The default is 10 seconds.

The following two examples check the name server 194.25.2.129, by requesting it for the IP address of the computer www.swobspace.de. The second example ends with a WARNING, since the reply of the name server for www.swobspace.de returns a different IP address from 1.2.3.4 in the ANSWER SECTION:

```
nagios@linux:nagios/libexec$ ./check_dig -H 194.25.2.129 -l \
    www.swobspace.de
DNS OK - 2,107 Sekunden Antwortzeit (www.swobspace.de. 1800  IN   A   21
2.227.119.101)
nagios@linux:nagios/libexec$ ./check_dig -H 194.25.2.129 -l \
    www.swobspace.de -a 1.2.3.4
DNS WARNING - 0,094 Sekunden Antwortzeit (Server nicht gefunden in ANSWE
R SECTION)
```

Example 1 is implemented as a command object as follows:

```
define command{
    command_name   check_dig
    command_line   $USER1$/check_dig -H $HOSTADDRESS$ -l $ARG1$
}
```

In order to test the specific name server linux01, you look for an address that Nagios should always be able to resolve, such as www.google.com:

```
define service{
    service_description   DNS/dig
    host_name             linux01
    check_command         check_dig!www.google.com
    ...
}
```

6.6 Querying the Secure Shell Server

Monitoring of Secure Shell servers (irrespective of whether they use protocol version 1 or 2) is taken over by the plugin check_ssh (included in the standard distribution). It is quite a simple construction and just evaluates the SSH handshake. User name and password are not required for the test.

Not to be confused with check_ssh is the plugin check_by_ssh (see Chapter 9 from page 205), which starts plugins remotely on a different computer.

-H *address* / --hostname=*address*
> Host name or IP address of the computer to which the plugin should set up an SSH connection.

-p *port* / --port=*port*
> This specifies an alternative port. The default is 22.

-r *version* / --remote-version=*version*
> The version details for the tested Secure Shell must match the specified text instead of *version*, otherwise a WARNING will be sent (see example below). If the version details contain spaces, the string must be enclosed by double quotes.

-t *timeout* / --timeout=*timeout*
> After *timeout* (by default, 10) seconds the plugin breaks off the test and returns the CRITICAL state.

The following example in turn tests the Secure Shell daemons on the local computer and on wobgate, to see whether the current SSH version from Debian Etch is being used:

```
nagios@linux:nagios/libexec$ ./check_ssh -H localhost \
    -r 'OpenSSH_4.3p2 Debian-9'
SSH OK - OpenSSH_4.3p2 Debian-9 (protocol 2.0)
nagios@linux:nagios/libexec$ ./check_ssh -H wobgate -r \
    'OpenSSH_4.3p2 Debian-9'
SSH WARNING - OpenSSH_3.8.1p1 Debian-8.sarge.6 (protocol 2.0) version mi
smatch, expected 'OpenSSH_4.3p2 Debian-9'
```

The latest version of SSH is not in use on wobgate.

In heterogeneous environments with various Linux distributions, you will usually use version checking "manually" only for plugin calls, and only rarely integrate them into the Nagios configuration. Instead, it is normally sufficient to use command and service definitions using the following simple pattern:

```
define command{
    command_name  check_ssh
    command_line  $USER1$/check_ssh -H $HOSTADDRESS$
}


define service{
    service_description  SSH
    host_name            linux01
    check_command        check_ssh
    ...
}
```

Otherwise you run the risk of having to adjust the version number in the command object after every security update.

6.7 Generic Network Plugins

Sometimes no plugin can be found that is precisely geared to the service to be monitored. For such cases, two generic plugins are available: check_tcp and check_udp. Both of them test whether a service is active on the target port for the protocol in question. Although this does not yet guarantee that the service running on the port really is the one in question, in an environment that one adminstrator looks after and configures, this can be sufficiently guaranteed in other ways.

Both plugins send a string to the server and evaluate the reply. This is at its most simple for text-based protocols such as POP or IMAP: these two "specific" plugins, which are tailor-made for these two mail services (see Section 6.3.2 from page 115), use nothing more than symbolic links to check_tcp, which has already completed the corresponding question-and-answer game with relevant default settings.

If you know the protocol to be tested and you configure a "quiz" that will fit this (no easy task for binary protocols), a check becomes considerably more than just a port scan. In this way the generic plugins can also be substituted for specific missing plugins.

6.7.1 Testing TCP ports

check_tcp is concentrated on TCP-based services. In line with its generic nature, it has a large number of options:

-H *address* / --hostname=*address*
    This is the IP address or host name of the computer whose port should be tested.

-p *port* / --port=*port*
This specifies the target port. In contrast to the plugins that are formed as a symbolic link to check_tcp, this detail is always required.

-w *floating_point_dec* / --warning=*floating_point_dec*
This sets the warning limit for the response time in seconds.

-c *floating_point_dec* / --critical=*floating_point_dec*
This sets a time limit like -w but specifies the critical limit value.

-s "*string*" / --send="*string*"
This is the string that the plugin should send to the server.

-e "*string*"/ --expect="*string*"
This is the string that the reply of the server should contain. The plugin does not restrict its search here to the first line.

-E / --escape
This allows the use of the escape sequences \n, \r, \t or simply \ for -s and -e. In all cases -E must be placed in front of the options -s and -e on which it should have an influence.

-A / --all
If you specify multiple reply strings with -e, the plugin with -A will only return OK if all required reply strings were found. Without this option it is enough for a positive return if just one of several strings is found.

-M *return_value* / --mismatch=*return_value*
How should the plugin react if a returned string does not match what is specified with -e? The default is warn, which means that a WARNING is given. With crit, a false return value could be categorized as CRITICAL, and with ok, as OK.

-q "*string*" / --quit="*string*"
This is the string that requests the service to end the connection.

-m *bytes* / --maxbytes=*bytes*
The plugin closes the connection if it has received more than *bytes*.

-d *floating_point_decimal* / --delay=*floating_point_decimal*
This is the time period in seconds between sending a string and checking the response.

-t *timeout* / --timeout=*timeout*
After *timeout* (the default is 10) seconds the plugin stops the test and returns the CRITICAL status.

-j / --jail

> Setting this displays the TCP output. For text-based protocols such as POP or IMAP, this is usually "human-readable", but for binary protocols you generally cannot decipher the output, so that -j is appropriate.

-r *return_value* / --refuse=*return_value*

> This switch specifies what value the plugin returns if the server rejects the TCP connection. The default is crit (CRITICAL). With ok as the *return_value*, you can test whether a service is available that should not be accessible from outside. The third possible value, warn, ensures that a WARNING is given.

-D *days* / --certificate=*days*

> This is the time span in days for which a server certificate must at least be valid for the test to run successfully. It is relevant only for SSL connections. Note that there is a danger of confusion: in the check_http plugin this same option is -C (see page 123). If the time span drops below the time period specified for the server certificate, the plugin returns a WARNING.

-S / --ssl

> SSL/TLS should be used for the connection. The plugin cannot handle STARTTLS[13].

The following example checks on the command line whether a service on the target host 192.168.1.89 is active on port 5631, the TCP port for the Windows remote-control software, PCAnywhere:

```
nagios@linux:nagios/libexec$ ./check_tcp -H 192.168.1.89 -p 5631
TCP OK - 0,061 second response time on port 5631 | time=0,060744s;0,
000000;0,000000;0,000000;10,000000
```

For all services for which the computer name and port detail are sufficient as parameters for the test, the command object is as follows:

```
define command{
    command_name   check_tcp
    command_line   $USER1$/check_tcp -H $HOSTADDRESS$ -p $ARG1$
}
```

To monitor the said PCAnywhere on the machine Win01, the following service definition would be used:

[13] See footnote on page 117.

```
define service{
   service_description pcAnywhere
   host_name           Win01
   check_command       check_tcp!5631
   ...
}
```

6.7.2 Monitoring UDP ports

It is not so simple to monitor UDP ports, since there is no standard connection setup, such as the *three-way-handshake* for TCP, in the course of which a connection is opened, but data is not yet transferred. For a stateless protocol such as UDP there is no regulated sequence for sent and received packets. The server can reply to a UDP packet sent by the client with a UDP packet, but it is not obliged to do this.

If you find an unoccupied port, the requested host normally sends back an ICMP port unreachable message, which evaluates the plugin. If there is no reply, there are two possibilities: either the service on the target port is not reacting to the request, or a firewall is filtering out network traffic (either the UDP traffic itself or the ICMP message). This is why you can never be sure with UDP whether the server behind a particular port really is offering a service or not.

In order to force a positive response where possible, you normally have to send data to the server, with the option -s, containing some kind of meaningful message for the underlying protocol. Most services will not respond to empty or meaningless packets. This is why you cannot avoid getting to grips with the corresponding protocol, since you will otherwise not be in a position to send meaningful data to the server, to prompt it into giving a reply at all.

Ever since Nagios plugin version 1.4.4, check_udp has been a symlink to check_tcp, so that check_udp has the same options as check_tcp (see page 132). -p *port*, -s *string*, and -e *string* are obligatory entries, even though the integrated online help declares these to be optional.

The following example tests whether a service on the target host 192.168.1.13 is active on the time server (NTP) Port 123. The NTP daemon only replies to packets containing a meaningful request (e.g., to ones whose contents begin with w):

```
nagios@linux:nagios/libexec$ ./check_udp -H 192.168.1.13 -p 123 -s "w" \
   -e ""
UDP OK - 0.001 second response time on port 123 []|time=0.000586s;;;0.00
0000;10.000000
```

The reply remains empty, so the reply string is specified as -e "". The NTP server does not respond to packets with data not in the protocol form. Normally NTP expects a relatively complex packet[14] containing various information. The w used here was found out by trial and error: It does not contain really meaningful data, but it does provoke the server into giving a response.

The command line command shown above is implemented as follows as a command object:

```
define command{
    command_name   check_udp
    command_line   $USER1$/check_udp -H $HOSTADDRESS$ -p $ARG1$ -s $ARG2$
}
```

Here we pass on the port as the first argument; all the other switches of the plugin are accessed through $ARG2$.

Checking an NTP time server is then taken over by the following service definition:

```
define service{
    service_description
    host_name            timesrv
    check_command        check_tcp!123!-s "w" -e ""
    ...
}
```

As in the command line example, Nagios sends the string w to the service to provoke a positive response.

6.8 Monitoring Databases

Nagios provides three plugins for monitoring databases: check_pgsql for PostgreSQL, check_mysql for MySQL, and check_oracle for Oracle. The last will not be covered in this book.[15] They all have in common the fact that they can be used both locally and over the network. The latter has the advantage that the plugin in question does not have to be installed on the database server. The disadvantage is that you have to get more deeply involved with the subject of authentication, because configuring a secure *local* access to the database is somewhat more simple.

---

[14] The protocol version NTPv3 is described in RFC 1305: http://rfc.sunsite.dk/rfc/rfc1305.html.

[15] The plugin check_oracle assumes the installation of an Oracle Full Client on the Nagios server; it does not work together with the Instant Client and expects its users to have an extensive knowledge of Oracle. To explain all this here is far beyond the scope of this book.

For less critical systems, network access by the plugin can be done without a password. To do this, the user `nagios` is set up with its own database in the database management system to be tested, which does not contain any (important) data. Areas accessed by this user can be isolated from other data, stored in the DBMS, through the database's own permissions system.

Of course, there is nothing stopping you from setting up a password for the user `nagios`. But if you cannot make use of SSL-encrypted connections, this will be transmitted in plain text for most database connections. In addition, it is stored unencrypted in the Nagios configuration files. In this respect the password does offer some protection, but it is not really that secure.

As an additional measure, you should certainly restrict the IP address from which a user `nagios` user can access the database on the Nagios server.

The plugins introduced here have only read access to the database. `check_mysql` additionally allows a pure connection check, without read access. A write access to the database is not available in any of the plugins mentioned. For Oracle there is a plugin on Nagios Exchange[16] called `check_oracle_writeaccess.sh`, which also tests the writeability of the database.

6.8.1 PostgreSQL

With the `check_pgsql` plugin you can establish both local and network connections to the database. Local connections are handled by PostgreSQL via a Unix socket, which is a purely local mechanism. An IP connection is set up by `check_pgsql` if a target host is explicitly passed to it. The plugin performs a pure connection test to a test database but does not read any data from it.

In order that PostgreSQL can be reached over the network, you must start the `postmaster` program, either with `-i`, or by setting the parameter `tcpip_socket` in the configuration file `postgresql.conf` to the value `true`.

Configuring a monitor-friendly DBMS

In order to separate the data that the user `nagios` (executing the plugin) gets to see more clearly from other data, you first set up a database user with the same name, and a database to which this user is given access:

```
postgres@linux:~$  createuser --no-adduser --no-createdb nagios
postgres@linux:~$  createdb --owner nagios nagdb
```

Of particular importance when creating a database user with the command `createuser` is the option `--no-adduser`. To PostgreSQL, the ability to be

---

[16] http://www.nagiosexchange.org/153;3

allowed to create users automatically means that you are the superuser, who can easily get round the various permissions set.[17] But `nagios` should not be given superuser permissions under any circumstances.

`createdb` finally creates a new, empty database called `nagdb`, which belongs to `nagios`.

Access to the database can be restricted in the file `pg_hba.conf`. Depending on the distribution, this can be found either in `/etc/postgresql` or in the subdirectory `./data` of the database itself (for example, `/var/lib/pgsql/data` for SUSE). The following extract restricts access by the database user `nagios` to a specific database and to the IP address of the Nagios server (instead of the IP address to be completed by *ip-nagios*):

```
#type db      user     ip-address   ip-mask          method options
local nagdb   nagios                                 ident sameuser
host  nagdb   nagios   ip-nagios    255.255.255.255  ident sameuser
```

The first line is a comment describing the function of the columns. The second line allows the database user `nagios` access to the database `nagdb` over a local connection. Even though the authentication method here is called `ident`, you do not need a local ident daemon for Linux and BSD variants (NetBSD, FreeBSD, etc.).

The last line describes the same restriction, but this time it is for a TCP/IP connection to the Nagios server. But now PostgreSQL asks the ident daemon of the Nagios server which user has set off the connection request. This means that an ident daemon must be installed on *ip-nagios*. In this way the DBMS tests whether the user initiating the connection from the Nagios server really is called `nagios`. It will not permit another user (or a connection from a different host).

Normally the ident protocol is only partially suited for user authentication. But in the case of the Nagios server you can assume that a host is involved that is under the control of the administrator who can ensure that an ident daemon really is running on port 113.

There is a huge range of different ident daemons. `pidentd`[18] is widely used and is included in most Linux distributions. Normally it is already preconfigured and just needs to be started. But how it is started depends on the distribution; usually `inetd` or `xinetd` takes over this task. A glance at the documentation (should) put you straight.

After modifying the configuration in `pg_hba.conf` you must stop the DBMS so that it can reload the configuration files. This is best done with the command

```
linux:~ #  /etc/init.d/postgresql reload
```

---

[17] Permissions in PostgreSQL are given by the database command GRANT.

[18] http://www.lysator.liu.se/~pen/pidentd/.

(a restart is not necessary). If the configuration of the inetd/xinetd was modified, this daemon is reinitialized in the same way.

The test plugin check_pgsql

check_pgsql has the following options:

-H *address* / --hostname=*address*
> If given this option, the plugin establishes a TCP/IP connection instead of making contact with a local DBMS through a Unix socket.

-P *port* / --port=*port*
> In contrast to the plugins discussed until now, check_pgsql uses a capital P to specify the port on which PostgreSQL is running. In its default value it is connected to port 5432. This option is only useful if PostgreSQL allows TCP/IP connections.

-d *database* / --database=*database*
> Specifies the name of the database to which the plugin should connect. If this detail is missing, it uses the standard database template1.

-w *floating_point_dec* / --warning=*floating_point_dec*
> This is the warning time in seconds for the performance time for the test.

-c *floating_point_dec* / --critical=*floating_point_dec*
> This is the critical limit for the performance time of the test in seconds.

-l *user* / --logname=*user*
> This is the name of the user who should establish contact to the database.

-p *passwd* / --password=*passwd*
> This switch sets the password for access to the database. Since this must be stored in plain text in the service definition, a potential security problem is involved. It is preferable to explicitly define a restricted, password-free access to the database in the PostgreSQL configuration for the user nagios.

-t *timeout* / --timeout=*timeout*
> After 10 seconds have expired, the plugin stops the test and returns the CRITICAL status. This option allows the default value to be changed.

To test the reachability across the network of the database nagdb set up specially for this purpose, this is passed on as a parameter together with the target host (here: linux01):

```
nagios@linux:nagios/libexec$ ./check_pgsql -H linux01 -d nagdb
CRITICAL - no connection to 'nagdb' (FATAL: IDENT authentication failed
for user "nagios")
```

The fact that the check went wrong in the example is clearly due to the ident authentication. This happens, for example, if you forget to reload the ident daemon after the configuration has been modified. Once the error has been rectified, the plugin—hopefully—will work better:

```
nagios@linux:nagios/libexec$ ./check_pgsql -H linux01 -d nagdb
OK - database nagdb (0 sec.)|time=0,000000s;2,000000;8,000000;0,000000
```

If the database parameter is omitted, check_pgsql will address the database template1:

```
nagios@linux:nagios/libexec$ ./check_pgsql -H linux01
CRITICAL - no connection to 'template1' (FATAL: no pg_hba.conf entry fo
r host "172.17.129.2", user "nagios", database "template1", SSL off)
```

A similar result is obtained if you run the test with the correct database, but with the wrong user:

```
wob@linux:nagios/libexec$ ./check_pgsql -H linux01 -d nagdb
CRITICAL - no connection to 'nagdb' (FATAL: no pg_hba.conf entry for ho
st "172.17.129.2", user "wob", database "nagdb", SSL off)
```

You should certainly run the last two tests, just to check that the PostgreSQL database really does reject corresponding requests. Otherwise you will have a security leak, and we recommend that you remove settings in the configuration that are too generous.

If you have created a separate database for the check, there is no reason why you shouldn't write this explicitly in the command definition, instead of using parameters, with $ARG1$:

```
define command{
    command_name    check_pgsql
    command_line    $USER1$/check_pgsql -H $HOSTADDRESS$ -d nagdb
}
```

Then the service definition for linux01 is as simple as this:

```
define service{
    service_description    PostgreSQL
    host_name              linux01
    check_command          check_pgsql
    ...
}
```

6.8.2 MySQL

With the `check_mysql` plugin, MySQL databases can be tested both locally and across the network. For local connections, it makes contact via a Unix socket, and not via a real network connection.

MySQL configuration

In order that the database can be reached across the network, the `skip-networking` option in the configuration file `my.cnf` must be commented out. The database should then be running on TCP port 3306, which can be tested with `netstat -ant`, for example:

```
user@linux:~$ netstat -ant | grep 3306
tcp   0   0 0.0.0.0:3306   0.0.0.0:*   LISTEN
```

To set up the password-free access to the database relatively securely, a separate `nagdb` database is created here that does not contain any critical data, and for which the user `nagios` is given restricted access from the Nagios server. To do this, you connect yourself, as the database user `root`, to the database `mysql`, and there you create the database `nagdb`:

```
user@linux:~$  mysql --user=root mysql
mysql> CREATE DATABASE nagdb;
```

If the command `mysql --user=root mysql` functions without the need to enter a `root` password, then you have a serious security problem. In that case, anyone—at least from the database server—is able to obtain full access to the database. If this is the case, it is essential that you read the security notes in the MySQL documentation.[19]

Recreating a user and the access restrictions can be done in one and the same step:

```
mysql> GRANT select ON nagdb.* TO nagios@ip-nagios;
```

The command sets up the user `nagios`, if it does not exist. It may only accept connections from the Nagios server with the IP address *ip-nagios* and obtains access to all tables in the database `nagdb`, but may execute only the SELECT command there (no INSERT, no UPDATE or DELETE); that is, user `nagios` only has read access.

---

[19] To be found at `http://dev.mysql.com/doc/mysql/de/Security.html`.

The test plugin `check_mysql`

`check_mysql` has fewer options than its PostgreSQL equivalent—apart from -H, it does not implement any standard flags and has neither a warning not a critical limit for the performance time of the test. For the database-specific options, it uses the same syntax as `check_pgsql`, except for the user entry:

-H *address* / --hostname=*address*
> This sets the host name or IP address of the database server. If the option -H is omitted, or if it is used in connection with the argument `localhost`, `check_mysql` does not set up a network connection but uses a Unix socket. If you want to establish an IP connection to `localhost`, you must explicitly specify the IP address 127.0.0.1.

-P *port* / --port=*port*
> This is the TCP port on which MySQL is installed. In the default, port 3306 is used.

-d *database* / --database=*database*
> This is the name of the database to which the plugin should set up a connection. If this option is omitted, it only makes a connection to the database process, without addressing a specific database.

-u *user* / --username=*user*
> This is the user in whose name the plugin should log in to the DBMS.

-p *passwd* / --password=*passwd*
> This switch is used to provide the password for logging in to the database.

To set up a connection to the database `nagdb` as the user `nagios`, both parameters are passed on to the plugin:

```
nagios@linux:nagios/libexec$ ./check_mysql -H dbhost -u nagios -d nagdb
Uptime: 19031  Threads: 2  Questions: 80  Slow queries: 0  Opens: 12
Flush tables: 1  Open tables: 6  Queries per second avg: 0.004
```

In contrast to PostgreSQL, with MySQL you can also make contact without establishing a connection to a specific database:

```
nagios@linux:nagios/libexec$ ./check_mysql -H dbhost
Uptime: 19271  Threads: 1  Questions: 84  Slow queries: 0  Opens: 12
Flush tables: 1  Open tables: 6  Queries per second avg: 0.004
```

With a manual connection to the database, with `mysql`, you can then subsequently change to the desired database, using the MySQL command use:

```
user@linux:~$ mysql -u nagios
mysql> use nagdb;
Database changed
mysql>
```

With this plugin, a subsequent database change is not possible. Here you must decide from the beginning whether you want to contact a database or whether you just want to establish a connection to the MySQL database system.

To test a nagdb database set up explicitly for this purpose, you can do without parameters when creating the corresponding command object, and explicitly specify both user and database:

```
define command{
   command_name   check_mysql
   command_line   $USER1$/check_mysql -H $HOSTADDRESS$ -u nagios -d nagdb
}
```

This simplifies the service definition:

```
define service{
   service_description   MySQL
   host_name             linux01
   check_command         check_mysql
   ...
}
```

6.9 Monitoring LDAP Directory Services

For monitoring LDAP directory services, the check_ldap plugin is available. It runs a search query that can be specified anonymously or with authentication. It has the following parameters to do this:

-H *address* / --hostname=*address*
: This is the host name or IP address of the LDAP server.

-b *base_dn* / --base=*base_dn*
: This is the top element (*Base Domain Name*) of the LDAP directory, formed for example from the components of the domain name: dc=swobspace,dc=de.

-p *port* / --port=*port*
: This is the port on which the LDAP server is running. The default is the standard port 389.

-a "*ldap-attribute*" / --attr="*ldap-attribute*"
> This switch enables a search according to specific attributes. Thus
> -a "(objectclass=inetOrgPerson)" searches for all nodes in the
> directory tree containing the object class inetOrgPerson (normally
> used for telephone and e-mail directories, for example).
>
> Specifying attributes in the check is less useful than it may seem. If
> you search through an LDAP directory for nonexistent attributes, you
> will normally receive an answer with zero results, but no errors.

-D *ldap_bind_dn* / --bind=*ldap_bind_dn*
> This specifies a bind DN[20] for an authenticated connection, such as:
>
> ```
> uid=wob,dc=swobspace,dc=de
> ```
>
> Without this entry, the plugin establishes an anonymous connection.

-P *ldap_passwd* / --pass=*ldap_passwd*
> This is the password for an authenticated connection. It only makes
> sense in conjunction with the option -D.

-t *timeout* / --timeout=*timeout*
> After *timeout* seconds have expired (10 seconds if this option is not
> given), the plugin stops the test and returns the CRITICAL status.

-2 / --ver2
> Use LDAP version v2 (the default). If the server does not support this
> protocol version, the connection will fail. In OpenLDAP from version
> 2.1, v3 is used by default; to activate protocol version v2, the following
> line is entered in the configuration file slapd.conf:
>
> ```
> allow bind_v2
> ```
>
> Many clients, such as Mozilla and the Thunderbird address book, are
> still using LDAP version v2.

-3 / --ver3
> Use LDAP version v3. For many modern LDAP servers such as Open-
> LDAP, this is now the standard, but they usually also have parallel
> support for the older version v2, since various clients cannot yet im-
> plement v3.

-w *floating_point_dec* / --warning=*floating_point_dec*
> If the performance time of the plugin exceeds *floating_point_dec*
> seconds, it issues a warning.

---

[20] A bind DN serves to identify the user and refers to the user's nodes in the directory tree,
specifying all the overlying nodes. The bind DN in LDAP corresponds in its function
more or less to the user name when logging in under Unix.

-c *floating_point_dec* / --critical=*floating_point_dec*
> If the performance time of the plugin exceeds *floating_point_dec* seconds, it returns CRITICAL.

-T / --starttls
> Uses the STARTTLS intended in LDAPv3.[21]

-S / --ssl
> Uses SSL encrypted LDAP (LDAPS) from LDAPv2 and at the same time sets the port used for this, port 636. Whenever possible you should choose STARTTLS. LDAP with STARTTLS uses the same port as LDAP without SSL encryption; in many cases this allows the unencrypted LDAP access to be configured as a fallback for LDAP with STARTTLS. Such a fallback is not possible for LDAPS due to the different ports.

In the simplest case it is sufficient to query whether the LDAP server really does own the base DN specified with -b:

```
nagios@linux:nagios/libexec$  ./check_ldap -H ldap.swobspace.de \
    -b "dc=swobspace,c=de"
LDAP OK - 0,002 seconds response time|time=0,002186s;;;0,000000
```

This query corresponds to the following command object:

```
define command{
    command_name   check_ldap
    command_line   $USER1$/check_ldap -H $HOSTADDRESS$ -b $ARG1$
}
```

Since an LDAP server can handle many LDAP directories with different base DNs, it is recommended that you configure this with parameters:

```
define service{
    service_description   LDAP
    host_name             linux01
    check_command         check_ldap!dc=swobspace,dc=de
    ...
}
```

If authentication is involved, things get slightly more complicated. On the one hand the plugin is given the bind-DN of the nagios user, with -D. On the other hand, the following example protects the necessary password from curious onlookers by storing this as the macro $USER3$ in the file resource.cfg, which may be readable only for the user nagios (see Section 2.14, page 79):

---

[21] See footnote on page 117.

```
define command{
   command_name check_ldap_auth
   command_line $USER1$/check_ldap -H $HOSTADDRESS$ -b $ARG1$ -D $ARG2$
-P $USER3$
}
```

Accordingly, the matching service definition contains the base DN and bind DN as arguments, but not the password:

```
define service{
   service_description   LDAP
   host_name             linux01
   check_command check_ldap_auth!dc=swobspace,dc=de!uid=nagios,\
   dc=swobspace,dc=de
   ...
}
```

6.10   Checking a DHCP Server

To monitor DHCP services, the plugin check_dhcp is available. It sends a DHCPDISCOVER via UDP broadcast to the target port 67 and waits for an offer from a DHCP server in the form of a DHCPOFFER, which offers an IP address and further configuration information.

Because check_dhcp does not send a DHCPREQUEST after this, the server does not need to reserve the sources and to confirm this reservation with DHCPACK, nor does it need to reject the request with DHCPNACK.

Granting the plugin root permissions

There is a further restriction to the check_dhcp: it requires full access to the network interface and must therefore run with root privileges.

In order for the user nagios to be able to run the plugin with root permissions, the plugin must belong to the user root and the SUID bit must be set. If you install the plugins from a current tarball, the permissions will be set correctly. Several distributions disable the SUID bit, as it represents a potential danger—it is possible that general root permissions may slip in via buffer overflows in uncleanly programmed code. Here the program owner must be changed manually to the user root so that the SUID bit can be set with chmod. When this is done, only the group nagios, apart from root, is allowed to run the plugin:

```
linux:nagios/libexec # chown root.nagios check_dhcp
linux:nagios/libexec # chmod 4750 check_dhcp
```

```
linux:nagios/libexec # ls -l check_dhcp
-rwsr-x--- 1 root nagios 115095 Jan  8 12:15 check_dhcp
```

The chown command assigns the plugin to the user root and to the group nagios, to whom nobody else should belong apart from the user nagios itself. (The user in whose name the Web server is running should be a member of a different group, such as nagcmd, as is described in Chapter 1 from page 37.)

In addition the chmod ensures that nobody apart from root may even read the plugin file, let alone edit it.

Applying the plugin

check_dhcp only the following options:

-s *server_ip* / --serverip=*server_ip*
> This is the IP address of a DHCP server that the plugin should explicitly query. Without this entry, it is sufficient to have a functioning DHCP server in the network to pass the test satisfactorily. So you have to decide whether you want to test the general availability of the DHCP service or the functionality of a specific DHCP server.

-r *requested_ip* / --requestedip=*requested_ip*
> With this option the plugin attempts to obtain the IP address *requested_ip* from the server. If this is not successful because it is already reserved or lies outside the configured area, check_dhcp reacts with a warning.

-i *interface* / --interface=*interface*
> This selects a specific network interface through which the DHCP request should pass. Without this parameter, the plugin always uses the first network card to be configured (in Linux, usually eth0).

-m *mac_address* / -mac=*mac_address* (from version 1.4.10)
> Uses the specified MAC address in DHCP queries instead of that of the Nagios server. This explicit detail is required if the DHCP server only assigns IP addresses to specific MAC addresses, and the MAC address of the Nagios server is not one of these.

-u / --unicast (from version 1.4.10)
> Sends a unicast message instead of a broadcast.[22] The IP address to which the DHCP request is addressed is specified with -s *server_ip*.

---

[22] A unicast message is addressed to exactly one IP address, whereas a broadcast message is meant for all stations in the local network.

-t *timeout* / --timeout=*timeout*

> After 10 seconds have expired (the default), otherwise *timeout* seconds, the plugin stops the test and returns the CRITICAL state.

With a configurable warning or critical limit for the performance time, the plugin is of no use. Here you must, where necessary, explicitly set a timeout, which causes the CRITICAL return value to be issued.

The following example shows that the DHCP service in the network is working:

```
nagios@linux:nagios/libexec$  ./check_dhcp -i eth0
DHCP ok: Received 1 DHCPOFFER(s), max lease time = 600 sec.
```

The plugin includes only the *lease time* as additional information, that is, the time for which the client would be assigned an IP address. If you want to see all the information contained in DHCPOFFER, you should use the option -v ("verbose").

In the next example the plugin explicitly requests a specific IP address (192.168.1.40), but this is not available:

```
nagios@linux:nagios/libexec$  ./check_dhcp -i eth0 -r 192.168.1.40
DHCP problem: Received 1 DHCPOFFER(s), requested address (192.168.1.40)
was not offered, max lease time = 600 sec.
nagios@linux:nagios/libexec$  echo $?
1
```

The result is a WARNING, as is shown by the output of the status, with $?.

If you want to test both the availability of the DHCP service overall and the servers in question individually, you need two different commands:

```
define command{
    command_name   check_dhcp_service
    command_line   $USER1$/check_dhcp -i eth0
}
```

check_dhcp_service grills the DHCP service as a whole by sending a broadcast, to which any DHCP server at all may respond.

```
define command{
    command_name   check_dhcp_server
    command_line   $USER1$/check_dhcp -i eth0 -s $HOSTADDRESS$
}
```

check_dhcp_server on the other hand explicitly tests the DHCP service on a specific server.

To match this, you can then define one service that monitors DHCP as a whole and another one that tests DHCP for a specific host. Even if the first variation is in principle not host-specific, it still needs to be assigned explicitly to a computer for it to run in Nagios:

```
define service{
    service_description    DHCP Services
    host_name              linux01
    check_command          check_dhcp_service
    ...
}

define service{
    service_description    DHCP Server
    host_name              linux01
    check_command          check_dhcp_server
    ...
}
```

6.11 Monitoring UPS with the Network UPS Tools

There are two possibilities for monitoring uninterruptible power supplies (UPS): the *Network UPS Tools* support nearly all standard devices. The apcupsd daemon is specifically tailored to UPS's from the company APC, described in Section 7.10 from page 182. The plugin check_ups included in Nagios only supports the first implementation.

The following rule generally applies: no plugin directly accesses the UPS interface. Rather they rely on a corresponding daemon that monitors the UPS and provides status information. This daemon primarily serves the purpose of shutting down the connected servers in time in case of a power failure. But it also always provides status information, which plugins can query and which can be processed by Nagios.

Both the solution with the Network UPS Tools and that with apcupsd are fundamentally network-capable, that is, the daemon is always queried via TCP/IP (through a proprietary protocol, or alternatively SNMP). But you should be aware here that a power failure may affect the transmission path, so that the corresponding information might no longer even reach Nagios. Monitoring via the network therefore makes sense only if the entire network path is safeguarded properly against power failure. In the ideal scenario, the UPS is connected directly to the Nagios server. Calling the check_ups plugin is no different in this case from that for the network configuration, since even for local use it communicates via TCP/IP—but in this case, with the host localhost.

The Network UPS Tools

The Network UPS Tools is a manufacturer-independent package containing tools for monitoring uninterruptible power supplies. Different specific drivers take care of hardware access, so that new power supplies can be easily supported, provided their protocols are known.

The remaining functionality is also spread across various programs: while the daemon upsd provides information, the program upsmon shuts down the computers supplied by the UPS in a controlled manner. It takes care both of machines connected via serial interface to the UPS and, in client/ server mode, of computers supplied via the network.

http://www.networkupstools.org/ lists the currently supported models and provides further information on the topic of UPS. Standard distributions already contain the software, but not always with package names that are very obvious: in SuSE and Debian they are known by the name of nut.

To query the information provided by the daemon upsd, there is the check_ ups plugin from the Nagios Plugin package. It queries the status of the UPS through the network UPS Tools' own network protocol. A subproject also allows it to query the power supplies via SNMP.[23] However, further development on it is not taking place at the present time.

For purely monitoring purposes via Nagios (without shutting down the computer automatically, depending on the test result), it is sufficient to configure and start the upsd on the host to which the UPS is connected via serial cable. The relevant configuration file in the directory /etc/nut is called ups.conf. If you perform the query via the network, you must normally add an entry for the Nagios server in the (IP-based) access permissions. Detailed information can be found directly in the files themselves or in the documentation included, which in Debian is in the directory /usr/share/doc/nut, and in SuSE, in /usr/share/doc/packages/nut.

Provided that the Network UPS Tools include a suitable driver for the uninterruptable power supply used, the driver and communication interface are entered in the file ups.conf:

```
# -- /etc/nut/ups.conf

[upsfw]
    driver = apcsmart
    port = /dev/ttyS0
    desc = "Firewalling/DMZ"
```

In the example, a UPS of the company APC is used. Communication takes place on the serial interface /dev/ttyS0. A name for the UPS is given in

---

[23] http://eu1.networkupstools.org/server-projects/

square brackets, with which it is addressed later on: desc can be used to describe the intended purpose of the UPS in more detail, but Nagios ignores this.

Next you must ensure that the user with whose permissions the Network UPS Tools are running (such as the user nut from the group nut) has full access to the interface /dev/ttyS0:

```
user@linux:~$ chown nut:nut /dev/ttyS0
user@linux:~$ chmod 660 /dev/ttyS0
```

In order for Nagios to access information from the UPS via the upsd daemon, corresponding data is entered in an Access Control List in the upsd configuration file upsd.conf:

```
# -- /etc/nut/upsd.conf

# ACL aclname ipblock
ACL all 0.0.0.0/0
ACL localhost 127.0.0.1/32
ACL nagios 172.17.129.2/32

ACCEPT localhost nagios
REJECT all
```

With the keyword ACL you first define hosts and network ranges with their IP address. You must always specify a network block here: /32 means that all 32 bits of the netmask are set to 1 (this corresponds to 255.255.255.255), which is therefore a single host address. It is not sufficient just to specify the IP address here.

An ACCEPT entry allows access for the computer specified in the ACL aclname. ACCEPT rules may be used more than once. The final REJECT entry then refuses access to all other hosts.

To conclude the configuration, you should make sure that the UPS daemon is started with every system start. In SuSE this is done via YaST2; in Debian this is taken care of during the installation.

The check_ups plugin

The monitoring plugin itself has the following options:

-H address / --host=address
    This is the computer on which upsd is installed.

-u identifier / --ups=identifier
    This is the name for the UPS in ups.conf, specified in square brackets.

-p *port* / --port=*port*
> This is the number of the port on which the upsd is running. The default is TCP port 3493.

-w *whole_number* / --warning=*whole_number*
> This switch defines a warning limit as a whole number. If no variable is given (see -v), *whole_number* means a response time in seconds; otherwise the value range of the variable (e.g., 80 for 80% in BATTPCT). Specifying multiple warning limits is currently not possible: the plugin then only uses the last variable and the last warning limit.

-c *whole_number* / --critical=*whole_number*
> This option specifies a critical limit in connection with a variable (see -v).

-v *variable* / --variable=*variable*
> With this option, specific values of the UPS can be queried. The limit values then referred to this parameter. check_ups currently supports only the following variables:
>
> LINE: input voltage of the UPS.
>
> TEMP: Temperature of the USV.
>
> BATTPCT: Remaining battery capacity in percent.
>
> LOADPCT: Load on the UPS in percent.
>
> If this option is missing, the plugin only checks the status of the UPS (online or offline).
>
> Since -v thus has another value, check_ups does not know the obligatory option --verbose (see Table 6.2 on page 108), even in its long form.

-T / --temperature
> This command issues temperature values in degrees Celsius instead of Fahrenheit.

-t *timeout* / --timeout=*timeout*
> After *timeout* seconds have expired, the plugin stops the test and returns the CRITICAL state. The default is 10 seconds.

The following example tests the above defined local UPS with the name upsfw. The -T switch ensures that the output of the temperature is given in degrees Celsius:

```
user@linux:nagios/libexec$  ./check_ups -H localhost -u upsfw -T
UPS OK - Status=Online Utility=227.5V Batt=100.0% Load=27.0% Temp=30.6C|
voltage=227500mV;;;0 battery=100%;;;0;100 load=27%;;;0;100 temp=30degF;;
;0
```

If a variable is not used, the plugin returns a CRITICAL if the UPS is switched off (Status=Off) or has reached low battery capacity (Status=On Battery, Low Battery). check_ups issues a warning if at least one of the three states On Battery, Low Battery, or Replace Battery applies, but this is not sufficient for a CRITICAL status (for example, because of correspondingly set variables). With On Battery the power supply is provided by the battery, with Low Battery the UPS is online with a low battery state, and with Replace Battery, the battery must be replaced.

If none of these points apply, the plugin issues an OK for the following states:

- In the normal online state

- If the UPS is being calibrated (Calibrating)

- If it is currently being bypassed and the power supply is provided directly from the power supply grid (On Bypass)

- If the UPS is overloaded (Overload)

- If the voltage in the power grid is too high and the UPS restricts the voltage to the normal value (Trimming)

- If the voltage in the power grid is too low and is supplemented by the UPS (Boosting)

- If the UPS is currently being charged (Charging)

- If the UPS is currently being discharged (e.g., during a programmed maintenance procedure) (Discharging)

Transformed into a command object, the above test for any host looks like this:

```
define command{
    command_name   check_ups
    command_line   $USER1$/check_ups -H $HOSTADDRESS$ -u $ARG1$ -T
}
```

The corresponding service definition for the computer linux01, to which the UPS is connected, and for the above defined UPS upsfw, would then look like this:

```
define service{
    service_description   UPS
    host_name             linux01
    check_command         check_ups!upsfw
    ...
}
```

If `check_ups` is to determine the UPS status by means of the current load, the relevant information is taken from the variable LOADPCT:

```
user@linux:nagios/libexec$  ./check_ups -H linux01 -u upsfw -T -v \
    LOADPCT -W 60 -c 80
UPS WARNING - Status=Online Utility=227.5V Batt=100.0% Load=61.9%
Temp=30.6C|voltage=227500mV;;;0 battery=100%;;;0;100 load=61%;60000;
80000;0;100 temp=30degC;;;0
```

With 61 percent, the UPS has a heavier load than specified in the limit value -w, but it does not yet reach the critical area above 80 percent, so there is just a warning. If two error criteria occur, such as a warning limit for a queried variable being exceeded and a critical state simultaneously, because the UPS is losing power (On Battery and Low Battery simultaneously), the most critical state has priority for the return value of the plugin, so here, `check_ups` would return CRITICAL, and not the WARNING which results from the query of LOADPCT.

6.12 Health Check of an NTP Server with `check_ntp_peer`

The plugin `check_ntp_peer`, which is included from plugin version 1.4.11, tests the quality of an NTP server. If you want to check the time deviation of a local server against an NTP server, you need to use the plugin `check_ntp_time`, described in Section 7.7.1 on page 177.

Several parameters characterize the quality: the *offset* describes the time difference from other NTP servers (the reference servers). *Jitter* is a measurement of the fluctuations in the packet delay to a remote reference server, and *stratum* specifies the topological distance from the next atomic clock. Stratum 0 is the atomic clock itself, stratum 1 refers to an NTP server directly connected to an atomic clock. Stratum 2 is an NTP server that obtains its time from an NTP server with stratum 1. The further an NTP server is away from the atomic clock, the higher the stratum value. The imprecision of the server also increases the higher this value is.

These parameters can also be queried with the program ntpq, by giving the IP address of the NTP server. The option -p reveals the reference server from which the queried NTP server obtains its time details. The option -n prevents name resolution on the reference servers, thus accelerating the execution of ntpq:

```
nagios@linux:nagios/libexec$ ntpq -np 192.168.1.13
remote           refid         st t when poll reach   delay  offset jitter
==============================================================================
127.127.1.1     .LOCL.         10 l   26   64  377    0.000  0.000  0.001
*81.169.141.30   81.169.172.219  3 u    1  128  377   27.515 -4.411  1.219
+217.160.215.119 212.82.32.26    3 u  125  128  377   17.834  1.505  1.069
```

The remote column specifies the reference server that uses the queried NTP server. 127.127.1.1 here is a special case, and stands for the local system clock. The stratum value (column st), with 10, is relatively high, but the local system clock only plays a role if no other NTP source can is reachable. The other two quality parameters, offset and jitter, are located in the last two columns.

In the simplest case you can run check_ntp_peer, specifying only the NTP server to be checked (option -H):

```
nagios@linux:nagios/libexec$  ./check_ntp_peer -H 192.168.1.13
NTP OK: Offset -0.004411 secs|offset=-0.004411s;60.000000;120.000000;
```

Without further details the plugin checks the time deviation from the reference servers, and the stratum and jitter are not taken into account. All threshold details from check_ntp_peer are specified in the format described in Section 24.1.5 from page 557The plugin has the following options:

-H *address* / -host=*address*
> This is the name or IP address of the NTP server to be checked.

-p *port* / --port=*port*
> This is the UDP port on which the NTP server is listening. The default is port 123.

-q / --quiet
> This returns UNKNOWN instead of WARNING or CRITICAL if the NTP server is not synchronized.

-w *threshold* / -warning=*threshold*
> This is the warning threshold for the time deviation. A warning is issued if the time deviation between the NTP server and at least one of the reference servers is greater than the specified number of seconds. The default is 60 seconds.

-c *seconds* / -critical=*seconds*
> This is the critical threshold for the time deviation. If the time of one of the reference servers used deviates by more than *seconds* seconds (in the default: 120) from that of the NTP server, the state becomes CRITICAL.

-W *threshold* / -swarn=*threshold*

This is the warning threshold based on the stratum value. A warning is issued if no reference server is available whose stratum value matches the specified threshold. This means that -W 1:2 causes a WARNING if no reference server is available with stratum 1 or stratum 2. Without the detail of this parameter the stratum value is not included in the check.

-C *threshold* / -scrit=*threshold*

This is the critical threshold based on the stratum value. See -W.

-j *threshold* / -jwarn=*threshold*

This is the warning threshold for the jitter in milliseconds, given in the threshold format. The plugin returns OK if at least one reference server displays a jitter within the specified range. If this option is not given, the jitter is not included in the evaluation; there is no default.

-k *threshold* / -jcrit=*threshold*

This is the critical threshold for the jitter in milliseconds in the threshold format.

Testing Local Resources

The plugins introduced in this chapter, originating from the `nagios-plug-ins` package,[1] test local resources that do not have their own network protocol and therefore cannot be easily queried over the network. They must therefore be locally installed on the computer to be tested. Such plugins on the Nagios server can test only the server itself—with command and service definitions as described in Chapter 6.

To perform such local tests from a central Nagios server on remote hosts, you require further utilities: the plugins are started via a secure shell, or you use the *Nagios Remote Plugin Executor* (NRPE). Using the secure shell is described in Chapter 9 from page 205, and Chapter 10 (page 213) is devoted to NRPE.

The definition of command and service depends on the choice of mechanism. If you want to test for free hard drive capacity with the `check_by_ssh`

---

[1]   This edition is based on version 1.4.11.

plugin installed on the Nagios server, which remotely calls `check_disk` on the target server (see Section 7, page 157), then a special command definition is required for this, which differs somewhat from the definitions given in Chapter 6 (page 105). What command and service definitions for remotely executed local plugins look like is described in the aforementioned chapters on NRPE and SSH.

For the remote query of some local resources you can also use SNMP (see Chapter 11 from page 227), but the checks are then restricted to the capabilities of the SNMP daemon used. Local plugins are usually more flexible here and provide more options for querying.

7.1 Free Hard Drive Capacity

The question of when the hard drive(s) of a computer may threaten to overflow is answered by the `check_disk` plugin. It has the following options for specifying thresholds:

`-w` *limit* / `--warning=`*limit*

The plugin will give a warning if the free hard drive capacity drops below this limit, expressed as a percentage or as an integer. If you specify percentage, the percent sign % must also be included; floating point decimals such as 12.5% are possible. Integer values represent the absolute free space in the unit that defines the `--units` switch. The default is `--units=MB`, or megabytes.

`-c` *limit* / `--critical=`*limit*

If the free hard drive capacity level falls below this as a percentage or integer (see `-w`), `check_disk` displays the CRITICAL status. The critical limit must be smaller than the warning limit.

`-W` *limit* / `-iwarning=`*limit*

The number of free inodes in the file system as a percentage; `check_disk` issues a warning if this drops below the limit.

`-K` *limit* / `-icritical=`*limit*

Like `-W`, except that this is the critical threshold.

`-u` *unit* / `--units=`*unit*

In what unit do you specify integer limit values? kB, MB, GB, and TB are all possible.

`-k` / `--kilobytes`

With this switch, limit values given as whole numbers with `-c` and `-w` are to be interpreted as KB. This is the same as `--units=kB`.

`-m` / `--megabytes`
> With this switch, whole number limit values with `-c` and `-w` are interpreted by the plugin as MB (the default). This is the same as `--units=MB`.

Before one of the following path selectors is specified, at least one threshold must be given (`-w`, `-c`, `-W`, or `-K`).

`-p` *path_or_partition* / `--path=`*path* or `--partition=`*partition*
> This specifies the root directory in file systems or the physical device in partitions (e.g., `/dev/sda5`). From version 1.4 `-p` can be called multiple times. If the path is not specified, the plugin tests all file systems (see also `-x` and `-X`).

`-E` / `--exact-match`
> This demands that the root of the file system is included for all paths or partitions specified with `-p`, otherwise the plugin will issue an error:
>
> ```
> nagios@linux:nagios/libexec$ df /usr/local
> Filesystem  1K-blocks     Used Available Use% Mounted on
> /dev/md2    9843168  7062980   2280172  76% /usr
> ```
>
> `/usr/local` is not a file system, but a directory within the `/usr` file system on the partition `/dev/md2`. If you call the plugin with the switches `-p /usr/local` and `-E`, you will receive an error, since `/usr/local` is not itself the root of the file system as required by `-E`:
>
> ```
> nagios@linux:nagios/libexec$ ./check_disk -w 10% -E -p/usr/local
> DISK CRITICAL: /usr/local not found
> ```

`-x` *path* / `--exclude_device=`*path*
> This switch excludes the mount point specified as *path* from the test. This option assumes that paths are specified with `-p` and that they may be run in a plugin call multiple times.

`-X` *fs_typ* / `--exclude-type=`*fs_typ* (from 1.4)
> This switch excludes a specific file system type from the test. It is given the same abbreviation as in the `-t` option of the `mount` command. In this way *fs_type* can take the values `ext3`, `reiserfs`, or `proc`, for example (see also `man 8 mount`). This option can be used several times in a plugin command.

`-R` *regexp* / `--eregi-path=`*regexp*, `--eregi-partition=`*regexp*
> From version 1.4.8: a regular expression that selects all paths or partitions with which it matches. Upper/lower case is ignored here. The following example checks all partitions that end with `md0` thru `md2`:

```
nagios@linux:nagios/libexec$ ./check_disk -w 10% -r 'md[0-2]$'
DISK OK - free space: / 281 MB (31% inode=80%); /usr 2226 MB (24% i
node=77%);| /=626MB;861;;0;957 /usr=6897MB;8650;;0;9612
```

The swap partition /dev/md1 is ignored here.

-r *regexp* / --ereg-path=*regexp*, --ereg-partition=*regexp*

From version 1.4.8: a regular expression to check partitions and/or paths. Like -R, except that it is now case-sensitive.

-A / --all

From version 1.4.10: checks all partitions and file systems. The equivalent of -R '.*'.

-I *regexp* / --ignore-eregi-path=*regexp*,
--ignore-eregi-partition=*regexp*

From version 1.4.10: a regular expression that excludes paths or partitions that match it from the check. Upper/lower case is ignored.

-i *regexp* / --ignore-ereg-path=*regexp*,
--ignore-ereg-partition=*regexp*

From version 1.4.10: like -I, except that it is now case-sensitive.

In addition the plugin has the following options:

-e / --errors-only

With this switch, the plugin shows only the file systems or partitions that are in a WARNING or CRITICAL state.

-M / --mountpoint

From version 1.4 on, check_disk by default displays the file system path (e.g., /usr). With -M you are told instead what physical device (e.g., /dev/sda5) is involved.

-C / --clear

From version 1.4 on, -p can be used multiple times. If you want to test several file systems at the same time, but using different limit values, -C can be used to delete old limit values that have been set:

```
-w 10% -c 5% -p / -p /usr -C -w 500 -c 100 -p /var
```

The order is important here: the limit values are valid for the file system details until they are reset with -C. Then new limits must be set with -w and -c.

-l / --local

Only checks local file systems, others–file systems mounted via NFS, for example–are ignored.

-L / --stat-remote-fs (ab Version 1.4.10)

Checks local file systems for the specified thresholds, but checks network file systems only for availability. With this switch you can test, for example, whether a *stale file handle* exists for a path connected via NFS.[2]

-g *group_name* / --group-type=*group_name*

Refers to the thresholds of the sum of all specified partitions and paths. Without this switch the plugin compares each path and each partition separately with the thresholds. -g requires a name to be given, which the plugin includes as additional information in the output:

```
nagios@linux:nagios/libexec$ ./check_disk -g CLUSTER -w 10%\
    -r 'md[0-3]'
DISK OK - free space: CLUSTER 7437 MB (38% inode=86%);| CLUSTER=11
719MB;18163;;0;20182
```

This option must be placed *in front of* the path specification to which it refers.

-t *timeout* / --timeout=*timeout*

After *timeout* seconds have expired the plugin stops the test and returns the CRITICAL status. The default is 10 seconds.

Here is a somewhat more extensive example of the use of check_disk:

```
user@linux:nagios/libexec$ ./check_disk -w 10% -c 5% -p / -p /usr \
    -p /var -C -w 5% -c 3% -p /net/emil1/a -p /net/emil1/c -e
DISK WARNING - free space: /net/emil1/c 915 MB (5%);| /=146MB;458;483;0;
509 /usr=1280MB;3633;3835;0;4037 /var=2452MB;3633;3835;0;4037 /net/emil1
/a=1211MB;21593;22048;0;22730 /net/emil1/c=17584MB;17574;17944;0;18499
```

Everything is in order on the file system /, /usr, and /var, since more space is available on them—as can be seen from the performance data—than the limit value of 10 percent (for a warning), and certainly more than 5 percent (for the critical status). The file systems /net/emil1/a and /net/emil1/c encompass significantly larger ranges of data, which is why the limit values are set lower, after the previous ones have been deleted with -C.

-e ensures that Nagios shows only the file systems that really display an error status. In fact the output of the plugin *before* the | sign, with /net/emil1/c, only displays one single file system. The performance information after the pipe can only be seen on the command line—it contains all

---

[2] The error message NFS stale file handle indicates the non-availability of the NFS path.

file systems tested, as before. This is slightly confusing, because a Nagios plugin restricts its output to a single line, which has been line wrapped here for this printed version.

7.2 Utilization of the Swap Space

The check_swap plugin tests the locally available swap space:

-w *limit* / --warning=*limit*

The warning limit can be specified as a percentage or as an integer, as with check_disk, but the integer value is specified in *bytes*, not in kilobytes!

If at least 10 percent should remain free, specify -c 10%. The integer specification refers to the remaining free space, too.

-c *limit* / --critical=*limit*

Critical limit, similar to the warning limit.

-a / --allswaps

Tests the threshold values for each swap partition individually.

The following example tests to see whether at least half of the swap space is available. If there is less than 20 percent free swap space, the plugin should return a critical status. After the | sign the program again provides performance data, which is logged by Nagios but not displayed in the message on the Web interface:

```
user@linux:nagios/libexec$  ./check_swap -w 50% -c 20%
swap OK: 100% free (3906 MB out of 3906 MB) |swap=3906MB;1953;781;0;3906
```

7.3 Testing the System Load

The load on a system can be seen from the number of simultaneously running processes, which is tested by the check_load plugin. With the help of the uptime program, it determines the average value for the last minute, the last five minutes, and the last 15 minutes. uptime displays these values in this sequence after the keyword load average:

```
user@linux:~$  uptime
 16:33:35 up  7:05, 18 users,  load average: 1.87, 1.38, 0.74
```

check_load has only two options (the two limit values), but these can be specified in two different ways:

-w *limit* / --warning=*limit*

>   This option specifies the warning limit either as a simple floating point decimal (5.0) or as a comma-separated triplet containing three floating point decimals (10.0,8.0,5.0).

>   In the first case, the limit specified applies to all three average values. The plugin issues a warning if (at least) one of these is exceeded. In the second case the triplet allows the limit value to be specified separately for each average value. Here as well, check_load issues a warning as soon as one of the average values exceeds the limit defined for it.

-c *limit* / --critical=*limit*

>   This specifies the critical limit in the same way as -w specifies the warning limit. These critical limit values should be higher than the values for -w.

-r / --percpu (from Version 1.4.9)

>   Divides the system load determined by the number of existing CPU kernels, to get a better idea of the load per CPU kernel.

In the following example Nagios would raise the alarm if more than 15 processes were active on average in the last minute, if more than 10 were active on average in the last five minutes, or if eight were active on average in the last 15 minutes. There is a warning for average values of ten, eight, or five processes:

```
user@linux:local/libexec$ ./check_load -w 10.0,8.0,5.0 -c 15.0,10.0,8.0
OK - load average: 1.93, 0.95, 0.50| load1=1.930000;10.000000;15.000000;
0.000000 load5=0.950000;8.000000;10.000000;0.000000 load15=0.500000;
5.000000;8.000000;0.000000
```

7.4   Monitoring Processes

The check_procs plugin monitors processes according to various criteria. Usually it is used to monitor the running processes of just one single program. Here the upper and lower limits can also be specified.

nmbd, for example, the name service of Samba, always runs as a daemon with two processes. A larger number of nmbd entries in the process table is always a sure sign of a problem; it is commonly encountered, especially in older Samba versions.

Services such as Nagios itself should only have one main process. This can be seen by the fact that its parent process has the process ID 1, marking it as a child of the init process. It was often the case, in the development phase of Nagios 2.0, that several such processes were active in parallel after a failed restart or reload, which led to undesirable side effects. You can test to see whether there really is just one single Nagios main process active, as follows:

```
nagios@linux:nagios/libexec$ ./check_procs -c 1:1 -C nagios -p 1
PROCS OK: 1 process with command name 'nagios', PPID = 1
```

The program to be monitored is called nagios (option -C), and its parent process should have the ID 1 (option -p). Exactly one Nagios process must be running, no more and no less; otherwise the plugin will issue a CRITICAL status. This is specified as a range: -c 1:1.

Another example: between one and four simultaneous processes of the OpenLDAP replication service slurpd should be active:

```
nagios@linux:nagios/libexec$ ./check_procs -w 1:4 -c 1:7 -C slurpd
PROCS OK: 1 process with command name 'slurpd'
```

If the actual process number lies between 1 and 4, the plugin returns OK, as is the case here. If it finds between five and seven processes, however, a warning will be given. Outside this range, check_procs categorizes the status as CRITICAL. This is the case here if there are either no processes running at all, or more than seven running.

Instead of the number of processes of the same program, you can also monitor the CPU load caused by it, its use of memory, or even the CPU runtime used. check_procs has the following options:

-w *start*:*end* / --warning=*start*:*end*
> The plugin issues a warning if the actual values lie *outside* the range specified by the start and end value. Without further details, it assumes that it should count processes: -w 2:10 means that check_procs gives a warning if it finds less than two or more than ten processes.

> If you omit one of the two limit values, zero applies as the lower value, or infinite as the upper limit. This means that the range :10 is identical to 0:10; 10: describes any number larger than or equal to 10. If you just enter a single whole number instead of a range, this represents the maximum. The entry 5 therefore stands for 0:5.

> If you swap the maximum and minimum, the plugin will give a warning if the actual value lies *within* the range, so for -w 10:5 this will be if the value is 5, 6, 7, 8, 9, or 10. You may always specify only one interval.

-c *start*:*end* / --critical=*start*:*end*
> This specifies the critical range, in the same way as for the warning limit.

-m *type* / --metric=*type*
> This switch selects one of the following metrics for the test:
>
> PROCS: number of processes (the default if no specific type is given)
>
> VSZ: the virtual size of a process in the memory (*virtual memory size*), consisting of the main memory space that the process uses exclusively, plus that of the shared libraries used. These only take up memory space once, even if they are used by several different processes. The specification is given in bytes.
>
> RSS: the proportion of main memory in KB that the process actually uses for itself (*Resident Set Size*), that is, VSZ minus the shared memory.
>
> CPU: CPU usage in percent. The plugin here checks the CPU usage for each individual process for morning and critical limits. If one of the processes exceeds the warning limit, Nagios will issue a warning. In the text output the plugin also shows how many processes have exceeded the warning or critical limit.
>
> ELAPSED: The overall time that has passed since the process was started.

-s *flags* / --state=*flags*
> This restricts the test to processes with the specified status flag.[3] The plugin in the following example gives a warning if there is more than one zombie process (status flag: Z):
>
> ```
> nagios/libexec@linux: $ ./check_procs -w 1 -c 5 -s Z
> PROCS OK: 0 processes with STATE = Z
> ```
>
> Things become critical here if more than five zombies "block up" the process table. Several states can be queried at the same time by by adding individual flags together, as in -s DSZ. Now Nagios cancels the processes that are in at least one of the states mentioned.

-p *ppid* / --ppid=*ppid*
> This switch restricts the test to processes whose parent processes have the *parent process ID* (*ppid*). The only PPIDs that are known from the beginning, and that do not change, are 0 (started by the kernel, and usually only concerns the init process) and 1 (the init process itself).

-P *pcpu* / --pcpu=*pcpu*
> This option filters processes according to the percentage of CPU they use:

---

[3] The following states are possible in Linux: D (uninterruptible waiting, usually a *Disk Wait*), R (running process), S (wait status), T (process halted), W (paging, only up to kernel 2.4), X (a finished, killed process), and Z (zombie). Further information is provided by man ps.

```
nagios/libexec@linux: $ ./check_procs -w 1 -c 5 -P 10
PROCS OK: 1 process with PCPU >= 10,00
```

The plugin in this example takes into account only processes which have at least a ten percent share of CPU usage. As long as there is just one such process (-w 1), it returns OK. If there are between two and five such processes, the return value is a WARNING. With at least six processes, each with a CPU usage of at least ten percent, things get critical.

-r *rss* / --rss=*rss*
> This option filters out processes that occupy at least *rss* bytes of main memory. It is used like -P.

-z *vsz* / --vsz=*vsz*
> This option filters out processes whose VSZ (see above) is at least *vsz* bytes. It is used like -P.

-u *user* / --user=*user*
> This option filters out processes that belong to the specified user (see example below).

-a "*string*" / --argument-array="*string*"
> Filters out commands whose argument list contains *string*. -a .tex, for example, refers to all processes that work with *.tex files; -a -v to all processess that are called with the -v flag.

-C *command* / --command=*command*
> This causes the process list to be searched for the specified command name. *command* must exactly match the command specified, without a path (see example below).

-t *timeout* / --timeout=*timeout*
> After *timeout* seconds have expired, the plugin stops the test and returns the CRITICAL status. The default is 10 seconds.

The following example checks to see whether exactly one process called master is running on a mail server on which the Cyrus IMAPd is installed. No process is just as much an error as more than one process:

```
user@linux:nagios/libexec$ ./check_procs -w 1:1 -c 1:1 -C master
CRITICAL - 2 processes running with command name master
```

The first attempt returns two processes, although only a single Cyrus Master process is running. The reason can be found if you run ps:

```
user@linux:~$ ps -fC master
UID      PID PPID  C STIME TTY      TIME CMD
cyrus    431    1  0 2004  ?    00:00:28 /usr/lib/cyrus/bin/master
root    1042    1  0 2004  ?    00:00:57 /usr/lib/postfix/master
```

The Postfix mail service also has a process with the same name. To keep an eye just on the master process of the IMAPd, the search is additionally restricted to processes running with the permissions of the user `cyrus`:

```
user@linux:nagios/libexec$ ./check_procs -w 1:1 -c 1:1 -C master -u \
    cyrus
OK - 1 processes running with command name master, UID = 96 (cyrus)
```

7.5   Checking Log Files

Monitoring log files is not really part of the concept of Nagios. On the one hand, the syslog daemon notices critical events there immediately, so that an error status can be correctly determined. But if the error status continues, this cannot be seen in the log file in most cases.

Correspondingly the plugins described here can determine only whether other, new entries on error events are added. In order to communicate information on a continuing error behavior to Nagios via a log file, the service monitored must log the error status regularly—at least at the same intervals as Nagios reads the log file—and repeatedly. Otherwise the plugin will alternate between returning an error status, and then an OK status, depending on whether the (continuing) error has in the meantime turned up in the log or not.

Under no circumstances may Nagios repeat its test. The parameter `max_check_attempts` (see page 63) must have the value 1. Otherwise Nagios would first assign the error status as a soft state, would repeat the test, and would almost always arrive at an OK, since it only takes into account new entries during repeat tests. `max_check_attempts = 1` ensures that Nagios diagnoses a hard state after the first test.

For events that log an error just once, Nagios has *volatile services*, described in Section 14.5.2 from page 309. For services defined in this way, the system treats every error status as if it was occurring for the first time (causing a message to be sent each time, for example).

Nagios periodically performs (active) checks with the plugins introduced here. If the entry sought does not reoccur, the plugin returns an OK. This is desired in many cases, and the administrator does not need to worry about the earlier error event. But if an error event needs to be handled in all cases, a simple Nagios check is no longer sufficient, since it will be easily overlooked due to the OK of a subsequent check. A slightly different approach, in which an administrator has to explicitly confirm every error result, is introduced in Chapter 23 on page 531.

7.5.1   The standard plugin `check_log`

With `check_log`, Nagios provides a simple plugin for monitoring log files. It creates a copy of the tested log file each time it is run. If the log file has changed since the previous call, `check_log` searches the newly added data for simple text patterns. The plugin does not have any longer options and just has the states OK and CRITICAL:

-F *logfile*
> This is the name and path of the log file to be tested. It must be readable for the user `nagios`.

-O *oldlog*
> This is the name and path of the log file copy. The plugin just examines the difference between *oldlog* and *logfile* when it is run. Afterward it copies the current log file to *oldlog*. *oldlog* must contain the absolute path and be readable for the user `nagios`.

-q *query*
> This is the pattern searched for in examining the log file. Not found means OK; a match returns the CRITICAL status.

It is recommended that you generally do not use messages of the type *recovery notification* (OK after an error state).

An OK in a repeated test just means that no new error in events have occurred since the last test. The `notification_options` parameter (see page 64) in the service definition should therefore not contain an `r`.

The following command examines the file /var/log/auth for failed logins:

```
nagios@linux:local/libexec$  ./check_log -F /var/log/auth \
    -O /tmp/check_log.badlogin -q "authentication failure"
(1) < Jan  1 18:47:56 swobspace su[22893]: (pam_unix) authentication
failure; logname=wob uid=200 euid=0 tty=pts/8 ruser=wob rhost= user=root
```

This produces one hit. The plugin does not show its return value in the text, but it can be displayed in the shell with `echo $?`. In the example, a 2 for CRITICAL is returned.

If you examine the log file for several different events, you must specify a separate *oldlog* for each log file:

```
./check_log -F /var/log/messages -O /tmp/check_log.pluto -q "pluto"
./check_log -F /var/log/messages -O /tmp/check_log.ntpd -q "ntpd"
```

Even if you are searching in the same original log file, you cannot avoid using two different `oldlogs`: otherwise `check_log` would not work correctly.

7.5.2 The modern variation: `check_logs.pl`

As an alternative, The Nagios Exchange[4] provides a completely new plugin for monitoring log files. `check_logs.pl` represents a further development of the Perl plugin `check_log2.pl`, which is included in the `contrib` directory for Nagios plugins but is not installed automatically.

`check_logs.pl` can examine several log files simultaneously for events, in contrast to `check_log` and `check_log2.pl`. It requires a configuration file to do this.

It does have a simple command line mode, but this functions only if you specify a single log file and a single regular expression simultaneously. But the really interesting feature of `check_logs.pl` is that you can perform several examinations in one go. This is why we will not spend any more time describing the command line mode.

Initially we create a configuration file with roughly the following contents, preferably in the directory `/etc/nagios`:

```
# /etc/nagios/check_logs.cfg
$seek_file_template='/var/nagios/$log_file.check_log.seek';

@log_files = (
    {'file_name' => '/var/log/messages',
     'reg_exp' =>'ntpd',
    },
    {'file_name' => '/var/log/warn',
     'reg_exp' =>'(named|dhcpd)',
    },
);
1;
```

The Perl variable `$seek_file_template` contains the path to the file in which the plugin saves the current position of the last search. `check_logs.pl` remembers here at what point in the log file it should carry on searching the next time it is run. This means that the plugin does not require a copy of the processed log file. Instead of the variable `$log_file`, it uses the name of the log file to be examined in each case and creates a separate position file for each log file.

[4] http://www.nagiosexchange.org/54;279

What exactly `check_logs.pl` is to do is defined by the Perl array `@log_files`. The entry `file_name` points to the log file to be tested (with the absolute path), and `reg_exp` contains the regular expression,[5] for which `check_logs.pl` should search the log file. In the example above this is just a simple text called `ntpd` in the case of the `/var/log/messages` log file, but there is an alternative in the case of `/var/log/warn`: the regular expression `(named|dhcpd)` matches lines that contain either the text `named` or the text `dhcpd`.

The only specification that the plugin itself requires when it is run is the configuration file (option `-c`) :

```
nagios@linux:local/libexec$ ./check_logs.pl -c \
/etc/nagios/check_logs.cfg
messages => OK; warn => OK;
```

```
nagios@linux:local/libexec$ ./check_logs.pl -c \
/etc/nagios/check_logs.cfg
messages => OK; warn => (4): Jul  2 14:33:25 swobspace dhcpd:
Configuration file errors encountered -- exiting;
```

The first command shows the basic principle: in the text output the plugin for each log file announces separately whether it has found a matching event or not. In the above example it didn't find anything, so it returns OK. In the second command the plugin comes across four relevant entries in the `warn` log file, but it doesn't find any in `/var/log/messages`. Because of this, the plugin returns a WARNING; OK is given only if no relevant events were found in any of the log files checked. In its output line, after `(4):`, the plugin remembers the last of the four lines found.

7.5.3 The Swiss Army knife: `check_logfiles`

If you have many requirements from a log file check and the tools introduced so far do not meet your needs, then you really should take a look at the plugin `check_logfiles` by Gerhard Lauẞer. As well as sophisticated search options, it can handle any rotation methods you please, so that no information will be lost after a rotation. Its range of functions can be extended by scripts, which can be used to restart applications that have crashed, to send SNMP traps, or send passive check results to an NSCA daemon via `send_nsca` (Section 14.4, page 305).

For simple tasks the plugin can be operated easily from the command line, but to use it in more advanced ways you will need to have some knowledge of Perl: the configuration file that is needed to make use of all the features uses the Perl syntax.

---

[5] In the form of Perl-compatible regular expressions (PCRE, see `man perlre`), since `check_logs.pl` is a Perl script.

The plugin[6] is unpacked in a suitable directory, for example in /usr/local/src:

```
linux:local/src # tar xvzf /pfad-zu/check_logfiles-2.3.1.2.tar.gz
...
linux:local/src # cd check_logfiles-2.3.1.2
linux:check_logfiles-2.3.1.2 # ./configure \
    --with-seekfiles-dir=/var/tmp \
    --with-protocols-dir=/var/tmp
...
linux:check_logfiles-2.3.1.2 # make && make install
...
```

The installation is done with the three commands configure && make && make install. --with-seekfiles-dir specifies the directory in which check_logfiles writes status information, and --with-protocol-dir specifies the directory in which check_logfiles explicitly retains matches it has found. When doing this you should select a directory that is not deleted directly after every reboot. Logging can be switched off in the configuration, depending on the check defined.

On the command line, check_logfiles offers the following options:

--tag=*designator*
> Indicates individual checks, to make better distinction between them. The names of the variables in the performance data also start with this designator, so that the values can later be reassigned to a check. Specifying --tag is optional, but the author of the plugin generally recommends its use.

--logfile=*logfile*
> Specifies the name and path of the log files to be examined. check_logfiles takes note of the last line of the file to be considered during each check, so that it can continue at the same place the next time it is called. In addition, check_logfiles saves other information such as inode and timestamp, so that it can detect log file rotations.

--rotation=*rotation method*
> Specifies the rotation procedure for the log file: loglog0log1gz is used if if you want to turn *logfile* into *logfile*.0 and turn this into *logfile*.1.gz.
>
> loglog0gzlog1gz means that *logfile* is first compressed to *logfile*.0.gz and is later renamed *logfile*.1.gz.
>
> loglogdate8gz states that *logfile* will be converted into *logfile*.*YYYYMMDD*.gz.

---

[6] http://www.consol.de/opensource/nagios/check-logfiles

loglog0log1 describes the rotation method that turns *logfile* into *logfile*.0 and creates the file *logfile*.1 in the next rotation step.

hpux in turn describes the variation " *logfile* is turned into OLD*logfile*".

If a suitable rotation method is missing, you can specify a regular expression that matches the archived files instead. For Debian, you therefore specify --rotation='*logfile*\.(0|[0-9]+\.gz). This is in case the ending .0 is missed during the initial rotation of the file, and if all older archived files end in .*number*.gz.

--criticalpattern=*regexp*
Regular expression in Perl syntax that triggers a CRITICAL. More detailed information on this is provided by man perlre.

--warningpattern=*regexp*
Like --criticalpattern, except that the regular expression here triggers a WARNING.

--noprotocol
Switches off logging of matches to a separate file.

--syslogserver
Restricts the evaluation of log files of a syslog server to lines that the server itself has entered.

--syslogclient=*clientname*
Restricts the evaluation of log files of a syslog server to lines that originate from the syslog client *clientname*.

-f *configfile*
Specifies a configuration file that allows a more extensive configuration than that allowed by just a few command line parameters. A knowledge of Perl is essential for this (see page 173).

-d
Switches on debugging. Useful for searching for errors; this option should not be used during normal operation.

check_logfiles is initialized when it is first called so that it can orient itself. The plugin only takes into account log entries that are subsequently appended to the log file, so it cannot evaluate already existing details.

For demonstration purposes we will first use the logger program to generate an entry in the file /var/log/messages:[7]

---

[7] We are assuming here that the daemon facility is logged with the info priority in /var/log/messages. This is dependent on the distribution, however. In Debian, such entries land in /var/log/daemon.log.

```
user@linux:~$ logger -p daemon.info hellowob
```

The log file now contains the following entry:

```
Dec 16 17:46:06 swobspace wob: hellowob
```

A simple call of check_logfiles returns the following result:

```
nagios@linux:nagios/libexec$ ./check_logfiles --tag=hellowob \
    --logfile=/var/log/messages --criticalpattern='hellowob'
CRITICAL - (1 errors in check_logfiles.protocol-2007-12-16-17-46-08) - D
ec 16 17:46:06 swobspace wob: hellowob |hellowob_lines=2 hellowob_warni
ngs=0 hellowob_criticals=1 hellowob_unknowns=0
```

All variables in the performance data are appended to the hellowob tag so that the respective events can be referenced again, if check_logfiles is to simultaneously search for several different entries.

Re-running check_logfiles again returns an OK, since none of the 32 newly added entries (hellowob_lines=32) contains the text being sought:

```
nagios@linux:nagios/libexec$ ./check_logfiles --tag=hellowob \
    --logfile=/var/log/messages --criticalpattern='hellowob'
OK - no errors or warnings |hellowob_lines=32 hellowob_warnings=0 hellow
ob_criticals=0 hellowob_unknowns=0
```

Configuration Files

Configuration files for check_logfiles basically contain an array consisting of search instructions, each of which are written as an anonymous hash:

```
@searches = (
    { search_instruction_1 },
    { search_instruction_2 },
    ...
    { search_instruction_n },
)
```

The array is called @searches; each instruction enclosed in {} is a search instruction. A configuration file for the hellowob example could look like this:

```
@searches = (
    {
        tag             => 'hellowob',
        logfile         => '/var/log/messages',
        criticalpatterns => 'hellowob',
```

```
        rotation        => 'debian',
        options         => 'noprotocol,nocase',
    },
)
```

The instructions tag and `rotation` correspond to the command line parameters of the same name. The instructions `criticalpatterns` and `warningpatterns` are notated here –in contrast to the equivalent command line parameter–in the plural. The configuration file also allows multiple details:

```
    criticalpatterns => ['VIRUS found', 'hellowob'],
```

Instead of a scalar, an anonymous array may also be specified within square brackets. Here are some more instructions for `@searches`:

archivedir
: Archive directory for rotated log files. The default is the directory in which the log file is located.

type
: Specifies the type of log file: `rotation` is accepted by default if the parameter `rotation` is set. `simple` describes log files without rotation, `check_logfiles` does not continue searching for archived files. `virtual` indicates files that should always be searched from the beginning, such as sockets or files from the `/proc` directory in Linux. For AIX, the option `errpt` is also available: instead of a real file, the plugin now searches for the output of the `errpt` command.

criticalpatterns
: Like the command line option `--criticalpattern`, except that now a number of expressions may be specified as an array:

```
    criticalpatterns => ['.*hallowob.*', '.*hellowob.*', '!dontcryforme'],
```

The exclamation mark ensures a CRITICAL if no line is found with the text `dontcryforme`.

criticalexceptions
: Like `criticalpatterns`, except as an exception: If a line matches an expression from `criticalpatterns`, a CRITICAL would be triggered. If an expression from `criticalexceptions` also matches this very same line, this then stops the critical state. The instruction is used to intercept special cases.

criticalthreshold
: Sets a threshold. The value 5, for example, means that only every fifth match from `criticalpatterns` is really counted as CRITICAL. Below this threshold, the result remains OK.

warningpatterns
:   Like `criticalpatterns`, except for warnings.

warningexceptions
:   Like `criticalexceptions`, except for warnings.

warningthreshold
:   Like `criticalthreshold`, except for warnings.

okpatterns
:   Sometimes errors can rectify themselves. In such cases the administrator does not want to be woken up by unnecessary alarms.

    `okpatterns` cancels all previous WARNINGs and CRITICALs. It is possible to specify multiple details (see `criticalpatterns`).

script
:   Allows a script to be executed in case a match is found. To following instructions supplement this: `scriptparams` passes additional command line options to the script, `scriptstdin` allows to specify strings that are expected by the script on STDIN, and `scriptdelay` forces `check_logfiles` to take a break after the script has been executed.

options
:   This instruction allows further settings options to be made, the meanings of which can be negated by placing the prefix `no` in front of the option:

    script Executes the specified script. The default is `noscript`.

    smartscript Controls whether the return value of the script and its output should be included in the match list. The default is `nosmartscript`.

    supersmartscript Defines whether the return value and the output of the script should replace previous matches (the default is `nosupersmartscript`). The return value 0 (OK) of the script would, for example, suppress a found match, by overwriting the return value that is normally returned by `check_logfiles`.

    protocol Controls whether matches are to be retained in a separate log file. (The default is `protocol`).

    count Should matches be counted or not? `count` is the default. If this option is switched off with `nocount`, you can still use `check_logfiles` to just execute scripts.

    syslogserver Corresponds to the option `--syslogserver` (the default is `nosyslogserver`).

syslogclient=string Like --syslogclient, except that an additional filter may be specified, for example, to search only for the files of a specific client (nosyslogclient is the default).

perfdata Should performance data be displayed? The default is perfdata.

logfilenocry If a log file does not exist, check_logfiles outputs UNKNOWN, in accordance with the default, logfilenocry. The parameter nologfilenocry tells the plugin to omit an error message if the log file is missing.

case nocase ignores upper/lower case. The default, with case, is the opposite of this.

sticky=seconds With this option check_logfiles notices an error state for the amount of time specified. Normally a subsequent check that does not find any more matches would return an OK, so that the administrator might overlook an important entry.

Let us assume that you only accept the truce when there have been no more matches in the log file for two hours. Then the check with sticky=7200 will announce an error state for up to two hours. Only after this period has expired will check_logfiles return to an OK, provided that in the meantime no new entry restarts the two-hour time limit.

If the search pattern contains okpattern, check_logfiles returns an OK directly after a match, that is, before the specified time has expired.

savethresholdcount If an event does not attain the number of matches required in the *threshold options, no error is announced. The question here is how the matches overall should be handled. savethresholdcount (the default) saves the number of matches until the next check and adds these together until the threshold is reached and an error is triggered. The parameter nosavethresholdcount prevents the event counter from always being reset to zero between two checks.

It is beyond the scope of this book to describe all the possible applications of check_logfiles. For this reason, we refer to the documentation, available in German and English, on the check_logfiles Web site.[8]

---

[8] http://www.consol.com/opensource/nagios/check-logfiles

7.6 Keeping Tabs on the Number of Logged-In Users

The plugin `check_users` is used to monitor the number of logged-in users:

```
user@linux:nagios/libexec$ ./check_users -w 5 -c 10
USERS CRITICAL - 20 users currently logged in |users=20;5;10;0
```

It has just two options:

-w *number* / `--warning=`*number*
> This is the threshold for the number of logged-in users after which the plugin should give a warning.

-c *number* / `--critical=`*number*
> This is the threshold for a critical state, measured by the number of logged-in users.

The performance data after the | is as usual visible only on the command line; Nagios does not include it in the Web interface.

7.7 Checking the System Time

7.7.1 Checking the system time via NTP

The two plugins `check_ntp` and `check_ntp_time` compare the clock time of the local computer with that of an available NTP server in the network. If the Nagios server keeps time via NTP accurately enough, so that it can serve as a reference itself, then it can also be used as a network plugin, provided that the host to be checked in the network has an NTP daemon installed.

From plugin version 1.4.11, the plugins `check_ntp_time` and `check_ntp_peer` (Section 6.12, page 154) replace `check_ntp`, which contains the functions of both: the comparison of the local system time with an NTP server described here and the health check of the NTP server itself. The options here apply both to `check_ntp` and to `check_ntp_time`.

In the simplest case, `check_ntp` is called, specifying the computer (here: ntpserver) whose time should be compared with that of the local computer:

```
nagios@linux:nagios/libexec$ ./check_ntp_time -H ntpserver
NTP OK: Offset -0.009505749214 secs|offset=-0.009506s;60.000000;120.0000
00;
```

The deviation determined here amounts to just 9.5 milliseconds, a good value. How much deviation can be tolerated depends on the particular intended use. If you want to compare the log file entries of several different computers, they ought to be NTP-synchronized. Then you can certainly use -w 1 -c 2, that is, assign a deviation of two seconds as critical. In environments in which Kerberos is used for authentication, time synchronization of all hosts involved is also important, but not quite as critical: Microsoft's Active Directory under Windows Server 2003 tolerates a maximum deviation of five minutes, and only when there are larger deviations do real problems arise.

check_ntp_time and check_ntp have the following options:

-H address / --host=address
> This is the NTP server with which the plugin should compare the local system time.

-p port / --port=port
> The UDP port on which the NTP server runs. The default is port 123.

-w threshold / --warning=threshold
> This is the warning limit, specified in the standard threshold format (Section 24.1.5, page 557). The warning is given if the fluctuation of the local system time is larger than the threshold specified. The default is 60 seconds.

-c threshold / --critical=threshold
> Critical threshold in seconds, specified in the standard threshold format (Section 24.1.5, page 557). If the local system time deviates more than the given number of seconds (in the default setting 120 seconds) from that of the NTP server, the status becomes CRITICAL.

-q / --quiet (only check_ntp_time)
> Returns UNKNOWN instead of CRITICAL if the NTP server–for whatever reason–does not provide an offset.

7.7.2 Checking system time with the time protocol

Apart from the *Network Time Protocol* NTP there is another protocol, older and more simple: the *Time Protocol* described in RFC 868, in which communication takes place via TCP port 37. On many Unix systems the corresponding server is integrated into the inet daemon, so you do not have to start a separate daemon. With check_time, Nagios provides an appropriate test plugin.

check_time can also be used as a network plugin, in a similar way to
check_ntp, but this again assumes that the time service is available for every client. In most cases it will therefore be used as a local plugin that compares its own clock time with that of a central time server (here: timesrv):

```
nagios@linux:nagios/libexec$ ./check_time -H timesrv -w 10 -c 60
TIME CRITICAL - 1160 second time difference| time=0s;;;0 offset=1160s;10
;60;0
```

The performance data after the | sign, not shown in the Web interface,
contains the response time in seconds, with time (here: zero seconds);
offset describes by how much the clock time differs from that of the time
server (here: 1160 seconds). The other values, each separated by a semicolon, provide the warning limit, the critical threshold, and the minimum
(see also Section 19.1 from page 404). Since we have not set any threshold
values with the options -W or -C, the corresponding entries for time are
empty.

check_time has the following options:

-H *address* / --hostname=*address*
   This is the host name or IP address of the time server.

-p *port* / --port=*port*
   This is the TCP port specification, if different from the default 37.

-u / --udp
   Normally the time server is queried via TCP. With -u you can use UDP
   if the server supports this.

-w *integer* / --warning-variance=*integer*
   If the local time deviates more than *integer* seconds from that of
   the time server, the plugin returns a WARNING. *integer* is always
   positive, and this covers clocks that are running both slow and fast.

-c *integer* / --critical-variance=*integer*
   If there is more than *integer* seconds difference between the local
   and the time server time, the return value of the plugin is CRITICAL.

-W *integer* / --warning-connect=*integer*
   If the time server needs more than *integer* seconds for the response,
   a WARNING is returned.

-C *integer* / --critical-connect=*integer*
   If the time server does not respond within *integer* seconds, the
   plugin reacts with the return value CRITICAL.

7.8 Regularly Checking the Status of the Mail Queue

The check_mailq plugin can be used to monitor the mail queue of a mail server for e-mails that have not yet been delivered. check_mailq runs the program mailq of the mail service installed. Unfortunately each MTA interprets the mail queue differently, so the plugin can evaluate only mail queues from mail services that the programmer has taken into account. These are, specifically: sendmail, qmail, postfix, and exim. The check_mailq plugin has the following options:

-w *number* / --warning=*number*
> If there are at least *number* mails in the mail queue, the plugin gives a warning.

-c *number* / --critical=*number*
> As soon as there are at least *number* of mails in the queue waiting to be delivered, then the critical status has been reached.

-W *number_of_domains* / --Warning=*number_of_domains*
> This is the warning limit with respect to the number of recipient domains of a message waiting in the mail queue. Thus -W 3 generates a warning if there are any mails in the queue that are addressed to three or more different recipient domains.

-C *number_of_domains* / --Critical=*number_of_domains*
> This is the critical threshold with respect to the number of recipient domains (like -W).

-M *daemon* / --mailserver=*daemon* (from version 1.4)
> This specifies the mail service used. Possible values for *daemon* are sendmail (the default), qmail, postfix, and exim.

-t *timeout* / --timeout=*timeout*
> After *timeout* seconds, the plugin stops the test and returns the CRITICAL status. The default here—as an exception—is 15 seconds (usually it is 10 seconds).

In the following example, Nagios should give a warning if there are at least five mails in the queue; if the number reaches ten, the status of the MTAs Postfix used here becomes CRITICAL:

```
user@linux:nagios/libexec$ ./check_mailq -w 5 -c 10 -M postfix
OK: mailq reports queue is empty|unsent=0;5;10;0
```

Since the queue is empty, check_mailq returns OK here.

7.9 Keeping an Eye on the Modification Date of a File

With the `check_file_age` plugin you can monitor not only the last modification date of a file, but also its size. In the simplest case it is just run with the name and path of the file to be monitored:

```
user@linux:nagios/libexec$ ./check_file_age /var/log/messages
WARNING - /var/log/syslog/messages is 376 seconds old and 7186250 bytes
```

Here the plugin gives a warning, since the warning limit set is 240 seconds and the critical limit, 600 seconds. The last modification of the file was 376 seconds ago—that is, inside the warning range.

The file size is taken into account by `check_file_age` only if a warning limit for the file size (option `-W`) is explicitly specified. The plugin could then give a warning if the file is smaller than the given limit (in bytes). The defaults for the warning and critical limits here are both zero bytes.

`check_file_age` has the following options:

`-w` *integer* / `--warning-age=`*integer*
: If the file is older than *integer*[9] (the default is 240) seconds, the plugin issues a warning.

`-c` *integer* / `--critical-age=`*integer*
: A critical status occurs if the file is older than *integer* (default: 600) seconds.

`-W` *size* / `--warning-size=`*size*
: If the file is smaller than *size* bytes, the plugin gives a warning. If the option is omitted, 0 bytes is the limit. In this case `check_file_age` does not take the file size into account.

`-C` *size* / `--critical-size=`*size*
: A file size smaller than *size* bytes sets off a critical status. The default is 0 bytes, which means that the file size is ignored.

`-f` *file* / `--file=`*file*
: The name of the file to be tested. The option may be omitted if you instead—as in the above example—just give the file name itself as an argument.

---

[9] Because `check_file_age` is a Perl script, it does not matter in this case whether an integer or a floating point decimal is specified. Fractions of a second do not play a role in the file system.

7.10 Monitoring UPSs with `apcupsd`

To monitor uninterruptible power supplies (UPS) from the company APC there is the possibility, apart from the Network UPS Tools described in Section 6.11 from page 149 of using the `apcupsd` daemon, optimized specifically for use with these UPSs. The software can be obtained from `http://www.apcupsd.com/` and is licensed under the GPL, despite the fact that it is vendor-dependent.

The principal function here is the capacity to be able to shut down systems in the event of power failure, rather than a mere monitoring function with Nagios. For this latter purpose, it is easier to configure the Network UPS Tools.

Nearly all Linux distributions contain a working `apcupsd` package,[10] so you don't have to worry about installing it. Nagios does not include an `apcupsd` plugin, but there is a very simple and effective script available for download at `http://www.negative1.org/check_apc/`: `check_apc`.[11] It is also licensed under the GPL, but it has no network capabilities. The plugin cannot be given a host when it is run, and it also does not support any other types of options. Instead of this, internal commands control its functionality, which are given as the first argument.

Executing `check_apc status` tests whether the UPS is online. If this is the case, the plugin returns the OK status, in all other cases it returns CRITICAL:

```
user@linux:nagios/libexec$ ./check_apc status
UPS OK - ONLINE
```

`check_apc load` *warn crit* checks the load currently on the UPS and displays it as a percentage of the maximum capacity. A warning is given if the load is greater than the warning limits specified in *warn* (in the following example, 60 percent), CRITICAL if the load is greater than *crit* (here 80 percent):

```
user@linux:nagios/libexec$ ./check_apc load 60 80
UPS OK - LOAD: 39%
```

The load status of the UPS is checked by the command `check_apc bcharge` *warn crit*. Here the warning limit *warn* and the critical limit *crit* are also given in percent. The value 100 means "fully loaded." The plugin accordingly gives a warning if the load is smaller than the warning limit, and a CRITICAL if the load is smaller than the critical limit:

```
user@linux:nagios/libexec$ ./check_apc bcharge 50 30
UPS OK - Battery Charge: 100%
```

[10] At least SuSE and Debian use this package name.
[11] It can also be obtained at: `http://www.nagiosexchange.org/54;615`.

You can find out how long the saved energy will last with check_apc time *warn crit*. Here check_apc gives a warning if the remaining time is less than *warn* minutes, and a CRITICAL if the remaining time is less than *crit* minutes:

```
user@linux:nagios/libexec$ ./check_apc time 20 10
UPS OK - Time Left: 30 mins
```

7.11 Nagios Monitors Itself

If necessary, Nagios can even monitor itself: the included plugin, check_nagios, tests, on the one hand, whether Nagios processes are running and, on the other hand, the age of the log file nagios.log in the Nagios var directory, for example, /var/nagios/nagios.log.

Despite this, the question needs to be asked: if Nagios itself is not running, then the system simply cannot perform the plugin, which in turn cannot deliver an error message. The solution to this problem consists in having two Nagios servers, each of which addresses the locally installed plugin on the opposite server, with the help of NRPE (see Chapter 10 from page 213).

If you have just one Nagios server you can also run check_nagios alone via cron and have the return value checked using a shell script. In this case, you take action yourself, as shown in Section 7.11.1, so that you are suitably informed of this.

The plugin has the following options:

-C */path/to/nagios* / --command=*/path/to/nagios*
 This is the complete nagios command, including the path (e.g., -C /usr/local/nagios/bin/nagios).

-F */path/to/logfile* / --filename=*/path/to/logfile*
 This is the path to where the Nagios log file nagios.log is saved. The file is located in the Nagios var directory.

-e *integer* / --expires=*integer*
 This is the maximum age of the log file. If there have been no changes to the file for longer than *integer* minutes, check_nagios issues a warning.

 You should make sure that this time specification is large enough: if no errors are currently occurring, Nagios will not log anything in the log file. The only reliable way to obtain a regular entry is with the parameter retention_update_interval in the configuration file nagios.cfg (see page 601). The default value is 60 minutes.

In the following example the log file should not be older than 60 minutes (this corresponds to the default *retention update interval*; see page 601):

```
user@linux:nagios/libexec$ ./check_nagios -e 60 \
    -F /var/nagios/nagios.log -C /usr/local/nagios/bin/nagios
NAGIOS OK: 1 process, status log updated 184 seconds ago
```

With one running Nagios process and a log file last changed 183 seconds (about three minutes) ago, everything is in order here. If the -e parameter is omitted, the plugin always gives a warning.

7.11.1 Running the plugin manually with a script

The following example script demonstrates how the plugin is called outside the Nagios environment. It starts check_nagios initially as Nagios does and then evaluates the return value. If the status is not 0, it sends an e-mail to the administrator nagios-admin@example.com, using the external mailx program:

```
#!/bin/bash

NAGCHK="/usr/local/nagios/libexec/check_nagios"
PARAMS="-e 60 -F /var/nagios/nagios.log -C /usr/local/nagios/bin/nagios"

INFO=`$NAGCHK $PARAMS`
STATUS=$?

case $STATUS in
    0) echo "OK : " $INFO
       ;;
    *) echo "ERROR : " $INFO | \
          /usr/bin/mailx -s "Nagios Error" nagios-admin@example.com
       ;;
esac
```

The script can be run at regular intervals via a cron job—such as every 15 minutes. But then it will also "irritate" the administrator every quarter of an hour with an e-mail. There is certainly room for improvement in this respect—but that would go beyond the scope of this book.

7.12 Hardware Checks with LM Sensors

Modern mainboards are equipped with sensors that allow you to check the "health" of the system. In the lm-sensors[12] project it is also possible in

---

[12] http://www.lm-sensors.nu/

Linux to query this data via I2C or SMBus (*System Management Bus*, a I2C special case).

To enable this, the kernel must have a suitable driver. Kernel 2.4.x normally requires additional modules, which are included in the software.[13] With a little luck, your distribution may include precompiled modules (e.g., SUSE). Kernel 2.6, however, already includes many drivers; here you just compile the entire branch below I2C Hardware Sensors Chip support.

It would take too much space here to detail the installation of the necessary modules. We will therefore only go into detail for the check_sensors plugin, and assume that the corresponding kernel driver is already loaded as a module. Help is provided during operation with the sensors-detect program from the lm-sensors package, which does a number of tests and then tells you which modules need to be loaded. If all requirements are fulfilled, running the sensors program will produce an output similar to the following one, and shows that the onboard sensors are providing data:

```
user@linux:~$ sensors
fscher-i2c-0-73
Adapter: SMBus I801 adapter at 2400
Temp1/CPU:      +41.00 C
Temp2/MB:       +45.00 C
Temp3/AUX:      failed
Fan1/PS:          1440 RPM
Fan2/CPU:            0 RPM
Fan3/AUX:            0 RPM
+12V:           +11.86 V
+5V:             +5.10 V
Battery:         +3.07 V
```

The output depends on the hardware, so it will be slightly different for each computer. Here you can see, for example, the CPU and motherboard temperatures (41 and 45 degrees Celsius), the rotation speed of the fans, and the voltages on the 12- and 5-volt circuits and on the battery. Depending on the board design and the manufacturer, some details may be missing; in this example, only the fan for the power supply FAN1/PS[14] provides information; Fan3/AUX refers to an additional fan inside the computer box that, although it is running, is not recorded by the chipset.

Apart from the standard options -h (help function), -v (*verbose*), which displays the response of the sensors, and -V, which shows the plugin version, the plugin itself has no special options. Warning and critical limits must be set via the lm-sensors configuration. check_sensors only returns the status given by the onboard sensors:

---

[13] http://secure.netroedge.com/~lm78/download.html

[14] PS stands for *power supply*; but the names displayed can be edited in /etc/sensors.conf.

```
user@linux:nagios/libexec$ ./check_sensors
sensor ok
```

If this is called with the -v option, you can see more clearly whether the test works:

```
user@linux:nagios/libexec$ ./check_sensors -v
fscher-i2c-0-73 Adapter: SMBus I801 adapter at 2400 Temp1/CPU: +40.00 C
Temp2/MB: +45.00 C Temp3/AUX: failed Fan1/PS: 1440 RPM Fan2/CPU: 0 RPM
Fan3/AUX: 0 RPM +12V: +11.86 V +5V: +5.10 V Battery: +3.07 V
sensor ok
```

The output line is only wrapped for printing purposes; the plugin displays verbose information on a single line.

Alternatively you can use SNMP to access the sensor data: the NET-SNMP package (see Chapter 11.2 from page 234) provides the data delivered by lm-sensors, and with the SNMP plugin check_snmp, warning limits can also be set from Nagios. This solution is described in Section 11.3.1 from page 246.

Plugins for Special Tasks

A number of plugins do not really fit into the category of local checks versus remote checks because they themselves do not detect operating states but manipulate the results of other checks or summarize them into new results. These include the plugin check_dummy, which always returns a fixed result in order to create a well-defined environment for test scenarios.

negate (which negates the return value) and urlize (which adds a hyperlink to the text output) manipulate the outputs. Summarizing and processing check results is the task of check_cluster and check_multi. Whereas check_cluster only combines and evaluates existing states, check_multi calls the specified plugins itself and combines their results.

8.1   The Dummy Plugin for Tests

For tests expected to end with a defined response, the check_dummy plugin can be used. it is given a return value and the desired response text as parameters, and it provides exactly these two responses as a result:

```
nagios@linux:nagios/libexec$ ./check_dummy 1 "Debugging"
WARNING: Debugging
nagios@linux:nagios/libexec$ echo $?
1
```

The output line contains the defined response, preceded by the status in text form. the return value can again be checked with echo $?: 1 stands for WARNING.

Alternatively you can give check_dummy a 0 (OK), an 2 (CRITICAL) or a 3 (UNKNOWN) as the first argument. The second argument, the response text, is optional.

8.2   Negating Plugin Results

In some situations you may want to test the opposite of what the standard plugin normally tests, such as an interface that should *not* be active, a Web page or a host that should normally *not* be reached. In these cases the program negate, included in the Nagios plugins, provides a way of negating the return value of the original check.

Like plugins, negate has an option to specify a timeout in seconds, with -t, after which it should abort the operation. The actual command line must always contain the complete path to the plugin:

```
negate plugin command
negate -t timeout plugin command
```

negate changes the return value of 2 (CRITICAL) to 0 (OK) and vice versa. The return codes 1 (WARNING) and 3 (UNKNOWN) remain unchanged.

The following example carries out check_icmp on the host 192.0.2.1, which in normal cases should not be reachable:

```
nagios@linux:nagios/libexec$ ./negate \
    /usr/local/nagios/libexec/check_icmp -H 192.0.2.1
CRITICAL - 192.0.2.1: rta nan, lost 100%| rta=0.000ms;200.000;500.000;0;
pl=100%;40;80;;
nagios@linux:nagios/libexec$ echo $?
0
```

The plugin itself returns a CRITICAL in this case with a corresponding text. negate "inverts" the return value; 2 (CRITICAL) turns into 0 (OK). Since the text originates from the plugin and is not changed, the information CRITICAL remains here. For Nagios itself, however, nothing but the return value is of any interest.

8.3 Inserting Hyperlinks with urlize

The program urlize represents the text output of a plugin as a hyperlink, if required, so that clicking in the Nagios Web interface on the test result takes you to another Web page. Like negate, urlize functions as a wrapper around the normal plugin command and is included with the other Nagios plugins.

As the first argument it expects a valid URL to which the hyperlink should point. This is followed by the plugin command, including its path:

```
urlize url plugin command
```

To avoid problems with spaces in plugin arguments, you can set the complete
plugin command in double quotation marks.

The hyperlink around the normal plugin output can be easily recognized when running the command manually:

```
nagios@linux:nagios/libexec$ ./urlize http://www.swobspace.de \
    /usr/local/nagios/libexec/check_http -H www.swobspace.de
<A href="http://www.swobspace.de">HTTP OK HTTP/1.1 200 OK - 2802 bytes
    in 0.132 seconds |time=0.132491s;;;0.000000 size=2802B;;;0</A>
```

In version 1.4 urlize also embeds the performance output in the link text, but Nagios cut this off before the representation in the Web interface, together with the end tag. But most browsers do not have any problem with the missing </A>.

8.4 Checking Host or Service Clusters as an Entity

Plugins normally check an individual host or service, compare the result with the specified thresholds, and then return an appropriate result. On systems with redundant designs (such as in clusters) you can also check the respective host or service individually. In addition, a check of the virtual host or service provides a clue as to whether or not the virtual system as a whole is reachable. The plugin `check_cluster` allows more complex values to be queried.

As an example, we will take a host cluster consisting of five identical single systems. One of these hosts may fail without any problem, but if a second one fails, the plugin should issue a WARNING. If a third host should fail, a CRITICAL should certainly be signalled.

The special feature of `check_cluster` is that it does not actively perform a check itself but determines the return value from already-existing status values from the desired hosts or services. To do this it uses on-demand macros (see Section D.2 from page 632). Whereas the standard macros always refer to the current host or service, which obviously makes little sense for `check_cluster`, on-demand macros allow access to all existing information on other hosts or services.

For `check_cluster` we require the status of various hosts or services. These can be determined through the on-demand macros $HOSTSTATEID:*host*$ and $SERVICESTATEID:*host*:*service_description*$. They both provide the respective status in numerical form: 0 for OK; for hosts, 1 for DOWN and 2 for UNREACHABLE; for services, 1 for WARNING, 2 for CRITICAL, and 3 for UNKNOWN).[1] In each case the host name must be specified, and for $SERVICESTATEID$ the service description of the host or service from which Nagios is to obtain the values must also be given.

The plugin has the following options:

-s / --service
Handles the status values as the results of service checks, that is, 0 as OK, 1 as WARNING and 2 as CRITICAL

-h / --host
Handles the status values as the results of host checks, that is, 0 as UP, 1 as DOWN, and 2 as UNREACHABLE

-l *label* / --label=*label*
Inserts the text specified with *label* into the text output

-d *statusliste* / --data=*statusliste*
Comma-separated list of the states from which the total result should be determined; here the already mentioned macros are used:

--data=$HOSTSTATEID:srv1$,$HOSTSTATEID:srv2$,$HOSTSTATEID:srv3$

-w *schwellwert* / --warning=*schwellwert*
Warning threshold in the threshold format,[2] with respect to the number of error states. So by specifying -w 0:2, a maximum of two er-

---

[1] See Appendix D from page 625.
[2] For the specification of thresholds, see Section 24.1.5 on page 557.

ror states are allowed for an OK result. From the third error state, a WARNING is issued.

-c *threshold* / --critical=*threshold*
    Like --warning, but refers to the critical threshold

The following call simulates the failure of two out of a total of five existing Web servers. A third server displays a WARNING. This means that we have a total of three error states:

```
nagios@linux:local/libexec$ ./check_cluster -s -d 0,2,1,0,2 -w 0:2 -c 0:3
CLUSTER WARNING: Service cluster: 2 ok, 1 warning, 0 unknown, 2 critical
```

The check issues a WARNING because the warning threshold is exceeded (even though the critical threshold is not). The definition of the check_cluster command is kept simple:

```
define command{
    command_name   check_cluster
    command_line   $USER1$/check_cluster -l $ARG1$ $ARG2$
}
```

The command expects a label as the first argument, and the plugin prefixes it to the text output. Everything else is defined in the second argument in the host or service definition:

```
define service{
    host_name mycluster
    service_description Web Cluster
    command  check_cluster!Web Cluster!--service -d $SERVICESTATEID:srv1:
HTTP$,$SERVICESTATEID:srv2:HTTP$ -w 0:0 -c 0:1
}
```

The service Web Cluster checks the service states of the two services srv1: HTTP and srv2:HTTP. As long as they are both working without errors, the command returns OK. If there is an error state, the result will be a WARN-ING, and if both services have errors, CRITICAL is returned.

This completes the possibilities of check_cluster. If you are not satisfied with simply evaluating the number of existing error states, you should take a closer look at the plugin check_multi, which also allows AND and OR operations.

8.5 Summarizing Checks with `check_multi`

There are various reasons for grouping different checks into a single one. On one hand it simplifies work for Nagios, because the system now only needs to manage 1,000 procedures instead of maybe 20,000—this increases performance significantly in many cases. If you summarize checks remotely, Nagios now performs 1 instead of 20 network queries, which results in better network performance. The Nagios administrator may also have an easier time, as the configuration is more concise.

The method originally planned for load distribution and reducing checks was via distributed Nagios instances. There are certainly productive installations in which a Nagios instance performs only 50 checks and transmits these to a central Nagios installation. If there are some several hundred Nagios instances, this method does ease the load on the central Nagios installation but not on the administrator, who has a considerable amount of work managing such configurations.

The plugin check_multi, by Matthias Flacke, takes a different approach. It performs (almost) any number of checks decentrally and returns just a sum total of the results to the Nagios server (Figure 8.1). The plugin is executed remotely; it is called either via NRPE (Section 10 from page 213) or via the plugin check_by_ssh (Section 9.1 from page 206).

Figure 8.1:
Summarizing checks
with check_multi

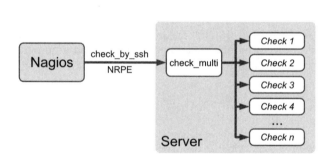

Information is lost during this process—ultimately, there can be only one return value for each check_multi call. But you gain clarity with the configuration of services, and you acquire—unexpectedly—a nice feature: The checks that must be performed are listed in an NRPE-like configuration file on the corresponding target system on which check_multi is also installed. This makes it possible to delegate certain tasks, such as the maintenance of threshold values, to other (non-Nagios) administrators. They require write access to the relevant check_multi configuration file but do not need to continue grappling—apart from correctly running the plugins used—with a Nagios configuration.

To be able to pass on as much information as possible, check_multi makes regular use of the multiple-line plugin output format that was introduced

with Nagios 3.0 (see Section 8.5.1). This restricts the use of `check_multi`
essentially to Nagios 3.0. Starting from `check_multi` in version 0.14, there
have been approaches to support Nagios 2.x. These are only of limited use,
however, since the entire amount of information for plugins in Nagios 2.x
is about 300 bytes, and only the first line of the plugin output is utilized.

8.5.1 Multiple-line plugin output

Starting with Nagios 3.0, an expanded output format for plugins has been
introduced. Instead of squeezing everything onto a single line, the output
may be spread over several lines:

```
normal text output | optional performance data
longtext, 1st line
longtext, 2nd line
...
longtext, n-th line | performance data, 2nd line
performance data, 3rd line
...
performance data, n-th line
```

The first line contains the standard text output, supplemented with performance data if required. This line can still be processed by Nagios 2.x, so it
shouldn't be longer than 300 bytes. In the following lines a plugin may sup-
ply other text information until the character | closes the text output and
allows other performance data to be written. Nagios 3.0 displays the entire
text information in the status information generated by `extinfo.cgi` on
the Web interface (see Section 16.2.2 from page 339).

When accessing text information via macros (See Appendix D.1 from page
627), Nagios splits up the information into two macros: $HOSTOUTPUT$
contains the first line of the text information of host checks (that is, the contents of the placeholder *normal text output*), and $LONGHOSTOUTPUT$
contains only the long text. For service checks the macros are called $SER-
VICEOUTPUT$ and $LONGSERVICEOUTPUT$. The LONG* variation of the
macro is available only in Nagios 3.0 and later; Nagios 2.x only knows the
short version.

The performance data from the first line and from the end is summarized
by Nagios 3.0 in the macros $HOSTPERFDATA$ and $SERVICEPERFDATA$.
There is no LONG* variation, as is the case for the output.

The entire output, including performance data, is a maximum of 8 KB long
in Nagios 3.0. If Nagios runs a plugin directly, as opposed to indirectly,
(for instance, via NRPE or `check_by_ssh`), you must ensure that the entire
8 KB really are passed across the entire transmission path. This is covered
in Section 8.5.2.

8.5.2 Installation requirements

check_multi does not put any restrictions on the size of its output. In order to support enough checks, you should ensure that all the resources used allow at least 8 KB of plugin output. For Nagios version 3.0, the developers have increased the buffer size to to 8 KB, so no adjustments are necessary. For scenarios involving remote use with NRPE or check_by_ssh, you may need to make manual adjustments.

Adjusting buffer sizes for NRPE

By default, NRPE (Section 10, page 213) transmits no more than 1,024 characters. To make proper use of check_multi, you need to adjust the buffer size in the source code. To do this, you set the appropriate values in the file include/common.h to 8192:

```
#define MAX_INPUT_BUFFER        8192
...
#define MAX_PACKETBUFFER_LENGTH 8192
```

Afterward, you must re-compile and re-install the NRPE daemon and the check_nrpe plugin.

Adjusting buffer sizes for check_by_ssh

The plugin check_by_ssh (Section 9.1 from page 206) can handle multiple-line output from plugins in versions 1.4.10 and later, so it can be used unchanged. A patch is required for older versions, which can be found on the check_multi homepage.[3]

8.5.3 Installation and testing

After downloading the plugin from the very extensive and well-documented homepage,[4] you should unpack it in a directory anywhere, and then change to that directory to carry out an initial test. In the subdirectory contrib of the source code there is a preconfigured file, check_multi.cmd, containing several example checks. When running the plugin, specify this file with the option -f; check_multi will perform all the checks defined there in one go. This output gives you a feeling of how the plugin functions:

---

[3] http://www.my-plugin.de/wiki/de/projects/check_multi/installation#c
heck_by_ssh

[4] http://www.my-plugin.de/wiki/de/projects/check_multi/start

```
user@linux:~$ ./check_multi -f contrib/check_multi.cmd
MULTI CRITICAL - 35 plugins checked, 7 critical (network_rsync, proc_acp
id, proc_httpd, system_syslog, system_users, nagios_system, dummy_critic
al), 2 warning (nagios_tac, dummy_warning), 2 unknown (network_if_eth1,
dummy_unknown), 24 ok
[ 1] network_ping PING OK - Packet loss = 0%, RTA = 0.06 ms
[ 2] network_interfaces OK: host 'localhost', interfaces up: 6, down: 0,
dormant: 0, excluded: 0, unused: 0
[ 3] network_if_eth1 Either a valid snmpkey key (-k) or a ifDescr (-d) m
ust be provided)
...
[16] system_load OK - load average: 0.89, 0.71, 0.71
[17] system_mail TCP OK - 0.000 second response time on port 25
[18] system_mailqueue OK: mailq is empty
[19] system_mysql Uptime: 5573  Threads: 1  Questions: 140  Slow queries
: 0 Opens: 137  Flush tables: 1  Open tables: 19  Queries per second avg
: 0.025
[20] system_ntp NTP OK: Offset -0.07118669868 secs
[21] system_portmapper OK: RPC program portmapper version 2 udp running
[22] system_rootdisk DISK OK - free space: / 287 MB (31% inode=81%);
[23] system_ssh SSH OK - OpenSSH_4.3p2 Debian-9 (protocol 2.0)
...
|MULTI::check_multi::plugins=35 time=10.92 network_interfaces::check_ifs
tatus::up=6,down=0,dormant=0,excluded=0,unused=0 system_load::check_load
::load1=0.890;5.000;10.000;0; load5=0.710;4.000;8.000;0; load15=0.710;3.
000;6.000;0; system_mail::check_tcp::time=0.000225s;;;0.000000;10.000000
system_mailqueue::check_mailq::unsent=0;2;4;0 system_ntp::check_ntp::off
set=-0.071187s;60.000000;120.000000; system_rootdisk::check_disk::/=620M
B;909;937;0;957 system_swap::check_swap::swap=3906MB;0;0;0;3906 system_u
sers::check_users::users=25;5;10;0 nagios.org_dns::check_dns::time=0.039
187s;;;0.000000 nagios.org_http::check_http::time=0.674044s;;;0.000000 s
ize=21530B;;;0
```

The first line of the output—starting with `MULTI CRITICAL`—summarizes all the executed checks. These lines (line-wrapped here for display purposes) are also processed by Nagios 2.x. The output from the individual checks begins on line 2 (starting with [1]), which looks exactly like the output of a single call of the plugin currently being run. The performance data is summarized by `check_multi`, but only at the the end, in a totals line—starting with |`MULTI::check_multi::plugins`. The individual variables are separated by spaces. The purpose for the variable names, along with their format (which takes some getting used to), is explained in Section 8.5.6 from page 198.

8.5.4 Configuration file

The format of the configuration file is based on that of NRPE (Section 10.3 from page 218). For `check_multi`, however, only the commands are defined. Here is an extract from the example file included, `check_multi.cmd`:

```
...
command[ network_interfaces ]   = check_ifstatus -H localhost
command[ system_load ]          = check_load -w 5,4,3 -c 10,8,6
command[ system_mail ]          = check_tcp -H localhost -p 25
command[ system_mailqueue ]     = check_mailq -w 2 -c 4
command[ system_mysql ]         = check_mysql -u admin
command[ system_ntp ]           = check_ntp -H ntp1.fau.de
command[ system_portmapper ]    = check_rpc -H localhost -C portmapper
command[ system_rootdisk ]      = check_disk -w 5% -c 2% -p /
command[ system_ssh ]           = check_ssh localhost
...
```

The command command[*Name_of_check*] specifies the name for the appropriate check. This is used in the text output and in the performance data.

After the equal sign comes the check to be executed. When calling the plugin, path details can be omitted if the plugins are located in the default path, /usr/local/nagios/libexec. Alternatively, you can include the plugin path with the option -l when running check_multi. You can also specify the absolute path in the configuration file, of course.

8.5.5 Command-line parameters

check_multi has the following options:

-f */path/to/config/file* / --filename=*/path/to/config/file*
>   This specifies the configuration file. So that Nagios can find it, you should always specify the complete path. This option does not have a default value; it can be given several times.

-l */path/to/the/plugins* / --libexec=*/path/to/the/plugins*
>   The default for calling plugins is the path /usr/local/nagios/lib-exec. If they are located in a different directory, this is specified here with the -l option.

-n *name* / --name=*name*
>   This is the name of a check that check_multi outputs in the text output and in the performance data. The default is an empty string. If you run check_multi on a machine several times with different checks, it is better here to use different names so that they are more clearly separated from each other.

-t *sekunden* / --timeout=*seconds*
>   This specifies the timeout for an individual check. The default is 10 seconds.

-T *seconds* / --TIMEOUT=*seconds*
> For all checks together, `check_multi` requires a further timeout parameter, which is defined with -T (the default is 60 seconds).
>
> This ensures that the call of `check_multi` will end within the time specified. The plugin does not start any new checks if the starting time and the timeout of a single plugin exceed the timeout of the entire `check_multi` call.[5] Such individual checks are given the status UNKNOWN; in the output, `check_multi` assigns them the message `plugin cancelled due to global timeout`.

-r *integer* / --report=*integer*
> This option controls the output behavior of `check_multi`. The placeholder *integer* can take on the following values:

> - 1 includes the service name for error states in parentheses in the plugin output:
>
>   ```
>   ..., 2 critical (network_rsync, proc_acpid), 1 warning (nagios_t
>   ac), 1 unknown (if_eth1), dummy_unknown), 24 ok
>   ```

> - 2 formats the output as HTML. Here the numbers of the individual checks (e.g., [3]) are stored along with the color of the respective return value (green for OK, yellow for WARNING, red for CRITICAL, and orange for UNKNOWN).
>
>   If you use `check_multi` recursively (a `check_multi` itself calls other instances of `check_multi`), the output of the subordinate checks are indented (see Figure 8.3 on page 202).

> - 4 shows the output of the individual check—if they exist—on STDERR.

> - 8 outputs the performance data in the multi-format (see Section 8.5.6 from page 198).

> - 16 has the same function as 1, except that states for which there are no check results (e.g., 0 unknown) are also included.

> - 32 outputs performance data in the classical format (see Section 8.5.6).

> - 128 extends the HTML format required by 2 by including a hyperlink to an installed PNP if performance data is available and the output is in multi-format (8). PNP is described in Section 19.6 from page 446.

> - 256 displays the output in XML formatting.

---

[5] Let us assume that 53 have passed since `check_multi` was called, but not all planned individual checks have yet been processed. The total from starting time and individual timeout (53 + 10 = 63) exceeds the timeout of the `check_multi` call, so `check_multi` does not start any further checks.

- 512 ensures that the output is Nagios 2.x compatible in order to bring the output below the 300-byte limit.

Indivudal values may be combined; the default is 13 (8 + 4 + 1).

-w *expression* / --warning=*expression*

This sets the status WARNING if *expression* is true, e.g., COUNT(WARNING) > 0 (the default). For all states, check_multi separately checks whether or not the corresponding status was determined. Eventually, the status with the highest priority wins out: CRITICAL trumps WARNING, trumps UNKNOWN, trumps OK. The definition and use of expressions is explained in Section 8.5.7 from page 199.

-c *ausdruck* / --critical=*expression*

If the expression is true, the status is set to CRITICAL. Eventually, the status with the highest priority wins out (see --warning and Section 8.5.7).

-u *expression* / --unknown=*expression*

If the expresion is true, the status UNKNOWN is set. The status with the highest priority (see --warning and Section 8.5.7) wins out.

-o *expression* / --ok=*expression*

If *ausdruck* is true, the status OK is set. Here the status with the highest priority also wins out (see --warning and Section 8.5.7).

-v / --verbose

This increases the verbosity of the plugin for debugging purposes. The option can be used up to three times; if specified three times, you will obtain the most detailed information.

8.5.6   Performance data and PNP

In the simple output form for performance data (which can be set with the option -r 32), check_multi simply lists all variables provided by the plugins:

```
...|rta=0.111ms;500.000;1000.000;0; pl=0%;5;10;; offset=0.002980s;60.000
000;120.000000;
```

The performance data for the plugin check_icmp (the average response time rta and the packet loss pl) in this example seamlessly follow the performance data of check_ntp in the form of deviation from the local system time (offset). You can't tell, at first glance, what information comes from which plugin—you have to consult the order in the configuration file and the outputs of the individual checks.

This is not particularly suitable for automatic processing. `check_multi` therefore provides an extended output with the default option `-r 8`, which is modified specifically to handle PNP (see Section 19.6 from page 446). When doing this, the plugin adds a service description and the name of the plugin used to the name of the variables. No deviation is made from the standardized format; the label is just given a more extensive form:

```
servicedescription::plugin::label=values [label=calues]
```

PNP requires information on the plugin executed so that it can select a suitable template for processing the graphics (see Section 19.6.5 from page 454). In addition, `check_multi` now also provides performance data referring to the overall processing:

```
|MULTI::check_multi::plugins=5 time=0.18 net_ping::check_icmp::rta=0.048
ms;500.000;1000.000;0; pl=0%;5;10;; system_ntp::check_ntp::offset=0.0022
66s;60.000000;120.000000;
```

First `check_multi` announces that it has called 5 plugins and has used a total of 0.18 seconds for processing. This is followed by the performance data for the other plugins, each supplemented with the service description and plugin name. If a plugin issues more than one variable, the service description and plugin name are not repeated.

8.5.7 Simple business process monitoring

In order to evaluate business processes, you generally want to know whether a particular process is working—for instance, whether or not a customer can perform online banking. Individual pieces of information on all hosts and services involved are not relevant from this perspective and are also not always useful if systems are designed redundantly in different forms.

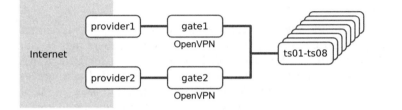

Figure 8.2:
For the terminal server farm to be reachable from the Internet, an OpenVPN access and a terminal server must be available.

One example is shown in Figure 8.2: Home office users access a terminal server farm via OpenVPN. For access from the Internet, two connections are available, and with gate1 and gate2, two OpenVPN gateways are available. The terminal server farm consists of the eight terminal servers ts01 through ts08.

In order for home office users to be able to work, at least one Internet connection (including the accompanying gateway) must be available, and the server farm must be reachable. The business process can be split into two processes: Our example looks at the Internet access separated from the server farm, and afterward it can connect the two results with one another.

The condition for a critical status for Internet access could be formulated as follows:

```
(gate1 > 1 || provider1 > 1) && (gate2 > 1 || provider2 > 1)
```

Access is unusable if the provider is unreachable or (||) the OpenVPN service is not available on the gateway. But it is sufficient if one of the two access points is functioning (thus the AND logical operator with &&). The syntax is taken from Perl and can equally be processed by check_multi. The configuration file for the Internet check therefore contains four commands and the logocal operators:

```
# openvpn.cmd
command[ gate1 ]      = check_nrpe -H gate1 -c check_openvpn
command[ provider1 ] = check_icmp -H provider1 -c 1000.0,60%
command[ gate2 ]      = check_nrpe -H gate2 -c check_openvpn
command[ provider2 ] = check_icmp -H provider2 -c 1000.0,60%

state[warning] = count(CRITICAL) > 0 || count(UNKNOWN) > 0
state[critical] = (gate1 > 1 || provider1 > 1) && (gate2 > 1 || provider
2 > 1)
```

The two gate* commands each check (via NRPE) whether the gateway of the OpenVPN service is running. The provider test sends ICMP echo packets to the dial-up router of the respective provider. You should take great care here to ensure that routing is correctly set up, that is, that the ICMP packets to the respective provider really are sent across the accompanying connection.

For a business process, a Boolean expression for individual states is defined in the configuration file, so depending on requirements, there may be one for CRITICAL, one for WARNING, and, if necessary, one for UNKNOWN as well. The syntax and the operators are passed on to Perl as specified and are described in detail in the Perl online documentation (man perlop). Before evaluating the expression, check_multi undertakes the following substitutions:

- If the expression contains the name of a check previously defined with command, the return value of this check will be used instead. Let's assume that check `gate1` returns 2 and check `provider1` returns 1. Then the partial expression shown above will become

```
state[critical] = (2 > 1 || 1 > 1) ...
```

Within the brackets, the first condition is true, and through the subsequent OR (|| in Perl syntax) the partial expression evaluates to true.

- The function `count` determines the number of all checks that provided the return value given as an argument.

- Instead of the numerical value of a status, the text form (UNKNOWN, WARNING, CRITICAL, WARNING, OK) can also be included in the expression (so you can write something like `gate1 > WARNING`). This detail is replaced by `check_multi` with the numerical value before the expression is evaluated.

The WARNING status is set in `openvpn.cmd` if at least one critical status occurs, at least one check delivers UNKNOWN, or at least one check returns WARNING. The CRITICAL status appears if both accesses should fail (because of the AND logical operator between the two partial expressions in brackets). The partial expressions on their own are true if either of the `gate` or `provider` checks delivers a CRITICAL (return value 2) or an UNKNOWN (return value 3). The condition for the UNKNOWN status can be omitted since UNKNOWN results always lead to the WARNING status.

The second partial process—the function of the terminal server farm—is described in the configuration file `terminalserver.cmd`:

```
# terminalserver.cmd
command[ ts01 ] = check_tcp -H ts01 -p 3389
command[ ts02 ] = check_tcp -H ts02 -p 3389
command[ ts03 ] = check_tcp -H ts03 -p 3389
command[ ts04 ] = check_tcp -H ts04 -p 3389
command[ ts05 ] = check_tcp -H ts05 -p 3389
command[ ts06 ] = check_tcp -H ts06 -p 3389
command[ ts07 ] = check_tcp -H ts07 -p 3389
command[ ts08 ] = check_tcp -H ts08 -p 3389

state[ warning ] = count(CRITICAL) > 0 || count(UNKNOWN) > 0 || count(WA
RNING) > 0
state[ critical ] = ts01 >= CRITICAL || count(CRITICAL) > 3
```

The individual checks here consist of only a primitive TCP check of the RDP port 3389 in order to keep the example relatively simple. WARNING should be indicated if at least one CRITICAL or at least one UNKNOWN occurs so that the administrator has the opportunity to fix the problem at an early stage. The condition for the CRITICAL status stipulates that `ts01` must not be CRITICAL because a very specific application is running there which is not available on the other servers. In addition, no more than three terminal servers may fail, as otherwise the load on the other servers may increase so heavily that useful work would no longer be possible.

Figure 8.3:
Recursive output of
check_multi on the
Extended Info page
of the Nagios Web
interface

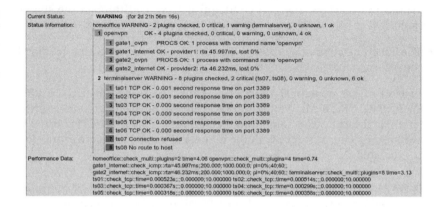

The two checks of the partial processes are summarized by a check_multi call into a single result (the lines are wrapped for display purposes):

```
# homeoffice.cmd
command[ openvpn ] = check_multi -f /etc/nagios/check_multi/openvpn.cmd
-r31
command[ terminalserver ] = check_multi -f /etc/nagios/check_multi/termi
nalserver.cmd -r31
```

So that the Extended Info page of Nagios (Figure 8.3) is more presentable, the details of the respective plugin names are omitted (through the missing option -n; the recursive HTML output of check_multi adds the name of the check called anyway). The -r 31 detail sets all reporting functions from 1 to 16, including HTML formatting (-r 2). Special conditions for a status are not formulated, so a WARNING of a partial process leads to a WARNING in the overlying check, and a CRITICAL leads to a CRITICAL.

Figure 8.3 shows the two partial processes quite clearly separated. The serial numbers of the checks are stored with the respective status colors, which are unfortunately not visible in this black-and-white book. A complex color example of recursive display in the Extended Info Web page can be found on the homepage of the plugin.[6]

For the sake of completeness, here is the definition of command and service for Nagios. The former is kept deliberately simple, and all the details for the command line are repeated in the service definition:

[6] http://www.my-plugin.de/wiki/de/projects/check_multi/screenshot#ser-
vice_extended_info_rekursiv

```
define command{
   command_name check_multi
   command_line $USER1$/check_multi $ARG1$
}

define service{
host_name            elix01
service_description homeoffice
check_command  check_multi!-f /etc/nagios/check_multi/homeoffice.cmd -n
homeoffice -r 31
...
}
```

If the mapping of business processes with `check_multi` isn't enough for you, you should take a look at the somewhat more complex addon *Nagios Business Process View and Nagios Business Impact Analysis* from the Sparda-Datenverarbeitung eG, Nuremberg, Germany, which is available on the Nagios-Exchange.[7]

In contrast to `check_multi`, which appears as the only Nagios service and which also needs to be managed only once by Nagios, this addon uses services already defined in Nagios, which means that Nagios performs each individual check as usual. It retrieves the results of individual checks, links these, and displays them on its own Web interface.

When doing so, the result of such links—business processes, so to speak—can be redefined in Nagios as a separate service so that it is possible, for instance, to use the notification logic of Nagios. Furthermore, the addon includes a mode with which it can simulate a "what would happen if" scenario. Individual services are set to an expected status, and the effects can be seen via the Web interface.

`check_multi` and the Nagios Business Process View and Nagios Business Impact Analysis addon are thus not in competition. Depending on the intended use, either `check_multi` will reduce the complexity of the services represented in Nagios and therefore will reduce the number of checks performed, or the addon will allow a more detailed view of overall events, though it does demand that all services are individually mapped in Nagios.

---

[7] http://www.nagiosexchange.org/22;1088

Executing Plugins via SSH

Local plugins, that is, programs that only run tests locally because there are no network protocols available, must be installed on the target system and started there. They check processes, CPU load, or how much free hard disk capacity is still available, among other things.

But if you still want to execute these plugins from the Nagios server, it is recommended that you use the secure shell, especially if any kind of Unix system is installed on the machine to be tested—a Secure Shell daemon will almost always be running on such a target system, and you do not require any special permissions to run most plugins. The Nagios administrator needs nothing more than an account, which he can use from the Nagios server. On the server itself, the check_by_ssh plugin must be installed.

In heterogeneous environments the Secure Shell itself often create conditions that may cause problems: depending on the operating system, an

SSH daemon may be in use that returns a false return code[1] or is so old
that it cannot handle the SSH protocol version 2.0. In this case it is better
to install the current OpenSSH version.[2] In pure Linux environments with
up-to-date and maintained installations, such problems generally do not
occur.

9.1 The check_by_ssh Plugin

check_by_ssh is run on the Nagios server and establishes a Secure Shell
connection to a remote computer so that it can perform local tests on it.
The programs run on the remote machine are to a large extent local plugins (see Chapter 7 from page 157); the use of check_by_ssh is not just
restricted to these, however.

The plugin sends a complete command line to the remote computer and
then waits for a plugin-compatible response: a response status between
0 (OK) and 3 (UNKNOWN), as well as a one-line text information for the
administrator (page 105).

If you run network plugins via check_by_ssh in order to perform tests
on other computers, these are known as *indirect checks,* which will be explained in the context of the *Nagios Remote Plugin Executor* in Section 10.6
from page 224.

The following example shows how check_by_ssh can be used to check the
swap partition on the target computer:

```
nagios@linux:nagios/libexec$ ./check_by_ssh -H target_computer \
    -i /etc/nagios/.ssh/id_dsa \
        -C "/usr/local/nagios/libexec/check_swap -w 50% -c 10%"
SWAP OK: 100% free (972 MB out of 972 MB) |swap=972MB;486;97;0;972
```

The command is similar to that for a secure shell, in the form of

```
ssh -i private_key target_computer "command"
```

The fact that a separate private key—not the default private key in the home
directory—is used, is optional and is described in detail in section 9.2 from
page 208. The command to be run is specified in check_by_ssh—in contrast to the secure shell ssh— with the option -C, the plugin is always specified with an absolute path.

check_by_ssh has the following options:

---

[1] In the nagios-users mailing list it was reported that Sun_SSH_1.0 returns a return
code of 255 instead of 0, which makes it unsuitable for the deployment described here.
[2] http://www.openssh.org/

-H address / --hostname=address
> The host name or IP address of the computer to which the plugin should set up an SSH connection.

-C command / --command=command
> The command to be run on the remote computer, that is, the plugin with its complete path and all the necessary parameters:

```
-C "/usr/local/nagios/libexec/check_disk -w 10% -c 5% -e -m"
```

-1 / --proto1
> Force version 1 of the secure shell protocol.

-2 / --proto2
> Force version 2 of the secure shell protocol.

-o ssh_option / --ssh-option=ssh_option (from version 1.4.6)
> Passes an SSH option to the secure shell on the target host. To specify multiple options, use of the switch is repeated.

-i keyfile / --identity=keyfile
> Which file should be used instead of the standard key file containing the private key of the user nagios? For one option, which is recommended, see Section 9.2.3, page 210.

-p port / --port=port
> This specifies the port if the Secure Shell daemon on the target server is not listening on the standard TCP port 22.

-l user / --logname=user
> User name on the target host. [-S number / --skip-stdout=number (from version 1.4.9)]
> Ignores the specified number of lines at the beginning of the output to STDOUT. If this option is omitted, the entire output is ignored.

-E number / --skip-stderr=lines (from version 1.4.9)
> Like --skip-stdout, but refers only to the output of STDERR.

-w floating_point_decimal /
--warning=floating_point_decimal
> If the response to the command to be executed takes more than *floating_point_decimal* seconds, the plugin will issue a warning.

-c floating_point_decimal /
--critical=floating_point_decimal
> The critical value in seconds concerning the response time of the command to be executed.

-f[3]

    Starts a background process without opening an interactive terminal (tty).

-t *timeout* / --timeout=*timeout*

    After *timeout* seconds have expired, the plugin stops the test and returns the CRITICAL status. The default is 10 seconds.

In addition to this, check_by_ssh has parameters available, -O, -s and -n, enabling it to write the result in *passive mode* to the *interface for external commands* (see section 13.1 from page 292). The mode is named this way because Nagios does not receive the information itself but reads it indirectly from the interface.

This procedure has the advantage of being able to run several separate commands simultaneously over a single SSH connection. This may cause the command definition to be rather complicated, however. Since the plugins themselves are called and executed as programs on the target server, it hardly matters whether the SSH connection is established once or three times. For this reason it is better to use a simple command definition rather than the passive mode.

But if you still want to find more information about this, you can look in the online help, which is called with check_by_ssh -h.

9.2 Configuring SSH

So that Nagios can run plugins over the secure shell remotely and automatically, it—or, strictly speaking, the user nagios on the Nagios server—must not be distracted by any password queries. This is avoided with a login via a Public Key mechanism.

9.2.1 Generating SSH key pairs on the Nagios server

The key pair required to do this is stored by the key generator ssh-keygen by default in the subdirectory .ssh of the respective user's home directory (for the user nagios, this therefore corresponds to the installation guide in Chapter 1.2 from page 39, that is, /usr/local/nagios). If it is also sent on its way with the -f *private_keyfile* option (without path specification), it will land in the current working directory, which in the following example is /etc/nagios/.ssh:

```
nagios@linux:~$ mkdir /etc/nagios/.ssh
nagios@linux:~$ cd /etc/nagios/.ssh
```

---

[3] There is currently no long form for this option.

```
nagios@linux:/etc/nagios/.ssh$ ssh-keygen -b 1024 -f id_dsa -t dsa -N ''
Generating public/private dsa key pair.
Your identification has been saved in id_dsa.
Your public key has been saved in id_dsa.pub.
The key fingerprint is:
02:0b:5a:16:9c:b4:fe:54:24:9c:fd:c3:12:8f:69:5c nagios@nagserv
```

The length of the key here is 1024 bits, and DSA is used to encrypt the keys. -N ' ' ensures that the private key in id_dsa does not receive separate password protection: this option forces an empty password.

9.2.2 Setting up the user nagios on the target host

Similar to the configuration on the Nagios server, the group and the user nagios are also set up on the computer to be monitored:

```
target_computer:~ # groupadd -g 9000 nagios
target_computer:~ # useradd -u 9000 -g nagios -d /home/nagios -m \
    -c "Nagios Admin" nagios
target_computer:~ # mkdir /home/nagios/.ssh
```

The target computer is given the directory /home/nagios as the home directory, where a subdirectory .ssh is created. In this the administrator (or another user[4]) saves the public key generated on the Nagios server /etc/nagios/.ssh/id_dsa.pub, in a file called authorized_keys:

```
linux:~ # scp /etc/nagios/.ssh/id_dsa.pub \
    target_computer:/home/nagios/.ssh/authorized_keys
```

Now the user nagios does not require its own password on the target server. You just need to make sure that on the target server the .ssh directory, together with authorized_keys, belongs to the user nagios:

```
target_computer:~ # chown -R nagios.nagios /home/nagios/.ssh
target_computer:~ # chmod 700 /home/nagios/.ssh
```

9.2.3 Checking the SSH connection and check_by_ssh

With this configuration you should first check whether the secure shell connection is working properly. The test is performed as the user nagios, since Nagios makes use of this during the checks:

---

[4] ... but not the user nagios, because when an account is created, useradd first sets an invalid password here, which we do not change into a valid one. This means that you cannot currently log in to the target computer as nagios.

```
nagios@linux:~$ ssh -i /etc/nagios/.ssh/id_dsa target_computer w
18:02:09 up 128 days, 10:03,  8 users,  load average: 0.01, 0.02, 0.00
USER     TTY     FROM           LOGIN@  IDLE   JCPU   PCPU WHAT
wob      pts/1   linux01:S.1    08Sep04 1:27   4.27s  0.03s -bin/tcsh
...
```

The -i option explicitly specifies the path to the private key file. If the command w to be run on the target computer does not provide any output or if the opposite SSH daemon requests a password, then the login via public key is not working. In this case you must first find and eliminate the error before you can move on to testing check_by_ssh.

In this next step, you run the local plugin on the target computer, with check_by_ssh, which later on is run automatically, from the command line of the Nagios server. Make sure that the plugin paths are correct in each case. The path to the private key file of the user nagios on the server is specified with -i:

```
nagios@linux:~$ /usr/local/nagios/libexec/check_by_ssh \
   -H target_computer -i /etc/nagios/.ssh/id_dsa \
   -C "/usr/local/nagios/libexec/check_disk -w 10% -c 5% -e -m"
DISK CRITICAL [2588840 kB (5%) free on /net/linux04/b] [937152 kB (5%)
free on /net/linux04/c]
```

In the example, check_by_ssh should start the /usr/local/nagios/lib-exec/check_disk plugin on the target computer with the options -w 10% -c 5% -e -m. If this does not work, then this is first run locally on the target host with the same parameter. By doing this you can rule out that the problem lies in the plugin command itself and not in the secure shell connection.

9.3 Nagios Configuration

The matching command object is again defined in the file checkcommands. cfg; similar to check_local_disk, it should be named check_ssh_disk:

```
# check_ssh_disk command definition
define command{
    command_name    check_ssh_disk
    command_line    $USER1$/check_by_ssh -H $HOSTADDRESS$ \
                    -i /etc/nagios/.ssh/id_dsa \
                    -C "$USER1$/check_disk -w $ARG1$ -c $ARG2$ -p $ARG3$"
}
```

The command line stored in command_line first runs check_by_ssh; $USER1$ contains the local plugin path on the Nagios server. Next come the arguments—the IP address of the target host (parameter -H), the private key file (parameter -i) and finally, with the -C parameter, the complete command that the target host should carry out. If the plugin path on the target host and on the Nagios server are identical, then you can also use the $USER1$ macro in it; otherwise the plugin path on the target computer is given explicitly.

Setting up the command is no different here to the one in `check_local_disk` in Section 7.1 on page 158. This means that apart from the warning and critical limits, we explicitly specify a file system or a hard drive partition, with the -p parameter.

The command `check_ssh_disk` defined in this way is applied as follows, here on a computer called `linux02`:

```
define service{
    host_name         linux02
    service_description FS_root
    ...
    check_command     check_ssh_disk!10%!5%!/
    ...
}
```

The service object defined in this way ensures that Nagios checks its / file system. The warning limit lies at 10 percent, the critical limit at 5 percent.

If you use the `check_by_ssh` plugin with `check_ssh_disk`, as in the example here, you must make sure that the plugin path is identical on all target hosts. This is also worth doing for reasons of simplicity, though it is not always possible in practice. The following service definition, for this reason, gives the plugin path to the target computer as an additional argument:

```
define service{
    host_name         linux02
    service_description FS_root
    ...
    check_command     check_ssh_disk!/usr/lib/nagios/plugins!10%!5%!/
    ...
}
```

In order for this to work, you must change the command line in the command definition, passed on with -C, as follows:

```
-C "$ARG1$/check_disk -w $ARG2$ -c $ARG3$ -p $ARG4$"
```

Caution: this causes the numbers of each of the $ARGx$ macros for -w, -c, and -p to be shifted by one.

The Nagios Remote Plugin Executor (NRPE)

The *Nagios Remote Plugin Executor* (or in short, NRPE) as the name suggests, executes programs on a remote host. These are usually plugins that test the corresponding computer locally and therefore must be installed on it. The use of NRPE is not restricted to local plugins; any plugins at all can be executed, including those intended to test network services—for example, to indirectly test computers that are not reachable from the Nagios server (as shown in Section 10.6 from page 224).

While a genuine user account must be available on the remote computer when the secure shell is used (see Chapter 9), which can also be used to do other things than just start plugins, NRPE is restricted exclusively to explicitly configured tests. If you want to, or are forced to, do without a login shell on the target host, it is better to use NRPE, even if there is somewhat more configuration work involved than with the secure shell. In addition to the Nagios configuration and the installation of the check_nrpe plugin on the Nagios server, the following tasks remain on the target system:

- The program nrpe must be installed.

- The inet daemon there (inetd or xinetd) must be configured with administrator privileges.

- All the plugins called via NRPE must be installed.

10.1   Installation

NRPE and the plugins are installed from the sources, or you can fall back on the packages provided by the distributor. You should use at least version 2.0 of NRPE, since this is incompatible with its predecessors. Starting with version 2.6, NRPE has the switch -u. If the NRPE service on the target system is not reachable, the plugin check_nrpe on the Nagios server returns an UNKNOWN for this switch. Starting with version 2.8, NRPE supports the multi-line output of plugins that was introduced with Nagios 3.0 (see Section 8.5.1 from page 193). At the time this book went to press, the current version was 2.12, dated 26. 03. 2008.

All established distributions include the plugin collection from at least version 1.4. Whether you need the most up-to-date version depends on your expectations of the respective plugins.

10.1.1   Distribution-specific packages

SuSE Linux 10.3 includes the packages nagios-nrpe-2.10-4.1.i586.rpm, nagios-plugins-1.4.10-12.1.i586.rpm, and nagios-plugins-extras -1.4.10-12.1.i586.rpm. nagios-nrpe contains both the daemon and the plugin check_nrpe. nagios-plugins-extras installs several additional plugins, such as database checks, FPing test or Radius test, which can be omitted, depending on your specific monitoring needs.

For the sake of simplicity, the design packages are installed via YAST2[1] or rpm -ihv *package*. the second method is also open to Fedora users.

For Fedora Core and Red Hat Enterprise Linux, Dag Wieers has made available corresponding Nagios packages of several versions.[2]

Debian/Sarge distributes the NRPE daemon and the NRPE plugin check_ nrpe in two different packages called nagios-nrpe-server and nagios- nrpe-plugin, which can be installed separately via apt-get install

---

[1] On the command line, using yast -i *package*.

[2] http://dag.wieers.com/

package. If you want to do without local documentation, you can omit the package `nagios-nrpe-doc` and just add the plugin package `nagios-plug-ins` to the target hosts.

The paths for the program `nrpe`, the configuration file `nrpe.cfg`, and the plugin directory are listed in Table 10.1.

Distribution	NRPE program	Configuration file	Plugins
Self-compiled[3]	`/usr/local/sbin/nrpe`	`/etc/nagios/nrpe.cfg`	`/usr/local/nagios/libexec`
SuSE	`/usr/bin/nrpe`	`/etc/nagios/nrpe.cfg`	`/usr/lib/nagios/plugins`
Debian	`/usr/sbin/nrpe`	`/etc/nagios/nrpe.cfg`	`/usr/lib/nagios/plugins`
Fedora[4]	`/usr/sbin/nrpe`	`/etc/nagios/nrpe.cfg`	`/usr/lib/nagios/plugins`

Table 10.1:
Installation paths for
NRPE and plugins

10.1.2 Installation from the source code

The plugins are installed on the computers to be monitored exactly as described in Section 1.4 from page 43 for the Nagios server.

The NRPE source code is obtained from the Nagios homepage.[5] The directory `/usr/local/src`[6] is ideal for unloading the sources.

```
linux:~ #  mkdir /usr/local/src
linux:~ #  cd /usr/local/src
linux:local/src #  tar xvzf /path/to/nrpe-2.11.tar.gz
```

In the new directory that has been created, you run the `configure` command:

```
linux:local/src # cd nrpe-2.11
linux:src/rnpe-2.11 # ./configure --sysconfdir=/etc/nagios --enable-ssl
```

The recommended path specifications are listed in Table 10.1. The only difference from the default settings are for the directory in which the NRPE configuration file is stored (`configure` option `--sysconfdir`).

---

[3] Recommended.
[4] From the packages provided by Dag Wieers.
[5] http://www.nagios.org/download/
[6] The subdirectory `src` may need to be created first.

Accordingly, we can leave out the entry for `--with-nrpe-user` and `--with-nrpe-group` in the `configure` command. Both options are relevant only if the `nrpe` program is running as a daemon, and they can be overwritten in the configuration file. If the inet daemon is used, you should specify the user with whose permissions `nrpe` should start in the configuration file for the inet daemon.

`--enable-ssl` ensures that NRPE communicates over an SSL-encrypted channel. This will only work, of course, if both `nrpe` on the target host and `check_nrpe` on the Nagios server have both been compiled accordingly.

The command `make all` compiles the programs `nrpe` and `check_nrpe`, but it does *not* copy them from `/usr/local/src/nrpe-2.11/src` to the corresponding system directories. Since there is no `make install`, you must do this yourself, following the details in Table 10.1: you need to have `nrpe` on the computer to be monitored and the `check_nrpe` plugin on the Nagios server.

If the Nagios server and the target host used the same platform, you can compile both programs on one computer (e.g., the server) and then copy `nrpe` together with its configuration file to the computer to be monitored, instead of separately compiling `check_nrpe` on the Nagios server and `nrpe` on the target system.

10.2   Starting via the inet Daemon

It is best to start the program `nrpe` on the machine to be monitored via the inet daemon rather than as a separate daemon, since the Nagios server only performs the tests occasionally, and `nrpe` does not need to load any large resources.

If you have a choice, you should use the more modern `xinetd`. But to keep work to a minimum, the inet daemon will normally be used, as it is already running on the target system. In order that NRPE can be started as a service via `inetd` or `xinetd`, the `nrpe` service is defined in the file `/etc/services`:

```
nrpe    5666/tcp   # Nagios Remote Plugin Executor NRPE
```

Even if this has been installed as a package, you should still check to see whether this entry exists. By default, NRPE uses TCP port 5666.

10.2.1   `xinetd` configuration

If `xinetd` is used, a separate file is stored in the directory `/etc/xinetd.d` for each service to be started, so for `nrpe` it is best to create a file called `nrpe` or `nagios-nrpe`:

```
# /etc/xinetd.d/nrpe
# description: NRPE
# default: on
service nrpe
{
    flags            = REUSE
    socket_type      = stream
    wait             = no
    user             = nobody
    group            = nogroup
    server           = /usr/local/sbin/nrpe
    server_args      = -c /etc/nagios/nrpe.cfg --inetd
    log_on_failure   += USERID
    disable          = no
    only_from        = 127.0.0.1 ip_of_the_nagios_server
}
```

The values printed in italics are passed on to your own environment; instead of the placeholder `ip_of_the_nagios_server` you should enter, for example for `only_from`, the IP address of your own Nagios server. The NRPE access from outside is then restricted to this computer and to `localhost` (127.0.0.1). The latter address allows local tests; multiple IP addresses are separated by a space. However, this restrictive configuration functions only if `xinetd` has been compiled with support for the TCP wrapper (this is normally the case).

Under no circumstances should NRPE run with the permissions of a privileged user—`nobody` is therefore a sensible value. The `server` parameter specifies the complete path to the program `nrpe`; for `server_args` you should enter the matching path to the configuration file. After this modification, the configuration of `xinetd` is reloaded, with

```
linux:~ # /etc/init.d/xinetd reload
```

10.2.2 `inetd` configuration

In the standard `inetd`, the following line is added to the configuration file `/etc/inetd.conf`:

```
nrpe  stream  tcp  nowait  nobody /usr/sbin/tcpd /usr/local/sbin/nrpe  -c
/etc/nagios/nrpe.cfg --inetd
```

The line has been split up for reasons of space, but in the configuration file this must all be in a single line. Here the TCP wrapper `tcpd` is used. If this is not intended, you simply leave out this entry.[7] Here you should also explicitly enter the user `nobody`, the complete path to the binary `nrpe`, and the configuration file, also with its complete path. These strings, printed above in italics, should be adjusted to your own system, where necessary. After the configuration change, `inetd` is reloaded:

```
linux:~ # /etc/init.d/inetd reload
```

10.2.3 Is the Inet daemon watching on the NRPE port?

A simple test shows whether the inet daemon wants to respond to queries on port 5666:

```
linux:~ # netstat -lnt | grep ':5666'
...
tcp  0  0 0.0.0.0:5666  0.0.0.0:*  LISTEN
...
```

The program `netstat` uses option `-l` to display all the ports on which a service is waiting for incoming queries, that is, a service which is in the LISTEN state. Option `-n` suppresses the name resolution of hosts and ports and speeds up the display of information, and `-t` restricts the otput to TCP ports.

The test shows only whether the inet daemon was properly configured and newly started, for instance, whether the `nrpe` service is correctly entered in `/etc/services`. It does not clarify whether the paths to the NRPE daemon and its configuration file are correct. Errors like this are announced by the inet daemon only when a concrete access attempt takes place on NRPE port 5666. The subsequent complete function test is carried out only after the NRPE daemon has been configured. This is described in Section 10.4 from page 221.

10.3 NRPE Configuration on the Computer to Be Monitored

When compiling NRPE, the file `nrpe.cfg` is created in the source directory, which contains several parameters as well as the commands to run NRPE. These are copied manually to the configuration directory, which normally first has to be created on the target computer:

---

[7] inetd does not have a built-in method to allow access to services only from specific IP addresses. This function is added in the TCP wrapper `tcpd`. The access configuration is then taken over by the files `/etc/hosts.allow` and `/etc/hosts.deny`. More information on this is given by `man host_access`.

```
linux:src/rnpe-2.11 #  mkdir /etc/nagios
linux:src/rnpe-2.11 #  cp nrpe.cfg /etc/nagios/.
```

Distribution-specific packages are unpacked from the location specified in Table 10.1 on page 215.

nrpe is given the permissions of the user at runtime specified in the inet daemon configuration, which in our case is that of nobody. Therefore nrpe.cfg needs to be readable for this user. As long as the file does not contain any passwords (these really should not be used) or other critical information, then read permissions for all can be allowed.

The configuration file contains many comments; the following command displays the active parameters:[8]

```
user@linux:~$  egrep -v '^#|^$' nrpe.cfg | less
server_port=5666
allowed_hosts=127.0.0.1
nrpe_user=nobody
nrpe_group=nogroup
dont_blame_nrpe=0
debug=0
command_timeout=60
...
```

The parameters server_port, allowed_hosts, nrpe_user, and nrpe_group are only relevant if nrpe is working as a daemon. When the inet daemon is used, the program ignores these values since they have already been determined by the (x)indetd configuration.

The entry dont_blame_nrpe=0 prevents nrpe from accepting parameters, thus closing a potential security hole. debug=1 allows extensive logging, useful if you are looking for errors (debug=0 switches off the output for debugging information), and command_timeout specifies a timespan in seconds after which nrpe abruptly interrupts a plugin that has hung. Comments in the configuration file explain all these parameters as well.

After this, the commands are defined that are to be executed by NRPE. The configuration file nrpe.cfg already contains some, but first they all have to be commented out, and only those commands activated that really are intended for use.

The keyword command is followed in square brackets by the name with which check_nrpe should call the command. After the equals sign (=), the corresponding plugin command is specified, with its complete path:[9]

---

[8] The regular expression ^#|^$ matches all lines that either begin with a comment sign # or that consist of an empty line. The option -v ensures that egrep shows all lines that are *not* matched by this.

[9] The check_users command is explained in Section 7.6 from page 177, check_load is explained in Section 7.3 from page 162, and Section 7.4 from page 163 deals with check_procs.

```
command[check_users]=/usr/local/nagios/libexec/check_users -w 5 -c 10
command[check_load]=/usr/lib/nagios/libexec/check_load -w 8,5,3 -c 15,10,7
command[check_zombies]=/usr/lib/nagios/libexec/check_procs -w :1 -c :2 -s Z
```

With the path, care must be taken that this really does point to the local plugin directory. In the directory specified here, /usr/local/nagios/libexec, the self-compiled plugins are located[10]; and for installations from distribution packages the path is usually /usr/lib/nagios/plugins.

From the Nagios server, the command just defined, check_users is now run on the *target computer* via check_nrpe:

```
nagios@linux:nagios/libexec$ ./check_nrpe -H target_host -c check_users
```

10.3.1 Passing parameters on to local plugins

The method described so far has one disadvantage: for each test on the target system, a separately defined command is required for this. Here is the example of a server on which the plugin check_disk (see Section 7.1 from page 158) is required to monitor nine file systems:

```
command[check_disk_a]=path/to/check_disk -w 5% -c 2% -p /net/linux01/a
command[check_disk_b]=path/to/check_disk -w 4% -c 2% -p /net/linux01/b
command[check_disk_c]=path/to/check_disk -w 5% -c 2% -p /net/linux01/c
command[check_disk_d]=path/to/check_disk -w 5% -c 2% -p /net/linux01/d
command[check_disk_root]=path/to/check_disk -w 10% -c 5% -p /
command[check_disk_usr]=path/to/check_disk -w 10% -c 5% -p /usr
command[check_disk_var]=path/to/check_disk -w 10% -c 5% -p /var
command[check_disk_home]=path/to/check_disk -w 10% -c 5% -p /home
command[check_disk_tmp]=path/to/check_disk -w 10% -c 5% -p /tmp
```

To avoid all this work, NRPE can also be configured so that parameters may be passed on to check_nrpe:

```
dont_blame_nrpe=1
...
command[check_disk]=path/to/check_disk -w $ARG1$ -c $ARG2$ -p $ARG3$
```

In order for this to work, the NRPE configure script must be run with the option
--enable-command-args. The reason for this inconvenient procedure is that passing parameters on is a fundamental risk, since it cannot be ruled out that a certain choice of parameters could cause an (as yet unknown) buffer overflow, allowing the target system to be penetrated.

---

[10] ...provided you have followed the instructions in the book.

If you still decide on this, despite all the security risks, you should use a TCP wrapper (see Section 10.2.2, page 217), to ensure that only the Nagios server itself is allowed to send commands to NRPE.

If the plugin provides the corresponding options, there is sometimes a third method, however: the above-mentioned problem can also be solved by getting check_disk, if necessary, to test all file systems with one single command:

```
user@linux:nagios/libexec$  ./check_disk -w 10% -c 4% -e -m
DISK WARNING [2588840 kB (5%) free on /net/linux1/b] [937160 kB (5%) free
 on /net/linux1/c]
```

The -e parameter persuades the plugin to display only those file systems that produced a warning or an error. One restriction remains: the warning and critical limits are, by necessity, the same for all file systems.

10.4 NRPE Function Test

For a concluding function test, the plugin check_nrpe on the Nagios server is called. The command -H *target host* returns the IP address specified for the server on which the NRPE service has just been installed:

```
nagios@linux:nagios/libexec$ ./check_nrpe -H swobspace
CHECK_NRPE: Error - Could not complete SSL handshake.
```

The error message given here occurs very frequently and causes confusion almost as often because although problems may occur with the SSL handshake, the cause is to be found elsewhere in most cases. You only have an SSL problem if the SSL versions used by the plugin check_nrpe and the NRPE daemon addressed are incompatible or if one of the two software packages was compiled without SSL and the other was compiled with SSL.

Otherwise, the cause will lie elsewhere: The problem could be caused by an error in the configuration file, the inet daemon being unable to find the NRPE program or configuration file, or access permissions for the file nrpe.cfg that are not sufficient. You would also receive the error message mentioned if the Nagios server cannot access the NRPE service at all via the inetd configuration. In this case, you need to check the parameter only_from for xinetd or the same restrictions via the tcpd for inetd.

You can search for the exact cause of error in the syslog files, particularly in the file messages, and depending on the distribution, also in warn.log, daemon.log, or another log file:

```
linux:~ # grep nrpe /var/log/messages
...
```

```
nrpe[19844]: Unable to open config file '/etc/nagios/nrpe.cfg' for readi
ng
nrpe[19844]: Config file '/etc/nagios/nrpe.cfg' contained errors, aborti
ng...
...
```

In this example, the file `nrpe.cfg` is either not in the path being searched or `nrpe` cannot open it. Since `nrpe` is running with the permissions of the user `nobody`, it must also be able to read the configuration file.

A successful call of `check_nrpe` will then provide the version of the installed NRPE service:

```
nagios@linux:nagios/libexec$ ./check_nrpe -H swobspace
NRPE v2.11
```

10.5   Nagios Configuration

Commands that "trigger" local plugins on remote computers via `check_nrpe` are defined as before in the file `checkcommands.cfg` on the Nagios server.

10.5.1   NRPE without passing parameters on

If no parameters are passed on to the target plugin, things will look like this:

```
define command{
    command_name check_nrpe
    command_line $USER1$/check_nrpe -H $HOSTADDRESS$ -c $ARG1$
}
```

As the only argument, Nagios passes the command here that NRPE is to execute. If the `check_nrpe` plugin on the Nagios server is located in a different directory to the other plugins, you must enter the correct path instead of $USER1$.

A service to be tested via NRPE uses the command just defined, `check_nrpe`, as `check_command`. As an argument, the command is specified that was defined in `nrpe.cfg` on the target system (here: `linux04`):

```
define service{
    host_name              linux04
    service_description FS_var
    ...
```

```
    check_command  check_nrpe!check_disk_var
    ...
}
```

10.5.2   Passing parameters on in NRPE

In order to address the command defined in Section 10.3.1 on page 220

```
command[check_disk]=path/to/check_disk -w $ARG1$ -c $ARG2$ -p $ARG3$
```

from the Nagios server, the check_nrpe is given the corresponding arguments through the option -a:

```
define command{
    command_name check_nrpe
    command_line $USER1$/check_nrpe -H $HOSTADDRESS$ -c $ARG1$ -a $ARG2$
}
```

So that $ARG2$ can correctly transport the parameters for the remote plugin, these are separated by spaces in the service definition. in addition, you should ensure that the order is correct:

```
define service{
    host_name           linux04
    service_description FS_var
    ...
    check_command  check_nrpe!check_disk!10% 5% /var
    ...
}
```

The locally installed check_disk on linux04 distributes the three strings 10%, 5%, and /var to its own three macros $ARG1$, $ARG2$, and $ARG3$ for the command defined in nrpe.cfg.

10.5.3   Optimizing the configuration

If the NRPE commands are given identical names on all target systems, then all NRPE commands with the same name can be included in a single service definition. When doing this you can make use of the possibility of specifying several hosts, or even an entire group of hosts:

```
define service{
    host_name           linux04,linux02,linux11
    service_description FS_var
    ...
```

```
        check_command   check_nrpe!check_disk_var
        ...
}
```

With the command check_disk_var, defined at the beginning of Section
10.3.1 on page 220, Nagios now checks the /var file systems on the computers linux04, linux02, and linux11. If other file systems are to be
included in the test, a separate service is created for each one, thus avoiding the security problem involved in passing parameters on. If you use
the option of testing all file systems at the same time, with the check_disk
plugin (see Section 7.1), then ultimately, one single service definition is sufficient to monitor all file systems on all Linux servers— provided you have
a corresponding NRPE configuration on the target system:

```
define service{
    hostgroup_name          linux-servers
    service_description Disks
    ...
    check_command   check_nrpe!check_disk
    ...
}
```

10.6   Indirect Checks

NRPE executes not just local plugins, but any plugins that are available. If
you use network plugins via NRPE, these are referred to as *indirect checks*,
as illustrated graphically in Figure 10.1.

Figure 10.1:
Indirect checks with
NRPE

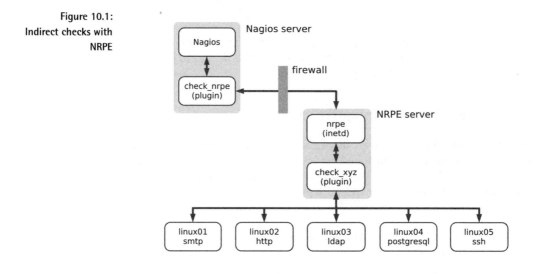

If every network service was tested directly across the firewall, it would have to open all the required ports. In the example, these would be the ports for SMTP, HTTP, LDAP, PostgreSQL, and SSH. If the checks are performed indirectly from a computer that is behind the firewall, on the other hand, then it is sufficient just to have the port for NRPE (TCP port 5666) open on the firewall. As long as it is configured via NRPE, the NRPE server behind the firewall can perform any tests it wants.

Whether the effort involved in indirect checks is greater than that for direct ones is dependent on the specific implementation: if this means that you would have to "drill holes into your firewall," then the additional work on the NRPE server may be worthwhile. But if the ports involved are open anyway, then the direct test can usually be recommended; this would make additional configuration work on an NRPE host unnecessary.

Collecting Information Relevant for Monitoring with SNMP

SNMP stands for *Simple Network Management Protocol*, a protocol defined above all to monitor and manage network devices. This means being able to have not only read access, but also write access to network devices, so that you can turn a specific port on a switch on or off, or intervene in other ways.

Nearly all network-capable devices that can also be addressed via TCP/IP can handle SNMP, and not just switches and routers. For Unix systems there are SNMP daemons; even Windows servers contain an SNMP implementation in their standard distribution, although this must be explicitly installed. But even uninterruptible power supplies (UPSs) or network-capable sensors are SNMP-capable.

If you are using Nagios, then at some point you can't avoid coming into contact with SNMP, because although you usually have a great choice of querying techniques for Unix and Windows systems, when it comes to hardware-specific components such as switches, without their own sophisticated operating system, then SNMP is often the only way to obtain information from the network device. SNMP certainly does not have a reputation of being easy to understand, which among other things lies in the fact that it is intended for communication between programs, and machine processing is in the foreground. In addition, you generally do not make direct contact with the protocol and with the original information, since even modems or routers provide a simple-to-operate interface that disguises the complexity of the underlying SNMP.

If you want to use SNMP with Nagios, you cannot avoid getting involved with the information structure of the protocol. Section 11.1 therefore provides a short introduction to SNMP. Section 11.2 from page 234 introduces NET-SNMP, probably the most widely used implementation for SNMP on Unix systems. On the one hand it shows how to obtain an overview of the information structure of a network device with command-line tools, and on the other it describes the configuration of the SNMP daemon in Linux. Finally, Section 11.3 from page 246 is devoted to the concrete use of SNMP with Nagios.

11.1   Introduction to SNMP

Although SNMP contains the P for "protocol" in its name, this does not stand for a protocol alone, but is used as a synonym for the *Internet Standard Management Framework*. This consists of the following components:

- Manageable network nodes that can be controlled remotely via SNMP. A specific implementation of an SNMP engine, whether by software or hardware, is referred to as an *agent*.

- At least one SNMP unit consisting of applications with which the agents can be managed. This unit is referred to as a *manager*.

- A protocol with which agent and manager can exchange information: the *Simple Network Management Protocol* (SNMP).

- A well-defined information structure, so that any managers and agents can understand each other: the so-called *Management Information Base*, or in short, MIB.

The framework assigns the manager the active role. The agent itself just waits passively for incoming commands. In addition, so-called *traps* extend the application possibilities of SNMP: these are messages that the agent actively sends to a single manager or a whole group of managers, for example if predefined limit values are exceeded or if functions of the network device fail.

As agents, SNMP engines implemented by the manufacturer are used for hardware-specific devices (switches, routers). For Linux and general Unix systems, the NET-SNMP implementation is available (see Section 11.2), for Windows servers there is equivalent software already included with the operating system.

In combination with Nagios, there are two possibilities. With respect to Nagios in the active role, corresponding Nagios plugins, as the manager, ask the agents for the desired information. The other way round, Nagios can also passively receive incoming SNMP traps using utilities and process these. Section 14.6 from page 312 is devoted to this topic.

An understanding of the SNMP information structure, the so-called *Management Information Base* (MIB), is critical if you want to use SNMP with Nagios successfully. For this reason this section will focus on this. The protocol itself is only mentioned briefly to illustrate the differences between different protocol versions.

If you want to get involved more deeply with SNMP, we refer you to the numerous *Request for Comments* (RFCs) describing SNMP. The best place to start would be in RFC 3410, "Introduction and Applicability Statements for Internet Standard Management Framework", and RFC 3411: "An Architecture for Describing Simple Network Management Protocol (SNMP) Management Frameworks." Apart from an introduction and numerous cross-links, you will also find references there to the original documents of the older versions, today referred to as SNMPv1 and SNMPv2.

11.1.1 The Management Information Base

The SNMP information structure consists of a hierarchical namespace construction of numbers. Figure 11.1 shows an extract from this. The tree structure is similar to those of other hierarchical directory services, such as DNS or LDAP.

Its root is called 1 (iso) and stands for the *International Organization for Standardization*. The next level, 3 (org) shown in Figure 11.1 provides a space for general, national and international organizations. Beneath this is 6 (dod) for the U.S. *Department of Defense*. The general (IP-based) internet owes its assignment as a subitem 1 (internet) of dod to its origin as a military project.

If you bring together the corresponding numbers from left to right and separate them with the dot, then for the internet node in the tree, you arrive at the designation 1.3.6.1. Such nodes are referred to in general as *object identifiers* (OID). Their syntax is used not only in SNMP but also in the definition of LDAP objects and attributes, for example.

The OID 1.3.6.1 is not exactly easily readable for humans, which is why other notation methods have gained acceptance: both iso.org.dod.internet and the combination iso(1).org(3).dod(6).internet(1) is allowed. Because this would quickly make readable descriptions infinitely long if the tree were deep enough, another abbreviated notation method has become established: as long as the term remains unique, you may simply write internet instead of 1.3.6.1.

The important thing here is that the communication between manager and agent is exclusively of a numerical nature. Whether the manager also allows text input or is capable of issuing information as text instead of as a numeric OID depends on the implementation in each case. The information on individual nodes is provided by the manufacturer of the SNMP agent as a Management Information Base (MIB) in file form.

Figure 11.1:
SNMP namespace
using the example of
the MIB–II interfaces

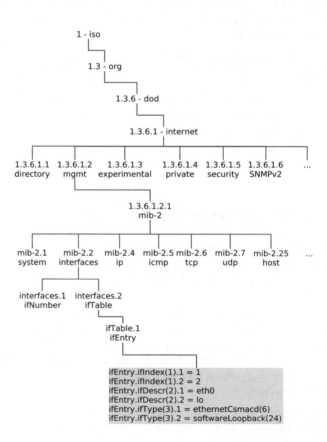

The data stored in the MIB includes contact information (who designed the MIB; usually the manufacturer of the device will be given here), the definition of individual subnodes and attributes, and the data types used. If an MIB file also describes the individual subnodes and attributes, this puts the manager in a position to supply the user with additional information on the meaning and purpose of the entry in question.

Below `internet`, the next level is divided into various namespaces. The management node `1.3.6.1.2` is especially important for SNMP, that is, `iso(1).org(3).dod(6).internet(1).mgmt(2)`. The namespace here is described by RFC 1155, "Structure and Identification of Management Information for TCP/IP-based Internets."

In order for manager and agent to be able to understand each other, the manager needs to know how the agent structures its data. This is where the *Management Information Base, Version II* comes into play. SNMP requests information from the agents on their implementation; with this, every manager can access the most important parameters of the agent, without a previous exchange of MIB definitions. The *Management Information Base II*, or MIB-II (or mib-2) for short, can be found in the namespace at `1.3.6.1.2.1` or `iso(1).org(3).dod(6).internet(1).mgmt(2).mib-2(1)`. Since it is well-defined and unique, OIDs lying beneath that are usually described in short, starting with MIB-II or mib-2.

Manufacturer-specific information can also be defined in your own Management Information Base. Corresponding MIBs are located beneath `internet.private.enterprise`. Once an OID has been described in an MIB, the meaning of this entry may never be changed. The description format for an MIB is standardized by RFC 1212, which is the reason that special MIBs, included by a vendor for its agents, can be integrated into almost any manager.

MIB-II

MIB-II, the Management Information Base , which is obligatory for all SNMP agents, contains several information groups. The most important of these are summarized in Table 11.1. The notation `mib-2.x` stands for `1.3.6.1.2.1.x`.

Group	OID	Description
system	mib-2.1	Information on the device, (e.g., the location, contact partner, or uptime)
interfaces	mib-2.2	Information on the network interfaces (Name, interface type, status, statistics etc.)

Table 11.1:
MIB-II groups (a selection)

continued:

Group	OID	Description
at	mib-2.3	Assignment of physical addresses (e.g., of MAC addresses) to the IP address (*Address Translation Table*)
ip	mib-2.4	Routing tables and IP packet statistics
icmp	mib-2.5	Statistics on individual ICMP packet types
tcp	mib-2.6	Open ports and existing TCP connections
udp	mib-2.7	ditto for UDP
host	mib-2.25	Information on storage media, devices, running processes and their use of resources

How you specifically handle information stored in the MIB-II can be explained using the example of the *interfaces* group: Figure 11.1 shows how they are split up into the two OID `interfaces.ifNumber` and `interfaces.ifTable`. This is because one network node initially reveals an unknown number of interfaces. This number is taken up by `ifNumber`. Before looking at these interfaces more closely, a manager can get the information from `ifNumber` about how many there really are.

`ifTable` then contains the actual information on the different interfaces. To obtain this information for a specific interface, the manager queries all the entries in which the last number is the same, like this:

```
ifEntry.ifIndex.1 = INTEGER: 1
ifEntry.ifDescr.1 = STRING: eth0
ifEntry.ifType.1 = INTEGER: ethernetCsmacd(6)
ifEntry.ifMtu.1 = INTEGER: 1500
ifEntry.ifSpeed.1 = Gauge32: 100000000
ifEntry.ifPhysAddress.1 = STRING: 0:30:5:6b:70:70
ifEntry.ifAdminStatus.1 = INTEGER: up(1)
ifEntry.ifOperStatus.1 = INTEGER: up(1)
```

`ifIndex` describes the device-internal index—SNMP always starts counting from 1, switches start counting here from 100. `ifDescr` contains the name of the interface, here `eth0`—this is obviously a Linux machine. It can be assumed from the next four entries that a normal 100-Mbit Ethernet interface is involved.

The interface type `ifType` is given as `ethernetCsmacd`,[1] that is, Ethernet. `ifMtu` specifies the *Maximum Transfer Unit*, which in local networks is always 1,500 bytes for Ethernet. The interface speed `ifSpeed` is 100,000,000

---

[1] *Carrier Sense* (CS) means that each network interface checks to see whether the line is free, based on the network signal (in contrast to Token Ring, for example, where the network card may use the line only if it explicitly receives a token); *Multiple Access* (MA) means that several network cards may access a common network medium simultaneously.

bits here, that is, 100 Mbit. And `ifPhysAddress` contains the physical network address, also called the MAC address.

`ifAdminStatus` reveals whether the admin has switched the interface on (up) or off (down) via the configuration. `ifOperStatus` on the other hand specifies the actual status, since even interfaces activated by an administrator are not necessarily connected to a device, or even switched on.

There is a similar picture for the second interface:

```
ifEntry.ifIndex.2 = INTEGER: 2
ifEntry.ifDescr.2 = STRING: lo
ifEntry.ifType.2 = INTEGER: softwareLoopback(24)
ifEntry.ifMtu.2 = INTEGER: 16436
ifEntry.ifSpeed.2 = Gauge32: 10000000
ifEntry.ifPhysAddress.2 = STRING:
ifEntry.ifAdminStatus.2 = INTEGER: up(1)
ifEntry.ifOperStatus.2 = INTEGER: up(1)
...
```

This is not an Ethernet card here, however, but a local loopback device.

11.1.2 SNMP protocol versions

The first SNMP version and *Internet Standard Management Framework* were described back in 1988 in RFCs 1065–1067; the current documentation on this version, named SNMPv1, can be found in RFC 1155–1157. It is still used today, since higher versions are fundamentally backward-compatible.

The big disadvantage of SNMPv1 is that this version allows only unsatisfactory authentication in precisely three stages: no access, read access, and full access for read and write operations. Two simple passwords, the so-called *communities*, provide a little protection here: they divide users into one community with read permissions, and the second one with read and write permissions. No further differentiation is possible. If this was not enough, the community is transmitted in plain text, making it an easy prey for sniffer tools.

Further development on the second version, SNMPv2, was intended to solve problems concerning the display of value ranges, error events, and the performance if there are mass requests (RFC 1905). This RFC was never fully implemented, however. The only relatively complete implementation that was used in practice is known as the *Community-based SNMPv2*, or SNMPv2c for short (RFC 1901–1908). The current version, SNMPv3 (RFC 3411–3418), has the status of an Internet standard. Agents with SNMPv3 implementations always understand requests from SNMPv1.

Apart from extended protocol operations, there are no fundamental differences between SNMPv1 and SNMPv2c. This is probably also the reason why SNMPv2 could not really gain a foothold. The hoped-for increase in security was certainly missing in this version. It is only the extensions of the framework in SNMPv3 which allow more precise access control, but this is much more complicated than the two community strings in SNMPv1. RFC 3414 describes the *user-based security model* (USM), RFC 3415 the *view-based access control model* (VACM).

When accessing an SNMP agent, you must tell all tools, including plugins, which protocol version is to be used. In Nagios you exclusively require read access. If this is restricted to the required information and you only allow the access from the Nagios server, you need have no qualms about doing without the extended authentication of SNMPv3. It is only important that you configure the agent—if possible—so that it completely prevents write accesses, or at least demands a password. You should never use this: since it is transmitted in plain text, there is always a danger that somebody may be listening, and misuse the password later on.

In NET-SNMP, write accesses can be completely prevented, access can be restricted to specific hosts, and information revealed can be limited. For other agents implemented in hardware such as switches and routers, you must weigh up whether you really need SNMPv3, assuming the manufacturer has made this available. SNMPv1, however, is available for all SNMP devices.

We will therefore only explain access via SNMPv1 below, and assume that this is generally read access only. If you still want to get involved with SNMPv3, we refer you to the NET-SNMP documentation.[2]

11.2 NET–SNMP

Probably the most widely used SNMP implementation for Linux and other UNIX systems is NET-SNMP[3] and was originally conceived at Carnegie-Mellon University. Wes Hardaker, a system administrator at the University of California in Davis, continued developing the code and first published it under the name UCD-SNMP (Version 3.0).

With version 5.0 the project finally got the name NET-SNMP. But various distributions still call the package UCD-SNMP, in part because it contains version 4.2, in part because the maintainer has simply not gotten around to renaming it.

NET-SNMP consists of a set of command line tools, a graphical browser (tkmib), an agent (snmpd, see Section 11.2.2 on page 238) and a library, which now forms the basis of nearly all SNMP implementations in the Open Source field.

---

[2] http://net-snmp.sourceforge.net/docs/FAQ.html#How_do_I_use_SNMPv
[3] http://net-snmp.sourceforge.net/

All common distributions include corresponding packages. In SuSE this is called `net-snmp` and contains all the components; Debian packs the tools in the package `snmp`, and the daemon in the package `snmpd`. At the time of going to press, version 5.4.1 was the current version, but an older 5.x version will do the job for our purposes. Their outputs differ to some extent, but the exact options can be looked up where necessary in the man page.

11.2.1 Tools for SNMP requests

For read access, the programs `snmpget`, `snmpgetnext` and `snmpwalk` are used. `snmpget` specifically requests a single OID and returns a single value from it. `snmpgetnext` displays the next variable existing in the Management Information Base, including its value:

```
user@linux:~$ snmpget -v1 -c public localhost ifDescr.1
IF-MIB::ifDescr.1 = STRING: eth0
user@linux:~$ snmpgetnext -v1 -c public localhost ifDescr.1
IF-MIB::ifDescr.2 = STRING: lo
user@linux:~$ snmpgetnext -v1 -c public localhost ifDescr.3
IF-MIB::ifType.1 = INTEGER: ethernetCsmacd(6)
```

The option `-v1` instructs `snmpget` to use SNMPv1 as the protocol. With `-c` you specify the read community an; in this case then, the password is `public`. This is followed by the computer to be queried, here `localhost`, and finally there is the OID whose value we would like to find out.

The NET-SNMP tools are masters of OID abbreviation: without special instructions, they always assume that an OID is involved which lies inside the MIB-II. For unique entries such as `ifDescr.1`, this is sufficient. But whether the various SNMP plugins for Nagios can also handle this depends on the specific implementation; it is best to try out cases on an individual basis. To be on the safe side, it is better to use complete OIDs, either numerical in readable form. The latter is obtained if you instruct `snmpget` to display the full OID:

```
user@linux:~$ snmpget -v1 -On -c public localhost ifDescr.1
.1.3.6.1.2.1.2.2.1.2.1 = STRING: eth0
user@linux:~$ snmpget -v1 -Of -c public localhost ifDescr.1
.iso.org.dod.internet.mgmt.mib-2.interfaces.ifTable.ifEntry.ifDescr.1 =
STRING: eth0
```

The `-On` option provides the numerical OID, `-Of` the text version. In this way you can easily find out the complete OID, for plugins which cannot handle the abbreviation. It is important to remember here: each OID always starts with a period. If you omit this, there will always be a plugin which doesn't work properly.

In order to obtain the entire information stored in the MIB-II, it is better to use snmpwalk. As the name suggests, the program takes a walk through the Management Information Base, either in its entirety or in a specified part of the tree. If you would like to find out about all the entries beneath the node mib-2.interfaces (Figure 11.1 on page 230), you simply give snmpwalk the required OID:

```
user@linux:~$ snmpwalk -v1 -c public localhost mib-2.interfaces
IF-MIB::ifNumber.0 = INTEGER: 3
IF-MIB::ifIndex.1 = INTEGER: 1
IF-MIB::ifIndex.2 = INTEGER: 2
IF-MIB::ifIndex.3 = INTEGER: 3
IF-MIB::ifDescr.1 = STRING: eth0
IF-MIB::ifDescr.2 = STRING: lo
IF-MIB::ifDescr.3 = STRING: eth1
IF-MIB::ifType.1 = INTEGER: ethernetCsmacd(6)
...
```

snmpwalk hides the exact structure slightly (links to ifTable and ifEntry are missing, for example, see Figure 11.1), so that it is better to use -Of:

```
user@linux:~$ snmpwalk -v1 -Of -c public localhost mib-2.interfaces
...mib-2.interfaces.ifNumber.0 = INTEGER: 3
...mib-2.interfaces.ifTable.ifEntry.ifIndex.1 = INTEGER: 1
...mib-2.interfaces.ifTable.ifEntry.ifIndex.2 = INTEGER: 2
...mib-2.interfaces.ifTable.ifEntry.ifIndex.3 = INTEGER: 3
...mib-2.interfaces.ifTable.ifEntry.ifDescr.1 = STRING: eth0
...mib-2.interfaces.ifTable.ifEntry.ifDescr.2 = STRING: lo
...mib-2.interfaces.ifTable.ifEntry.ifDescr.3 = STRING: eth1
...mib-2.interfaces.ifTable.ifEntry.ifType.1 = INTEGER: ethernetCsmacd(6)
```

The three dots ... in the version here abbreviated for print stand for .iso.org.dod.internet.mgmt.

As the next step, you could take a look around your own network and query the Management Information Bases available there. Normally you will get quite far with the read community public, since this is often the default setting. So you should also try out the community string private, which is the default set by many vendors. An extremely dubious practice, by the way: anyone who knows a bit about SNMP and who has access to the network can use this to manipulate device settings, such as switching off certain ports or the entire switch. But even with all the other default passwords, you should take the trouble to change them. Entire password lists can be found on the Internet, sorted by vendors and devices—easily found through Google.

Whether you also change the preset read community (such as public) depends on the information available on it and on your own security requirements. But the read-write community should under no circumstances retain the default setting. In addition it is recommended that you switch off

SNMP completely for devices that are neither queried nor administrated via SMNP, just to be on the safe side.

Taking a graphic walk with `mbrowse`

A graphical interface is often recommended for interactive research and for initial explorations of the Management Information Base, such as the SNMP browser `mbrowse`[4] (see Figure 11.2). This is not a component of NET-SNMP, but most Linux distributions provide an `mbrowse` package for installation.

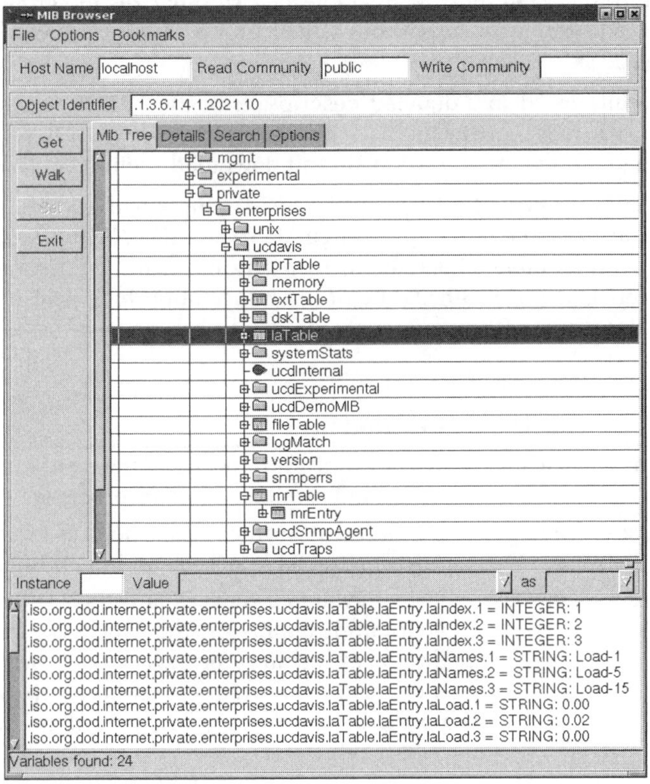

Figure 11.2:
SNMP browser
`mbrowse`

If you highlight an entry and click on the Walk button, the lower window displays the same output as `snmpwalk`. The graphical display, however, allows better orientation—it is easier to see in which partial tree you are currently located. It is also interesting that `mbrowse` shows the numeric OID of each selected object, in `Object Identifier`.

---

[4] `http://www.kill-9.org/mbrowse/`

11.2.2   The NET–SNMP daemon

The NET-SNMP daemon `snmpd` works as an SNMP agent for Linux and other Unix systems; that is, it answers requests from a manager and also provides a way of making settings to the Linux system via write accesses, such as manipulating the routing table.

Supported Mangement Information Bases

The agent initially provides information on the MIB-II described in RFC 1213 (Section 11.1.1 from page 229), but also the host extensions belonging to this from RFC 2790 (host MIB). Table 11.2 summarizes the groups of the host MIB, and the most important MIB-II groups are introduced in Table 11.1 (page 231).

If you are interested in a detailed description of the MIB-II, including the host MIB, we refer you to `http://www.snmplink.org/`. There you can surf through a huge number of MIBs and download them if you wish.

In addition to the basic MIB-II, the NET-SNMP implementation has its own extension at `private.enterprises.ucdavis` (UCD-SNMP-MIB). The directives given in table 11.3 refer to instructions in the configuration file `snmpd.conf` (see page 240). Some of the information here is also given in the Host Resources MIB.

	Group	OID	Description
Table 11.2: Components of the Host Resources MIB `mib-2.host` (RFC 2790)	hrSystem	host.1	System time and uptime of the host, logged-in users, and number of active processes
	hrStorage	host.2	Details on all storage media such as swap, hard drives, removable media, and main memory
	hrDevice	host.3	List of available devices and their properties: apart from details on the processor, network interfaces, printer and DVD-/CD-ROM drives, there is also information on hard drives, their partitioning, file systems, mount points and file system types
	hrSWRun	host.4	All running processes including PID and command line parameters
	hrSWRunPerf	host.5	CPU usage and memory usage for the processes from hrSWRun
	hrSWInstalled	host.6	Installed software; the information originates from the RPM database (unfortunately this does not work in Debian).

Group	OID	Directive	description	
prTable	ucdavis.2	`proc`	details of running processes	Table 11.3:
memory	ucdavis.4	–	Memory and Swap space load, as in the program `free`	Extract from the
extTable	ucdavis.8	`exec`	Information on self-defined commands in the configuration file[5]	UCD-SNMP-MIB
dskTable	ucdavis.9	`disk`	Information on file systems, see example in the text	
laTable	ucdavis.10	`load`	System load	
ucdExperimental	ucdavis.13	–	Experimental extension containing an entry with lm-sensor information, among other things	
fileTable	ucdavis.15	`file`	Information on files to be explicitly monitored	
version	ucdavis.100	–	Details on the NET-SNMP version and the parameters with which the daemon was compiled	

While `mib-2.host` only specifies absolute values, such as for file systems, UCD-SNMP-MIB also allows threshold values to be set for agent pages, which then explicitly generate an error value (`dskErrorFlag`) with error text (`dskErrorMsg`):

```
user@linux:~$ snmpwalk -v1 -c public localhost ucdavis.dskTable |\
    grep '.2 ='
UCD-SNMP-MIB::dskIndex.2 = INTEGER: 2
UCD-SNMP-MIB::dskPath.2 = STRING: /net/swobspace/b
UCD-SNMP-MIB::dskDevice.2 = STRING: /dev/md6
UCD-SNMP-MIB::dskMinimum.2 = INTEGER: -1
UCD-SNMP-MIB::dskMinPercent.2 = INTEGER: 10
UCD-SNMP-MIB::dskTotal.2 = INTEGER: 39373624
UCD-SNMP-MIB::dskAvail.2 = INTEGER: 1694904
UCD-SNMP-MIB::dskUsed.2 = INTEGER: 35678636
UCD-SNMP-MIB::dskPercent.2 = INTEGER: 95
UCD-SNMP-MIB::dskPercentNode.2 = INTEGER: 1
UCD-SNMP-MIB::dskErrorFlag.2 = INTEGER: 1
UCD-SNMP-MIB::dskErrorMsg.2 = STRING: /net/swobspace/b: less than 10% fr
ee (= 95%)
```

The `grep '.2 ='` filters all entries on the second device from the `snmpwalk` output, the Linux software-RAID `/dev/md6`. The entry `dskPercent` shows

---

[5] Any executable programs can be used here.

the current load of this data medium. An error exists if `dskErrorFlag` contains the value 1 instead of 0; `dskErrorMsg` adds a readable message to the error message. It can be assumed from this that the agent is being configured so that it will announce an error if free capacity falls below 10 percent.

The configuration file `snmpd.conf`

Configuring the agent is done in the file `snmpd.conf`, which is either located in the directory `/etc` directly (the case for SUSE) or in `/etc/snmp` (Debian), depending on the distribution.

Authentication and security   As the first step towards a finely tuned access control, you first need to define who should have access to which community:

```
# (1) source addressesQuelladressen
com2sec  localnet  192.168.1.0/24 public
com2sec  localhost 127.0.0.1      public
com2sec  nagiossrv 192.168.1.9    public
```

`com2sec` links the source IP addresses to a community string (the SNMP password). This keyword is followed by an alias for the IP address range, the address range itself, and then a freely selectable community string, for which we will use `public` here, to keep things simple.[6] `192.168.1.0/24` refers to the local network; the Nagios server itself has the IP address `192.168.1.9`. If you set access permissions for the alias `localnet` later on, they will apply to the entire local network `192.168.1.0/24`, but if you reference `nagiossrv` when doing this, they will only apply to the Nagios server itself.

Then the defined computers and networks are assigned via their aliases to groups which have different security models:

```
# (2) assignment of group - security model - source-IP alias
group Local     v1        localhost
group Nagios    v1        nagiossrv
```

The keyword `group` is followed first by a freely selectable group name: here we define the group `Local` with the security model `v1`, which belongs to the address range defined as `localhost`, and the group `Nagios` with the same security model contained in the Nagios server.

You can choose from `v1` (SNMPv1), `v2c` (community-based SNMPv2), and `usm` (the *User Model* from SNMPv3) as the security model. If you assign

---

[6] See also page 236.

a computer or a network several security models at the same time, then separate entries with the same group name are required:

```
group Nagios    v1      nagiossrv
group Nagios    usm     nagiossrv
```

With the definition of views (keyword `view`) the view from the outside can be restricted precisely to partial trees of the Management Information Base. Each view here is also given a name for referencing:

```
#(3) View definition for partial trees of the SNMP namespace
view all     included  .1
view system included  .iso.org.dod.internet.mgmt.mib-2.system
```

The reference `included` includes the following partial tree in the view. Thus the view `all` covers the entire tree (`.1`). If you want to exclude certain partial trees in this, then the keyword `excluded` is used:

```
view all     included  .1
view all     excluded  .iso.org.dod.internet.private
```

The partial tree beneath `private` in `all` is now blocked, such as the MIB ucdavis (`private.enterprises.ucdavis`).

One interesting feature is the mask; it specifies in hexadecimal notation which nodes correspond exactly to the subtree:

```
view all     included  .iso.org.dod.internet.mgmt       F8
```

All places of the queried OID, for which the mask contains a 1 in binary notation, must be identical in the queried partial tree to the OID specified here, `.iso.org.dod.internet.mgmt`, otherwise the daemon will refuse access and not provide any information. `.iso.org.dod.internet.mgmt` is written numerically as `.1.3.6.1.2`.

Thanks to the mask F8,[7] binary 11111000, the first five places from the left in the OID must always be `.iso.org.dod.internet.mgmt`. If somebody queried an OID (such as the `private` tree `.1.3.6.1.4`), which deviates from this, the agent would remain silent and not provide any information. If you leave out the mask detail, FF will be used.

If you have defined the alias, community, security model, and view, you just need to bring them together for the purpose of access control. This is done with the `access` instruction:

---

[7] $F = 1 \cdot 2^3 + 1 \cdot 2^2 + 1 \cdot 2^1 + 1 \cdot 2^0 = 1111, \ 8 = 1000$

```
# (4) Definition of the access control
access Local            any      noauth  exact  all    none   none
access NagiosGrp        any      noauth  exact  all    none   none
```

The access restrictions are bound to the group. The `context` column remains empty (`'"'`), since only SNMPv3 requires it.[8] As the security model, you then normally choose `any`, but you may define a specific model with `v1`, `v2c` or `usm`, since several different security models may be assigned to a group, as shown in the discussion of "Authentication and Security" at the beginning of this Section. The fifth column specifies the security level, which is also of interest only for SNMPv3. In the other two security models (we are only using `v1`), `noauth` is given here. The fourth last column also has just one meaning in SNMPv3. But since you must enter a valid value forSNMPv1 and SNMPv2c as well, then `exact` is chosen here.

The last two columns specify which view should be used for which access (read or write). In the example, the groups `Local` and `NagiosGrp` obtain read access for the view `all`, but no write access. The final column defines whether the agent should send SNMP traps—that is, active messages, to the manager—for events that occur within the range of validity of the view. Section 14.6 from page 312 goes into more detail about SNMP traps.

With the configuration described here, you can now exclusively access the Nagios server and `localhost` via SNMPv1 for information. The server access can be restricted further by defining a view that makes only parts of the MIB visible. But you should only try this once the configuration described is working, to avoid logical errors and time-consuming debugging.

System and local information   The partial tree `mib-2.system` provides information on the system itself and on the available (that is, implemented) MIBs. With `syslocation` you can specify where a system is located in the company or on the campus, and after the keyword `syscontact` you enter the e-mail address of the administrator responsible:

```
# (5) mib-2.system
syslocation Server room Martinstr., 2nd rack from the left
syscontact root <wob@swobspace.de>
```

As long as you do not redefine the parameters `sysname` and `sysdescr` at this point, the corresponding MIBs in the default will reveal the host name and/or the system and kernel specification, corresponding to `uname -a`:

```
user@linux:~$ snmpwalk -v1 -c public localhost system
system.sysDescr.0 = STRING: Linux swobspace 2.6.10 #20 SMP Mon Dec 27
11:55:25 CET 2004 i686
```

---

[8] Corresponding descriptions on SNMPv3 would go beyond the bounds of this book.

```
system.sysObjectID.0 = OID: NET-SNMP-MIB::netSnmpAgentOIDs.10
system.sysUpTime.0 = Timeticks: (1393474) 3:52:14.74
system.sysContact.0 = STRING: root <wob@swobspace.de>
system.sysName.0 = STRING: swobspace
system.sysLocation.0 = STRING: Serverraum Martinstr., 2. Rack von links
...
```

Defining processes to be monitored   Processes that you want to monitor using SNMP are specified with the `proc` directive, and if required you can specify the minimum or maximum number of processes:

```
# (6) Processes: enterprises.ucdavis.procTable
# proc process maximum minimum
# proc process maximum
# proc process
proc sshd
proc nmbd 2 1
proc smbd
proc slapd
```

If the entry for maximum and minimum is missing, at least one process must be running. If only the minimum is omitted, NET-SNMP will define this with zero processes. The corresponding entries end up in the MIB `ucdavis.prTable`; in case of error you will receive an error flag (`prError-Flag` and an error description (`prErrMessage`) (which unfortunately you cannot define yourself):

```
user@linux:~$ snmpwalk -v1 -c public localhost prTable
...
prTable.prIndex.4 = INTEGER: 4
prTable.prNames.4 = STRING: slapd
prTable.prMin.4 = INTEGER: 0
prTable.prMax.4 = INTEGER: 0
prTable.prCount.4 = INTEGER: 0
prTable.prErrorFlag.4 = INTEGER: 1
prTable.prErrMessage.4 = STRING: No slapd process running.
...
```

`ucdavis.prTable` only reveals the configured processes; on the other hand it allows `mib-2.host.hrSWRun` and `mib-2.host.hrSWRunPerf` in general to query all running processes. If you want to prevent this, the view must exclude the area you do not want.

Your own commands   With the `exec` directive you can specify commands in the extension `ucdavis.extTable`, which the agent will execute in the corresponding queries. The result then appears in the relevant entries. In the following example the agent calls `/bin/echo` if it is asked for `ucdavis.ext-Table`:

```
# (7) your own commands: enterprises.ucdavis.extTable
# exec name command arguments
exec echotest /bin/echo hello world
```

The program to be executed must appear with its absolute path in the configuration. Running `snmpwalk` provides only the following:

```
user@linux:~$ snmpwalk -v1 -c public localhost extTable
extTable.extEntry.extIndex.1 = INTEGER: 1
extTable.extEntry.extNames.1 = STRING: echotest
extTable.extEntry.extCommand.1 = STRING: /bin/echo hello world
extTable.extEntry.extResult.1 = INTEGER: 0
extTable.extEntry.extOutput.1 = STRING: hello world
...
```

`extTable.extEntry.extResult` contains the return value of the command executed, and `extTable.extEntry.extOutput` contains the text output.

With the `exec` directive you can thus query everything that a local script or program can find out. This could be a security problem, however: if the programs used are susceptible to buffer overflows, this feature could be misused as a starting point for a denial-of-service attack.

Monitoring hard drive capacity   The `disk` directive is suitable for monitoring file systems. The keyword `disk` is followed by the path for a mount point, and then the minimum hard drive space in KB or in percent that should be available. If you omit the capacity entry, at least 100 MB must be available; otherwise an error message will be given.

In the following example the free capacity in the / file system should not drop below 10%, and on /usr, at least 800 MB[9] should remain free:

```
#(8) File systems: enterprises.ucdavis.dskTable
#disk mount point
#disk mount point minimum_capacity_in_KB
#disk mountpoint minimum_capacity_in_percent%
disk / 10%
disk /usr 819200
disk /data 50%
```

As far as the data partition /data is concerned, the alarm should be raised if free capacity falls below 50%. `dskErrorFlag` in this case contains the value 1 instead of 0, and `dskErrorMsg` contains an error text:

```
...
UCD-SNMP-MIB::dskPercent.3 = INTEGER: 65
```

[9]   1024KB ∗ 800

```
UCD-SNMP-MIB::dskErrorFlag.3 = INTEGER: 1
UCD-SNMP-MIB::dskErrorMsg.3 = STRING: /data: less than 50% free (= 65%)
...
```

dskPercent reveals a current load of 65%. Instead of the partial tree configured here, ucdavis.dskTable, mib-2.host.hrStorage also provides an overview of all file systems, even those not explicitly defined. These are missing percentage details, however, and you do not receive an error status or error message, as supplied by ucdavis.dskTable.

You should think hard about whether you set the warning limit in the NET-SNMP or in the Nagios configuration. In the first case you must configure the values on each individual host. If you query the percentage load, however, with the check_snmp plugin (see section 11.3.1 from page 246), then you set warning and critical limits centrally on the Nagios server, saving yourself a lot of work if you make changes later on. The includeAllDisks directive adds all existing file systems to the dskTable table:

```
includeAllDisks 10%
```

It requires a minimum limit to be specified in percent, and also returns error values. An absolute specification in KB is not possible here. If you set warning and error limits centrally for check_snmp; (see Section 11.3.1 from page 246) the error attributes dskErrorFlag and dskErrorMsg are not queried, so that the value set here as the minimum limit can be ignored.

System load   The load directive queries the CPU load. As the limit values, you specify the average values for one minute, and optionally for five and 15 minutes:

```
# (9) System Load: enterprises.ucdavis.laTable
# load max1
# load max1 max5
# load max1 max5 max15
load 5 3 2
```

If the values are overstepped, laErrorFlag will contain the status 1 (otherwise: 0) and laErrMessage will have the text of the error message.

In a system that exceeds one of the specified limits, snmpwalk returns the following:

```
user@linux:~$ snmpwalk -v1 -c public localhost laTable
...
UCD-SNMP-MIB::laNames.1 = STRING: Load-1
UCD-SNMP-MIB::laNames.2 = STRING: Load-5
UCD-SNMP-MIB::laNames.3 = STRING: Load-15
```

```
UCD-SNMP-MIB::laLoad.1 = STRING: 5.31
UCD-SNMP-MIB::laLoad.2 = STRING: 2.11
UCD-SNMP-MIB::laLoad.3 = STRING: 0.77
...
UCD-SNMP-MIB::laLoadInt.1 = INTEGER: 530
UCD-SNMP-MIB::laLoadInt.2 = INTEGER: 210
UCD-SNMP-MIB::laLoadInt.3 = INTEGER: 77
UCD-SNMP-MIB::laLoadFloat.1 = Opaque: Float: 5.310000
UCD-SNMP-MIB::laLoadFloat.2 = Opaque: Float: 2.110000
UCD-SNMP-MIB::laLoadFloat.3 = Opaque: Float: 0.770000
UCD-SNMP-MIB::laErrorFlag.1 = INTEGER: 1
UCD-SNMP-MIB::laErrorFlag.2 = INTEGER: 0
UCD-SNMP-MIB::laErrorFlag.3 = INTEGER: 0
UCD-SNMP-MIB::laErrMessage.1 = STRING: 1 min Load Average too high (=5.31)
UCD-SNMP-MIB::laErrMessage.2 = STRING:
UCD-SNMP-MIB::laErrMessage.3 = STRING:
```

From `laLoadInt.1` we are told the one-minute average value for the system load as an integer, from `laLoad.1` as a string, and from `laLoad‐Float.1` as a floating-point decimal. `laErrorFlag.1` contains the corresponding error status, `laErrMessage.1` the corresponding error message. The same applies for the other two averages.

You can also use the `check_snmp` plugin here to query the floating-point decimal values just as accurately, and specify limit values centrally.

11.3   Nagios's Own SNMP Plugins

Among the standard Nagios plugins there are three programs with which data can be obtained via SNMP: a generic plugin that queries any OIDs you want, and two Perl scripts that are specialized in interface data of network cards and the ports of switches, routers and so forth. In addition to this, the directory `contrib` contains the source code of other SNMP plugins that are not automatically installed. Apparently these are no longer maintained and cannot run without major adjustments to the code.

`http://www.nagiosexchange.org/` also provides some useful specialized plugins, some of which are introduced in Section 11.4 from page 255. The following descriptions are limited, for reasons of space, to SNMPv1/2 queries; for SNMPv3-specific options, we refer you to the online help for the corresponding plugin.

11.3.1   The generic SNMP plugin `check_snmp`

With `check_snmp` a generic plugin is available that queries all available information via SNMP, according to your requirements. However, its operation does require a degree of care, since as a generic plugin, it has no idea of specifically what data it is querying.

For this reason as well, its output looks quite meager; specialized plugins provide more convenience here. But since these don't exist for every purpose, check_snmp is then quite justified. It calls the program snmpget auf, which means that the NET-SNMP tools must be installed.

It provides the following options:

-H *address* / --host=*address*
This is the host name or IP address of the SNMP agent to be queried.

-o *OID* / --oid=*OID*
This is the object identifier to be queried, either as a complete numerical OID or as a string, which is interpreted by snmpget (e.g., system.sysName.0).

Attention: in contrast to snmpwalk, you must always specify the end nodes containing the information.

-p *port* / --port=*port*
This is the alternative port on which the SNMP agent is running. The default is UDP port 161.

-C *password* / --community=*password*
This is the community string for read access. The default value is public.

-w *start*:*end* / --warning=*start*:*end*
If the queried value lies within the range specified by *start* and *end*, check_snmp does not give out a warning. For -w 0:90 it must therefore be larger than 0 and smaller than 90.

-c *start*:*end* / --critical=*start*:*end*
If the query value lies outside the range, the plugin gives out CRITICAL. If the warning and critical limits overlap, the critical limit always has priority.

-s *string* / --string=*string*
The contents of the queried OID must correspond exactly to the specified *string*, otherwise check_snmp will give out an error.

-r *regexp* / --ereg=*regexp*
This option checks the contents of the queried OID to see whether the regular expression *regexp*[10] is matched. If this is the case, the plugin returns OK, otherwise CRITICAL.

[10] POSIX regular expression, see man 7 regex.

-R *regexp* / --erexi=*regexp*
> As -r, except that there is no case distinction.

-l *prefix* / --label=*prefix*
> A string that is placed in front of the plugin response. The default is SNMP.

-u *string* / --units=*string*
> SNMP only has simple values, not units. A string that is specified instead of *string* is extended by the plugin in the text output so that it serves the value as a unit. Because only text is involved here, you can also specify apples or pears, for example, as "units".

-d *delimiter* / --delimiter=*delimiter*
> This character separates the OID in the snmpget output from the value. The default is =.

-D *delimiter* / --output-delimiter=*delimiter*
> The plugin is able to query several OIDs simultaneously. The result values are separated with *delimiter*, which in the default is a space.

-m *mibs* / --miblist=*mibs*
> This specifies the MIBs that should be loaded for snmpget. The default is ALL. -m +UCD-DEMO-MIB[11] loads *in addition*, -m UCD-DEMO-MIB (without the + sign) *only* loads the specified MIB.[12]

-P *version* / --protocol=*version*
> Defines the SNMP protocol version. The values for *version* are 1 or 3. Without this option, SNMPv1 is used.

SNMP provides almost unlimited possibilities, so the following examples can merely convey a feeling for other plugins used.

Testing hard drive capacity via SNMP

The following command queries the load of a file system and to do this accesses the partial tree ucdavis.dskTable of a locally running NET-SNMP agent:

```
nagios@linux:local/libexec$ ./check_snmp -H swobspace -C public \
    -o dskTable.dskEntry.dskPercent.2 -w 0:90 -c 0:95 -u percent
SNMP WARNING - *95* percent
```

---

[11] UCD-DEMO-MIB is an MIB included for demonstration purposes.
[12] See also the online help, with man snmpcmd.

The query applies to the percentage load of the file system with the index number 2. As long as no more than 90 percent of the hard drive space is then occupied, the test should return OK; here a warning will be returned if it is between 91 and 95 percent, and critical status if it goes beyond this. Thanks to the -u option, check_snmp adds the description percent to the output of the figure determined.

Nevertheless, the plugin does not tell the whole truth: a test check with df shows a 96 percent load, which comes from the fact that this program correctly rounded up the actual 95.8 percent load, while integer values in SNMP are seldom rounded up, but simply cut off. So you just have to live with slight inaccuracies as long as the MIB does not provide any floating-point decimals.

If you would like things to be more detailed, you can use the option -l: -l 'SNMP-DISK: /net/swobspace/b' causes other, self-defined information to be added to the output of the above command:

```
SNMP-DISK: /net/swobspace/b WARNING - *95* percent
```

The above query can be more generally run through a command object such as the following:

```
define command{
   command_name   check_snmp
   command_line   $USER1$/check_snmp -H $HOSTADDRESS$ -C $USER3$
 -P 1 -o $ARG1$ -w $ARG2$ -c $ARG3$ -l $ARG4$
}
```

This definition assumes that the value being queried is numerical, and not Boolean (see page 251), otherwise specifying a warning and critical value simultaneously would make no sense. We store the community here in the macro $USER3$.[13] this is followed by the protocol version (-P 1 stands for SNMPv1), the OID, the warning and critical limits, and a prefix.

The call for this command in service definitions is then made in the form

```
check_snmp!oid!warn!critical!prefix
```

If you want to specifically monitor the load of the file system with the index number 2 on the computer swobspace through dskTable, then the following definition would be used:

```
define service{
   service_description   SNMP-DISK-a
   host_name             swobspace
```

[13] The $USERx$ macros are defined in the resource file resource.cfg.

```
    check_command check_snmp!dskTable.dskEntry.dskPercent.2!0:90!0:95!DIS
K: /net/swobspace/a
    ...
}
```

Even though the check_command line is wrapped here, in practice all parameters must be on a single line, separated by an exclamation point !
(without spaces before or after the delimiter).

Measuring temperature via lm-sensors

The next test checks the CPU temperature of the host. For the sensor, the
package lm-sensors[14] is used here, which accesses corresponding chips
on modern mainboards. As soon as lm-sensors is active, it allows the NET-
SNMP agents to read out the corresponding information from the partial
tree ucdavis.ucdExperimental.lmSensors:

```
nagios@linux:local/libexec$ ./check_snmp -H localhost -C public \
    -o lmTempSensorsValue.1 -w 25000:45000 -c 20000:48000  \
    -u 'degrees Celsius (* 1000)' -l 'Temp1/CPU'
Temp1/CPU OK - 41000 degrees Celsius (* 1000)
```

The output depends on the chipset: here you must multiply the query values by the factor 1000. Accordingly, you have no other alternative but to
adjust the warning and critical limits to the main board you are using. In
the example, the CPU temperature, 41 degrees Celsius, is "on a green light":
if it were to drop below 25 degrees or rise above 45 degrees, it would cause
a warning, while below 20 or above 48 degrees, this would be critical.

Regular expressions and comparing fixed strings

You can check whether the text swobspace occurs in the system name as
follows:

```
nagios@linux:local/libexec$ ./check_snmp -H localhost -C public \
    -o system.sysName.0 -r swobspace
SNMP OK - "swobspace"
```

Instead of defining the string being searched for, with -r as the regular
expression, you could also use the -s option. Then the text must match
exactly, however, which may be quite tricky, since everything counts that
snmpget outputs after the delimiter, =.

[14] http://www.lm-sensors.nu/

Monitoring network interfaces

The final example queries whether the first network interface of a Cisco router is in operation:

```
nagios@linux:local/libexec$ ./check_snmp -H cisco1 -C public \
   -o ifOperStatus.1 -w 1:1 -l 'SNMP: Port Status for Port 1 is: '
SNNP: Port Status for Port 1 is:  OK - 1
```

The information sought can be found in ifOperStatus. Here we are querying port 1. While ifOperStatus gives out the operating status, ifAdmin-Status reveals whether the interface is administratively switched on or off.

When specifying the warning limit here, we use the range 1:1, so that the plugin gives out a warning if the interface is physically switched off, and the return value is thus 0. We will do without the definition of a critical status here, since there are only two states, "on" or "off." If the plugin returns a CRITICAL when the interface is switched off, you should use -c 1:1 and omit -w entirely.

If you just want to query the status of network interfaces, you should certainly take a look at the plugins check_ifstatus and check_ifoper-status, described below, which provide slightly more operating convenience.

If MIB-II or MIB ucdavis do not provide the desired information, you could also take a look at the MIB provided by the manufacturer. You can find out from mib-2.system in which partial tree the overall MIB is hidden:

```
user@linux:~$ snmpwalk -v1 -c public konica01 system
system.sysDescr.0 = Konica IP Controller
system.sysObjectID.0 = OID: enterprises.2364
...
```

The example involves a network-capable Konica photocopying machine called konica01. system.sysObjectID.0 reveals that enterprises.2364 serves as the entry point for device specific details. With snmpwalk you can then obtain further information:

```
user@linux:~$ snmpwalk -v1 -c public konica01 enterprises.2364
...
enterprises.2364.1.2.6.1.1.5.1.1 = "Ready to Print"
...
```

In the concrete case of this photocopier, you can query the current device status through enterprises.2364.1.2.6.1.1.5.1.1. Manufacturers usually store information on the implemented MIBs, so that you are not restricted to just guessing.

11.3.2   Checking several interfaces simultaneously

Active network components such as switches usually have quite a large number of ports, and it would be very time-consuming to check every single one of them. Here the check_ifstatus plugin is very useful, since it tests all ports simultaneously. It retrieves the information necessary for this via SNMP, and has the following options:

-H *address* / --host=*address*
   This is the host name or IP address of the SNMP agent to be queried.

-C *password* / --community=*password*
   This sets the community string for read access.

-p *port* / --port=*port*
   This parameter is the alternative port on which the SNMP agent is running. The default is UDP port 161.

-v *version* / --snmp_version=*version*
   This parameter specifies the SNMP version (1, 2, or 3) for the query.

-x *list* / --exclude=*list*
   Use this to specify a comma-separated list of interface types that should not be queried (see example below).

-u *list* / --unused_ports=*list*
   Use this to specify a comma-separated list of all ports that should be excluded from the test. Like -x, the list consists of the indices of the interfaces which are determined from ifIndex: -u 13,14,15,16.

-M *bytes* / --maxmsgsize=*bytes*
   This is the maximum size of the SNMP data packets; the default is 1472 bytes.

With exclusion lists it is possible to exclude certain interface types or port numbers from the test, perhaps because these are not occupied, or are connected to PCs or other devices that are not always running.

With the following query we can find out, for example, which interface types are gathered together on the Cisco switch here named cisco01:

```
user@linux:~$ snmpwalk -v1 -c public cisco01 ifType
...
interfaces.ifTable.ifEntry.ifType.12 = ethernetCsmacd(6)
interfaces.ifTable.ifEntry.ifType.13 = other(1)
interfaces.ifTable.ifEntry.ifType.14 = propVirtual(53)
...
```

If the interface types other(1) and propVirtual(53) should now be excluded, the plugin is sent off with the two figures, separated by a comma, as the exclusion list -x 1,53:

```
nagios@linux:local/libexec$ ./check_ifstatus -C public -H cisco01 \
    -x 1,53
CRITICAL: host 'cisco01', interfaces up: 2, down: 10, dormant: 0,
excluded: 4, unused: 0<BR>GigabitEthernet0/2: down
<BR>GigabitEthernet0/3: down <BR>GigabitEthernet0/4: down
<BR>GigabitEthernet0/10: down <BR>GigabitEthernet0/5: down
<BR>GigabitEthernet0/11: down <BR>GigabitEthernet0/6: down
<BR>GigabitEthernet0/7: down <BR>GigabitEthernet0/8: down
<BR>GigabitEthernet0/9: down <BR> |up=2,down=10,dormant=0,excluded=4,unu
sed=0
```

In reality, this plugin also does *not* display its output over several lines, as the line wrap here may suggest. The fact that this information appears on the Nagios Web interface in a relatively clear form is because the HMTL formatting element <BR> is thrown in. This causes the output for each port to be displayed on a separate line. The | character defines the beginning of the performance data, which does not appear at all in the Web interface.

A query of this type is implemented as a command object as follows:

```
define command{
    command_name    check_ifstatus
    command_line    $USER1$/check_ifstatus -H $HOSTADDRESS$ -C
        $USER3$
 -x $ARG1$
}
```

Here the macro $USER3$ is also used to define the community string in the file resource.cfg. Altogether, 32 $USERx$ macros are available, of which the first two usually contain path details, and the others can be used in any way you want.

If you would prefer to exclude ports rather than interface types, you can use the -u option instead of -x in the definition.

If Nagios is to monitor the switch cisco01, as shown above, excluding the two interface types 1 and 53, the corresponding service definition begins as follows:

```
define service{
    service_description    Interfaces
    host_name              cisco01
    check_command          check_ifstatus!1,53
    ...
}
```

11.3.3   Testing the operating status of individual interfaces

To test an individual interface, you can use either the generic plugin check_
snmp or check_ifoperstatus, which specifically tests the operating status
(ifOperStatus) of the network card. The advantage of this over the generic
plugin consists above all in its ease of use: instead of an index for the port,
you can also specify its description here—for example, eth0.

check_ifoperstatus has the following options:

-H address / --host=address
:   This is the host name or IP address of the SNP agent to be queried.

-C password / --community=password
:   This parameter gives the community string for read access.

-p port / --port=port
:   As long as the SNMP agent is not running on UDP port 161, the port
    is specified with this option.

-k ifIndex / --key=ifIndex
:   ifIndex is the number of the network interface to be queried (such as
    the network card of a computer or the port of a switch).

-d ifDescr / --descr=ifDescr
:   Instead of the index key, the plugin processes the name of the inter-
    face from ifDescr (see below).

-v version / --snmp_version=version
:   This specifies the SNMP version (1, 2, or 3) for the query.

-w return_value / --warn=return_value
:   This option selects the return value if the interface is dormant. The
    return_value can be i (ignore the dormant status and return OK!),
    w (WARNING) or c (CRITICAL, the default).

-D return_value / --admin-down=return_value
:   What value (i, w or c) should the plugin return if the interface has
    been shut down administratively? The default, w, issues a warning, c
    returns CRITICAL, and i returns OK.

-M bytes / --maxmsgsize=bytes
:   This is the maximum size of the SNMP data packets; the default is
    1472 bytes.

On a system called igate, on which snmpwalk finds the following interfaces ...

```
...
interfaces.ifTable.ifEntry.ifDescr.3 = ipsec0
interfaces.ifTable.ifEntry.ifDescr.4 = ipsec1
...
interfaces.ifTable.ifEntry.ifDescr.7 = eth0
interfaces.ifTable.ifEntry.ifDescr.8 = eth1
interfaces.ifTable.ifEntry.ifDescr.9 = eth2
interfaces.ifTable.ifEntry.ifDescr.10 = ppp0
```

the first Ethernet card is tested either with -k 7 or with -d eth0. Since the plugin in the second case has to query all ifDescr entries to determine the index itself, this variation generates a somewhat higher network load. It can be especially useful if not all network interfaces are active on a host, causing its index to change.

The plugin itself reveals which index this port currently has:

```
nagios@linux:local/libexec$ ./check_ifoperstatus -H igate -c public \
    -d eth0
OK: Interface eth0 (index 7) is up.
```

As the command object in the Nagios configuration, the call looks like this:

```
define command{
    command_name   check_ifoperstatus
    command_line   $USER1$/check_ifoperstatus -H $HOSTADDRESS$ -C $USER
3$ -d $ARG1$
}
```

The $USER3$ macro again contains the community string, defined in the file resource.cfg. The service definition for igate specifies the name of the interface to be tested as a plugin argument:

```
define service{
    service_description   Interface eth0
    host_name             igate
    check_command         check_ifoperstatus!eth0
    ...
}
```

11.4   Other SNMP-based Plugins

Apart form the SNMP plugins from the Nagios Plugin package, the Nagios community provides a large variety of other plugins for special purposes. Most of them can be found at http://www.nagiosexchange.org/ in the category **Check Plugins | SNMP**.[15]

---

[15] http://www.nagiosexchange.org/SNMP.51.0.html

11.4.1 Monitoring hard drive space and processes with `nagios-snmp-plugins`

One of these is the package `nagios-snmp-plugins`,[16] which exists not only as source code but also as an RPM package (for Red Hat and Fedora). It contains two very easy-to-use plugins: `check_snmp_disk` and `check_snmp_proc`.

Both absolutely require the NET-SNMP agent as the partner on the other side (see Section 11.2.2 from page 238) and use `ucdavis.dskTable` and `ucdavis.prTable` to test the processes and file systems specified in the configuration file `snmpd.conf`. Its options are restricted to specifying the host and the community string:

-H *address* / --host=*address*
> This is the host name or IP address of the NET-SNMP agent to be queried.

-C *password* / --community=*password*
> This is the community string for read access.

The next example tests the available capacity of the /data file system; `public` is again used as the community string:

```
nagios@linux:local/libexec$ ./check_snmp_disk -H swobspace -C public
/data: less than 50% free (= 95%) (/dev/md6)
```

The configuration of the NET-SNMP agent specifies, with the `disk` directive (page 244), 50% as the threshold for this file system. In this case the plugin accordingly returns a CRITICAL. It can only distinguish between an error and OK; it does not have a WARNING status.

Using `check_snmp_proc` is just as easy:

```
nagios@linux:local/libexec$ ./check_snmp_proc -H localhost -C public
No slapd process running.
```

The plugin again tests the processes defined in the configuration of the NET-SNMP agent with the `proc` directive (page 243). The process `slapd` is missing here, which is why a CRITICAL is returned. The return value is revealed by `echo $?`.

The corresponding command objects are defined in a similar unspectacular way:

[16] `ftp://ftp.hometree.net/pub/nagios-snmp-plugins/`

```
define command{
    command_name    check_snmp_proc
    command_line    $USER1$/check_snmp_proc -H $HOSTADDRESS$ -C $USER3$
}

define command{
    command_name    check_snmp_disk
    command_line    $USER1$/check_snmp_disk -H $HOSTADDRESS$ -C $USER3$
}
```

This definition also assumes that the community string is stored in the $USER3$ macro in the file resource.cfg. In order to query the NET-SMTPD on the computer linux01 for its hard drive load, the following service object is defined:

```
define service{
    service_description    DISK
    host_name              linux01
    check_command          check_snmp_disk
    ...
}
```

11.4.2 Observing the load on network interfaces with check-iftraffic

The MIB-II contains only numbers that provide information on the load on network interfaces, but no average values for the used bandwidth, for example. If the vendor has not specifically made such an entry available in his MIB, then you will always have to make a note of the last counter status and the timestamp, so that you can work out the relative usage yourself.

http://www.nagiosexchange.org/ introduces two plugins that take over this task. The Perl-based plugin check_traffic[17] writes the query values into a *round-robin database* (RRD, see page 408), which makes it somewhat more complex to handle.

The same purpose is achieved, but with more simple means, by the check_iftraffic.pl plugin.[18] It has the following options:

-H *address* / --host=*address*
    address is the host name or IP address of the NET-SNMP agent that is to be queried.

-C *password* / --community=*password*
    password is the community string for read access. The default is public.

---

[17] http://nagios.sourceforge.net/download/contrib/misc/check_traffic/
[18] http://www.nagiosexchange.org//51;37

-i *ifDescr* / --interface=*ifDescr*
> From the interface name *ifDescr* the plugin determines the index so that it can access other values (e. g., the counter states).

-b *integer* / --bandwith=*integer*
> This is the maximum bandwidth of the interface in bits (see -u).

-u *unit* / --units=*unit*
> This is the unit for bandwidth specification with -b. Possible values are g (Gbit), m (Mbit), k (kbit) and the default b (bit): -b 100 -u m corresponds to 100 Megabits (Fast Ethernet).

-w *integer* / --warning=*integer*
> If traffic exceeds this warning limit in percent (default: 85 percent), the plugin issues a WARNING.

-c *integer* / --critical=*integer*
> This is the critical threshold in percent (default: 92 percent).

The plugin saves the timestamp and counter status of the interface queried in files in /tmp, to which it adds the prefix traffic. So if you are using a different user ID than nagios for the manual test on the command line, you should delete the files /tmp/traffic_*interface*_*computer* before activating the appropriate Nagios service.

The following command line example queries the Fast Ethernet network interface eth0 on the computer linux01, which in theory has a bandwidth of 100 Mbit:

```
nagios@linux:local/libexec$ ./check_iftraffic.pl -H linux01 -i eth0 \
    -b 100 -u m
Total RX Bytes: 60.32 MB, Total TX Bytes: 26.59 MB<br> Average Traffic:
1.14 kB/s (0.0%) in, 777.93 B/s (0.0%) out | inUsage=0.0,85,98 outUsage
=0.0,85,98
```

The amount of data transmitted here is reported separately by the plugin, depending on the direction, and here it announces 60.32 (RX, "received") and 26.59 MB (TX, "transmitted"). The text contains the HTML element
 (line break), to display the output in the Nagios Web interface on two lines. This is followed by the average transmission rate, again separated for incoming and outgoing data traffic. The performance data (see Section 19.1, page 404) after the | sign contain only the average load as a percentage, each separated by incoming and outgoing values. The numbers 85 and 98 are the default values for the warning and critical limits.

The corresponding command object is implemented as follows:

```
define command{
    command_name   check_iftraffic
```

```
      command_line  $USER1$/check_iftraffic.pl -H $HOSTADDRESS$ -C $USER3$
-i $ARG1$ -b $ARG2$ -u m
}
```

If the definition is taken over literally, you must define the community string in the $USER3$ macro. If you only generally use public as the password, it is better to write -C public instead of -C $USER3$.

To simplify the call of the command within the following service definition, we set the unit to Mbit/second (-u m).

```
define service{
   service_description    Traffic load eth0
   host_name              linux01
   check_command          check_iftraffic!eth0!100
   ...
   max_check_attempts     1
   normal_check_interval  5
   retry_check_interval   5
   ...
}
```

check_iftraffic calculates the bandwidth used by comparing two counter states at different times. Because Nagios does not test exactly down to the second, the check interval you choose should not be too small. The *Multi Router Traffic Grapher*,[19] which displays the bandwidth used in graphic form, normally works at five-minute intervals.

If you select max_check_attempts other than 1, you should make sure that the retry interval (retry_check_interval) is the same as the normal check interval. For max_check_attempts 1 this makes no difference, but you have to define a retry_check_interval at some time or other.

11.4.3 The manubulon.com plugins for special application purposes

The Nagios Exchange, with the SNMP plugins to be found under http:// www.manubulon.com/nagios/ (see Table 11.4), also includes some that are customized to a specific application, such as querying hard drive space. They are relatively simple to use.

Plugin	Description	
check_snmp_storage.pl	Query of storage devices (hard drives, swap space, main memory, etc.)	Table 11.4: The manubulon.com-SNMP plugins

[19] http://www.mrtg.org/

continued:

Plugin	Description
check_snmp_int.pl	Interface status and load
check_snmp_process.pl	processes: status, CPU and memory usage
check_snmp_load.pl	System load
check_snmp_mem.pl	main memory and swap usage
check_snmp_vrrp.pl	querying a Nokia-VRRP cluster[20]
check_snmp_cpfw.pl	querying a Checkpoint firewall-1[21]
check_snmp_env.pl	tests environment parameters of switches such as temperature, power supply unit, and fan (Cisco, Foundry, and others)
check_snmp_win.pl	Queries Windows services via SNMP

We will introduce two of the plugins—check_snmp_storage.pl and check_snmp_load.pl—in detail here.

Keeping checks on storage media with check_snmp_storage

While the check_snmp_disk plugin, introduced in Section 11.4.1 from page 256, only checks the file systems entered in the NET-SNMP configuration, check_snmp_storage.pl is capable of querying any storage media—even swap space or main memory—without previous configuration on the target host. check_snmp_storage.pl tests the partial tree mib-2.host here, while check_snmp_mem.pl uses ucdavis.memory, so that it remains restricted to NET-SNMP.

The fact that you do not have to battle with OIDs, but instead can work with descriptions of the swap space type to specify the type of the storage medium, provides a certain level of convenience. These can be queried with snmpwalk as follows:

```
user@linux:~$ snmpwalk -v1 -c public swobspace hrStorageDescr
hrStorageDescr.2 = STRING: Real Memory
hrStorageDescr.3 = STRING: Swap Space
hrStorageDescr.4 = STRING: /
...
hrStorageDescr.11 = STRING: /net/swobspace/b
```

When the plugin is called, the text specified after the STRING: is sufficient or—if unique—a part of this:

---

[20] The abbreviation VRRP stands for *Virtual Router Redundancy Protocol*.
[21] http://www.checkpoint.com/products/firewall-1/

```
nagios@linux:local/libexec$ ./check_snmp_storage.pl -H swobspace \
    -C public -m /net/swobspace/b -w 90 -c 95
/net/swobspace/b : 91 %used (34842MB/38451MB)  (< 90) : WARNING
nagios@linux:local/libexec$ ./check_snmp_storage.pl -H swobspace \
    -C public -m "Swap" -w 50 -c 75 -f
Swap Space : 0 %used (0MB/3906MB)  (< 50) : OK | 'Swap Space'=0MB;1953;
2930;0;3906
```

In the second example, it is sufficient to specify Swap, in order to query the data for Swap Space, since the pattern is unique. The -f option ensures that check_snmp_storage.pl will include performance data in its output.

-w and -c specify in normal fashion the warning or critical limits in percent of the available memory space. The following overview lists all the options:

-H *address* / --host=*address*
> This is the host name or IP address of the NET-SNMP agent that is to be queried.

-C *string* / --community=*string*
> This is the community string for read access.

-p *port* / --port=*port*
> *port* specifies an alternative port if the SNMP agent is not running on the default UDP port 161.

-m *string* / --name=*string*
> *string* contains a description of the device to be queried, corresponding to its description in hrStorageDescr (see above), such as -m "Swap Space" for swap devices, -m "Real Memory" for the main memory, or -m "/usr" for the partition mounted under /usr in the file tree.

-w *percent* / --warn=*percent*
> A warning is given in the default if the proportion of used memory is larger than the specified threshold. Other warning limits can be defined with the -T parameter.

-c *crit* / --critical=*crit*
> In the default, the status is categorized as critical if the proportion of used memory is larger than the specified critical limit. Other critical limits can also be specified with the -T parameter.

-T *option* / --type=*option*
> What do the critical and the warning thresholds refer to?
>
>   - pu (*percent used*): used capacity in percent
>   - pl (*percent left*): free capacity in percent

- bu (*bytes used*): used capacity in megabytes

- bl (*bytes left*): free capacity in megabytes

The default is -T pu.

-r / --noregexp
> Normally the description in the -m parameter is treated as a regular expression. For example, /var here stands for all file systems containing /var, for example /var and /var/spool/imap, provided that these are really two independent file systems. The -r option switches off the regular expression capability, so that specifying /var will then match this file system exactly, but not /var/spool/imap, for example.

-s / --sum
> Instead of performing individual tests for several specified storage media, the total occupied space is added up and compared to the total capacity. It is then determined whether thresholds are exceeded.

-i / --index
> With -m, a text is normally specified, which turns up again in the description hrStorageDescr. With the -i option, the index table is used instead of the description. Here the Regexp capability also applies: -m 2 matches all the entries containing the number 2 in the index (that is, 2, 12, 20, etc.). It then makes sense to use the -r option at the same time.

-e / --exclude
> Now all the memories that are matched by the -m specification are excluded from the test, the remaining ones are included in the test.

-f / --perfparse
> This option provides an additional output of performance data that is not shown in the Web interface but can be evaluated by additonal tools (see Chapter 19).

Testing system load with check_snmp_load

The plugin compares either the average system load in form of averages of 1 min, 5 min, and 15 min, or the CPU load in percent.

-H *address* / --host=*address*
> This is the host name or IP address of the NET-SNMP agent to be queried.

-C *string* / --community=*string*
> This is the community string for read access.

-p *port* / --port=*port*
> *port* is the alternative UDP port on which the SNMP agent is running. The default is UDP port 161.

-w *warning_limit* / --warn=*warning_limit*
> The warning limit is given either as a simple integer value in percent (e.g., 90) or as an integer triplet separated by commas, which defines the thresholds for the system load average for one, five, and 15 minutes (e.g., 8,5,5). The percentage load, on the other hand, always refers to the CPU load of the last minute.
>
> If the plugin queries a NET-SNMP agent, you *must* additionally specify the −L option in the second variation, for the percentage, −N.

-c *critical_limit* / --crit=*critical_limit*
> This specifies a critical limit; the syntax is the same as that for -w.

-L / --linux
> This option specifies that the plugin queries the system mode of a Linux system via NET-SNMP.

-A / --as400
> This option specifies that the CPU loaded on an AS/400 machine is queried.

-I / --cisco
> This option specifies that the CPU load of a Cisco network component is involved.

-N / --netsnmp
> If the plugin queries the percentage CPU load of a Linux system via NET-SNMP, the −N option must be specified.

-f / --perfparse
> This option ensures the output of performance data that is not displayed in the Web interface, but can be evaluated by additional tools (see Chapter 19).

The following example queries the system load on the computer swobspace via NET-SNMP and specifies threshold values for the one-, five-, and fifteen-minute averages:

```
nagios@linux:local/libexec$ ./check_snmp_load.pl -H swobspace \
    -C public -w 1,2,3 -c 3,5,6 -L
Load : 0.05 0.07 0.06 : OK
nagios@linux:local/libexec$ ./check_snmp_load.pl -H swobspace \
```

```
      -C public -N -w 80 -c 90 -f
CPU used 3.0 : < 80 : OK | cpu_prct_used=3%;80;90
```

The second example involves the percentage CPU load on the same machine. Here we additionally request performance data, which as usual repeats not only the measured value but also the thresholds.

The Nagios Notification System

What would be the point of system and network monitoring if it did not inform the right contact partner when things went wrong? Hardly any system or network administrator can afford to keep an eye on the Nagios Web interface continually and wait for changes in status to occur. A practical working system must inform the admin actively (push information), so that the admin has time to devote to other things and needs to intervene only when Nagios raises the alarm.

Whether a notification system does its job in practice or not is ultimately decided by how well it can be adjusted to the requirements of a specific situation. What may already be a critical error for one person may, for another, not be normal but still tolerable, and nothing is worse than being bombarded with supposed error messages that are not even seen as errors in a certain environment. An excess of wrong information can make the administrator careless, and at some point the real problems get lost in a flood of false messages.

Nagios provides a sophisticated notification system allowing your own environment to be fine-tuned to your own requirements. The wide range of settings at first seem confusing, but once you have understood the basic principle, everything becomes much clearer.

The efforts to keep Nagios small and modular also apply to the notification system: sending a message is again left by the system to external programs: from a simple e-mail through SMS, down to hardware solutions—such as a real traffic light on the server cabinet—anything is possible.

12.1 Who Should be Informed of What, When?

In order for Nagios to send meaningful messages, the administrator must answer four questions:

- When should the system generate a message?

- When should it be delivered?

- Whom should the system inform?

- How should the message be sent?

Figure 12.1:
An overview of the
notification system

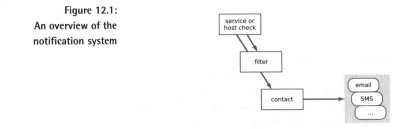

Figure 12.1 gives a rough outline of the concept. The service and host check generate the message, which then runs through various filters,[1] which usually refer to the time. The *contact* refers to the person whom Nagios should inform. If the message has passed all tests, the system hands it to an external program, which informs the respective contact.

---

[1] Strictly speaking, filters defined in the host or service prevent a message from being created, instead of filtering already generated messages. To keep things simple, however, we pretend that Nagios has created a message that is then discarded by a corresponding filter.

12.2   When Does a Message Occur?

Each message is preceded by a host or service check, which determines the current status. In the following two cases it generates a message:

- One hard state changes to another hard state.

- One computer or service remains in a hard error state. (The test therefore confirms a problem that already exists.)

To remind you: the `max_check_attempts` parameter (see Sections 2.3 and 2.5) defines in host and service objects how often a test should be repeated before Nagios categorizes a new status as "hard." If it is set to 1, this is immediately the case and is followed by the corresponding message. With a value greater than 1, the system repeats the test that number of times, and only if they all come to the same new result—such as determining the CRITICAL error status—does the status finally change to the new hard state, thus triggering a new notification.

As long as Nagios has not exhausted the specified number of repeats, a soft state exists. If the old status reoccurs before these have finished, the administrator remains uninformed unless he looks at the Web interface or in the log file. Ultimately the administrator is only interested in genuine unsolved problems. On the other hand, to assess availability as such, it normally does matter if a service is not available for minutes on end, which is why the soft states are also taken into account in the evaluation.

12.3   The Message Filter

Even if you define on a systemwide basis that Nagios may bring attention to errors not just through the Web interface and log files but also via e-mail and/or SMS, filter parameters in the host and service definition may in individual cases cancel out these basic decisions. In all cases the final word is had by the filters defined for the relevant contact. Which parameters play a role on each of these three levels (systemwide, host/service, contact), is described in Figure 12.2.

If a filter stops a notification, the filter chain ends "in a vacuum," so to speak—filter options further down in the hierarchy remain unaccounted for—and Nagios does not generate any message.

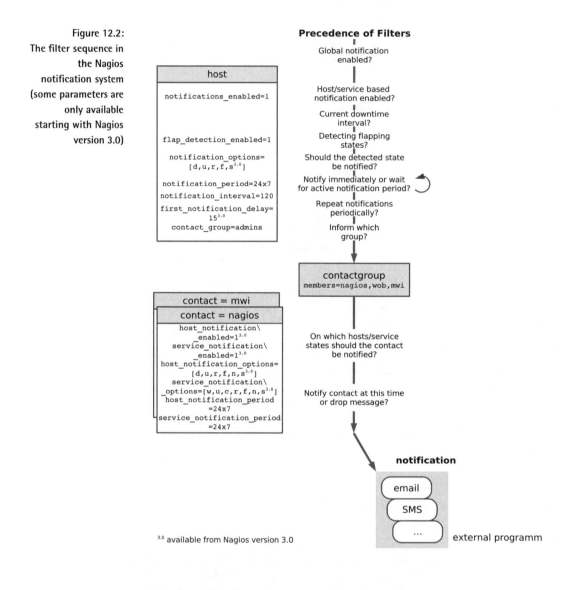

Figure 12.2:
The filter sequence in
the Nagios
notification system
(some parameters are
only available
starting with Nagios
version 3.0)

12.3.1 Switching messages on and off systemwide

With the `enable_notifications` parameter in the central configuration file `nagios.cfg`, you can in principal define whether Nagios should send messages at all. Only if it is set to 1 will the notification system work:

```
enable_notifications=1
```

12.3.2 Enabling and suppressing computer and service-related messages

When defining a host or service, various parameters can influence the messaging system. Here you can define, for example, at what time Nagios should send messages, whether the contact person is regularly informed of error states, and about which states or changes in state he should be informed (just CRITICAL, or WARNING as well, etc.).

The switch `notifications_enabled` determines whether this specific computer or service is important enough for the admin to be informed of errors not just through the Web interface, but also in other ways as well. If this is so, the parameter must be set to 1:

```
notifications_enabled=1
```

This is also the case in the default, so that you have to set the value explicitly to 0 at this point to stop separate notifications.

Taking downtimes into account

At times when a specific service or host is intentionally not available, Nagios should certainly not send any error messages through the network. The configuration of corresponding maintenance periods (*downtime scheduling*) is only possible through the Web interface and is described in Section 16.3 from page 359.

What states and changes of state are worth a notification?

If a regular test shows that service or computer is changing its data continuously, this is called *flapping* in Nagios (see also Appendix B from page 611). If the `flap_detection_enabled` parameter is set to 1, the system tries to detect this situation.

Whether Nagios sends a message in this case depends on the `notification_options` filter. This decides on which states or changes of state Nagios will inform the contact involved. In host definitions it can have the following combinations of values, separated by commas: d (switched off or crashed, *down*), u (*unreachable*), r (computer again reachable, *recovered*), and f (quickly alternating state, *flapping*). Starting with Nagios 3.0, there is an additional value s, which is used to send notifications if a planned maintenance period is about to start, end, or is canceled.

For service objects, `notification_options` recognizes the following states: c (CRITICAL), w (WARNING), u (UNKNOWN, unknown problem), r (service again reachable, *recovered*), and f (*flapping*). From Nagios 3.0

onward, the value s is also available for sending notifications on planned maintenance periods.

Nagios correspondingly informs the admin of the state of the service whose definition is contained in the line

```
notification_options=c,r
```

only if this is critical or was recreated after an error state. Messages involving a WARNING or flapping are discarded by the system.

If notification_options is set to n (*none*), Nagios will generally not send a message concerning this computer or service.

When should Nagios send messages?

At what time should a message be sent? This can be defined with the notification_period parameter:

```
notification_period=24x7h
```

notification_period expects a time object (see Section 2.10 from page 74) as the value; 24x7h is such a value and stands for "round the clock."

Outside the specified time period, Nagios suppresses possible messages, but does not simply discard them, in contrast to the other filters. Instead of this, the system places the message in a kind of queue and sends it as soon as the notification period begins (*rescheduling*). This means that the relevant contact will certainly get to hear about the problem. Nagios also ensures that the admin receives the message only once, even if multiple messages on the same event were generated outside the time period.

notification_period is the only time-controlled filter in which a message is not lost, despite filtering. With all the other time filters, the message never reaches its destination outside the specified period of time.

With an *interval check*, Nagios can be instructed to report at regular intervals on problems that persist for a longer time:

```
notification_interval=120
```

If a state persists that Nagios should normally report, corresponding to the notification_option parameter—CRITICAL, for example—for a long time, the system would grant this wish, in the example, every 120 time units (normally, minutes). In other words it suppresses the notification that is generated anyway with every check, after a corresponding notification until the specified time has elapsed. If nothing has changed in the state until then, it then sends the corresponding notification.

If you set `notification_interval` to 0, Nagios will send a notification of this only once. You should be careful when doing this, however: filters defined for the contact can also reject messages. If you normally generate just one single message, which might arrive at the relevant admin outside the admin's chosen contact time period, then the admin will never be told anything about the problem, even if it persists into working hours.

Starting with Nagios 3.0, the parameter `first_notification_delay` allows the delayed sending of a notification. With the setting

```
first_notification_delay=15
```

Nagios sends notification only after 15 time units (usually minutes) have expired. If the system administrator responsible for handling the problem posts an acknowledgement within the delay period (Section 16.1.2 from page 332), the notification will not be sent, but if the administrator does not react in time, then Nagios sends the first notification once the delay period has expired. This option is useful for avoiding unneeded notifications when administrators use the Web interface to check on the system periodically during their regular working hours.

Whose concern is the message?

The contact group defined in the host or service object does not itself belong to the message filters, but it still decides on who is informed and who is not:

```
contact_group=admins
```

What contacts belong to the specified group (here: `admins`) is defined by the corresponding `contact_group` object in its definition object (see also Section 2.8 from page 72):

```
# -- /etc/nagios/global/contactgroups.cfg
define contactgroup{
    contactgroup_name   admins
    alias               administrators
    members             nagios,wob,mwi
}
```

The specified contact group, though, merely makes a rough preselection: which of the contacts specified in it actually receive the message depends on the filter functions in the definition of the individual contact. In this way you can ensure that one employee is only notified during normal office hours, another one round-the-clock, and that one of them is kept up to date about all changes in status, and the other one is informed only of a selection (for example, only CRITICAL but not WARNING).

12.3.3 Person-related filter options

When defining the contact objects, the method is also specified in which Nagios delivers the notification in specific cases (see Section 12.4 from page 275). It can be described separately for host and service problems. Several parallel methods are also possible, such as via e-mail *and* SMS.

Since the contact-related filters are specifically for the corresponding contact object, it can certainly be useful to define several contacts for one and the same recipient that differ in individual parameters, such as a contact object that keeps the person informed via e-mail of all problems during normal working hours, and a second one for SMS messages concerning critical events outside working hours.

What should Nagios inform you about?

The events for which somebody should be informed can be specified not only by host or service, but also by contact. Host and service-related states are defined separately here:

```
host_notification_options=d,u,r
service_notification_options=c,r,u
```

The possible values are the same as those for the host-service parameter `notification_options` (page 269).

From Nagios 3.0 onward you can normally switch notifications for host and service on and off via an additional parameter:

```
host_notifications_enabled=1
service_notifications_enabled=1
```

The value 0 prevents the corresponding messages, and the value 1 ensures that the messages are sent. At first glance this corresponds to the value n (no notification) for the accompanying option parameter.

The two *_notifications_enabled parameters can also be switched on and off with the external commands ENABLE/DISABLE_CONTACT_HOST_NO-TIFICATIONS and ENABLE/DISABLE_CONTACT_SVC_NOTIFICATIONS[2] via the interface for external commands (Section 13.1 from page 292). This can be done with a script where the contact is concerned, without having to alter the preset *_notification_options.

---

[2] See http://www.nagios.org/developerinfo/externalcommands/.

When do messages reach the recipient?

The final filter in the filter chain again refers to time periods. If a message is produced in the time period specified here, Nagios notifies the contact; otherwise it discards the message. The notification window can again be set separately for hosts and services, and as a value it expects a `timeperiod` object defined elsewhere:

```
host_notification_period=24x7
service_notification_period=workhours
```

12.3.4 Case examples

Letting you know once, but doing this reliably

What should you do if only a single message should be sent for each change in status of the service, but this message must always reach the relevant recipient during working hours? We can illustrate the solution to this problem through the example of the `admins` contact group to which the contact `wob` is assigned, ...

```
define contactgroup{
   contactgroup_name  admins
   alias              Local Site Administrators
   members            wob
}
```

...and to the `PING` service for the computer `linux01`:

```
define service{
   host_name              linux01
   service_description    PING
   check_command          check_ping!100.0,20%!500.0,60%
   max_check_attempts     3
   normal_check_interval  2
   retry_check_interval   1
   check_period           24x7
   notification_interval  0
   notification_period    workhours
   notification_options   w,u,c,r,f
   contact_groups         admins
}
```

`notification_interval` 0 normally forces Nagios not to produce any repeat messages. The `notification_period` ensures the desired time period through the `timeperiod` object `workhours`: if Nagios raises the alarm at other times, the inbuilt *rescheduling* is used, that is, the notification is sent on its way only if the specified time period again applies. It is definitely not discarded.

In order for Nagios to be active in all changes of state, the notification_ options must always cover all possible events for services.

To guarantee that the contact wob always receives the messages, it is essential that the service_notification_period in the corresponding contact object is 24x7:

```
define contact{
    contact_name                 wob
    alias                        Wolfgang
    host_notification_period     24x7
    host_notification_options    d,u,r
    service_notification_period  24x7
    service_notification_options w,u,c,r,f
    ...
}
```

A restricted time filter at this position could, under certain circumstances, lead to the loss of each of the individual messages. The same applies for the values of service_notification_options: only if all are entered here as well will no message be lost.

Informing different admins at different times

If you want to inform different persons at different times about different events, you may not restrict either the notification_period or the notification_options of a host or service:

```
define service{
    ...
    notification_interval  120
    notification_period    24x7
    notification_options   w,u,c,r,f
    ...
}
```

Filtering takes place exclusively for individual contacts. For this to work on a time level you must ensure that Nagios generates a message regularly (here every 120 time units, normally minutes) if error states persist.

If admin A is to be informed only during his working hours, and then only of changes to critical or OK states, A's contact object will be sent with the following parameters:

```
define contact{
   ...
   service_notification_period      workhours
   service_notification_options     c,r
   ...
}
```

There is also a second and not quite so obvious difference to the first example: let us assume that the service reports the CRITICAL status at 7:30 in the morning, which will persist for several hours. The workhours object is defined so that it describes the time from Monday to Friday between 8:00 and 18:00. In the above example, Nagios holds back the message (rescheduling), until the time period defined in it has been reached. The administrator therefore receives a corresponding message at 8:00.

In the case described here, no rescheduling takes place, Nagios generates a corresponding message every two hours, which is filtered out if the contact is currently taking a "break." The system correspondingly discards the message at 7:30, but allows the next message two hours later to pass through. The administrator therefore does not receive the corresponding information until 9:30, provided that the problem still exists at this point in time.

Which of the two solutions is more suitable depends on specific requirements. For an e-mail notification, for example, it makes little difference if the administrator receives mails round-the-clock but reads them only when sitting in his office. A filter for Nagios messages in the mail client, sorting them in reverse chronological order (the most current mail first) makes sense in this case. Sitting in front of the screen, the administrator can also take a quick look at the Web interface when problems are announced, to check whether anything has changed.

If the methods of differentiation described so far are not sufficient, then escalation management, described in Section 12.5, may be of further help.

12.4   External Notification Programs

Which external programs deliver the messages is defined by the contact definition.

Here there are again two parameters to define the commands to be used, one for services and one for hosts:

```
define contact{
   ...
   service_notification_commands   notify-by-email,notify-by-sms
   host_notification_commands      host-notify-by-email,host-notify-by-sms
   email                           nagios-admin@localhost
   pager                           +49-1234-56789
```

```
        address1              root@example.com
        address2              123-456789
        ...
}
```

Both *_notification_commands allow comma-separated lists, so it is permitted to specify more than one command at the same time. The message is then sent simultaneously to the recipient in all the ways defined. The names of the command objects describe these ways: via e-mail and via SMS.

To achieve a better overview, the corresponding commands are not defined together with the plugin commands in the file checkcommands.cfg, but in a separate object file, misccommands.cfg. Nagios loads these like any other file with object definitions, which is why any name can be chosen for them.

The other parameters, email, pager, address1, and address2, can be regarded as variables. The delivery commands access the values set in these through macros. Whether pager contains a telephone number for SMS delivery or an e-mail address pointing to an e-mail SMS gateway is immaterial for the contact definition. The decisive factor is that the value matches the corresponding command that references this variable.

12.4.1 Notification via e-mail

In defining the notify-by-email command, a name and the command line to be executed is specified, as with every other command object. Only its length is unusual, which is why it has had to be line-wrapped several times for this printed version:

```
define command{
   command_name     notify-by-email
   command_line     /usr/bin/printf "%b" "***** Nagios *****\n\n Notificat
ion Type: $NOTIFICATIONTYPE$\n\nService: $SERVICEDESC$\nHost: $HOSTALIAS
$\nAddress: $HOSTADDRESS$\nState: $SERVICESTATE$\n\nDate/Time: $LONGDATE
TIME$\n\nAdditional Info:\n\n$SERVICEOUTPUT$" | /usr/bin/mail  -s "** $N
OTIFICATIONTYPE$ alert - $HOSTALIAS$/$SERVICEDESC$ is $SERVICESTATE$ **"
$CONTACTEMAIL$

}
```

The printed-out command object comes from the included example file misccommands.cfg-sample. The command line defined in it can be reduced in principle to the following pattern:

```
printf text | mail -s "subject" e-mail_address
```

With the help of the macro, `printf` generates the message text, which is passed on to the mail program through a pipe. What is caused by the macros specifically used is revealed in Table 12.1.[3] Using this, the jumbo line shown above produces messages that look something like this:

```
To: wob@swobspace.de
Subject: ** PROBLEM alert - mail-WOB/SMTP is CRITICAL **
Date: Fri, 14 Jan 2005 16:22:47 +0100 (CET)
From: Nagios Admin <nagios@swobspace.de>

***** Nagios  *****

Notification Type: PROBLEM

Service: SMTP
Host: mail-WOB
Address: 172.17.168.2
State: CRITICAL

Date/Time: Fri Jan 14 16:22:47 CET 2005

Additional Info:

CRITICAL - Socket timeout after 10 seconds
```

Macro	Description
$CONTACTEMAIL$	Value of the `email` parameter from the contact definition
$LONGDATETIME$	Long form of data specification, e.g., `Fri Jan 14 16:22:47 CET 2005`
$HOSTALIAS$	Value of the `alias` parameter from the host definition
$HOSTADDRESS$	Value of the `address` parameter from the host definition
$HOSTNAME$	Value of the `host_name` parameter from the host definition
$HOSTOUTPUT$	Text output of the last host check
$HOSTSTATE$	State of the host: UP, DOWN, or UNREACHABLE

Table 12.1:
Macros used in
`notify-by-email`
and
`host-notify-by-email`

---

[3] A complete list of all macros is contained in the original documentation at `http://localhost/nagios/docs/macros.html` (normally to be found in the file system under `/usr/local/nagios/share/docs/macros.html`). For Nagios 3.0 the corresponding file `macrolist.html` can also be found in this directory.

continued:

Macro	Description
$NOTIFICATIONTYPE$	Type of notification: PROBLEM (CRITICAL, WARNING, or UNKNOWN), RECOVERY (OK after error state), ACKNOWLEDGEMENT (an admin has confirmed the error state; see Section 16.1.2, page 332), FLAPPINGSTART or FLAPPINGSTOP
$SERVICEDESC$	Value of the description parameter in the service definition
$SERVICEOUTPUT$	Text output of the last service check
$SERVICESTATE$	State of the service: OK, WARNING, CRITICAL, UNKNOWN

For the command host-notify-by-email, the command line looks similar, except that now host-related macros are used:

```
/usr/bin/printf "%b" "***** Nagios  *****\n\nNotification Type:
$NOTIFICATIONTYPE$\nHost: $HOSTNAME$\nState: $HOSTSTATE$\nAddress:
$HOSTADDRESS$\nInfo: $HOSTOUTPUT$\n\nDate/Time: $LONGDATETIME$\n" |
/usr/bin/mail -s "Host $HOSTSTATE$ alert for $HOSTNAME$!" $CONTACTEMAIL$
```

It generates e-mails with the following content:

```
To: wob@swobspace.de
Subject: Host UP alert for wob-proxy!
Date: Fri, 14 Jan 2005 17:50:21 +0100 (CET)
From: Nagios Admin <nagios@swobspace.de>

***** Nagios  *****

Notification Type: RECOVERY
Host: wob-proxy
State: UP
Address: 172.17.168.19
Info: PING OK - Packet loss = 0%, RTA = 69.10 ms

Date/Time: Fri Jan 14 17:50:21 CET 2005
```

12.4.2 Notification via SMS

While the infrastructure necessary for sending e-mails[4] is usually available anyway, programs for sending SMS messages such as yaps,[5] smssend,[6] or

---

[4] Apart from the /usr/bin/mail client, a local mail server is required.
[5] http://www.sta.to/ftp/yaps/
[6] http://zekiller.skytech.org/smssend_menu_en.html

smsclient[7] usually have to be additionally installed. yaps and smsclient require a local modem or ISDN card and "telephone" directly with the cell phone provider (e.g., T-Mobile), smssend establishes a connection to the Internet servers of the cellphone provider and sends the SMS message on this route. With yaps and smsclient you can also use a mail gateway that generates and sends an SMS message from an e-mail.

Whichever method you choose, you should be aware of possible interference in sending messages: a connection between the Nagios server and the Internet passes through many hosts, routers, and firewalls. Especially if Nagios is itself monitoring one of the computers involved, things get interesting: if this machine is down, then a message sent via smssend will no longer work either. The same thing applies for e-mail-SMS gateways. Whether a self-made construction is involved, with yaps or smsclient, each of which represents its own SMS gateway, or a telecom installation with a sophisticated unified messaging solution, if the actual sender of the SMS is many nodes removed from the Nagios server (because you have a networked telephone installation with several locations, for example), the chances increase that the message will not reach its destination because of an interrupted connection.

For this reason the best solution is an smsclient or yaps installation on the Nagios server itself with a direct telephone access. In larger, networked telephone systems you can also consider giving the telephone access a dedicated, direct line from the telephone system. Whether this is ISDN or analog is just a question here of the technology used.

To represent the programs mentioned here, we will take a closer look at smsclient, which can be configured very simply, and has an active community. On its homepage you can also find a link to a mailing list whose members will be pleased to help in case you have questions.

Setting up smsclient

While Debian has its own precompiled smsclient package, for SuSE and other distributions you have to compile the software yourself. For historical reasons the program itself is called sms_client; a short subtext is provided with man sms_client.

The installation from the source code follows the usual procedure:

```
linux:~ # cd /usr/local/src
linux:local/src # tar xvzf /path/to/sms_client-2.x.y
linux:local/src # cd ./sms_client-2.x.y
linux:src/sms_client-2.x.y # ./configure
linux:src/sms_client-2.x.y # make && make install
```

[7] http://www.smsclient.org/

The only point worth mentioning here is that the "homemade" `configure` procedure manages without `autoconf` and `automake`.

The configuration files listed in Table 12.2 are now located in the directory /etc/sms; the Debian package installs it to /etc/smsclient.

File	Description
sms_addressbook	Definition of aliases and groups
sms_config	Main configuration file
sms_daemons	Configuration file for the daemon mode of smsclient, in which this can be reached via a proprietary protocol. Is not required.
sms_modem	Modem configuration
sms_services	Supported provider

The file `sms_services` lists the supported providers and at the same time assigns them to the protocol used. The precise telephone number dialed is specified by the corresponding service file in the directory `services` (if you have compiled this yourself) or `/usr/lib/smsclient/services` (for Debian). In case of doubt, you should request the telephone number of your own mobile cell provider. The mailing list can also be of assistance here.

In the file `sms_config` you set a default provider, which the program uses for calls when the provider is not specifically given:

```
SMS_default_service  = "d1"
```

Only the configuration of the modem is now missing in the file `sms_modem`. In principle, however, any modem that functions under Linux can be used. In the following example we address an ISDN card with the Isdn4Linux-HiSax driver:

```
MDM_lock_dir       = "/var/lock"    # directory for the lock files
MDM_device         = "ttyI0"        # device name of the modem
...
MDM_command_prefix = "AT"
MDM_init_command   = "Z&E<MSN>"
MDM_dial_command   = "D"
MDM_number_prefix  = "0"            # outside line, if required
...
```

/dev/ttyI0 is used as the device here; for MDM_init_command, your own MSN is used. This applies particularly to private branch exchanges, which allow a connection only if your own MSN has been correctly specified.

Since Isdn4Linux does not recognize tone or pulse dialing, we use only D instead of the usual DT as the `MDM_dial_command`. If the ISDN connection requires an outside line as part of a phone exchange, you should enter the corresponding prefix; otherwise this string remains empty.

`smsclient` requires write permissions both for the device used and for the log file `/var/log/smsclient.log`:

```
linux:~ # touch /var/log/smsclient.log
linux:~ # chgrp dialout /usr/bin/sms_client
linux:~ # chgrp dialout /dev/ttyI0 /var/log/smsclient.log
linux:~ # chmod 2755 /usr/bin/sms_client
linux:~ # chmod  664 /dev/ttyI0 /var/log/smsclient.log
```

To test this, you should now send—preferably as the user `nagios`, who will later use `smsclient`—an SMS message to your own cellphone (here to be reached at the number 01604711):

```
nagios@linux:~$ sms_client 01604711 "Text"
Dialing SMSC 01712521002...
WARNING: read() Timeout
Connection Established.
Login...
SMSC Acknowledgment received
Login successful
Ready to receive message
Received Message Response: Message 3003123223 send successful - message
submitted for processing<CR>
Successful message submission
Disconnect...
Disconnected from SMSC
Hangup...
d1 Service Time: 17 Seconds
[000] d1:01604711 "Text"
Total Elapsed Time: 17 Seconds
```

Getting Nagios to work together with `smsclient`

If the second argument is missing in `smsclient`, which contains the message text, the program will read it from STDIN:

```
nagios@linux:~$ /bin/printf "%b" message | sms_client  number
```

Based on the command `notify-by-email`, described from page 276, we will use the second variation here for defining the `notify-by-sms` command:

```
# 'notify-by-sms' command definition
define command{
```

```
    command_name    notify-by-sms
    command_line    /usr/bin/printf "%.150s" "$NOTIFICATIONTYPE$ $HOSTNAM
E$[$HOSTADDRESS$]/$SERVICEDESC$ is $SERVICESTATE$ /$SHORTDATETIME$/ $SER
VICEOUTPUT$" | /usr/bin/smsclient $CONTACTPAGER$

}
```

As usual, the entire command_line is written on a single line. Nagios obtains the telephone number (or alias) through the macro $CONTACTPAGER$, which reads out the value of the pager parameter from the contact definition. Since an SMS here may not be longer than 150 characters, we will considerably abbreviate the information, compared to the e-mail message. To be on the safe side (you never know how long the plugin output ($SERVICEOUTPUT$) really is), the printf format specification .150 (instead of %b) cuts off the text after 150 characters. Although we then do without the line breaks in the message, by means of \n, an SMS is never formatted cleanly, due to its limited display. Thus notify-by-sms generates a one-line message of the following type:

```
PROBLEM elimail[172.17.130.1]/UPS is CRITICAL /2005-03-30 17:00:53/ Conn
ection refused
```

12.5   Escalation Management

Whenever the administrators responsible cannot find a solution in the specified time when important components fail, although Service Level Agreements or other contracts commit the IT department to do this,[8] Nagios's ability to escalate notifications makes allowances for conflicts, at least on an organizational level. It can be used to provide multilevel support. For example, Nagios first informs the *First Level Support* (usually the *Help Desk*). If the problem still persists after one day, then the *Second Level Support* is notified, and so on.

Nagios also makes a distinction here between host- and service-related escalation stages. In essence, both function identically.

In the escalation, Nagios does not count in time units, but in how many messages it has already sent out. In the following example the system should report on error states of the Database service on linux01 every 120 minutes,[9] and this, round-the-clock:

```
define service{
    host_name              linux01
```

---

[8]   These can also be internal specialist departments.
[9]   To be precise, every 120 time units, whereby the default time unit is 60 seconds.

```
    service_description    Database
    notification_period    24x7
    notification_interval 120
    ...
    contact_groups         admins
}
```

The corresponding messages always go to a contact group, so without escalation, that is to admins.

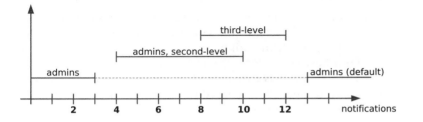

Figure 12.3:
Nagios escalates,
depending on the
number of messages
already sent

After the fourth notification, Nagios should switch on the first stage of escalation (as illustrated in Figure 12.3) and, in addition to admins, should notify the second-level contact group. The eighth message triggers the second level, at which Nagios informs the contact_group third-level.

As shown in Figure 12.3, escalations may certainly overlap. It can also be seen from the graphics that the contact group defined in the service object only applies as long as Nagios does not escalate. As soon as an escalation stage is switched on, the system puts the default contact group out of action.

If the original contact group—here admins—should also receive a message in the first escalation level, then this must be additionally specified in the escalation definition. If several levels overlap, Nagios informs all the groups involved. In Figure 12.3 the eighth to the tenth messages accordingly go both to admins and to second-level and third-level, while only the latter receives message numbers 11 and 12. From message number 13, Nagios keeps only the contact group admins informed, since escalation is no longer defined here.

The latter takes place via separate serviceescalation (for services) and hostescalation objects (for computers). For a service escalation object, Nagios requires the beginning and the end of exceptional circumstances to be defined, apart from service details (consisting of the service_description and host_name) parameters and the name of the contact groups responsible:

```
define serviceescalation{
    host_name               linux01
    service_description     Database
    first_notification      4
    last_notification       10
    notification_interval 60
    contact_groups          admins,second-level
}
```

The escalation level defined here starts, as desired, with message No 4 and ends with message No 10. If `last_notification` is given the value 0, the escalation only ends if the service changes back to the OK state.

In addition you must specify the `notification_interval` parameter for service escalations: this changes the notification interval (previously 120 according to the service definition) to 60 time units. This parameter is also mandatory for a host escalation. The only difference in the definition of a `hostescalation` object is that instead of the host name, you can also specify one or more host groups (in addition the `service_description` parameter is dropped, of course).

The second escalation step is defined in the same way:

```
define serviceescalation{
    host_name               linux01
    service_description     Database
    first_notification      8
    last_notification       12
    notification_interval 90
    contact_groups          third-level
}
```

If there are overlapping escalations with different `notification_inter-vals`, Nagios chooses the smallest defined time unit in each case. Nagios therefore sends messages 8 to 10 at intervals of 60 minutes, numbers 11 and 12 at intervals of 90 minutes, and then the original interval of 120 minutes again applies.

With `escalation_period` and `escalation_options` there are two more setting parameters specially for escalations. Both have the same function as `notification_period` and `notification_options` in the host or service definition, but they refer only to the escalation case.

In contrast to `notification_interval`, `escalation_period` *does not replace* the `notification_period`, but acts in addition to this. From the intersection of `notification_period` and `escalation_period`, the actual time period is deduced. Suppose that `notification_period` refers to the time between 7:00 A:M and 5:00 P.M., and `escalation_period` to the period from 8:00 A.M. to 8:00 P.M.. Then Nagios will only send out messages in the escalation level between 8:00 A.M. and 5:00 P.M.. You must always remember here that it is only the number of messages that have already been sent that decides whether an escalation level exists. `escalation_period` and `escalation_options` only have an effect as additional filters.

Before these two parameters are used, you should carefully consider what it is you want to achieve with them. To restrict the escalation to a specific time period could under certain circumstances result in it being omitted entirely. If you restrict them to weekdays, for example, this would mean that if the `Database` service failed during the weekend, Nagios would inform the contact group `admins` only on Monday morning: over the weekend the system has already sent more than 12 messages, so it no longer even uses its escalation mechanism. If there is a time restriction via `escalation_period`, you should set `last_notification` to 0 to ensure that the escalation really does take place.

Every case of error is followed at some point in time by a recovery. An intelligent mechanism ensures that Nagios only notifies those contacts of the corresponding recovery who are in charge, depending on the active escalation level, and who also received the last notification to be sent.

12.6 Accounting for Dependencies between Hosts and Services

If you test services with local plugins (see Chapter 7) via NRPE (see Chapter 10), all these tests will come to nothing the moment the Plugin Executor fails. With *service dependencies* you can prevent Nagios from flooding the appropriate administrator with messages on the dependent services. Instead of this, the system informs him specifically of the NRPE failure.

Aa with such service dependencies, Nagios also has *host dependencies*, which suppress messages, depending on individual hosts. Both variations can also be used to specifically "switch off" tests.

12.6.1 The standard case: service dependencies

Let us take as an example the host `linux01`, illustrated in Figure 12.4, on which locally installed plugins, controlled via NRPE, monitor hard drive space (`Disks` service, see page 224), the number of logged-in users (`Users` service), and the system load (`Load` service). If NRPE were now to fail, Nagios would announce the CRITICAL state for all three services, although their actual state is unknown, and the real problem is the "NRPE daemon."

In order to solve this contradiction, NRPE is monitored as a separate service and describes the dependencies in a `servicedependency` object.

Figure 12.4:
The three
above-mentioned
services depend on
NRPE

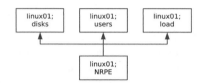

To define the additional service check for NRPE, we make use of the possibility of calling the check_nrpe plugin (see page 214) (almost) without any
parameters at all. It then simply returns the version of the NRPE daemons
being used:

```
nagios@linux:~$ /usr/local/nagios/libexec/check_nrpe -H linux01
NRPE v2.0
```

The command defined in Section 10.5 on page 222, check_nrpe, requires
further arguments and therefore cannot be used for our purposes. For this
reason we set up a new command object, test_nrpe, which exclusively
tests NRPE:

```
define command{
    command_name    test_nrpe
    command_line    $USER1$/check_nrpe -H $HOSTADDRESS$
}
```

With this, an NRPE service can now be defined:

```
define service{
    host_name               linux01
    service_description NRPE
    check_command           test_nrpe
    ...
}
```

The dependencies of the three local services of NRPE are described by the
following servicedependency object.

```
define servicedependency{
    host_name                       linux01
    service_description             NRPE
    dependent_host_name             linux01
    dependent_service_description   Disks,Users,Load
    notification_failure_criteria   c,u
    execution_failure_criteria      n
}
```

host_name and service_description define the master service, the failure of which leads to the failure of the services named in dependent_service_description on the computer specified in dependent_host_name. Multiple entries, separated by commas, are possible for all four parameters mentioned. You should bear in mind, however, that each dependent service is dependent on every possible master service.

The remaining parameters influence service checks and notifications: notification_failure_criteria specifies for which states of the master service notifications involving an error of the dependent services (e.g., Disks) should not appear. Possible values are u (UNKNOWN), w (WARNING), c (CRITICAL), p (PENDING, i.e., an initial check is planned but was so far not yet carried out), o (OK), and n (None).

u,c in the example above means that Nagios does not inform the administrators responsible of "errors" in the services Disks, Users, and Load on linux01 if the master service is in the CRITICAL or UNKNOWN state. With an o for OK, the logic can be reversed: here there is no message if there is an error in the dependent service, as long as the master service is in an OK state. Accordingly, n means that Nagios provides a notification irrespective of the status of the master service.

The execution_failure_criteria parameter controls tests, depending on the state of the master service. The details u (UNKNOWN), w (WARNING), c (CRITICAL), p (PENDING), o (OK), and n (None), as with notification_failure_criteria, refer to states of the master service for which there should be no check. In the example, n is specified, so that Nagios tests Disks, Users, and Load even if NRPE fails.

Nagios therefore suppresses messages, but since it still carries out the service checks on the dependent services, the Web interface always shows the current status of these.

The details for notification_failure_criteria interact with the *Freshness mechanism* of passive tests (see Section 13.4 from page 295). If check_freshness is used in the service definition, and if Nagios considers the most recently determined status to be out of date, it will carry out active tests even if it ought to suppress them, according to the service dependency.

Inheritance

Nagios does not automatically inherit dependencies. An example of this is shown in Figure 12.5: on the internal side of a firewall, the system should query various resources via SNMP. For security reasons, the test is performed indirectly via NRPE, that is, the Nagios server runs the SNMP plugins, which are installed on a host inside the file, indirectly via NRPE.

Figure 12.5:
Multilevel
dependencies for
services

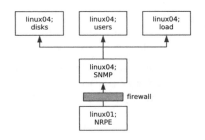

Figure 12.5:
Multilevel
dependencies for
services

The following two `servicedependency` objects describe a dependency between the SNMP (Master) service and the Disks service (dependent service) on the host linux04, as well as between the NRPE service on linux01 and the SNMP service on linux04:

```
define servicedependency{
    host_name                      linux04
    service_description            SNMP
    dependent_host_name            linux04
    dependent_service_description  Disks
    notification_failure_criteria  c,u
    execution_failure_criteria     c,u
}

define servicedependency{
    host_name                      linux01
    service_description            NRPE
    dependent_host_name            linux04
    dependent_service_description  SNMP
    notification_failure_criteria  c,u
    execution_failure_criteria     c,u
}
```

If the NRPE daemon on linux01 fails, Nagios would only recognize the defined dependencies between NRPE and SNMP, but not the implicit dependency between NRPE and Disks. To take these into account as well, the parameter `inherits_parent` is inserted in the definition of the service dependency between Disks and SNMP:

```
    inherits_parent                1
```

With this, Nagios tests whether the master service itself (here SNMP) is dependent on another service, thanks to a corresponding `servicedependency`. If the NRPE service on linux01 fails (CRITICAL state), Nagios leaves out the check of `Disks` on `linux04`, thanks to `execution_failure_cri-teria c,u`, and also does not send any notification of the most recently detected status of `Disks`.

Other application cases

Dependency definitions between services are particularly useful if a great deal depends on a single service, so that the actual problem is in danger of disappearing under a flood of error messages. Apart from the already described use in combination with NRPE, this applies for all services that the Nagios server cannot test directly and for which it must use tools instead (NRPE, SNMP, or even NSCLIENT for Windows, see Section 20.2.1). If a simple connection to the utility cannot be established and a constant value (version number, system name) cannot be queried, you can still use a generic plugin to address the corresponding port.

Another example of using service dependencies are the applications that depend on a database: a Web application with dynamic Web pages fails if the underlying database (which may be located somewhere in the network on another host) is not working. A precisely defined dependency between the database service and dynamic Web application also ensures here that the administrator is notified of the actual cause.

Additional functions in Nagios 3.0

Nagios 3.0 includes two innovations: On one hand, the parameter `depend-ency_period` now allows a time restriction to be placed on the dependency. The default is 7x24h, that is, round the clock.

On the other hand, Nagios 3.0 makes it easier to define the dependencies between services and dependent services on the same host. Specifying `dependent_host_name`, as was done in the previous examples, can be omitted if this is identical to `host_name`. An example of this so-called *same-host dependency* is described in Section H.1.6 on page 683.

12.6.2   Only in exceptional cases: host dependencies

Host dependencies function in principle exactly like service dependencies; the `hostdependency` object is also capable of suppressing messages.

There are a number of subtle differences in the detail, however. Only explicitly configured regular host checks can be suppressed in which checked intervals are defined as for services. This type of host check should be used only in exceptional circumstances, however, since it can have a significant influence on the performance of Nagios. Normally Nagios decides for itself when it will perform a host check (see Section 4.1 from page 92).

In nearly all cases the `parents` parameter in the host definition is better at describing the dependencies between hosts. As long as Nagios can test individual hosts directly, the system can distinguish much better between DOWN and UNREACHABLE (see Section 4.1 from page 92). If you do not want any notification for particular hosts, dependent on the network topology, then you should be informed only for DOWN, but not for UNREACHABLE.

Host dependencies should be used only when Nagios can no longer distinguish between DOWN and UNREACHABLE. This is usually the case when indirect checksthe host check is performed indirectly (e. g., in the figure shown on page 224).

Passive Tests with the External Command File

Apart from active service and host checks, Nagios also makes use of passive tests (and combinations of both types of test). While the system itself defines the time for active checks when they are performed, and then initiates them, Nagios in passive mode only processes incoming results.

For this to work, an interface is required that allows test results from the outside to be passed on to Nagios, as well as commands that perform checks and feed in the results through the interface. Normally remote hosts send their test results, determined by shell scripts, via the *Nagios Service Check Acceptor* (NSCA), which is introduced in the next chapter (page 299), to the Nagios server.

Passive checks are used in particular with distributed monitoring, in which noncentral Nagios servers send all their results to a central Nagios instance. This subject is discussed in Chapter 15. Another field in which they are used is in the processing of asynchronous events, the time of which Nagios cannot define itself. One example of this is a backup script that sends a result to Nagios (OK or CRITICAL) when it has completed a data backup, and another example is processing SNMP traps (see Section 14.6).

13.1 The Interface for External Commands

The interface for external commands, known in Nagios jargon as *External Command Files*, consists of a named pipe (FIFO)[1] in the subdirectory rw of the Nagios var directory:

```
user@linux:~$ ls -lF /var/nagios/rw
prw-rw----  1 nagios nagcmd 0 Dec 19 10:56 nagios.cmd|
```

The pipe, marked in the ls output with p, correctly sets up the make in-stall-commandmode command during installation. For reasons of security it is essential that you ensure that only the group nagcmd can read from and write to the pipe. Anyone who has access here can control Nagios remotely via commands, and can, if they want, shut it down entirely.

Commands that Nagios accepts from the External Command File have the following form:

```
[timestamp] command;arguments
```

As the timestamp in square brackets, Nagios expects the current time in epoch seconds, that is the number of seconds which have elapsed in the UTC time zone since January 1, 1970. This is followed by a space, then a command followed by a matching number of arguments, separated by a semicolon.

The interface makes extensive use of this mechanism, allowing its users to make various settings via mouse click. A detailed description of all possible commands is provided by the online documentation.[2] An example script for each command can be found there, which can be copied to a file with cut-and-paste and used after a few path adjustments have been made.

In this chapter we will limit ourselves to the two processing commands with which computers deliver the results of passive checks to the Nagios server, PROCESS_SERVICE_CHECK_RESULT and PROCESS_HOST_CHECK_RESULT.

---

[1] A named pipe is a buffer to which a process can write something, which can then be read by another process. Whatever is written first is also read first: *First In, First Out* (FIFO). Since this involves space in the main memory, a named pipe does not need any space on the hard drive.

[2] http://www.nagios.org/developerinfo/externalcommands/

For reasons of security, the processing of external commands must be explicitly switched on in the main configuration file `nagios.cfg` with the directive `check_external_commands=1`:

```
# /etc/nagios/nagios.cfg
...
check_external_commands=1
command_check_interval=-1
command_file=/var/nagios/rw/nagios.cmd
...
```

The `command_check_interval` determines that Nagios checks the interface for existing commands every so many seconds. -1 means "as often as possible." `command_file` specifies the path to the named pipe.

13.2   Passive Service Checks

In order for Nagios to be able to accept passive service checks via the interface, this must be explicitly allowed in the global configuration and in the corresponding service definition. The corresponding entry in `nagios.cfg` is

```
# /etc/nagios/nagios.cfg
...
accept_passive_service_checks=1
...
```

In the service definition you can select whether you want to perform active checks in parallel to the passive ones. Active checks are only possible, of course, if Nagios can query the information itself. The following example allows passive checks and stops all active ones:

```
define service{
    host_name               linux01
    service_description     Disks
    passive_checks_enabled  1
    active_checks_enabled   0
    check_command           check_dummy
    check_period            none
    ...
}
```

An exception is normally made for *freshness checks* (see Section 13.4 from page 295)—here Nagios makes use of the command defined in `check_command`. To ban active checks entirely, the `check_period` parameter is set to none. The check command does not play a role in this case, so you can just enter a dummy check here, for example (which like all other commands has to be defined, of course).

On the computer to be tested passively (in this example, linux01) you must ensure, via NSCA (see Chapter 14), that it contacts the Nagios server through the interface for external commands. There it writes the command for passive service checks in the following one-line form:

```
[timestamp] PROCESS_SERVICE_CHECK_RESULT;host-name;service;
return value;plugin output
```

The timestamp can be created in a shell script, for example with date:

```
user@linux:~$ date +%s
1112435763
```

A simple script that passes on the result of a passive service check on the Nagios server itself to the Nagios installed there, could look like this:

```
#!/bin/bash
EXTCMDFILE="/var/nagios/rw/nagios.cmd"
TIME=`date +%s`
HOST=$1
SRV=$2
RESULT=$3
OUTPUT=$4
CMD="[$TIME] PROCESS_SERVICE_CHECK_RESULT;$HOST;$SRV;$RESULT;$OUTPUT"

/bin/echo $CMD >> $EXTCMDFILE
```

When it is run it expects the parameters in the correct sequence:

```
name_of_script linux01 Disks 0 'Disks ok: everything in order :-)'
```

After the host and service names, the test status follows as a digit, and finally the output text. If the service name contains spaces, then it should also be set in quotation marks.

13.3 Passive Host Checks

Passive host checks follow the same principle as passive service checks, except that they involve computers and not services. To allow them globally, the accept_passive_host_checks parameter is set in nagios.cfg to 1:

```
# /etc/nagios/nagios.cfg
...
accept_passive_host_checks=1
...
```

In addition, the host definition for the computer to be monitored passively must allow this kind of host check:

```
define host{
    host_name              linux01
    passive_checks_enabled 1
    active_checks_enabled  0
    check_period           none
    check_command          check_dummy
    ...
}
```

In this example it simultaneously forbids active checks.

The command to be sent through the external interface with which the computer delivers its test results differs here only marginally from the syntax used in the service check command already introduced:

```
[timestamp] PROCESS_HOST_CHECK_RESULT;hostname;return value; plugin output
```

Active and passive host checks differ in one important respect: with passive checks, Nagios is no longer in a position to distinguish between DOWN and UNREACHABLE (see Section 4.1 from page 92). If you still want to take account of network topology dependencies when making notifications and to give specific information on the actual host that is down, you must make use of host dependencies in this case (see Section 12.6.2 from page 289).

13.4 Reacting to Out-of-Date Information of Passive Checks

It lies in the nature of passive checks that Nagios is content with the information delivered. Nagios has no influence over when and at what intervals the remote host delivers them. It may even be the case that the information does not arrive at all.

In order to classify the "knowledge state" of the server as out of date, Nagios has the ability to become active itself, with a *freshness check*. Like passive checks, freshness checking must be enabled both globally and in the relevant serviceable host object. To do this, you need to set the following global parameters in the file nagios.cfg:

```
# /etc/nagios/nagios.cfg
...
check_service_freshness=1
service_freshness_check_interval=60
check_host_freshness=0
host_freshness_check_interval=60
...
```

The value 0 in `check_host_freshness` and the value 1 in `check_service_freshness` ensure that Nagios carries out freshness checks only for services, and not for hosts. The check interval defines the intervals at which the server updates its information, in this case, every 60 seconds. When Nagios really becomes active in the case of a specific service or host depends on the threshold value, which you can set in the appropriate service or host definition with the `freshness_threshold` parameter:[3]

```
define service{
    host_name               linux01
    service_description     Disks
    passive_checks_enabled  1
    active_checks_enabled   0
    check_freshness         1
    freshness_threshold     3600
    check_command           service_is_stale
    ...
}
```

So in this example Nagios performs the freshness check for this service only if the last transmitted value is older than 3600 seconds (one hour). Then Nagios starts the command defined in `check_command`, even if active checks have been switched off in the corresponding host or service definition, or even globally.

If you define the command named here in the example, `service_is_stale`, so that Nagios really does check the service or host, then Nagios will perform active tests even if active checking is switched off, but always only if passive results are overdue for longer than the threshold value set.

If active checks are not possible or not wanted, you can ensure, using a pseudo-test, that Nagios will explicitly signal an error status, so that the administrator's attention is drawn to it. Otherwise Nagios will always display the last status to be received. If this was OK, then it will not necessarily be noticed that current results have not been arriving for some time. The following pseudo-test script delivers an appropriate error message with `echo`, and with `exit 2` delivers the return value for CRITICAL, so that the administrator can react accordingly:

---

[3] If you do not explicitly specify `freshness_threshold`, the value set for `normal_check_interval` will be used in the hard state, and if there is a soft state, the value `retry_check_interval` will serve as the default.

```
#!/bin/bash
/bin/echo "CRITICAL: no current results of the service"
exit 2
```

If you start the script from the plugin directory as service_is_stale.sh, the Nagios command service_is_stale will be defined as follows:

```
define command{
    command_name    service_is_stale
    command_line    $USER1$/service_is_stale.sh
}
```

If the results for the service Disks on linux01 fail to appear for longer than one hour, Nagios will run the script service_is_stale.sh, which always returns CRITICAL, irrespective of what data linux01 last sent. This CRITICAL status is only ended when the host passes on new and more positive results to the server through a passive check.

14

The Nagios Service Check Acceptor (NSCA)

In order to send service and host checks across the network to the central Nagios server, a transmission mechanism is required. This is provided by the *Nagios Service Check Acceptor* (NSCA). It consists of two components: a client program send_nsca, which accepts the results of a service or host check on the remote host and sends them to the Nagios server, and the NSCA daemon nsca, which runs on the server, receives data from the client, processes this for the External Command File interface (see Section 13.1), and passes this data on to it (Figure 14.1).

The Nagios Service Check Acceptor was originally developed to enable distributed monitoring in which decentralized Nagios servers can send their results to a central Nagios server (see Chapter 15 from page 317). In principle, the data that send_nsca sends to the Nagios server can come from any applications you like.

Sending commands across the network to the central Nagios instance is not insignificant, from a security point of view, since Nagios could be completely switched off using the External Command File. This is why NSCA sends the data in encrypted form, and clients must have the correct key to obtain access to the interface. This prevents an arbitrary network participant from being able to run any commands at all on the Nagios server.

Figure 14.1:
How the NSCA
functions

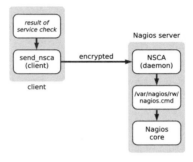

14.1 Installation

NSCA version 2.7.2, current at the time of going to press, was published in the spring of 2007; the chances are therefore quite high that the distribution you are using contains a current package. The source code[1] is quite easy to compile yourself, however. As a prerequisite, you need to have the library libmcrypt installed, together with the relevant header files,[2] or else the integrated encryption cannot be used.

In the unpacked source directory, you should run the included configure script, specifying the Nagios configuration and var directories:

```
linux:local/src # tar xvzf /path/to/nsca-2.7.2.tar.gz
...
linux:local/src # cd nsca-2.7.2
linux:src/nsca-2.7.2 # ./configure --sysconfdir=/etc/nagios \
   --localstatedir=/var/nagios
...
*** Configuration summary for nsca 2.7.2 07-03-2007 ***:

General Options:
-------------------------
NSCA port:  5667
```

_____

[1] http://www.nagios.org/download/
[2] The corresponding binary package usually contains -dev or -devel in its name.

```
NSCA user:  nagios
NSCA group: nagios
...
```

At the end it displays output, showing the permissions with which the NSCA user starts by default, if not otherwise specified in the configuration. Normally the NSCA daemon waits on TCP port 5667.

A final `make all` compiles the two programs `nsca` and `send_nsca`. They are now located in the subdirectory `src` and need to be copied manually to a suitable directory:

```
linux:src/nsca-2.7.2 # cp src/nsca /usr/local/sbin/.
linux:src/nsca-2.7.2 # scp src/send_nsca remote host:/usr/local/bin/.
```

`nsca` is copied to the Nagios server, preferably to the directory `/usr/local/sbin`. `send_nsca` belongs on the remote host that is to send its test results to the Nagios server. If this computer has a different operating system version or platform, it is possible that the client to run there will need to be recompiled. Both programs each require their own configuration file, which is best stored in the directory `/etc/nagios`:

```
linux:src/nsca-2.7.2 # cp nsca.cfg /etc/nagios/.
linux:src/nsca-2.7.2 # scp send_nsca.cfg remote_host:/etc/nagios/.
```

14.2 Configuring the Nagios Server

14.2.1 The configuration file `nsca.cfg`

For NSCA to work, the External Command File interface on the Nagios server must be activated in the configuration file `/etc/nagios/nagios.cfg` (Section 13.1, page 292) and the corresponding data entered in the NSCA configuration file `nsca.cfg`:

```
# /etc/nagios/nsca.cfg
server_port=5667
server_address=192.168.1.1
allowed_hosts=127.0.0.1
nsca_user=nagios
nsca_group=nagios
debug=0
command_file=/var/nagios/rw/nagios.cmd
alternate_dump_file=/var/nagios/rw/nsca.dump
aggregate_writes=0
append_to_file=0
```

```
max_packet_age=30
password=verysecret
decryption_method=10
```

The parameters `server_port`, `server_address`, `allowed_hosts`, `nsca_user`, and `nsca_group` take effect only if `nsca` is started as a daemon. If it is started as an inet daemon, the values set in its configuration apply to the NSCA server address and the port on which the NSCA is listening, the IP addresses of the hosts that are allowed to access the interface,[3] and the users and group with whose permissions the Service Check Acceptor runs.

The `debug` parameter makes it easier to search for errors, but it should normally be switched off (value 0). If it is set to 1, NSCA writes debugging information in the syslog.

The named pipe is defined by the entry `command_file`. If you specify an alternative output file, with `alternate_dump_file`, this serves as a fallback in case the named pipe given does not exist. Before version 2.0, Nagios removed the pipe each time it was shut down, but this should not happen anymore.

If it is set to 1, `aggregate_writes` ensures that NSCA collects all the incoming commands just once and then passes these on to the interface as a block. If the value at this position is 0, then NSCA sends on each incoming command immediately to the External Command File.

`append_to_file` can have the values 0 (opens the External Command File in write mode) or 1 (opens it in the append mode), and it should always be set to 0.[4]

Client messages older than `max_packet_age` seconds are discarded by NSCA, to avoid replay attacks. This value may not be larger than 900 seconds (15 minutes) and should be as small as possible.

The last two parameters refer to the encryption of the communication. `password` contains the actual key, which is identical for clients, and which must be entered in the configuration for the clients (see Section 14.3 on page 304). Because the key is written in the file in plain text, `nsca.cfg` should be readable only for the user with whose permissions the NSCA is running, which in our case is `nagios`:

```
linux:/etc/nagios # chown nagios.nagios nsca.cfg
linux:/etc/nagios # chmod 400 nsca.cfg
```

Finally, `decryption_method` defines the encryption algorithm. The default is 1 (XOR), which is almost as insecure as 0 (no encryption). 10 stands for

---

[3] If you want to define more than one IP address for `allowed_hosts`, they are separated by a comma.

[4] The append mode only makes sense if the External Command File is replaced for debugging purposes with a simple file.

LOKI97, which is regarded as secure.[5] The list of all possible algorithms is contained in the supplied configuration file, which contains many old algorithms and some newer ones, such as DES (2), Triple-DES (3), Blowfish (8), and Rijndael (AES).[6]

14.2.2 Configuring the inet daemon

If you want to start nsca with the inet daemon, the following entry is added in the file /etc/services:

```
nsca   5667/tcp   # Nagios Service Check Acceptor (NSCA)
```

xinetd configuration

If the newer xinetd is used, the file nagios-nsca is created in the directory /etc/xinetd.d with the following contents:

```
# /etc/xinetd.d/nsca
# description: NSCA
# default: on
service nsca
{
   flags           = REUSE
   socket_type     = stream
   wait            = no
   user            = nagios
   group           = nagios
   server          = /usr/local/sbin/nsca
   server_args     = -c /etc/nagios/nsca.cfg --inetd
   log_on_failure  += USERID
   disable         = no
   only_from       = 127.0.0.1 ip1 ip2 ... ipn
}
```

The values printed in bold type for the user and group with whose permissions the NSCA should run, and the path to the NSCA daemon nsca (parameter server) and the corresponding configuration file, are adjusted if necessary to your own environment. The line only_from, as an equivalent to the nsca.cfg parameter allowed_hosts, takes in all the IP addresses, separated by spaces, from which the NSCA may be addressed. Distributions that include NSCA as a finished package and install xinetd by default, include a ready-to-use xinetd configuration file, where you only need to adjust this last parameter.

[5] http://en.wikipedia.org/wiki/LOKI97

[6] Rijndael-128: 14; Rijndael-192: 15; Rijndael-256: 16

In order for the new configuration to become effective, the xinetd init script is run with the reload argument:

```
linux:~ # /etc/init.d/xinetd reload
```

inetd configuration

If the standard inetd command is run, the following line is added (line-wrapped for the printed version) in the configuration file /etc/inetd. conf:

```
nsca   stream  tcp  nowait  nagios /usr/sbin/tcpd
       /usr/local/sbin/nsca -c /etc/nagios/nsca.cfg --inetd
```

If you want to leave out the TCP wrapper tcpd, you just omit the string /usr/sbin/tcpd. In this case you must also explicitly specify the user (nagios) with whose permissions the NSCA starts, the complete path to the binary nsca, and the configuration file with its absolute path. So that the Internet daemon can take account of the modification, its configuration must be reloaded:

```
linux:~ # /etc/init.d/inetd reload
```

14.3   Client-side Configuration

The configuration file send_nsca.cfg on the client side must contain the same encryption parameters as the file on the Nagios server:

```
password=verysecret
decryption_method=10
```

Since the key is also written here in plain text, it should not be readable for just any user. For this reason it is best to create a user nagios and a group nagios on the client side:

```
linux:~ # groupadd -g 9000 nagios
linux:~ # useradd -u 9000 -g nagios -d /usr/local/nagios \
    -c "Nagios Admin" nagios
```

You should now protect the file send_nsca.cfg so that only the user nagios can read it, and ensure, using the SUID mechanism, that the program send_nsca always runs under the user ID of this user. If you now grant execute permission to the group nagios, only its members may execute the NSCA client program:

```
linux:~ # chown nagios.nagios /etc/nagios/send_nsca.cfg
linux:~ # chown nagios.nagios /usr/bin/send_nsca
linux:~ # chmod 400 /etc/nagios/send_nsca.cfg
linux:~ # chmod 4710 /usr/bin/send_nsca
linux:~ # ls -l /usr/bin/send_nsca
-rws--x--- 1 nagios nagios  83187 Apr  2 17:56 /usr/local/bin/send_nsca
```

14.4 Sending Test Results to the Server

The client program `send_nsca` reads the details of a host or service check from the standard input, which the administrator must format as follows:[7]

```
host-name\tservice\treturn value\toutput
host-name\treturn value\toutput
```

`send_nsca` sends this to the Nagios server. The first line describes the format for service checks and the second line, that for host checks. The placeholder `return value` is replaced by the status determined, that is, 0 for OK, 1 for WARNING, 2 for CRITICAL, and 3 for UNKNOWN. By `output`, a one-line text is meant, of the type that plugins provide as a support for the administrator. As the separator, a tab sign is used (\t).

In order to make a complete command from this that can be understood by the external command, the NSCA daemon first prefixes the timestamp and the matching command (`PROCESS_SERVICE_CHECK_RESULT` or `PROCESS_HOST_CHECK_RESULT`). This is why only these two commands can be sent using NSCA.

`send_nsca` itself has the following options:

-H `address`
> This is the host name or IP address of the Nagios server to be addressed by NSCA.

-d `delimiter`
> This is the delimiter for the input; the default is a tab sign. The following example page uses the semicolon as a *delimiter*.

-c `path/to_the/configuration_file`
> This parameter specifies the path to the configuration file `send_nsca.cfg`. Since no path has been compiled into the client, `send_nsca` expects by default to find the file in the current directory. For this reason it makes sense to specify the absolute path with this option.

---

[7] Normally you have to ensure that test scripts you have written yourself produce the correct output; if you use Nagios plugins, you must reformat their output accordingly. Since the latter can be run much better directly with NRPE, this should be the exception to the rule.

-p *port*

> This defines an alternative port if the default, the TCP port 5667, is not used.

-to *timeout*

> After *timeout* seconds (by default, 10) send_nsca aborts the connection attempt to the NSCA daemon, if no connection is established.

With simple test scripts such as the following one, the functionality of the NSCA can be tested. A service is chosen as the test object, which is in a state other than UNKNOWN (e.g., OK), in this case, nmbd on the host linux01:

```
#!/bin/bash
CFG="/etc/nagios/send_nsca.cfg"
CMD="linux01;nmbd;3;UNKNOWN - just one NSCA test"

/bin/echo $CMD | /usr/local/bin/send_nsca -H nagios  -d ';' -c $CFG
```

The script puts it, from Nagios's point of view, into the UNKNOWN status. After it is run, you should discover if the transfer was successful:

```
nagios@linux:~$ bash ./test_nsca
1 data packet(s) sent to host successfully.
```

As soon as Nagios processes the command and you have reloaded the page in your browser, the Web interface displays the UNKNOWN status for the selected service. With the next active check, the previous status will be recovered.

Because it is so simple to send Nagios check results with send_nsca, it is essential that you protect the NSCA from misuse, as already demonstrated. On the client, you should restrict access to the client program send_nsca and to its configuration file and you should make sure that you have secure encryption, and on the server explicitly define the sender and IP addresses that are to be allowed.

14.5 Application Example I: Integrating syslog and Nagios

Linux and Unix systems as a rule log system-relevant events through syslog. Sooner or later you will probably want Nagios to also inform the administrator of important syslog events. To do this, you require passive service checks, NSCA for transmitting the results to the Nagios server, and a method of filtering individual block entries.

If you are using `syslog-ng`[8] instead of the standard BSD syslog, you can make use of its ability to set filters and to format the output using templates. The use of NSCA compensates for the fact that the program cannot itself transmit data in encrypted form.

This connection to Nagios is supplemented by programs to evaluate log files, such as `logcheck`,[9] which is contained in almost every Linux distribution, but it does not replace them. This is because Nagios can send individual e-mails for each event, but not for a summary of events, as `logcheck` does (usually once per hour). In addition to this, the Web interface always displays the last event in each case.

14.5.1 Preparing `syslog-ng` for use with Nagios

Apart from the source code, the `syslog-ng` homepage[10] also provides a detailed manual, which is why we shall only discuss the basic principle at this point. The software differentiates between the `source`, `filter`, and `destination`. All three objects can be combined in any form; they are defined in the configuration file /etc/syslog-ng/syslog-ng.conf:

```
# /etc/syslog-ng/syslog-ng.conf
source local {
   unix-stream("/dev/log");
   internal();
   file("/proc/kmsg" log_prefix("kernel: "));
};

destination console_10 {
   file("/dev/tty10");
};

filter f_messages {
   not facility(auth, authpriv) and
   level(info .. alert);
};

log {
   source(local);
   filter(f_messages);
   destination(console_10);
};
```

This example defines three sources at the same time: `unix-stream` reads from the socket /dev/log, through which most programs send their messages to the syslog. `internal` is the name of the source `syslog-ng` feeds

---

[8] The "ng" stands here for *next generation*.
[9] http://sourceforge.net/projects/logcheck/
[10] http://www.balabit.com/products/syslog_ng/

with internal messages, and from the file /proc/kmsg syslog receives kernel messages. These are given the kernel: prefix, so that they can be be distinguished from normal log entries.

The destination definition ensures that all syslog output appears on the console tty10 (this can be displayed with (Alt)-(F10)).

filter defines what messages should reach this destination, if any. In the case of the f_messages filter, this is all messages matching the category (the level) info and that syslog does not provide with the stamp (the facility; see man syslog.conf and man 3 syslog) auth or authpriv. Alternatively syslog-ng filters according to a search pattern, with the instruction match("*pattern*"), according to the program doing the logging (program("*program name*")) and according to the source host (host ("*hostname*")).

Finally the keyword log links the source, filter, and destination. Multiple specifications are possible here, so several sources and destinations can be specified in a single statement:

```
log {
    source1); source2; ...
    filter1; filter2; ...
    destination1; destination2; ...
}
```

If you specify several filters in a log statement, syslog-ng only allows data through that matches all filter criteria (AND link).

To integrate this into Nagios, use is made of the option of defining a program as a target, which is called for every event:

```
destination d_nagios_warn {
    program("/usr/local/nagios/misc/send_syslog.sh"
    template("$HOST;syslog-ng;1;WARNING: $MSG\n") template_escape(no));
};

destination d_nagios_crit {
    program("/usr/local/nagios/misc/send_syslog.sh"
    template("$HOST;syslog-ng;2;CRITICAL: $MSG\n") template_escape(no));
};
```

The template directive formats the output so that it is suitable for send_nsca, using a semicolon as the delimiter: host and service names (syslog-ng) are followed by the state (1 = WARNING; 2 = CRITICAL), and then the actual output text is given. Apart from $HOST and $MSG, syslog-ng has a series of further macros, which are described individually in the documentation on the homepage. The parameter template_escape protects quotation marks in the text and is intended principally for SQL commands, so in this case it can be set to no.

The following script `send_syslog.sh` uses the bash function `read` to read from the standard input line by line, and for each line read it calls up `send_nsca`, which sends on the data—as described in this chapter—as a passive test result to Nagios:

```
#!/bin/bash
while read -r line; do
    echo $line | /usr/bin/send_nsca -H nagsrv -d ';' \
            -c /etc/nagios/send_nsca.cfg \
            1>/usr/local/nagios/var/send_syslog.log 2>&1
done
```

Because a semicolon is used as a delimiter, we specify this explicitly with the option `-d`. The status report that each `send_nsca` command displays on the standard output is diverted by the script into a separate log file (`/usr/local/nagios/var/send_syslog.log`).

Thanks to the `program` instruction in the syslog configuration, `syslog-ng` starts the script automatically. This is also the reason that the `send_nsca` command is in an endless loop: this means that `syslog-ng` does not run an external program every time there is a relevant event.

14.5.2 Nagios configuration: volatile services

In Nagios slang, "volatile" refers to services that show an error state only once. This refers to devices, for example, that automatically reset the state when an error is queried—which means that the error cannot be reproduced. The same applies for syslog entries: if a check following an error state returns an error, this will always be a second event. So we don't have a continuing error state here, but a problem that has again occurred.

For continuing error states, Nagios normally does not send any further messages for the time being. With the `is_volatile` parameter, however, it treats every error as if it had just occurred. Nagios logs the state, sends a notification, and implements the event handler—provided it is defined—(see Appendix C from page 619).

For `syslog-ng`, this means that each entry is seen as an independent event. In order that Nagios sees things in this way as well, the corresponding service definition contains the `is_volatile` parameter:

```
define service{
    host_name               linux01
    service_description     syslog-ng
    active_checks_enabled   0
    passive_checks_enabled  1
    check_freshness         0
    is_volatile             1
```

```
max_check_attempts       1
normal_check_interval    1
retry_check_interval     1
check_command            check_dummy!3!active check
check_period             none
contact_groups           localadmins
notification_options     w,c,u
notification_interval    480
notification_period      24x7
}
```

Since the Nagios server should not test anything on its own, `active_checks _enabled` 0 switches off active service checks. However, *freshness checking* (see Section 13.4 from page 295) can always cause Nagios to perform active tests. To prevent this, we set the `check_freshness` parameter in this case explicitly to 0.

This service definition does not really require the parameters `check_command` and `check_period`, but since these are mandatory parameters, they must still be specified: as `check_command`, the plugin `check_dummy` (see Section 8.1 on page 188) is used.

It is also important that `max_check_attempts` is set to 1, so that a transmitted error state immediately triggers a hard state. With a value larger than 1, Nagios would wait for further error results here before categorizing the problem state as a hard state.

The `notification_options` parameter ensures that the system informs the specified contact group of all error states (WARNING, CRITICAL, and UNKNOWN). The `notification_interval`, which defines the interval between two notifications for a continuing error state, is actually superfluous, since Nagios, thanks to `is_volatile` 1, provides notification of every event immediately, irrespective of what the previous state looked like. But since it is a mandatory parameter, `notification_interval` still has to be specified.

14.5.3 Resetting error states manually

Events that are taken into account by the syslog filter always inform you of only one current state, which is why the syslog service in Nagios never displays an OK state on its own (Figure 14.2).

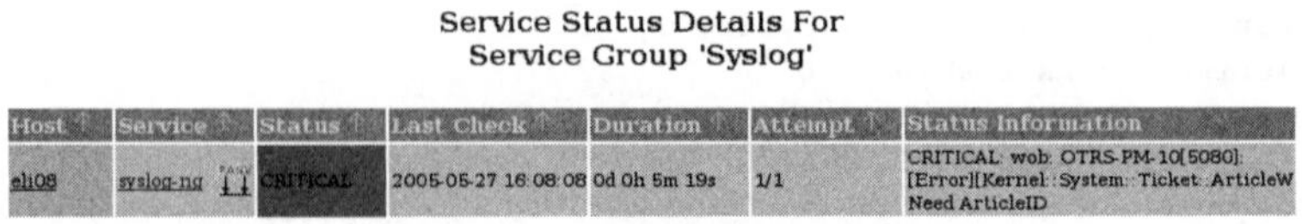

Figure 14.2:
The syslog-ng
service in an error
state

Service Status Details For
Service Group 'Syslog'

Host	Service	Status	Last Check	Duration	Attempt	Status Information
eli08	syslog-ng	CRITICAL	2005-05-27 16:08:08	0d 0h 5m 19s	1/1	CRITICAL: wob: OTRS-PM-10[5080]: [Error][Kernel::System::Ticket::ArticleW Need ArticleID

This problem can be solved with the Web interface, which allows a passive check result to be generated manually.

If you click on the service name in Figure 14.2, the extended status information will be shown (Figure 14.3). There you will find the entry Submit passive check result for this service, with which a test result can be sent manually (Figure 14.4). In this way the syslog-ng service can be reset to its normal state. Since the Web interface always shows only the most recent error state, but not individual error messages, you must look through the e-mail messages to see whether other errors have occurred apart from those errors displayed by Nagios in the Web interface.

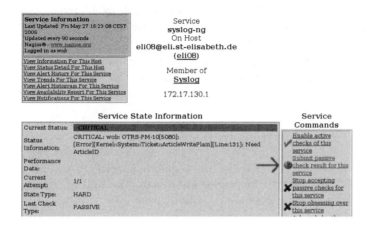

Figure 14.3:
The arrow points to the possibility of "generating" a passive test result for the syslog-ng service

You can also define your own service for each syslog event, of course. This may sometimes be quite time-consuming, but it does allow you to separate various messages and their processing states in the Web interface. If the filter in syslog-ng is restricted so that a syslog service object always refers to just one resource to be monitored, you can also leave out the is_volatile parameter.

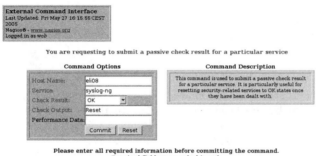

Figure 14.4:
Creating a passive check result syslog-ng

14.6 Application Example II: Processing SNMP Traps

Asynchronous messages that are sent by an SNMP agent (see Section 11.1 from page 228) to a central management unit, called *traps* in SNMP jargon, can be processed by Nagios in a way similar to the Nagios Service Check Acceptor (NSCA). In addition, it allows SNMP traps to be accepted on a host other than the Nagios server itself.

Processing SNMP traps with Nagios is particularly worthwhile if the system monitors the network almost completely, and only a few devices or services restrict their communication just to SNMP and SNMP traps. Nagios, or the Open Source tool OpenNMS,[11] are no substitutes for real commercial SNMP management systems.

In many cases, SNMP traps are vendor-specific, so that you cannot avoid getting to grips with the appropriate documentation and the vendor-specific MIB (*Management Information Base*; see Section 11.1.1 from page 229).

14.6.1 Receiving traps with `snmptrapd`

In order to receive SNMP traps, you require a special Unix/Linux daemon that generates messages for Nagios from them. The software package NET-SNMP, described in Section 11.2.2 from page 238, includes the daemon `snmptrapd`.

In the following scenario, `snmptrapd` is installed on a third host (neither the computer generating the trap, nor the Nagios server). It evaluates the information received by means of a script and forwards it with NSCA to the Nagios server.[12]

In the `snmptrapd` configuration file `/etc/snmp/snmptrapd.conf`, each trap type is given a separate entry, the syntax of which corresponds to one of the following lines:

```
traphandle oid program
traphandle oid program arguments
traphandle default program
traphandle default program arguments
```

The keyword `traphandle` is followed either by the object identifier of the desired trap, or by the keyword `default`. In the second case the entry

---

[11] http://www.opennms.org/

[12] If you install the `snmptrapd` on the Nagios server itself, you do not need NSCA and you can send a correspondingly formatted command, as described in Section 13.2 from page 293 directly to the interface for external commands.

applies to all traps that do not have their own configuration entry. Finally the program that should run if a relevant trap arrives is specified.

In addition you can also include arguments used with this program. But you must be a bit careful when doing this. Quotation marks are passed on by snmptrapd as characters and spaces are always used as delimiters. This means that you cannot pass on any arguments containing spaces, which you should bear in mind when assigning name services in Nagios.

snmpdtrapd gives this program information via the standard output in the following format:

```
hostname
ip-address
oid value
...
```

The first line contains the *fully qualified domain name* of the host that sends the message and the second, its IP address. Then one or more OID-value pairs are given, each on a separate line. A particular event is very often linked to a unique OID-value pair, so that the program can often omit the evaluation of the OID-value pair entirely.

In the following snmptrapd.conf example, the lines are wrapped for readability. Each traphandle instruction *must* be entered on a single line:

```
# snmptrapd.conf
traphandle SNMPv2-MIB::coldStart /usr/local/nagios/libexec/eventhandler/
handle-trap SNMP cold-start
traphandle NET-SNMP-AGENT-MIB::nsNotifyRestart /usr/local/nagios/libexec
/eventhandler/handle-trap SNMP restart
traphandle NET-SNMP-AGENT-MIB::nsNotifyShutdown /usr/local/nagios/libexe
c/eventhandler/handle-trap SNMP shutdown
traphandle default /usr/local/nagios/libexec/eventhandler/handle-trap SN
MP unknown
```

The traps used here are sent by the SNMP agent snmpd from the NET-SNMP package by default, as long as a destination was specified in snmpd.conf:

```
# snmpd.conf
trapsink name_or_ip_of_the_nagios-server
```

If a trap arrives with the OID SNMPv2-MIB::coldStart, for example, snmp-trapd starts the script handle-trap with the argument cold-start. In this way it does not have to search first for the necessary information from the OID-value pairs. However, this shortcut only works with trap OID names that describe their function.

14.6.2 Passing on traps to NSCA

The script `handle-trap`, which is run by `snmptrapd`, breaks down the information passed on and hands it over, correctly formatted, to `send_nsca`:

```
#!/bin/bash

NAGIOS="nagsrv"
LOGFILE="/usr/local/nagios/var/handle-trap.log"

read HOST && echo "host: $HOST" >> $LOGFILE
read IPADDR && echo "ip: $IPADDR" >> $LOGFILE

case $IPADDR in
   192.168.201.4)
      HOSTNAME="irouter"
   ;;
   *)
      # silent discard from unknown hosts
      exit 0
   ;;
esac

if [ -z "$1" ]; then
   echo "usage: $0 <service> <key>"
   echo "usage: $0 <service> <key>" >> $LOGFILE
   exit 1
else
   SERVICE="$1"
fi

if [ ! -z "$2" ]; then
   SWITCH="$2"
fi


case $SWITCH in
   "cold-start")
      OUTPUT="snmpd: Cold Start"
      STATE=0
      ;;
   restart)
      OUTPUT="snmpd: Restart"
      STATE=1
      ;;
   shutdown)
      OUTPUT="snmpd: Shutdown"
      STATE=2
      ;;
   *)
      OUTPUT="Unknown Trap"
      STATE=1
```

```
        ;;
esac

CMD="$HOSTNAME;$SERVICE;$STATE;$OUTPUT"

echo "$CMD" >> $LOGFILE

echo "$CMD" |  /usr/bin/send_nsca -H $NAGIOS -d ';' \
               -c /etc/nagios/send_nsca.cfg >> $LOGFILE 2>&1
```

First it saves the log file and the name of the Nagios server nagsrv, each in
a separate variable. The first case statement specifies the host name used
by Nagios for the IP address passed on (and temporarily stored in IPADDR).
HOST normally contains the fully qualified domain name, which also cannot
be used directly, and sometimes also just contains one IP address, so that
it is better to use the latter here. The explicit test also allows it to discard
traps from undesired hosts. Finally, matching traps land without further
authentication on the Nagios server.[13]

The following if statement determines whether a service name was also
given to the script. If this is the case, then it is saved in the SERVICE variable. If there was a second argument, the procedure is similar. Depending
on the value, the next case $SWITCH instruction defines the output text
and the desired status for Nagios.

The command for NSCA is finally assembled and the CMD variable is passed
on by the script to send_nsca. As in previous examples, a semicolon is used
as the delimiter, which must be specified in send_nsca with the option -d.

14.6.3   The matching service definition

As in the syslog-ng example (page 309), we again define the service on
the Nagios server as a purely passive one:

```
define service{
    host_name               irouter
    service_description     SNMP
    active_checks_enabled   0
    passive_checks_enabled  1
    check_freshness         0
    max_check_attempts      1
    is_volatile             1
    ...
}
```

[13]   Although SNMPv3 does provide authentication for SNMP traps, this would go beyond
the scope of this book.

Since soft states do not make any sense in a single trap message, we should set max_check_attempts back to 1. Whether the parameter is_volatile is used or not depends on the purpose to which the service is put. As long as you define a separate service for each error category, there is no problem in omitting is_volatile. But if you form different error categories using a single service, you should set is_volatile 1, because in this case the previous error will seldom have anything to do with the new one. Section 14.5.2 on page 309 is devoted to the subject of volatile services.

Distributed Monitoring

Passive service and host checks can be used to create a scenario in which several noncentral Nagios instances send their results to a central server. In general they transfer their results using the Nagios Service Check Acceptor (see Chapter 14); the central Nagios instance receives them through the External Command File interface and continues processing them as passive checks (see Chapter 13 from page 291).

What is now missing is the mechanism that prepares each test result of a noncentral Nagios instance to be sent with NSCA. For such cases, Nagios provides the commands OCSP ("Obsessive Compulsive Service Processor") and OCHP ("Obsessive Compulsive Host Processor"), two commands designed specifically for distributed monitoring. In contrast to *event handler* (see Appendix C from page 619), which shows changes in status and only passes on check results if the status has changed, these two commands obsessively pass on every test result (Figure 15.1).

Figure 15.1:
Distributed
monitoring with
Nagios

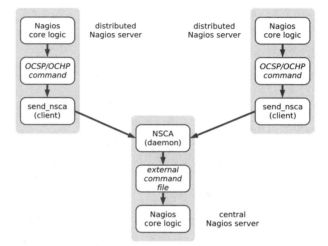

15.1   Switching On the OCSP/OCHP Mechanism

In order to use OCSP/OCHP, several steps are necessary. The mechanism is initially switched on (only) on the noncentral Nagios servers in the global configuration file /etc/nagios/nagios.cfg, where a global command for hosts (OCHP) and services (OCSP) is defined. This causes the noncentral Nagios instance to send every result to the central server.

In the service and host definitions you can additionally set whether the corresponding service or host should use the mechanism or not. For the central Nagios server to be able to use the results transferred, each service or host on it must finally be defined once again.

You should only switch on the two parameters obsess_over_services and obsess_over_hosts in nagios.cfg if you really do want distributed monitoring:

```
# /etc/nagios/nagios.cfg
...
obsess_over_services=1
ocsp_command=submit_service_check
ocsp_timeout=5
obsess_over_hosts=1
ochp_command=submit_host_check
ochp_timeout=5
```

Every time a new test result arrives on the Nagios server, it calls the command object defined with `ocsp_command` or `ochp_command`. This causes an additional load on resources.

The two timeouts prevent Nagios from spending too much time on one command. If processing does not terminate (because the command itself does not receive a timeout and the central Nagios server does not react), then the process table of the noncentral Nagios instance would fill very quickly, and might overflow.

If you want to selectively exclude test results for specific services and hosts from transmission to the central Nagios server, the following parameters are used:

```
define host{
    ...
    obsess_over_hosts=0
    ...
}

define service{
    ...
    obsess_over_services=0
    ...
}
```

With a value of 1 the local Nagios instance sends the results of the host or service check to the central server, but with a value of 0, this does not happen. The 1 is the default for both `obsess_over_hosts` and `obsess_over_services`; if results are *not* to be transferred, then you have to specify the two parameters. This is always recommended if the central location is only responsible for particular things, and the remaining administration is carried out on site.

15.2 Defining OCSP/OCHP Commands

Defining the two commands with which the noncentral instances send their results to the Nagios main server in most cases involves scripts that are based on `send_nsca` (see also the example on page 306). For services, such a script would look like the following one, in this case called `submit_service_check`:

```
#!/bin/bash
# Script submit_service_check

PRINTF="/usr/bin/printf"
CMD="/usr/local/bin/send_nsca"
```

```
CFG="/etc/nagios/send_nsca.cfg"
HOST=$1
SRV=$2
RESULT=$3
OUTPUT=$4

$PRINTF "%b" "$HOST\t$SRV\t$RESULT\t$OUTPUT\n" | $CMD -H nagios -c $CFG
```

When run, the command expects four parameters on the command line in the correct order: the host monitored, the service name, the return value for the plugin opened (0 for OK, 1 for WARNING, etc.), and the one-line info text that is issued by the plugin. To format the data we use the printf function (man printf). The newly formatted string is finally passed on to send_nsca.

The equivalent script for OCHP (stored here in the file submit_host_check) looks something like this:

```
#!/bin/bash
# Script submit_host_check

PRINTF="/usr/bin/printf"
CMD="/usr/local/bin/send_nsca"
CFG="/etc/nagios/send_nsca.cfg"
HOST=$1
RESULT=$2
OUTPUT=$3

$PRINTF "%b" "$HOST\t$RESULT\t$OUTPUT\n" | $CMD -H nagios -c $CFG
```

The only thing missing is the specification of the service description.

It is best to store the two scripts, in conformity with the Nagios documentation, in a subdirectory eventhandlers (which normally needs to be created) in the plugin directory (usually /usr/local/nagios/libexec, but for some distributions this will be /usr/lib/nagios/plugins). You can retrieve this from the definition of the matching command object using the macro $USER1$. This is best defined in the misccommands.cfg file:

```
define command{
    command_name submit_service_check
    command_line $USER1$/eventhandlers/submit_service_check $HOSTNAME$ '$
SERVICEDESC$' $SERVICESTATEID$ '$SERVICEOUTPUT$'


define command{
    command_name submit_host_check
    command_line $USER1$/eventhandlers/submit_host_check $HOSTNAME$ $HO
STSTATEID$ '$HOSTOUTPUT$'
```

If you use a separate file for this, you must make sure that Nagios will load this file by adding an entry to /etc/nagios/nagios.cfg. The single quotes surrounding the $SERVICEDESC$ macro and the two output macros in the command_line line are important. Their values sometimes contain empty spaces, which the command line would interpret as delimiters without the quotes.

15.3 Practical Scenarios

One application for distributed monitoring is the monitoring of branches or external offices in which a noncentral Nagios installation is limited to running service and host checks and sending the results to the central instance. The noncentral instances do not need further Nagios functions, such as the notification system or the Web interface.

On the other hand, if administrators look after the networks at the distributed locations, while the central IT department only looks after special services, then the noncentral Nagios server is set up as a normal, full-fledged installation and selectively forwards only those check results over the OCSP/OCHP mechanism to the central office for which the specialists there are responsible.

Whatever the case, you must ensure that the host and service definition is available both noncentrally and centrally. This can be done quite simply using templates (Section 2.11 on page 75) and the cfg_dir directive (Section 2.1, page 55): you set up the definition so that the configuration files can be copied 1:1.

15.3.1 Avoiding redundancy in configuration files

In the following example we assume that the noncentral servers only perform host and service checks and send the results to the central server, and do not provide any other Nagios functions. The following directories are set up on the central host:

```
/etc/nagios/global
/etc/nagios/local
/etc/nagios/sites
/etc/nagios/sites/bonn
/etc/nagios/sites/frankfurt
/etc/nagios/sites/berlin
...
```

Each of the configurations used for a location lands in the directory /etc/nagios/sites/*location*. After global, all the definitions follow that can be used identically at all locations (e.g., the command definitions in checkcommands.cfg). The directory local takes in specific definitions for the central server definitions. These include the templates for services and hosts, where distinction must be made between central and noncentral.

This directory is also created separately on the noncentral servers: only the folders global and sites/*location* are copied from the central instance to the branch offices.

The three directories are read in with the cfg_dir directive in /etc/nagios/nagios.cfg:

```
# -- /etc/nagios/nagios.cfg
...
cfg_dir=/etc/nagios/global
cfg_dir=/etc/nagios/local
cfg_dir=/etc/nagios/sites
...
```

Only settings that are identical for the noncentral and central page are used in the service definition:

```
# -- /etc/nagios/sites/bonn/services.cfg
define service{
    host_name          bonn01
    service_description HTTP
    use                bonn-svc-template
    ...
    check_command      check_http
    ...
}
```

The location-dependent parameters are dealt with by the templates.

15.3.2 Defining templates

In order that service definitions are identical on both the central and noncentral servers, the local templates must have the same names as the central ones. In addition you should ensure that the obligatory parameters (see Chapter 2 from page 53) are also all entered, even if they are not even required at one of the locations, because together, the template and service definitions must cover all obligatory parameters.

The following example shows a service template for one of the noncentral locations:

```
# -- On-Site configuration for the Bonn location
define service{
```

```
name              bonn-svc-template
register          0

max_check_attempts        3
normal_check_interval     5
retry_check_interval      1
active_checks_enabled     1
passive_checks_enabled    1
check_period              24x7
obsess_over_services      1
notification_interval     0
notification_period       none
notification_options      n
notifications_enabled     0
contact_groups            dummy
}
```

The parameters that are important for the noncentral page are printed in bold type. Besides the parameters that refer to the test itself, the parameter obsess_over_services must also not be left out. This ensures that the check results are sent to the central server.

notifications_enabled switches off notification in this case, since the local admins do not need to worry about error messages from services that are centrally monitored. Alternatively this can be done globally in the non-central /etc/nagios/nagios.cfg.

register 0 ensures that the template is used exclusively as a template, so that Nagios does not interpret it as a separate service definition.

The counterpart with the same name on the central server looks something like this:

```
# -- Service template for the central Nagios server
define service{
    name              bonn-svc-template
    register          0

    max_check_attempts        3
    normal_check_interval     5
    retry_check_interval      1
    active_checks_enabled     0
    passive_checks_enabled    1
    check_period              none
    check_freshness           0
    obsess_over_services      0
    notification_interval     480
    notification_period       24x7
    notification_options      u,c,r
    notifications_enabled     1
    contact_groups            admins
}
```

The parameter `passive_checks_enabled` is of importance here, as well as the configuration of the notification system. On the central side, the parameters involving the test itself come into play only if freshness checking is used (see Section 13.4 from page 295). This works only if the central Nagios server is itself in a position to actively test all services if there is any doubt. Since the `check_command` in this simple template solution is given in the location-dependent service definition, which is identical on the noncentral and central servers, this will work only if the same command object can be used both centrally and noncentrally—if the object definitions in `global/checkcommands.cfg` match on both sides.

In the example, however, we completely switch off active tests of services at the Bonn location, with `check_period none` and `check_freshness` set to 0. The system described so far can also be applied to host checks, of course.

Part III

The Web Interface and Other Ways to Visualize Nagios Data

The Classical Web Interface

On the right is the navigation area with the unmistakable black background, and the remaining area is for displaying the CGI scripts called (Figure 16.1)–the Nagios Web interface is that simple. The start screen provides access to the program documentation—extremely useful if you just want to look up something quickly.

Provided you have the correct access rights, the Web interface allows much more than just looking up information. You can run a series of commands and control Nagios actively: from setting a single command, to switching messages on and off, to restarting the server.

A separate book would be needed to describe all the features completely. This is why we will just describe the concept here on which the CGI programs are based,[1] in this way giving you a picture of the extensive range of options available.

---

[1] There is a good reason that we refer here to CGI programs and not to CGI scripts: all CGI programs for Nagios 2.x and 3.0 are C programs.

Many functions use the very same CGI program. If you move the mouse up and down in the navigation area shown in Figure 16.1 and observe the status display of the browser when doing this, which reveals the URLs to be called, you will see that in the **Monitoring** section up to the **Show Hosts:** entry field, the CGI program `status.cgi` is always called, with just four exceptions. Only the parameters are different. Things are similar for the CGI program `cmd.cgi`, with which general commands can be run. The parameters passed specify whether a comment is to be read, or a message enabled or disabled, or if Nagios is to be restarted.

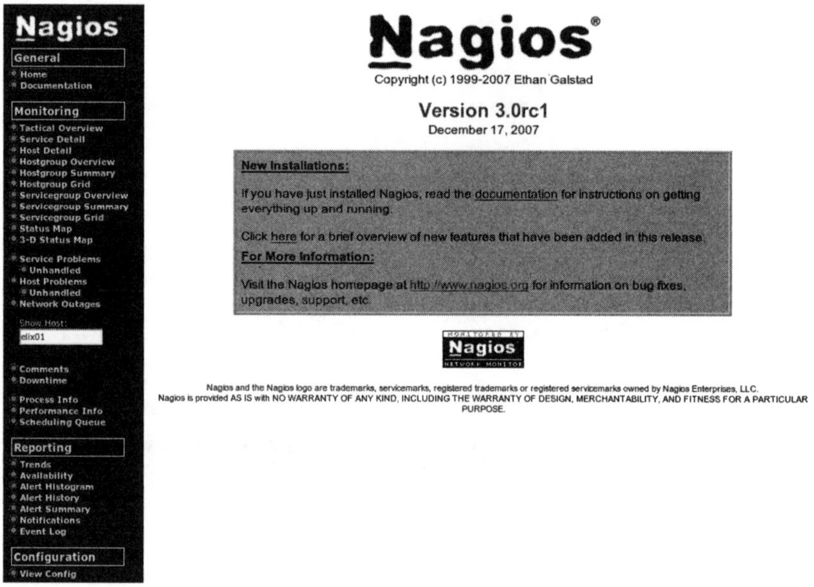

Figure 16.1:
The subitem
Unhandled under
both the Service
Problems and Host
Problems menu items
has only been on the
start page of the
Nagios Web interface
since Nagios 3.0.

CGI program	Description
`status.cgi`	Status display in various forms; by far the most important CGI program (Figures 16.10 to 16.15, page 334.)
`statusmap.cgi`	Topological representation of the monitored host (see Figure 16.27, page 347)
`statuswrl.cgi`	Topological representation in 3D format; requires a VRML-capable browser and allows interactive navigation in a virtual space (Figure 16.29, page 349)
`statuswml.cgi`	Simple status page for WAP devices (cellphone)

Table 16.1:
overview of CGI
programs

continued:

CGI program	Description
extinfo.cgi	Additional information on a host or service, with the possibility of running commands (Figure 16.4, page 331)
cmd.cgi	Running commands (Figure 16.23, page 343)
tac.cgi	Overview of all services and hosts to be monitored, the **Tactical Overview** (see Figure 16.26 on page 346)
outages.cgi	Network nodes that cause the failure of partial networks (Figure 16.30, page 350)
config.cgi	Display of Nagios object definitions (Figure 16.31, page 351)
avail.cgi	Availability report (e.g., "98 percent of all systems OK, 2 percent WARNING", see Figure 16.32, page 352)
histogram.cgi	Histogram of the number of events occurring (Figure 16.34, page 353)
history.cgi	Display of all events that have ever occurred (Figure 16.35, page 355)
notifications.cgi	Overview of all sent notifications (Figure 16.36, page 355)
showlog.cgi	Display of all log file entries (Figure 16.37, page 356)
summary.cgi	Report of events, which can be compiled by host, service, error category and time period (Figure 16.39, page 358)
trends.cgi	Time axis recording the states that have occurred (Figure 16.40, page 359)

Table 16.1 shows an overview of all the CGI programs included in the package. They all check to see whether the person running the requested action is allowed to do so. Normally a user can only access the hosts and services for which he is entered as the contact. In addition there is the possibility of assigning specific users more comprehensive rights, so that they are basically allowed to display all hosts and services, for example, or to request system information. Settings for other users are made in the cgi.cfg configuration file, and the authentication parameters are described in Appendix A.2, page 606.

16.1 Recognizing and Acting On Problems

A suitable starting point for the administrator is the **Service Problems** page, which can be reached through the menu item, shown in Figure 16.2. You can see all problems at a glance. If there is just a service-related problem, but not a host-related one, the host name in the **Host** column has a gray background, but a red background means the host itself is the source of the trouble.

Figure 16.2:
The menu item
Service Problems
brings current
problems to
attention

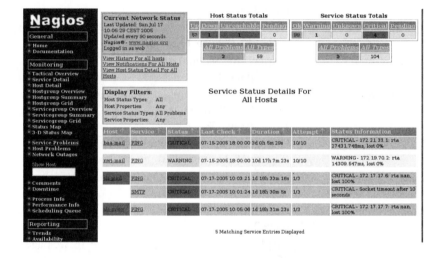

The hosts `sls-mail` and `sls-proxy`, which have failed in Figure 16.2, can be seen again in the **Host Problems** menu item (Figure 16.3): `sls-mail` cannot be reached (UNREACHABLE), so the real problem therefore exists in the failure of the host `sls-proxy`. This dependency is illustrated in the **Outages** menu item (Figure 16.30, page 350) or the **Status Map** (Figure 16.27, page 347). In Figure 16.27 the two failed hosts are shown with a red background, and you can also clearly see which host is dependent on the other (always from the point of view of the central Nagios host).

Figure 16.3:
The Host Problems
menu item reveals
this display

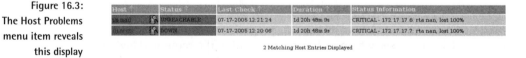

16.1.1 Comments on problematic hosts

The administrator clarifies the problem with the external office by telephone: the DSL connection has failed. He announces this failure to the provider responsible. To stop his colleagues from going to the same trouble again, the admin enters a corresponding comment on the failed host. To do this he clicks in the status display on the host name, which takes him to an information page for this specific host (Figure 16.4), the options of which are described in more detail in Section 16.2.2, page 339.

Figure 16.4:
extinfo.cgi
provides additional
information on the
selected host

Nagios

General
- Home
- Documentation

Monitoring
- Tactical Overview
- Service Detail
- Host Detail
- Hostgroup Overview
- Hostgroup Summary
- Hostgroup Grid
- Servicegroup Overview
- Servicegroup Summary
- Servicegroup Grid
- Status Map
- 3-D Status Map
- Service Problems
- Host Problems
- Network Outages

Show Host:

- Comments
- Downtime
- Process Info
- Performance Info
- Scheduling Queue

Reporting
- Trends
- Availability
- Alert Histogram
- Alert History
- Alert Summary
- Notifications
- Event Log

Configuration
- View Config

Host Information
Last Updated: Sun Jul 17 10:20:03 CEST 2005
Updated every 90 seconds
Nagios® - www.nagios.org
Logged in as wob

View Status Detail For This Host
View Alert History For This Host
View Trends For This Host
View Alert Histogram For This Host
View Availability Report For This Host
View Notifications This Host

Host
proxy SLS
(sls-proxy)

Member of
eli-vpn-proxies

172.17.17.7

Host State Information

Host Status:	DOWN
Status Information:	CRITICAL - 172.17.17.7: rta nan, lost 100%
Performance Data:	rta=0.000ms;1000.000;1000.000;0; pl=100%;100;100;;
Current Attempt:	5/5
State Type:	HARD
Last Check Type:	ACTIVE
Last Check Time:	07-17-2005 10:15:06
Status Data Age:	0d 0h 4m 57s
Next Scheduled Active Check:	N/A
Latency:	0.000 seconds
Check Duration:	10.008 seconds
Last State Change:	07-15-2005 15:35:06
Current State Duration:	1d 18h 44m 57s
Last Host Notification:	07-15-2005 15:35:06
Current Notification Number:	1
Is This Host Flapping?	N/A
Percent State Change:	N/A
In Scheduled Downtime?	NO
Last Update:	07-17-2005 10:19:49

Active Checks:	ENABLED
Passive Checks:	ENABLED
Obsessing:	ENABLED
Notifications:	ENABLED
Event Handler:	ENABLED
Flap Detection:	ENABLED

Host Commands
- Locate host on map
- Disable active checks of this host
- Re-schedule the next check of this host
- Submit passive check result for this host
- Stop accepting passive checks for this host
- Stop obsessing over this host
- Acknowledge this host problem
- Disable notifications for this host
- Delay next host notification
- Schedule downtime for this host
- Disable notifications for all services on this host
- Enable notifications for all services on this host
- Schedule a check of all services on this host
- Disable checks of all services on this host
- Enable checks of all services on this host
- Disable event handler for this host
- Disable flap detection for this host

Host Comments
- Add a new comment
- Delete all comments

Entry Time	Author	Comment	Comment ID	Persistent	Type	Expires	Actions

This host has no comments associated with it

Using the **Add a new comment** link at the bottom of the page, the CGI program cmd.cgi (Section 16.2.3, page 343), which by passing on a corresponding parameter is already prepared for this task,[2] allows a comment to be recorded (Figure 16.5). The host name is already shown, the check mark in the **Persistent** box ensures that the comments will also "survive" a Nagios restart. The user name filled out in the **Author (Your Name):** field can be edited, as can the actual comment in the **Comment** field.[3]

---

[2] cmd_type=1&host=sls-proxy. More on the parameters in Section 16.2.3 following, page 343.

[3] Starting with Nagios 3.0, amending the author name can be prevented by using the parameter lock_author_name (see page 609).

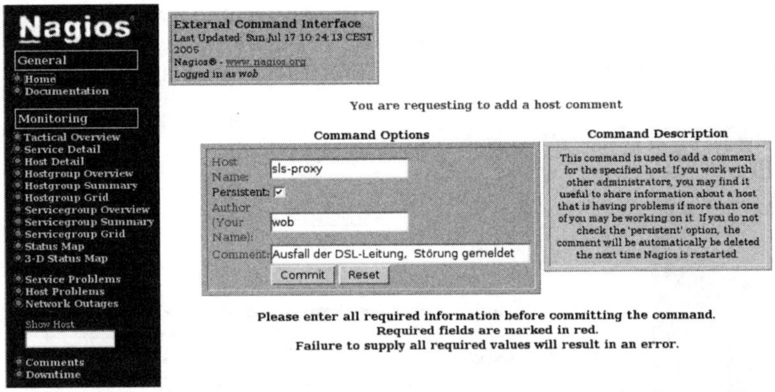

Figure 16.5:
Entering a comment
for a host

The administrator confirms the entry with the **Commit** button. Returning to the status overview, for example with the **Service Problems** menu item, the administrator will see a speech bubble next to the host name, indicating that a comment exists for this host (Figure 16.6). Clicking on the icon opens the corresponding information page and takes the admin directly to the comment entries (Figure 16.7). Clicking on the icon of the trash can in the **Actions** column deletes these individually, if required.

Figure 16.6:
A speech bubble
displays the
existence of
comments

Figure 16.7:
A click on Delete all
comments deletes all
comments at once

16.1.2   Taking responsibility for problems

Acknowledgements (so spelled on the Web interface) are oriented more closely to the workflow than simple comments. An acknowledgement signals to other administrators that somebody is already working on a problem, so nobody else needs to get involved with it for the time being. In the status overview, a small laborer icon symbolizes this form of taking responsibility (Figure 16.8), and Nagios additionally notifies the relevant contacts.

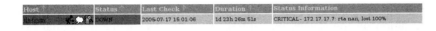

Figure 16.8:
A laborer icon shows that an admin has already taken on responsibility for the problem (acknowledgement)

To issue such a statement, the link **Acknowledge this Host Problem** is used on the extended info page for the host in question. As well as the fields used for entering a normal comment, there are two checkboxes in this case, **Sticky Acknowledgement** (Figure 16.9)—if checked, this option prevents period notification if the error status persists—and **Send Notification**. If the latter is also checked, Nagios notifies the other administrators.

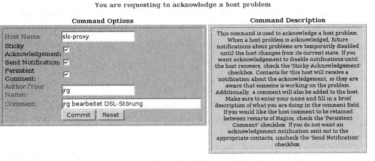

Figure 16.9:
Entry dialog for a host acknowlegement

The effect of **Persistent Comment** is different in Nagios 2.x and Nagios 3.0: In Nagios 2.x the comment is only preserved on a reboot if the checkbox has been marked. Unfortunately, using this to save comments in case of a reboot has the disadvantage that the comment does not disappear automatically when the problem has been solved. On the other hand, Nagios 3.0 normally retains all comments after a reboot. If the check mark for **Persistent Comment** is deleted, Nagios will remove the comment automatically as soon as the problem has been rectified. If the check mark is set, the comment must be removed manually if it is no longer needed, as in Nagios 2.x.

What we are demonstrating here, using a faulty host state, can also be applied to faulty services. The CGI programs are the same, and through the passing of parameters they receive information on whether a host or service is involved, and react accordingly; only the host field receives company in the form of a **Service** entry.

16.2   An Overview of the Individual CGI Programs

At the time of going to press, this chapter was the most extensive documentation on the Nagios Web interface, especially for the individual CGI scripts. But for reasons of space, we shall not go into every detail. If you want to know more, you must take a look at the source code of the scripts or look at the nagios-users[4] mailing list. Some of these are also read by the Nagios developers, and many a question is answered there for which there is currently no documentation.

16.2.1   Variations in status display: status.cgi

By far the most important CGI program, status.cgi is responsible for the status display. What it shows is determined by three parameter groups. The first one defines whether the Web page generated displays all hosts, a specific host, or a service group:

```
http://nagiosserver/nagios/cgi-bin/status.cgi?host=all
http://nagiosserver/nagios/cgi-bin/status.cgi?hostgroup=all
http://nagiosserver/nagios/cgi-bin/status.cgi?servicegroup=all
```

With host you can select individual hosts, and all in this case stands for *all hosts*. hostgroup enables a specific host group to be displayed, and again you can use all to stand for *all host groups*. Finally, servicegroup tells the CGI program to display either the individual service group given as a value, or all service groups, given with all.

Figure 16.10:
The overview
output style

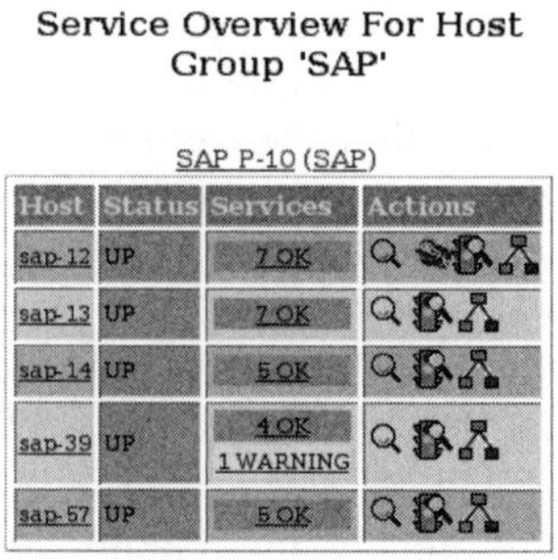

Service Overview For Host
Group 'SAP'

SAP P-10 (SAP)

Host	Status	Services	Actions
sap-12	UP	7 OK	
sap-13	UP	7 OK	
sap-14	UP	5 OK	
sap-39	UP	4 OK / 1 WARNING	
sap-57	UP	5 OK	

The outputs of host=all and hostgroup=all are only different in their style, which is defined by the second parameter group. For host=all, style=detail is the default setting, and for hostgroup=all, it is style=

[4] http://lists.sourceforge.net/mailman/listinfo/nagios-users

`overview.status.cgi?host=all&style=overview` therefore delivers the same result as `status.cgi?hostgroup=all`.

Hosts that do not belong to a host group only appear in the detail view `host=all&style=detail` or `hostgroup=all&style=hostdetail`. All other display styles always show entire host groups from which individual hosts may be missing. `status.cgi` provides five possible output styles: `overview` represents the hosts in a table, but summarizes the services according to states (Figure 16.10). For the host group SAP, you would call the corresponding display with the URL

`http://nagiosserver/nagios/cgi-bin/status.cgi?hostgroup=SAP&style=overview`

The `style` value `summary` compresses the output of `overview`: `status.cgi` only displays one host group for each line (Figure 16.11 shows this for Nagios 2.x, Figure 16.12 for Nagios 3.0). For Nagios 3.0, error states are distinguished as **unhandled** (no acknowledgement set) or **acknowledged**.

Status Summary For Host
Group 'SAP'

Host Group	Host Status Totals	Service Status Totals
SAP P-10 (SAP)	6 UP	27 OK 2 WARNING

Figure 16.11:
The summary output
style of Nagios 2.x

Status Summary For Host Group 'SAP'

Host Group	Host Status Summary	Service Status Summary
SAP P-10 (SAP)	6 UP	39 OK 1 WARNING : UNHANDLED 1 CRITICAL : 1 Acknowledged

Figure 16.12:
The summary output
style of Nagios 3.0

The `grid` style provides an extremely attractive summary in which you can see the status of each individual service by means of the color with which it is highlighted (Figure 16.13). `detail` shows each service in detail on a separate line. The `hostdetail` output style is limited just to host information, providing detailed information with one line for each host (Figure 16.15).

Status Grid For Host Group
'SAP'

SAP P-10 (SAP)

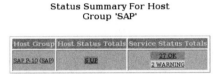

Host	Services	Actions
sap-12	PING SAP Dialog Network Time SAP Dialog Response Time SAP-3200 SAP-3300 SAP-3600 SAP_AS_12	Q⊗&♂
sap-13	PING SAP Dialog Network Time SAP Dialog Response Time SAP SpoolNumbers SAP-3201 SAP-3301 SAP_AS_13	Q&♂
sap-14	PING SAP Dialog Network Time SAP Dialog Response Time SAP-3202 SAP_AS_14	Q&♂
sap-39	PING SAP Dialog Network Time SAP Dialog Response Time SAP-3203 SAP_AS_39	Q&♂
sap-57	PING SAP Dialog Network Time SAP Dialog Response Time SAP-3204 SAP_AS_57	Q&♂

Figure 16.13:
The grid output style

Figure 16.14:
The detail output
style

Service Status Details For
Host Group 'SAP'

Host	Service	Status	Last Check	Duration	Attempt	Status Information
sap-12	PING	OK	2005-07-17 15:58:21	0d 14h 41m 40s	1/3	OK- 10.128.254.12: rta 39.244ms, lost 0%
	SAP Dialog Network Time	OK	2005-07-17 15:59:05	0d 0h 0m 22s	1/2	P10 p10db012_P10_00 Dialog FrontEndNetTime 415 msec
	SAP Dialog Response Time	OK	2005-07-17 15:58:49	0d 22h 56m 59s	1/2	P10 p10db012_P10_00 Dialog ResponseTime 81 msec
	SAP-3200	OK	2005-07-17 15:58:33	1d 21h 48m 57s	1/3	TCP OK- 0.031 second response time on port 3200
	SAP-3300	OK	2005-07-17 15:58:38	1d 21h 48m 57s	1/3	TCP OK- 0.031 second response time on port 3300
	SAP-3600	OK	2005-07-17 15:58:22	1d 21h 49m 57s	1/3	TCP OK- 0.031 second response time on port 3600
	SAP_AS_12	OK	2005-07-17 15:59:06	1d 21h 49m 8s	1/3	OK- SAP server p10db012_P10_00 available.
sap-13	PING	OK	2005-07-17 15:58:50	2d 2h 51m 31s	1/3	OK- 10.128.254.13: rta 92.678ms, lost 0%
	SAP Dialog Network Time	OK	2005-07-17 15:54:34	1d 21h 48m 18s	1/2	P10 p10ap013_P10_01 Dialog FrontEndNetTime 617 msec
	SAP Dialog Response Time	OK	2005-07-17 15:56:39	1d 21h 46m 38s	1/2	P10 p10ap013_P10_01 Dialog ResponseTime 31 msec
	SAP SpoolNumbers	OK	2005-07-17 15:57:23	1d 21h 39m 46s	1/2	P10 Spool SpoolNumbers UsedNumbers 35 %
	SAP-3201	OK	2005-07-17 15:59:07	5d 9h 56m 14s	1/3	TCP OK- 0.031 second response time on port 3201
	SAP-3301	OK	2005-07-17 15:58:51	5d 9h 56m 14s	1/3	TCP OK- 0.030 second response time on port 3301
	SAP_AS_13	OK	2005-07-17 15:58:35	1d 21h 50m 43s	1/3	OK- SAP server p10ap013_P10_01 available

Figure 16.15:
The hostdetail
output style

Host Status Details For Host
Group 'SAP'

Host	Status	Last Check	Duration	Status Information
sap-12	UP	2005-07-17 15:54:15	7d 6h 37m 34s	OK- 10.128.254.12 responds to ICMP. Packet 1, rta 39.340ms
sap-13	UP	2005-07-15 18:14:49	20d 8h 32m 20s	OK- 10.128.254.13 responds to ICMP. Packet 1, rta 39.156ms
sap-14	UP	2005-07-17 07:59:13	20d 8h 34m 23s	OK- 10.128.254.14 responds to ICMP. Packet 1, rta 39.223ms
sap-39	UP	2005-07-17 16:37:36	20d 8h 34m 22s	OK- 10.128.254.39 responds to ICMP. Packet 1, rta 39.472ms
sap-57	UP	2005-07-17 01:22:55	20d 8h 34m 22s	OK- 10.128.254.57 responds to ICMP. Packet 1, rta 39.389ms

5 Matching Host Entries Displayed

The third and final parameter group allows you to influence, through *selectors*, what states and what properties are shown by status.cgi, such as all services in an error state for which no acknowledgement has yet been set by an administrator (see Section 16.1.2, page 332). States are passed on with the hoststatustypes or servicestatustypes parameter, properties with hostprops and serviceprops. All four parameters demand numerical values after the equals sign, and these are summarized in Tables 16.2, 16.3, and 16.4.

Table 16.2:
Possible values for
hoststatustypes

Value	Description
1	PENDING (a result of the very first test planned for this host is not yet available)
2	UP
4	DOWN
8	UNREACHABLE

The third and final parameter group allows *selectors* to be used to influence what states and properties are displayed by status.cgi, fofr instance all services in an error state for which no administrator has yet set an acknowledgement (see Section 16.1.2, page 332). Conditions are passed with the parameter hoststatustypes or servicestatustypes, and properties with the hostprops and serviceprops parameters. All four parameters require numerical values after the equals sign, and these are summarized in tables 16.2, 16.3 and 16.4.

Value	Description
1	PENDING (Service was originally planned for a check, but so far no result is available)
2	OK
4	WARNING
8	UNKNOWN
16	CRITICAL

Table 16.3:
Possible values for
servicestatus-
types

Value	Description
1	Scheduled downtime (downtime planned)
2	No Scheduled downtime (no downtime planned)
4	Acknowledgement (status confirmed by the admin)
8	No acknowledgement
16	Host/Service check disabled
32	Host/Service check enabled
64	Event Handler disabled
128	Event Handler enabled
256	Flap Detection disabled
512	Flap Detection enabled
1024	Host/Service oscillates (flapping)
2048	Host/Service does not oscillate
4096	Hosts or services currently excluded from a notification
8192	Notification enabled
16384	Passive host/service checks disabled (Chapter 13, page 291)
32768	Passive host/service checks enabled
65536	Hosts/services for which there is at least one result determined for each passive test
131072	Hosts/services for which there is at least one active check result

Table 16.4:
Possible values for
host and
serviceprops

continued:

Value	Description
262144	Hosts/services in the hard state (from Nagios 3.0)
524288	Hosts/services in the soft state (from Nagios 3.0)

If you want to query several states or properties simultaneously, you just add the specified values together: `status.cgi?host=all&servicestatustypes=28` shows all services with an error status: WARNING, UNKNOWN, and CRITICAL, that is, $4+8+16=28$. This query is identical to the **Service Problems** menu item in the navigation area.

`status.cgi?hostgroup=all&hoststatustypes=12&style=hostdetail` corresponds to the **Host Problems** menu item in the navigation area. It queries all hosts which are either DOWN or UNREACHABLE (here $4+8=12$). Since only host information should be shown, but no service information, the output style is in the form of `hostdetail`.

`status.cgi?host=all&servicestatustypes=24&serviceprops=10` is the variation of the first example: only the states UNKNOWN and CRITICAL ($8+16=24$) are shown, and only those that neither show a planned downtime, nor have already been confirmed ($2+8=10$).

The CGI program specifies the filter parameter each time in a separate checkbox. Figure 16.16 shows this for the third example.

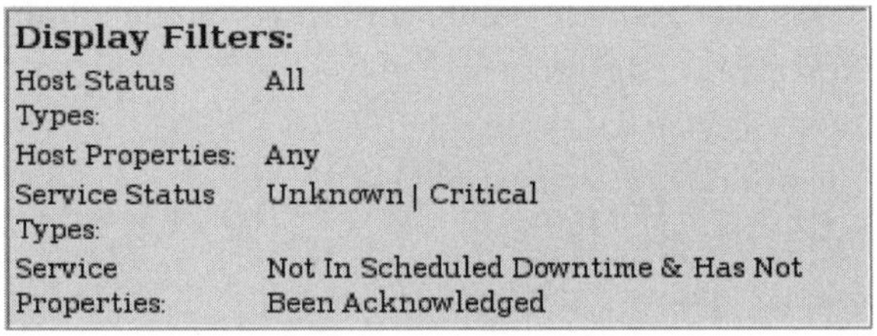

Figure 16.16:
This information box
shows what states
and properties
`status.cgi` should
display

Display Filters:

Host Status Types:	All
Host Properties:	Any
Service Status Types:	Unknown	Critical
Service Properties:	Not In Scheduled Downtime & Has Not Been Acknowledged

If you want, you can define your own navigation area to your own requirements or just use the existing one. The main page consists of one frame, and the navigation area itself is defined by a normal HTML file: `/usr/local/nagios/share/side.html`.[5]

One example of a changed `side.html` is provided on the Nagios Demo page[6] at Netways;[7] another is the Nuvola style, shown in the figure on page 369.

---

[5] If you have kept to the installation in this book.
[6] http://nagios-demo.netways.de/
[7] http://www.netways.de/

16.2.2 Additional information and control center: `extinfo.cgi`

If called with the `host` or `service` parameter, `extinfo.cgi` not only provides detailed information on a specific host (Figure 16.4, page 331) or service, it also serves as a control center for hosts and services (parameter
`hostgroup`) and for service groups (`servicegroup`). Depending on the
object class for which it is called, you can run various commands from
here.

In the area on the left, the status of the host is extensively documented
and in the box on the right—overwritten with **Host Commands**—there is a
selection of commands that can be run. The latter commands call `cmd.cgi`
(Section 16.2.3, page 343) and only function if the interface for external
commands (Section 13.1, page 292) is active. The lower area of the page
allows you to enter object-specific comments, read them, and delete them
again. The Web page that `extinfo.cgi` generates for services also follows
this pattern.

Corresponding pages for service and host groups (Figure 16.17), on the
other hand, allow only group-specific commands to be run and do not show
any additional information. Each command applies to the entire group,
sparing you from a lot of mouse clicking. **Disabling notifications for all hosts
in this hostgroup**, for example, ensures that Nagios does not send any more
messages for hosts in this host group.

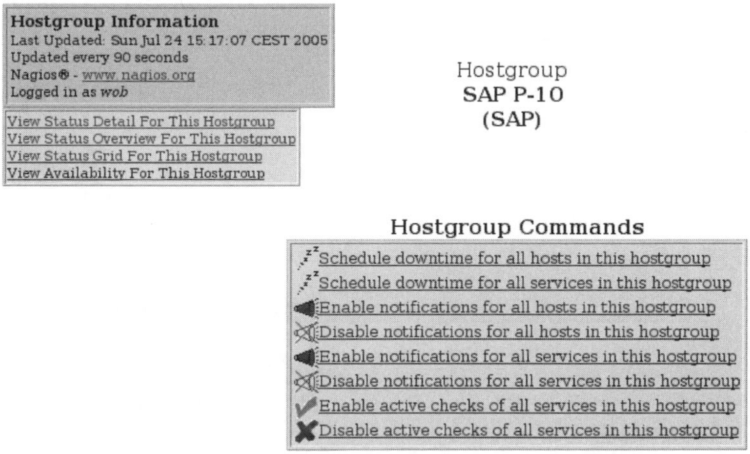

Figure 16.17:
Command center for
the SAP host group:
`extinfo.cgi?type=`
`5&hostgroup=SAP`

Apart from hosts, services, and corresponding groups, the CGI program has
other display functions, enabled by the CGI parameter `type`:

```
http://nagsrv/nagios/cgi-bin/extinfo.cgi?type=value
```

Depending on the value specified, further parameters are required, so to display the service you also have to include the host name and service designation:

extinfo.cgi?type=0

Shows information (such as starting time and process ID) for the Nagios process itself and all global parameters (normally notifications are sent, performance data processed, etc.; see Figure 16.18). In the **Process Commands** box the global parameters can be changed, and Nagios can also be stopped and restarted.

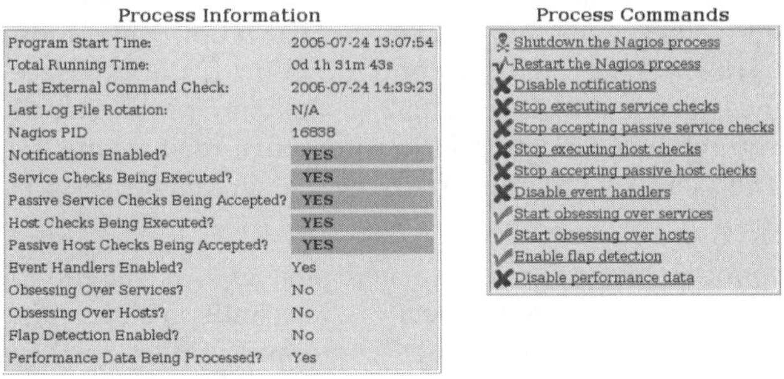

Figure 16.18:
Information on the
Nagios process and
global settings:
extinfo.cgi?type=
0

extinfo.cgi?type=1&host=*host*

Shows commands and information on the *host* (see Figure 16.4, page 331).

extinfo.cgi?type=2&service=*service*

The same for the *service*.

extinfo.cgi?type=3

Shows all available host and service comments on a single page (Figure 16.19).

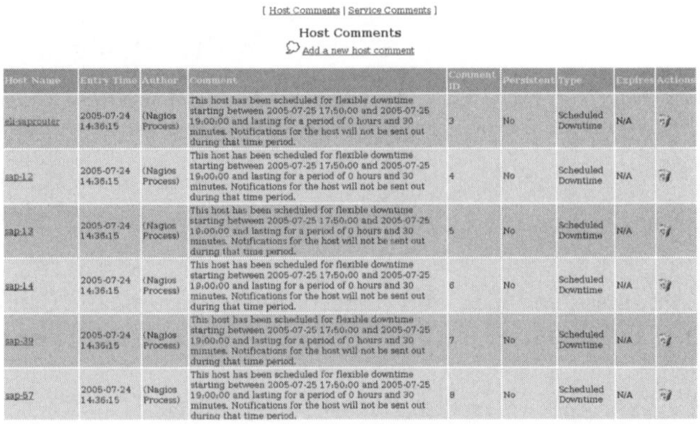

Figure 16.19:
Overview of all
existing comments:
extinfo.cgi?type=
3

`extinfo.cgi?type=4`

Provides information on the performance of Nagios, separated according to host and service, as well as active and passive checks (Figure 16.20).

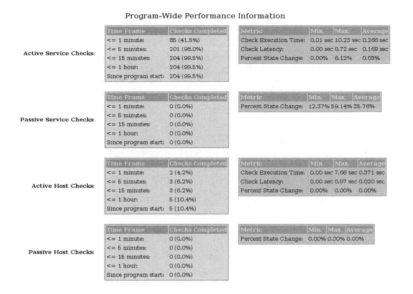

Program-Wide Performance Information

	Time Frame	Checks Completed
Active Service Checks:	<= 1 minute:	85 (41.5%)
	<= 5 minutes:	201 (98.0%)
	<= 15 minutes:	204 (99.5%)
	<= 1 hour:	204 (99.5%)
	Since program start:	204 (99.5%)

Metric	Min.	Max.	Average
Check Execution Time:	0.01 sec	10.23 sec	0.266 sec
Check Latency:	0.00 sec	0.72 sec	0.169 sec
Percent State Change:	0.00%	6.12%	0.03%

	Time Frame	Checks Completed
Passive Service Checks:	<= 1 minute:	0 (0.0%)
	<= 5 minutes:	0 (0.0%)
	<= 15 minutes:	0 (0.0%)
	<= 1 hour:	0 (0.0%)
	Since program start:	0 (0.0%)

Metric	Min.	Max.	Average
Percent State Change:	12.37%	59.14%	35.76%

	Time Frame	Checks Completed
Active Host Checks:	<= 1 minute:	2 (4.2%)
	<= 5 minutes:	3 (6.2%)
	<= 15 minutes:	3 (6.2%)
	<= 1 hour:	5 (10.4%)
	Since program start:	5 (10.4%)

Metric	Min.	Max.	Average
Check Execution Time:	0.00 sec	7.66 sec	0.371 sec
Check Latency:	0.00 sec	0.97 sec	0.020 sec
Percent State Change:	0.00%	0.00%	0.00%

	Time Frame	Checks Completed
Passive Host Checks:	<= 1 minute:	0 (0.0%)
	<= 5 minutes:	0 (0.0%)
	<= 15 minutes:	0 (0.0%)
	<= 1 hour:	0 (0.0%)
	Since program start:	0 (0.0%)

Metric	Min.	Max.	Average
Percent State Change:	0.00%	0.00%	0.00%

Figure 16.20: Information on the performance: `extinfo.cgi?type=4`

The middle column reveals how many of the planned tests Nagios has already performed in the last 1, 5, 15, and 60 minutes. As long as there are checks for which `normal_check_interval` is more than five minutes, the first two values can never reach 100 percent.

The right-hand columns define the actual value for this page: **Check Execution Time** specifies the minimum, maximum, and average time which Nagios requires to perform active host and service checks. **Check Latency** measures the distance between the planned start and the actual running time of a test. If this delay is considerably larger than one or two seconds, Nagios probably has a performance problem. One possible cause is that the system is processing performance data too slowly, but low-performance hardware may also play a role here. Searching for the cause can sometimes turn out to be very difficult, and the original documentation[8] provides a number of tips on the subject.

`extinfo.cgi?type=5&hostgroup=hostgroup`

Shows command center for a host group (Figure 16.17 on page 339).

---

[8] `/usr/local/nagios/share/docs/tuning.html`

`extinfo.cgi?type=6`
: Shows all planned maintenance periods for hosts and services (Figure 16.21).

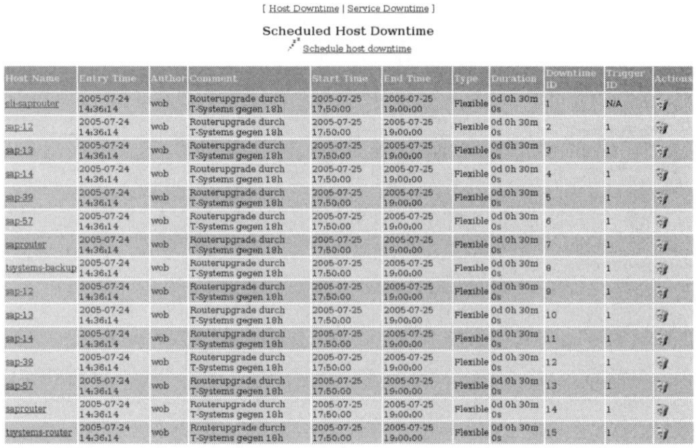

[Host Downtime | Service Downtime]

Scheduled Host Downtime

Schedule host downtime

Host Name	Entry Time	Author	Comment	Start Time	End Time	Type	Duration	Downtime ID	Trigger ID	Actions
eli-saprouter	2005-07-24 14:36:14	wob	Routerupgrade durch T-Systems gegen 18h	2005-07-25 17:50:00	2005-07-25 19:00:00	Flexible	0d 0h 30m 0s	1	N/A	
sap-12	2005-07-24 14:36:14	wob	Routerupgrade durch T-Systems gegen 18h	2005-07-25 17:50:00	2005-07-25 19:00:00	Flexible	0d 0h 30m 0s	2	1	
sap-13	2005-07-24 14:36:14	wob	Routerupgrade durch T-Systems gegen 18h	2005-07-25 17:50:00	2005-07-25 19:00:00	Flexible	0d 0h 30m 0s	3	1	
sap-14	2005-07-24 14:36:14	wob	Routerupgrade durch T-Systems gegen 18h	2005-07-25 17:50:00	2005-07-25 19:00:00	Flexible	0d 0h 30m 0s	4	1	
sap-39	2005-07-24 14:36:14	wob	Routerupgrade durch T-Systems gegen 18h	2005-07-25 17:50:00	2005-07-25 19:00:00	Flexible	0d 0h 30m 0s	5	1	
sap-57	2005-07-24 14:36:14	wob	Routerupgrade durch T-Systems gegen 18h	2005-07-25 17:50:00	2005-07-25 19:00:00	Flexible	0d 0h 30m 0s	6	1	
saprouter	2005-07-24 14:36:14	wob	Routerupgrade durch T-Systems gegen 18h	2005-07-25 17:50:00	2005-07-25 19:00:00	Flexible	0d 0h 30m 0s	7	1	
tsystems-backup	2005-07-24 14:36:14	wob	Routerupgrade durch T-Systems gegen 18h	2005-07-25 17:50:00	2005-07-25 19:00:00	Flexible	0d 0h 30m 0s	8	1	
sap-12	2005-07-24 14:36:14	wob	Routerupgrade durch T-Systems gegen 18h	2005-07-25 17:50:00	2005-07-25 19:00:00	Flexible	0d 0h 30m 0s	9	1	
sap-13	2005-07-24 14:36:14	wob	Routerupgrade durch T-Systems gegen 18h	2005-07-25 17:50:00	2005-07-25 19:00:00	Flexible	0d 0h 30m 0s	10	1	
sap-14	2005-07-24 14:36:14	wob	Routerupgrade durch T-Systems gegen 18h	2005-07-25 17:50:00	2005-07-25 19:00:00	Flexible	0d 0h 30m 0s	11	1	
sap-39	2005-07-24 14:36:14	wob	Routerupgrade durch T-Systems gegen 18h	2005-07-25 17:50:00	2005-07-25 19:00:00	Flexible	0d 0h 30m 0s	12	1	
sap-57	2005-07-24 14:36:14	wob	Routerupgrade durch T-Systems gegen 18h	2005-07-25 17:50:00	2005-07-25 19:00:00	Flexible	0d 0h 30m 0s	13	1	
saprouter	2005-07-24 14:36:14	wob	Routerupgrade durch T-Systems gegen 18h	2005-07-25 17:50:00	2005-07-25 19:00:00	Flexible	0d 0h 30m 0s	14	1	
tsystems-router	2005-07-24 14:36:14	wob	Routerupgrade durch T-Systems gegen 18h	2005-07-25 17:50:00	2005-07-25 19:00:00	Flexible	0d 0h 30m 0s	15	1	

Figure 16.21: Overview of all planned maintenance periods: `extinfo.cgi?type=6`

`extinfo.cgi?type=7`
: Shows an overview of all planned tests, sorted by the next implementation time (see Figure 16.22). Next to this, `extinfo.cgi` also lists the time of the last check.

  The **Active Checks** column shows if the respective tests are active or not, and in the `Actions` column the planned check can be deleted or moved to a different time.

`extinfo.cgi?type=8&servicegroup=`*`servicegroup`*
: Shows the command centre for a service group, identical in structure to the command center of a host group.

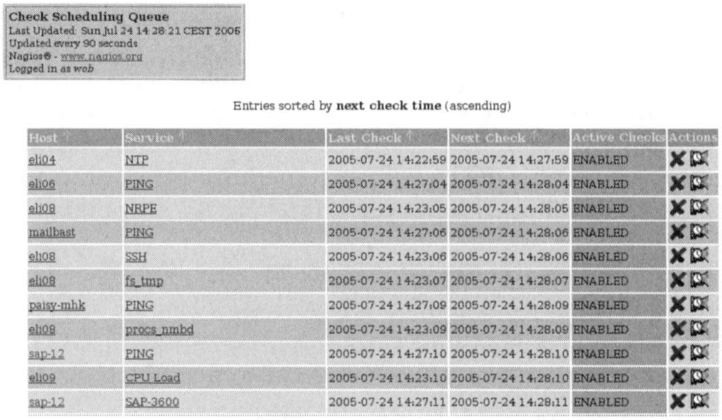

Check Scheduling Queue
Last Updated: Sun Jul 24 14:28:21 CEST 2005
Updated every 90 seconds
Nagios® - www.nagios.org
Logged in as *wob*

Entries sorted by **next check time** (ascending)

Host	Service	Last Check	Next Check	Active Checks	Actions
eli04	NTP	2005-07-24 14:22:59	2005-07-24 14:27:59	ENABLED	
eli06	PING	2005-07-24 14:27:04	2005-07-24 14:28:04	ENABLED	
eli08	NRPE	2005-07-24 14:23:05	2005-07-24 14:28:05	ENABLED	
mailbast	PING	2005-07-24 14:27:06	2005-07-24 14:28:06	ENABLED	
eli08	SSH	2005-07-24 14:23:06	2005-07-24 14:28:06	ENABLED	
eli08	fs_tmp	2005-07-24 14:23:07	2005-07-24 14:28:07	ENABLED	
paisy-mhk	PING	2005-07-24 14:27:09	2005-07-24 14:28:09	ENABLED	
eli08	procs_nmbd	2005-07-24 14:23:09	2005-07-24 14:28:09	ENABLED	
sap-12	PING	2005-07-24 14:27:10	2005-07-24 14:28:10	ENABLED	
eli09	CPU Load	2005-07-24 14:23:10	2005-07-24 14:28:10	ENABLED	
sap-12	SAP-3600	2005-07-24 14:27:11	2005-07-24 14:28:11	ENABLED	

Figure 16.22: All planned tests, sorted by their planned implementation time: `extinfo.cgi?type=7`

16.2.3 Interface for external commands: cmd.cgi

As a real all-rounder, `cgi.cmd`, with some 100 functions, covers nearly all the possibilities that the interface provides for external commands. The `cmd_typ` parameter defines which of these the CGI program should run. The command

```
http://nagiosserver/nagios/cgi-bin/cmd.cgi?cmd_typ=6
```

switches off active service checks for a specific service (Figure 16.23). In order to describe the desired service uniquely, you must specify the host and service description. If you run the CGI program manually, the Web form shown queries these values, and if `cmd.cgi` is started by another CGI program, the required data is passed through CGI parameters. Possible parameters here are `host`, `service`, `hostgroup`, and `servicegroup`, which are followed by an equals (=) sign and then the appropriate Nagios object.

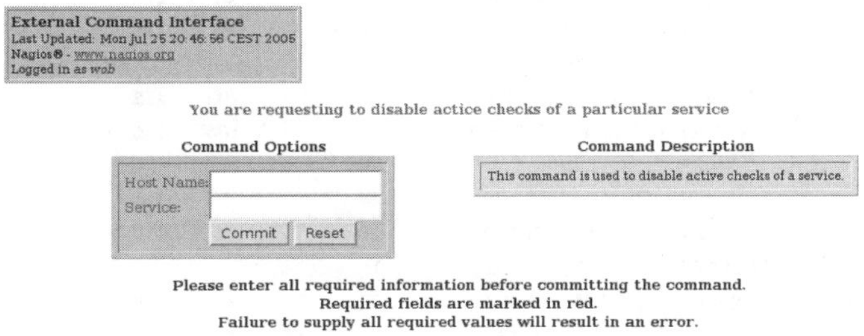

Figure 16.23:
Disabling a service check with
`cmd.cgi?cmd_typ=6`

Figure 16.24 lists the most important commands which refer to a host or service, and Figure 16.25 shows those that refer to the control of global parameters (corresponding to the values in the main configuration file `nagios.cfg`). The source code file `include/common.h` contains a complete list of all possible values, including ones that are planned but not yet implemented.

The first column in Figures 16.24 and 16.25 describes the function of the command: `ADD_HOST_COMMENT` adds a comment to a host, and `DISABLE_ACTIVE_SVC_CHECK` switches off active checks for a service (in abbreviated form: `SVC`).

The columns after this specify the object type to which the respective function refers. To add a comment with `ADD_HOST_COMMENT`, you must specify the host in question. For this reason the function code 1 is shown in the **Host** column. A specific active service check can only be switched off if the matching service is named, so the function code 6 is to be found in the **Service** column. With 16 you switch off all active service checks on a host to be specified; there are also corresponding codes for all active service checks for a host or service group.

With ACKNOWLEDGE_PROBLEM, an administrator confirms that he is taking care of a specific problem. 33 (**Host** column) refers to a host problem, and 34 (**Service** column) to a service problem. The gray fields mean that there is no corresponding function for host and service groups. The Web form that opens with cmd_typ=33 (Figure 16.9, page 333) then allows a comment to be entered.

Figure 16.24:
The most important
host and service
related codes for
cmd.cgi?cmd_typ=

command	host	service	hostgroup	servicegroup
ADD_HOST_COMMENT	1			
DEL_HOST_COMMENT	2			
DEL_ALL_HOST_COMMENT	20			
ADD_SVC_COMMENT		3		
DEL_SVC_COMMENT		4		
DEL_ALL_SVC_COMMENT		21		
ENABLE_ACTIVE_SVC_CHECK	15	5	67	113
DISABLE_ACTIVE_SVC_CHECK	16	6	68	114
SCHEDULE_SVC_CHECK	17	7		
ENABLE_ACTIVE_HOST_CHECK	47		103	115
DISABLE_ACTIVE_HOST_CHECK	48		104	116
SCHEDULE_HOST_CHECK	96			
ENABLE_HOST_NOTIFICATIONS	24		65	111
DISABLE_HOST_NOTIFICATIONS	25		66	112
DELAY_HOST_NOTIFICATIONS	10			
ENABLE_SVC_NOTIFICATIONS	28	22	63	109
DISABLE_SVC_NOTIFICATIONS	29	23	64	110
DELAY_SVC_NOTIFICATIONS	19	9		
ACKNOWLEDGE_PROBLEM	33	34		
REMOVE_ACKNOWLEDGE	51	52		
ENABLE_PASSIVE_HOST_CHECKS	92		107	119
DISABLE_PASSIVE_HOST_CHECKS	93		108	120
ENABLE_PASSIVE_SVC_CHECKS		39	105	117
DISABLE_PASSIVE_SVC_CHECKS		40	106	118
SCHEDULE_HOST_DOWNTIME	55		84	121
DEL_HOST_DOWNTIME	78			
SCHEDULE_SVC_DOWNTIME		56	85	122
DEL_SVC_DOWNTIME		79		
ENABLE_EVENT_HANDLER	43	45		
DISABLE_EVENT_HANDLER	44	46		
ENABLE_FLAP_DETECTION	57	59		
DISABLE_FLAP_DETECTION	58	60		

Functions that refer to global parameters (Figure 16.25) can normally only be switched on or off. So the value 11 in the **Start** column for NOTIFICA-TIONS means that this command code switches on all notifications globally, while 12 switches them off globally.

If you are not quite certain whether the determined function does what you really wanted, it is best to run cmd.cgi manually with the corresponding function code, such as shown here:

```
http://nagiosserver/nagios/cgi-bin/cmd.cgi?cmd_typ=12
```

The Web page generated in this way always has a small gray box available next to the required entry fields that explains the corresponding command (Figure 16.23, on the right side of the page).

global parameters	START/ ENABLE	STOP/ DISABLE
NOTIFICATIONS	11	12
SVC_CHECKS	35	36
ACCEPTING_PASSIVE_SVC_CHECKS	37	38
HOST_CHECKS	88	89
ACCEPTING_PASSIVE_HOST_CHECKS	90	91
EVENT_HANDLER	41	42
FLAP_DETECTION	61	62
PERFORMANCE_DATA	82	83

Figure 16.25: cmd.cgi command codes for global parameters

16.2.4 The most important things at a glance: tac.cgi

As a "tactical overview," tac.cgi provides a wealth of information on a single Web page, displayed in a summary (Figure 16.26). On the left-hand side of the page you can see, in order of priority, first the failure of entire network ranges (**Network Outages**), followed by the status of hosts and services, and at the bottom tac.cgi lists whether individual monitoring features such as notifications and event handlers are active.

Up to this final section, everything is concentrated on displaying problems. Provided everything is OK, the CGI merely shows the number of unproblematic services or hosts, highlighted in light gray (and announces 47 Up, for example, in the Hosts box). In problem cases it distinguishes between open problems, which nobody has looked at yet (highlighted in red, e.g., 2 Unhandled Problems for **Services | Critical**), and those for which an adminstrator has already taken responsibility through an acknowledgement (pink background, like 1 Acknowledged for **Services | Unknown**). If host or service checks are disabled, these are also shown with a pink background, since they are problems that do not require the immediate attention of the admin (e.g., 2 Disabled for **Services | Ok**).

Enabled features in the lower parts are marked by tac.cgi in green, and disabled ones, in red. The vertically written green **Enabled** in **Notifications** means that notifications are enabled globally, whereas the red background on the other hand, 2 Services Disabled, means that they were explicitly switched off for two individual services.

For all the problems displayed you are taken to a single overview specifically showing the hosts and services in question.

On the right-hand side of the page the upper box summarizes the extinfo. cgi?type=4 (see page 341) Nagios performance data, which can be shown in detail. The bar graph beneath it shows the health of the entire network monitored as a percentage. If you move the mouse over one of the bars, you will also see the percentage as a number.

16.2.5 The topological map of the network: statusmap.cgi

statusmap.cgi (Figure 16.27) provides a view of the dependencies between the monitored hosts. Starting from the central Nagios server in the middle, lines connect all hosts that the server reaches directly—and whose host definitions do not need the parents parameter to be specified (see Section 2.3, page 62.).

The graphics also reveal the hosts to which Nagios has only indirect access through other hosts. So between sls-mail and the Nagios server in Figure 16.27 lie the hosts sls-proxy, hspvip, and pfint. sls-proxy, as the comment **Down** and the red (instead of green) background suggest, has failed. Since sls-mail depends on this, it is in an UNREACHABLE state, which statusmap.cgi also marks with a red background.

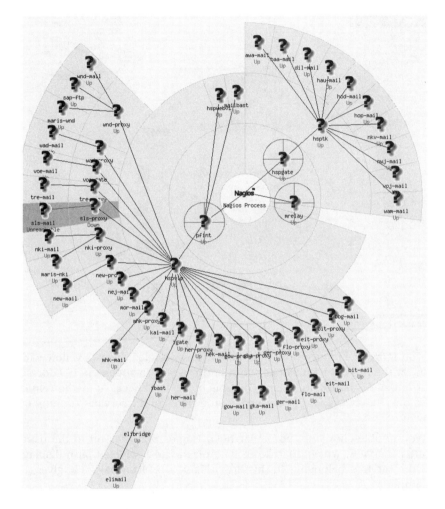

Figure 16.27:
Dependencies of
monitored hosts
shown graphically

How Nagios arranges the hosts in the graphics is defined by the parameter
`default_statusmap_layout` (page 608) in the configuration file `cgi.cfg`.
The layout can also be changed with a selection window in the Web interface (at the top right in Figure 16.28). The figure shows the demo system of
Netways,[9] whose appearance depends on user-specific coordinates, which
in this case you have to specify individually for each host (see page 365).
The question mark icon supplied by Nagios has been replaced with nicer
pictures by the operator of the site. Coordinates and icons are defined with
the `hostextinfo` object, described in more detail in Section 16.4.1).

[9] http://netways.de/Demosystem.1621.0.html

Figure 16.28:
Statusmap with
self-defined
coordinates and
icons

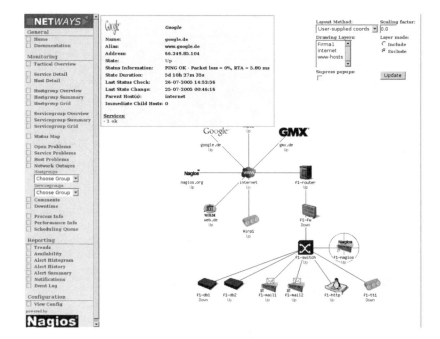

If you move the mouse onto a particular host, Nagios opens a yellow window at the top left with status information, which includes the IP address, current status information, and the time of the last check. At the bottom of this box, `statusmap.cgi` summarizes the states of the services running on this host.

If you double-click on a particular host, Nagios branches off to the usual status overview, which apart from data on the host selected, also displays all the services belonging to this host (Figure 16.14 on page 336 gives an example).

16.2.6 Navigation in 3D: `statuswrl.cgi`

`statuswrl.cgi` allows Nagios to move through a 3D representation of the network plan (Figure 16.29). In this you can zoom on to hosts, move the overall view, rotate it, etc.

A VRML-capable browser is necessary for the display.[10] Although the original documentation[11] provides links to the corresponding plugins, two of

---

[10]   The *Virtual Reality Markup Language* (VRML), version 2.0/1997, is used to describe the virtual "space."

[11]   `/usr/local/nagios/share/docs/cgis.html#statuswrl_cgi`

them are out of date, and only *Cortona*[12] could be reached at the time of going to press. This plugin does not work under Linux, however; in Windows it works with Internet Explorer, and also with Netscape, Mozilla, and Firefox.[13] A good overview of VRML software, organized according to operating system and browser, is provided by the National Institute of Standards and Technology (NIST) on its Web site.[14]

Of the VRML plugins for Linux, *OpenVRML*,[15] and *freeWRL*[16] are the most likely to be used. The standard Linux distributions usually do not include a finished package. OpenVRML is included in Fedora in Extras; on the homepage of freeWRL there are binary packages for Fedora and Ubuntu. You should not try compiling the software yourself unless you are an experienced system administrator or software developer: there are a large number of pitfalls. If you have never worked with the Java compiler before and have not compiled complex software packages such as Mozilla or Firefox yourself, then you should leave it alone.

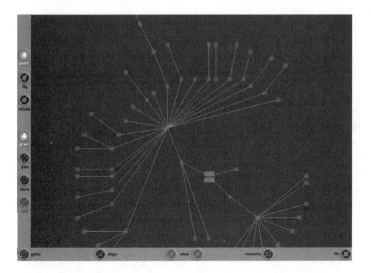

Figure 16.29:
This picture marks the beginning of the tour through your own network

But all of this is no reason to despair, since the use of 3D navigation is questionable anyway, especially as the 2D view of the normal status map displays all the information required, and displaying simple flat graphics in the browser takes up considerably less time than CPU-intensive 3D rendering. Before you rush into the adventure of compiling software yourself, we

---

[12] http://www.parallelgrafics.com/products/cortona/
[13] For Firefox you have to install it manually, select **Custom** instead of **Typical** in the installation routine, and in **not supported browsers** specify the plugin directory of the browser.
[14] http://cic.nist.gov/vrml/vbdetect.html
[15] http://www.openvrml.org/
[16] http://freewrl.sourceforge.net/

recommend that you decide for yourself, using the Cortona plugin, whether it is worth the effort of compiling a project like OpenVRML.

16.2.7 Querying the status with a cell phone: `statuswml.cgi`

In order to make the information provided by Nagios accessible for WAP[17]-capable devices without a fully functional browser, `statuswml.cgi` generates a Web page in the WML format,[18] which can be displayed with a cellphone—provided that the Nagios server is reachable in the Internet. Apart from the status query for hosts and services, it also allows the CGI program to switch off tests and notifications and to confirm existing problems with acknowledgements.

You should think carefully before you make Nagios accessible over the Internet: Nagios makes available much sensitive data that can be misused by hackers. In case of doubt, you're better off doing without it. Without direct Internet access, `statuswml.cgi` is useless, since a cellphone cannot use protected access methods such as a VPN tunnel. This is why we shall not introduce `statuswml.cgi` in great detail at this point.

16.2.8 Analyzing disrupted partial networks: `outages.cgi`

The CGI program `outages.cgi` only shows those network nodes in a host overview that are responsible for the failure of a partial network: In contrast to a status overview, as in Figure 16.15, page 336, `outages.cgi` specifies in the **# Hosts Affected** column how many services and hosts this affects in each case (Figure 16.30).

Figure 16.30:
As long as
sls-proxy fails,
Nagios cannot reach
any hosts lying
behind it

With the icons in the **Actions** column you call other CGI programs that selectively filter out information on the host shown here. From left to right, they show the status display in the detail view (traffic light), the topological network view (network tree), the 3D view (**3-D**), the trend display (graph), the log file entries for the host (spreadsheet), and the display of notifications which have been made (megaphone).

---

[17] *Wireless Access Protocol.*
[18] The *Wireless Markup Language* contains a part of HTML, heavily reduced in its functionality.

16.2.9 Querying the object definition with `config.cgi`

`config.cgi` shows a tabular overview of the definition of all objects for a type that can be specified (Figure 16.31)—the type of object involved can be defined in the selection field in the top right corner. Where the consideration itself contains Nagios objects (in the host view **Host Check Command**, **Default Contact Group**, and—not visible in the picture—**Notification Period**), a link takes you directly to the configuration view of this object type.

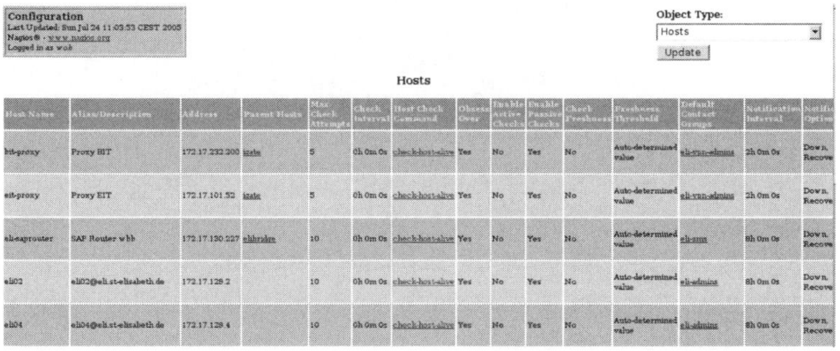

Figure 16.31: `config.cgi` displays the current configuration of the selected object class—here hosts—(extract)

The CGI program does not provide any way of changing anything in the settings. In addition, only users who are entered in the parameter `authorized_for_configuration_information` (configuration file `cgi.cfg`, p. 607) have access to this view.

16.2.10 Availability statistics: `avail.cgi`

If you are monitoring systems, then you also take an interest in their availability. `avail.cgi` first asks if you are interested in **Hosts**, **Services**, **Hostgroups**, and **Servicegroups**. After you have selected a time period, you will see an overview, as in Figure 16.32. For **Services** and **Hosts** you can also have the availability data presented through **All Hosts** or **All Services** as a CSV file.

`avail.cgi` shows the hosts involved separately from the services. How long a service or host remained in a particular state can be seen from the corresponding colored column—green for OK, yellow for WARNING, red for CRITICAL (service), DOWN and UNREACHABLE (host)—in percent. The column that shows how much time the status of a service was UNKNOWN is shown in orange. Incomplete log files are shown in the **Undetermined** column. If there is a value larger than zero, then there are periods for which Nagios cannot make a statement concerning the state.

Below each table, the **Average** line specifies the average of the individual values. In Figure 16.32 the hosts involved were available 99.965 percent of the time.

`avail.cgi` shows the availability twice in each case: first as an absolute value for the evaluation period, and then (in brackets) with respect to the time during which data actually was available. As long as the **Time Undetermined** column displays `0.000%`, the two availability values match.

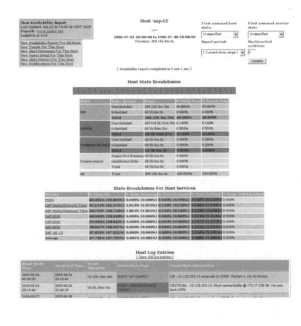

If you click on one of the hosts or services displayed, a detailed view will appear. Figure 16.33 shows such a view for the host `sap-12`.

On a bar diagram that shows the states over the selected period in color, there is detailed information on the host itself, followed by statistics on the availability of the service that is monitored on this host. This includes an extract from the log file, which only shows the relevant entries for the availability of the host; that is, HOST UP, HOST DOWN, or HOST UNREACHABLE. The log file entries are cut off by avail.cgi to save space.

16.2.11 What events occur, how often?—histogram.cgi

If the state of a host or service changes, this is called an *event*. The CGI program histogram.cgi shows the frequency of this in different views. If you select **Day of the Month** as the **Breakdown type**, it illustrates what event took place on which day of the month, and how often (Figure 16.34). The red graph in services stands for CRITICAL, the orange one for UNKNOWN, yellow for WARNING, and green for OK. The curve for hosts in the DOWN state is marked by histogram.cgi in red, that for UNREACHABLE hosts in wine-red, and the green line stands, as usual, for OK.

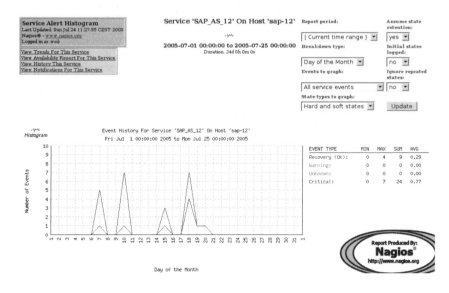

Figure 16.34:
How many events of what type were there on which day?

If you choose the variation **Day of Week**, the Web page shows on which day of the week most events occur, so you can find out whether Monday really is always the worst day. In addition to this you can have the frequency presented by day (**Hour of Day**) or by the month of a year (**Month**). With **Report Period** you can adjust the report period. With **Assume state retention** you can adjust whether the previously existing states are retained and included in the evaluation (yes) or not (no).

If you have configured Nagios so that it explicitly logs the states of the monitored hosts and services for a restart or when the log file is changed,[19] and if you set Initial states logged to yes, the script includes this explicitly in the evaluation. A no ignores the entry; histogram.cgi then assumes that the state after a system start is identical to that which existed directly before the restart.[20]

Ignore repeated states makes allowances if a state persists for a long time and therefore delivers the same result again and again. If you set yes here, the script evaluates it once instead of many times.

If you select the item **Hard and soft states** in **State types to graph:**, histogram.cgi also counts soft states. If a service changes from OK to CRITICAL, for example, while retry_check_interval is set to 4,[21] then histogram.cgi counts a total of four results, three soft and one hard. If you only evaluate hard states, the statistics evaluate the value 1. If an error is rectified, there are no soft states; therefore the value for CRITICAL is usually larger that that for RECOVERY if you include soft states in the evaluation.

16.2.12   Filtering log entries after specific states: history.cgi

The history.cgi script allows the states of a type (soft or hard) to be extracted selectively from the log file using the selection field **State type options** (at the top right in Figure 16.35), and specific events to be extracted (all, all related to hosts, all service events, only host-recovery, only host-down, etc.) using **History detail level for all hosts**. The entries to be shown can be restricted through parameters to individual hosts, services, or host or service groups when the CGI program is called. So the command

```
histogram.cgi?host=sap-12
```

only displays log file entries for the host sap-12. If the output should be restricted to a specific host, then the service description needs to be specified as well:

```
histogram.cgi?host=sap-12&service=PING
```

Selecting a host and service group is done in the same way:

```
histogram.cgi?hostgroup=SAP
histogram.cgi?servicegroup=SAP-Services
```

---

[19] Parameter log_initial_state in nagios.cfg; see page 597.
[20] The subtle difference here lies in retain_state_information (see page 601). If this parameter is set to 0, Nagios forgets the previous state. Without log_initial_state = yes, Nagios accepts an OK after the restart.
[21] Nagios thus repeats the test four times before it categorizes the state as "hard."

The period that `history.cgi` views depends on the archiving interval of the log file. The script always refers to the contents of an archive file. If you set the parameter `log_rotation_method` (page 597) in the configuration file `nagios.cfg` to `d` for daily archiving, the Web page presents the entries for one day. Using the arrows (at the top in Figure 16.35) you can then scroll up and down through the days.

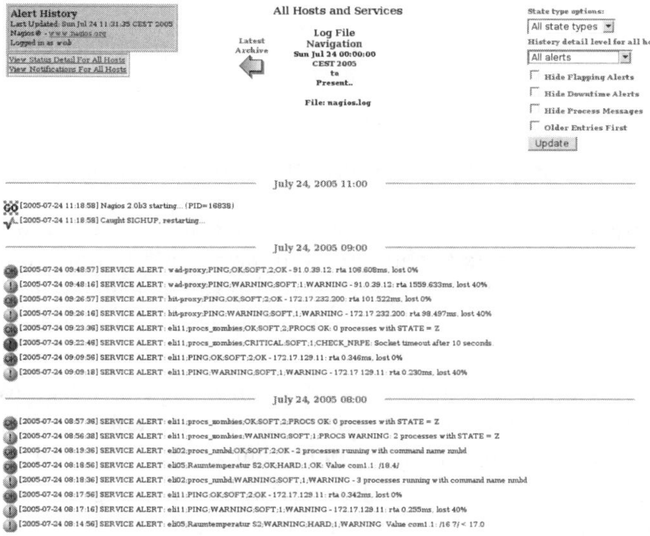

Figure 16.35: `history.cgi` filters the information from the log file

16.2.13   Who was told what, when?—`notifications.cgi`

Another filtered view of the log file is offered by `notifications.cgi`: It shows all sent messages. Here the view can aso be restricted to a specific message group, through the selection field at the top right in Figure 16.36: to all notifications involving hosts, to all which are about services in a critical state, and so on.

Figure 16.36: `notifications.cgi` answers the question of who gets messages when, about what

If you just want to see messages here concerning particular hosts and services, you must again specify this with parameters when running the CGI program:

```
notifications.cgi?host=host
notifications.cgi?host=host&service=service name
notifications.cgi?contact=contact
```

Apart from `host` and `service`, you can also select a particular contact, but selecting host or service groups is not possible.

16.2.14   Showing all log file entries: `showlog.cgi`

The CGI program `showlog.cgi` shows the log file as it is, with the few colored icons added to help you find your way: a red button marks critical service states or DOWN/UNREACHABLE hosts, a yellow button marks WARNINGs, and a green one, OK. Other buttons refer to information entries or Nagios restarts (Figure 16.37).

You only have a single option here: the chronological order. Normally `showlog.cgi` shows the newest entries first. If you enable the check mark in **Older Entries First:** (top right), the oldest entries will be shown first.

The period represented here also depends on the archiving method: if you archive once a day, you will obtain just one day for each Web page. To reach the entries for other days you must make your way through the individual archive files of the log file using the arrows at the top of the picture.

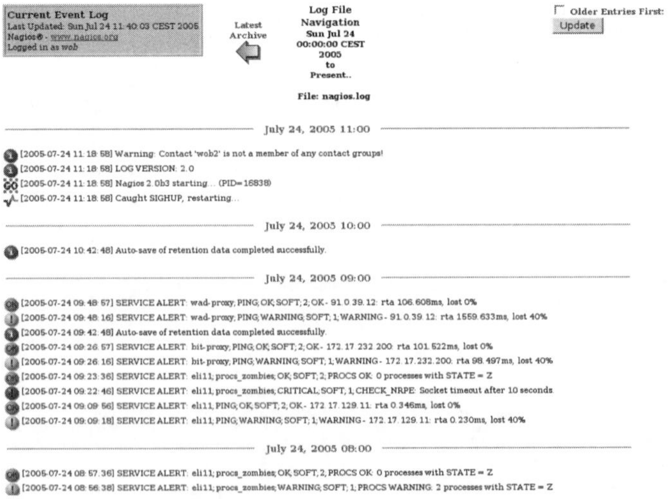

Figure 16.37:
A blue button marks information entries, the graph changing from red to green stands for Nagios restarts, and the icon marked GO with a green checked background represents restarts of the monitoring system

16.2.15   Evaluating whatever you want: `summary.cgi`

If the display and selection options are introduced so far are not sufficient for you, you can create your own report with `summary.cgi`, which generates the selection dialog shown in Figure 16.38. The upper section, **Standard Reports:**, provides a quick summary in which just one fixed report type can be selected. Clicking on the button directly below this generates the report.

The second section is more sophisticated. The field **Report Type:** with the report type **Most Recent Alerts** provides an individual listing of the last n of individual events. The number n is defined further down in the selection dialog in **Max List Items:**.[22] **Report Type:** can also be used to show all events individually on a separate line, with **Most Recent Alerts**, or you can have statistics displayed, for the number of events that have occurred overall, for each host group, etc., with **Alert Totals**, **Alert Totals by Hostgroups**, etc.

One particularly interesting report type is **Top Alert Producer:** such reports show in a hit list of who has caused most trouble during the report period.

In **Report Period:** you can either choose the desired report period from predefined intervals (this week, the past seven days, this month, last week, last month, etc.), or you can specify `CUSTOM REPORT PERIOD` and define any period you choose. If you forget to specify `CUSTOM REPORT PERIOD` explicitly, the CGI program ignores the dates you have set and selects what is currently entered in **Report Period**.

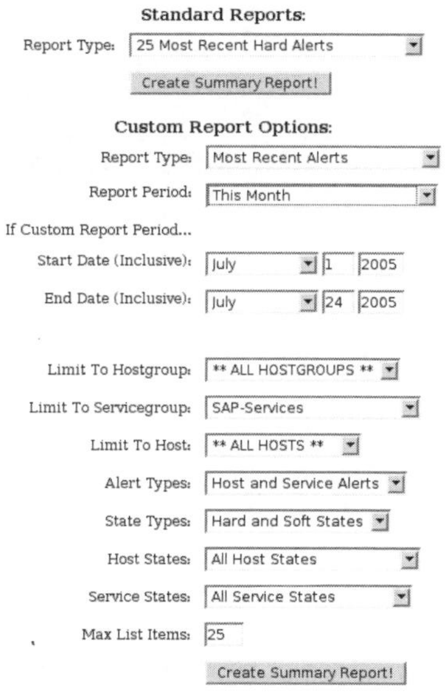

Figure 16.38:
Selection template
for parameters in
`summary.cgi`

***

22   If the number of events in the report period is less than specified in **Max List Items:**, the report covers all the events that have happened during this period.

The details that follow the report period filter according to host, services or their groups, state types, and/or individual states (e.g., only services in a CRITICAL state). It is important to specify **Max List Items** at the end: summary.cgi always shows only as many entries as are specified here. The default is a little small; if you want all the entries in the selected period to be shown, you should enter 0 as the value. The largest value that can be given explicitly here is 999. The **Create Summary Report!** button then generates the requested report (Figure 16.39).

The header of the report contains details of the report period and the selection made. The detail directly above the table is interesting: **Displaying most recent 25 of 3721 total matching alerts** shows that the selection criteria matched a total of 3721 entries, but that the CGI script restricted the output to the 25 most current entries, thanks to **Max List Items:**.

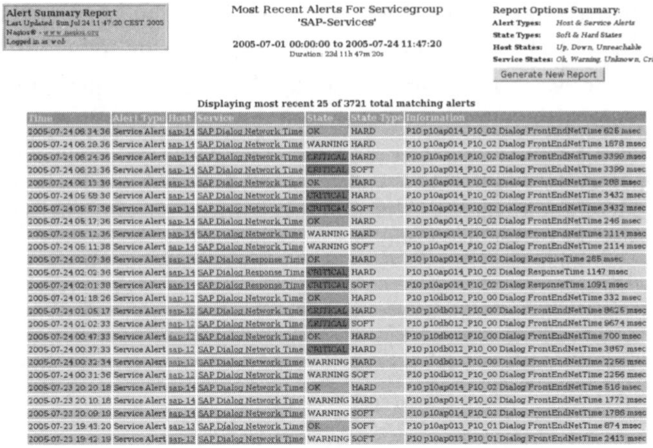

Figure 16.39:
An individual report, as generated by summary.cgi

16.2.16 Following states graphically over time: trends.cgi

A rapid overview of what state occurred when for a particular host or service is provided by the graphic output of trends.cgi (Figure 16.40). After selecting a specific host or service, you can define a period, as with summary.cgi. The states are color-coded by trends.cgi, which makes the overview easier to follow.

The zoom function of the CGI program is an interesting detail. If you click in the colored area on a particular section, the selected area is enlarged or reduced in size by the zoom factor specified at the top right. Negative entries (-1, -2, -3, and -4 are possible) expand the report period instead of reducing it.

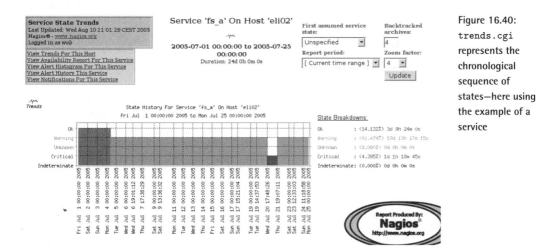

Figure 16.40: trends.cgi represents the chronological sequence of states—here using the example of a service

16.3 Planning Downtimes

In every system environment maintenance work accumulates from time to time that the administrator can normally plan, so that users can be informed accordingly beforehand. Nagios refers to such maintenance windows as *Scheduled Downtime*; the administrator enters these either in the information page for the host or service generated by extinfo.cgi (Figure 16.4, page 331) or for the corresponding host or service group (Figure 16.17, page 339). In doing this, extinfo.cgi makes use of cmd.cgi (Section 16.2.3, page 343), which can also be called selectively:

```
http://nagiosserver/nagios/cgi-bin/cmd.cgi?cmd_typ=55
```

opens the import template for maintenance times for a single host. The values for cmd_typ are summarized by Figure 16.24 on page 344.

A further method of recording maintenance periods is provided by addons, which, like the CGI programs, use the external command interface, but which can be automated, in contrast to the interactive Web interface. Such addons can also be found on the Nagios Exchange.[23]

For scheduled downtimes, Nagios prevents notifications from being sent. This ensures that the administrator is not flooded with false alarms. When

---

[23] http://www.nagiosexchange.org/Downtimes.38.0.html.

checks are made to see whether messages should be sent, a downtime is the third item in the list (Figure 16.2, page 268). In addition, `avail.cgi` (Section 16.2.10, page 351.) takes account of the downtime when evaluating the availability of individual hosts and services, and assigns error states that occur during these times not as error states, but as OK.

Maintenance periods can overlap. If one maintenance window lasts from 8:00 A.M. till 12:00 P.M., and a second one involving the same host or service, from 10:00 A.M. to 2:00 P.M., then Nagios does not send any error messages between 8:00 A.M. and 2:00 P.M., and the whole period is also ignored in the availability statistics.

16.3.1 Maintenance periods for hosts

What data is required to record the maintenance window can be explained quite clearly using the Web interface. Figure 16.41 shows the input template for the downtime of a host (`cmd.cgi?cmd_typ=55`).

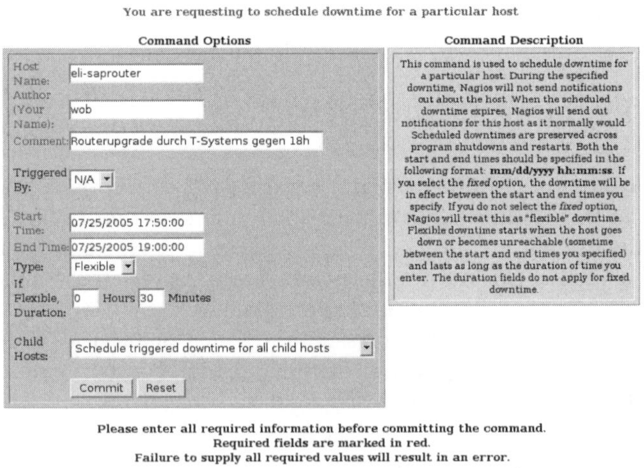

Figure 16.41:
The downtime for a
host in the Web
interface is recorded
using this dialog

The first line defines the host, and in the second line Nagios automatically enters the login with which you have logged in to the Web interface. In the input field after the **Comment:** keyword, you can describe the reason for the planned downtime. Specifying the trigger shows whether it was generated indirectly through another entry. When recording a new downtime, you should leave the value **N/A** (*not available*, that is, no trigger) as it is.

In the next four lines you have the option of entering two different downtime types: fixed ones (**Type: Fixed**) or variable periods (**Flexible**). The first has a fixed start and a fixed end. In this case Nagios ignores the period entry in hours and minutes in the **Flexible Duration:** fields completely.

A flexible downtime starts when the first-ever event occurs in the period specified. From this point in time Nagios plans the downtime for the length of time that was specified here in hours and minutes. This may certainly exceed the end point specified in **End Time:**.

If further hosts are dependent on the computer specified in **Host Name:** (perhaps because a router is involved, which other host objects have entered as **parents**), you have the possibility of extending the downtime to all dependent hosts with the last item, **Child Hosts:**. **Schedule triggered downtime for all child hosts** passes on flexible downtimes to all "child hosts," **Schedule non-triggered downtime for all child hosts** does the same for fixed downtimes, and **Do nothing with child hosts** ignores dependencies, so that Nagios does not plan for any downtime for any hosts other than the one specified here.

How this hereditary behavior takes effect in Figure 16.41 is shown by the overview of all scheduled downtimes in Figure 16.21 on page 342. The first line contains the downtime just described for the host **eli-saprouter** with the **Downtime ID** number 1. Entries that are caused by inheriting this timeout contain the **Downtime ID** of the downtime causing them in the **Trigger ID** column: for `sap-12` this is 1, since the maintenance of `eli-saprouter` also affects this host.

Nagios simultaneously generates a comment entry when planning a downtime, which is automatically removed when this period has passed. This is why a speech bubble appears in the status display. During the downtime Nagios supplements this with a "snoring sign," which is meant to represent a sleep state (Figure 16.42).

Host	Service	Status	Last Check	Duration	Attempt	Status Information
eli-saprouter	PING	OK	2005-07-31 12:02:50	34d 3h 66m 11s	1/3	OK- 172.17.130.227: rta 1.324ms, lost 0%

Figure 16.42:
The snoring sign zzzzz shows that the downtime for the host has begun

16.3.2 Downtime for services

Downtimes for services differ from those for hosts in two small details. Apart from host name, the service description must be included, and the possibility of inheritance is excluded, since there are no corresponding dependencies for services.

A downtime for a host does not automatically apply to the services running on it. But since they are also not available if the host is down, it is recommended that you plan the same downtime for all dependent services. It can be quite strenuous to enter all the services individually. It is much easier to do this using a host group (`cmd_typ=85`), as shown in Figure 16.43. With this you can define the downtime for services in a specific host group with a single command, and much more as well: a check mark in **Schedule**

Downtime For Hosts Too at the same time defines the same downtime for all hosts belonging to this group.[24]

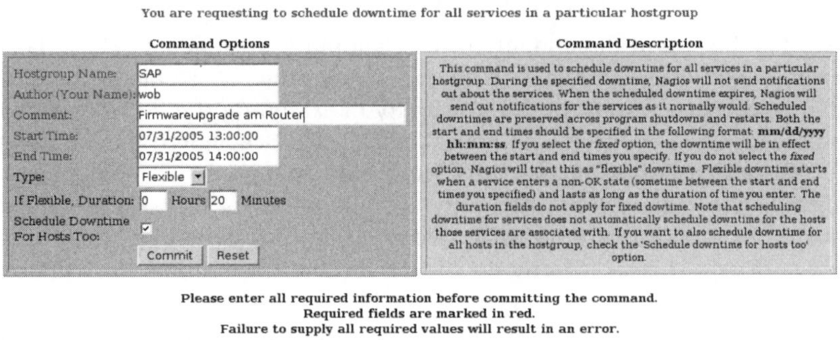

Figure 16.43:
One downtime for all
services of a host
group

16.4 Additional Information on Hosts and Services

With the extended information for hosts and services, you can incorporate additional information in the Web interface and also brighten up its appearance somewhat, using suitable icons. Two separate objects hold this information in Nagios 2.x: hostextinfo and serviceextinfo. Starting with Nagios 3.0, the additional information is defined directly in the host and service objects. Although Nagios 3.0 still evaluates the hostextinfo and serviceextinfo objects, it issues a warning message when checking the configuration and considers these objects to be obsolete.

It is planned to leave these out of Nagios entirely, by version 4 at the latest. Those using Nagios 3.0 for the first time should specify the information introduced below directly in the host and service definitions and leave out hostextinfo and serviceextinfo right from the start. If you are changing from Nagios 2.x to Nagios 3.0, you don't need to worry about this, and you can continue using existing instances of these objects.

To make this clearer, below we will use the terms hostextinfo and serviceextinfo object *information*. For Nagios 2.x, the term refers to the *object* of the same name, whereas for Nagios 3.0 it refers to the corresponding *details* given in the host and service objects. The parameters themselves are identical for Nagios 2.x and 3.0. The object information only influences the Web interface and has no effect on the capabilities of Nagios.

---

[24] Up until (at least) Nagios version 3.0rc1, the check mark has no effect, however; there you have to enter the downtime of the hosts separately by running cmd.cgi?cmd_typ=84 again.

16.4.1 Extended host information

Object information for hosts allow you to enhance the display of hosts in the Web interface through additional functions in the form of links and enhancement features in the form of icons and coordinates:

```
# Nagios 2.x              # Nagios 3.0
define hostextinfo{       define host{
    host_name       linux01
    notes           Samba Primary Domaincontroller
    notes_url       /hosts/linux01.html
    action_url      /hosts/actions/linux01.html
    icon_image      base/linux40.png
    icon_image_alt  Linux Host
    vrml_image      base/linux40.png
    statusmap_image base/linux40.gd2
    2d_coords       120,80
    3d_coords       70.0,30.0,40.0
}
```

The only obligatory parameter when these are defined is the specification of the host, with host_name; everything else is optional:

host_name

> This is the name of the host object whose Web pages are to be expanded by the following properties.

notes

> Use this for additional information that extinfo.cgi takes into account in its information pages. (The entry specified in the above example, **Samba Primary Domaincontroller**, can be found in Figure 16.44 below the Linux icon.)

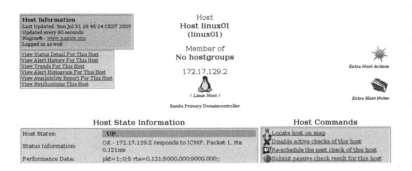

Figure 16.44: extinfo.cgi also shows an alternative text here for the Linux icon (beneath the Tux in brackets) and the additional information from the parameter notes (beneath the alternative text)

notes_url

> This is the URL of a (HTML) file with additional information on the host in question, to which you are linked by an icon in the form of a red, slightly opened manual, both in the status overview (Figure 16.45) and in the info page generated by extinfo.cgi (Figure 16.44). If the documentation on the host involved is stored in the Intranet, then maintenance contracts, hotline numbers, system configuration, etc. are then just a mouse click away.
>
> The parameter may contain an absolute path (from the view of the Web server) or a complete URL (http://...).

Figure 16.45:
This detail view
shows an icon each
for notes_url
(open, read booklet),
action_url (pink
star), and icon_
image (here, Linux
penguin)

Service Status Details For Host
'linux01'

Host	Service	Status	Last Check	Duration	Attempt	Status Information
linux01	LPD	OK	2005-07-31 16:43:18	0d 0h 0m 25s	1/3	TCP OK - 0.000 second response time on port 515

1 Matching Service Entries Displayed

action_url

> This is a link pointing to an action to be run for the host, which executes a CGI program such as cmd.cgi, for example, with just a mouse click. Since a link in the browser is always just a link, this does not have to be a command, and you can just as easily link another Web page. Both in the status overview (Figure 16.45), and on the extinfo.cgi info page (Figure 16.44) it is hidden behind the pink star.
>
> As a value, absolute paths from the view of the Web server or complete URLs can be used.

icon_image

> This is an icon to enhance the Web interface, but also to provide help: if you systematically use pictures here that represent the operating system (e.g., the Tux for Linux, the Windows window for Microsoft operating systems, the Sun logo for Solaris computers, etc.), this helps you to keep an overview of the operating systems in the status view—especially if you have a large number of hosts (Figure 16.45). extinfo.cgi also uses this icon (Figure 16.44).
>
> Icons should be approximately 40x40 pixels large and be available as a GIF, JPEG, or PNG file. If you specify a relative path (or none at all), then this begins with the directory /usr/local/nagios/share/images/logos/.[25]

---

[25] If you have kept to the paths suggested in this book.

icon_image_alt

>   This alternative text for the icon appears if the browser does not
>   show a picture (for example for reading devices or output devices
>   for Braille). From the icon and the icon text details, Nagios generates
>   the following HTML code:

```
<IMG SRC=icon_image ALT=icon_image_alt>
```

vrml_image

>   This is an image symbolizing the host in the 3D representation of
>   statuswrl.cgi. Permissible formats are again GIF, JPEG, or PNG.
>   You should avoid slides, since the image is placed on a cube, and the
>   transparent parts in the 3D interface may lead to unexpected results.

statusmap_image

>   This is the image with which statusmap.cgi (see Section 16.2.5,
>   page 346) symbolizes the host in its topological map. The Nagios
>   demo page of Netways,[26] (Figure 16.28 on page 348) shows a nice
>   example.

>   Although GIFs, JPEGs, and PNGs are allowed, it is better to use the
>   GD2 format, because then Nagios requires less computer time to gen-
>   erate the status map. Using the program pngtogd2, which ought to
>   be available as a component of the utilities for Thomas Boutells GD
>   library in most Linux distributions, PNG files can be easily converted.
>   Again the image size of 40x40 pixels is recommended.

2d_coords

>   This parameter specifies coordinates for a user-defined layout of the
>   topological map. Details are given in pixels, with the origin, (0,0),
>   at the top left, and values must be positive: a positive x
>   value counts the number of pixels from the origin to the right, a pos-
>   itive y value from the origin downwards.

>   Figure 16.28 works with fixed coordinates for individual hosts. Nagios
>   ignores 2d_coords details if the status maps a different layout to the
>   user-defined one.

3d_coords

>   These are the coordinates for the 3D representation. Positive and
>   negative floating-point numbers are allowed. (0.0,0.0,0.0) is used
>   as the origin. In the start view, statuswrl.cgi scales the 3D image
>   so that all existing hosts appear on the screen. Where the starting
>   point lies on the screen can therefore not be predicted.

---

[26] http://nagios-demo.netways.de/

On The Nagios Exchange there is a wide range of finished icons in the category **Logos and Images**.[27] It is best to unpack these into separate subdirectories, and then the individual packages will not get in each other's way:

```
linux:~ # cd /usr/local/nagios/share/images/logos
linux:images/logos # tar xvzf imagepak-base.tar.gz
base/aix.gd2
base/aix.gif
base/aix.jpg
base/aix.png
base/amiga.gd2
...
```

`imagepak-base.tar.gz` contains a basic selection of icons, which can be supplemented as you please with other packages. The `base` subdirectory created, as with the object definition at the beginning of this chapter, must also be included.

16.4.2 Extended service information

Extended service object information is more or less identical to the host equivalents, so that we will only mention the differences. In addition to the host name, the service description in `service_description` is obligatory, but the details on the 2D (status map) and 3D views are omitted:

```
# Nagios 2.x                  # Nagios 3.0
define serviceextinfo{        define service{
...
   host_name                  linux01
   service_description LPD
   notes                      Linux Print Services
   notes_url                  /hosts/linux01-lpd.html
   action_url                 /hosts/linux01-lpd-action.html
   icon_image                 base/hp-printer40.png
   icon_image_alt             Linux Print Server
}
```

In contrast to extended host information, the status overview for this example only shows the printer icon specified in `icon_image`, but not the two icons defined in `notes_url` and `action_url` for the two links `notes_url` and `action_url`. They only appear in the page generated by `extinfo.cgi` with the same icons as for the extended host information (Figure 16.44, page 363).

---

[27] http://www.nagiosexchange.org/Image_Packs.75.0.html

16.5   Configuration Changes through the Web Interfaces: the Restart Problem

The CGI program `cmd.cgi` (Section 16.2.3, page 343) enables a series of changes to be made to the current configuration through the Web interface.[28] In this way notifications or active checks can be switched on and off, for example.

Nagios does not save such changes in the accompanying configuration file, but notes the the current status in a separately defined file, with the parameter `state_retention_file` in `nagios.cfg` (see page 604). But what happens if you restart Nagios after many changes using the Web interface?

Whether Nagios retains the interactive changes made after a restart or forgets them is dependent on the parameter `retain_state_information` in the configuration file `nagios.cfg` (page 601). The default 0 tells the system to forget interactive changes. For Nagios to remember this, you have to set

```
# /etc/nagios/nagios.cfg
...
retain_state_information=1
...
```

But this causes a new problem: settings made in the Web interface do not have priority over the details in the configuration files. If you change the `active_checks_enabled` parameter there for a service, a direction of the parameter in the configuration file is ignored, since the current, temporarily stored setting in the file defined with `state_retention_file` will always "win out." This behavior affects all parameters for external commands that can be changed in the interface, and therefore also via the CGI program `cmd.cgi`. The original documentation of Nagios[29] labels these with a red star.

Two approaches provide a remedy in this case: on the one hand you can set the parameter `retain_state_information` to 0 shortly before a restart. Then Nagios forgets all the changes when it restarts and reads the configuration files in from scratch. This procedure is recommended only in exceptional cases, as in large environments it will hardly be possible to go through all the interactive changes in the configuration files. Alternatively you can get into the habit, whenever you make changes in the configuration file, of making them a second time in the Web interface. Although this means slightly more work, there is never a danger that current, and perhaps very important settings, will be lost.

---

[28] The CGI program makes use of the External Command File interface when doing this.
[29] Nagios 2.x: `/usr/local/nagios/share/docs/xodtemplate.html`, Nagios 3.0: `/usr/local/nagios/docs/objectdefinitions.html`

Two additional parameters in the host and service definitions provide opportunities for fine-tuning:

```
define host{
    ...
    retain_status_information    1
    retain_nonstatus_information 1
    ...
}
define service{
    ...
    retain_status_information    1
    retain_nonstatus_information 1
    ...
}
```

`retain_status_information` specifies whether the current state of a host or service should survive the Nagios restart: 1 means that the system temporarily stores the state, and 0, that it forgets it. 1 is certainly the more sensible value for states, and you should depart from this only in cases that can be justified.

`retain_nonstatus_information`, on the other hand, refers to all information that describes *no* status. This includes, for example, whether active checks are switched on or off, whether passive checks are allowed or not, or whether admins are to be informed of status changes for this object. With a value of 1, the system stores this information temporarily and uses it again after a restart, whereas with a value of 0, Nagios forgets the current settings and reads the settings from the configuration file when it restarts.

16.6   Modern Layout with the Nuvola Style

The classical view of the Nagios Web interface described so far uses only a few of the CGI configuration options. However, it is hardly possible to pack any more items into the navigation bar on the left, which has become somewhat amateurish in appearance. One solution to this is the Nuvola style, shown in Figure 16.46.

The layout for the actual CGI program—this example shows a view of the service problems with `status.cgi` on the right of the picture—is not only in color, but there are also new icons. On the left of the picture you can see the rather elegant navigation, spiced up with corresponding icons. The real highlight, though, is the use of a Javascript-based menu tree: The individual entries (such as the sections **Home**, **Monitoring**, **Reporting**, and **Configuration**) can be opened and closed via mouse click.

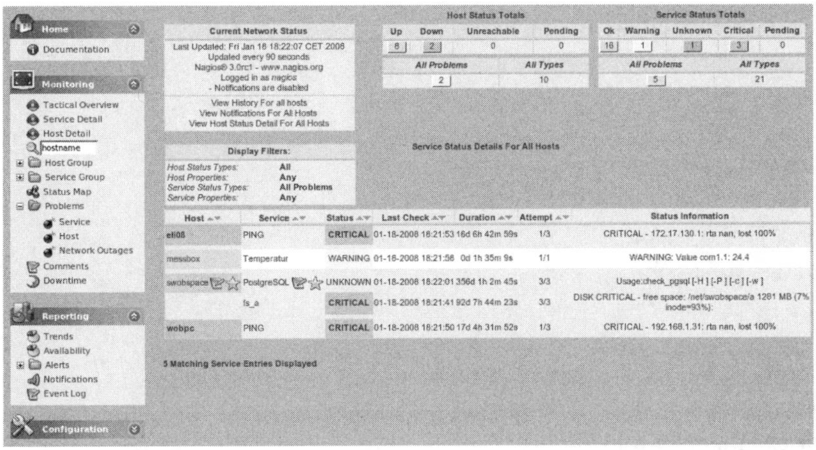

Figure 16.46:
Nagios in the Nuvola
style: shown here are
the Service Problems

Before installing the Nuvola style it is essential that you back up the directory /usr/local/nagios/share so that you can restore the old setup if you don't like the new one.

The current version 1.0.3 of Nuvola from NagiosExchange[30] at the time of going to press is from September 2005, but it does work very well with Nagios 3.0 as well. The contents are unpacked into a suitable empty directory:

```
linux:~ # cd /usr/local/src; mkdir nuvola; cd nuvola
linux:src/nuvola # tar xvzfpfad/zu/nagios-nuvola-1.0.3.tar.gz
...
linux:src/nuvola # cd html
```

The sources contain files (index.html, main.html) and directories (stylesheets, images) that already exist in Nagios, and they overwrite the originals during installation. In addition, the Nuvola style includes a new subdirectory, side, which contains the actual Javascript code for the tree navigation:

```
linux:nuvola/html # tree
.
|-- config.js
|-- images
|   |
... ...
|-- index.html
|-- main.html
|-- side
```

[30] http://www.nagiosexchange.org/75;252

```
|   |-- apytmenu.css
|   |-- apytmenu.js
|   |-- apytmenu_data.js
... ...
|   |-- dtree.css
|   |-- dtree.js
|   |-- dtree_data.js
... ...
|   |-- icons
|   |   |
... ...
|-- side1.html
'-- stylesheets
    |
... ...
5 directories, 175 files
```

The contents of the directory html are simply copied to /usr/local/share, for example, with rsync:

```
linux:nuvola/html # rsync -av . /usr/local/nagios/share/.
...
```

For the new navigation to appear, the file side1.html must be installed. If you just rename it to side.html, though, the make install of a new Nagios version will just overwrite it again. So it is better to use a separate index file instead, such as index1.html, and run the Nagios Web interface from this:

```
http://nagiosserver/nagios/index1.html
```

To do this, you copy the index.html file included in Nuvola to the Nagios share directory with the name index1.html:

```
linux:nuvola/html # cp index.html/usr/local/nagios/share/index1.html
```

In the file index1.html you replace side.html with side1.html so that the Javascript navigation is called:

```
...
document.write('<FRAME SCROLLING="no" SRC="side1.html" NAME="side"
...
...
```

If, like the author of this book, you consider it to be going over the top to change the styles of all the CGI programs, you can just pick out the improved navigation and supplement and redesign this as you think fit. Instead of making a complete copy of the directory html, you just select the files you require:

```
linux:nuvola/html # cp -r side /usr/local/nagios/share/.
linux:nuvola/html # cp side1.html config.js/usr/local/nagios/share/.
linux:nuvola/html # cp index.html/usr/local/nagios/share/index1.html
```

You change the file `index1.html` as we have just shown and check the `cgipath` variable in `config.js`:

```
...
var cgipath = "/nagios/cgi-bin/";
...
```

Nuvola uses a ready-made menu tree library, which is available in a commercial version called `apytmenu`,[31] which will not be discussed here, or in a free variation, dTree.[32] dTree is the default setting in `config.js` (`treeType ='dtree'`) and is included in full. Configuration of the menu and trees is done in the file `dtree_data.js` in the directory `side`. The basic principle can be briefly explained using the **Home** menu as an example:

```
general = new dTree('general');
general.header( 'Home', 'icon', ... );
general.add(0,-1);
general.add(1, 0,'Documentation','docs/index.html', ... );
document.write(general);
```

The `dTree` function generates a new menu tree. Its parameter is a freely selectable identifier (in this case, `general`), which is used to reference the tree. `general.header` sets the title of the menu to Home. The function requires other parameters as well, including an icon (as shown).

The first `general.add` call anchors the tree still to be created. The first two parameters of the `add` function refer to the number of the node to be added, followed by its parent node. The topmost node is called 0, and beneath this is the entry `Documentation`, to which the number 1 is assigned. If `Documentation` itself is to have subnodes, the invocations would be written as follows:

```
general.add(2, 1, 'new_entry', ...);
general.add(3, 1, 'new_entry', ...);
general.add(4, 1, 'new_entry', ...);
```

Finally `document.write` builds the entire menu tree. The `header` function has the following parameters:

```
menu_name.header(title,icon,height,background  image,background color,open);
```

[31] http://dhtml-menu.com/
[32] http://www.destroydrop.com/javascripts/tree/

title contains the heading and can also be set up as a URL. A mouse click on the heading opens the hyperlink specified.

icon specifies the path to a small graphic that is displayed in front of the heading.

height specifies the height of the background beneath the heading. Following this, the property of this background can be specified either as a background image, with *backgroundimage*, or as a color (*background color*).

Finally *open* specifies whether the menu tree should be open (1) or closed (0) at the start. Arguments specifying textual values are enclosed in single quotes, and numerical arguments are written directly, as shown in the examples.

The add function is invoked in a similar way:

```
menu_name.add(id, pid, name,
url, title, target, icon,
iconOpen, open, css);
```

id is the node number, and *pid* is the number of the node beneath which the entry should be integrated. *name* defines the name of the node in the menu, and *url* defines the hyperlink to be called. *title* and *target* optionally specify a page title and the target frame for displaying the page called via *url*. Both parameters normally remain empty here; the default for the target—correctly for Nagios—is the frame *main*.

icon defines the mini-graphic that is placed in front of the menu entry, and *iconOpen* optionally contains another icon that is used in its place when the menu entry is open. *open* again defines whether the entry should be opened (value 1) or closed (value 0) on starting, and *css* optionally allows an alternative CSS definition. For all optional parameters, the following applies: If they are at the end, they can be omitted, but if they are followed by other details, their omission must be marked by a pair of single quotation marks (' ').

The included file *dtree_data.js* contains four extensive menus. If you have little experience with handling Javascript, it is best to save this template and adjust it in small steps. In case of error, information is very sparse and usually misleading, so it is particularly important that you note exactly what has been changed from one step to the next in order to be able to quickly isolate the error.

At this point we would like to mention the dTree homepage[33] once again, which provides examples with extracts of code, along with a description of the programming interface.

---

[33] http://www.destroydrop.com/javascripts/tree/

Those who are not satisfied with the possibilities of the Nagios Web interface described in this chapter should take a look at NagVis (Chapter 18 from page 389). The addon enables a freely definable interface and supplements the standard CGIs in an impressive manner. However, a prerequisite for NagVis is the installation of the database interface NDOUtils (Chapter 17 from page 375), which sets the installation hurdle slightly higher.

Flexible Web Interface with the NDOUtils

The Web interface of Nagios 2.x ansd 3.0, introduced in Chapter 16 from page 327, has a crucial disadvantage for large environments with hundreds of hosts: It cannot be scaled up. As long as you only observe error states and work intensively with acknowledges, you will manage fine with the CGI-based Web interface. But if you try to display several thousand services, you will have to be prepared to wait—it does not matter what their states are. Setting up the page can take a long time, and then practical work is hardly possible.

Nagios extensions struggle with the CGI Web interface because this directly evaluates Nagios internals, such as object configuration, status data, and log files. This means that every extension that is used to supplement or replace the Web interface must follow this logic.

The solution to this is called NDOUtils (*Nagios Data Objects Utilities*). These consist of a handful of tools that write all data—from configuration through events and check results to historical records—to a database and make them available via a uniform database model.

The mechanism that connects the NDOUtils to Nagios is called *Nagios Event Broker* (NEB). This adds a modular interface to Nagios. The NEB loads the extensions as modules when Nagios starts so that the modules can be used without having to recompile Nagios. This approach is similar to that of the Apache modules, which are loaded when required and add new functions to the Web server.

The NDOUtils form the basis for the future Web interface of Nagios, implemented with PHP, which should see the light of day starting with Nagios 4.x. With NagVis (see Chapter 18 from page 389), however, there is already an alternative Web interface that is based on the NDOUtils.

17.1 The Event Broker

The NEB provides an interface between Nagios and external modules based on shared libraries. An external, application-dependent module makes *callback functions* available. The Nagios kernel itself calls the accompanying callback function from the loaded module for every event: If there is no matching function, nothing happens. What actions the callback function executes is left to the imagination of the developer: Either it does something itself or it passes on configuration, status, and event data to an external application, as outlined in Figure 17.1.

For the transfer of data to external tools, Unix sockets or network sockets can be used, although it is also possible to use the file system. The application further processes information (saves it in a database, for example, or sends it as messages via SNMP traps, writes it to the syslog, etc.).

Figure 17.1:
An external
application
communicates with a
loaded NEB module

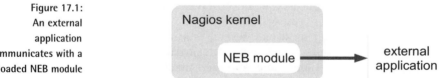

When a callback function is called, Nagios waits for it to finish. This means that long execution times hinder the system. For this reason callback functions should always leave time-consuming processing steps to an external application and be restricted to sending on the necessary information as quickly as possible.

Building event broker modules is something that should be left to experienced programmers; mere mortals must be content with using ready-made modules. An NEB module can be integrated via the instruction `broker_module` in the main configuration file `nagios.cfg`:

```
# /etc/nagios/nagios.cfg
...
broker_module=module-with-path arguments
event_broker_options=-1
```

Whether you pass on arguments to the module or not depends on its concrete implementation. The parameter `event_broker_options` controls what information Nagios passes on to event broker modules. With the option -1 it is all of them, while the value 0 prevents any information from being passed on. An alternate approach, of selectively passing on specific information, is provided by the file `broker.h` from the Nagios sources:

```
/* broker.h from the Nagios sources */
...
/*************** EVENT BROKER OPTIONS ****************/

#define BROKER_NOTHING                  0
#define BROKER_EVERYTHING               1048575

#define BROKER_PROGRAM_STATE            1          /* DONE */
...
#define BROKER_DOWNTIME_DATA            512        /* DONE */
...
#define BROKER_STATUS_DATA              4096       /* DONE */
...
#define BROKER_RETENTION_DATA           32768      /* DONE */
#define BROKER_ACKNOWLEDGEMENT_DATA     65536
```

Broker Option	Value	Explanation
BROKER_PROGRAM_STATE	1	Is the program Nagios running?
BROKER_DOWNTIME_DATA	512	Details of planned maintenance periods
BROKER_STATUS_DATA	4096	Current status information of all checks
BROKER_RETENTION_DATA	32768	Data which is buffered for a restart of Nagios
BROKER_ACKNOWLEDGEMENT_DATA	65536	Confirmations that have been made on error states of host and service checks

Table 17.1:
Data to be
transferred to NagVis

NagVis 1.1, introduced in Chapter 18, requires the information listed in Table 17.1. The corresponding numerical values add up to 102913, so that `event_broker_options` can be modified as follows so that is tailor-made for NagVis:

```
# /etc/nagios/nagios.cfg
...
event_broker_options=102913
```

Information on the event broker is currently very sparse. The only descriptions of the interface are a quite old documentation from Nagios 2.0 and the *Nagios Event Broker API*[1].

17.2 The Database Interface

As a concrete and practically-oriented application of the event broker concept, the Nagios data object utilities, or NDOUtils, save all configuration and event data to a database. In order to be able to make use of the database, further applications are required. For Nagios 4.x, this will in all probability be a newly designed, PHP-based Web interface. Whether this Nagios version will immediately manage all the configuration data in the database was still a matter of speculation at press time (when Nagios 3.0 was not quite finished).

For the database, the NDOUtils currently support only MySQL; the use of PostgreSQL is planned, but is not yet implemented in version 1.4, introduced here.

Since the NDOUtils addons provide a database interface that is relatively simple to use, it is expected that their use with Nagios 3.x will increase. NagVis (discussed in the next chapter from page 389) already provides a powerful NDO-based front end that in many cases can replace the status map, which remains relatively simple and is discussed in Section 16.2.5 from page 346.

Figure 17.2 shows the various paths by which Nagios data can be imported into the NDOUtils database. Export of data from Nagios is handled by the event broker module ndomod. It can either operate a TCP or Unix socket, or write the data to a file. If Nagios is installed on the same computer as the NDOUtils database, the Unix socket interface will provide the best performance and the greatest security (Unix sockets cannot be addressed from a network, in contrast to TCP sockets). The socket of the ndo2db daemon that ultimately writes the data to a database is queried.

[1] http://www.nagios.org/developerinfo

The method using a file involves the utility FILE2SOCK, which reads in the file and also delivers data to the nd02db daemon via a TCP or Unix socket. FILE2SOCK can also read data from the standard input.

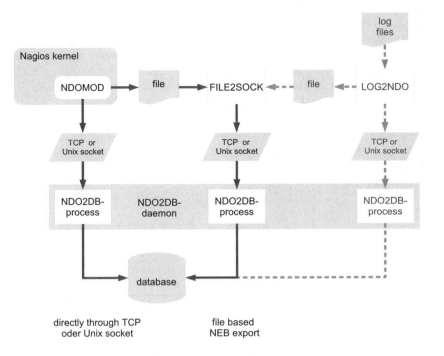

Figure 17.2:
How can you integrate Nagios data into the NDOUtils database?

For each database you need exactly one ndo2db daemon. If several different clients have access to the socket interface, it will start several processes to handle these.

The program LOG2NDO is one of the NDOUtils. It reads log files from Nagios 2.x and 3.0 and passes this data to the ndo2db daemon—either directly via the socket interface or via a file that has to be separately imported with FILE2SOCK. If you want to integrate such historical data into the database, you will have to make plenty of storage space available, because the log files are compressed when they are archived but are saved in the database in uncompressed form. Thus the log files occupy more space when they are managed using the database.

FILE2SOCK and LOG2NDO are primarily used to import historical data. The data later required by NagVis is updated by Nagios at very short intervals. Since historical data is not required here, we shall not describe these two programs in any more detail.

17.3   The Installation

Since there are problems with INSERT statements in some tables of the NDOUtils database when MySQL in version 4.0 is used, it is better to use MySQL 5 right from the start.[2] In addition to the MySQL server package (in Debian, "Etch" `mysql-server-5.0`) and the libraries that are usually selected automatically during the installation of the server package, you also require the accompanying development package (in Debian, "Etch" `libmysqlclient15-dev`) in order to be able to compile the NDOUtils.

One consequence of the far-reaching integration of the NDOUtils into Nagios is that the version must exactly match that of the Nagios version used. Both Nagios and the NDOUtils define their version status in the source code with the macro CURRENT_OBJECT_STRUCTURE_VERSION. The macro can be found in the file `./include/objects.h` in the Nagios source code (for Nagios 3.0, in this example):

```
linux:src/nagios-3.0rc1 # fgrep CURRENT_OBJECT_STRUCTURE_VERSION \
    include/objects.h
#define CURRENT_OBJECT_STRUCTURE_VERSION  307
```

The NDOUtils package contains two include files, one for Nagios 2.x and one for Nagios 3.x:

```
linux:src/ndoutils-1.4b7 # fgrep CURRENT_OBJECT_STRUCTURE_VERSION \
    include/*/objects.h
include/nagios-2x/objects.h:#define CURRENT_OBJECT_STRUCTURE_VERSION 2
include/nagios-3x/objects.h:#define CURRENT_OBJECT_STRUCTURE_VERSION 307
```

If the CURRENT_OBJECT_STRUCTURE_VERSION value of Nagios does not match one of the two values in the NDOUtils source code, the NDOUtils module will unload itself and refuse to perform. The procedure is documented in the log file `nagios.log` with an entry like the following (the two different versions are marked in bold type):

```
[1186152181] ndomod: NDOMOD 1.4b4 (06-19-2007) Copyright (c) 2005 -2007
Ethan Galstad (nagios@nagios.org)
[1186152181] ndomod: I've been compiled with support for revision 303 of
the internal Nagios object structures, but the Nagios daemon is currentl
y using revision 304. I'm going to unload so I don't cause any probl...
```

---

[2] The author has tested version 5.0.23, but there are also reports of NDOUtils working successfully with MySQL 4.1.x.

17.3.1 Compiling the source code

The up-to-date NDOUtils code can be downloaded from the Nagios Web page[3] and then unpacked to a suitable directory:

```
linux:~ # cd /usr/local/src/nagios
linux:src/nagios # tar xvzf /path/to/ndoutils-1.4b7.tar.gz
...
linux:src/nagios # cd ndoutils-1.4b7
linux:nagios/ndoutils-1.4.b7 # ./configure --sysconfdir=/etc
...
linux:nagios/ndoutils-1.4.b7 # make
...
```

We start the `configure` run with the switch `--sysconfdir=/etc` in order to install the configuration files for the module and daemon to match the convention in this book, that is, to the directory `/etc/nagios`. The `make` call compiles the program code, and the installation is then done manually:

```
linux:nagios/ndoutils-1.4.b7 # cd ./src
linux:ndoutils-1.4.b7/src # cp ndo2db-3x ndomod-3x.o log2ndo file2sock \
    /usr/local/nagios/bin/
```

For Nagios 2.x the daemon `ndo2db-2x` and the module `ndomod-2x.o` are copied to `/usr/local/nagios/bin` instead of the 3.x versions.

17.3.2 Preparing the MySQL database

In the MySQL database system, we require a database storing appropriate access options for the user `nagios`. In order to set this up, we first log in to MySQL as the user `root`:

```
user@linux:~$ mysql --user=root -p
Enter password: root-passwort_for_the_db
Welcome to the MySQL monitor.  Commands end with ; or \g.
Your MySQL connection id is 1861
Server version: 5.0.32-Debian_7etch1 Debian etch distribution

Type 'help;' or '\h' for help. Type '\c' to clear the buffer.

mysql>
```

The switch `-p` ensures that the password is requested. The following command tests whether a password is set or not:

[3] http://www.nagios.org/download/

```
user@linux:~$ mysql --user=root
```

If the login triggered by this works without an error message, then the `root` password is missing. This should be specified with the command

```
user@linux:~$ /usr/bin/mysqladmin -u root password 'secret'
```

You should replace `secret` with your own secure password.[4]

The database (it is given the name `nagios`) is created with the SQL command `CREATE DATABASE`, and it is then given the required permissions with GRANT:

```
mysql> CREATE DATABASE nagios;
Query OK, 1 row affected (0.01 sec)
mysql> GRANT USAGE ON *.* TO 'nagios'@'localhost' IDENTIFIED BY 'secret'
    WITH MAX_QUERIES_PER_HOUR 0
    MAX_CONNECTIONS_PER_HOUR 0
    MAX_UPDATES_PER_HOUR 0 ;
Query OK, 0 rows affected (0.00 sec)
mysql> GRANT SELECT , INSERT , UPDATE , DELETE ON `nagios`.*
    TO 'nagios'@'localhost';
Query OK, 0 rows affected (0.01 sec)
mysql> FLUSH PRIVILEGES;
Query OK, 0 rows affected (0.00 sec)
mysql> quit
```

The `GRANT USAGE` command defines the user, along with his password, and specifies that for him there are no restrictions in the number of queries, database connections, or database updates per hour. For the password, something slighty more secure than `secret` is chosen, but it must be written here in plain text. `GRANT USAGE` does not yet give any access permissions to the tables of the `nagios` database. This is handled by the second GRANT command. The changes to the permissions of the `nagios` user are activated with FLUSH PRIVILEGES.

The NDOUtils require SELECT, INSERT, UPDATE, and DELETE permissions. For NagVis and other applications, which only read data from the database, the SELECT permission is sufficient.

In the next step the tables are generated in which the NDOUtils will later save data. A finished SQL script in the db subdirectory of the NDOUtils sources is provided for this purpose, and needs only to be executed:

```
user@linux:src/ndoutils-1.4b7$ cd db
user@linux:ndoutils-1.4b7/db$ mysql -u root -p nagios < mysql.sql
```

---

[4] Further notes on the secure adminstration of MySQL can be found in the online documentation at http://www.mysql.org/doc/refman/5.0/en/security-guidelines.html and possibly in the documentation delivered with the distribution under /usr/share/doc/.

The script should run without error in all cases (meaning without any messages). The tables created can be shown with the SQL command show tables.

Various distributions install MySQL by default with logging switched on. With the (usually binary) log files, the current status of the database can be replicated or restored. In combination with the NDOUtils, however, these log files grow very quickly. If you are using the database only for the NDOUtils, you will need such tools only in rare cases, and you can therefore comment out all the *log* parameters in the my.cnf configuration file and restart MySQL—this time without logging.

17.3.3 Upgrading the database design

Since the NDOUtils are actively undergoing development, larger changes to the database structure cannot be ruled out. For an upgrade, it is possible that the database design must also be changed. The NDOUtils provide a script for this purpose, upgradedb in the subdirectory db, which automatically adjusts the tables:

```
linux:~ # cd /usr/local/src/nagios/ndoutils-1.4b7/db
linux:ndoutils-1.4b7/db # ./upgradedb -u root -p password \
-h localhost -d nagios
Current database version: 1.4b5
** DB upgrade required for 1.4b7
     Using mysql-upgrade-1.4b5.sql for upgrade...
** Upgrade to 1.4b7 complete
```

The script detects the existing NDOUtils version and adjusts the tables accordingly. Among other things, it uses the SQL command ALTER TABLE, for which the MySQL user nagios, created in the last section, does not have sufficient permissions. The script therefore needs to be run as the MySQL user root.

17.4 Configuration

The NDOUtils are configured at three different locations. The file ndomod.cfg specifies the settings for the Event Broker module. ndo2db.cfg controls the daemon ndo2db, which accepts data from the Broker and writes to the database. An entry in /etc/nagios/nagios.cfg finally ensures that Nagios loads the Event Broker module ndomod when it starts.

The NDOUtils source code in the subdirectory ./config provides a template for each of the two configuration files. The command

```
linux:src/ndoutils-1.4b7 # cp config/ndo*.cfg /etc/nagios/.
```

copies these, in accordance with the convention used in this book, to the directory /etc/nagios.

17.4.1 Adjusting the Event Broker configuration

The template for ndomod.cfg can almost be used unchanged; you need to adjust only the path to the var directory:

```
# /etc/nagios/ndomod.cfg
instance_name=default
output_type=unixsocket
output=/var/nagios/ndo.sock
# tcp_port=5668
output_buffer_items=5000
buffer_file=/var/nagios/ndomod.tmp
# file_rotation_command=rotate_ndo_log
# file_rotation_interval=14400
# file_rotation_timeout=60
reconnect_interval=15
reconnect_warning_interval=15
data_processing_options=-1
config_output_options=2
```

instance_name refers to the instance in the database to be used. Provided that you map only one Nagios instance in the database, it is no problem to keep to the default settings. Assuming that Nagios and the ndo2db daemon are running on the same host, a Unix socket can be used as the output_type, the name of which is defined by the output parameter. tcp_port is used only for output_type=tcpsocket and is therefore commented out.

In case the ndomod module cannot release data via the socket interface (because the daemon has just restarted, for instance), these are saved temporarily in the file buffer_file. The number of entries to be saved in this in the output_buffer_items parameter should not be set too low. A tried-and-tested rule of thumb here is to take the number of all defined host and service objects and multiply this by five. This is an empirical value: When reloaded, or when Nagios is restarted, the NDOUtils write the start state for each host and each service to the database, along with all planned and started checks. These might be supplemented by the results of new or still running checks.

The file_rotation_* parameters are required only for output_type= file, which requires the use of the additional daemon FILE2SOCK. For reasons of performance it is recommended, however, that you use the socket interface instead of the file-based one. The file interface also makes the configuration more complex, due to additional daemons.

The parameters `reconnect_interval` and `reconnect_warning_inter-val` are also intended for cases where a connection using the ndo2db daemon could not be established. They specify in seconds how often Nagios should try to make contact with them and how often a warning should appear in the log file if a connection is not established. These two parameters should be left as they are in the default.

17.4.2 Configuring database access

There is also little to adjust in the template for the configuration file of the ndo2db daemon. Apart from the path to the socket interface, the relevant password for write access to the database must be specified here:

```
# /etc/nagios/ndo2db.cfg
ndo2db_user=nagios
ndo2db_group=nagios
socket_type=unix
socket_name=/var/nagios/ndo.sock
# tcp_port=5668
db_servertype=mysql
db_host=localhost
db_port=3306
db_name=nagios
db_prefix=nagios_
db_user=nagios
db_pass=secret
max_timedevents_age=1440
max_systemcommands_age=1440
max_servicechecks_age=1440
max_hostchecks_age=1440
max_eventhandlers_age=10080
```

The two `ndo2db_*` parameters specify the user and group with whose permissions the daemon runs after the start. `socket_type` and `socket_name` must be set to the configuration in `ndomod.cfg`.

The only database type that can currently be specified `db_servertype` is `mysql`; for `db_port` the standard port of MySQL (3306) is normally entered. The database name in `db_name` must match the name selected in the `CREATE DATABASE` command (in this case, `nagios`), and the database user and password must also be given in the same way as described when setting up the database. The value of the parameter `db_prefix` should not be changed under any circumstances, otherwise the name of the tables to be created in the `mysql.sql` script must also be adjusted.

The parameters beginning with `max_*` define in minutes how long the NDO-Utils data on system commands, planned events, service and host checks, and event handlers[5] should be kept in the database. The value 1440 corresponds to one day. If you are using the NDOUtils only with NagVis, you won't need longer times. Short intervals go easy on the database, as well as the hard disk.

17.4.3 Starting the ndo2db daemon

When everything is configured, the ndo2db daemon is first called manually:

```
/usr/local/nagios/bin/ndo2db-3x  -c /etc/nagios/ndo2db.cfg
```

Later on it is recommended that you create an init script by copying and modifying the script /etc/init.d/skeleton, provided in the distribution. The daemon must match the Nagios version: ndo2db-3x works together with Nagios version 3.x, ndo2db-2x with version 2.x. After it has started you should look to see whether the socket specified in the configuration exists:

```
linux:~ # ls -l /var/nagios/ndo.sock
srwxr-xr-x 1 nagios nagios 0 Jul 18 21:16 /var/nagios/ndo.sock
```

If the message Socket already in use appears when the daemon is run, then either the daemon is already running or the socket ndo.sock was not removed when the daemon was stopped. In this case you should delete it manually before restarting it.

17.4.4 Loading the Event Broker module in Nagios

In order for Nagios to load the Event Broker module of the NDOUtils when it is started, the following entry is added to the configuration file /etc/nagios/nagios.cfg:

```
# /etc/nagios/nagios.cfg:
...
# === NDO ===
broker_module=/usr/local/nagios/bin/ndomod-3x.o config_file=/etc/nagios/
ndomod.cfg
```

In this example the module for Nagios version 3.x is used; if you are using Nagios 2.x, you enter ndomod-2x.o instead. A reload activates the module:

```
linux:~ # /etc/init.d/nagios reload
```

---

[5] For event handlers, see Appendix C on page 619

Shortly after the reload, all host and service objects should be recorded in
the database:

```
user@linux:~$ mysql --user=nagios -p nagios
mysql> select name1,name2 from nagios_objects WHERE objecttype_id=2 ;
+--------+-----------------+
| name1  | name2           |
+--------+-----------------+
| AHDC01 | CPU_LOAD        |
| AHDC01 | DISK_C          |
| AHDC01 | DISK_D          |
...
```

The table nagios_objects contains all the objects, and objecttype_id=2
shows all the services. Alternatively the object type 1 refers to hosts, 3 to
host groups, and 4 to service groups. A complete description of the tables
is provided in the file NDOUTILS DB Model.pdf, included in the NDOUtils
in the subdirectory ./docs.

NagVis

NagVis[1] is an addon for Nagios that displays host and service states against a background image selected by the user. This must be available in the PNG format; the choice is yours whether you use a map, a diagram of your own system documentation, a photo of the server room, or a schematic diagram of the system environment as a background, as shown in Figure 18.1.

Via the Web interface, you can place objects wherever you want on the background. NagVis displays different icons, depending on the state of the object: red for the CRITICAL state, yellow for WARNING, green for OK, and a question mark on a gray background for UNKNOWN. If an acknowledgment was set, this is indicated by a green button with a picture of a worker on it.

There are different icons for hosts and services; in the default template, host icons are rectangular, and service icons are round. A finished NagVis

[1] http://www.nagvis.org/

display—NagVis refers to this as a *map*—is shown in Figure 18.2. Further examples—such as using a geographical map, or a photo of the server room, as a background—are provided on the NagVis homepage.[2]

Figure 18.1:
Schematic diagram
of a system
environment as a
template for NagVis

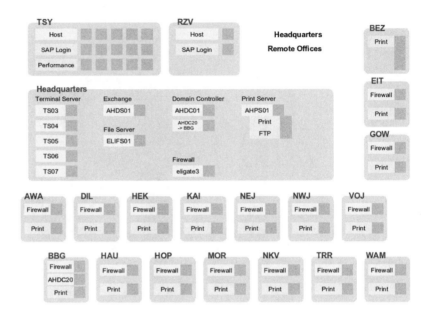

In addition to hosts and services, host and service groups can also be integrated into a NagVis display, as well as additional maps. Thus a geographical overview map could be used for the start page, which has an icon for each location monitored that links to a detailed NagVis map specifically for that location.

If an icon contains several states, as is the case for host and service groups, for instance, NagVis displays the state with the highest priority. CRITICAL has a higher priority than WARNING, WARNING trumps UNKNOWN, UNKNOWN gets more attention than an acknowledgment, and OK has the lowest priority of all. If any host in a host group assumes the CRITICAL state, this is shown accordingly for the entire host group.

For hosts and host groups, NagVis offers you the choice of having only host states considered in determining the state that is displayed, or having the services dependent on these hosts are included as well (see page 394). In the latter case, a red stop light is displayed if even a single service of a host is in the critical state.

---

[2] http://www.nagvis.org/screenshots

Of particular interest is NagVis's ability to evaluate only hard states (page 394). For routine work with the Web interface, it turns out to be quite useful if not every temporary soft CRITICAL state immediately generates a red light.

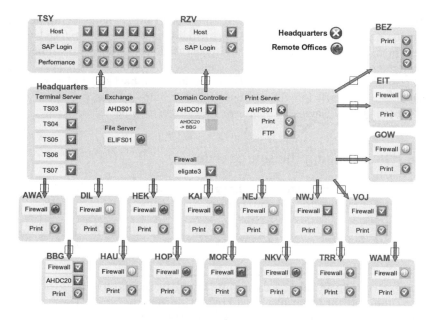

Figure 18.2:
Displaying the
system environment

It will especially please fans of object-oriented programming that NagVis makes full use of object-oriented concepts. For example, the system inherits defaults from the global configuration for individual maps and settings on the map level and passes these on to individual objects, with the option of overwriting settings locally always available. This simplifies the configuration to a considerable extent, and NagVis also indicates in the graphical editor (also called the *Web user interface* or WUI) which settings are object-specific and which have been inherited (Figure 18.8 on page 399).

NagVis is published under the GNU Public License Version 2 (GPLv2); the description below refers to version 1.3.

18.1 Installation

NagVis makes use of NDOUtils and is implemented in PHP. Therefore, besides an NDO database in running order, as described in Chapter 17 from page 375, you need a Web server with PHP 4.2 or higher, as well as the packages php-mysql for access to the NDO database and php-gd to be able to draw lines.[3] Depending on the distribution and the PHP version used, the package names may vary slightly. For Debian "Etch" and PHP5 you need the packages libapache2-mod-php5, php5, php5-common, php5-gd, and php5-mysql.

NagVis does not necessarily have to be installed on the same computer as Nagios and the NDOUtils, although in many cases they are packed onto one host. The configuration of the NDO database—NagVis documentation refers to this as the *backend*—can refer (as described on page 395) to any system you please. NagVis even allows the backend to be selected separately for each individual object so that maps can be generated that combine several Nagios installations in a single graphic.

18.1.1 Installing the source code

The NagVis source code, from http://www.nagvis.org/downloads, is unpacked in a directory of your choice:

```
linux:~ # tar xvzf /pfad/zu/nagvis-1.3.tar.gz
...
```

If a previous installation exists, you should back this up first. Then you copy the directory that has been created (in our case, nagvis-1.3) with the name nagvis to /usr/local/nagios/share:

```
linux:~ # mv nagvis-1.3 /usr/local/nagios/share/nagvis
linux:~ # ls -F /usr/local/nagios/share/nagvis
INSTALL LICENCE README config.php etc/ index.php nagvis/ var/ wui/
```

The duplicated directory name nagvis can sometimes lead to confusion, but it is correct:

```
/usr/local/nagios/share/nagvis
/usr/local/nagios/share/nagvis/nagvis
/usr/local/nagios/share/nagvis/wui
```

/usr/local/nagios/share/nagvis represents the main directory of the NagVis installation, while the subdirectory nagvis contains the NagVis application, together with its configuration. Finally the subdirectory wui contains the graphic editor that enables NagVis maps to be edited via the browser.

---

[3] You can manage without using the GD libraries if the parameter usedgdlibs in the NagVis configuration file config.ini.php (see page 393) is set to 0.

At present, the correct access permissions for directories and files must be set manually. To do this, you first need to determine the user with whose permissions the Web server is running (see also Section 1.2, page 39):

```
linux:~ # grep "^User" /etc/apache2/apache2.conf
User www-data
linux:~ # id www-data
uid=33(www-data) gid=33(www-data) Groups=33(www-data),9001(nagcmd)
```

The first grep command looks for the corresponding user in the configuration file for the Web server—in this case, Apache2—and then the id command searches for the primary group of this user. This can be found after the gid= specification. The access permissions are now set accordingly:

```
linux:~ # chown www-data.www-data -R /usr/local/nagios/share/nagvis
linux:~ # chmod 664 /usr/local/nagios/share/nagvis/etc/nagvis.ini.php
linux:~ # chmod 775 /usr/local/nagios/share/nagvis/nagvis/images/maps
linux:~ # chmod 664 /usr/local/nagios/share/nagvis/nagvis/images/maps/*
linux:~ # chmod 775 /usr/local/nagios/share/nagvis/etc/maps
linux:~ # chmod 664 /usr/local/nagios/share/nagvis/etc/maps/*
linux:~ # chmod 775 /usr/local/nagios/share/nagvis/var
linux:~ # chmod 664 /usr/local/nagios/share/nagvis/var/*
```

Before the Web user interface can be used, you must create the central configuration file and ensure that access to NagVis is only possible after successful authentication.

18.1.2 Initial configuration

A template for the central NagVis configuration file config.ini.php can be found in the directory /usr/local/nagios/share/nagvis/etc, which only needs to be renamed and modified:

```
linux:~ # cd /usr/local/nagios/share/nagvis/etc
linux:nagvis/etc # cp config.ini.php.dist config.ini.php
linux:nagvis/etc # chown www-data.www-data config.ini.php
linux:nagvis/etc # chmod 664 config.ini.php
```

The commands chown and chmod ensure that the correct access permissions are set for the Web user (here, www-data) and his group.

Apart from the configuration of the backend (that is, the NDO database), the included config.ini.php already has usable defaults. The following description is therefore limited to introducing the most important parameters:[4]

---

[4] The complete documentation can be found at http://www.nagvis.org/docs/1.3/ nagvis_config_format_description.

```
[global]
language="german"
refreshtime=60
```

In the [global] section you can set the language with language; the default is english. refreshtime defines every how many seconds the display in the brower is refreshed.

The section [defaults] specifies defaults that are inherited by the defined objects from the map configuration. The values can be overwritten via the map, if required. It is best to define settings here that are identical for the majority of objects, in order to avoid the repeated work of defining them explicitly in the object definitions:

```
[defaults]
backend="ndomy_1"
icons="std_medium"
recognizeservices=1
onlyhardstates=1
```

backend specifies which NDO database is used as the default backend. The name for this can be anything you like, but the backend itself must still be defined in a separate section (see page 395). If you are just getting started, it is best to keep the name supplied, ndomy_1.

The parameter icons defines the icon set from the directory ./nagvis/ nagvis/images/iconsets that is to be used. Four sets are included: std_ small, std_medium, std_big, and folder. Other icons can be downloaded from the NagVis homepage,[5] or you can create them yourself.[6]

The setting recognizeserivces=1 ensures for hosts and host groups that the current states of the accompanying services are included when the overall state is being determined. The value 0 switches off this behavior.

onlyhardstates=1 on the other hand instructs NagVis to take only hard states into account. The default 0 also includes soft states.

The [wui] section allows settings to be made for the NagVis editor:

```
[wui]
autoupdatefreq=25
maplocktime=5
```

autoupdatefreq determines how often (in number of seconds) the Web user interface automatically saves changes, while maplocktime specifies the number of minutes after which any further changes to a map that is

---

[5] http://www.nagvis.org/downloads
[6] A corresponding guide can be found at http://www.nagvis.org/docs/extending/ iconsets.

currently being edited should be blocked, from the time of the last change. This is intended to prevent several users from simultaneously editing the same map.

The paths to the NagVis installation from the perspective of the file system (base) and—separately for NagVis data and NagVis CGIs—from the perspective of the browser, are specified in Section [paths]:

```
[paths]
base="/usr/local/nagios/share/nagvis/"
htmlbase="/nagios/nagvis"
htmlcgi="/nagios/cgi-bin"
```

The defaults listed here match the standard installation described above.

The configuration for the backend, that is, for accessing the NDO database, follows at the bottom of the file:

```
[backend_ndomy_1]
backendtype="ndomy"
dbhost="localhost"
dbport=3306
dbname="nagios"
dbuser="nagios"
dbpass="verysecret"
dbprefix="nagios_"
dbinstancename="default"
maxtimewithoutupdate=180
```

This name of this section must contain the name specified with the backend parameter under [defaults], according to the pattern [backend_*value_ of_backend*]. The default here is ndomy_1. If the backend parameter value does not match any of the defined backend sections, NagVis will refuse to work.

backendtype defines the type of backend, and for now ndomy—an NDO database based on MySQL—is the only possible value.

dbhost and dbport specify the host name or IP address and the accompanying TCP port for access to the database. dbname contains the name of the NDO database, and dbuser and dbpass give the user and the password for access.

The values defined by default for dbprefix and dbinstancename are set for a NDOUtils standard installation. Provided that you have not changed the parameter instance_name in the file ndomod.cfg (see Chapter 17.4.1 from page 384) and db_prefix in the file ndo2db.cfg (see Chapter 17.4.2 from page 385), you can use the values given here.

One parameter to which you should pay particular attention is maxtime withoutupdate: This defines how much time in seconds is allowed for the status update of Nagios to appear. If the time specified here is exceeded, NagVis assumes that the data is obsolete and displays this as an error. If NagVis accesses NDO databases that are distributed across several servers, it is essential that the clock times of the servers be synchronized with one another, otherwise NagVis will refuse to work if it comes across a time difference greater than `maxtimewithoutupdate` seconds.

At this point we shall mention another problem involving data exchange between the NDO database and NagVis: NagVis evaluates the current program status. Nagios versions prior to 3.0b1, however, only write this to the NDO database *after* the nightly change of the log files. Starting with version 3.0b1, Nagios updates the status every five seconds, so that NagVis always has up-to-date information.

18.1.3 User authentication

NagVis demands authentication from the user. Without user authentication, it will just issue an error message.[7]

If the `share` directory of Nagios is not accessible for authentication, as in the Apache configuration on page 48, you should change this in the Apache configuration file `/etc/apache2/conf.d/nagios`. The authentication data are best taken from the CGI directory (see Section 1.5 from page 47).

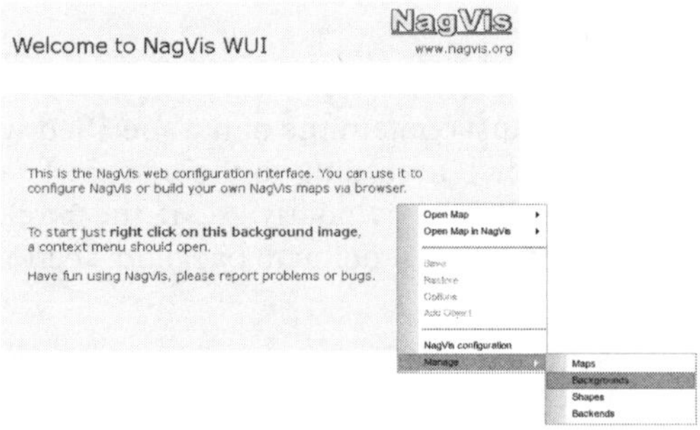

Figure 18.3:
After a right mouse click on the graphic displayed, the menu will appear

18.2 Creating NagVis Maps

The NagVis configuration interface is accessed through the URL `http://nagiosserver/nagios/wui/index.php`. Here you replace *nagiosserver* with your own Nagios host name (Figure 18.3 shows the start page).

---

[7] The FAQ entry `http://www.nagvis.org/docs/general/faq#how/to/run/nagvis/without/authentication/` describes a way of using NagVis without authentication, but you should avoid this, for reasons of security.

It is operated through a menu that opens when you click the right mouse button. For browsers that overlay the NagVis menu with their own menu, a second click with the right mouse button will cause the browser menu to disappear.

If you don't have a suitable background graphic available in PNG format, you can create a new, empty background image via the menu item **Manage | Backgrounds**, as shown in Figure 18.4. In this example, a gray image of size 800x600 pixels is created.

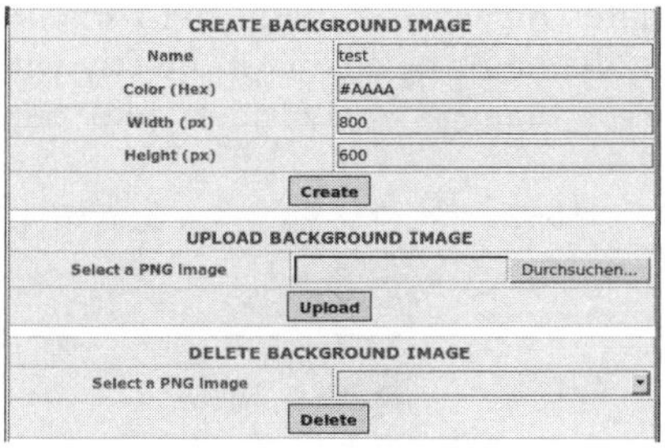

Figure 18.4:
Creating a new,
empty background

This image is displayed on screen in its original size, that is, not scaled. To avoid scrolling, it should not be too large, with the proper size depending on the screen resolution and taking into account possible window frames.

Later on the image size can only be altered to a limited extent: although you can upload or create a background image at any time, objects that have already been placed are not affected by any changes in the size or other characteristics of the background, and so they may not fit properly into a new background image. The only option then is to reposition all the objects. The best approach is to experiment at first with just a few objects in the definitive environment before you set up an extensive map.

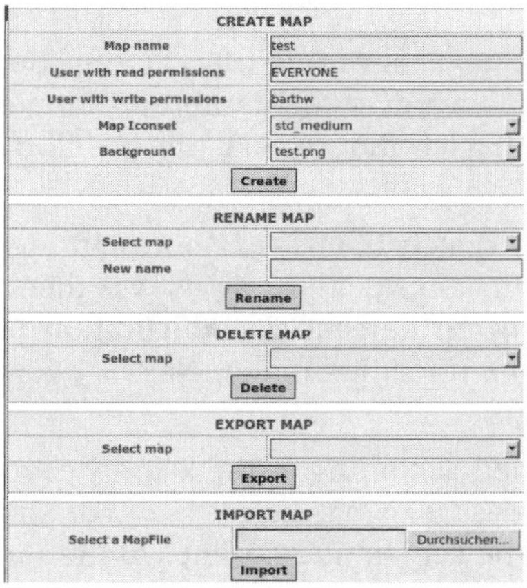

Figure 18.5:
If the entry for Map
Iconset remains
empty, NagVis uses
the defaults from the
central
configuration.

You now create a new map for the generated or uploaded image. Via the menu entry **Manage | Maps** (Figure 18.3) you navigate to the dialog shown in Figure 18.5. There you define the name of the map and select the background image. If every authenticated user should see the map, you enter EVERYONE as **User with read permissions**. For the User with write permissions, on the other hand, you would probably enter a specific user, or several user names, separated by commas. Defining the icon sets is optional at this point, although the example shown specifies them.

Newly created maps are automatically opened by NagVis in editing mode. You can reach this later on via the menu item **Open Map** in the context menu of the opening dialog or by calling it directly with the URL http:// nagiosserver/nagios/nagvis/wui/index.php?map=*mapname*.

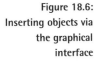

Figure 18.6:
Inserting objects via
the graphical
interface

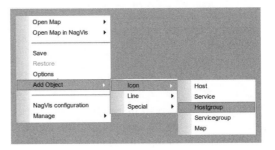

The *mapname* for the map created in Figure 18.5 is Test. In the map itself you now insert objects using the right mouse button (see Figure 18.6). An object can be an icon, a line, or a special object. Icons and lines represent the current state of a host or service and can also stand for entire host or service groups. Icons can only reflect the overall state of a map. Special objects are graphics representing stateless objects (which might be icons as well, for example) or text boxes, which can also be provided with a hyperlink.

To insert a host group you select **Add Object | Icon | Hostgroup** in the menu. Then you place the mouse over the desired position and define the destination of the icon with a left mouse click (the position can be changed later on).

When this is done a dialog opens, as shown in Figure 18.7. The entry **backend_id** can remain empty, and NagVis will then use the value of the backend parameter from the central configuration file config.php.ini. In the **hostgroup_name** pulldown menu, NagVis allows you to select from all defined host groups.

Icons can be positioned according to the **x** and **y** coordinates by either entering numerical values or using the mouse. For simple icons, the point (x,y) corresponds to the center, and for lines to the start or end points. The z coordinate is only used when icons overlap. The value 0 describes the underlying image at the rear and is reserved for the background, and the object with the highest z value is right at the front. If the z coordinate is explicitly left empty when the object is inserted, it automatically receives the value 1.

backend_id	
hostgroup_name	AH
x	65
y	64
z	
recognize_services	Yes
only_hard_states	Yes

Figure 18.7:
Defining a host
group in the
graphical interface

The parameter `recognize_services` allows the `recognizeservices` setting from the `config.ini.php` (see page 394) to be overridden, and `only_hard_states` does the same for the parameter `onlyhardstates` (page 394).

The object inserted in this way always appears in the graphical editor in the form of the OK icon from the icon set chosen; the Web interface takes no account of its actual state.

If you move the mouse over the icon, a hover menu opens, as shown in Figure 18.8. It clearly distinguishes which settings are inherited and which ones have been specified directly in the object. If you follow the **Change** link there, the settings can be changed again.

Hostgroup	
Configured	
hostgroup_name	AH
x	65
y	64
recognize_services	1
only_hard_states	1
Inherited	
backend_id	eli
z	1
iconset	std_medium
hover_menu	1
hover_template	default
hover_delay	0
url_target	_self
label_show	0
label_text	[name]
label_x	-20
label_y	+20
label_width	auto
label_background	transparent
label_border	#000000
hover_childs_show	1
hover_childs_sort	s
hover_childs_order	asc
hover_childs_limit	10
Change	**Delete**

Figure 18.8:
If you move the
mouse over the
inserted object, a
hover menu opens

When your work is finished, don't forget to save your changes via the context menu entry **Save** (see Figure 18.3 on page 396). The menu item **Open Map in NagVis** will then take you to the finished view, which now does display the actual states.

In Figure 18.9 a text box has been added to the host group icon. The field displayed beneath this is a hover menu, which shows information on the object and its state if you move the mouse over the object. This example shows that two hosts of the host group display a Not OK state and that this has already been confirmed with an acknowledgment.

Figure 18.9:
Object in the final
view with text box
and hover menu

Headquarters		
	Hostgroup	
Hostgroup Name	Headquarters	
Alias		
Summary State	CRITICAL (Acknowledged)	
Summary Output	There are 1 CRITICAL, 1 WARNING, 8 UP Hosts.	
Host Name	State	Output
eligate3	CRITICAL (Acknowledged)	The Host is UP. There are 1 CRITICAL, 13 OK Services.
ELIFS01	WARNING (Acknowledged)	The Host is UP. There are 1 WARNING, 8 OK Services.
ELITS05	UP	The Host is UP. There are 11 OK Services.
ELITS06	UP	The Host is UP. There are 11 OK Services.
ELITS04	UP	The Host is UP. There are 11 OK Services.
ELITS07	UP	The Host is UP. There are 11 OK Services.
ELITS03	UP	The Host is UP. There are 11 OK Services.
AHPS01	UP	The Host is UP. There are 37 OK Services.
AHDC01	UP	The Host is UP. There are 23 OK Services.
AHDS01	UP	The Host is UP. There are 30 OK Services.

The finished map can be called directly via the URL `http://nagiosserver/nagios/nagvis/nagvis/index.php?map=mapname`.

18.2.1 Editing the configuration in text form

NagVis stores the entire configuration of a map in text files, which can also be edited with a text editor. The files are located in the directory `/usr/local/nagios/share/nagvis/etc/maps/`. If you are using a background image with a known raster, you can insert several objects in the WUI and continue editing the map in the editor using the coordinates just determined. This is how the map shown in Figure 18.2 was created. The background image (Figure 18.1) was created with OpenOffice in order to obtain a reproducible raster; the OpenOffice drawing is subsequently exported as a PNG file.

The configuration options for the text files, which altogether are very extensive, are described in the online documentation.[8]

_____
[8] `http://www.nagvis.org/docs`

18.2.2 Adding NagVis maps to the Nagios Web interface

NagVis maps can also be integrated into the Nagios Web interface. Figure 18.10 shows these after a third frame has been added to the `index.html` page, which binds a 32-pixel-high map beneath the main window. No matter what the administrator is currently working on, the most important states (here these are the host groups) are always displayed directly and can be reached with a single mouse click. There are no limits to your user interface dreams when using NagVis!

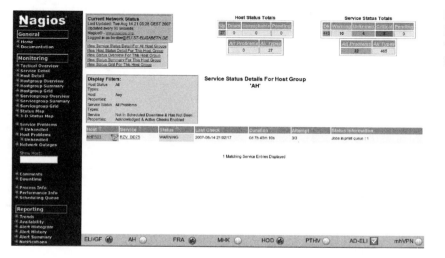

Figure 18.10:
NagVis map as a "footnote" in the Nagios Web interface

Graphic Display of
Performance Data

When Nagios reports to the administrator quickly and selectively on problems that have occurred, it can basically only distinguish between OK states and error states, sparing the admin a flood of information on problematic services and hosts. The graphic display of measured values over a time period cannot be integrated into this "traffic light approach," but it is available through third-party software. Nagios supports external processing of values with an interface created specifically for this. The data processed through it is referred to in Nagios jargon as *performance data*.

Nagios has two different classes of performance data. The first is Nagios-internal performance data, statistics on the performance times of tests and on the difference between the actual test time and the planned time (the *latency*). The second class includes performance data that the plugin passes on with the test result. This involves everything that the plugin can measure: response times, hard drive usage, system load, and so on. These are the very things that are of interest to an administrator, which is why the book concentrates on how they are processed.

Nagios extracts this data and either writes it to a file where it can be processed by other programs, or passes it on directly to the external software that is run after every service or host check.

19.1   Processing Plugin Performance Data with Nagios

Performance data provided by service and host checks can be processed only if the corresponding plugin delivers it in a predefined format. As shown here using the check_icmp plugin (Section 6.2, page 108), it is preceded by a | sign and is not shown in the Web interface:

```
nagios@linux:libexec/nagios$ ./check_icmp -H vpn01
OK - eli02: rta 96.387ms, lost 0%| rta=96.387ms;200.000;500.000;0; pl=0%;
40;80;;
```

This standardized form is provided by most plugins only after version 1.4.[1] The performance data itself consists of one or more variables in the following form:

```
name=value;warn;crit;min;max
```

The variable *name* may contain spaces, but then it must be surrounded by single quotation marks. After the equals sign comes first the measured value as an integer or floating-point decimal, with or without a unit. Possible units are % (percentage), s (time in seconds), B (data size in bytes), or c (counter, an incremental counter).

This is followed, separated by a semicolon, by the warning and critical limits, and then the minimum and maximum value. Percentage values can be left out by the plugin. You can also specify 0 for minimum/maximum, as well as for the warning or critical limit, if there is no such threshold value. If there are several variables, these are separated with spaces, as in the check_icmp example. However, in contrast to this, the final specification should *not* end with a semicolon, according to the Developer Guidelines.

---

[1]   Some tools such as Nagiosgraph and NagiosGrapher make use of the fact that the remaining text normally contains performance data as well. If they are correspondingly configured, they are able to extract the performance data contained there. In this way they can further process data that does not conform to the standard format.

19.1.1 The template mechanism

Nagios has two methods of processing performance data: either the system saves the data to a file using a *template*, or it executes an external command. If you just want to write data consistently to a log file, the template procedure is somewhat easier to configure.

In order that Nagios can process performance data at all, the parameter

```
# /etc/nagios/nagios.cfg
...
process_performance_data=1
...
```

must be set to 1. The file to which Nagios writes the host or service performance data is specified by the parameters `host_perfdata_file` and `service_perfdata_file`:

```
# /etc/nagios/nagios.cfg
...
# host_perfdata_file=/var/nagios/host-perfdata.dat
service_perfdata_file=/var/nagios/service-perfdata.dat
# host_perfdata_file_template=[HOSTPERFDATA]\t$TIMET$\t$HOSTNAME$\t$HOST
EXECUTIONTIME$\t$HOSTOUTPUT$\t$HOSTPERFDATA$
service_perfdata_file_template=[SERVICEPERFDATA]\t$TIMET$\t$HOSTNAME$\t$
SERVICEDESC$\t$SERVICEEXECUTIONTIME$\t$SERVICELATENCY$\t$SERVICEOUTPUT$\
t$SERVICEPERFDATA$
...
```

If `host_perfdata_file` is commented out, as in this example, Nagios does not save any performance data of host checks. But since they are only used if all service checks fail, it lies in the nature of host checks that they only provide data sporadically and at irregular intervals. This is why it is not worth evaluating them in most cases.

The `*_perfdata_file_template` parameters define the output format. The definition shown above, `service_perfdata_file_template`, delivers (one-line) log file entries in the following pattern:

```
[SERVICEPERFDATA]     1114353266     linux01 PING   0.483  0.104 OK
 - 10.128.254.12: rta 100.436ms, lost 0% rta=100.436ms;3000.000;6000.000
;0; pl=0%;40;80;;
```

Each line begins with a [SERVICEPERFDATA] "stamp," followed by the test time in epoch seconds ($TIMET$), the host name and service description ($HOSTNAME$ and $SERVICEDESC$), the time Nagios requires for the test ($SERVICEEXECUTIONTIME$), and the latency between the planned and actual time of performance ($SERVICELATENCY$), each separated by a tab.

Then Nagios writes the output for the Web interface to the log file (\$SER-VICEOUTPUT\$) and finally the actual performance data (\$SERVICEPERF-DATA\$). \t in the parameter definition ensures that a tab separates the individual details from each other in the log. With the *_perfdata_file_mode parameters you can define whether Nagios appends the data to an existing file (a) or overwrites the existing file (w):

```
# /etc/nagios/nagios.cfg
...
host_perfdata_file_mode=a
service_perfdata_file_mode=a
...
```

This is suitable for external programs that can read the data from a (previously set up) named pipe. This method provides better performance and does not require any space on the hard drive. If the processing software is not running, however, the data may be lost: Nagios does try for a time to continue writing to the pipe, but aborts this process after a timeout if the data cannot be read out.

Programs that read from a log file generally delete it afterwards, to prevent the file system from overflowing. If the program does not retrieve any data, the file will grow quickly, but nothing will be lost as long as there is still space on the file system.

It is best to run external evaluation software as a permanent service. But you can also configure Nagios so that it regularly triggers a program for further processing:

```
# /etc/nagios/nagios.cfg
...
# host_perfdata_file_processing_interval=0
# service_perfdata_file_processing_interval=0
# host_perfdata_file_processing_command=process-host-perfdata-file
# service_perfdata_file_processing_command=process-service-perfdata-file
...
```

With the *_perfdata_file_processing_interval parameters you set an interval in seconds after which Nagios will carry on running the corresponding *_perfdata_file_processing_command at specific intervals. This command is defined as a normal Nagios command object:

```
# misccommands.cfg
...
define command{
    command_name    process-service-perfdata-file
    command_line    /path/to_the/evaluation_program
}
...
```

As long as the external software itself looks after the further processing of the file with the performance data, you do need to use the *_perfdata_file_processing_* parameters.

19.1.2 Using external commands to process performance data

As an alternative to the template method, Nagios can also directly call a command that takes over further processing of data. This is done directly after each test result; so after each individual check, an external program is started. If you have a large number of services to be checked, this can, depending on the software, considerably degrade performance.

The command itself is defined with the process_perfdata_command parameter instead of the perfdata_file parameter:

```
# /etc/nagios/nagios.cfg
...
process_performance_data=1
service_perfdata_command=process-service-perfdata
...
```

In the same way as with service performance data, you can also process the results of host checks, using the host_perfdata_command parameter. process-service-perfdata itself again refers to a normal Nagios command object:

```
# misccommands.cfg
...
define command{
    command_name    process-service-perfdata
    command_line    /pfad/zum/programm "$LASTSERVICECHECK$||$HOSTNAME$||$
SERVICEDESC$||$SERVICEOUTPUT$||$SERVICEPERFDATA$"
}
...
```

This opens the external program, which is given the necessary information as arguments. This should include at least the timestamp of the last service check ($LASTSERVICECHECK$), the host name ($HOSTNAME$), and the service description ($SERVICEDESC$), as well as the actual service performance data ($SERVICEPERFDATA$). The delimiter depends on the program used: this example uses ||, as is used by the Nagiosgraph program.

19.2 Graphs for the Web with Nagiosgraph

With the program Nagiosgraph from `http://nagiosgraph.sf.net/`, performance data supplied by plugins can be displayed graphically in a Web interface in chronological form. The software consists of two Perl scripts. The script `insert.pl` writes the Nagios performance data to a round-robin database, a ring buffer in which the newest data overwrites the oldest.[2] The advantage of this is the small amount of space required, which can be defined beforehand.

The trick consists of saving data in various resolutions, depending on its age: older data with a lower resolution (e.g., one measurement value per day), current data with a high resolution (e.g., one measurement every five minutes). When setting up the database, you also define how long the data is retained. This defines space requirements right from the beginning.

Provided that Nagiosgraph detects the performance data, the program creates a separate round-robin database for each new service, when it appears for the first time. The `map` configuration file included describes just a few services, so that usually some manual work—and a basic knowledge of Perl—is required.

The second Nagiosgraph script `show.cgi`, a CGI script, represents the information from the database in a dynamic HTML page. To do this, it is run (after configuration is completed) in the form

```
http://nagsrv/path/to/show.cgi?host=host&service=service_description
```

Nagiosgraph then displays four graphs (a daily, a weekly, a monthly, and a yearly summary) for the desired service.

19.2.1 Basic installation

An installed RRDtool package, which is contained in most Linux distributions, is a prerequisite for Nagiosgraph. Alternatively you can obtain the current source code from `http://www.rrdtool.org/`.[3] For reasons of performance, it is recommended here that you also install the included Perl module RRDs.

The Nagiosgraph tar file itself is preferably unpacked in the directory `/usr/local/nagios`:

```
nagios@linux:local/nagios$ tar xvzf nagiosgraph-0.5.tar.gz
nagiosgraph/INSTALL
nagiosgraph/README
```

---

[2] Further information on this topic can be found at `http://www.rrdtool.org/`.
[3] To install, see page 421.

```
nagiosgraph/README.map
nagiosgraph/insert.pl
nagiosgraph/insert_fast.pl
nagiosgraph/map
nagiosgraph/nagiosgraph.conf
nagiosgraph/show.cgi
nagiosgraph/testcolor.cgi
nagiosgraph/testentry.pl
```

insert.pl extracts the data transferred by Nagios and inserts this into the RRD database. If this does not exist, however, the script will create it. Alternatively insert_fast.pl can take on this task. This script uses the Perl module RRDs, which is considerably more efficient than calling up rrdtool as an external program each time, which is what insert.pl does.

Another Perl script called testentry.pl helps if you are testing your own map entries. But since you have to write these directly into this file, you can also change the map file itself (as shown below)—provided you have made a backup copy first. The CGI script testcolor.cgi looks more like a developer's utility left over in the package, rather than a tool that is of any use for users.

Apart from the already mentioned map configuration file, there is a second one, nagiosgraph.conf, and its path must be defined correctly in both insert.pl (or insert_fast.pl) and show.cgi, so it is recommended that you check this:

```
my $configfile = '/usr/local/nagios/nagiosgraph/nagiosgraph.conf';
```

19.2.2 Configuration

The configuration file nagiosgraph.conf

All other relevant paths—such as those to the map file and to the rrdtool—are adjusted in nagiosgraph.conf:

```
rrdtool = /usr/bin/rrdtool
rrddir  = /var/lib/rrd/nagiosgraph
logfile = /var/nagios/nagiosgraph.log
mapfile = /usr/local/nagios/nagiosgraph/map
debug   = 2
colorscheme = 4
```

Nagiosgraph creates the RRD databases in the rrddir directory. Here the user nagios must have write access and the user with whose rights the Web server is running must have read access:

```
linux:~ # mkdir -p /var/lib/rrd/nagiosgraph
linux:~ # chown nagios.nagcmd /var/lib/rrd/nagiosgraph
linux:~ # chmod 755 /var/lib/rrd/nagiosgraph
```

The log file, for which both users need write access (the Web user because the CGI script also records information to the log file), is also critical:

```
linux:~ # touch /var/nagios/nagiosgraph.log
linux:~ # chown nagios.nagcmd /var/nagios/nagiosgraph.log
linux:~ # chmod 775 /var/nagios/nagiosgraph.log
```

How verbose Nagiosgraph is can be adjusted with debug. The possible debug levels are documented in the configuration file included: 2 means "errors," 4 "information"—here Nagiosgraph is already so verbose that you must watch out that the file system does not overflow. Except for debugging purposes (such as when setting up the system), it is better to choose 2.

With colorscheme, which can accept values from 1 to 8, you can influence the amount of color in the graphs—it is best to try out the options to see which color scheme matches your personal taste best.

Nagios configuration

Nagiosgraph grabs the performance data directly from Nagios. For this reason nagios.cfg does not require any *_perfdata_file_* parameters.

```
# /etc/nagios/nagios.cfg
...
process_performance_data=1
service_perfdata_command=process-service-perfdata
...
```

process_performance_data switches on processing of performance data in general; service_perfdata_command refers to the Nagios command object that contains the external command:

```
# misccommands.cfg
...
define command{
  command_name    process-service-perfdata
  command_line    /usr/local/nagios/nagiosgraph/insert_fast.pl "$LASTSERV
ICECHECK$||$HOSTNAME$||$SERVICEDESC$||$SERVICEOUTPUT$||$SERVICEPERFDATA$"
}
...
```

The definition of the parameter command_line must be written on one line (without the backslashes \), as usual.

So that the CGI script can run directly from the Nagios Web interface, a `serviceextinfo` object is defined:

```
define serviceextinfo{
    service_description PING
    host_name       *
    notes_url       /nagiosgraph/show.cgi?host=$HOSTNAME$&service=PING
    icon_image      graph.gif
    icon_image_alt  show graphics
}
```

If the graphic defined in `icon_image` is in the directory `/usr/local/nagios/share/images/logos`, the Web interface marks the `PING` services for all hosts in the status display with this.[4] Here the strength of `show.cgi` can be seen: only because this script is called explicitly with host and service names is a definition like the one above possible. Instead of an individual host name, you can also specify a host group, or, as in this example, a `*`. A requirement for this is that `PING` really is defined as a service for every host.

The `$HOSTNAME$` macro then automatically inserts the appropriate host. The additional information for a specific service type (which must have the same service description in all hosts) can therefore be catered for with just one single definition.

Apache configuration

So that the Apache Web server can accept the CGI script as it is, a `ScriptAlias` is created, for example:

```
ScriptAlias /nagiosgraph/ /usr/local/nagios/nagiosgraph/
```

This entry is best placed in the configuration file discussed in Section 1.5 (page 47), `nagios.conf`. Only after Apache is reloaded can the CGI script be run from the URL specified on page 408.

Adjustments to the map

Depending on the service, the round-robin database may also save several series of measurements, which can be requested individually through the CGI script:

```
http://nagsrv/path/to/show.cgi?host=host&service=service_description&db=
database,entry1,entry2&db=database,entry3
```

---

[4]   A more detailed description of the `serviceextinfo` object is contained in Section 16.4.2, page 366.

The database used here contains at least three different series of measurements, the first two of which are shown together in one graphic, while the third is shown in a separate graphic. What is shown together and what is separate depends on the standardization. It makes little sense to display the percentage load of a hard drive and the absolute value in bytes in the same graphic, since the Y axis can only have one scale. It is better here to display percentage values in one graphic and absolute byte values in a second one. On the other hand you can display the various average values of the system load (for one, five, and 15 minutes) in a single graphic. If you leave out all db= specifications, Nagiosgraph always displays all measured values for a service in a single graphic.

What individual databases and measured values display is defined by the map file. To understand how the instructions contained there influence the extraction of data, you just need to switch the debugging level to 4 and take a look at the output in the log file nagiosgraph.log. Each time the insert function is run, Nagiosgraph rereads the configuration files, so that this does not cause any kind of reset.

In the following extract from the log file the three dots mark sections which we will not print, for the sake of clarity:

```
... INSERT info:... servicedescr:PING
... INSERT info:... hostname:linux01
... INSERT info:... perfdata:rta=99.278ms;3000.000;7000.000;0; pl=0%;60;
80;;
... INSERT info:... lastcheck:1114853435
... INSERT info:... output:OK - 172.17.4.11: rta 99.278ms, lost 0%
```

The output is from the check_icmp plugin. The host name, service description, performance data, (perfdata:) and the standard output line (output:) each have their own line. In the performance data the plugin announces the *round trip average* with the variable rta, and the number of packets that have gone missing with pl (*packet loss*).

The map file contains Perl instructions that filter these outputs and extracts the corresponding data if there are hits. Each of them starts with a search instruction:

```
/perfdata:rta=([.\d]+)ms.+pl=(\d+)%/
```

The classic Perl search function consists of the two forward slashes / with a search pattern in the form of a regular expression in between. Round pairs of brackets enclose partial patterns with which the text found in this way can later be accessed using the variables $1, $2, etc.

The pattern in the first bracket thus matches a single digit (\d) or a dot,[5] and the next + states that there can be several of them (or none at all). In

---

[5] A pair of square brackets contains alternatives.

the second round brackets, though, one or more digits are allowed, but no period. In concrete terms $1 delivers the numerical value of the response time, $2 provides the packet loss in percent.

The full instruction in the map file links two Perl statements with the and operator:

```
# -- check_icmp
# perfdata:rta=100.424ms;5000.000;9000 .000;0; pl=0%;40;80;;
/perfdata:rta=([.\d]+)ms.+pl=(\d+)%/
and push @s, [ 'ping',
               [ 'rta',     'GAUGE', $1 ],
               [ 'losspct', 'GAUGE', $2 ],
             ];
```

If the first one—the search function—is successful, then it is the turn of the push statement. It adds the expression in square brackets following to the array @s. The instruction ends with a semicolon. If the search function provides no result, the map instruction will not save any entry in the @s array. The expression to be included in the array has the following format:

```
[ db-name,
   [name_of_data_source, type, value ],
   [name_of_data_source, type, value ],
   ...
]
```

The file name for a Nagiosgraph database file consists of the host name, service description, and the database name together, for example, linux01_PING_ping.rrd. The desired string for the database name is entered instead of the placeholder *db-name* into the map file (in this case, ping).

The name of the data source can be chosen freely, but should contain an indication of the data that is stored here, such as rta for the response time or losspct for percentage of packets that have been lost.

What *type* you specify is determined by the RRD tools. GAUGE stands for simple measured values that are displayed simply as they are. DERIVE is recommended by Nagiosgraph author Soren Dossing for processing counters, such as in querying a packet counter on the network interface. Counters grow incrementally and, when they run over, start again at zero. What is of interest here is the difference between two points in time. The RRD database determines these automatically if the data source type DERIVE is specified.

The database name, data source, and type should always be placed in single quotation marks in the map file, so that no name conflicts can occur with keywords reserved in Perl.

The measured value itself is determined using Perl methods, and the place-holder *value* is substituted with the corresponding instructions. In the simplest case, you take over the values found with the search pattern in the performance data with $1, $2, etc. (see example above), or calculate new values from these by multiplying[6] by 1024 or by calculating the percentage:

```
# -- check_nt -v USEDDISKSPACE
# perfdata:C:\ Used Space=1.71Gb;6.40;7.20;0.00;8.00
/perfdata:.*Used Space=([.\d]+)Gb;([.\d]+);([.\d]+);([.\d]+);([.\d]+)/
and push @s, [ 'disk',
              [ 'used', 'GAUGE', $1*1024 ],
              [ 'usepct', 'GAUGE', ($1/$5)*100 ],
              [ 'freepct', 'GAUGE', (($5-$1)/$5)*100 ],
            ];

# -- check_disk (unix)
# perfdata:/=498MB;1090;1175;0;1212
m@perfdata:..*/([^ =]+)=([.\d]+)MB;([.\d]+);([.\d]+);([.\d]+);([.\d]+)@
and  push @s, [ $1,
               [ 'used', 'GAUGE', $2*1024**2 ],
               [ 'warn', 'GAUGE', $3*1024**2 ],
               [ 'crit', 'GAUGE', $4*1024**2 ],
             ];
```

The first entry evaluates the query of hard drive space on a Windows server with `check_nt` (see Section 20.2.1, page 476). The performance data also contains, apart from the occupied space in $1, the size of the data carrier in $5. This can be used to calculate the percentage that is available (`freepct`) and the percentage used (`usepct`).

The second example evaluates data obtained on a Unix host, with `check_disk`, by multiplying the free hard drive space specified in MB by 1024^2 to convert it to bytes. The critical and warning limits always remain constant, which leads to horizontal lines, as seen in Figure 19.1: the lower line at 12.1 GB represents the warning limit, the middle line the current load, and the top line at 18.1 GB, the critical limit. The keys for the individual graphs each list minimum, maximum, and average as a numerical value. This differentiation for the two limit values is not of any use, but it cannot be avoided, since Nagiosgraph does not know that these are constant values: it treats warning and critical limits just like any other measured values.

If a plugin does not provide any performance data, but values that are used in normal output, the search function can be applied to the output (`/output:.../`) instead of to the performance data. Help is provided, for example, by the Nagiosgraph Forum at `http://sourceforge.net/forum/forum.php?forum_id=394748`.

---

[6] This turns kilobytes into bytes.

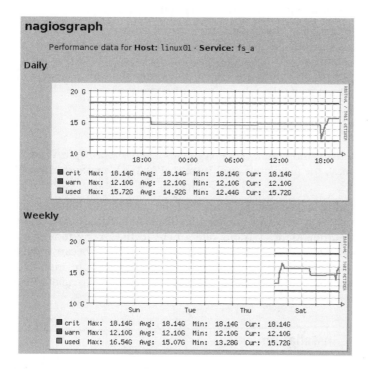

Figure 19.1:
Used space and limit values for the file system /net/linux01/a on the host linux01, as Nagiosgraph represents them

Changes to the map are critical. It is therefore recommended that you copy the file first and edit the copy, and then perform a syntax check, using `perl -c`:

```
nagios@linux:libexec/nagios$ cp map map.new
nagios@linux:libexec/nagios$ vi map.new
nagios@linux:libexec/nagios$ perl -c map.new
nagios@linux:libexec/nagios$ mv map.new map
```

If the syntax check is in order, you can install the new file as map.

19.3 Preparing Performance Data for Evaluation with Perf2rrd

Another tool which transfers Nagios performance data to an RRD database is the Java application Perf2rrd. This requires an installed Java Runtime Environment (1.4.2, or preferably 1.5). Since the virtual machine generates a noticeable load on less powerful computers, and also requires a large amount of memory, the requirements made of the Nagios server by Perf2rrd are significantly higher than those made by Nagiosgraph.

On the other hand there is no more work after the installation as far as generating the RRD databases is concerned, because Perf2rrd uses the template mechanism of Nagios (see Section 19.1, page 404). For each service and each variable contained in the template, the tool creates a separate RRD database using the following naming pattern:

```
host+service_description+variable_name.rrd
```

So to evaluate the `check_icmp` variables `rta` (*round trip average*) and `pl` (*packet loss*), the file names are `linux01+PING+pl.rrd` and `linux01+PING +rta.rrd`.

Perf2rrd only looks after the storage of data in an RRD database and does not provide any tools to graphically display the data saved there. The Perf2rrd author Marc DeTrano refers here to the `drraw` tool (see Section 19.4, page 420). It can be advantageous to use this, because on the one hand `drraw` allows far more than just the one display provided by Nagios-graph, and on the other hand you do not have to struggle with regular expressions in Perl.

19.3.1   Installation

For the installation you should get hold of the archive in tar format from `http://perf2rrd.sf.net/`, and copy it, preferably to the `/usr/local` hierarchy:

```
linux:~ # cd /usr/local
linux:usr/local # tar xvzf /path/to/perf2rrd-1.0.tar.gz
...
perf2rrd/run
...
```

The executable program that is later run is a script called `run`, which in turn calls the Java bytecode interpreter, `java`. Besides this the directory contains the Java class files and other utilities, with which you can recompile the included shared library `librrdj.so`, if required. This is normally not necessary for the newer distributions.

In order for `run` to be able to find the `java` program, it must be located in `/usr/bin`. If this is not the case (because you have installed the Java archive from `http://www.sun.com/`, for example), then you should set a link:

```
linux:~ # ln -s /usr/local/jre1.5.0_02/bin/java /usr/bin/java
```

A short test shows whether or not Perf2rrd starts correctly:

```
nagios@linux:local/perf2rrd$ ./run
perf2rrd starting
Using Nagios Config: /etc/nagios/nagios.cfg
Using RRD Repository: /var/log/nagios/rrd
Unable to create RRD Repository
```

The error message issued in the last line is not a problem at the moment, since we have saved the RRD databases in a different directory anyway (page 420).

19.3.2 Nagios configuration

Perf2rrd searches in the Nagios configuration for all the data it requires: to what file Nagios should write the performance data, the write mode used for this,[7] and the format of the template:

```
# /etc/nagios/nagios.cfg
...
process_performance_data=1
...
service_perfdata_file=/var/nagios/service-perfdata.dat

service_perfdata_file_template=$TIMET$\t$HOSTNAME$\t\
    $SERVICEDESC$\t$SERVICEEXECUTIONTIME$\t$SERVICELATENCY$\t\
    $SERVICEOUTPUT$\t$SERVICEPERFDATA$

service_perfdata_file_mode=w
...
```

The named pipe used here, thanks to service_perfdata_file_mode=w, must be created manually—Perf2rrd 1.0 in Nagios 2.0 has problems with the normal file interface (service_perfdata_file_mode=a):

```
linux:~ # mknod /var/nagios/service-perfdata.dat p
linux:~ # ls -l /var/nagios/service-perfdata.dat
prw-r--r-- 1 nagios nagios 0 May 1 10:49 /var/nagios/service-perfdata.dat
```

In the template the introductory [SERVICEPERFDATA] stamp is missing (see Section 19.1), since Perf2rrd 1.0 does not parse this correctly. Changes to the Nagios configuration require a reload:

```
linux:~ # /etc/init.d/nagios reload
```

[7] With a, Nagios appends the data to a normal log file; with w it makes it accessible through a named pipe. See Section 19.1, page 404.

Finally you create the directory for the RRD databases:

```
linux:~ # mkdir /var/lib/rrd/perf2rrd
linux:~ # chown nagios.nagios /var/lib/rrd/perf2rrd
```

19.3.3 Perf2rrd in practice

Loading the Java Virtual Machine each time Perf2rrd is started requires considerable resources. For this reason you should not use the method of starting Perf2rrd with the parameter `service_perfdata_file_processing_command` at specific intervals of Nagios, and also should not use the *one-shot mode*, with `./run -o`, in which the software processes one file at a time. In theory this would make it possible to run Perf2rrd regularly with a cron job. Instead, it is recommended that you keep the program running permanently.

When using this for the first time, we recommend that you switch on the debugging mode, which will show any problems that occur. The option `-d` specifies the directory in which the tools should create and update the RRD databases:

```
nagios@linux:local/perf2rrd$ ./run -d /var/lib/rrd/perf2rrd -x
perf2rrd starting
Using Nagios Config: /etc/nagios/nagios.cfg
Using RRD Repository: /var/lib/rrd/perf2rrd
Debug Mode is on
Reading perfdata from named pipe.
Perf Data File is : /var/nagios/service-perfdata.dat
I believe we are using Nagios ver. 2
Object Cache File is : /var/nagios/objects.cache
Nagios interval_length 60
called update with: .../eli02+PING+rta.rrd 1114938329:0.079
called update with: .../eli02+PING+pl.rrd 1114938329:0.0
/var/lib/rrd/perf2rrd/sap-14+SAP-3202+time.rrd created.
called update with: .../sap-14+SAP-3202+time.rrd 1114938688:0.030775
...
```

The output of the Nagios configuration file, the RRD repository, and the data transfer mode (`named pipe`) is followed by the time unit used by Nagios (and set with the `interval_length` parameter). Normally this is 60 seconds, that is, a check interval of 5 is five minutes long. It is extremely important that this parameter is correctly recognized, since Perf2rrd determines the *step interval* of the RRD database by multiplying the `normal_check_interval` and `interval_length` parameters together.

All measured values that occur during a step interval are averaged by the database. If this time period is too small, it is possible that the database will never issue any values, since it expects considerably more data than it obtains for saving.

While Nagiosgraph works with a fixed five-minute interval, Perf2rrd adjusts itself to the Nagios configuration. The software only takes into account the interval when creating the RRD database, however; changing the Nagios configuration later on has no further consequences. The only thing you can do here to alter this is delete the RRD database and set it up again.

Perf2rrd in permanent operation

Operating Perf2rrd on a named pipe has one disadvantage: if Nagios restarts, it closes the pipe before opening it again. Unfortunately when the pipe closes, Perf2rrd closes as well.

This can be prevented by the use of the Daemon Tools by Daniel J. Bernstein. They monitor programs and restart them, if these programs should ever stop. They are themselves started through an /etc/inittab entry by the init process, and are restarted if they were to shut themselves down at some point. The Daemon Tools tar file can be obtained from http://cr. yp.to/daemontools/install.html and it is unpacked in the directory /usr/local/src:

```
linux:~ # cd /usr/local/src
linux:local/src # tar xvzf /path/to/daemontools-0.76.tar.gz
admin
admin/daemontools-0.76
admin/daemontools-0.76/package
admin/daemontools-0.76/package/README
...
admin/daemontools-0.76/src
```

This creates the directory admin/daemontools-0.76, with the subdirectories package and src. From there you should run the install script, which compiles and installs the program:

```
linux:local/src # cd admin/daemontools-0.76
linux:admin/daemontools-0.76 # package/install
```

The binaries land in the newly created directory daemontools-0.76/command and remain there. The installation routine also sets up symbolic links pointing to them from the—also newly created—folder /command.

The install script also includes the following line in the file /etc/inittab, which ensures that the Daemon Tools run permanently:

```
SV:123456:respawn:/command/svscanboot
```

The program `svscanboot` searches regularly for new or crashed daemons. For this purpose it scans the `/service` directory, which is also created during the installation. Just one symbolic link is required to have Perf2rrd monitored:

```
linux:~ # ln -s /usr/local/perf2rrd /service/perf2rrd
```

The Daemon Tools search in this directory for a script called `run` and start it. In order for `run` to be able to find the path to the RRD repository, an actual command-line option is entered in the script file instead of `$*`:

```
# exec java -cp $classpath perf2rrd $*
exec java -cp $classpath perf2rrd -d /var/lib/rrd/perf2rrd
```

Starting and ending Perf2rrd is now taken over by the program `svc`:

```
linux:~ # /command/svc -d /service/perf2rrd
linux:~ # /command/svc -u /service/perf2rrd
```

The `-d` option (for *down*) stops the service specified, and `-u` (*up*) starts it again. It is not necessary to run it at the beginning, since the Daemon Tools regularly scan the `/service` directory for new services and automatically start them. This is important insofar as the Nagios-2.0 beta versions, on which this book is based, had problems if the configured named pipe was not read. Then it might not deliver any more data at all until a reload or restart. Whether this problem has been fixed in the final version 2.0 of Nagios could not be clarified at the time of going to press.

19.4 The Graphics Specialist `drraw`

From the RRD databases, generated for example by Perf2rrd or Nagios-graph, the CGI script `drraw` creates interactive graphics—simple ones relatively quicky, whereas for more complex ones you need to know a bit more about the RRDtools.[8]

19.4.1 Installation

For the `drraw` installation, you need to obtain the current tar file from `http://www.taranis.org/drraw/` and unpack it to its own subdirectory in the CGI hierarchy[9] on the Web server:

---

[8] Apart from the documentation on the homepage `http://www.rrdtool.org/`, the tutorial included (`man rrdtutorial`) is a useful starting point, as well as the man page `man rrdgraph`.

[9] Which directory this is depends on the distribution or Apache configuration you are using.

```
linux:~ # cd /usr/lib/cgi-bin
linux:lib/cgi-bin # tar xvzf /path/to/drraw-2.1.1.tar.gz
drraw-2.1.1/
...
drraw-2.1.1/drraw.cgi
drraw-2.1.1/drraw.conf
drraw-2.1.1/icons/
...
```

The directory created by this is then renamed to drraw:[10]

```
linux:lib/cgi-bin # mv drraw-2.1.1 drraw
```

drraw.cgi itself requires, apart from Perl, the Perl CGI module (CGI.pm), and the RRDtools, from at least version 1.0.47; nothing will work below version 1.0.36. If your distribution does not include a current version, you should obtain the sources from http://www.rrdtool.org/ and compile them yourself:

```
linux:~ # cd /usr/local/src
linux:local/src # tar xvzf /path/to/rrdtool-1.0.49.tar.gz
...
linux:local/src # cd rrdtool-1.0.49
linux:src/rrdtool-1.0..49 # ./configure
...
linux:src/rrdtool-1.0..49 # make
...
linux:src/rrdtool-1.0..49 # make install
...
linux:src/rrdtool-1.0..49 # make site-perl-install
...
```

The CGI script drraw.cgi uses the Perl module RRDs, which after the installation with make site-perl-install, is found automatically.

19.4.2 Configuration

The drraw configuration is contained in the file drraw.conf:

```
linux:cgi-bin/drraw # egrep -v '^#|^$' drraw.conf
...
%datadirs = ('/var/lib/rrd'  => '[RRDbase]',
            );
$vrefresh = '120';
@dv_def  = ( 'end - 6 hours', 'end - 28 hours', 'end - 1 week', 'end - 1
```

---

[10] A symbolic link would also be possible, but then Apache must be configured so that it follows symbolic links, which is normally not automatically the case.

```
month', 'end - 1 year' );
@dv_name = ( 'Past 6 Hours', 'Past 28 Hours', 'Past Week', 'Past Month',
'Past Year' );
@dv_secs = ( 21600, 100800, 604800, 2419200, 31536000 );
$saved_dir = '/var/lib/drraw/saved';
$tmp_dir = '/var/lib/drraw/tmp';
...
```

The extract shown specifies the RRD repository (here: /var/lib/rrd) as the most important detail, but several directories can also be specified:

```
%datadirs = ('/var/lib/rrd'   => '[RRDbase]',
             '/data/rrd'       => '[RRDdata]',
             );
```

The text in square brackets (e.g., [RRDbase]) appears later on the Web interface, which allows a distinction to be made between various different repositories. The variables @dv_def, @dv_name, and @dv_secs influence the layout and number of graphics.

The configuration shown above generates one graphic more than the standard configuration. This represents the past six hours: the extended statement 'end--6 hours' in @dv_def describes the time period for rrdtool (see man rrdgraph), in @dv_name the representation is given a suitable title with 'Past 6 Hours', and @dv_secs contains the six hours, converted into (21600) seconds, displayed by drraw as a time period in a separate graphic.

The repository must be readable for the user with whose rights the Web server is running, and the directories specified in $saved_dir and $tmp_dir must also be readable. If a user other than www-data runs this, the following command must be adapted accordingly:

```
linux:~ # mkdir -p /var/lib/drraw/{saved,tmp}
linux:~ # chown -R www-data.www-data /var/lib/drraw
```

Data arrives in the temporary directory $temp_dir, whose contents can be deleted at any time, whereas in $saved_dir drraw stores configuration data which the program needs in order to access already created graphics later on. This data must not be lost.

drraw implements a simple access protection in three stages: read-only (0), restricted editing (1), and full access (2). Users logged in to the Web server automatically obtain level 2. Nonauthorized users are treated as guests and assigned level 0. To avoid the hassle with authentication at the beginning, you can grant the user guest full access via the following directive in the configuration file:

```
%users = ( 'guest' => 2 );
```

19.4.3 Practical application

The CGI script in the CGI directory of the Web server can be addressed through the URL `http://nagiosserver/cgi-bin/drraw/drraw.cgi`.

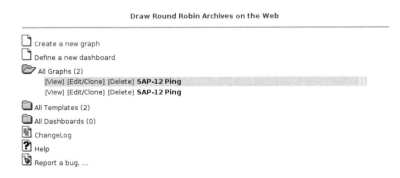

Figure 19.2:
The `ddraw` start menu

New graphics are generated in the menu item **Create a new graph** in the start picture, which is shown in Figure 19.2. The dialog shown in Figure 19.3 allows the appropriate RRD database to be selected. Using a regular expression[11] in the **Data Source filter regexp** field, the data sources available can be further restricted; this expression can also be a simple literal text, such as `sap-12`.

Figure 19.3:
Selecting the data source

Once you have chosen an RRD database, you just need to specify the *round-robin archive* (RRA) to be used. Each of these archives saves data in a partic-

---

[11] POSIX regular expression; see `man 7 regex`.

ular form, processed with a consolidation function: the AVERAGE function averages all measurement data that accumulates in a measurement period, MIN saves only the minimum value of the data in an interval, and MAX saves only the maximum. Since the original data is lost, the archives must be specified when the round-robin database is created; maximum values can only be recalled later if this was taken into account at the time.

If you cannot remember what archives exist, you can display them using the button RRD Info for selected DB. Clicking on the Add DB(s) to Data Sources button takes you to a dialog where you first have to scroll down a bit to reach the item Data Source Configuration (Figure 19.4). There you can fine-tune the desired graph—now or later. You can define your own colors, and whether a line or a surface will be shown. You should only make use of the other possibilities if you are familiar with the concepts of the RRDtools and the way they work.[12]

The **Update** button provides a preview of the finished graphic, which at the same time reveals the rrdtool options used (Figure 19.5). When you save, with **Save Graph**, you obtain a link in the form

```
http://nagiosserver/cgi-bin/drraw/drraw.cgi?Mode=view;Graph=11149589.4932
```

with which the graphic can be accessed at any time. Alternatively you can now find the graphic in the drraw starting menu under **All Graphs**.

Figure 19.4:
Fine–tuning the
graphic
configuration

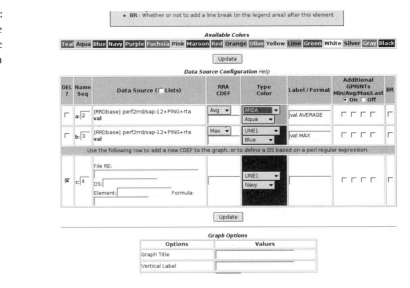

<hr>

[12] There are a number of tutorials on the homepage of the RRDtools author, To-
bias Oetiker, at http://people.ee.ethz.ch/~oetiker/webtools/rrdtool/tut/
index.en.html.

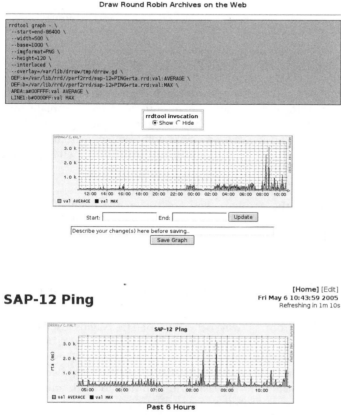

Figure 19.5:
Preview and
specifying the
`rrdtool` options

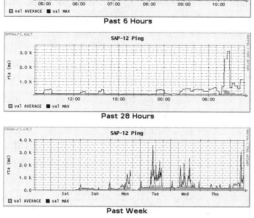

Figure 19.6:
The finished graphic
represents different
time periods

The link mentioned when you save a graphic can be recorded in a `service-extinfo` object, making it directly accessible through the Nagios interface:

```
define serviceextinfo{
    service_description PING
    host            sap-12
    notes_url /nagiosgraph/drraw/drraw.cgi?Mode=view;Graph=11149589.4932
    icon_image      graph.gif
    icon_image_alt  View graphics
}
```

With templates and dashboards, `drraw` includes other features, which cannot be discussed in detail here, for reasons of space. Templates allow several sources of the same type to be shown in the same graphic. What these are can be specified in **Create a new Graph** (see Figure 19.3). Since you can only add one source at a time there, you must click the **Add** button for each separate source, before moving on to the next one.

A dashboard presents a display containing several preview graphics. If you click on one of the graphics, you are shown the detailed representation. The interactive menu **Create a Dashboard** contains brief instructions where you can obtain help on the two features.

19.5   Automated to a Large Extent: NagiosGrapher

NagiosGrapher from Netways, the host of The Nagios Exchange Platform `http://www.nagiosexchange.org/`, is a powerful representation tool for performance data, but already a very powerful one. This also saves data in round-robin databases and uses the RRDtools for processing and representation. It claims to be easy to install and to work automatically to a large extent in contrast to the "competition." The latter promise has so far not been kept; as in Nagiosgraph, you have to configure search patterns in order to interpret the plugin output or performance data correspondingly. The RRD databases are generated by NagiosGrapher automatically; in addition to this, the tool `serviceextinfo` also generates entries.

As soon as it once recognizes the performance data, you don't have to worry any more about integrating it into Nagios. A reload is sufficient to make the `serviceextinfo` entries generated in the meantime usable in Nagios. The entries are created "intelligently," so that if you click on the corresponding icon in the service summary (see Figure 19.7 on page 434), you are taken directly to the graphic display of the performance data.

As far as functionality and installation efforts are concerned, NagiosGrapher lies somewhere between Nagiosgraph and Perf2rrd: the initial configuration needed is somewhat more than for Nagiosgraph, but the possibilities of variations in the graphic output are considerably larger, and you do not have to generate each graphic individually, as is the case with Perf2rrd/drraw.

19.5.1 Installation

In addition to the RRDtools (in version 1.2, at least) and the program `auto-conf`, NagiosGrapher requires a series of Perl modules: `CGI`, `CGI::Carp`, `Calendar::Simple`, `Carp`, `Data::Dumper`, `File::Basename`, `File::Copy`, `GD`, `IO::Handle`, `Image::Magick`, `POSIX`, `RRDs`, `Storable`, `Time::HiRes`, `Time::Local`, and `URI::Escape`.

There are two alternatives for installing them, namely from the packages included in the distribution or from CPAN. On Debian "Etch" and comparable Debian-based systems, you have all the modules if you select the packages `autoconf`, `rrdtool`, `perl-modules`, `libcalendar-simple-perl`, `libgd-gd2-perl`, `perlmagick`, `librrds-perl`, and `liburi-perl` for installation. In other distributions you must search for the above-mentioned modules, preferably using the graphic package installer in the distribution. You can see whether you have installed all the required modules by running `make testdeps` after the `configure` command. Installing each of the most current module versions from the CPAN is done with the command `make fixdeps`.

The NagiosGrapher sources can be obtained from NagiosExchange,[13] and they are unpacked into the directory `/usr/local/src`:

```
linux:~ # cd /usr/local/src
linux:local/src # tar xvjf /path/to/NagiosGrapher-1.6.1.tar.bz2
...
linux:local/src # cd NagiosGrapher-1.6.1
linux:src/NagiosGrapher-1.6.1 # autoconf
```

The command `autoconf` generates a `configure` script. Before you run this, edit the file `config.layout`, which provides various *layouts*. In the NagiosGrapher documentation, this term means the definition of all installation paths that are required.

`config.layout` contains a series of distribution-dependent suggestions that need to be changed in certain aspects in order to comply with the conventions in this book. For this purpose it is best if you copy the section that matches your distribution and rename it to <Layout nagiosbook> and modify a number of entries.[14] For Debian "Etch," the following entries apply (the changed values are shown in bold print):

```
# config.layout
<Layout nagiosbook>
    prefix:             /usr/local/nagios
    nagios_config:      /etc/nagios
```

---

[13] http://www.nagiosexchange.org/42;195
[14] Starting from NagiosGrapher 1.7, the file `config.layout` already contains the entry `<Layout nagiosbook>`.

```
        nagios_config_cgi:    /etc/nagios/cgi.cfg
        nagios_images:        ${prefix}/share/images
        nagios_images_logos:  ${prefix}/share/images/logos
        nagios_folder_cgi:    ${prefix}/sbin
        nagios_contribution:  ${prefix}/contrib
        perl_inc:             ${prefix}/perl/lib
        ng_config:            /etc/nagios
        ng_config_sub:        ${ng_config}/ngraph.d
        ng_daemon:            /var/nagios_grapher
        ng_srvext_file:       /etc/nagios/serviceextinfo.cfg
        ng_srvext_dir:        /etc/nagios/serviceext
        ng_interface_pipe:    /var/nagios/rw/ngraph.pipe
        ng_perffile_path:     /var/nagios/
        ng_logfile:           /var/nagios/ngraph.log
        ng_rrd:               /var/lib/rrd/nagios_grapher
        ng_rrd_font: /usr/share/fonts/truetype/ttf-dejavu/DejaVuSansCondensed
.ttf
     ng_cgi:                  /nagios/cgi-bin
     ng_logos:                /nagios/images/logos
     ng_pid_file:             ${ng_daemon}/nagios_grapher.pid
     init_script_dir:         /etc/init.d
     logrotate_conf_dir:      /etc/logrotate.d
</Layout>
```

The path for the Perl modules defined in the parameter `perl_inc` corresponds in this case to the directory suggested by Ton Voon for the Perl module `Nagios::Plugin` (see page 561).

The new layout is included in the `configure` script:

```
linux:src/NagiosGrapher-1.6.1 # ./configure --with-layout=nagiosbook
...
```

You can run `make testdeps` to check whether all dependencies, especially the ones for the Perl modules, have been met:

```
linux:src/NagiosGrapher-1.6.1 # make testdeps
/usr/bin/perl ./tools/testdeps.pl
Checking Data::Dumper ... found
...
Checking IO::Handle ... found
Checking URI::Escape ... found
Checking Calendar::Simple ... not installed!
make: *** [testdeps] Error 1
```

If an error occurs, as in this example, you must install the appropriate module (here `Calendar::Simple`). This can be done from the CPAN with the command

```
linux:src/NagiosGrapher-1.6.1 # make fixdeps
...
```

For Debian-based distributions, the package naming scheme is quite simple: The Perl module Calendar::Simple is turned into the package lib-calendar-simple-perl, which is installed with apt-get or aptitude:

```
linux:src/NagiosGrapher-1.6.1 # apt-get install libcalendar-simple-perl
...
```

Running make testdeps again shows whether all requirements have now been met.

An already installed NagiosGrapher is updated with make update, since the make install, intended for a new installation, does not take account of already existing configuration files and simply overwrites them.[15] make install creates all the necessary directories, ensures that the correct access permissions are set, and copies all the files to where they should go:

```
linux:src/NagiosGrapher-1.6.1 # make install
mkdir -p /etc/nagios/serviceext
chown -R nagios /etc/nagios/serviceext
mkdir -p /var/lib/rrd/nagios_grapher
chown -R nagios /var/lib/rrd/nagios_grapher
...
================================================================
Just a few steps to run the grapher ...
...
```

The output of make ends with some instructions on the configuration of NagiosGrapher and of Nagios, which we will examine in more detail on page 430 and page 443.

A core component of NagiosGrapher is the daemon collect2.pl, which is started via the startup script nagios_grapher in /etc/init.d:

```
linux:~ # /etc/init.d/nagios_grapher start
```

So that the daemon starts automatically on system start, corresponding symlinks are set in distributions that use the system V init. On Debian/Ubuntu this is done by the system script update-rc.d:

```
linux:~ # update-rc.d nagios_grapher defaults 98
```

OpenSUSE includes the script insserv for this purpose:

```
linux:~ # insserv nagios_grapher
```

[15] Even when running make update, it doesn't hurt for you to back up the configuration files beforehand.

In Fedora this task is performed by `chkconfig`:

```
linux:~ # chkconfig --add nagios_grapher
linux:~ # nagios on
```

19.5.2 Configuration

The configuration file `ngraph.ncfg`

The configuration file `ngraph.ncfg` contains a global `config` section with paths and general settings. This is followed by an include instruction with the parameter `cfg_dir`, which, as in Nagios, integrates all the configuration files located in the directory specified. In contrast to Nagios, the configuration files for NagiosGrapher all end in `.ncfg`.

It can be seen even from a quick glance that the syntax complies with the convention used by Nagios:

```
# /etc/nagios/ngraph.ncfg
define config {
    interface        file
    perffile_path    /var/nagios/
    pipe             /var/nagios/rw/ngraph.pipe
    port             5667
    buffer           1024
    pidfile          /var/nagios_grapher/nagios_grapher.pid

    user             nagios
    group            nagios

    step             300
    heartbeat        AUTO

    rrdpath          /var/lib/rrd/nagios_grapher/
    tmppath          /tmp/nagiosgrapher/

    fontfile         /usr/share/fonts/truetype/ttf-dejavu/DejaVuSansCon
densed.ttf

    serviceext_type  MULTIPLE
    serviceextinfo   /etc/nagios/serviceextinfo.cfg
    serviceext_path  /etc/nagios/serviceext

    url              /nagios/cgi-bin/graphs.cgi
    #notes_url       /wiki/index.php/$HOSTNAME$#$SERVICEDESC$
    notes_url

    nagios_config    /etc/nagios
    cgi_config       /etc/nagios/cgi.cfg
```

```
    icon_image_tag      dot.png' border="0"></a><A TARGET="_blank" HREF="g
raphs.cgi?###URL###"><img src='###IMAGESRC###' '
    icon_image_src      /nagios/images/logos/graph.png
    icon_image_script /nagios/cgi-bin/rrd2-system.cgi?###URL###&start=-5
400&title=Actual&width=20&height=20&type=AVERAGE&only-graph=true
    icon_image_static true

    log_file            /var/nagios/ngraph.log
    log_level           1023

    rrd_color_background ffffff
    rrd_color_font        333333
    rrd_color_arrow       ff0000
    rrd_color_frame       ffffff
    rrd_color_grid
    rrd_color_canvas      ffffff
    rrd_color_shadea      c0c0c0
    rrd_color_shadeb      c0c0c0

    fe_use_browser_all    false
    fe_use_browser_for    nagiosadmin
    fe_use_browser_url    false
    fe_use_timefilter     true
    use_authentication    true
    ...
}

# Includes
cfg_dir=/etc/nagios/ngraph.d
```

The `config` section contains the following parameters:

`interface`

> This defines the type of connection to Nagios. Possible connections are pipe, `network`, and `file`. For the `pipe` type, Nagios and the `collect2.pl` daemon communicate via a named pipe (see the `pipe` parameter); for the `network` type, Nagios sends the performance data via the UDP transport protocol over a network socket (see parameter `port`).

> In contrast to the interface types just described, the `file` type (available from version 1.7) makes use of the template mechanism,[16] which means that Nagios writes the performance data to a file which is periodically evaluated by the daemon `collect2.pl`. This makes possible, for the first time, bulk processing of performance data, thus saving resources. The default interface type is `pipe` up to version 1.6, and `file` from version 1.7.

---

[16] See Section 19.1.1 on page 405

`perffile_path`

> This defines the directory for the file to which Nagios writes all performance data via the template mechanism.

`pipe`

> This defines a named pipe to which Nagios writes data with the program `fifo_write` and from which the collector script `collect2.pl` reads them out again. The named pipe is created automatically by `make install` from version 1.6.1.

`port`

> This specifies the UDP port for the `network` communication type. The default is 5667.

`buffer`

> This determines the size of the buffer for sending performance data via UDP in bytes. The default is 1024 bytes.

`pidfile`

> This defines the file to which NagiosGrapher writes its own process ID on starting.

`user, group`

> These define the user and group with whose permissions the daemon `collect2.pl` runs. Here it makes sense to specify the user and group with whose permissions Nagios is working.

`step`

> This defines the step size in seconds for the RRD database. All values recorded during this period are summarized by the RRDtools in a single value. `step` therefore also describes the smallest time resolution of data in the RRD database. The value only has an effect on newly created RRD databases, and a modification made later on has no effect on existing databases.

`heartbeat`

> The heartbeat defines a time period in seconds, during which the RRD database always expects data. If no measured value at all arrives during this period, NagiosGrapher generates an invalid entry (`nan`, *not a number*).
>
> In order for valid entries to materialize in the above example, at least one measured value must arrive every 600 seconds. Since the resolution is 60 seconds, the database contains ten entries for the period of the "heartbeat." If one of these values is missing, NagiosGrapher simply replaces it with the last valid one. If just one measured value arrives in ten minutes, it will be recorded ten times in the database.

rrdpath

> This specifies the directory for the RRD databases. It must be writable for the user nagios and (along with the database files) readable for the Web server user. The directory is created automatically during the installation of NagiosGrapher.

tmppath

> This defines where NagiosGrapher temporarily saves internal XML files.

fontfile

> This specifies the font file for the font used by the RRDtools for labeling the graphics.

serviceext_type

> This describes how the serviceextinfo objects are created. With the SINGLE type, NagiosGrapher writes everything to the file specified in serviceextinfo.

> Nagios 2.0 can also read directories recursively, and in this case it is better to use the MULTIPLE type. Then NagiosGrapher creates a separate file for each host with the corresponding serviceextinfo object. The directory is specified with the serviceext_path parameter. This must be made known to Nagios through the cfg_dir directive.

url

> This contains the path to the CGI script graphs.cgi from the point of view of the Web server (a path starting from the server root) or of the browser (that is, the complete URL).

notes_url

> NagiosGrapher automatically generates serviceextinfo objects; it is useful to also be able to set the parameter notes_url (Section 16.4.2 from page 366), for example, to generate a service-related link to a Wiki entry.

nagios_config

> This reveals to NagiosGrapher where the standard configuration file of Nagios is located.

cgi_config

> This specifies the Nagios CGI configuration file. NagiosGrapher uses this to find out who, apart from the contact groups, has the right to query information on all hosts.

icon_image_tag

> This parameter corresponds to the entry that is later to be found in the serviceextinfo object as the icon_image parameter. In the serviceextinfo object, NagiosGrapher replaces the text ###URL###

with the host and service names. The entry ###IMAGESRC###, on the other hand, is replaced by NagiosGrapher with the contents of the parameter icon_image_src.

Here the program outwits Nagios with a trick: dot.png is a graphic that is one pixel in size, which is invisible on the screen. To create a second, visible icon, graph.png, around it, a hyperlink is set to the CGI script graphs.cgi.

Normally if you click on an image specified in icon_image, Nagios will take you to the Extended info page, and the graphic can be reached at url (Nagios: notes_url) only with another mouse click. With the trick used here, you can do this directly.

The specification following icon_image_tag must be written on a single line. Figure 19.7 shows the icon graph.png, which is visible on the Nagios interface, thanks to the automatically generated serviceextinfo objects.

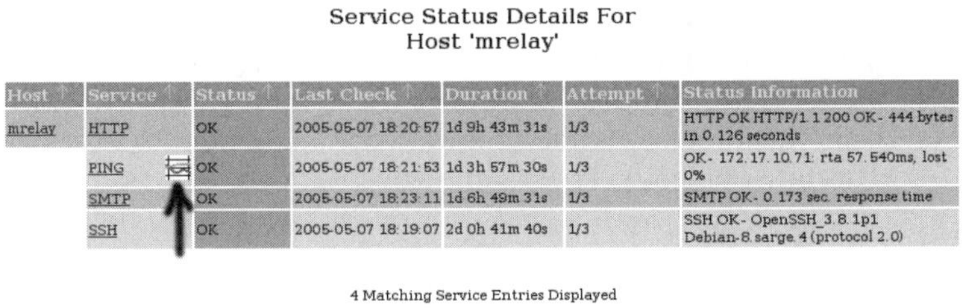

Figure 19.7:
The NagiosGrapher
icon (arrow) in the
Nagios Web interface
indicates a
time-related
evaluation for this
service

Service Status Details For
Host 'mrelay'

Host	Service	Status	Last Check	Duration	Attempt	Status Information
mrelay	HTTP	OK	2005-05-07 18:20:57	1d 9h 43m 31s	1/3	HTTP OK HTTP/1.1 200 OK - 444 bytes in 0.126 seconds
	PING	OK	2005-05-07 18:21:53	1d 3h 57m 30s	1/3	OK - 172.17.10.71: rta 57.540ms, lost 0%
	SMTP	OK	2005-05-07 18:23:11	1d 6h 49m 31s	1/3	SMTP OK - 0.173 sec. response time
	SSH	OK	2005-05-07 18:19:07	2d 0h 41m 40s	1/3	SSH OK - OpenSSH_3.8.1p1 Debian-8.sarge.4 (protocol 2.0)

4 Matching Service Entries Displayed

icon_image_static

> This specifies whether the icon integrated in Figure 19.7 is generated statically or dynamically. Possible values are true (static icon) or false (dynamically generated icon).

icon_image_src

> This specifies a static icon, which NagiosGrapher integrates into icon_image_tag.

icon_image_script

> This defines a script that generates a mini-view of a graph rather than a dynamic icon.

log_file

> This defines the log file to which the NagiosGrapher writes information. If you want log rotation, you have to set it up yourself, as NagiosGrapher does not clean up automatically. Because Nagios requries write permissions for the file, it is better stored in the Nagios var directory (in this case: /var/nagios).

`log_level`

This parameter specifies what information the log file should contain. Possible values are 1 (detected services and values), 2 (performance data delivered by Nagios which has not been recognized by Nagios-Grapher), 4 (program states), 8 (information on the `serviceextinfo` object), 16 (RRD actions), and 32 (input which is read from the pipe). For more extensive debugging, there are the values 64 (details of how regular expressions are parsed) and 128 (advanced information on how the configuration files are parsed).

If you want to log several of these information types, you just add the relevant values together, so the most extensive output is obtained with 255; page 445 shows an example of this. It is recommended that you only use these log levels for debugging purposes, and you should normally use 0 or 4.

`rrd_color_*`

The `rrd_color` options bring color to the Web interface (Figure 19.8): `rrd_color_background` defines the background color for the entire image, `rrd_color_font` the font color, `rrd_color_arrow` the color of the arrow tips, `rrd_color_frame` the frame color for the keys, `rrd_color_grid` the grid color, and `rrd_color_canvas` the background of the diagram itself. `rrd_color_shadea` defines the colors for the top and left of the frame, and `rrd_color_shadeb` does so for the right and bottom of the frame. Colors are specified as RGB values in hexadecimal notation, with a preceding #, as is the norm for Web pages. Changes to these options take effect immediately the next time the Web page is reloaded.

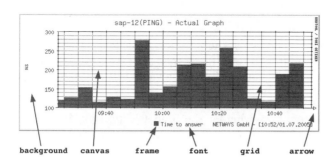

Figure 19.8:
The influence of the
`rrd_color_*` color
options

`fe_use_browser_all`

From version 1.2, NagiosGrapher provides a method of switching from the display of a specific service to that of other services for any host at all. To do this it integrates a selection window into the `graphs.cgi` display (see Figure 19.9).

The value 1 activates the pulldown menus `host` and `service`, 0 hides them.

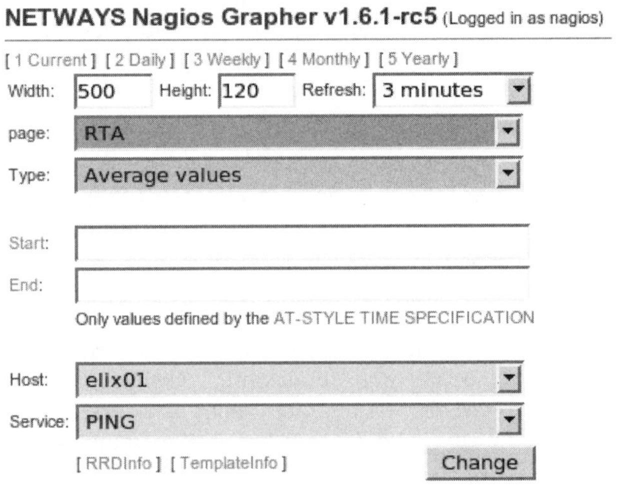

Figure 19.9:
Whether
NagiosGrapher shows
the `host` and
services fields is
determined by the
`fe_use_browser`
parameters

NETWAYS Nagios Grapher v1.6.1-rc5 (Logged in as nagios)

[1 Current] [2 Daily] [3 Weekly] [4 Monthly] [5 Yearly]

Width:	500	Height: 120	Refresh: 3 minutes
page:	RTA		
Type:	Average values		

Start:

End:

Only values defined by the AT-STYLE TIME SPECIFICATION

Host: elix01

Service: PING

[RRDInfo] [TemplateInfo]   Change

`fe_use_browser_for`

This option allows particular users to use the host/service selection. Several users can be specified, separated by commas. So that only the users specified here can see the selection fields for `host` and `service`, `fe_use_browser_all` must also be set to 0 at the same time.

`fe_use_browser_url`

This option allows the selection fields for `host` and `service` to be inserted through the URL `graphs.cgi?browser=1`, provided the value is 1. This is not possible if the value is 0.

`fe_use_timefilter`

This controls whether the time selection via **Start** and **End** appears in the browser menu (see Figure 19.9 on page 436). The value `true` displays the selection, `false` hides it.

`use_authentication`

This defines whether NagiosGrapher should take the result of authentication by Nagios into account or not. The value `true` allows the observer only to access hosts and services for which he is responsible as the contact. The value `false` switches off authentication entirely, so that everyone has access to everything.

The `cfg_dir` configuration parameter already mentioned on page 430 defines a directory containing additional configuration files, in particular the definition of the various graphs:

```
cfg_dir=/etc/nagios/ngraph.d
```

NagiosGrapher examines it recursively for configuration files of any name; they just need to end in `.ncfg`. The parameter must stand outside the `config{}` block; there has to be an = sign between the parameter and the value.

Configuring the graphics—the basic principle

`ngraph` objects are used to define what data is to be extracted and written to an RRD database, but the objects also contain information on the display form. Like Nagios, NagiosGrapher saves the information temporarily in a cache file, which is why the data collection script `collect2.pl` must be restarted after every change to a configuration file with `/etc/init.d/nagios_grapher restart`. `collect2.pl` also updates the object cache when this is done.

During its installation, NagiosGrapher provides a number of templates for `ngraph` objects; these can be found in the subdirectories `standard` and `extra` below `/etc/nagios/ngraph.d/templates`. These templates all end in `.ncfg_disabled` so that they are not considered by NagiosGrapher. In order to use them, the file extension is renamed:

```
nagios@linux:nagios/ngraph.d$ cp \
    templates/standard/check_ping.ncfg_disabled ./check_ping.ncfg
```

The example in `check_ping.ncfg_disabled`, however, only works with `check_ping` and not with `check_icmp` (see page 111). So that NagiosGrapher can graphically display the average response time `rta` (*round trip average*) and the `pl` (*packet loss*) from the performance data of the `check_icmp` plugin,

```
nagios@linux:libexec/nagios$ ./check_icmp -H linux01
OK - linux01: rta 96.387ms, lost 0%| rta=96.387ms;200.000;500.000;0; pl=
0%;40;80;;
```

the following `ngraph` objects are used:

```
# check_icmp.ncfg
...
# Ping Packet loss
define ngraph{
```

```
            service_name            PING
            graph_perf_regex        pl=([0-9]*)%
            graph_value             Loss
            graph_units             %
            graph_legend            Packet Loss
            graph_legend_eol        none
            page                    Packet Loss
            rrd_plottype            LINE2
            rrd_color               ff0000
}
# Ping RTA
define ngraph{
            service_name            PING
            graph_perf_regex        rta=([0-9]*\.[0-9]*)
            graph_value             RTA
            graph_units             ms
            graph_legend            Time to answer
            page                    RTA
            rrd_plottype            AREA
            rrd_color               00a000
}
```

service_name

> This consists of a regular expression,[17] with which the NagiosGrapher identifies the service to be displayed in the data passed on. If the service description in service objects that use the same plugin is provided with the same prefix, one ngraph definition is enough for all: Disk_ matches both Disk_usr, as well as Disk_var or Disk_tmp. In order for this to work, the performance data must be structured identically, which is always the case if the same plugin is used.

graph_perf_regex

> With this regular expression, NagiosGrapher finds the value being searched for in the performance data. The pattern in the round brackets must match the value itself.
>
> If a plugin does not provide any performance data, you can use graph _log_regex instead. The search pattern specified there is applied by NagiosGrapher to the normal text output of the plugin.

graph_value

> The name of the variable in the RRD database must be unique for each service and may not contain empty spaces or special characters (exception: _ is allowed).

graph_units

> This parameter defines the unit of the y axis.

---

[17] Since we have a Perl script on our hands, this is, of course, a Perl regexp.

`graph_legend`

    This contains the key for the variables.

`graph_legend_eol`

    This determines whether and how a line break should be inserted into the legend after the entry for these graphs. Possible values: `left` (line break, line is left-aligned), `right` (line break, line is right-aligned), `center` (line break, line is centrally aligned), `justify` (line break, fully aligned), and `none` (no line break, left-aligned). You can append to all values the number of empty spaces to be added, separated from it by a colon: `none:20` does not create a line break, but the entry is followed by 20 empty spaces.

`graph_legend_max`

    This defines a column width for the legend. Instead of formatting this manually with empty spaces, using `graph_legend_eol`, this parameter specifies how wide the column for a legend entry should be. Entries that are longer are truncated.

`page`

    This optional parameter ensures that NagiosGrapher displays the variables in different diagrams if the standardization does not match. All values which are to be used in a single graphic are given the same `page` entry. For the selection of the "page" to be displayed, the CGI script contains its own `page` entry field (see Figure 19.10).

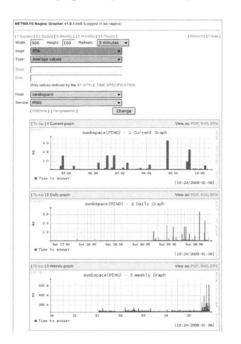

Figure 19.10:
The average response time to pings, represented by NagiosGrapher

For the two `check_icmp` outputs, it is recommended that the percentage of Loss, which is in the value range from 0 to 100, be separated from RTA, which can be several thousand milliseconds.

If you leave out the `page` parameter, both graphs—the one for Packet Loss and that for RTA—are displayed in one graphic.

`rrd_plottype`
> This parameter defines which drawing function the RRDtools should use:
>
> - LINE1: simple line,
> - LINE2: double line,
> - LINE3: extra-fat line,
> - AREA: filled out surface,
> - STACK: adds the current value to the previous one. In this case the display (line or surface) depends on the previous value.

`rrd_color`
> This is the color of the graph in RGB hexadecimal notation (*rrggbb*).

Figure 19.10 shows how NagiosGrapher displays the average response time RTA for the PING service on the host `sap-13`. The respective output page `page` can be selected at the top of the Web form. In addition you can adjust the `width:` and `height:` of an individual graphic, as well as the `Refresh` rate.

Starting with version 1.7, NagiosGrapher also has a zoom function: If you click on one of the graphics in Figure 19.10, you can see it in greater detail. You can select a time period in the diagram with the mouse, and NagiosGrapher will display the diagram for this period after the mouse button has been released.

Advanced options of graphic reprocessing

You may not always want the measured values to be displayed directly. With the *CDEF* feature of the RRDtools you can add new values that are calculated from the ones recorded.

As an example, we will use the output of the `check_disk` plugin (section 7.1, page 158), which determines amount of a file system occupied:

```
DISK OK - free space: /usr 287 MB (19%);| /usr=1225MB;1359;1465;0;1511
```

The used space is shown as an dark grey area, the free capacity as a light grey one. The performance data provides the current used space (1225MB) and uncritical warning limits, as well as the minimum and maximum (the size of the file system). The capacity that is still free is determined as the difference between the maximum and the current occupied space. In addition, the unit of MB is somewhat unfortunate: the graphic would show 10 GB as 10k MB. For this reason you first determine the value that the plugin returns, so that you can then scale it as you wish:

```
# (1) readout current occupancy of hard drive space,
#      but do not show it as a graphic
define ngraph{
    service_name          fs_
    graph_perf_regex      =([.]+)MB;[.]+;[.]+;[.]+;[.]+
    graph_value           disk_used
    graph_units           Bytes
    graph_legend          used space
    rrd_plottype          AREA
    rrd_color             00a000
    hide                  yes
}
```

The regular expression specified after `service_name` matches all service descriptions that start with `fs_` (short for *file system*), that is, `fs_root`, `fs_usr`, `fs_var`, `fs_tmp`, etc. The parameter `hide` ensures that the CGI script does not show the graphs. Instead, NagiosGrapher just stores the data in a database.

In the second step, the values determined are standardized with the RRD feature CDEF:

```
# (2) display used hard drive space in scaled form
define ngraph{
    service_name          fs_
    type                  CDEF
    graph_value           DISK_USED
    graph_legend          used space
    graph_calc            disk_used,1024,1024,*,*
    rrd_plottype          AREA
    rrd_color             666666
    hide                  no
}
```

`type` identifies the entry as a CDEF definition, which calculates new values from already existing ones. `graph_value` must be unique, which is why the entry here is given its own name.

`graph_calc` finally processes the data. This parameter expects the instructions in reverse Polish notation (RPN).[18] In this, the values to be processed are pushed, in turn, onto a stack, to be removed and operated on later.

---

[18] An introduction to RPN can be found at http://people.ee.ethz.ch/~oetiker/
      webtools/rrdtool/tut/rpntutorial.en.html.

Adding $2+3$ is noted in RPN accordingly as $2,3,+$. In the example we multiply the variable defined on page 441, `disk_used`, by 1024^2 so that the result is in bytes. `hide no` now ensures that this value is displayed.

To display available space according to the same pattern, we first determine the entire space available (`disk_max`), which NagiosGrapher should not display, calculate the difference between `disk_max` and the above `disk_used` value, and convert the result to bytes:

```
# (3) defining the space available,
#     but not displaying it in the graphic
define ngraph{
    service_name        fs_
    graph_perf_regex    =[.]+MB;[.]+;[.]+;[.]+;([.]+)
    graph_value         disk_max
    graph_legend        max space
    rrd_plottype        LINE2
    rrd_color           0000a0
    hide                yes
}
# (4) calculate and display free space
define ngraph{
    service_name        fs_
    type                CDEF
    graph_value         DISK_MAX
    graph_legend        free space
    rrd_plottype        STACK
    rrd_color           CCCCCC
    graph_calc          disk_max,disk_used,-,1024,1024,*,*
    hide                no
}
```

The corresponding formula is $(\text{disk\_max}-\text{disk\_used})\times 1024^2$. The plot type STACK ensures that the value determined from the previous `disk_used` value is placed on top of this. Figure 19.11 shows a corresponding output: The lower part of the screen represents the current used space on the file system for the past six hours and the past day and week, and the top part shows the remaining free hard drive space. The graph also contains a monthly and a yearly view, not shown here.

At this point it should again be emphasized that with this definition, NagiosGrapher automatically records all services that begin with `fs_` and are matched by the search pattern, writes the data to an RRD database, and generates a corresponding `serviceextinfo` entry, which appears automatically in the Web interface after a Nagios reload (see Figure 19.7 on page 434).

After changes have been made to the configuration file `ngraph.ncfg`, the file collector `collect2.pl` must also be restarted:

```
linux:~ # /etc/init.d/nagios_grapher restart
```

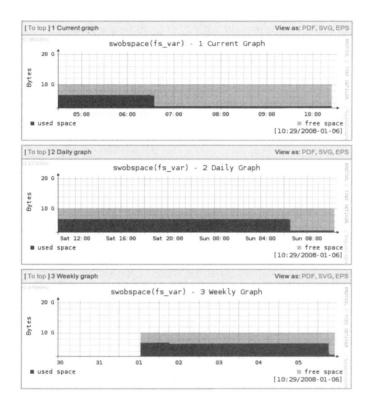

Figure 19.11:
Displaying the
calculated load data

Nagios configuration

Nagios passes on data for NagiosGrapher through the command interface,
that is, each individual result leads to an external command being started.
Correspondingly, the Nagios main configuration file contains the following
parameter:

```
# /etc/nagios/nagios.cfg
...
process_performance_data=1
service_perfdata_command=process-service-perfdata
...
```

The definition of the command object process-service-perfdata—
which is best achieved by creating a separate file with the name process_
service_perfdata_ngraph.cfg—depends on the interface type used.

For interface pipe, the program fifo_write is used, whereas for interface network, NagiosGrapher requires the program udpecho.

The definition of the command with fifo_write is as follows:

```
# process_service_perfdata_ngraph.cfg
...
define command{
   command_name   process-service-perfdata
   command_line   /usr/local/nagios/contrib/fifo_write /var/nagios/rw/ngr
aph.pipe '$HOSTNAME$\t$SERVICEDESC$\t$SERVICEOUTPUT$\t$SERVICEPERFDATA$\
n' 3

}
...
```

process-service-perfdata calls the script fifo_write.pl, which is given three arguments as parameters: the named pipe, a string with the performance details, and a timeout in seconds. The latter ensures that the script aborts the action if the data cannot be written within three seconds. The command_line must, as usual, be writen on one line.

For the program udpecho, the definition of the command is somewhat simpler:

```
# process_service_perfdata_ngraph.cfg
...
define command{
   command_name   process-service-perfdata
   command_line   /usr/local/nagios/contrib/udpecho
}
...
```

udpecho does not need any parameters: It retrieves the required information from the environment variables NAGIOS_HOSTNAME, NAGIOS_SERVICE-DESC, NAGIOS_SERVICEOUTPUT, and NAGIOS_SERVICEPERFDATA. Nagios has to make these available with enable_environment_macros=1 (see page 592) so that udpecho can provide NagiosGrapher with usable data.[19]

For the file interface type, the command process-service-perfdata has another meaning: It is not called for every check result, but rather shifts the file into which Nagios writes all performance data via the template mechanism:

```
# process_service_perfdata_ngraph.cfg
...
define command{
   command_name   process-service-perfdata
```

[19] Environment macros are described in Section D.1.8 from page 631.

```
   command_line  mv /var/nagios/service-perfdata /var/nagios/service-per
fdata.$TIMET$
}
...
```

The current timestamp is simply appended to the file name `service-perf-data`. The daemon `collect2.pl` searches for all files called `service-perfdata.time_stamp` from the specified directory and processes these.

What data is written to the file by Nagios is specified by `service_perfdata_file_template` in `nagios.cfg`:

```
# /etc/nagios/nagios.cfg
...
service_perfdata_file_processing_command=process-service-perfdata
service_perfdata_file=/var/nagios/service-perfdata
service_perfdata_file_template=$HOSTNAME$\t$SERVICEDESC$\t$SERVICEOUTPUT
$\t$SERVICEPERFDATA$\t$TIMET$
service_perfdata_file_mode=a
service_perfdata_file_processing_interval=60
...
```

Compared to the variation with `fifo_write.pl`, Nagios now also passes on a timestamp for each check. This is necessary because the data are not processed immediately, but periodically at intervals of `service_perfdata_file_processing_interval`—this is 60 seconds in our example.

If you want to squeeze a little more performance out of this, you can select a temporary file system such as `/dev/shm` for the `service-perfdata*` files. The file then is not written to the hard drive, but remains in the main memory of the Nagios server.

As usual, changes to the Nagios configuration require a reload:

```
linux:~ # /etc/init.d/nagios reload
```

The success of this can be clearly observed in the log file if you set the loglevel to 255 (see page 435).[20] For the sake of clarity we will omit the timestamp at the beginning of the line:

```
CFG: buffer => '1024'
CFG: cgi_config => '/etc/nagios/cgi.cfg'
...
PRG: Starting up collect2.pl (PID: 25003) ...
PRG: using UDP socket (port: 5667)
...
NET: got udp message from localhost:32783
```

---

[20] In general: $2^n - 1$ with $n \geqslant 8$

```
PIPE: swobspace     PING    OK - 192.168.1.9: rta 0.104ms, lost 0%  rt a
=0.104ms;200.000;500.000;0; pl=0%;20;60;;
REGEX: 2 blocks for 'PING' found.
REGEX: graph_value=RTA
REGEX: output=perfdata
REGEX: regex=m/rta=([0-9]*[0-9]*)/i
REGEX: perfdata=rta=0.104ms;200.000;500.000;0; pl=0%;20;60;;
REGEX: match=0.104
REGEX: graph_value=Loss
REGEX: output=perfdata
REGEX: regex=m/.*pl=([0-9]*)/i
REGEX: perfdata=rta=0.104ms;200.000;500.000;0; pl=0%;20;60;;
REGEX: match=0
VALUES: [swobspace][PING]: RTA=0.104 Loss=0
RRD: rrdtool update /var/lib/rrd/nagios_grapher/swobspace/f66ffe61c885 d
e2d8b6d0c41ff444b39.rrd --template=RTA:Loss N:0.104:0
...
```

The label PRG identifies program states, such as the restart here. PIPE re-
produces in full all the data taken from the named pipe (host name, service
description, plugin output, and performance data, each separated by a tab).
REGEX shows how the search for matching entries takes place and how the
values are extracted from them. RRD reveals the commands performed with
rrdtool and VALUES shows the recognized values(PING).

19.6   Smooth Plotting with PNP

PNP is not PerfParse—with this recursive acronym, which is an allusion to
the PerfParse tool (not described in this book)—the authors of PNP, Jörg
Linge and Hendrik Bäcker, are clearly heralding the virtues of their own
tool for processing performance data: It is allegedly very easy to install (in
contrast to PerfParse) and can be used (almost) without configuration, yet
provides extensive configuration options for advanced usage.

Besides providing the usual graphs for a specific check, PNP also creates
an overview of all graphs belonging to one host. An AJAX-based input field
allows host names to be typed in. The names are auto-completed during
input, and a match list of alternative completions is displayed. The graphics
have a sophisticated appearance and can be exported to PDF format.

PNP takes the performance data directly from the area reserved for the
plugin output, that is, only plugins that display performance data in the
standard format can be used. In contrast to NagiosGrapher, no data can
be extracted from the normal text output. To compensate for this slight
limitation, PNP outputs the performance data for all plugins automatically.
If PNP does not recognize the plugin, it uses a generic template.

On the PNP homepage[21] you can find addresses of English mailing lists[22] and a German-language forum, where you can, however, ask questions in English.[23] The English homepage is /cmdhttp://www.pnp4nagios.org/pnp/.

The following description refers to PNP version 0.4; older versions do not have all the features described here.

19.6.1 Installation

The requirements for installation are quite minimal: Apache, Perl (without any special modules), PHP4 from version 4.3.0 or PHP5, and all the RRDtools.[24] If possible you should install the Perl module RRDs from the Perl package included with your distribution (e. g., `librrds-perl` in Debian). The Perl script `process_perfdata.pl`, which forwards Nagios performance data to PNP, then accesses the RRD databases directly, without running an external program.

The PNP source code is downloaded from the homepage[25] and is unpacked appropriately in the directory `/usr/local/src`:

```
linux:~ # cd /usr/local/src/
linux:local/src # tar xvzf /path/to/pnp-0.4.tar.gz
...
linux:local/src # cd pnp-0.4
linux:src/pnp-0.4 # ./configure --sysconfdir=/etc/pnp
...
```

Finally, `make all` compiles the necessary C programs, and `make install` installs PNP in full. In the `configure` command, `--sysconfdir=/etc/pnp` allows for the later installation of the configuration examples in `/etc/pnp`, in accordance with the conventions used in this book. Other `configure` options are shown with `./configure --help`.

19.6.2 The standard configuration

During the installation of PNP a variety of data is placed in the configuration directory (in this case `/etc/pnp`), including `config.php`, the configuration file for the Web interface. There you must first check to see if the paths to `rrdtool` and to the performance data directory are correctly set:

---

[21] http://www.pnp4nagios.org/pnp/
[22] https://lists.sourceforge.net/mailman/listinfo/pnp4nagios-users (generally on PNP usage) and https://lists.sourceforge.net/mailman/listinfo/pnp4nagios-devel (feature requests, bugs, patches, and the like)
[23] http://nagios-portal.de/forum/board.php?boardid=58
[24] http://www.rrdtool.org/, see also page 421.
[25] http://www.pnp4nagios.org/pnp/

```
# /etc/pnp/config.php
...
$conf['rrdtool'] = "/usr/bin/rrdtool"
$conf['rrdbase'] = "/usr/local/nagios/share/perfdata"
...
```

/etc/pnp also contains example configurations for the data collector pro-
cess_perfdata.pl, in the files process_perfdata.cfg-sample and rra.
cfg-sample. Neither of these are absolutely essential: PNP also functions
correctly without any adjustments. But in order to use the data collector
you need to rename the files process_perfdata.cfg and rra.cfg and
modify them accordingly. If the Perl module RRDs is installed, then it is
activated in the file process_perfdata.cfg with USE_RRDS=1:

```
# /etc/pnp/process_perfdata.cfg
TIMEOUT = 5
USE_RRDs = 1
RRDPATH = /usr/local/nagios/share/perfdata
RRDTOOL = /usr/bin/rrdtool
CFG_DIR = /etc/pnp/
RRA_CFG = /etc/pnp/rra.cfg
RRA_STEP = 60
LOG_FILE = /var/nagios/pnp-perfdata.log
LOG_LEVEL = 0
```

The second change (here in bold type) to the sample file refers to the Nagios
directory for log files, which in this book is named /var/nagios.

rra.cfg is used as a template for the RRD databases to be newly created. If
an existing database is to be modified, it must be deleted; but then all existing data will be lost. The template is a good compromise between length of
storage and time resolution: This causes data with a time resolution of one
hour to be stored for up to four years, such an RRD database that is about
400 KB in size. Information on settings for RRD databases is provided by
the command man rrdcreate.

In the directory /etc/pnp there is also the configuration file npcd.cfg for
the *Nagios Performance Data C Daemon* npcd and a subdirectory check_
commands for so-called *custom templates*. Both will be discussed on page
453.

Adjusting the Nagios configuration

There are a number of ways in which Nagios can pass on performance data
to the PNP data collector process_perfdata.pl. The simplest way is for
the system to run a separate program for each event, called service-perf-
data-pnp. To do this, performance data processing is switched on in the
file /etc/nagios/nagios.cfg with the parameter process_performance

_data, and the command to be executed is defined with `service_perf-data_command`:

```
# /etc/nagios/nagios.cfg
...
illegal_macro_output_chars='~$&|"<>
# -- perfdata
process_performance_data=1
service_perfdata_command=service-perfdata-pnp
...
```

The performance data of various plugins contains names that are set in single quotes. So that these do not get lost in the plugin output, a single quote may *not* be used in the parameter `illegal_macro_output_chars`.[26]

The command `service-perfdata-pnp` runs `process_perfdata.pl`:

```
# /etc/nagios/global/commands/service-perfdata-pnp.cfg
define command{
    command_name service-perfdata-pnp
    command_line /usr/bin/perl /usr/local/nagios/libexec/process_perfdat
a.pl
}
```

The embedded Perl interpreter ePN (see Appendix G on page 669) cannot execute this Perl script, which is why it is called explictly with `/usr/bin/perl`. If ePN is not compiled into Nagios, you can leave out the `/usr/bin/perl` path.

The performance data is taken here by `process_perfdata.pl` via the environment variable `NAGIOS_SERVICEPERFDATA`, so that environment variables in general must not be switched off.[27]

19.6.3 The PNP Web interface

If you run `http://nagios_server/nagios/pnp/index.php` you will be taken to the PNP overview page (see Figure 19.12). This displays the data of the first host, in alphabetical order, that is found by PNP. The input field at the top right is implemented with AJAX and shows a hit list, matching the text entered so far, from which the desired host is selected. The accompanying overview page presents all services in a 24-hour view.

This can also be accessed directly via `http://nagiosserver/nagios/pnp/index.php?host=hostname`. If you replace *hostname* with elix01, you will arrive at the overview page for the host of that name (Figure 19.12).

---

[26] Performance data is provided by the macro `$SERVICEPERFDATA$`; see page 628.

[27] This has only been possible since Nagios 3.0, with the `enable_environment_macros` parameter (see page 592). More on environment variables in Section D.1.8 from page 631.

Figure 19.12:
All services of
elix01 on one page

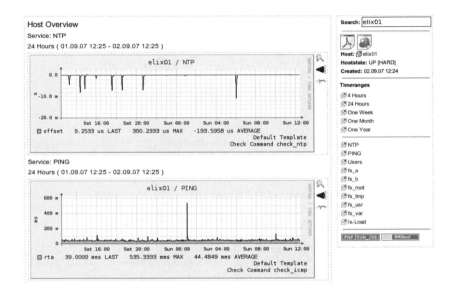

A mouse click on a service graph or on the accompanying link on the right in the overview causes the selected display to be shown in a different time resolution (Figure 19.13): four hours, one day, and (not shown) one week, one month, and one year. The periods presented here by PNP are defined in the configuration file config.php:

```
$views[0]["title"] = "4 Hours";
$views[0]["start"] = ( 60*60*4 );

$views[1]["title"] = "24 Hours";
$views[1]["start"] = ( 60*60*24 );

$views[2]["title"] = "One Week";
$views[2]["start"] = ( 60*60*24*7 );

$views[3]["title"] = "One Month";
$views[3]["start"] = ( 60*60*24*30 );

$views[4]["title"] = "One Year";
$views[4]["start"] = ( 60*60*24*365 );
```

The specific title labels can be chosen freely, so you could also use text in other languages. The images themselves cannot be localized, however.

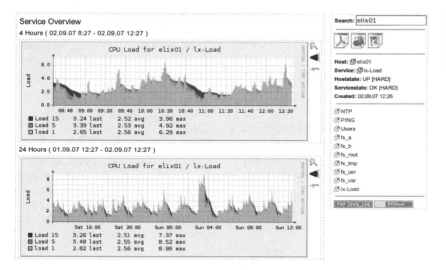

Figure 19.13:
System load in PNP:
host elix01, service
lx-load

The **start** details specify for how many seconds *before* a defined reference point the graphic will begin. Normally the current time is used as a reference point, but this can also be selected using the calendar included. To do this, you click the calendar icon (see Figure 19.14), select the end time after **Time** with a mouse click, and then select the day. Selecting the time takes some getting used to: One click increases the value displayed by one, and holding down the (Shift) key at the same time reduces the time value displayed. You can also hold down the left mouse button and drag the mouse to the left to increase the value, or drag to the right to decrease it.

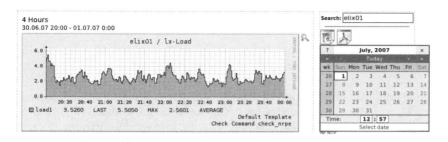

Figure 19.14:
PNP's calendar
function

In order to display a specific service directly, just add the detail svc=*servicename* to the URL, so that you have http://*nagiosserver*/nagios/ pnp/index.php?host=*hostname*&svc=*servicename*.

A particular feature of PNP is that each graphic can be addressed directly, without using HTML or PHP pages. You require the two optional parameters display and view: http://*nagiosserver*/nagios/pnp/index.php ?host=*host*&svc=*servicename*&display=image&view=0. display can currently handle only the value image, and for view you enter the index defined in config.php: view=0 refers to the time period that was defined there with $views[0]["start"] (so this is the default, with a four-hour overview).

Integrating PNP into the Nagios Web interface

To display a single service directly from the Nagios Web interface, in Nagios 3 you need to integrate the following URL as action_url in the service definition:

```
# Nagios 3
define service {
    hostname              hostname
    service_description   servicename
    ...
    action_url            /pnp/index.php?host=$HOSTNAME$&srv=$SERVICEDESC$
}
```

In Nagios 2.x you require the object serviceextinfo to achieve the same purpose:

```
# Nagios 2.x
define serviceextinfo {
    hostname              hostname
    service_description   servicedesc
    ...
    action_url            /pnp/index.php?host=$HOSTNAME$&srv=$SERVICEDESC$
}
```

19.6.4 Bulk processing of performance data

The standard configuration discussed calls the command defined in service_perfdata_command for each check. Since the embedded Perl interpreter ePN (see Appendix G on page 669) cannot execute process_perfdata.pl, Nagios has to restart the Perl interpreter for every service whose performance data is to be processed. This takes a toll on resources and, depending on the capabilities of the host and the number of services to be processed, has a negative influence on the performance of Nagios (to measure Nagios performance, see Appendix F from page 653). Nagios then really is brought to its knees, which means that the latency time that passes between the planned starting point and the actual start of a check increases considerably, and Nagios's timetable (the *scheduling*) gets out of control.

One solution to this is offered by PNP's bulk mode in combination with the *Nagios Performance Data C Daemon* (NPCD).[28] When this is used, Nagios writes the performance data—formatted by templates (defined in `service_perfdata_file_template`)—to a file that is regularly renamed by a command in `service_perfdata_file_processing_command`. NPCD now runs the Perl script `process_perfdata.pl` only once for each file.

`service_perfdata_file_template` defines the format in which the data is written to the file specified in `service_perfdata_file`:[29]

```
# /etc/nagios/nagios.cfg
...
service_perfdata_file_template=DATATYPE::SERVICEPERFDATA\tTIMET::$TIMET$
\tHOSTNAME::$HOSTNAME$\tSERVICEDESC::$SERVICEDESC$\tSERVICEPERFDATA::$SE
RVICEPERFDATA$\tSERVICECHECKCOMMAND::$SERVICECHECKCOMMAND$\tHOSTSTATE::
$HOSTSTATE$\tHOSTSTATETYPE::$HOSTSTATETYPE$\tSERVICESTATE::$SERVICEST
ATE$\tSERVICESTATETYPE::$SERVICESTATETYPE$

service_perfdata_file=/var/nagios/service-perfdata
service_perfdata_file_mode=a
service_perfdata_file_processing_interval=30
service_perfdata_file_processing_command=service-perfdata-npcd
...
```

`service_perfdata_file_mode` specifies how Nagios handles the file: The value a stands for *append*. Thus Nagios appends new results to an already existing file. Every 30 seconds (as specified in `service_perfdata_file_processing_interval`) the *File Processing Command* `service-perfdata-npcd` starts. It shifts the file, renames it, and adds the current timestamp, using the Nagios macro `$TIMET$`:

```
define command{
   command_name  service-perfdata-npcd
   command_line  /bin/mv /var/nagios/service-perfdata /var/nagios/perfsp
ool/service-perfdata-$TIMET$
}
```

Renaming and shifting doesn't use up any time. So Nagios can immediately resume its normal tasks and leave further processing of performance data to the external NPCD daemon. NPCD has its own configuration file, in `npcd.cfg`, which is copied during installation to the directory `/etc/pnp`:

```
user=nagios
group=nagios
```

---

[28] The C in the name alludes to the considerably faster performance speed of a C program compared to a Perl script, for which Nagios has to restart the Perl interpreter each time.

[29] This is just a single line, which has been line-wrapped here for display purposes.

```
log_type=syslog
log_level=0
perfdata_spool_dir=/var/nagios/perfspool/
perfdata_file_run_cmd=/usr/local/nagios/libexec/process_perfdata.pl
perfdata_file_run_cmd_args=-b
npcd_max_threads=1
```

The first two entries specify with which user and which group membership NPCD is to be started. The daemon can currently only log its work in the syslog. Future versions should also allow this to be written to a separate file. `log_level=0` ensures that NPCD itself behaves quietly and passes on all errors only to the syslog daemon.

The parameter `perfdata_spool_dir` renames the directory to be monitored. It must already exist; the NPCD does not create it automatically. Thanks to the argument -b given in `perfdata_file_run_cmd_args`, `process_perfdata.pl` starts in bulk mode.

The NPCD installs itself during the "make install" command for PNP to the directory /usr/local/nagios/bin. Running `make install-init` causes an additional startup script to be placed in /etc/init.d, in which you have to check the path to the configuration file:

```
...
CONF=/etc/pnp/npcd.cfg
...
```

With the help of this, the daemon is started with the following command:

```
linux:~ # /etc/init.d/npcd start
```

Depending on your distribution, the init script in the rc directories is linked to the relevant runlevel:

```
linux:~ # ln -s /etc/init.d/npcd.sh /etc/init.d/rc2.d/S99npcd
linux:~ # ln -s /etc/init.d/npcd.sh /etc/init.d/rc3.d/S99npcd
linux:~ # ln -s /etc/init.d/npcd.sh /etc/init.d/rc5.d/S99npcd
```

19.6.5 How should the graphic appear?

The appearance of PNP graphics is determined by templates. The examples included are located in the directory /usr/local/nagios/share/pnp/templates.dist. You should not touch these, as they will be overwritten at the next update. The directory `templates` is intended for some templates. PNP takes the name of the check that was defined in the `command_name` and searches here for a matching template called *command_name*.php.

If PNP cannot find this either in ./templates or in ./templates.dist, it uses the default template default.php.

Sometimes there is already a suitable template in templates.dist (for example, check_ping.php for the plugin check_icmp), the name of which does not match the command name (in the case of check_icmp, we have defined this as command_name check_icmp). Then you must create a symlink in ./templates to the desired file:

```
linux:~ # cd /usr/local/nagios/share/pnp/templates
linux:pnp/templates # ln -s ../templates.dist/check_ping.php \
check_icmp.php
```

A simple template which can be used for all plugins that transmit a simple response time is response.php:

```
<?php
#
# For all plugins that provide response times
# $Id: response.php 53 2006-06-07 07:16:50Z linge $
#

$opt[1] = "--vertical-label \"Response Time\"  \
          --title \"Response Time For $hostname / $serviced
esc\" ";

$def[1] =   "DEF:var1=$rrdfile:$DS[1]:AVERAGE " ;
$def[1] .= "AREA:var1#00FF00:\"Response Times \" " ;
$def[1] .= "LINE1:var1#000000:\"\" " ;
$def[1] .= "GPRINT:var1:LAST:\"%3.4lg %s$UNIT[1] LAST \" ";
$def[1] .= "GPRINT:var1:MAX:\"%3.4lg %s$UNIT[1] MAX \" ";
$def[1] .= "GPRINT:var1:AVERAGE:\"%3.4lg %s$UNIT[1] AVERAGE \" ";
?>
```

The variable $opt[1] defines the options for rrdtool, and the variable $def[1] defines the RRD graph. If you want to create your own templates, you will need to get involved with rrdtool in more detail. The definition of a graphic is explained in detail by man rrdgraph, and further information can be found on the homepage.[30]

Custom Templates

PNP is based on the name of the defined command object. If this is not informative enough, as in the case of command_name check_nrpe, then so-called *custom templates* in the directory /etc/pnp/check_commands are used. These must contain the name of the original command, however, which in our example is check_nt.cfg:

[30] http://www.rrdtool.org/

```
#
# Adapt the Template if check_command should not be the PNP Template
#
# check_command check_nt!MEMUSE!80%!90%
# _____0_____|    |    |  |
# _____1_____|    |  |
# _____2_____|  |
# _____3_____|
#
CUSTOM_TEMPLATE = 0,1
#
```

If check_nt is not given MEMUSE as the first parameter, the actual command for the plugin check_nt, only this parameter will differentiate whether memory usage or CPU load, for instance, is measured. The parameter CUSTOM_TEMPLATE puts together the command that PNP uses when searching for templates: The example below puts together check_nt (entry number 0) and MEMUSE (entry number 1). This means that PNP will search for a template with the name check_nt_MEMUSE.php. With CUSTOM_TEMPLATE = 1, PNP would search for MEMUSE.php. A suitable symlink is now set in the directory ./templates:

```
linux:~ # cd /usr/local/nagios/share/pnp/templates
linux:pnp/templates # ln -s ../templates.dist/check_nt_mem.php\
check_nt_MEMUSE.php
```

19.7 Other Tools and the Limits of Graphic Evaluation

Apart from the tools introduced here, http://www.nagiosexchange.org/ provides further tools for the graphic evaluation of performance data. Many of these are also based on the RRDtools and round-robin databases, the consequence of which is that they are not much use for exact evaluations over several years, just like the ones described here.

Several tools, such as the current APAN[31] version, save their data in an SQL database, thus enabling long-term statistics without data loss.

PerfParse[32] is very extensive, and it stores data in a MySQL or PostgreSQL database and also includes its own wide range of evaluation tools. Because it uses various current libraries which are not included in every distribution, the installation hurdles are quite high. Nevertheless, those for whom

---

[31] http://apan.sf.net/.
[32] http://perfparse.sf.net/

the RRD-based tools do not offer enough should look to see if the PerfParse tools can provide the missing functionality that is required.

For all the options it offers, the graphical display of Nagios performance data also has its limits. If you check WAN connections with a ping to a remote host and measure the average response time, all the pretty graphics don't mean much if the check interval is only every five minutes. You will receive only a momentary snapshot every five minutes, which does not provide any serious clues to the traffic load of the connection over a period of time.

To be able to sensibly assess the load of a Unix computer reported by a plugin every one, five, and 15 minutes, the check interval should be one minute. Less critical data are such things as used hard drive space or temperature. Equally noncritical is the display of network traffic, for which the plugin displays the values as a counter. RRD-based tools can automatically detect the difference between two measurements and display them; it makes no difference here whether the check interval is one, two, or five minutes; no data is lost.

If the measuring precision of Nagios leaves something to be desired, you can deploy other tools in parallel, such as Cricket[33] or Cacti.[34] If the external tool—like Munin[35]—works with RRD databases, you can check these for critical values, so that they are included in the sophisticated Nagios notification system. Alternatively the external tool can provide an interface with which recorded data can be further processed. These can be passed on as a passive test result to Nagios, for example using NSCA (see Chapter 14).

But an additional tool always has the disadvantage of adding to the configuration effort. Whether this is justified, or whether Nagios performance monitoring is sufficient, depends on the information required in a particular situation.

---

[33] http://cricket.sourceforge.net/
[34] http://www.cacti.net/
[35] http://munin.projects.linpro.no/

Part IV

Special Applications

20

Monitoring Windows Servers

You don't always deal with a homogeneous server landscape consisting of just Linux or Linux/Unix computers. As long as you are just monitoring pure network services, operating systems make no difference. But if you want to query local, non-network-capable resources, that is a different matter altogether.

With Unix-based systems such as Mac OS X, you can normally use the tools described so far (local plugins, NRPE, NSCA). In Windows you have to find other solutions. To some extent, local plugins can be run and/or compiled in an environment emulating Unix (for example, Cygwin[1]).

Because of the different philosophies of the operating system families, there are peculiarities as well, features in one operating system that are not comparable with anything in the other operating system. So although the Windows event log fulfils much the same purpose as syslog in Unix, it is queried

---

[1] http://www.cygwin.com/

in a completely different way, seen from a technical point of view. Here you cannot simply compile the Unix plugin in Windows and then use it.

One monitoring approach for Windows servers is to use SNMP, for which Microsoft includes a native implementation that just needs to be installed. Since the SNMP query of a Windows agent does not differ in principle from that of other SNMP agents, we refer you to Chapter 11, page 227. The Microsoft implementation, however, does not always work reliably where the display of figures—particularly CPU load and hard drive space—is concerned.

Figure 20.1:
`check_nt` queries
local Windows
resources about the
NSClient mechanism.

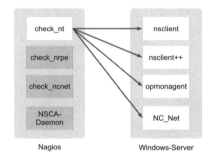

Nagios   Windows-Server

But local Windows resources can also be queried if you install a service on the Windows server that can be addressed over the network. Previously, only a single tool was available, NSClient, but today you have a choice of various programs: NSClient, NSClient++, OpMon Agent, or NC_Net. For all of them, basic parameters such as CPU and hard disk load, memory usage or Windows counters are queried with the `check_nt` plugin (see Figure 20.1), which is one of the standard Nagios plugins.

Figure 20.2:
`check_nrpe` uses
the NRPE mechanism
to execute checks via
NSClient++, OpMon
Agent, and NRPE_NT.

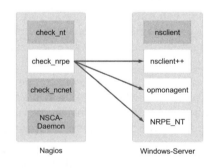

Nagios   Windows-Server

In addition, NSClient++ and OpMon Agent support NRPE (see Chapter 10 from page 213). Querying the locally installed plugins is done by `check_nrpe` (Figure 20.2).

NC_Net in turn allows passive checks, the results of which are sent to the Nagios server by the NSCA (Chapter 14, page 299). If you query the data with `check_ncnet` (Figure 20.3) instead of the standard plugin `check_nt`, an extended set of commands is available (Section 20.3.3, page 480).

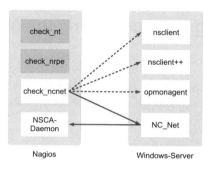

Figure 20.3:
`check_ncnet` allows passive checks.

Finally, there is also a purely NRPE service for Windows: NRPE_NT, which is configured the same as in Unix. Due to the additional NRPE functionality of NSClient++ and OpMon Agent, however, this has lost some of its significance.

20.1 Agent-less Checks via WMI

With *Windows Management Instrumentation*, or WMI for short, Microsoft provides an interface that allows network-wide querying of system properties, assuming that the user doing the query has sufficient permissions. The WMI query is made from a central Windows system; NRPE is used for communication between the Nagios server and the WMI proxy (Figure 20.4). Just a single Windows server is required, on which one NRPE service and all the desired plugins are installed in the form of WMI scripts—although to do this, you have to be familiar with the Microsoft WMI world.

Figure 20.4:
Using the WMI interface with Nagios

Extensive configuration examples can be found at the NagiosExchange[2] under Categories | Check Plugins | Operating Systems | Windows | Windows NRPE, for instance, under the entry wmi agentless plugins.[3] We will not go into further details of the WMI interface here.

20.2 Installing and Configuring the Additional Services

In contrast to the WMI approach, the additional services NSClient, NSClient++, OpMon Agent, and NC_Net must be installed on every single Windows server.

20.2.1 NSClient

NSClient, as the oldest package, has been widely tested and is in widespread use, but it is no longer being actively developed. The last current version is from October 2003; the package can be downloaded from the Nagios Exchange.[4] It also runs in Windows NT, Windows 2000 and Windows XP.

For Windows 2003, in particular Windows 2003 R2, the original package is no longer suitable, because numerous error messages in the form

```
PDH.dll Collect CPU - ERROR:...
```

land in the event log, which lengthens the execution time considerably. At the NagiosExchange a recompiled version can be found in the package nsclient_-_no_pdh.zip,[5] which does not have this problem.

For the NSClient installation, you unpack the archive nsclient_201.zip or nsclient_-_no_pdh.zip. This creates subdirectories named according to the architecture: Win_NT4_Bin for Windows NT and Win_2k_XP_Bin for Windows 2000 and higher. Copy the contents of the appropriate folder to the directory C:\Programs\NSClient and install NSClient from there as a service:

```
C:\Programs\NSClient> pNSClient.exe /install
C:\Programs\NSClient> net start nsclient
```

---

[2] http://www.nagiosexchange.org
[3] http://www.nagiosexchange.org/66;235
[4] http://www.nagiosexchange.org/49;65
[5] http://www.nagiosexchange.org/49;508

Running pNSClient.exe /install installs the service, and the switch /uninstall removes the service again. You should make sure that the operating system starts automatically using the services management.

NSClient has two parameters: port and password, with the defaults 1248 (port) and none (password). The values can only be changed (with regedit) in the registry under HKEY_LOCAL_MACHINE\SOFTWARE\NSClient\Parms.

20.2.2 NC_Net

NC_Net, by Tony Montibello, is one of the successors to NSClient, and its calls are also compatible with NSClient. Thus, NSClient can simply be replaced with NC_Net on the Windows server, without the need to change the Nagios configuration. Development on NC_Net is very active. The current version at the time this book went to press, version 4.x, is based on the DOT.NET framework, version 2.0. This is included by default only starting from Windows Server 2003 R2, but even there it is not installed automatically. For those who cannot or who don't want to install the new framework, the older NC_Net version 2.28 runs under DOT.NET 1.1 and is very stable and well established.

NC_Net Version 2.28 is available on the NC_Net homepage,[6] and all newer versions can be found at SourceForge.[7] Make sure that any previous version installed is first uninstalled. Since NC_Net uses the Microsoft Installer, you do this through the software administration utility. Even an NSClient that might exist should be removed first.

Double clicking on the file NC_Net_setup.msi installs the service, but you should check in the service management that it really is running, and whether or not automatic is entered as the starting type.

NC_Net has the same parameters as NSClient, with password and port, but these can also be specified in the services management under properties in the Start parameters line:

```
port 4711 password password
```

20.2.3 NSClient++

NSClient++ combines two query methods. On one hand, it is compatible with NSClient and can make queries as usual with check_nt. On the other hand, it contains a built-in NRPE service which can be configured and used

---

[6] http://www.shatterit.com/NC_Net
[7] http://sourceforge.net/projects/nc-net

like NRPE_NT (see Chapter 20.4.1 from page 488). NSClient++ provides all the NSClient functions via loadable modules, as well as other features such as event log querying or WMI queries via NRPE. In contrast to NRPE_NT, it is not essential to have external plugins for querying the CPU and hard disk load if you are using the modules.

NSClient++ is being actively developed; the homepage[8] provides not only a download area and documentation in the form of a Wiki, but also a bug-tracking system which allows you to report any errors and to make requests, including tracing open tickets.

Installation

The current NSClient++ version can be downloaded as a zip file from the homepage[9] or from SourceForge.[10] The contents of this file are unpacked, for instance in D:\Program Files\Nagios\nsclient++, and from there they are installed as a service, and the program is started:

```
D:\Program Files\Nagios\nsclient++> NSClient++/install
D:\Program Files\Nagios\nsclient++> NSClient++/start
```

If you want to use the classical net start command instead of the administrative tools to start and stop the service, you need to know that it is called nsclientpp (and not nsclient++):

```
D:\> net start nsclientpp
D:\> net stop nsclientpp
```

Configuration

NSClient++ requires a configuration file NSC.ini located in the same directory where the NSClient++-EXE file resides. The NSC.ini included in the distrubution needs to be edited in all cases.

This file is divided into a number of sections:

```
[modules]
; loadable modules
[Settings]
; general settings
[log]
; Logging and debugging
[NSClient]
```

[8] http://trac.nakednuns.org/nscp/
[9] http://trac.nakednuns.org/nscp/downloads
[10] http://sourceforge.net/projects/nscplus/

```
; Parameters for NSClient-compatible queries
[Check System]
; Fine-tuning configuration for system checks (CPU, memory, ...)
[NRPE]
; Parameters for NRPE
[NRPE Handlers]
; NRPE commands
```

Each section begins with a keyword in square brackets, and comment lines start with a semicolon. The section [modules] loads the individual modules. The following modules are currently available:

```
[modules]
FileLogger.dll
CheckDisk.dll
CheckSystem.dll
NSClientListener.dll
NRPEListener.dll
; SysTray.dll
; CheckHelpers.dll
; CheckWMI.dll
```

The internal module FileLogger.dll logs the work of NSClient++ to a file and does not provide any checks.

CheckDisk.dll checks the file size and hard disk usage, and CheckSystem. dll checks the CPU, the memory, counters, uptime, and service and process states.

NSClientListener.dll ensures compatibility with NSClient. If this module is not loaded, queries with check_nt will fail. The module NRPEListener.dll implements the NRPE service. This means you can choose whether you use NSClient++ as an NSClient or as an NRPE_NT replacement, or whether you use both functions at the same time.

SysTray.dll installs a systray icon on the server for access to NSClient++.

CheckHelpers.dll is a test module that always provides a specific return value (e. g., OK) and is not required for normal operation.

CheckWMI.dll provides queries for the WMI interface, but it is not yet completely finished.

The global section [Settings] contains settings that apply across section boundaries, including the password parameters and allowed_hosts, which are inherited by the sections [NSClient] (page 468) and [NRPE] (page 493), unless these options are set differently there:

```
[Settings]
; obfuscated_password=Jw0KAUUdX1AAUwASDAAB
; password=secret-password
```

```
allowed_hosts=
use_file=1
```

obfuscated_password, like password, is currently used only by the NS-Client-compatible part of NSClient++, and not for NRPE. Both parameters set the password for check_nt. obfuscated_password obscures this, so that it does not appear in plain text in the INI file. However, this is not real encryption. An obfuscated_password is generated by running nsclient++ /encrypt. This utility asks for a password, which it then displays in obscured form.[11]

The parameter allowed_hosts controls which IP addresses may access NSClient++. If it is left empty, there are no access restrictions. You can specify several IP addresses by separating them with commas, but it is not possible to use host names here.

Finally, use_file controls whether the configuration file is to be used at all (use_file=1). If the value 0 is entered here, NSClient++ searches in the registry for the settings. Configuration via the registry is currently still experimental, and it poses a security risk due to lack of sufficient protection, and so we will not look at it in more detail.

The next section is devoted to logging:

```
[log]
debug=0
; file=NSC.log
date_mask=%Y-%m-%d %H:%M:%S
```

With debug=1, debugging—which is disabled by default, using the value 0—can be switched on. file specifies the log file. If you omit this parameter or (as shown here) comment it out, NSClient++ writes its error messages to nsclient.log, in the same directory in which the binary file lies. The software does this even if debugging is switched off. With date_mask you can specify the date format of the timestamp with which every log message begins. This format corresponds to what is described in man date.

The [NSClient] section sets a number of options concerning compatibility with NSClient. Although nothing else can be configured here, NSClient functions (see Chapter 20.3 from page 472) are only available if the NSClientListener.dll module, CheckDisk.dll, and CheckSystem.dll (see page 467) have been loaded.[12]

The parameter allowed_hosts overrides the setting in the [Settings] section. In this way, NSClient++ can use a configuration for working with check_nt that is different from the one used for NRPE:

---

[11] The algorithm used is not documented, hence the utility should be treated with mistrust.

[12] The MEMUSE command (see page 476) thus requires the module CheckSystem.dll.

```
[NSClient]
; allowed_hosts=
port=12489
; bind_to_address=
```

The `port` and `bind_to_address` parameters specify the socket on which NSClient++ accepts `check_nt` queries. The default for the port is 1248, which regularly leads to problems on some Windows servers (e. g., Exchange servers) (see also page 471). You should therefore change to a higher port number (e. g., 12489).

`bind_to_address` specifies the IP address of the intended host, on which the service will listen. This parameter is only needed if the computer has more than one network interface and a specific IP address is to be set.

The `[Check System]` section allows system checks to be fine-tuned. Normally you won't need to configure anything here:

```
[Check System]
; CPUBufferSize=1h
; CheckResolution=10
```

CPUBufferSize determines how long NSClient++ stores information on the CPU load. The allowed value range starts at one second (`1s`), with a maximum of ten weeks (`10w`). To save data for a long period, however, you need a large amount of memory. The default value of one hour is enough for most purposes.

CheckResolution specifies the resolution of the stored measurement values in tenths of a second. The value 10 therefore means that a value is determined every second. CheckResolution currently influences only CPU measurement values.

Other parameters for the `[Check System]` section are rarely required and are documented in the Wiki.[13]

Configuration of the NRPE services in the two sections `[NRPE Handlers]` and `[NRPE]` is dealt with in Section 20.4.3 from page 493, and the internal functions of NSClient++ that can be called via NRPE are described in Section 20.4.4 from page 495.

20.2.4 OpMon Agent

OpMon Agent is nothing more than a further development of the original NSClient code by the company OPServices.[14] It can therefore be considered to be a succcessor to the NSClient program. Like its predecessor, the software is published under the GNU Public License.

---

[13] http://trac.nakednuns.org/nscp/wiki/Documentation
[14] http://www.opservices.com.br/

To install it, you unpack the current zip file from `http://www.opservices.com.br/downloads/` to `C:\Program Files\Nagios\opmonagent` and enter the following commands:

```
C:\Program Files\Nagios\opmonagent> opmonagent/install
C:\Program Files\Nagios\opmonagent> net startopmonagent
```

OpMon Agent also stores its configuration in an INI file. The original `opmonagent.ini` looks like this:

```
[OPMONAGENT]
enable=1
password=None
port=5667
allow_from=127.0.0.1,192.168.10.2,192.168.2.1
autodetect_counters=1
use_counters=W2K
max_connections=300
debuglevel=0

[NRPE]
enable=1
port=5666
command_timeout=60
allow_from=127.0.0.1,192.168.10.1,192.168.2.1
```

The NSClient functionality is configured in the `[OPMONAGENT]` section. `enable=1` allows queries via `check_nt`, but if this parameter is set to 0, OpMon Agent ignores this.

`password` sets a password, and the value `None` means that no password is required. Otherwise, the password is written in plain text after the equals sign.

5667 is entered here as the standard port, but if you want to use the usual port 1248, you just change the entry and restart the service. `allow_from` restricts access to specific hosts.

`autodetect_counters=1` tries to automatically determine the exact name of the Windows performance counter, depending on the language setting of Windows and the exact Windows version. If you switch off this capability with the value 0, you must specify the name explicitly in `use_counters`. Possible values for this parameter are listed in the file `counters.def`, which is located in the same directory as `opmonagent.ini`.

`max_connections` restricts the number of possible simultaneous connections. A `debuglevel` value larger than 0 switches on debugging.

In the future, it should be possible to configure the NRPE functions of OpMon Agent, which will be introduced in a later version, in the `[NRPE]` section. The current version of OpMon Agent at the time this book goes to press, version 2.4, does not yet provide official support for NRPE.

20.2.5 Rectifying problems with port 1248

All NSClient-compatible services work by default on port 1248. This can
sometimes turn out to be a problem, because Windows operating systems
work intensively with RPCs (Remote Procedure Calls). Here ports are assigned dynamically, starting at port 1025. Thus, under certain circumstances—for servers with many services or many simultaneous connections, for example—port 1248 is often already occupied when NSClient is
started as a service. For Exchange servers, this happens fairly often after a
reboot. You should therefore change to a high, unproblematic port number,
such as 12489.

If you are not installing Nagios for the first time but are working with an
existing installation, you may not be able to easily change the port for all
hosts to be monitored. For Nagios 2.x, there is no choice but to define a
separate command for every port used. With Nagios 3.0, this can be done
more elegantly. The solution is to use self-defined variables (see Section
H.2 from page 685). In the host template (see Section 2.11, page 75) the
value is now globally specified as the standard port (in the example shown
here, 1248):

```
define host{
    name        host_t
    register    0
    ...
    _NSCLIENT_PORT 1248
    ...
}
```

For hosts that have already been converted to the new port, you overwrite
the _NSCLIENT_PORT variable with the new port:

```
define host{
    host_name   winsrv
    use         host_t
    ...
    _NSCLIENT_PORT 12489
}
```

For all other hosts, the value defined in the template applies. The definition
of the command object takes into account the desired port by evaluating
the variable, as shown here:

```
define command{
    command_name check_nt
    command_line $USER1$/check_nt -H $HOSTADDRESS$ -p $_HOSTNSCLIENT_POR
T$ -v $ARG1$ $ARG2$
}
```

This means that for each newly converted host, only the variable needs to be set in this way, and all the service definitions remain unchanged.

20.3 The `check_nt` Plugin

When installing the standard Nagios plugins, the `check_nt` plugin is automatically loaded to the hard drive. The checks that can be queried here correspond to the function range of NSClient provided in NSClient, NSClient++, OpMon Agent, and NC_Net. To make use of the extensions of NC_Net, you must download the extended source code (the file `check_nt.c`) from `http://www.shatterit.com/NC_Net` and compile it yourself.

The actual effect that the `check_nt` parameters have, described below, depends on the command that is specified with the `-v` option:[15]:

`-H` *address* / `--host=`*address*
: IP address or host name of the host on which the NSClient/NC_Net is installed.

`-v` *command* / `--variable=`*command*
: The command to be executed.

`-p` *port* / `--port=`*port*
: This defines an alternative port for NSClient/NC_Net (see section 20.2.5 on page 471). The default is TCP port 1248.

`-w` *integer* / `--warning=`*integer*
: This defines a warning limit. This option is not available for all commands.

`-c` *integer* / `--critical=`*integer*
: The critical limit option is also not available for all commands.

`-l` *parameter*
: This is used for passing parameters along, such as the drive for the hard drive check or the process name when checking processes.

`-d` *option*
: When checking services or processes, you can specify several services or processes simultaneously. Normally `check_nt` then only shows the defective ones (`-d SHOWFAIL`). To have all of them displayed you must specify `SHOWALL` as the *option*.

---

[15] You can read about them in more detail on page 473.

-s *password*
> A password for authentication is only required if NC_Net or NSClient starts the corresponding service with the password parameter.

-t *timeout* / --timeout=*timeout*
> After *timeout* seconds have elapsed, the plugin aborts the test and returns the CRITICAL state. The default is 10 seconds.

20.3.1 Generally supported commands

For the commands introduced here, it makes no difference whether you use NSClient, NSClient++, NC_Net or OpMon; they can be run with the unpatched check_nt.

Querying the client version

The version of the installed NSClient or NC_Net service is returned by running the command

```
check_nt -H address -v CLIENTVERSION
```

All other arguments are ignored:

```
nagios@linux:nagios/libexec$ ./check_nt -H winsrv -v CLIENTVERSION
NC_Net 2.21 03/13/05
```

The first edition of this book defined a separate command for each check_nt function. But this is not necessary at all, as Ethan Galstad has shown in the online documentation for Nagios:[16]

```
define command{
    command_name check_nt_nsclient
    command_line $USER1$/check_nt -H $HOSTADDRESS$ -v $ARG1$ $ARG2$
}
```

For Nagios 3.0 with NSClient ports defined in a host-dependent fashion (see Section 20.2.5, page 471), the command object check_nt would look like this:

```
define command{
    command_name check_nt
    command_line $USER1$/check_nt -H $HOSTADDRESS$ -p$_HOSTNSCLIENT_POR
T$ -v $ARG1$ $ARG2$
}
```

---

[16] http://nagios.sourceforge.net/docs/3_0/monitoring-windows.html

The command line to be executed expects two arguments: The macro $ARG1$ expands in each case into the command to be called, and the contents of $ARG2$ are dependent on the respective command and may be empty in certain circumstances:

```
define service{
    host_name           winsrv
    service_description NSClient
    check_command       check_nt!CLIENTVERSION
    ...
}
```

The command CLIENTVERSION does not have any other arguments, so the second argument is simply left out.

This unassuming service is extremely useful in describing dependencies. If NSClient/NC_Net fails on the Windows server, Nagios normally informs the administrator of all services that may have failed. By querying CLIENT-VERSION, it becomes clear that the problem lies in the unavailability of NSClient. If you define appropriate dependencies, Nagios can provide more precise information.[17] Here is an example for the NSClient application:

```
define servicedependency{
    host_name                     winsrv
    service_description           NSClient
    dependent_host_name           winsrv
    dependent_service_description Disks,Load,Memory
    notification_failure_criteria c,u
    execution_failure_criteria    n
}
```

With NSClient as a master service on which the other services are dependent, Nagios does not trouble the admins with messages from these other services, as long as NSClient is in a CRITICAL or UNKNOWN state.

In Nagios 2.x you must set dependency objects for each host individually. In Nagios 3.0 there are the *same host dependencies*: If you omit the entry dependent_host_name, the dependency defined here applies to the same host. This allows host groups to be used in a sensible manner:

```
# Nagios 3.0
define servicedependency{
    hostgroup_name                WINDOWS_SERVER
    service_description           NSClient
    dependent_service_description Disks,Load,Memory
    notification_failure_criteria c,u
    execution_failure_criteria    n
}
```

[17] This problem is similar to one with NRPE, which was solved through the definition of dependencies (see Section 12.6, page 285).

Here the Disks service in each case only depends on the NSClient service of the same host. When using host groups in Nagios 2.x, Disks would be dependent on all NSClient services on all hosts of the host group WINDOWS_ SERVER—and this is normally not what is wanted.

CPU load

How heavy the load is on the processor is revealed by the command CPU-LOAD:

```
check_nt -H address -v CPULOAD -l interval,warning limit,critical_limit
```

It expects a triplet of parameters, separated by commas, consisting of the length of the time interval that is to be averaged, in minutes, and the two thresholds for the warning and critical limits in percent:

```
nagios@linux:nagios/libexec$ ./check_nt -H winsrv -v CPULOAD -l 5,80,90
CPU Load 10% (5 min average) |   '5 min avg Load'=10%;80;90;0;100
```

So CPULOAD, with 5,80,90, forms the average over five minutes and issues a warning if the value determined exceeds 80 percent. If there is over 90% CPU load, the command returns CRITICAL.

The output here also contains additional performance data after the | sign, which Nagios ignores in the Web interface. If you are interested in average values over several intervals, you just add further triplet values following to the first one:

```
nagios@linux:nagios/libexec$ ./check_nt -H winsrv -v CPULOAD \
   -l 5,80,90,15,70,80
CPU Load 10% (5 min average) 10% (15 min average) |   '5 min avg Load'=10
%;80;90;0;100 '15 min avg Load'=10%;70;80;0;100
```

In this example CPULOAD checks two intervals: the past five minutes and the past 15 minutes. In the second case there are deviating limit values. The plugin always returns the more critical value; for example, it returns CRITICAL if one interval issues CRITICAL and the other just a WARNING.

The service definition therefore looks like this:

```
define service{
   host_name            winsrv
   service_description CPU Load
   check_command        check_nt!CPULOAD!-l 5,80,90,15,70,80
   ...
}
```

Main memory usage

When specifying the limit values, the command for monitoring the amount of main memory used—in contrast to CPULOAD—is based on the syntax of "normal" Nagios plugins:

```
check_nt -H address -v MEMUSE -w integer -c integer
```

MEMUSE returns the memory usage in percent. It should be remembered that Windows refers here to the sum of memory and swap files, that is, the entire available virtual memory. The command expects the warning and critical limits as percentages, given without a percent sign:

```
nagios@linux:nagios/libexec$ ./check_nt -H winsrv -v MEMUSE \
    -w 70 -c 90
Memory usage: total:4331.31Mb - used: 257.04Mb (6%) - free: 4074.27Mb (9
4%) | 'Memory usage'=257.04Mb;3031.91;3898.18;0.00;4331.31
```

On the example host, winsrv, only six percent of the virtual memory is used. The fact that the physical size of the main memory itself (here: 256 MB) is already exceeded is not shown in the output.

It does not necessarily make sense, however, to request the memory usage as in Unix: Windows regularly swaps program and data code from the main memory, even when it still has spare reserves. In Unix, programs and data land in the swap partition only if more space is required than is currently free. In this respect the load of the entire virtual memory in Windows is the more important parameter.

The command mentioned above is again packed into a service object:

```
define service{
    host_name           winsrv
    service_description MEM Usage
    check_command       check_nt!MEMUSE!-w 70 -c 90
    ...
}
```

Hard drive capacity

The load on a file system is tested by USEDDISKSPACE:

```
check_nt -H address -v USEDDISKSPACE -l drive letter -w integer -c integer
```

in Windows fashion, the file system is specified as drive letters, the limit values in percent:

```
nagios@linux:nagios/libexec$ ./check_nt -H winsrv -v USEDDISKSPACE\
    -l C -w 70 -c 80
C: - total: 4.00 Gb - used: 2.06 Gb (52%) - free 1.94 Gb (48%) | 'C: Use
d Space'=2.06Gb;2.80;3.20;0.00;4.00
nagios@linux:nagios/libexec$ echo $?
0
```

In the example, check_nt should issue a Warning if drive C is more than 70 percent full, and a CRITICAL if the load exceeds 80%. The current value lies at 52 percent, so check_nt therefore returns an OK, which you can check with echo $?.

The corresponding service object would look something like this:

```
define service{
    host_name           winsrv
    service_description Disk_C
    check_command       check_nt!USEDDISKSPACE!-l C -w 70 -c 80
    ...
}
```

Uptime

How long ago the last reboot was performed is revealed by the command UPTIME:

```
check_nt -H address -v UPTIME
```

Defining a warning or critical limit is not possible, which is why such a query is only for information purposes (the plugin returns either OK, or UNKNOWN if it is used wrongly):

```
nagios@linux:nagios/libexec$ ./check_nt -H winsrv -v UPTIME
System Uptime - 17 day(s) 9 hour(s) 54 minute(s)
```

so the host winsrv has already been running for 17 days. A suitable definition of the corresponding service object looks like this:

```
define service{
    host_name           winsrv
    service_description UPTIME
    check_command       check_nt!UPTIME
    ...
}
```

Status of services

The current status of Windows services can be checked with SERVICESTATE:

```
check_nt -H address -v SERVICESTATE -d SHOWALL -l service1,service2,...
```

The optional -d SHOWALL ensures that the output text lists all services. If you leave this option out, the plugin provides information only on those services that are *not* running.

To find the name of the service description to be specified for NSClient after the -l option is quite a challenge. It is not the *display name* which is displayed by the services management (e.g., Routing and RAS), that is being sought, but the registry entry that corresponds to this. Accordingly you search with the Registry editor regedit in the partial tree HKEY_LOCAL_ MACHINE\SYSTEM\CurrentControlSet\Services for the node with the corresponding display name. It contains the service description being sought, which in the case of Routing and RAS is something like Remote-Access.

If you use NC_Net, you have an easier task: the software accepts both the service description and the display name, in which no distinction is made between upper and lower case. The following two examples use the display name:

```
nagios@linux:nagios/libexec$ ./check_nt -H winsrv1 -v SERVICESTATE \
    -l "RemoteAccess"
RemoteAccess: Stopped
nagios@linux:nagios/libexec$ ./check_nt -H winsrv2 -v SERVICESTATE \
    -l "Routing and RAS"
All services are running
```

In the first case the service name was used; in the second case, the display name was used. The service first queried is not running, as the output Stopped shows, and check_nt returns 2 (CRITICAL) as the return value. The service addressed with the second command is working, which is why the plugin does not display it if the -d SHOWALL option is not given. The return value here is 0 (OK). Several services (separated by commas) can also be queried in a single query. The worst-case result here dictates the return value. A matching service object looks something like this:

```
define service{
    host_name              winsrv
    service_description Routing and RAS
    check_command          check_nt!SERVICESTATE!-l RemoteAccess
    ...
}
```

Status of processes

As with the services, PROCSTATE monitors running processes:

```
check_nt -H address -v PROCSTATE -d SHOWALL -l process1,process2,...
```

The process name, which almost always ends in .exe, is best determined in the process list of the task manager; upper and lower case are also ignored here:

```
nagios@linux:nagios/libexec$ ./check_nt -H winsrv -v PROCSTATE \
WinVNC.exe,winlogon.exe,notexist.exe
 notexist.exe: not running
```

As with the services, you can also specify a list of several processes, separated by commas. Without -d SHOWALL, PROCSTATE shows only those processes that are *not* running, in this example, notexist.exe. A corresponding service definition might look like this:

```
define service{
    host_name               winsrv
    service_description  WinVNC
    check_command           check_nt!PROCSTATE!-l winvnc.exe
    ...
}
```

Age of files

It is worth monitoring the time since the last modification of critical files with FILEAGE, particularly for log files and other files that change regularly:

```
check_nt -H address -v FILEAGE -l path -w integer -c integer
```

FILEAGE can be used to check the age of a file, for instance a log file to which data should be written regularly. The file name is specified with the full path, and backslashes must be written twice: C:\\xyz.log. If the thresholds, specified in minutes, are exceeded, the plugin issues a WARNING or a CRITICAL. However, it gives the age of the file, by default, in epoch seconds:[18]

```
nagios@linux:nagios/libexec$  ./check_nt -H winsrv -v FILEAGE \
    -l "C:\\test.log" -w 1 -c 20
1113158517

nagios@linux:nagios/libexec$ echo $?
1
```

[18] That is, in seconds elapsed since 01. 01. 1970.

The status can again be checked with echo $?. Here as well, the service definition does not hold any secrets:

```
define service{
    host_name            winsrv
    service_description Log file
    check_command        check_nt_fileage!C:          xyz.log!60!1440
    ...
}
```

Querying Windows counters and instances

The duo of NSClient and check_nt provides two other functions: querying Windows counters with COUNTER and querying Windows performance counter objects with INSTANCES. Querying performance counters varies in small details from service to service, however (such as using a double backslash rather than a single backslash in the counter name). For this reason, we shall describe both in the discussion of the extended functions of NC_Net from page 481. If you want to use counters with OpMon Agent, NSClient, or NSClient++, we recommend that you take a look at the original documentation of each service.

When using NSClient++, it is recommended that you use the internal function CheckCounter, which is described on page 501.

20.3.2   Advanced functions of NC_Net

NC_Net's range of functions is expanding constantly; this chapter describes the possibilities that go beyond NSClient for version 2.28. These can only be used with the modified check_nt plugin. The extended version is based on the original check_nt version 1.4.1. But it is possible that both plugins will continue to be developed in different ways, and thus diverge.

We will therefore rename the NC_Net version to check_ncnet, so that we can keep the two separate and run them at the same time. Thus, check_nt examples in this book demonstrate functions that are available for all NSClient-compatible services; if check_ncnet is used, the NC_Net functionality in combination with the extended plugin is available.

20.3.3   Installing the check_ncnet plugin

check_ncnet exists only in the source code; it consists of a single file that unfortunately has the same name as the original plugin check_nt.c. The file ends up on the hard drive during the installation of NC_Net, but it can also be downloaded separately from http://www.shatterit.com/nc_net.

The source can currently be compiled without problems only in combination with the entire Nagios plugin package (see Section 1.4, page 43). To do this, you overwrite the existing file check_nt.c in the subdirectory plugins with the extended version. To be on the safe side, the old check_nt binary should be renamed; then you run make check_nt to recompile the source file. Afterward, you copy the binary under the name check_ncnet to the libexec directory of Nagios, along with the other plugins:

```
linux:~ # cp check_nt.c /usr/local/src/nagios-plugins-1.4/plugins
linux:~ # cd /usr/local/src/nagios-plugins-1.4/plugins
linux:nagios-plugins-1.4/plugins # mv check_nt check_nt_orig
linux:nagios-plugins-1.4/plugins # make check_nt
...
linux:nagios-plugins-1.4/plugins # mv check_nt check_ncnet
linux:nagios-plugins-1.4/plugins # cp check_ncnet \
   /usr/local/nagios/libexec/.
```

Windows Performance Counter

Through so-called Performance Counters, Windows provides values for everything in the system that can be expressed in numbers: hard drive usage, CPU usage, number of logins, number of terminal server sessions, the load on the network interface, and many more things. check_ncnet queries these with the command ENUMCOUNTER:

```
check_ncnet -H address -v ENUMCOUNTER -l category1,category2
```

If you omit the -l parameter, ENUMCOUNTER will display a list of all performance counter categories:

```
nagios@linux:nagios/libexec$ ./check_ncnet -H winsrv -v ENUMCOUNTER
... Processor; ... Terminal services; .NET CLR loading procedure; tot
al RAS services; Process; ...
```

Otherwise, it shows all counters in the category specified with -l. Several categories are separated with commas. The Terminal services category contains three counter objects in all:

```
nagios@linux:nagios/libexec$ ./check_ncnet -H winsrv -v ENUMCOUNTER \
   -l Terminal services
Terminal Services: Total Sessions; Active Sessions; Inactive Sessions
```

```
nagios@linux:nagios/libexec$ ./check_ncnet -H winsrv -v ENUMCOUNTER \
    -l "Terminal Services","Process"
Terminal Services: Total Sessions; Active Sessions; Inactive Sessions -
Process: % Processor Time; % User Time; % Privileged Time; Virtual Bytes
Peak; Virtual Bytes; Page Faults/sec; Working Set Peak; Working Set; ...
```

The precise object name is important for later use, in which the % sign (as, for example, in % Processor Time) is part of the name. If the counter or category name contains spaces, you must remember to place it within quotation marks when formulating the the request.

The description stored in the Windows Performance Counter objects are shown, by the way, with the command ENUMCOUNTERDESC.

Several counter categories contain instances, which you must specify when querying a counter object. For this reason you should always check first, using the INSTANCES function, whether the category you want works with instances:

```
check_ncnet -H address -v INSTANCES -l category1,category2
```

For the terminal services, this is not the case:

```
nagios@linux:nagios/libexec$ ./check_ncnet -H winsrv -v INSTANCES \
    -l "Terminal Services"
  Terminal Services:
```

Typical categories with instances are Processor or Process:

```
nagios@linux:nagios/libexec$ ./check_ncnet -H winsrv -v INSTANCES \
    -l "Process"
  Process: svchost#6,svchost,Idle,explorer,services,...
```

Here it becomes apparent what is meant by instances: Windows views every running process as an instance in the Process Performance Counter category. As can be seen on page 481, the counter object (% Processor Time), which contains the percentage use of processor time), is in this category. It can be queried only for individual instances, such as for the explorer process, or for all processes together. In case of the latter you specify _Total instead of an instance.

In order to access a Windows Performance Counter, therefore, you always need to give the following details:

```
\category\counter object
\category(instance)\counter object
```

The instance is specified only if the category has instances available. There must be no space between the category name and the first bracket. The corresponding query command is called COUNTER; the placeholder *name* is replaced by the combination just described:

```
check_nt -H adresse -v COUNTER -l name,formatbeschreibung -w ganzzahl
-c ganzzahl
```

This function asks after the Windows Performance Counter object that is specified after the -l option with its exact name. The warning and critical limits given as integer values refer to the size measured: if an object is involved that has a percentage figure (e.g., the processor load), just imagine a percent sign added to it; the numbers of processes, sessions, etc., are just values that are not specified in units.

The number of active sessions is checked with the Active Sessions object, for which there are no instances:

```
nagios@linux:nagios/libexec$ ./check_ncnet -H winsrv -v COUNTER \
    -l "\Terminal Services\Active Sessions"
1
nagios@linux:nagios/libexec$ ./check_ncnet -H winsrv -v COUNTER \
    -l "\Process(Idle)\% Processor Time"
98
```

Because the Idle instance always looks at the difference between used and spare processor load, so that the sum of the two is always 100 percent, querying the _Total pseudo-instance in the second example does not make much sense.

Normally COUNTER does not format its output. This can be changed by following the object name with a description in the printf format,[19] separated from it with a comma:

```
nagios@linux:nagios/libexec$ ./check_ncnet -H winsrv -v COUNTER \
    -l "\Process(Idle)\% Processor Time","Idle Process: %.2f %%"
Idle Process Usage is: 54.00 % | 'Idle Process Usage is: %.2f %%'=54.000
000%;0.000000;0.000000;
```

Not only does this cause the output to be clearer, it also returns additional performance data. A corresponding service definition might look like this:

```
define service{
  host_name          winsrv
  service_description Terminal Sessions
  check_command check_nt!COUNTER!-v "\Terminal Services\Active Sessions"
```

---

[19] man 3 printf

```
-w 20 -c 30
  ...
}
```

Listing processes and services

To find out the names of processes, you can work your way through the Task Manager—or have a list of all running processes displayed with ENUMPRO-CESS:

```
nagios@linux:nagios/libexec$ ./check_ncnet -H winsrv -v ENUMPROCESS
System Idle Process; System; smss.exe; csrss.exe; winlogon.exe;
services.exe; lsass.exe; svchost.exe; svchost.exe; svchost.exe;
...
```

The equivalent command for listing all installed services is ENUMSERVICE:

```
check_ncnet -H host -v ENUMSERVICE -l typ,short
```

The optional -l restricts the output to specific categories (see Table 20.1):

```
nagios@linux:nagios/libexec$ ./check_ncnet -H winsrv -v ENUMSERVICE
    \ -l manual,short
ALG; AppMgmt; BITS; COMSysApp; dmadmin; EventSystem; HTTPFilter;
LPDSVC; MSIServer; Netman; Nla; NtFrs; NtLmSsp; NtmsSvc; RasAuto;
...
```

With the short option, ENUMSERVICE displays the service names as they are entered in the registry; if you leave out the keyword, it shows the display names.

<table>
<tr><td>Table 20.1:
Limiting options for
ENUMSERVICE</td><td>**Type**</td><td>**Description**</td></tr>
<tr><td></td><td>all</td><td>all services</td></tr>
<tr><td></td><td>running</td><td>all currently active services</td></tr>
<tr><td></td><td>stopped</td><td>all services which have been stopped</td></tr>
<tr><td></td><td>automatic</td><td>services starting automatically</td></tr>
<tr><td></td><td>manual</td><td>services which must be started manually</td></tr>
<tr><td></td><td>disabled</td><td>disabled services</td></tr>
</table>

Querying the Windows event log

With the EVENTLOG command, the Windows Event Log can be queried:

```
check_ncnet -H adress -v EVENTLOG -w integer -c integer -l eventlog,
event_type,interval,source_filter,description_filter, id_filter
```

Using it does take some getting used to, however:[20] the first three parameters to follow –l select the events to be taken into account by type and by time.

The placeholder *eventlog* is replaced with one of the three log areas application, security, and system that you want to look at. If EVENTLOG is to include all three, you just specify any; but you cannot choose only two of the three areas.

For the *event type* you can choose from error, Warning, Information, or any for all three.

In place of *interval* you specify a time interval in minutes: 5 limits the selection to events which occurred in the last five minutes, for example; 1440 stands for a whole day.

The last three parameters in effect work as filters with which specific results can be determined from the preselection that all originate from a particular source (the *source_filter* placeholder), that contain a specific pattern in their descriptions (*description_filter*), or that have a specific event ID (*id_filter*).

Each of these filters consists of two parts: in the first an integer reveals how many search patterns are to follow (formulated as regular expressions in accordance with the .NET-Regexp class), and then the actual filter entries are specified, separated by commas. If one of the filters is not used, its placeholder is replaced with a 0, which searches for exactly zero search patterns. A source filter which only looks for NC_Net events would be called 1,NC_Net; if you want to search for NC_Net and Perflib events, it would be called 2,NC_Net,Perflib.

–l any,any,5,0,0,0 evaluates all entries from all event ranges from the last five minutes. –l application,error,1440,0,0,0 determines all events of the type error, which occurred in the event range application within the last 24 hours. With –l application,error,60,1,NC_Net,0,0, the time window is set to 60 minutes and filters the event source using the string NC_Net. Finally –l application,any,60,0,2,start,stop,0 searches the event description for two keywords: start and stop.

With the warning and critical limits you can specify how many matching entries are needed before the plugin returns a WARNING or CRITICAL

---

[20] According to his own comments, author Tony Montibello wanted to change the syntax for defining services in version 2.25. But up to and including version 2.28, this resolution has not yet been implemented.

value. If you leave out these two parameters, Nagios shows OK as long as *no* events occurred; otherwise, it shows CRITICAL.

The following example asks how many messages there were within the last 24 hours in the `applications` area:

```
nagios@linux:nagios/libexec$ ./check_ncnet -H winsrv -v EVENTLOG \
    -l "Application,any,1440,0,0,0"
9 Errors with ID: 13001;2003;1010;6013;1111;262194;26;262194;26 LAST - I
D 262194;Not all data for the file "\Device\LanmanRedirector" were sa
ved.  Possible causes are computer hardware or the network connection. P
lease specify a different file path.
```

The service we defined below searches for errors in all classes in the `System` area which occurred in the past five minutes. (When specifying the time period you should generally ensure that it correlates with the time period in `normal_check_interval`.) The service examines the descriptions of the entries found for the text `data loss`. The source and ID filters are not used here:

```
define service{
    host_name        winsrv
    service_description Eventlog data loss
    check_command    check_ncnet!EVENTLOG!-l System,any,5,0,1,data loss,0
    is_volatile          1
    normal_check_interval 5
    max_check_attempts   1
    ...
}
```

Log files have the characteristic of pointing out a problem only once under certain circumstances, even if the problem continues. You must therefore ensure that Nagios immediately makes a notification the first time the event occurs, and leaves out repeated tests and soft states. This can be achieved with `max_check_attempts 1`: this immediately sets off a hard state, and notification is given right away.

But if the hard state remains, this would mean in practice that new errors might occur in the meantime (the next test after five minutes no longer records the old states), while the state has not changed; the admin would only be informed again after the `notification_interval` has expired. For such cases, Nagios has available the `is_volatile` parameter (see Section 14.5.2, page 309), with which the system provides notification on every single error.

Displaying and manipulating the NC_Net configuration

The `ENUMCONFIG` function displays the current settings of NC_Net in a readable form:

```
nagios@linux:nagios/libexec$ ./check_ncnet -H winsrv -v ENUMCONFIG
Date: 16.04.2005 18:15:10;
Version: NC_Net 2.21 03/13/05;
NC_Net Config Path: c:\Programs\shatter it\nc_net\config\;
Startup Config: c:\Programs\shatter it\nc_net\config\startup.cfg;
Debug Log: c:\Programs\shatter it\nc_net\config\deb.log;
...
Port: 1248;
Pass: None;
...
```

Date shows the current query date, Version the NC_Net version used. NC_Net Config Path describes the path to the configuration directory, Startup Config the configuration file used. Debug Log specifies the log file containing the debugging output, but only if the MYDEBUG true parameter is set in the configuration file. Port reveals the port on which NC_Net is listening, and Pass shows whether a password has been used for the connection (None: no password).

There is also the command CONFIG to manipulate the configuration of the NC_Net installation over the network. For reasons of security you should use this for test purposes only, and otherwise keep the function switched off. Accordingly you should keep the following default set in the configuration filestartup.cfg:

```
lock_passive_config true
lock_active_config true
```

This means that the configuration cannot be changed from the outside.

Other functions

NC_Net's range of functions is growing all the time, and to describe all the functions in detail would need a separate book. We'll just mention a few quite useful commands:

FREEDISKSPACE

The equivalent of USEDDISKSPACE (page 476) expects the free hard drive capacity (instead of the used space) in percent for warning and critical limits

WMIQUERY

This function enables the SQL-capable WMI[21] database to be queried, which contains the .NET configuration data.

---

[21] Short for *Windows Management Instrumentation.*

WMICOUNTER
> Objects comparable to the Windows performance counters also exist in the WMI area (only .NET); they can be queried with this.

Passive Checks
> From version 2.0, NC_Net also supports passive checks based on the NSCA mechanism (see Chapter 14, page 299). A short documentation can be found in the included `passive.cfg` file.

More information can be found in the file `readme.html`, included in the installation, but it can also be viewed directly at `http://www.shatterit.com/nc_net/files/readme.html`.

20.4   NRPE for Windows

Besides NRPE_NT (an NRPE daemon ported to Windows), NSClient++ and now also OpMon Agent provide NRPE services. Its task is to execute plugins on the target system if a particular test is only possible locally and no suitable network protocol exists to query the resource concerned. As with the Unix version (see Section 10 on page 213), the desired plugins must be installed locally on the target system, apart from the daemon (in this case: NRPE_NT) and the tests must be entered in a local configuration file.

NRPE can also be used for other purposes: once installed on the Windows server, you can use the mechanism to run other scripts remotely, apart from Nagios plugins. If you want Nagios to restart a service remotely through the Eventhandler, this can be done just as easily with NRPE_NT.[22]

20.4.1   NRPE_NT, the classic tool

NRPE_NT can be used like the Nagios Remote Plugin Executor, introduced in Chapter 10—in reality, this is just the Windows version of the same tool. At the present time, however, it doesn't look as if this tool will continue to be actively developed.

The current zip archive from The Nagios Exchange, [23] SourceForge[24] or `http://www.miwi-dv.com/nrpent` is unpacked to a suitable directory, such as `D:\Programs\Nagios\nrpe_nt`:

```
D:\Programs\Nagios\nrpe_nt> unzip nrpe_nt.0.8-bin.zip
...
```

---

[22] To execute scripts remotely on a Windows server, you can also use the Windows version of the Secure Shell, a topic that is too large to go into in this book.

[23] `http://www.nagiosexchange.org/77;139`

[24] `http://sourceforge.net/project/showfiles.php?group_id=83239`

It contains a subdirectory `bin`, in which are found the daemon `NRPE_NT.exe`, two DLLs for using SSL (`libeay32.dll` and `ssleay32.dll`), an example of a simple plugin script (`test.cmd`), and the configuration file `nrpe.cfg`.

The service is installed from this directory with the command `nrpe_nt -i`, after which it just needs to be started, either in the Windows services manager or from the command line:

```
D:\Programs\Nagios\nrpe_nt\bin> nrpe_nt -i
D:\Programs\Nagios\nrpe_nt\bin> net start nrpe_nt
```

The configuration file `nrpe.cfg` is only slightly different from the Unix version of NRPE 2.0 (see Section 10.3, page 218): only the directive `include_dir` does not function in NRPE_NT.

The file in Windows also has the classical Unix text format,[25] so either you require a suitable editor (`notepad.exe` is not sufficient) or you must edit it in Linux and copy it afterwards to the test system.

Since there is no inet daemon in Windows, you must specify the port (standard: `server_port=5666`) and the hosts from which NRPE should be addressed (you should only enter the Nagios server here; for example: `allowed_hosts=172.17.129.2`)[26] in `nrpe.cfg`. The parameters `nrpe_user` and `nrpe_group` have no meaning in Windows, and the other parameters correspond to those discussed in Section 10.3.

In the definition of executable commands (here for the included test plugin) you must remember the Windows-typical syntax with hard drive letters and backslashes:

```
command[check_cmd]=D:\Programs\Nagios\nrpe_nt\plugins\test.cmd
```

In this example the plugins are in a separate subdirectory called `plugins`. After changes to the configuration file you should always restart NRPE_NT:

```
D:\Programs\Nagios\nrpe_nt\bin> net stop nrpe_nt
D:\Programs\Nagios\nrpe_nt\bin> net start nrpe_nt
```

Function test

Before putting NRPE_NT into service, you should check whether it is functioning correctly. To do this, run the plugin `check_nt` on the Nagios server as the user `nagios`, with just one host specification and no other parameters:

---

[25] The line break in Unix consists of only a line feed character, whereas Windows text files have a line break consisting of the two characters carriage return and line feed.

[26] This security measure, however, is restricted to a simple comparison of IP addresses.

```
nagios@linux:nagios/libexec$ ./check_nrpe -H winsrv
NRPE_NT v0.8/2.0
```

If the service has been correctly installed and configured, it will reply with a version number. Another simple test is performed by the included `test.cmd` plugin. It provides a short text and ends with the return value 1:

```
@echo off
echo hallo from cmd
exit 1
```

The command to be executed (defined in the previous section) is passed to the plugin `check_nt` with the `-c` option:

```
nagios@linux:nagios/libexec$ ./check_nrpe -H winsrv -c check_cmd
hallo from cmd
nagios@linux:nagios/libexec$ echo $?
1
```

The return value, determined with `echo $?`, must be 1 in this case, since the script exits with an `exit 1`.

20.4.2   Plugins for NRPE in Windows

A series of plugins can be found on the Internet that run in Windows and are suitable for use with NRPE. The first port of call is the subcategory **Check Plugins | Operating Systems | Windows NRPE** at the NagiosExchange.[27] Some of these are programs that are based on the same source code as their Unix equivalents, which was just recompiled for Windows. However, the portings also include Perl scripts that require Perl to be installed—and in most cases the script language must be installed in Windows first.

The Cygwin plugins

In the **Check Plugins | Windows**[28] category, The Nagios Exchange includes the `CygwinPlugins` package for downloading. It consists of Nagios standard plugins, which have been compiled for Windows with the help of the Cygwin Tools.[29] The package is based on the somewhat older plugin version

---

[27] http://www.nagiosexchange.org/NRPE_Plugins.66.0.html

[28] http://www.nagiosexchange.org/49;63.

[29] The Cygwin tools contain a large number of GNU tools, including a compiler, libraries, and shells—all for Windows. This means that many Unix programs can be ported to Windows directly. The necessary files normally require only the Cygwin DLL (`cygwin1.dll`).

1.3.1, but this is enough for most purposes. Apart from the executable plugins (*.exe) the package also contains all the necessary DLLs. It is therefore sufficient to unpack the zip archive into a directory:

```
D:\Tmp> unzip CygwinPlugins1-3-1.zip
D:\Tmp> dir NagPlug
check_dummy.exe  check_ssh.exe   check_udp.exe         cygwin1.dll
check_http.exe   check_tcp.exe   cygcrypto-0.9.7.dll   negate.exe
check_smtp.exe   check_time.exe  cygssl-0.9.7.dll      urlize.exe
```

For the sake of simplicity, just copy the contents of the directory that is created, NagPlug, to a separate plugin directory:

```
D:\Tmp\NagPlug> copy * D:\Programme\Nagios\plugins
```

The plugin functions in the same way as in Linux. Table 20.2 refers to the corresponding sections in this book.

Plugin	Page	Description
check_dummy.exe	188	Test plugin
check_http.exe	119	Reachability of a Web site
check_smtp.exe	113	Testing a mail server
check_ssh.exe	131	SSH availability
check_tcp.exe	132	Generic plugin
check_time.exe	178	Clock time comparison of two hosts
check_udp.exe	135	Generic plugin
negate.exe	188	Negates the return value of a plugin
urlize.exe	189	Turns the plugin output in the Nagios Web interface into a link

Table 20.2:
Cygwin Plugins for
NRPE_NT

As in Unix, each of the corresponding command definitions in the configuration file nrpe.cfg must be written on a single line:

```
command[check_web]=D:\Programme\nagios\plugins\check_http -H www.swobspa
ce.de
command[check_identd]=D:\Programme\nagios\plugins\check_tcp -H linux01 -
p 113
```

The first line checks whether a Web server is running on the HTTP standard port 80 of the host www.swobspace.de. The second line tests whether an identd daemon (TCP port 113) is active on the host linux01.

In the event that version 1.3.1 of the plugins is too old, or if you are missing plugins, you can also compile the plugins yourself under Windows in the

Cygwin environment if you have some basic knowledge of the development of C programs and how to handle Makefiles. However, not all recompiled plugins will function under Windows/Cygwin. For instance, `check_icmp` makes direct use of the network socket, whose construction in Windows is quite different from that of the Unix socket; thus, the plugin will not work in Windows unless changes are made to the code first. Notes on compiling under Cygwin, along with an already compiled binary archive of the plugin version 1.4.5, can be obtained at `http://www.psychoticwolf.net/blog/2007/07/nagios_plugins_for_windows.php`.

Perl plugins in Windows

Unfortunately the Cygwin plugins do not contain a `check_ping` or `check_icmp`. You can use the Perl script `check_ping.pl` instead, which is available for download on The Nagios Exchange in the `Networking` category.[30] It uses the Perl module `Net::Ping` for the network connection. In contrast to `check_tcp`, `check_ping.pl` sends several packets, so it can make a more precise assessment of response times and packet losses.

An up-to-date and simple to install Perl for Windows can be obtained from ActiveState[31]. To download the *Active Perl Free Distribution*, no registration is required, even if the download procedure would suggest otherwise. Of the versions offered, you should use the latest Perl version (currently 5.8.7), and only fall back on the older version 5.6.1 if this should cause problems.

The plugin script itself contains a `BEGIN` statement, which you must comment out for use in Windows:

```
# BEGIN{
#       push @INC, "/usr/lib/perl5/site_perl/...
# }
```

It sends a TCP echo request to port 7, alternatively you can also explicitly set a different port by adding the following line after the `Net::Ping->new` statement:

```
$p->port = 80;
```

This would cause a TCP ping to port 80 (HTTP). So that NRPE_NT can execute the script, you must explicitly start the Perl executable:

```
command[check_ping_eli02]=C:\Perl\bin\perl.exe D:\Programme\Nagios\plugi
ns\check_ping.pl --host 172.17.129.2 --loss 10,20 --rta 50,250
```

[30] http://www.nagiosexchange.org/Networking.53.0.html
[31] http://www.activestate.com/store/languages/register.plex?id=ActiveP
    erl

The command has been line-wrapped for the printed version, but in the configuration file the whole command must be written on a single line. With the `--host` parameter you specify a host name which can be resolved or an IP address, `--loss` is followed by a pair of values for the warning and critical limits for packet loss in percent, separated by a comma, (so values between 0 and 100 are possible here). The `--rta` option also demands a threshold value pair as an argument, for the average response time in milliseconds. Since this is a Perl script, it does not matter if these are specified as integers or floating comma decimals.

20.4.3 NRPE with NSClient++

NSClient++ contains its own NRPE service, so you don't need to install an additional NRPE service when using it. It is activated by loading the library `NRPEListener.dll` in the `[modules]` section of the configuration file `NSC.ini` (page 467). Configuration of the service is handled by the `[NRPE]` and `[NRPE Handlers]` sections. The first section contains the NRPE base configuration, and the second one defines the checks to be performed.

The default port in NRPE is port 5666, and the parameter `allow_arguments`, when set to 1, allows arguments to be passed and corresponds to the NRPE parameter `dont_blame_nrpe` (page 219):

```
[NRPE]
port=5666
allow_arguments=1
allow_nasty_meta_chars=1
use_ssl=1
; bind_to_address=
; allowed_hosts=
command_timeout=10
performance_data=1
```

`allow_nasty_meta_chars=1` allows the use of special characters `| ' &><' "\ [] {}` in `check_nrpe` arguments. These are not allowed if the value 0 is entered here instead of 1. `use_ssl` should only be switched off (that is, set to 0) if `check_nrpe` cannot be compiled with SSL support.

The `bind_to_address` und `allowed_hosts` parameters allow for NRPE settings that are different from the default. `command_timeout` interrupts an external command to be executed after the time specified (in seconds), but the timeout only has an effect on external commands. NRPE commands based on internal functions are unaffected by this. Finally, the `performance_data` parameter controls whether or not performance data should be returned. The default (value 1) is to return it, and it is not returned with the value 0.

In the [NRPE Handlers] section, the actual commands are defined. You can use the same syntax used in NRPE or a short notation, in which the keyword command is omitted entirely:

```
command[command_name]=command line
command_name=command line
```

Along with the usual plugin calls that make use of external plugins, there is the command inject. This runs an internal function (which is described in Section 20.4.4 from page 495):

```
[NRPE Handlers]
; -------------------------------------------
; external plugins
; -------------------------------------------
; NRPE-stylish:
;command[check_tcp]=C:\Plugins\check_tcp -H $ARG1$ -p $ARG2$
; shorter:
check_tcp=C:\Plugins\check_tcp -H $ARG1$ -p $ARG2$
;
check_smtp=C:\Plugins\check_smtp -H $ARG1$ -f wob@example.net
;
check_uptime=inject CheckUpTime ShowAll MinWarn=1d MinCrit=12h
```

In this example, check_uptime calls the internal function CheckUpTime by means of inject. If passing arguments via NRPE is allowed, you can greatly simplify the definition of inject commands:

```
check_inject=inject $ARG1$
```

Now you include the internal function, together with all required parameters, as an argument when calling check_nrpe:

```
nagios@linux:nagios/libexec$ ./check_nrpe -H winsrv -ccheck_inject \
    -a "checkUpTime ShowAll MinWarn=1d MinCrit=12h"
OK: uptime: 6d 7:19|'uptime'=544771000;86400000;43200000;
```

If you define the command object in Nagios just as generally, the exact formulation of the command will be shifted entirely to the service definition:

```
define command{
    command_name   check_inject
    command_line   $USER1$/check_nrpe -u -H $HOSTADDRESS$ -c check_inject
-a "$ARG1$"
}

define service{
```

```
    host_name           winsrv
    service_description Uptime
    check_command       check_inject!checkUpTime ShowAll MinWarn=1d MinCr
it=12h
    ...
}
```

There is a security issue that should be pointed out here, however. If you define `check_inject=inject $ARG1$` as described above, then you are opening a door to attackers who might be hoping for a buffer overflow in the code of NSClient++. In that event, the client will be able to run any command at all. You should therefore use this rather generous command only in secure environments, and even then you should restrict the hosts that are allowed to access NSClient++ via NRPE using `allowed_hosts`. On the other hand, such a free definition makes life much easier during the implementation phase, since you can try out all sorts of combinations and checks on the command line without having to adjust the configuration file NSC.ini to many hosts each time.

20.4.4 Internal NSClient++ functions

NSClient++ provides a series of internal functions that can be called by the `inject` command via NRPE, and usually also with the plugin `check_nt`. These are stored in several loadable modules. Table 20.3 gives an overview of which module is required for a particular function.

Module	Function
CheckDisk	CheckFileSize,
	CheckDriveSize
CheckSystem	CheckCPU,
	CheckUpTime,
	CheckServiceState,
	CheckProcState,
	CheckMem,
	CheckCounter
CheckEventLog	CheckEventLog
CheckHelpers	CheckAlwaysOK,
	CheckAlwaysCRITICAL,
	CheckAlwaysWARNING,
	CheckMultiple

Table 20.3:
Internal functions of
the NSClient++
modules

To use one of these functions with check_nt, you only need to ensure that the required modules are loaded in the [modules] section. Calling via NRPE and inject provides additional configuration options, however.

Thus, for the hard disk load check with check_nt, which uses the function CheckDriveSize internally, you can just have a warning and a critical threshold displayed:

```
nagios@linux:nagios/libexec$ ./check_nt -H winsrv -vUSEDDISKSPACE \
    -l C -w 80 -c 90
...
```

If, on the other hand, you access CheckDriveSize directly, you may specify higher and lower thresholds, and instead of using a hard drive letter, you can use a UNC path (see page 497).

Many of the parameters listed below are optional, at least if you go by the documentation in the Wiki. This convention does not seem to have been uniformly adhered to, however. Performance data, for instance, is obtained only if you specify a warning and a critical threshold. You can also omit one or both thresholds and the call will still function; what is missing is the performance data. The ShowAll and nsclient parameters are optional, provided that the function allows this.

For all other functions, you should test to see whether your configuration really fulfills the desired purpose and whether NSClient++ works without an error message before you deploy it in a production environment.

Checking file sizes with CheckFileSize

CheckFileSize tests the size of individual files or directories:

```
CheckFileSize MaxWarn=size MaxCrit=size
MinWarn=size MinCrit=size
File=path:alias ShowAll
```

The last ones here are processed recursively. You can also test drives if you specify File=C:*.*, for instance. The threshold parameters do require size values to be given, however. If you want to monitor how full a drive is in percent, you are better off using the command CheckDriveSize.

When specifying the threshold size values you can include a suffix: B for bytes, K for KB, M for MB, and G for GB (e.g., MaxWarn=2198M). A number without a suffix specifies a size in bytes.

The syntax allows several files and/or directories to be given. In this case, the File parameter follows the associated thresholds:

```
user@linux:nagios/libexec$ ./check_nrpe -H 172.17.129.25 \
   -c check_inject -a "CheckFileSize \
   MaxWarn=500M MaxCrit=1024MFile=E:\Exchsvr\mdbdata_log\*.* \
   MaxWarn=10G  MaxCrit=30G  File=F:\store02\priv2.edb
\
   File=G:\store03\pub3.edb ShowAll"

WARNING: E:\Exchsvr\mdbdata_log\*.*: 77M,
F:\store02\priv2.edb: 11.4G > w
arning, G:\store03\pub3.edb: 3.09G|
'E:\Exchsvr\mdbdata_log\*.*'=80740352
;524288000;1073741824;
'F:\store02\priv2.edb'=12234989568;10737418240;322
12254720;
'G:\store03\pub3.edb'=3316719616;10737418240;32212254720;
```

When monitoring directories, it is not sufficient to give just the directory names. Instead, as shown in the example for the directory E:\Exchsvr\ mdbdata_log\, you need to specify with *.* that all the files and subdirectories (together with their contents) contained in the directory must be included in the calculation.

Of course, you can also use wildcards, for example, *.log to find out the total size of all files ending in .log in a directory. The thresholds always refer to the total of all files and directories specified in the corresponding File parameter.

If there are several consecutive File specifications, the last thresholds that were specified before them are used. ShowAll displays the statuses of all files or directories specified, and if this parameter is not given, the display contains only files and directories with an error state.

The display contains the full path of the file and directories tested, which can become very confusing. CheckFileSize therefore allows the optional use of aliases. Calling

```
MaxWarn=500M MaxCrit=1024M File:TMP=C:\tmp\*.*
```

will display just the alias TMP instead of the full path:

```
OK: TMP: 0B|'TMP'=0;524288000;1073741824;
```

Checking how full drives are with CheckDriveSize

CheckDriveSize checks how full drives are. The thresholds can be given very flexibly here: You can either use the *Free parameters to determine the remaining free drive space or the *Used parameters to establish the used drive space:

```
CheckDriveSize MaxWarnFree=größe MaxCritFree=size
MinWarnFree=size Min
CritFree=size MaxWarnUsed=size
MaxCritUsed=size MinWarnUsed=size Min
CritUsed=size Drive=laufwerk FilterType=type
CheckAll CheckAllOthers Sho
wAll
```

When giving thresholds, you can again use sizes, or use the % suffix to obtain percentages. In contrast to CheckFileSize, the suffixes for size parameters must be written in lower case: b for bytes, k for KB, m for MB, and g for GB.

For the placeholder *disk* you can use either the respective disk letter or the UNC path of a network share: for example, Drive=\\WinSRV\C$. If CheckAllOthers is specified, NSClient++ checks all hard disks that have not been individually specified. CheckAll deals with all drives, so the Drive parameter can be omitted. An additional filter allows only certain drive types to be considered: FilterType=FIXED restricts itself to all drives that are permanently installed, while FilterType=REMOVABLE just considers removable drives. The filter FilterType=CDROM describes CD-ROM drives, and FilterType=REMOTE looks at all network drives. It is possible to combine several filters:

```
CheckDriveSize CheckAll FilterType=FIXED FilterType=REMOTE
```

checks all permanently installed local drives and all connected network drives.

Checking CPU load with CheckCPU

CheckCPU checks the processor load in percent, and thresholds are given here without the percentage sign:

```
CheckCPU warn=percentage crit=percentage
time=period ShowAll nsclient
```

The load is calculated over a period specified with the time parameter. If no suffix is given, the period is in seconds, otherwise the suffixes w for weeks, d for days, h for hours, m for minutes, and s for seconds are available. For longer periods, you must make sure that the parameter CpuBufferSize in the configuration file under [CheckSystem] has a sufficiently large value. The default period is one hour.

To display the CPU load over several different time intervals all at once, you can specify the time parameter multiple times:

```
CheckCPU warn=30 crit=80 time=1m time=5m time=15m
```

ShowAll influences the display of the plugin output (but not of the performance data; these have been omitted below):

```
OK CPU Load ok.
OK: 1m: 2%, 5m: 2%, 15m: 2%
OK: 1m: average load 2%, 5m: average load 2%, 15m: average load 2%
```

The first line shows the output without ShowAll, the second line shows it with this parameter. Here CheckCPU displays the values for each time interval individually. The third line demonstrates the parameter ShowAll=long. This does not give you more information, just more text.

The remaining parameter is nsclient, which displays the output in the style of the original NSClient and separates the details for the time intervals with the & sign: 2&2&2. Performance data is not displayed when using this parameter.

Determining the uptime with CheckUpTime

CheckUpTime shows how much time has passed since the system was started. As with CheckCPU, the thresholds can be set using a suffix (s, m, h, d, w):

```
CheckUpTime MaxWarn=time MaxCrit=time
MinWarn=time MinCrit=time ShowAll
nsclient Alias=string
```

ShowAll also displays the time even when there is no error state. nsclient changes the output to a simple value in seconds, without any other text. With Alias, the word Uptime can be replaced with a different text:

```
OK: uptime: 1d 20:11
OK: Running_Time: 1d 20:12
```

The first line shows a normal output with ShowAll; in the second line an additional Alias=Running_Time has been set.

Activity check with CheckServiceState

CheckServiceState checks whether services are active (started) or not (stopped). You can either check one or more individually listed services or use the CheckAll switch, which checks all services for which the autostart flag has been set and which should be running after every system start:

```
CheckServiceState service ShowFail CheckAll
exclude=servicename
CheckServiceState ShowFail ShowAll CheckAll exclude=servicename
```

Individual services can be explicitly checked for the desired state:

```
CheckServiceState MSExchangeSA=started MSSEARCH=stopped ShowFail
```

This call checks whether the MSExchangeSA service is running and the MSSEARCH service is not. If the state of either of the two services is different from what is specified, CRITICAL is displayed. ShowFail ensures that only services with errors appear in the output.

CheckAll normally includes all services with an autostart flag. Individual services can be excluded from this with exclude.

Monitoring processes with CheckProcState

CheckProcState checks the state of processes, and it functions in the same way as CheckServiceState, except that here there are fewer options available:

```
CheckProcState ShowAll ShowFail
CheckProcState ShowFail prozess
```

For single processes you can again specify the desired state (*process*=started or *process*=stopped); otherwise only ShowAll will be left to control the output. ShowFail is the default and can be omitted.

Checking memory load with CheckMem

CheckMem checks the load level of the memory. The type parameter is of interest here:

```
CheckMem MaxWarn=size MaxCrit=size
MinWarn=size MinCrit=size ShowAll
type=typ
```

type=page and type=paged show the entire memory (physical plus swap) and correspond to the value of check_nt -v MEMUSE. The difference between page and paged lies only in the routine used: The former uses the PDH library that is used by NSClient, and which originates from the days of Windows NT, whereas the latter uses the newer routines of Windows 2000 and Windows 2003. type=virtual refers to the swap memory used, and type=physical refers to the physical memory used.

The output of CheckMem only provides details of the entire memory available if there is an error state; for the OK state, only what is actually used of the specified category is shown.

As with `CheckFileSize`, suffixes for thresholds are written in upper case for this function: B, K, M, and G. Specifying percentages with the suffix % is also allowed.

Checking the performance counter with `CheckCounter`

With `CheckCounter` you can query Windows performance counters that record nearly all the parameters that Windows has to offer:

```
CheckCounter MaxWarn=number MaxCrit=number
MinWarn=number MinCrit=number ShowAll
Averages=value Counter=countername
```

With `Averages=true`, `CheckCounter` calculates averages for performance counters, which on their own do not provide averages. The value `false` switches this off, so that the query takes less time. The `Averages` parameter has no influence on performance counters that Windows already provides as an average.

The trick lies in finding the right performance counter. One starting point is the performance monitor itself, which is started in Windows via the `perfmon` program. If you insert a new performance counter in this for viewing, you will be shown all available objects (the performance counter categories) and performance indicators. All available counters are also shown by NSClient++ when it is run directly from the command line. Because of the large number of counters, it is best to redirect the output to a text file:

```
C:\Programme\Nagios\nsclient++> nsclient++CheckSystem listpdh > All.txt
```

`CheckCounter` takes as thresholds only whole numbers, since counters generally do not have units. This function allows an alias for the counter to be specified (see page 497):

```
CheckCounter "Counter:Logins=\Terminal services\Active
sessions" MaxWarn=2
0 MaxCrit=30 ShowAll
```

The quotation marks are important here. You must ensure that the parameter itself is within the quotation marks. If an alias is specified, NSClient++ replaces the performance counter in the output with the alias:

```
OK: Login: 1|'Login'=1;20;30;
```

Evaluating log entries with CheckEventLog

CheckEventLog searches through the event log for specific events and issues a WARNING or CRITICAL if the number of entries found exceeds the respective threshold. The function is very powerful and complex—and, regrettably, is not very easy to understand:

```
CheckEventLog  file=typ filter=value truncate=number
MaxWarn=number MaxCrit=
number descriptions filtermodetype=string
```

The Windows event log has various log files: for applications themselves (file=Application), for security aspects (file=Security), and for system parameters (file=System). There are some additional ones for domain controllers. If you want to search for events in more than one log file, you just repeat the file parameter:

```
file=Application file=Security file=System
```

The first filter parameter is used as a switch that is combined with filter expressions that are listed later on. filter=in includes all events that match the actual filter expression, filter=out excludes such events. filter=all demands that all filter expressions match the event (logical AND), but for filter=any, one single match (logical OR) is sufficient.

Writing the filter expression itself takes some getting used to: It starts with the keyword filter—an unfortunate choice, because the same keyword has already been used. This is followed by a mode: + or . ensure that the event is counted if the filter matches, whereas - excludes the event. For +, if the filter does not match, the event is excluded, even if filter=any is used and another filter expression demands that it be counted.

The mode is followed by the filter type. eventType describes whether an error or piece of information is involved (possible values for this are error, warning, info, auditSuccess, and auditFailure):

```
filter+eventType==warning
```

This expression includes all events in which the event type matches warning. The plus sign ensures that this filter is taken into account whatever the case, even if filter=any has been set.

The eventSource filter type specifies the source of the event (for example Print, Netlogon, or Service Control Manager). The following example searches for all events for which the source contains the partial string KCC:

```
filter.eventSource=substr:KCC
```

The generated and written filter types refer to time details: generated stands for the time at which the event entry was generated, written for the time at which the event was written to the log file:

```
filter-generated=>2d
```

This expression excludes all events that are more than two days old.

The message filter type refers to the text for the event entry and allows filtering according to text content:

```
filter.message=regexp:(hans|lisa)
```

Here a regular expression searches for events containing either the text hans or lisa.

With the eventID filter type you can filter according to the event number:

```
filter.eventID==7031
```

There is also the severity type, which is intended to filter according to the event priority. Since the author does not know of a suitable use for this, we will not look at it in any more detail.

It is not immediately clear when you need to write = for a filter expression and when == is needed. For expressions with purely text arguments (eventSource, message), a single equals sign is sufficient. For all other expressions which also allow a comparison, a relation symbol is part of the expression itself: =warning, =7031, >2d in the examples just mentioned. Together with the equals sign belonging to the filter type, this then looks like a double equals sign or a "greater than or equal to" sign—but this is not the case, there is no "greater than or equal to."

The following example searches in the System log file for crashes of the NSClient++ service:

```
user@linux:nagios/libexec$ ./check_nrpe -H 172.17.133.10 \
    -c check_inject -a 'CheckEventLog \
    file=System filter=in filter=all filter.eventID==7031 \
    filter.generated=<1d filter.message=substr:NSClientpp \
    MaxWarn=1 MaxCrit=2 descriptions'
Service Control Manager(error, 7031, error)[NSClientpp (Nagios) 0.2.7 20
07-03-06, 1, 60000, 1, Starten Sie den Dienst neu., ], : 1 > warning|''=
1;1;2;
```

Because of filter=in filter=all, all filter expressions must match simultaneously. The event number being looked for is 7031, the event should not be older than one day, and it should contain the substring NSClientpp in the text. If this is found, the test returns a WARNING, and if two or more matching events are found, the return value is CRITICAL. The `descriptions` switch here ensures that not only the name of the source, but the entire text is displayed. In addition, there is the `truncate` parameter, which restricts the entire output that is returned to `check_nrpe`.

When using `CheckEventLog`, the expression "practice makes perfect" applies. If you filter too unspecifically, so that `CheckEventLog` has to process too many event entries, strange side effects may occur. The message `UNKNOWN: No handler for that command` is sometimes shown, although the reason for this is actually a buffer overflow. In case of doubt, you should switch on debugging for NSClient++ (don't forget to stop/start) and examine the log file, which is in the same directory as the executable program and the INI file, for relevant error entries. Further information on `CheckEventLog` is contained in the Wiki.[32].

The debug functions `CheckAlwaysOK`, `CheckAlwaysWARNING`, and `CheckAlwaysCRITICAL`

The functions `CheckAlwaysOK`, `CheckAlwaysWARNING`, and `CheckAlwaysCRITICAL` are used for debugging purposes and always return the same status. Their use is relatively simple: The chosen debugging function is simply inserted in front of a normally defined function, such as `CheckFileSize`:

```
CheckAlwaysOK CheckFileSize ...
```

Summarizing several checks with `CheckMultiple`

If several checks need to be summarized into one single check, `CheckMultiple` is used:

```
CheckMultiple command=CheckFileSize ... command=CheckUpTime ... command=...
```

All individual checks are written one after another, each beginning with `command=`. Quotation marks in the style of `command=""` are not required. The highest error value that occurs in the individual checks is returned as the result.

---

[32] http://trac.nakednuns.org/nscp/wiki/CheckEventLog/CheckEventLog

Monitoring Room Temperature and Humidity

There are a number of sensors for monitoring room temperature and humidity. Most of them are integrated into the network as independent network devices, and are normally addressed via SNMP.

But you have to spend at least three hundred dollars on your first sensor. Searching for a cheaper and modular system, the author finally came across `http://www.pcmeasure.com/`; it has met all his requirements until now.

The fact that this chapter is restricted to this sensor is not meant to detract from other systems, but is down to the fact that this topic alone would be enough for a separate book.

21.1   Sensors and Software

A complete monitoring system for physical data normally consists of three components: a sensor (for temperature or humidity, for example), an adapter to connect to the serial or parallel port of a PC, and software to query the sensor.[1]

There are adapters for the PCMeasure system in variations from one to four sensors, which can be operated simultaneously. For the power supply the adapters need an available USB interface; alternatively a separate "USB power supply" is available. Instead of the adapter solution, there is also an optionally available Ethernet box with four sensor connections, which is somewhat more expensive, that can be expanded to accept 12 sensors.

The measurement querying software PCMeasure is available for both Linux and Windows.[2] Some features are exclusive to the Windows version, which is why it is slightly more expensive. For use with Nagios, the Linux version is totally sufficient, since only the measurement values are transmitted over a simple network protocol.

The sensors themselves are interesting: as well as those for temperature and humidity (as well as combinations of the two) there is also a contact sensor, a smoke and water alarm, a movement detector, and voltage detectors. These are normally connected with a twisted-pair cable (RJ45 connector); according to the FAQ,[3] they can be used up to 100 meters from the adapter or Ethernet box, provided you have good cables, that is, throughout a building.

21.1.1   The PCMeasure software for Linux

The tar archive pcmeasure.tar.gz with the Linux software is unpacked in its own directory, such as /usr/local/pcmeasure. The configuration file pcmeasure4linux.cfg is also installed here. The port entries in this file need to be adjusted so that only those ports are listed to which a sensor is actually connected:

```
[ports]
com1.1=01
```

com1 stands for the first serial port; if you are using the first parallel port instead, the entry before the period is lpt1. The digit following the port

---

[1] The PCMeasure Web site showed the following prices as of February 2008: simple temperature sensor 30101, $36; serial single-port adapter 30201 $51; Linux software, $38 (Windows: $53).

[2] The access data for the download comes with the invoice.

[3] http://www.pcmeasure.com/faq.php

refs to the adapter slot used by the sensor, so depending on how many adapters you have, this is a number from 1 to 4. The = sign is followed by the sensor type: 01 stands for a temperature sensor, 03 for a humidity sensor. An additional humidity sensor on the second slot of the same adapter would then be addressed as `com1.2=03`.

The query program `pcmeasure` requires the configuration file to be specified as an argument:

```
linux:local/pcmeasure # ./pcmeasure ./pcmeasure4linux.cfg
```

It runs as a daemon in the background and only ends if it is terminated with `kill`. In principle, any user can start it who has read permissions for the corresponding interface.

21.1.2 The query protocol

The software opens TCP port 4000 by default and accepts requests from the network. The protocol used is quite simple: you send a text in the format

```
pcmeasure.interface.slot<CR><LF>
```

(that is, with a DOS line ending) and you receive a response in the format

```
port;valid=validity;value=value;...
```

The *validity* placeholder is replaced by a 1 for a valid value or 0 for an invalid one. The port specification complies with the internal numbering system: `lpt1.1` corresponds to `port1`, `com1.1` to `port13`. Whether everything functions correctly or not can be tested with `telnet`:

```
user@linux:~$ telnet localhost 4000
Trying 127.0.0.1...
Connected to localhost.
Escape character is '^]'.
pcmeasure.com1.1
port13;valid=1;value=22.59;counter0=10627;counter1=14373;
Connection closed by foreign host.
```

The current temperature in this example is 22.59 °C, and the value is valid.

21.2 The Nagios Plugin `check_pcmeasure2.pl`

The plugin `check_pcmeasure2.pl`[4] allows a single sensor to be queried across a network. In exceptional cases—when measuring air pressure, for

---

[4] `http://www.nagiosexchange.org/60;575`

example—one call may also query two sensors. The plugin replaces `check_pcmeasure.pl` and uses the Perl module `Nagios::Plugin` to correctly represent the thresholds (see Section 24.1.5, page 557). The older `check_pcmeasure.pl` is still available under the same link, but is no longer maintained by the author.

Apart from the usual standard options, `-h` (online help), `-t` (timeout), `-V` (displays the version), and `-v` (*verbose*, additional information when looking for errors), `check_pcmeasure2.pl` has the following options:

`-H` *address* / `--host=`*address*
> This is the host name or IP address of the measuring computer on which the software is running and to which the sensors are connected, or the IP address or host name of the Ethernet box.

`-S` *sensor* / `--sensor=`*sensor*
> This switch defines the sensor, such as `com1.1` or `lpt1.2` (see above). When querying air pressure values, you need two sensors, which are separated by a comma when specified: `--sensor=com1.1,com1.2`.

`-p` *port* / `--port=`*port*
> This specifies an alternative TCP port for the software or for the Ethernet box. The default is port 4000.

`-w` *thresholds* / `--warning=`*thresholds*
> If the measured value lies outside the warning range specified here (e.g., `-w 18.0:22.0`, see Section 24.1.5 from page 557), `check_pcmeasure2.pl` sets off a warning.

`-c` *threshold* / `--critical=`*threshold*
> This defines the critical threshold; see `-w`.

`-T` *sensor type* / `--type=`*sensor type*
> This specifies the sensor type for sensors with special requirements. Types currently implemented are `brightness`, `barometer` (this needs two sensors to be specified in `--sensor`), and `standard` (the default).

`-R` *file* / `--rrd-database=`*file*
> This option specifies the round-robin database to save measured values independently of Nagios. The file must be writable for the user `nagios`. If this is missing, the plugin will create it again.
>
> In order to work with a round-robin database (see page 408) you need the Perl module RRDs used by the plugin, from the RRDtools.[5] The plugin automatically detects whether or not the module is available. If it is missing, it does not save the data separately.

---

[5] http://www.rrdtool.org/

In the following example the plugin asks for the temperature of the sensor connected to the host with the IP address 192.168.1.199:

```
nagios@linux:nagios/libexec$ ./check_pcmeasure2.pl -H 192.168.1.199 \
    -S com1.1 -w 18.0:22.0 -c 16.0:24.0
WARNING: Value com1.1: 23.5 |value=23.5;18.0:22.0;16.0:24.0;
```

Since the measured value lies above the warning limit of 22.0 °C, but below the critical limit of 24 °C, there is a WARNING. The interval details correspond to those in the figure on page 558.

The corresponding Nagios command can be specified with or without a round-robin database:

```
define command{
    command_name    check_temp_max
    command_line    $USER1$/check_pcmeasure2.pl -H $HOSTADDRESS$ -S $ARG1$
-w $ARG2$ -c $ARG3$
}
define command{
    command_name    check_temp_max_rrd
    command_line    $USER1$/check_pcmeasure2.pl -H $HOSTADDRESS$ -S $ARG1$
-w $ARG2$ -c $ARG3$ -R $ARG4$
}
```

Without a RRD, you only need to specify the maximum and critical warning limits, apart from the sensor details. In the second example the RRD file predefined in $ARG4$ saves the measured data. The following service uses the file /var/lib/rrd/temperatur-serverroom1.rrd for this purpose:

```
define service{
    host_name             linux01
    service_description   Room temperature
    max_check_attempts    1
    normal_check_interval 2
    check_command check_temp_max_rrd!com1.1!18.0:22.0!16.0:24.0!/var/lib
/rrd/temperatur-serverroom1.rrd

    ...
}
```

With max_check_attempts set to 1, Nagios does *not* repeat the query in case of an error at intervals of retry_check_interval. Instead the temperature is measured constantly every two minutes.

Since room temperatures normally change very slowly, you could use a normal_check_interval of five minutes. If you choose larger measuring intervals, you can set max_check_attempts to a value greater than 1 and repeat the measurement at shorter intervals in case of errors (e.g., retry_check_interval 1).

Monitoring SAP Systems

There are several ways of monitoring an SAP system. The simplest is just to check the ports on which the corresponding SAP services are running. Normally these are TCP ports 3200/3300 for system number 00, 3201/3301 for system number 01 etc. This can be done with the generic plugin described in Section 6.7.1, page 132. But it is possible that no user is able to log in even though the port is reachable, because SAP-internal services fail, making it impossible to work with the system.

To really test the complex interaction of various SAP components, you require a program that communicates on an application layer with the SAP system. There are two alternatives here: the more simple one uses the program `sapinfo`, which queries the available information without a direct login—like the SAP-GUI at the start. With somewhat more effort you can communicate with the SAP system over an SAP standard interface. This is no use, however, unless you have an SAP login with corresponding permissions. With the *Computing Center Management System* (CCMS), SAP provides its own internal monitoring system, which can also be queried with the RFC[1] interface, and which can be put to excellent use in Nagios, with the right plugins.

22.1 Checking without a Login: `sapinfo`

The program `sapinfo` is part of an optional software package for the development of client-side RFC interfaces. The Linux version which you require, RFC_OPT_46C.SAR, can be obtained either at ftp://ftp.sap.com/pub/linuxlab/contrib/, or you can log in to the *SAP Service Marketplace* at http://service.sap.com/ (a password is required for this) and use the search help there to look for the keyword RFC-SDK. Information is also provided by the SAP notes 413708 (at present the current RFC library), 27517 (installation of the RFC SDK), and 212876 (the new archiving tool SAPCAR).

22.1.1 Installation

SAP has its own archiving format in which the precompiled software is stored. To unpack programs you require the program SAPCAR, which can also be obtained through the FTP link mentioned or through the SAP Service Marketplace. It is operated in a way similar to tar:

```
linux:~ # mkdir /usr/local/sap
linux:~ # cd /usr/local/sap
linux:local/sap # /path/to/SAPCAR -xvf RFC_OPT_46C.SAR
SAPCAR: processing archive RFC_OPT_46C.SAR
x rfcsdk
x rfcsdk/bin
x rfcsdk/bin/sapinfo
...
```

The data contained in the archive lands in its own subdirectory, `rfcsdk`. If you run SAPCAR without any parameters, a short operating manual is displayed.

22.1.2 First test

The program `sapinfo` can be tested now without further configuration. To do this you require the so-called *connect string*; if the connection is running through an SAP gateway, this is a string such as /H/`ip_of_the_sap-gateway`/S/3297/H/`ip_of_the_sap_system`; without a gateway you simply specify an IP address or a host name that can be resolved, instead of this

---

[1] *Remote Function Call.*

complex expression. In case of doubt, the administrator responsible for the SAP system will reveal the exact connect string. In addition you must specify the system number,[2] in this example, 01:

```
nagios@linux:~$ cd /usr/local/sap/rfcsdk/bin
nagios@linux:rfcsdk/bin$ ./sapinfo ashost=10.128.254.13 sysnr=01

SAP System Information
---------------------------------------------

Destination          p10ap013_P10_01

Host                 p10ap013
System ID            P10
Database             P10
DB host              P10DB012
DB system            ORACLE

SAP release          620
SAP kernel release   640

RFC Protokoll        011
Characters           1100 (NON UNICODE PCS=1)
Integers             LIT
Floating P.          IE3
SAP machine id       560

Timezone             3600
```

The output provides various information on the SAP installation, including the SAP release (620), the SAP system ID (P10), the host on which the database is located, and the database system used, which in this case is Oracle.

With the `ashost` parameter you query a specific application server. For a message server, `sapinfo` requires the following details:

```
nagios@linux:rfcsdk/bin$ ./sapinfo r3name=P10 mshost=10.128.254.12 \
    group=ISH
```

The `r3name` parameter specifies the SAP system ID, `mshost` defines the IP address of the server, and `group` describes the logon group. As long as the PUBLIC group exists, you can leave this parameter out, and then the default, PUBLIC, will be used.

If the query ends with an error message such as

```
ERROR        service 'sapmsP10' unknown
```

---

[2] The SAP administrator will also know this.

then the definition of the sapmsP10 service is missing for the Nagios server[3] in /etc/services:

```
sapmsP10    3600/tcp
```

For the port you define the TCP port on which the message server is running. Which one this is depends on the particular SAP installation; the standard port is 3600.

22.1.3 The plugin check_sap.sh

The plugin check_sap.sh, a shell script based on sapinfo, is included in the standard Nagios Plugins package, but it is in the contrib directory and is not automatically installed. You can copy it manually to the plugin directory:

```
linux:~ #  cp /usr/local/src/nagios-plugins-1.4/contrib/check_sap.sh \
    /usr/local/nagios/libexec/.
```

Then you look in the plugin for the variable sapinfocmd and adjust the path for sapinfo:

```
sapinfocmd='/usr/local/sap/rfcsdk/bin/sapinfo'
```

If the plugin sapinfo is not found at the location given here, check_sap.sh will write an error message to STDERR, but if no error occurrs, you will receive an OK message on STDOUT and the return value 0:

```
./check_sap.sh: line 79: /usr/sap/rfcsdk/bin/sapinfo: No such file or di
rectory
OK - SAP server  available.
```

Like sapinfo, the plugin can be run in two ways: with the argument as it queries an application server, and with ms, a message server. The second argument in each case is the connect string, and if no SAP gateway is used, then it is the IP address or the host name of the host to be queried:

```
check_sap.sh as connect_string system_number
check_sap.sh ms connect_string SID logon_group
```

The first variation demands the two-digit system number of the application server as the third parameter, the counting of which starts at 00:

---

[3] Instead of P10, the appropriate system ID will always be shown here.

```
nagios@linux:nagios/libexec$ ./check_sap.sh as 10.128.254.13 01
OK - SAP server p10ap013_P10_01 available.
```

This means that the application server running on the host 10.128.254.13 is available.

When the message server is queried, the plugin displays the application server belonging to the specified login group (given as the fourth argument). If this information is missing, it determines the application server for the PUBLIC group.

For a message server, you specify the SAP system ID (*SID*), for example, P10,[4] instead of the system number:

```
nagios@linux:nagios/libexec$ ./check_sap.sh ms 10.128.254.12 P10 ISH
OK - SAP server p10ap014_P10_02 available.
```

In this example the message server running on 10.128.254.12 detects p10ap014_P10_02 as the application server for the logon group ISH and also reveals that this is reachable.

The following two command definitions assume that it is sufficient to use the IP address, and that no SAP connect string is required:

```
define command{
    command_name   check_sap_as
    command_line   $USER1$/check_sap.sh as $HOSTADDRESS$ $ARG1$
}
define command{
    command_name   check_sap_ms
    command_line   $USER1$/check_sap.sh ms $HOSTADDRESS$ $ARG1$ $ARG2$
}
```

If this is not the case, the command_line for querying an application server could look like this:

```
$USER1$/check_sap.sh as /H/sapgw/S/3297/H/$HOSTADDRESS$ $ARG1$
```

The following service definition can be used for all application servers:

```
define service{
   service_description   SAP_AS
   host_name             sap01
   check_command         check_sap_as!00
   ...
}
```

---

[4] The first instance of this has the system number 00, the second one, 01, etc.

Since there is only a single message server in an SAP system, it makes more sense to define a separate service for each logon group. The following example shows this for the group ISH:

```
define service{
    service_description    SAP_MS_ISH
    host_name              sap09
    check_command          check_sap_ms!P10!ISH
    ...
}
```

In this way you can test whether a user may log in without actually logging in. If there are interruptions between the database and the application server that make it impossible to log in, sapinfo provides a corresponding error message after a timeout. The author was able to observe several times that sapinfo and check_sap.sh reported an error in such a situation, while the TCP port-only test of the application server, check_tcp, returned an OK, although no user could log in any longer. So check_sap.sh, even without a login, provides more reliable information than a port-only check.

22.1.4 More up to date and written in Perl: check_sap.pl

check_sap.sh is not only getting on in years, it is apparently also no longer maintained, so once in a blue moon you just have to put up with the fact that it returns an OK, even when there is an error. The author of this book has therefore written his own version of the plugin in Perl and made this available on NagiosExchange.[5] As befits a reputable Perl plugin, it uses the Perl module Nagios::Plugin (more on this in Section 24.2 from page 560), parses the command line with Getopt::Long (Section 25.1, page 565), and includes integrated online help.

The plugin check_sap.pl also uses sapinfo (Section 22.1) and has the following options:

--ashost=connect_string

Tests the application server. A connect string (page 512) must be specified, which in the simplest case is the IP address of the application server. The test needs an SAP system number to be given at the same time, with --sap-sysnr.

--mshost=connect_string

Tests the message server. A connect string is expected, as with --ashost, and you also need to specify at least the SAP-SID of the

---

[5] http://www.nagiosexchange.org/21;744

system (e. g., P10). The test uses a logon group, and the default is PUBLIC. If this is not available in the SAP system, you must specify the group in question with `--group`.

`--sap-sysnr=system_number`
Defines the system number for the test of an application server. Normally the system number begins counting upwards from 00 for the first application server. In case of doubt, you should ask your SAP administrator for the correct system number.

`--sap-id=sid`
Defines the SAP-SID for the overall system for the test of the message server. In case of doubt, you should also ask your SAP administrator about this parameter.

`--group=logon group`
Defines the logon group that is to be used for the test of the message server. This must exist in the SAP system, otherwise the message server test will fail. The default is PUBLIC.

`--sapinfo=path_to_sapinfo`
Specifies the path to the program sapinfo. The default is /usr/lo-cal/sap/rfcsdk/bin/sapinfo.

`-h / --help`
Displays the online help.

`-V / --version`
Shows the version and the license conditions of the plugin (GPLv2).

`-v / --verbose`
Increases the verbosity of the plugin. This option can be given several times, to make the output increasingly extensive.

The following example tests an application server with the SAP system number 00:

```
nagios@linux:nagios/libexec$ ./check_sap.pl--ashost=10.128.254.12 \
    --sap-sysnr=00
CHECKSAP OK - system p10db012_P10_00 available
```

To test the message server you require the SID instead of the system number and, in our case, a logon group as well, since the default logon group PUBLIC does not exist in the P10 system:

```
nagios@linux:nagios/libexec$ ./check_sap.pl--mshost=10.128.254.12 \
    --sap-id=P10 --group=ISH
CHECKSAP OK - system p10ap014_P10_02 available
```

In contrast to the example given for `check_sap.sh`, the definition of the command is kept very general:

```
define command{
    command_name   check_sap
    command_line   $USER1$/check_sap.pl $ARG1$
}
```

Because of $ARG1$, a single command definition is sufficient for all checks, whether for application or message server, whether with or without an SAP connect string. The definition of the service for the test of an application server then looks like this:

```
define service{
    service_description   SAP_AS
    host_name             sap01
    check_command         check_sap!--ashost=$HOSTADDRESS$--sap-sysnr=00
    ...
}
```

The service obtains the IP address of the host from the accompanying host definition via the $HOSTADDRESS$ macro, so that the service definition works for an entire host group if you define the name of the host group with `hostgroup_name` instead of `host_name`. If an SAP connect string is required, you replace $HOSTADDRESS$ with the connect string:

```
check_sap!--ashost=/H/sapgw/S/3297/H/$HOSTADDRESS$ --sap-sysnr=00
```

In an SAP system there is just one message server, therefore the service check only makes sense for this one host. If there are several different logon groups, you define a separate service for each of these. The following example shows this for the group ISH:

```
define service{
    service_description   SAP_MS_ISH
    host_name             sap00
    check_command         check_sap!--mshost=$HOSTADDRESS$--sap-id=P10 -
-group=ISH
    ...
}
```

Here it is also possible to add a connect string that might be required.

22.2 Monitoring with SAP's Own Monitoring System CCMS

With SAP's own *Computing Center Management System* framework (CCMS), not only SAP systems, but also external applications can be monitored. Here local agents collect data from each of the hosts, which, since Release R/3 4.6C,[6] can be queried from a central component. The data examined includes not only SAP-specific features such as SAP buffers or batch jobs, but also operating system data such as memory and CPU usage, or disk IO and swapping. Even information on the database used or the average response times of applications can be queried.

The data of the CCMS can also be queried externally through RFC (*Remote Function Calls*, a standard SAP interface). Corresponding libraries for Unix and Windows platforms, with which a Linux program, for example, can query information from the CCMS over the network, are provided by SAP.

22.2.1 A short overview over the alert monitor

Within the SAP world you gain access to this data through the CCMS Alert Monitor (transaction RZ20) (Figure 22.1). The illustration shows so-called monitor connections that categorize various information in groups.

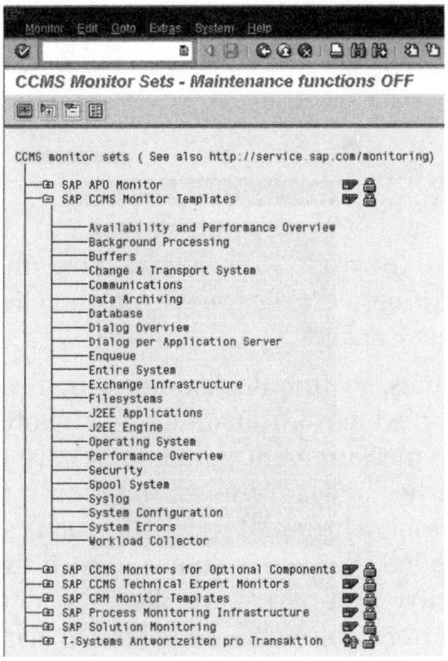

Figure 22.1:
The SAP CCMS Alert Monitor

---

[6] Central evaluation was not possible in earlier releases.

SAP provides several monitor collections with preconfigured values in its distribution. A trained SAP administrator can create and operate monitors at any time. We shall restrict ourselves here to the monitor collection SAP CCMS Monitor Templates and focus on the **Dialog Overview** monitor (Figure 22.2).

The dialog response times specified there (accessible through the *monitor attribute* Dialog Response Time) provide a measurable equivalent for performance problems corresponding to what the user feels is a "slow system." This value specifies the average processing time of a transaction (without network transmission time and without the time needed to render the information in the GUI of the client).

Figure 22.2:
The SAP CCMS
monitor dialog
Overview

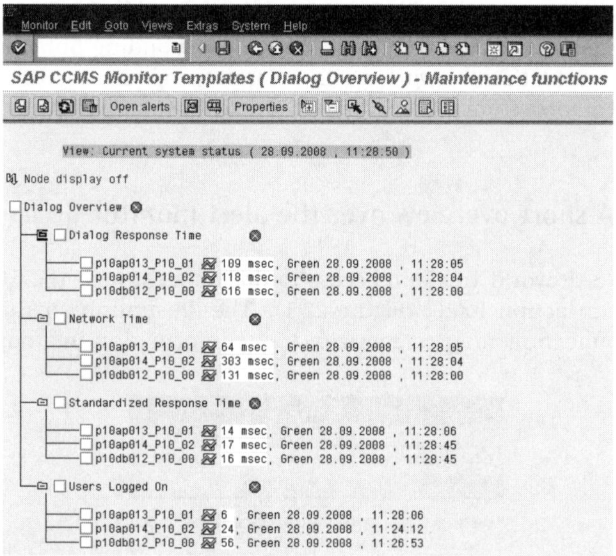

The monitor attribute Network Time reveals how much time the system needs to send data during a dialog stage from the client (the SAP GUI) to the SAP system and back again.

For each of the attributes, the monitor shows which context defined in the SAP system—normally, which SAP instance—is involved in the measured values specified. Most measurement parameters have a warning and a critical limit. If the value lies beneath the warning limit, the monitor displays the line in green; for monochrome devices the color is listed as text. If the warning limit is exceeded, yellow is shown, and if the critical limit is exceeded, red. If an entry of a partial tree lies outside the green limit, the monitor also sets the overlying nodes to yellow or red, so that the administrator can see that something is not right, even when the menus are not open.

You do not normally need to worry about the thresholds. The settings configured by SAP are sensible and should only be changed if there is a sound reason to do so.

The Nagios plugins for the CCMS query, described in Section 22.2.4 (page 525), return the status defined in the CCMS: OK if the traffic light is on green, WARNING for yellow, and CRITICAL for red. The thresholds are therefore set by the SAP system, and not by Nagios.

If you want to find out more about CCMS, we refer you to the documentation at
http://service.sap.com/monitoring (password required). There SAP provides detailed information on the installation and operation of CCMS. The SAP online help also has an extensive range of information available. If you just want a short summary of the subject and are more interested in the way the Nagios plugins work, you can find two informative PDF documents at http://www.nagiosexchange.org/Misc.54.0.html under the keyword SAP CCMS.

22.2.2 Obtaining the necessary SAP usage permissions for Nagios[7]

Retrieving information from the CCMS is done through RFC (*Remote Function Calls*), which requires a login on the SAP side. Luckily the user only needs a minimal set of permissions.

A new role is set up in the role generator (transaction PFCG) with a name that conforms to the company-internal conventions. It is not given any transaction assignment in the menu.

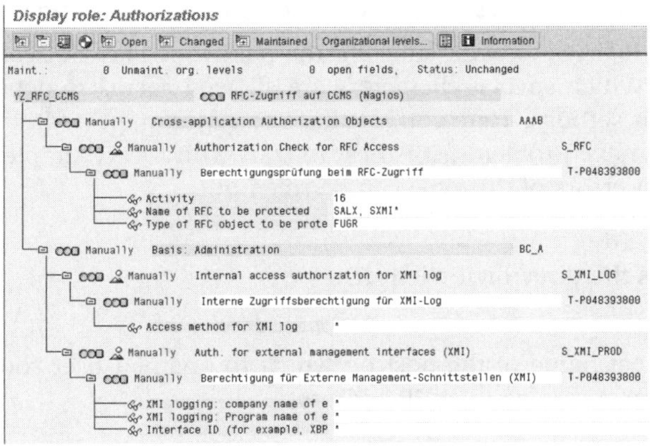

Figure 22.3:
For access from Nagios you require these SAP authorization objects

---

[7] This section is intended for SAP authorization administrators. If you do not maintain SAP authorizations yourself, you can skip this section.

When maintaining permissions, the following permission objects are added manually: S_RFC, S_XMI_LOG, and S_XMI_PROD (see also Figure 22.3).

Whether these permissions are sufficient or not can be tested with the plugin check_sap_cons described in Section 22.2.4, page 525 check_sap_cons. If a function group (such as SALG) is missing from the permission object S_RFC, the plugin shows name of this in plain text in the error message.

The login data is stored on the Nagios server in the file /etc/sapmon/ login.cfg. When doing this, various target hosts (called *RFC destinations* in SAP) can be configured simultaneously. Such a login configuration for a target system is called an *RFC template* in the language of the CCMS plugins (Section 22.2.4, page 525). It has the following form:

```
[LOGIN_template]
LOGIN=-d target -u user -p password -c client-id -h address
    -s system_number
```

The complete LOGIN definition must be written on a single line, and it is essential that it contain the following details:

-d target
> This is the name of the SAP system, also referred to as *SID* or *system ID*.

-u user -p password
> These parameters state the SAP user and corresponding password. Remember that a newly created dialog user has to change his or her password on first logon.
>
> In addition, there are problems with upper/lower case on some systems: In some cases the password must be written entirely in capitals.
>
> If the login is to work later on, the password may not contain the # sign. Which special characters are allowed seems to depend on the system settings. Here you just have to experiment a bit, if necessary. If you have problems, it is best to start with a very simple password, so that errors of this type can be ruled out.

-c client-id
> This is the three digit client ID.

-h address
> The host name of the host on which the named user should log in. This must resolve to an IP address.

-s system_number
> The SAP system number. The first SAP instance is normally 00, then increased incrementally.

Below, the *user* with the password *secret* should login from the client with the ID 020 to the host p10ap013 whose SAP installation has the system number 01:

```
[LOGIN_P10]
LOGIN=-d P10 -u user -p secret -c 020 -h p10ap013 -s 01
```

The RFC template name in square brackets consists of the text LOGIN_ and the SAP system ID (SID). The RFC template defined here belongs to the SAP system P10.

22.2.3   Monitors and templates

The interface provided by SAP that is used by the plugins is available in a simple and an extendable variant. Only additional functions enable all information from the CCMS to be retrieved, which is why we are omitting the description of the simple interface.[8]

For the extended interface, templates define the monitor data to be used. These are stored on the Nagios server in the file /etc/sapmon/agent.cfg and have the following format:

```
[TEMPLATE_name]
DESCRIPTION=description
MONI_SET_NAME=monitor collection
MONI_NAME=name_of_the_monitor
PATTERN_0=SID\context\monitor_object\attribute
```

The placeholders written in italics are replaced as follows:

name
> This is the name with which the plugins address the template. The name may consist of digits, letters, and the characters _ and -. When it is called by the plugin, the name must be written in lower case, irrespective of whether it is called TEST, Test, or test, for example. If you are having problems with alphanumerical names, it is better to select template names consisting of two digits when you are getting started, e. g., 00, 01, and so on.

description
> A freely selectable, simple text.

monitor collection
> This is the name of the monitor, set exactly as it is in the CCMS (including upper/lower case and spaces).

---

[8]   Information on this is provided by the PDF documents mentioned on page 521.

name_of_the_monitor

>The name of the monitor must also match the SAP name exactly.

context

>This pattern filters out the desired values from those contained in the monitor. In most cases you specify the identifier for the SAP instance, such as p10ap013_P10_01 (p10ap013 is the host name, P10 the SID of the SAP system, and 01 is the system number).

monitor_object

>This is the name of the desired monitor object, for example Dialog. Unfortunately the term demanded here rarely corresponds to the one shown in the SAP GUI. It is best to determine it using PATTERN_0=*, as described below.

attribute

>This is the variable to be queried. Each monitor object may contain severable variables. Dialog, for example, has, apart from the ResponseTime variable, the FrontendNetTime variable, which reveals the average processing time of a transaction, restricted to the network transmission time and processing time on the client.

The challenge here is in specifying the filter in PATTERN_0. It must exactly match the SAP-internal names, and these are not identical to the terms that are displayed in the CCMS Alert Monitor (Transaction RZ20).

It is best to start with PATTERN_0=*, which ensures that the entire tree appears. We shall call the template for this simply 00:

```
[TEMPLATE_00]
DESCRIPTION=Dialog response time
MONI_SET_NAME=SAP CCMS Monitor Templates
MONI_NAME=Dialog Overview
PATTERN_0=*
```

With this entry in /etc/sapmon/agent.cfg you query the complete list of all monitor entries, in this case those of the system with the ID P10, using the check_sap_cons plugin:

```
nagios@linux:nagios/libexec$ ./check_sap_cons 00 P10
...
P10 p10ap013_P10_01 Dialog ResponseTime 262 msec
P10 p10ap014_P10_02 Dialog ResponseTime 61 msec
P10 p10db012_P10_00 Dialog ResponseTime 11 msec
...
```

The entries contain the following information—with items separated by spaces:

SID context monitor_object attribute value

The information for the P10 system queried above first gives the SAP instance, such as p10ap013_P10_01, then the monitor object (Dialog) and the attribute (ResponseTime) together with values. In the SAP GUI (Figure 22.2) this latter is called Dialog Response Time, and since each empty space is significant, this is a completely different name.

In a template that is only interested in the response time of the instance p10ap014_P10_02, the PATTERN_0 is defined as follows:

```
PATTERN_0=P10\p10ap014_P10_02\Dialog\ResponseTime
```

If you want to query all the entries of a query level, you must use the wildcard *. The following example defines templates for the dialog response time, the network response time, and the average CPU load for all instances of the system P10:

```
[TEMPLATE_00]
DESCRIPTION=Dialog response time
MONI_SET_NAME=SAP CCMS Monitor Templates
MONI_NAME=Dialog Overview
PATTERN_0=P10\*\Dialog\ResponseTime

[TEMPLATE_01]
DESCRIPTION=network response time
MONI_SET_NAME=SAP CCMS Monitor Templates
MONI_NAME=Dialog Overview
PATTERN_0=P10\*\Dialog\FrontEndNetTime

[TEMPLATE_10]
DESCRIPTION=System load in five-minute average
MONI_SET_NAME=SAP CCMS Monitor Templates
MONI_NAME=Operating System
PATTERN_0="P10\*\CPU\5minLoadAverage"
```

22.2.4 The CCMS plugins

SAP demonstrates the use of the RFC interface to the CCMS with the CCMS plugins for SuSE. In Debian you can convert the RPM package nagios-plugins-sap-ccms-0.7.3[9] to a tar file with alien, or alternatively you can obtain the source RPM from a SuSE FTP mirror[10] and compile the source code yourself. This will give you the plugins listed in Table 22.1.

---

[9] It can be found at http://www.rpmseek.com/, for example, if you search there for nagios-plugins-sap-ccms.

[10] e.g., ftp://ftp5.gwdg.de/pub/linux/suse/opensuse/distribution/SL-OSS-factory/inst-source/suse/i586/nagios-plugins-sap-ccms-0.7.3-143.i586.rpm

Table 22.1:
The SAP-CCMS
plugins

Plugin	Description
check_sap	Output of the monitor data in HTML format
check_sap_cons	Ditto, but without HTML formatting and without hyperlinks for the output on the command line
check_sap_instance	Dialog response time and number of logged-in users on a particular application server (requires CCMS Ping[11])
check_sap_instance_cons	Ditto, as text output without HTML markup
check_sap_multiple	HTML-formatted output of data of a monitor template, which returns more than one value
check_sap_mult_no_thr	Output of multiple values with simple HTML formatting, without hyperlinks, in contrast to check_sap_multiple
check_sap_system	Shows the application servers of the SAP system and their states (requires CCMS Ping)
check_sap_system_cons	Like check_sap_system, only without HTML formatting

The plugins that end in _cons are especially suitable for test purposes: they simply pass the data on to the command line, without further formatting. The output of the others contains HTML formatting for a Nagios version modified by SAP; with Nagios 2.0 they usually lead to an incorrect view and are therefore useless.

Individual values are best retrieved with check_sap_cons. For Nagios 2.x the monitor definition must then really return only one single value. The remaining ones would be returned on additional lines, ignored by Nagios 2.x.

If you are using Nagios from version 3.0 onward, you can certainly formulate the monitor definition in such a way that check_sap_cons returns several values. Although the Web interface will only display the first line of these, the extended view, with extinfo.cgi, will show the rest of the output up to a length of 8 KB (see Figure 22.4).

---

[11] As components of the CCMS monitoring system, CCMS Ping monitors the availability of the application server belonging to the SAP system.

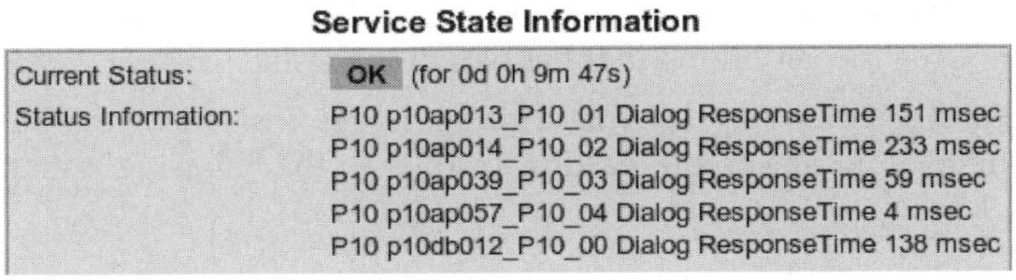

Service State Information

Current Status:	**OK** (for 0d 0h 9m 47s)
Status Information:	P10 p10ap013_P10_01 Dialog ResponseTime 151 msec
	P10 p10ap014_P10_02 Dialog ResponseTime 233 msec
	P10 p10ap039_P10_03 Dialog ResponseTime 59 msec
	P10 p10ap057_P10_04 Dialog ResponseTime 4 msec
	P10 p10db012_P10_00 Dialog ResponseTime 138 msec

Figure 22.4:
check_sap_cons
with a multiple-line
output in Nagios 3.0.

If Nagios 2.x is to display several return values, it is best to use check_sap_mult_no_thr, which provides these values with some HTML formatting elements that also work with Nagios 2.x. This causes all results to appear in the Web interface as well.

All plugins demand two arguments: check_sap, check_sap_cons, check_sap_multiple, and check_sap_mult_no_thr first require the name of the monitor template from the file /etc/sapmon/agent.cfg, such as 00, 00_sap13, 01, or 10 (see page 523), followed by the name of the RFC templates, as defined in /etc/sapmon/login.cfg (in the examples in this book we use the system ID P10).

For check_sap_system/check_sap_system_cons and check_sap_instance/check_sap_system_cons, the first argument changes: instead of the monitor template, check_sap_system demands the system ID (here, P10), and check_sap_instance demands the SAP instance, consisting of the host name, the SID, and the system number (for example, p10ap13_P10_01).

First steps with check_sap_cons

The plugin check_sap_cons is probably best suited to your first attempts. Only after this has worked for you properly on the command line should you move on to the actual Nagios configuration. The example on page 524 already showed how you determine the dialog response time with the monitor template 00, and the following example queries the network time which the SAP GUI requires till the result of the transaction appears in the SAP GUI, using the monitor template 01:

```
nagios@linux:nagios/libexec$ ./check_sap_cons 01 P10
P10 p10ap013_P10_01 Dialog FrontEndNetTime 383 msec
P10 p10ap014_P10_02 Dialog FrontEndNetTime 673 msec
P10 p10db012_P10_00 Dialog FrontEndNetTime 1491 msec
```

The definitions in the two templates can be found in Section 22.2.3 on page 523. In both examples, check_sap_cons returns multiple values, only the first line of which would be noticed by Nagios in the Web interface and in notifications. If the instance p10ap014_P10_02 displayed a critical status, but p10ap013_P10_01 did not, the plugin would return a CRITICAL, but the Web interface would only present the first line (like the notification), which would not give any reason to worry. This means that the admin would not see the very thing that has set off the critical state.

If `check_sap_cons` only returns error messages instead of the data you want, there could be several reasons for this. In the following example the login fails:

```
nagios@linux:nagios/libexec$ ./check_sap_cons 00 P10
<== RfcLastError
FUNCTION: SXMI_LOGON
RFC operation/code SYSTEM_FAILURE
ERROR/EXCEPTION
key     :
status  :
message : User account not in validity date
internal:
<== RfcClose
```

The reason is given in the `message:` field: the user currently does not have a valid account. If the following message were to be found there

```
message : User 910WOB has no RFC authorization for function group SXMI .
```

this would mean that the user `910WOB` does not have the necessary permission in the authorization object S_RFC. In order to grant it, that user should be assigned to the function group `SXMI`.

The plugins record such RFC error messages in the file `dev_rfc` in the current working directory. If Nagios runs the plugin, then it will generate this file in the Nagios home directory (`/usr/local/nagios`, if you have followed the installation description in this book).

In the next case the login works perfectly, but the plugin does not return any values:

```
nagios@linux:nagios/libexec$ ./check_sap_cons 01 P10
No information gathered! System up?
```

The error here lies in the monitor definition: often the name of the monitor set or the monitor is written wrongly, or the pattern does not match the monitor used. The intersection of monitor and pattern is then empty, and SAP also does not warn explicitly if the monitor or monitor set do not even exist.

Checking multiple values with `check_sap_mult_no_thr`

If Nagios is to represent multiple queried values in the Web interface, you should use `check_sap_mult_no_thr`:

```
nagios@linux:nagios/libexec$ ./check_sap_mult_no_thr 00 P10
<table>
    <tr><td CLASS='statusOK'>P10 p10ap013_P10_01 <br>
            Dialog ResponseTime 785 msec</td></tr>
    <tr><td CLASS='statusOK'>P10 p10ap014_P10_02 <br>
            Dialog ResponseTime 352 msec</td></tr>
    <tr><td CLASS='statusOK'>P10 p10db012_P10_00 <br>
            Dialog ResponseTime 22 msec</td></tr>
</table>
```

The output is given in a single line, which we have reformatted manually here so that it can be more easily read. With the HTML code, the plugin ensures that each value (thanks to the CLASS specifications) is shown on a separate line in the color matching its status. The status of the Nagios service changes to CRITICAL if at least one measured value is critical. Such a case is shown in Figure 22.5.

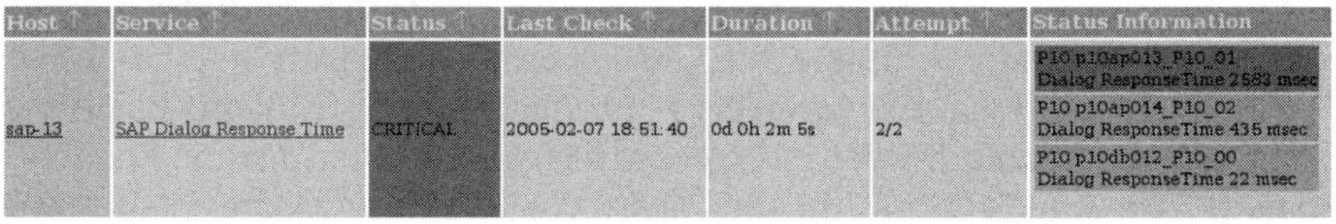

Figure 22.5:
check_sap_mult_no_thr
uses HTML markups
which Nagios 2.0
also understands

In this case as well you should remember that Nagios 2.x altogether processes no more than 300 bytes of the plugin output, and cuts off the rest. For HTML-formatted output, not only is information then missing, there are also side effects in the table layout in the Web interface. In case of doubt, you must share the test among several service checks. Starting with Nagios 3.0, this problem generally no longer occurs, as the limit of 8 KB for the plugin output is also usually sufficient to display extensive output.

In the definition of the Nagios command objects, the host name, exceptionally, does not play a role for the CCMS plugins. This means that the $HOSTADDRESS$ macro is not used:

```
define command{
    command_name    check_sap_ccms
    command_line    $USER1$/check_sap_mult_no_thr $ARG1$ $ARG2$
}
```

If you request several values simultaneously, they will normally belong to different hosts. This means that services can only be assigned to a host in one-to-one single value queries. Nevertheless, Nagios expects a specific host in the service definition:

```
define service{
    service_description    SAP Dialog Response Time
```

```
host_name              sap01
check_command          check_sap_ccms!00!P10
   . . .
}
```

22.2.5 Performance optimization

Since the monitor always transmits all the data it has available over the RFC interface, filtering always takes place on the client side through the plugin. For this reason it is not recommended that you query single values from a large monitor one after another: this consumes considerable resources.

You should either have a single service provide all the values,[12] or you should define a separate monitor yourself containing precisely those values you would like to test. This latter method is recommended by SAP.

If you want to check several monitors, or even single values of the monitor one after the other, you should keep an eye on the necessary network bandwidth. Within a local network this is normally not a problem, but it can place a considerable burden on narrow-bandwidth long-distance connections (ISDN, simple VPNs). In such cases you should measure the network traffic when starting operation, so that you can increase the check intervals accordingly in case of problems.

---

[12] Using a plugin predestined for the output of multiple values.

Processing Events with the EventDB

Events are fundamentally different from the other, usual host and service states in Nagios. The check of a service in a critical state returns a CRITICAL until the state of the service changes, irrespective of the number of checks and the repeat interval. An event, on the other hand, occurs only once, for instance in the form of a syslog entry or an SNMP trap.

If the events of an uninterruptible power supply (UPS) are logged via syslog to a log file, the message that the UPS has switched to battery because the voltage supply has failed will appear there only once. If you now test regularly whether a corresponding entry occurred within the last half hour, simple log file checks will not announce a match after this time has expired, so they will return an OK, since there is no critical event. But the UPS is still in a critical state. The critical state only really ends when the message arrives that the voltage supply has been restored.

Monitoring via SNMP traps comes close to the desired behavior: An alarm trap announces the failure of the voltage supply, the state of the service is set to CRITICAL, a subsequent OK trap announces the restoration of the voltage supply, and the state changes back to OK.

Events can be integrated into Nagios in various ways. A simple syslog integration is described in Section 14.5 from page 306, and another processing method for SNMP traps, also kept very simple, is dealt with in Section 14.6 from page 312. For Windows events it is often sufficient to test whether a specific event has occurred in the past 12 to 24 hours. The check can be made with NSClient++ and the module CheckEventLog (Section 20.4.4, page 502), for instance.

The procedure described in this chapter goes a little further. All events are collected in an event database. An administrator processes all these events and sets an acknowledge via a Web interface. Nagios now checks via plugin whether a defined number of events is exceeded for a specific group, so that the administrator will have to act—to set acknowledges and undertake further action, if necessary.

A similar approach is taken by nagtrap[1] (formerly SNMPTT Web Frontend, not to be confused with the SNMPTT GUI[2]). nagtrap is specialized for SNMP traps and is integrated directly into the Nagios Web interface. For reasons of space, we will not go into a detailed description here.

23.1 How the EventDB Works

The EventDB of NETWAYS[3] basically consists of four components: a syslog connection, which collects the events, a MySQL database to save the events, a Web interface for interactive processing, and a Nagios plugin, which connects the EventDB to Nagios. Figure 23.1 shows a diagram of the setup.

A central syslog service—syslog-ng is used because of its more flexible configuration—collects events from various sources. There are various software packages available for the integration of Windows event logs, one of which is described in Section 23.6 (page 545). The SNMP trap daemon installed on the syslog server, snmptrapd (Section 14.6.1, page 312), is able to pass the traps it receives on to the syslog. To provide more meaningful and readable messages from the cryptic OIDs, the *SNMP Trap Translator* (SNMPTT) is on hand to help out the snmptrapd, and this is described briefly in Section 23.7 from page 546.

syslog-ng allows existing events to be arranged in a self-defined format and to be sent to a named pipe. From this a daemon reads the incoming

---

[1] http://www.nagtrap.org/
[2] http://snmptt-gui.sourceforge.net/
[3] http://www.netways.de/

events and writes them to a MySQL database. Via a Web interface (Figure 23.2, page 539) the administrator confirms processed events with acknowledges. Nagios uses a plugin to test whether there are one or more non-confirmed entries for a specific event and informs the administrator accordingly about the notification functions.

It should also be mentioned that the EventDB is ideal for processing syslog entries, even when Nagios is not used at all. The Web interface of the EventDB provides a simple but effective interface that can be used to search the database quickly and easily for a particular event or for similar events, especially when events of the same type are collected from a large number of hosts.

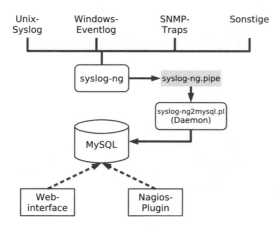

Figure 23.1:
syslog-ng collects data from various sources and writes these to a named pipe. A separate daemon reads the events from this and writes them to the database. From this they can be queried via Web interface or via Nagios plugin.

23.2 Installation

The current version of the EventDB can be obtained from NagiosExchange,[4] and the contents of the tar archive are unpacked in the directory /usr/local/src:

```
linux:~ # cd /usr/local/src
linux:local/src # tar xvzf /pfad/eventdb.tgz
eventdb/
eventdb/plugin/
eventdb/plugin/check_eventdb.pl
eventdb/agenten/
eventdb/agenten/syslog-ng/
eventdb/agenten/syslog-ng/syslog-ng2mysql
eventdb/agenten/syslog-ng/syslog-ng.conf
```

[4] http://www.nagiosexchange.org/36;1129

```
eventdb/agenten/syslog-ng/syslog-ng2mysql.pl
...
eventdb/db/
eventdb/db/create_tables.sql
eventdb/webinterface/
eventdb/webinterface/index.php
...
eventdb/cleanup/
eventdb/cleanup/eventdb-clean_database.sh
eventdb/cleanup/rotate_eventdb.sh
...
```

The Nagios plugin is located in the `plugin` subdirectory. The subdirectory `agenten` contains the integration with `syslog-ng`. In db there is a MySQL script that creates the necessary tables in the database. The `webinterface` directory contains the Web interface for the EventDB

23.2.1 Installation requirements

A prerequisite for the EventDB is `syslog-ng` in at least version 1.9.1, since the template mechanism required is only implemented from this version onward. For the database you require a current MySQL-5.0 server (included in the Debian package `mysql-server-5.0`, for example), and for the `syslog-ng2mysql.pl` daemon written in Perl, the module `DBD::MySQL` (in Debian, the package `libdbd-mysql-perl`).

The Web interface is implemented in PHP 5. This requires, along with Apache 2, the PHP-5 module for this server version (in Debian `libapache2-mod-php5`) and the PHP5-MySQL package (in Debian, `php5-mysql`).

An automatic installation routine that checks that all required packages are present is not included in EventDB.

If the SNMPTT, to be described later in Section 23.7, is to be integrated, then you will also require the daemons `snmpd` and `snmptrapd`, as well as the accompanying client programs. Debian provides these programs in the packages `snmpd` and `snmp`. The SNMP trap translator requires SNMP Perl (in Debian, included in the package `libsnmp-perl`), which must not be confused with `Net::SNMP`.

23.2.2 Preparing the MySQL database

After the installation of the MySQL-5 server package for the respective distribution, you set up the database `eventdb` and the database user `eventdb`:

```
linux:~ # mysql -p
mysql> CREATE DATABASE eventdb;
```

```
Query OK, 1 row affected (0.01 sec)

mysql> GRANT SELECT,INSERT,UPDATE,DELETE ON eventdb.* TO \
   'eventdb'@'localhost' IDENTIFIED by 'mypassword';
Query OK, 0 rows affected (0.00 sec)

mysql> quit
Bye
```

The GRANT command gives eventdb the necessary permissions to work with the event database; instead of the password set here, you use your own, secure password. Then you change to the directory where the source code has been unpacked (in this case, /usr/local/src/eventdb) and set up the necessary tables with the script create_tables.sql from the subdirectory db:

```
linux:~ # cd /usr/local/src/eventdb
linux:src/eventdb # mysql -p eventdb < db/create_tables.sql
```

If no errors occur when doing this, the prompt will appear, without any other output. What has been created by the script can then be displayed with show tables and describe *tablename*:

```
user@linux:~$ mysql -u eventdb -p eventdb
mysql> show tables;
+-------------------+
| Tables_in_eventdb |
+-------------------+
| comments          |
| events            |
+-------------------+
2 rows in set (0.00 sec)

mysql> describe events;
+--------------+---------------------+------+-----+---------------------+
| Field        | Type                | Null | Key | Default             |
+--------------+---------------------+------+-----+---------------------+
| uid          | int(11)             | NO   | PRI | NULL                |
| type         | varchar(50)         | NO   | MUL |                     |
| host         | varchar(50)         | NO   | MUL |                     |
| facility     | varchar(50)         | NO   | MUL |                     |
| priority     | varchar(20)         | NO   | MUL |                     |
| level        | varchar(10)         | NO   |     |                     |
| tag          | varchar(10)         | NO   |     |                     |
| program      | varchar(50)         | NO   |     |                     |
| datetime     | datetime            | NO   |     | 0000-00-00 00:00:00 |
| message      | blob                | NO   | MUL |                     |
| acknowledged | tinyint(1) unsigned | NO   |     | 0                   |
+--------------+---------------------+------+-----+---------------------+
11 rows in set (0.00 sec)
```

The MySQL command `show tables` shows the tables created. All events are saved in `events`. The `comments` table is just an auxiliary table, which is used for comments that the administrator might make when setting acknowledges.

23.2.3 Sending events to the database with `syslog-ng`

The configuration of `syslog-ng` has already been described in Section 14.5 from page 306, which is why we will deal here only with the adjustments for the EventDB. In order for the syslog daemon to be able to pass on data to the EventDB, we need suitable *destinations* and a log entry that uses these. To make the configuration more clear we will write our own template to the file `syslog-ng.conf`, which formats the output and which is referenced in the definition of the two destinations `d_eventdb` and `df_eventdb`:

```
template t_eventdb {
  template("$HOST\t$FACILITY\t$PRIORITY\t$LEVEL\t$TAG\t$YEAR-$MONTH-$DAY
\t$HOUR:$MIN:$SEC\t$PROGRAM\t$MSG\n");
  template_escape(no);
};
destination d_eventdb {
  pipe("/var/run/syslog-ng.pipe" template(t_eventdb));
};
destination df_eventdb {
  file("/var/log/eventdb" template(t_eventdb));
};
```

In the `TAG` variable there is a non-documented combination of `$FACILITY` and `$PRIORITY`, that is, of the type of program to be logged (daemon, authorization tool, kernel, cron daemon, printer, and so on; see also man 3 syslog) and the significance of the message. `$HOST` is a placeholder for the computer, `$YEAR-$MONTH-$DAY` for the date, `$HOUR:$MIN:$SEC` for the time, `$PROGRAM` for the program for which the message applies, and `$MSG` for the log message itself.

The `LEVEL` variable is actually unnecessary, since it contains the same value as `PRIORITY`. The database layout demands both values, however, which is why they must be specified. The entire template definition must be written on one line in the configuration file `syslog-ng.conf`; it is only line-wrapped here for printing purposes.

The destination `d_eventdb` is a named pipe that is fed with the data of the template. The destination `df_eventdb` is used for debugging purposes and can be used as a substitute or in parallel when you are searching for errors. The data here ends up in a normal log file. Since the same template is used, it produces exactly the same text as is contained in the named pipe.

The only things missing now are a source, a filter, and a log entry:

```
source local {
   unix-stream("/dev/log");
   internal();
};
source remote {
   udp( ip(0.0.0.0) port(514) );
};

filter f_warn {
   level(warn .. alert);
};

log {
   source(local); source(remote);
   filter(f_warn);
   destination(d_eventdb);
   # destination(df_eventdb);
};
```

The source `local` reads all local and system-internal events that arrive at the `syslog-ng`, but no kernel events. `remote` describes the classic method of receiving packets from remote syslog daemons via UDP port 514. The filter `f_warn` covers all events that have a priority (or level) of at least `warn`. Finally, `log` writes events from the two sources that are matched by the filter, to the destination `d_eventdb`.

The configuration shown uses `/var/run/syslog-ng.pipe` as a named pipe. Debian-based systems delete the contents of the directory `/var/run` when the system is booted, however. For this reason the named pipe must be newly created at each system start. The startup script included with Event-DB, `syslog-ng2mysql` in the directory `agenten/syslog-ng`, has been doing this since version 2007-11-30; for older installations you should add the following two lines at the beginning of the script:

```
FIFO="/var/run/syslog-ng.pipe"
test -p $FIFO || mkfifo $FIFO
```

Then you copy the script to `/etc/init.d` and ensure, depending on the distribution, that it is run automatically on system start, and certainly before `/etc/init.d/syslog-ng`.

The Perl daemon `syslog-ng2mysql.pl` is also located in the subdirectory `agenten/syslog-ng`. In this script you need to change the variables `$dbuser` and `$dbpass` to match your own MySQL installation:

```
my $db      = "eventdb";
my $dbhost  = "localhost";
```

```
my $dbuser  = "eventdb";
my $dbpass  = "mypasswd";
my $dbtable = "events";
```

Then you copy the file to /usr/local/sbin, where the init script expects it to be. With

```
linux:~ # /etc/init.d/syslog-ng2mysql start
linux:~ # /etc/init.d/syslog-ng restart
```

you restart the Perl daemon and perform a restart of the syslog daemon.

An initial overview of whether events end up in the database can be obtained by entering a simple select * command on the events table:

```
user@linux:~$ mysql -u eventdb -p eventdb
mysql> select * from events;
...
```

If nothing happens here, you can use the logger program to test whether the syslog daemon is writing entries at all to the log files (for further information, see man logger):

```
user@linux:~$ logger -p daemon.warn "hallo wob"
```

If no entries appear, despite the syslog working correctly, you should enable the destination df_eventdb and check to see if the output of the template appears correctly formatted.

23.3   Using the Web Interface

The Web interface for the EventDB consists of a single PHP file, index.php, which is included in the tarfile in the subdirectory webinterface. It accesses the database directly and therefore requires details of the database, such as user and password. You should check (and change) the following four lines of the file accordingly:

```
// Database
cset('db.user', 'eventdb');
cset('db.pass', 'mypasswd');
cset('db.host', 'localhost');
cset('db.name', 'eventdb');
```

Then you copy index.php to the (previously created) directory /usr/local /nagios/share/eventdb. The Web interface, as shown in Figure 23.2, can then be reached via the URL http://*nagios-server*/nagios/eventdb/index.php.

The Web interface is roughly divided into three areas: the selection window at the top, which allows data to be selectively filtered, the event display in the middle, and a third section which allows acknowledges to be commented.

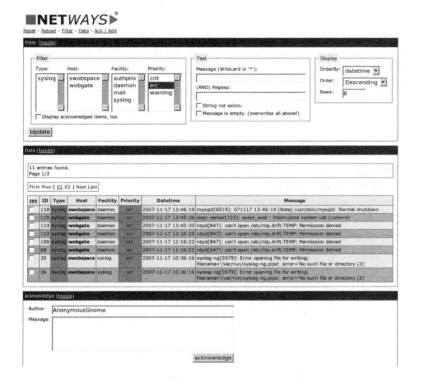

Figure 23.2:
The Web interface for the EventDB allows certain entries to be selected, and the administrator can also set acknowledges for each event via the Web interface.

The selection filter **Type** refers to the event source, which is normally **syslog**. If SNMP traps are being processed, another type, **snmptrap**, is included. With *Host* you specify the system of origin of the event by means of the host details in the syslog entries. The selection options for **Facility** and **Priority** also correspond to the naming convention used in syslog (see page 536).

If you set a check mark for **Display acknowledged items, too**, the Web interface will display all events. Normally you will just see the events for which there are no acknowledges.

Of more interest is the **Text** box in the center: At the top you can enter simple patterns. If you are looking for all the entries of the program pluto, for example, you just enter pluto* here. Distinction is made between upper and lower case. More options are provided by regular expressions, which can be specified in the second line: The entry (smbd|nmbd|winbind) searches for all entries in which either smbd, nmbd or winbind occur. The Regexp search is considerably slower, however. A check mark for **String not exists** negates the previous selection.

The option **Message is empty** can only be used on its own. It ignores all the other settings in the **Text** box and displays all events that do not contain any message text.

The **Display** box affects the presentation. You can select different sorting methods, and define the number of entries to be displayed. The default of 20 entries is too low for many purposes. If the Web interface displays a larger number by default, you should change the following line in the file index.php accordingly:

```
cset('page.maxrows', 20);
```

The data range shows normal syslog entries, together with the number of the dataset in the database in the **ID** column. For an acknowledgement, you can put a check mark in front of the entry, enter a comment in the lower section if necessary, and select the **acknowledge** button. Confirmed entries disappear when the Web page is reloaded.

If you want to confirm all entries shown simultaneously, select the **rev** header of the first table column, which inverts the current state of the selection fields. A subsequent acknowledge via the button confirms all entries at the same time.

The person responsible for an acknowledge is listed in the **Author** line. Once the user has logged in to the Web server, his user name will be given automatically there; otherwise, **AnonymousGnome** will appear as the author. This entry can be overwritten as you please.

23.3.1 Preselection of the filter with URL parameters

Specific parameters can be passed on to the Web interface through a URL so that a preselection is already made for the call:

```
http://nagios-server/nagios/eventdb/index.php?host[0]=swobspace
```

This example calls all non-confirmed entries assigned to the host swobspace. The entries for a multiple selection are represented by the Web interface as an array, which is why it must be specified in square brackets for the parameters host, type, facility, and priority. The entries for multiple hosts are queried with a consecutive index: index.php?host[0]= swobspace&host[1]=wobgate or index.php?host[0]=wobgate&host[1]=swobspace—the order of the menu entries in the Web interface does not have to match that of the indices.

The following CGI parameters can be specified, separated from one another by &:

type[*index*]=*type*
> corresponds to the **Type** filter.

host[*index*]=*host*
> ensures that the selection is in the **Host** field.

facility[*index*]=*facility*
> selects the **Facility** entry.

priority[*index*]=*priority*
> corresponds to the **Priority** selection.

message=*pattern*
> the placeholder *pattern* is replaced by the expression that you would write in the **Message** box. Special characters must first be compiled in HTML-compatible code. Thus, *Bad TCP* is turned into %2ABad%20TCP%2A:[5]

```
event.php?message=%2ABad%20TCP%2A
```

regexp=*regular_expression*
> allows a regular search expression to be given. As with message, special characters must also be given in an HTML-compatible form.

displayack=*value*
> also displays confirmed entries when set to true. The default is the opposite value, false.

message_notexists=*value*
> simulates setting the check mark in front of **String not exists**: the value true negates the message and regexp selection. The opposite value, false, is the default.

message_notext=*value*
> when set to true, shows only entries with an empty message. Here the default is also false.

order=*sorting*
> enables the sorting order to be defined: ASC for ascending, DESC for descending.

orderby=*criterion*
> defines the field by which sorting should be done: datetime, priority, host, facility, or uid (database index).

---

[5] A special character is converted to % followed by its hexadecimal value: a space corresponds to 20, a *, to 2A; see man ascii.

displayrows=*number*
>   defines the number of rows to be displayed.

23.4   The Nagios Plugin for the EventDB

Querying the EventDB from Nagios is done with the plugin check_event-
db.pl in the subdirectory plugin, which is copied to the directory /usr/
local/nagios/libexec/. It has the following options:

--db=*database_name*
>   The name of the EventDB. This is only specified if it is different from
>   the default eventdb.

--dbtable=*database_table*
>   The event table in the database. The default events is rarely changed.

--dbuser=*database_user*
>   This parameter must always be given, since none is set by default for
>   the database user.

--dbpassword=*database_password*
>   The same applies for the password for this user.

--dbhost=*database_host*
>   Details of the host on which the database is running. The default is
>   set to localhost.

-H *hostname* / --host=*hostname*
>   Host from which the message in the syslog really originates.

-p *priority* / --priority=*priority*
>   The desired syslog priority (or level), for example warning, err, or
>   crit. For other information, see man 3 syslog.

-f *facility* / --facility=*facility*
>   The syslog facility to be queried, such as cron, daemon, or auth (see
>   also man 3 syslog).

-m *text* / --message=*text*
>   The event text for which the plugin should look. It starts with the
>   name of the program from which the message originates. If you are
>   looking for entries from the program snmpd, you enter -m 'snmpd*'.
>   As wildcards, * (shell syntax) and % (SQL syntax) can be used equiva-
>   lently; the plugin replaces * with %.

-t *type* / --type=*type*
>   Event type, usually syslog.

-l *prefix* / --label=*prefix*
> Text placed in front of the plugin output in order to better identify a specific check.

-w *integer* / --warning=*integer*
> If the plugin finds at least *integer* matches it will issue a WARNING.

-c *integer* / --critical=*integer*
> If the plugin finds at least *integer* matches it will issue a CRITICAL.

The following plugin call looks for all error messages with the priority err from the daemon facility that originate from the snmpd and contain any type of message text. If the plugin finds one entry, it should issue a WARNING; if it find two or more, it should issue a CRITICAL:

```
nagios@linux:nagios/libexec$ ./check_eventdb.pl --dbuser=eventdb \
    --dbpassword=secret --facility daemon --priority err -m "snmpd%" \
    -w 1 -c 2 --label=syslog-snmpd
CRITICAL: syslog-snmpd 6 matches found!|matches=6
```

--label prefixes the actual result to the syslog-snmpd text, so that the statement can be more easily interpreted.

The command definition is kept really simple, due to the fact that the actual logic is stored in the service definition. The entire command_line must, as before, be written in a single line:

```
define command {
  command_name   check_eventdb
  command_line   $USER1$/check_eventdb.pl --dbuser=eventdb --dbpass=$USER
9$ $ARG1$
}
```

Database user and password are firmly joined together here. So that no password is visible at this point, we use the macro $USER9$ from the resources file (see page 601). All other parameters are specified by the service definition for $ARG1$, for example, as follows:

```
define service {
   host_name             nagios
   service_description syslog_snmpd
   check_command         check_eventdb!--facility daemon --priority err -m
"snmpd%" -w 1 -c 2 --label=syslog-snmpd
...
}
```

23.5 Maintenance

The MySQL database can, under some circumstances—depending on the number of connected systems and events passed on by the syslog—fill up very quickly. Then it is time to clean up. To do this you need to find all the entries that are older than a certain date, test whether an acknowledge exists for them, and delete them. The following SELECT statement demonstrates the principle:

```
user@linux:~$ mysql -u eventdb -p eventdb
mysql> SELECT * FROM events WHERE datetime < '2007-11-16'
    -> AND acknowledged;
```

The date is stored by MySQL in the format $YYYY-mm-dd\ HH:MM:SS$, which is why a simple string comparison works. If an admin has confirmed an entry, the acknowledged field will contain the value 1. The following simple cleanup script deletes all confirmed entries that are more than two weeks old:

```
#!/bin/bash
OLDDATE=`date --date '-2 weeks' "+%Y-%m-%d %H:%M:%S"`
MYSQL="mysql --user=eventdb --passwordmypassword eventdb"

$MYSQL --execute="DELETE FROM events WHERE datetime < '$OLDDATE' AND ackn
owledged;"
$MYSQL --execute="optimize table events;"
```

The script is run daily via cron, but not before it has been thoroughly tested. If you want to archive data before it is deleted, you need to export it *prior to* the DELETE statement. To do this, you add the SQL statement INTO OUTFILE to the SELECT command introduced above, between SELECT * and FROM. This saves data to a text file, with tabs as separators, as shown below:

```
SELECT *
   INTO OUTFILE '/var/backups/eventdb/$OLDDATE.txt'
   FIELDS TERMINATED BY '\t'
   FROM events WHERE datetime < '2007-11-16' AND acknowledged;
```

The EventDB tarfile contains the two example scripts eventdb-clean_database.sh and rotate_eventdb.sh in the cleanup subdirectory, which essentially call the functions just described. You should nevertheless carefully consider how you are going to clean up the database, and modify and test the scripts accordingly.

23.6 Sending Windows Events to Syslog

In order to integrate Windows systems into a syslog environment, you need a service that reads out the Windows event log and sends this on via the syslog protocol to the central Syslog server. This task is performed by the freely available and easy-to-install `evtsys` tool (an abbreviation of the project name *Eventlog to Syslog*), from the homepage of the Engineering Computer Network of Purdue University.[6] The Web page provides two binary packages for download, one for 32-bit and one for 64-bit systems (`evtsys_exe_32.zip` or `evtsys_exe_64.zip`), along with the source code.

The files `evtsys.exe` and `evtsys.dll` contained in the package are copied to the subdirectory `system32` of the system root of the Windows server (usually `C:\Windows\system32`). The service is then installed and activated with the command

```
C:\Windows\system32> evtsys -i -h syslogserver
C:\Windows\system32> net start evtsys
```

If the current `evtsys` version is to be installed on a system on which the service is already running, you must first de-install the old version entirely:

```
C:\Windows\system32> net stop evtsys
C:\Windows\system32> evtsys -u
```

`evtsys` sends all event log entries without exception to the central syslog server. Messages go the `daemon` facility, and possible priorities are `notice`, `warning`, and `err`.

In all cases you should make use of the extensive filter options of the `syslog-ng` on the syslog server, since the security messages from a single domain controller alone may total 1,000 or more entries per hour, even in small environments!

If you want to filter event log entries first on the Windows side, you will need to use other services. One tool that is free, but also rather old, and which may not work faultlessly from Windows 2003 R2 onward, is NTsyslog.[7] You will also find various commercial solutions on the Internet that can be purchased.

Another filter option for Windows is provided by the *Nagios EventLog Agent for Windows*, `nagevtlog`, by Steve Shipway,[8] which is also available on NagiosExchange.[9] But this is not compatble with the EventDB, since data is sent via NSCA to the Nagios server.

---

[6] https://engineering.purdue.edu/ECN/Resources/Documents/UNIX/evtsys/
[7] http://ntsyslog.sourceforge.net/
[8] http://www.steveshipway.org/software/f_nagios.html
[9] http://www.nagiosexchange.org/49;221

All services that provide filtering on the Windows side have one disadvantage: Unknown events may, under certain circumstances, not even end up in the syslog and must be individually supplemented in the configuration. Provided that the central syslog server can cope with the flood of data, the approach with a central filter is easier to maintain.

23.7   Making the Incomprehensible Legible with SNMPTT

The *SNMP Trap Translator (SNMPTT)*[10] translates numerical object identifiers, which are difficult to understand, to readable text by means of the accompanying MIB.[11] To install this, you unpack the SNMPTT sources from Sourceforge[12] to /usr/local/src:

```
linux:local/src # tar xvzf /pfad/snmptt_1.2.tgz
linux:local/src # cd snmptt_1.2
linux:src/snmptt_1.2 # cp snmptt snmptthandler snmpttconvertmib /usr/
sbin/.
linux:src/snmptt_1.2 # chmod +x /usr/sbin/snmptt*
linux:src/snmptt_1.2 # cp snmptt.ini /etc/snmp/.
```

The files snmptt, snmptthandler, and snmpttconvertmib contained in the archive are copied to /usr/sbin and made executable with chmod. The configuration file snmptt.ini is copied to the directory /etc/snmp, which was set up during the installation of the snmpd package.

SNMP traps are accepted by the snmptrapd. In order for this to forward them to snmptt, the following is entered in the snmptrapd.conf configuration file:

```
# /etc/snmp/snmptrapd.conf
traphandle default /usr/sbin/snmptt
```

So that all traps are forwarded to snmptt, the file may contain only this default rule. snmptt accepts the object identifier in a numerical form, which is why snmptrapd needs to be started with the -On option. Depending on the distribution, the snmptrapd startup script may need to be adjusted. For Debian the file /etc/default/snmpd is modified accordingly:

```
# /etc/default/snmpd (Debian)
...
```

---

[10]   http://www.snmptt.org/
[11]   For SNMP, see Chapter 11 from page 227; SNMP traps were described in Section 14.6 from page 312.
[12]   http://www.sourceforge.net/projects/snmptt

```
TRAPDRUN=yes
TRAPDOPTS='-Lsd -On -p /var/run/snmptrapd.pid'
```

The -Lsd option logs all traps for debugging purposes in parallel via syslog. This should be switched off later on, by replacing -Lsd with -t.

23.7.1 The configuration file snmptt.ini

To describe all the parameters of the central SNMPTT configuration file /etc/snmp/snmptt.ini would go beyond the scope of this book. We will just look at the sections and options that can be checked and which might need to be adjusted:

```
[General]
mode = standalone
net_snmp_perl_enable = 1
mibs_environment = ALL
...
[Logging]
log_enable = 1
log_system_enable = 1
unknown_trap_log_enable = 1
syslog_enable = 1
syslog_level = warning
...
[TrapFiles]
snmptt_conf_files = <<END
/etc/snmp/snmptt/snmptt.conf
/etc/snmp/snmptt/messbox.conf
END
```

The setting mode=standlone in the [General] section states that the snmptrapd calls snmptt directly. With mode=daemon, SNMPTT runs as a separate daemon. net_snmp_perl_enable=1 enables the use of the Perl module SNMP, which translates OIDs into meaningful text. Since the default 0 disables the module, this parameter certainly needs to be changed. mibs_environment=ALL integrates all installed MIBs. These must be free of errors, however, which is normally the case for MIBs installed from the distribution (for Debian, in the package libsnmp-base).

The parameter snmptt_conf_files in the [TrapFiles] section contains a list of configuration files that translate incoming SNMP traps and set off actions, if necessary. These are obtained from the MIB belonging to the device—how this is done is explained in Section 23.7.2.

The three variables log_enable=1, log_system_enable=1, and unknown_trap_log_enable=1 in the [Logging] section ensure that SNMPTT logs its activities to /var/log/snmptt*, which is very useful when searching for errors. By logging unknown traps, with `unknown_trap_log_enable=1`, you can see why SNMPTT does not translate a trap that it has received (for example, perhaps it contains OIDs other than those intended from the configuration file obtained from the MIB).

The two `syslog_*` parameters forward translated traps to the syslog daemon here with the syslog priority `warning` so that the data will then appear in the EventDB.

The parameters allowed in `snmptt.ini` and in the device-dependent configuration files are documented in detail on the SNMPTT homepage.[13]

23.7.2 Converting MIBs

The included program `snmpttconvertmib` converts existing MIBs into a configuration file which can be used by SNMPTT. The translator only translates files that are explicitly listed in configuration files which have been integrated with `snmptt_conf_files`.

`snmpttconvertmib` uses `snmptranslate`, so before using this you should check that the actual translation program works properly. To do this, run `snmptranslate -m ALL` without any other parameters. An online help will appear, starting with the following lines:

```
USAGE: snmptranslate [OPTIONS] OID [OID]...
```

No other error message should appear before this line; if one does, this means that the MIBs are not correctly installed. If the MIBs were installed directly from the distribution, no errors should occur.

The conversion process—depending on the quality of the MIB—ranges from very simple (for correctly formed MIBs) to almost impossible (for MIBs with many errors). A flawless MIB is provided by Debian, for example, in the file `rfc1628-UPS.mib`. This distribution stores the MIBs in the directory `/usr/share/snmp/mibs`.

Before you start looking for and installing MIBs from other sources, you should test the conversion with a "clean" MIB. The already mentioned UPS-MIB is converted as follows to an SNMPTT configuration file:

```
user@linux:~$ /usr/sbin/snmpttconvertmib \
    --in=/usr/share/snmp/mibs/rfc1628-UPS.mib \
    --out=rfc1628-UPS.conf
....
Done

Total translations:        4
```

_____

[13] http://www.snmptt.org/docs/snmptt.shtml

```
Successful translations:    4
Failed translations:        0
```

No error should appear in the summary at the end of the output, as is the case here. The contents of the new configuration file now appear as follows:

```
EVENT upsTrapOnBattery .1.3.6.1.2.1.33.2.1 "Status Events" CRITICAL
FORMAT UPS On Battery - Utility Power Failure: The UPS is operating on ba
ttery power (Minutes Remaining=%0 Seconds on Battery=$1)
...
```

The two decisive entries here are EVENT and FORMAT. The first contains the status (here: CRITICAL) together with the OID, while FORMAT defines the text with which a corresponding event is described in the syslog, and thus in the EventDB. More information can be found in the **ConvertMIB** documentation on the SNMPTT homepage.[14]

---

[14] http://www.snmptt.org/docs/snmpttconvertmib.shtml

Part V

Development

Writing Your Own Plugins

Plugins are independent programs—called by Nagios—that perform a check and return the result in standardized form. If there is neither a standard plugin for the task you want to perform, nor something appropriate in **Categories | Check Plugins** on NagiosExchange,[1] then the best solution is for you to write a plugin yourself.

The plugin needs only to be executable on the command line, and to return a short text output for the admin and a standardized return value. If you want to make it available on the Internet as well, you need to comply with various guidelines so that it will be widely used and accepted without the need for extensive support.

There is no restriction *in theory* on the programming language used. Exotic programming languages do restrict portability to other systems and platforms, however, and script languages need to be interpreted, so scripted

---

[1] http://www.nagiosexchange.org/Check_Plugins.21.0.html

plugins require more time to execute than compiled ones. But this should not stop anyone from using the language of his or her choice where rapid implementation is more important than portability and speed of execution. But if you are planning to run 2,000 or more checks at five-minute intervals using a script language, you will be forced to tackle the issue of performance.

Below we will be using the Perl programming language. This exists on almost every Unix system, and the many small tasks that a plugin has to perform, requiring simple text output, are within the classical domain of this script language. There are also numerous ready-made modules available via the CPAN,[2] which you can use to deal with emerging tasks in a modular fashion. There remains the problem of the drag on performance caused by the script language. However, with ePN, Nagios has its own integrated Perl interpreter, which considerably improves performance. A separate chapter is devoted to this, from page 669.

The central hub used when developing a Nagios plugin with Perl is the Perl module Nagios::Plugin by Tom Voon, which really simplifies concrete programming in many aspects. The module Pod::Usage is also used, which enables man pages embedded in the source code of the plugin to be formatted as online help.

24.1 Programming Guidelines for Plugins

Even if you just want to quickly throw something together, you will ultimately make life easier for yourself if you keep to the official *Developer Guidelines*[3] right from the beginning, as you will seldom be the only person involved with the resulting plugin.

The Developer Guidelines currently do not provide an option for processing multiple-line output with Nagios 3.0. The new Application Programming Interface (API) for Nagios 3 plugins is described on the Nagios homepage.[4]

24.1.1 Return values

Nagios expects from a plugin a standardized return value from 0 to 3, which describes the current state of the check performed. The differentiation between the values 0 (OK) and 2 (CRITICAL) is almost always defined by the adminstrator when defining the individual check via warning and critical thresholds—only for a few plugins does the plugin itself specify the thresholds.

[2] http://www.cpan.org
[3] http://nagiosplug.sourceforge.net/developer-guidelines.html
[4] http://nagios.sourceforge.net/docs/3_0/pluginapi.html

The return value 3 (UNKNOWN) is reserved for errors in operating the plugin (the wrong setting for options, nonexistent options) or internal plugin errors that may prevent the plugin from carrying out its work. The Development Guidelines cite the example here of a network socket which the plugin would like to open, but the call fails. Normal timeouts, on the other hand, should not be answered with UNKNOWN. There are certainly plugins which return WARNING when there is a timeout and only return CRITICAL if a specific threshold has been exceeded. In many cases CRITICAL makes more sense for a general timeout, since this can normally be interpreted as *service xyz won't work.*

Table 24.1 summarizes the return values and their meanings, arranged by service and host checks. For host checks, Nagios has the states OK, DOWN, and UNREACHABLE, where the difference between DOWN and UNREACHABLE reflects only the spatial arrangement: Is the failed host *itself* involved, or a host that lies *behind* a failed host? This is why it makes sense to distinguish only between return values for *state ok* (0) and *error state* (2).

Status	Service Check	Host Check
0	OK	UP
1	WARNING	UP or DOWN/UNREACHABLE[5]
2	CRITICAL	DOWN/UNREACHABLE
3	UNKNOWN	DOWN/UNREACHABLE

Table 24.1: Return values for Nagios plugins

How the return value 1 is handled in Nagios 3.0 depends on the parameter `use_aggressive_host_checking` (page 605): if this is set to 1, the return value 1 means DOWN/UNREACHABLE, otherwise Nagios will evaluate the host as UP.

24.1.2   Information for the administrator on the standard output

Nagios expects a text on the standard output that informs the administrator —in the Web interface, for instance—about the current state. This output should keep to specific form, however:

`TYPE_OF_CHECK STATUS - text information`

In practice this looks something like what is shown in the following three examples:

[5]   See text

```
SMTP OK - 0 second response time
CHECKSAP OK - system p10db012_P10_00 available
PROCS WARNING: 4 processes with command name 'pppoe'
```

The Web interface shows the return value itself only indirectly via the color, and the text contains the current state in a legible form. The contents of the text output should otherwise be based on what will provide the administrator with the most information for the check specifically carried out.

There are considerable differences between Nagios 2.x and Nagios 3.0 with respect to the requirements of the text output. For Nagios 2.x the text must be in one line, as shown in the examples. It will only process the first line of a multiple-line output. The entire text, including the performance data (we will discuss this on page 559) may not exceed a length of 300 bytes.

Nagios 3.0 processes output of up to a maximum length of 8192 bytes, and the output may contain several lines. The multiple-line format is described in Section 8.5.1 on page 193.

If you are programming a plugin that makes use of the advantages of Nagios 3.0 (multiple lines, text longer than 300 bytes), you need to realize that this plugin can only be used with limitations in Nagios 2.x. You should therefore carefully consider whether the multiple-line output format is the right approach for the specific problem. Remember that you can summarize the results of several individual checks with the check_multi plugin (see Section 8.5, page 191) and in this way reduce the number of individual checks performed—to optimize performance, say—without missing out on detailed text information. However, an individual check always provides just one return value, which in this case is a collective result. Another approach would be to start the test via a script and cron, and pass on individual results to Nagios as passive checks.

For this reason, it is recommended that you do without multiple-line output for general plugins and comply with the limitations of Nagios 2.x.

24.1.3 Onboard online help?

Classic Nagios plugins, including the core plugins, do not include separate man pages but are *self-documenting*: Help is obtained by calling with the switches -h or --help. This does not mean that there cannot be any other documentation, but the integrated help shold be be complete and all existing options described in detail, so that the plugin can be used without any further documentation.

Some plugins provide just a short help text with -h and the complete help text with --help. In this case, the output of -h should indicate that more information can be retrieved with the long form.

The help text should also be adjusted to the width of a normal terminal and not exceed 80 characters in length. It is quite often the case that an administrator is in the server room trying to solve a problem, faced with a simple console.

The help should always be written in English. For localization purposes, that is, output in different languages, `gettext` can be used. This tool translates text to be displayed using a simple file-based database. If no text exists for the target language, `gettext` displays the untranslated text, so it behaves in an error-tolerant manner. Further information can be found in the man page or info page for `gettext`.

For Perl scripts, man `perllocale`[6] is a good starting point. For a concrete application, we recommend the Perl module `Text::Domain`, which considerably simplifies localization.

24.1.4 Reserved options

The programming guidelines provide options that have the same meaning for all plugins. The most important of these are listed in Table 6.2 on page 108.

In addition there are several reserved options which are sometimes assigned twice in the short form. Thus, `-u` can stand for a user name (`--user`), but also for a URL (`--url`). The option `-p` in turn allows a TCP or UDP port (`--port`) to be specified, but also a password (`--password`). The user name can also be passed on with `-l` or `--logname`, and the password (in more general terms, the authentication string, which can also be a Kerberos realm) with `-a` or `--authentication`.

The fact that these options may have two different meanings is rather unfortunate, and is presumably for historical reasons. In case of doubt you should steer clear of such double assignments and use only the long form of the option whose meaning is clear. Many GNU and other Open Source programs behave in a similar fashion (e.g., `tar`, `rsync`,...). The main thing here is that a reserved option is not used for another purpose. The reserved option `-C`/`--community`, for instance, only makes sense in combination with SNMP queries. If the plugin has nothing to do with SNMP, you should not misuse it for other purposes.

24.1.5 Specifying thresholds

Thresholds determine whether a plugin returns OK or an error value (WARNING, CRITICAL). Thresholds always specify a range according to the pattern *from*:*to*.

---

[6] http://perldoc.perl.org/perllocale.html

The exclusion principle here takes some getting used to. A warning threshold in the form -w 10:20 means that a value within the specified range does *not* lead to a WARNING. The warning state includes all values from $-\infty$ to and including 9 and from 21 to ∞.

The interaction between warning and critical thresholds can best be explained by means of an example. Suppose Nagios is monitoring the temperature in the server room. Normally the temperature should lie between 18°C and 22°C. In each case, two degrees Centigrade above and below this range is set as the tolerance range, for which a WARNING should be shown. Below 16°C and above 24°C, Nagios should report a CRITICAL state.

Converted into thresholds, the scenario sketched in Figure 24.1 should look like this: -w 18:22 -c 16:24. The temperatures between 22°C and 24°C are not critical, but are only covered by the warning range. The temperature range above 24°C covers both threshold intervals, and there the stronger error value (CRITICAL) predominates.

Figure 24.1:
What happens with
the thresholds -w
18:22 -c 16:24?

To negate a value range, you just place a @ in front of it: -w @10:20 now ensures that a WARNING will be shown if the value determined is larger or equal to 10 and smaller or equal to 20. If the start value equals 0, this can be left out: -w 20 has the same effect as -w 0:20. An infinite final value does not need to be specified, but the colon after the start value must remain in place: -w 10:. The tilde (~) stands for negative infinity, and no provision is made for a separate sign for infinity (see Table 24.2).

Table 24.2:
Special syntax for
specifying thresholds

Threshold	Area covered
end	0:*end*
start:	*start*:∞
~:*end*	$-\infty$:*end*
@*start*:*end*	not *start*:*end*

24.1.6 Timeout

A plugin may not always perform its task in a reasonable amount of time. For instance, it may use df to access a volume mounted via NFS, the host of which is not currently available. Or, a firewall may reject the network packets from a network plugin, and the plugin was not designed to notice this. However, Nagios would like to receive a sensible reply from its plugins at some point in time; if any type of checks are hanging around in limbo somewhere, this consumes unnecessary resources and can really cause chaos for the Nagios scheduler.

Each plugin should therefore cancel its actions after a preset time—normally ten seconds—and return a corresponding error result to Nagios. The option -t (--timeout) enables a different timeout value to be specified when a plugin is called.

A modified timeout makes sense, for instance, if a plugin is run indirectly via NRPE (see Chapter 10 from page 213). The timeout of check_nrpe, which Nagios is running directly, should sensibly be somewhat longer than the timeout for the plugin itself, so that check_nrpe does not cancel the execution without learning something about the real cause.

24.1.7 Performance data

Performance data present result values in a standardized form, described from page 404, which enables these values to be processed automatically by external programs. They come after the normal text output, separated by the | sign.

As long as the plugin finds numerical values, it should always display these values as performance data. If an external program can process such data automatically, there is little configuration work for the administrator. There are some external programs that can, if necessary, fish out information from the normal text output, but because of the lack of standardization, this is always associated with extra work—and not every Nagios admin can handle Perl-compatible regular expressions perfectly. For this reason, every plugin programmer should always include performance data provided that the specific application allows this.

24.1.8 Copyright

A plugin should be furnished with a clear copyright notice that names the license and the author. For plugins written in languages that are compiled (such as C), the two items are stored in separate text files so that this information is not lost when the plugin is later distributed in binary form. The standard approach is to have one COPYING file containing the complete license in question (for example, the GNU Public License) and an AUTHORS file with the names of the authors.

For plugins written in script languages, it is sufficient to have the copyright notice in the source code itself, since the plugin is normally distributed in a readable form.

It is also useful to provide a brief output of the copyright when displaying the version number with the option --version.

If the plugin is based on already existing code, or if individuals have been involved in the form of patches or suggestions, the Developer Guidelines require the files ACKNOWLEDGEMENTS and THANKS. The first one is used if the code originally had a different author (or if parts of code are recycled), and the latter includes the names of those who have made contributions in the form of patches and sometimes in the form of important ideas.

24.2   The Perl Module `Nagios::Plugin`

If you want to create plugins in Perl with as little effort as possible, while at the same time conforming to the programming guidelines, the Perl module `Nagios::Plugin` is at hand to provide support to developers. We will introduce it here in version 0.21 from October 2007. In this version the main functions are well developed and should not undergo any major changes, apart from the message functions, which are still marked as being experimental.

This object-oriented module contains constants and variables to represent states; exit functions that use not only a Nagios-compatible exit code, but also the same formatting; and functions for testing thresholds and for the correct output of performance data. In addition, it provides functions for parsing the command line, as well as an integrated help function. On this last point, the module deviates from the standard Perl convention: There is already an extensive module for the command line with `Getopt::Long`, and for online help, Perl provides the Perl Online Documentation (POD).

24.2.1   Installation

`Nagios::Plugin` is one of the core plugins, but it can alternatively be installed via the CPAN. This anchors the module in the system in such a way that Perl finds it automatically. But the module does cause other modules to be installed as well, which is not always desirable on a certified system.

After the installation of the core plugins, `Nagios::Plugin` can be found in its own directory, together with all dependent modules. The existing Perl installation is not affected by this, but Perl does not find the module automatically in this way. Any plugins based on this must explicitly set the path to the base directory of the module themselves.

The method using the CPAN

The CPAN installation command for `Nagios::Plugin` checks existing dependencies and at the same time installs any modules required:

```
linux:~ # perl -MCPAN -e 'install Nagios::Plugin'
...
```

In some circumstances, modules that you have previously installed will be updated. If you are running `perl -MCPAN` for the first time, Perl will ask a number of questions that are answered interactively—apart from the selection of the download server, the suggested defaults can be used.

Together with the core plugins

Starting with version 1.4.10, the `nagios-plugins*` tar archive also contains the Perl module. It is included in the installation if you use the `--enable-perl-modules` switch (see Section 1.4, page 43) when running the `configure` command. The module is installed to the directory /usr/local/nagios/perl, complying with the conventions used in this book.

In order for a plugin to be able to find the module, you must explicitly set the path, via `use lib`. In his FAQ,[7] Ton Voon recommends using the Perl module FindBin:

```
use FindBin;
use lib "$FindBin::Bin/../perl/lib";
use Nagios::Plugin;
```

FindBin is a component of the Perl distribution and finds the path to the directory from which the plugin was called. In accordance with our conventions, this is the directory /usr/local/nagios/libexec. This path is queried with the variable $FindBin::Bin, and `use lib` then integrates the Nagios-specific Perl directory relative to this directory. Whether the Linux distributions will set up a Perl directory with an identical relative path remains to be seen. As long as you install the core plugins yourself, the three-line command will work as intended.

If `Nagios::Plugin` cannot be found in the path specified, Perl will search through all other standard paths. In this way the module will be found if it originates from the CPAN or (in the future) from distribution packages.

---

[7] http://www.nagiosplugins.org/faq/development/nagios-plugin-perl

Determining File and
Directory Sizes

For a specific example of a Perl plugin, we will look at check_du.pl.[1] It is used to determine the size of specified files or directories and to check whether the total size lies within preset thresholds. To do this, it calls the system program du:

```
user@linux:~$ du -cs /var/spool /var/log
26524    /var/spool
745640   /var/log
772164   total
```

---

[1] The plugin is available on the author's homepage at http://linux.swobspace.net/projects/nagios/perl-nagios-plugins.html.

When used with the -s option, du does not list all the individual subdirectories but just shows the total size. -c adds up individual values to reach a total size.

At the beginning, the plugin generates a new new Nagios::Plugin object with the new constructor so that it can make use of the functions of the module:

```perl
#!/usr/bin/perl -w
use strict;
use warnings;
use FindBin;
use lib "$FindBin::Bin/../perl/lib";
use Nagios::Plugin;

my $np = Nagios::Plugin->new(shortname => "CHECK_DU");
```

Various parameters can be used here. shortname contains the short name of the check to be performed, which will be later prefixed to all outputs:[2]

```
CHECK_DU OK - check size: 1128 kByte | size=1128kB;;
```

The contents of the first line after #! define the interpreter to be run, which is Perl. The option -w and the following use warnings—which both ensure extensive output, provided that Perl objects to something in the script—are duplicated here intentionally. In Perl versions prior to 5.6, there is no use warnings parameter, so you must comment out the statement and use -w. To make sure that no one forgets this, -w is included from the beginning. The instruction use strict enforces a strict syntactical check and forces the programmer to pre-declare all variables. Many simple errors are avoided when this is used.

The core function of the plugin is constructed in a relatively simple manner:

```perl
open ( OUT, "LANG=C /usr/bin/du -cs $what 2>&1 |" )
   or $np->nagios_die( "can't start /usr/bin/du" );

while (<OUT>) {
   print "$_" if ($verbose);
   chomp $_;
   $denied++ if ( /Permission denied/i );

   if ( /^(\d+)\s+total$/i ) {
      $size = $1;
      last;
   }
}
close (OUT);
```

---

[2] Other parameters are required for the online help functions of the module, which we will not use here. We will use the module Pod::Usage instead.

open calls the program du and handles the output as if this came from an opened file. If the call fails, `nagios_die` from the module `Nagios::Plugin` terminates execution of the plugin and issues an error message. Before the du program is called, `LANG=C` explicitly sets the language to the English default, so that the texts displayed by du do not depend on the specific environment.

The `while` loop reads the output line for line and checks whether all directories can be evaluated. If `Permission denied` appears in the text of the output, the plugin makes a note of this in the variable $denied, which at the end contains the number of nonreadable directories. If $verbose does not equal zero, the plugin sends all lines received by du to STDOUT for debugging purposes. chomp removes the end of line from the just-processed line called in $_.

From the line reporting the total size—identified by the text `total` at the end of the line of output—the plugin extracts the displayed number using the regular expression in the parentheses. This amount is what $1 now contains. If there is a match, `last` terminates the `while` loop, and then the close function closes the file handle correctly.

25.1 Splitting up the Command Line With `Getopt::Long`

The module `Getopt::Long` provides a function, `GetOptions`, that simplifies the fragmentation of the command line in the style of many GNU programs:

```
use Getopt::Long qw(:config no_ignore_case bundling);

GetOptions(
    "P|path=s"       => \$what,
    "w|warning=s"    => \$warn_threshold,
    "c|critical=s"   => \$crit_threshold,
    "t|timeout=s"    => \$timeout,
    "h|help"         => \$help,
    "V|version"      => \$printversion,
    "v|verbose+"     => \$verbose,
    "d|debug:+"      => \$debug,
) or die_with_help;
```

The instruction `qw(:config no_ignore_case)` configures the behavior of `GetOptions` so that a distinction is made between upper and lower case. `qw(:config bundling)` allows short options to be combined, as is normal for older Unix and GNU programs; instead of -a -b -c, the user can write -abc.

In the `GetOptions` option, you enumerate all the options of the plugin and pass a reference to a variable for each option. The variables used in the call of `GetOptions` had to be pre-declared because of the `use strict` parameter (e. g., with `my $what = '';`). This stores the arguments that have been passed on the command line with the corresponding option. The string on the left side defines under what name the option can be called. An option listed as

```
"P|path|directory=s"
```

can be called as `-P path`, `--path path`, `--path=path`, and also as `--directory=path`. All long forms can also be abbreviated, as long as the abbreviation is unambiguous. Examples of this are `--pf path`, `--pa path`, or `--dir=path`.

The instruction `=s` at the end states that the argument, which in this case is of the type string (`s`), must follow the option. Alternatives are `i` (integer), `o` (Perl integer, i.e., including octal and hexadecimal numbers), and `f` (floating-point decimal). If a colon is used instead of the equals sign, the argument is optional.

A plus sign following the option name, as in `v|verbose+`, allows the option to be specified multiple times on the command line. Each time it is used, the variable is incremented. If the user selects the option `--verbose`, `$verbose` will contain the value 1, but if he selects `--verbose --verbose` (or `--verbose -v`), it will contain 2, and so on. If you include the plus sign in combination with the colon (e. g., `d|debug:+`), the user can assign an integer to the variable when running the command: `--debug=5` sets the variable `$debug` to 5. If he calls just `--debug`, `$debug` will only have the value 1.

When calling `GetOptions` you should always check to see whether an error occurs, for instance through an error condition. In Perl this is written as follows:

```
GetOptions(...) or die_with_help;
```

In case of error, the Developer Guidelines demand that the reason for termination must be specified, along with a short online help. For this, we need to use the Perl Online Documentation and the module `Pod::Usage`.

25.2 The Perl Online Documentation

The Perl Online Documentation (POD) is a simple markup language, which is based on conventional man pages. It enables you to include the documentation for a Perl script in the script itself. The command `perldoc` *script* provides this ready-formatted:[3]

```
#!/usr/bin/perl -w
=head1 NAME

check_du.pl - Nagios plugin for checking size of directories and files

=head1 SYNOPSIS

 check_du.pl -P path/pattern [-v] [-w warning_threshold] [-c critical_th
reshold]
 check_du.pl [-h|-V]

=head1 OPTIONS

=over 4

=item -P|--path=expression

Path expression for calculating size. May be a shell expression like
/var/log/*.log

=item -w|--warning=threshold

threshold can be max (warn if < 0 or > max), min:max (warn if < min or >
max), min: (warn if < min), or @min:max (warn if >= min and <= max). All
values must be integer.

=item -c|--critical=threshold

see --warning for explanation of threshold format

...
=cut

... perlcode ...

=head1 AUTHOR
...
=cut
```

Each instruction begins with an equals sign as the first character in the line, as can be seen in the headings =head1 to =head4. The lines before and after an instruction are kept empty.

The instruction =over 4 starts a listing with an indentation of four characters, in which only =item may be used as a POD instruction. =cut ends

---

[3] The complete text is contained in the plugin check_du.pl at http://linux. swobspace.net/projects/nagios/perl-nagios-plugins.html .

the inserted documentation, after which you can continue with normal Perl code.

A Perl script may contain as many POD sections as you wish. Usually the important ones are set at the beginning of the script, and less important ones, such as the details for SEE ALSO-, AUTHOR- or BUGS for the man pages, are placed at the end.

Apart from `perldoc` there are programs such as `pod2html`, `pod2latex`, `pod2man`, `pod2text`, and `pod2usage`, which display the inline documentation in other formats. It should be pointed out, however, that POD basically displays an inline man page, and a man page converted to HTML will still have the appearance of a man page.

The individual sections of a man page are described by `man man`; important ones are `NAME`, `SYNOPSIS`, `DESCRIPTION`, `OPTIONS`, `FILES`, `SEE ALSO`, `BUGS`, and `AUTHOR`. If the plugin requires more extensive documentation, you can add your own sections. Syntax and construction of the POD format are described in detail by `man perlpod`, while `man perldoc` explains how the embedded help can be extracted.

25.2.1 The module `Pod::Usage`

`Pod::Usage` as a component of the Perl core distribution displays the inline documentation either in full or in extracts, and ends the script with a predefined exit code:

```
pod2usage(
    -msg     => $message_text,
    -exitval => $exit_status ,
    -verbose => $verbose      ,
    -output  => $filehandle   ,
);
```

You can specify an additional text, such as a note on the incorrect use of the plugin, with the switch -msg, which is displayed before the inline documentation.

-exitval determines the return code with which the script ends. For a Nagios plugin, the constant UNKNOWN, which is imported with `Nagios::Plugin`, should always be used here.

-verbose defines the amount of documentation displayed. With the value 0, pod2usage generates a short usage message. For -verbose => 1 the output includes the sections SYNOPSIS, OPTIONS, and ARGUMENTS, and for -verbose => 2 it includes the entire documentation. A special role is played by the value 99. This is used, together with the -sections switch, to specify which sections will be shown:

```
   -verbose => 99,
   -sections => "NAME|SYNOPSIS|OPTIONS|AUTHOR",
```

Individual sections are separated with a | sign. The switch -output finally defines where the information should end up—to STDOUT for verbose values of 0 or 1 and to STDERR for for 2 and higher. For the output of the complete online help you should therefore set this explicitly (otherwise the user would first have to redirect STDERR to STDOUT in order to be able to see the help):

```
   -output => \*STDOUT,
```

In the plugin you first check whether the GetOptions fails, for example because an invalid option has been specified. In case of an error, the instruction following or—in this case pod2usage—is executed:

```
GetOptions ( ...
) or pod2usage (
   -exitval => UNKNOWN,
   -verbose => 0,
   -msg     => "*** unknown option or argument found ***",
);
```

The return value is then UNKNOWN, since the plugin is used incorrectly. -verbose is set to 0, since a brief usage message is sufficient in this case. -msg explains more precisely to the user what he has done wrong; this message is placed before the usage message.

If the user requests the online help, the entire help text contained in the plugin is displayed:

```
pod2usage (
   -verbose => 2,
   -exitval => UNKNOWN,
   -output  => \*STDOUT,
) if ( $help );
```

Because pod2usage normally uses STDERR here, -output explicitly ensures that the output goes to STDOUT.

To display the version number, pod2usage can also be used. Many GNU programs include copyright information along with the version number. To do this, you create a POD section =head1 LICENSE and output this with verbose => 99:

```
=head1 LICENSE
```

```
This program is free software; you can redistribute it and/or
modify it under the terms of the GNU General Public License
as published by the Free Software Foundation; either version 2
of the License, or (at your option) any later version.

...

You should have received a copy of the GNU General Public License
along with this program; if not, write to the Free Software
Foundation, Inc., 51 Franklin Street, Fifth Floor, Boston,
MA  02110-1301, USA.

=cut
...
pod2usage(
    -msg      => "\n$0 -- version: $version\n",
    -verbose  => 99,
    -sections => "NAME|LICENSE",
    -output   => STDOUT,
    -exitval  => UNKNOWN,
) if ( $printversion );
```

Since the output for this verbose level goes to STDERR, you also use -output here to ensure that the output goes to STDOUT. The NAME and LICENSE sections may be located in the plugin file either before or after the pod2-usage call.

If the plugin expects mandatory details—in our case, the path to the directory subtree whose total size should be determined—the parameter is checked for existing values:

```
pod2usage(
    -msg      => "*** no path/pattern specified ***",
    -verbose => 0,
    -exitval => UNKNOWN,
) unless $what;
```

If the user calls the plugin without the --path option, the variable $what will remain empty and pod2usage will issue a corresponding message.

25.3   Determining Thresholds

The format of the thresholds, which was discussed in Section 24.1.5, page 557, is not easy to parse, which is why the functions from the module Nagios::Plugin are a welcome help:

```
$np->set_thresholds(
  warning  => $warn_threshold,
```

```
    critical => $crit_threshold,
);

$result = $np->check_threshold($size);

$np->nagios_exit($result, "check size: $size kByte");
```

The method `set_thresholds` has the task of setting the thresholds for the
`Nagios::Plugin` instance `$np`. `$warn_threshold` and `$crit_threshold`
contain the details that the user passed on to the options `--warning` and
`--critical` on the command line.

`check_threshold` compares the thresholds with the total size of the directory in `$size` and stores the return code in the variable `$result` (either
OK, WARNING, or CRITICAL). This can be used right away in the function
`nagios_exit`. `Nagios::Plugin` does all the work of parsing and checking.

25.4   Implementing Timeouts

To implement a hard timeout, the function `alarm()` is available in C, Perl,
and other programming languages, which normally calls the system functon of the same name (see `man 2 alarm`). For the Perl `alarm()` function,
the timeout is specified in seconds:

```
# ... GetOptions ...
alarm($timeout);
# ... core code ...
alarm(0);
# ... end
```

The `alarm($timeout)` call starts the alarm function, the argument 0 for
the second call stops it again. The first call should be used before time-
intensive processing steps, in network-based plugins before opening sockets, and similar situations where a long delay may occur. A good place is
after the command line has been processed via `GetOptions`.

At the end of the plugin it is recommended that you reset the alarm. This
may not be necessary for standalone programs, but if the Perl plugin is running in the Embedded Perl interpreter, some undesired side effects could
result if this step is not taken. By explicitly stopping the alarm, you are
certainly on the safe side.

What happens if the alarm is set off, which means that the timeout has
expired? Perl checks whether an accompanying signal handler is installed,
and executes it if this is the case. It is recommended that you make use
of this possibility and install your own signal handler, so that the plugin
behaves in compliance with the Developer Guidelines:

```
$SIG{ALRM} = sub {
    $np->nagios_die("Timeout reached");
}
```

The signal handler—an anonymous subroutine—is assigned the variable $SIG{ALRM}. The subroutine calls the function nagios_die from the Nagios::Plugin module. In case of a timeout, the plugin will terminate and send back the return code UNKNOWN with a suitable error message.

25.5   Displaying Performance Data

Displaying performance data with Nagios::Plugin is just as simple as processing thresholds. All you need to do is run the function add_perfdata with a few parameters, and the rest is handled by nagios_exit automatically:

```
$np->add_perfdata(
    label     => "size",
    value     => $size,
    uom       => "kB",
    threshold => $np->threshold(),
);
```

The parameter label defines the name of the variable. value contains the measured value, uom defines the unit of measurements, in this case KB. threshold expects a threshold object, which is generated with the function threshold(). The thresholds must already have been set, with set_thresholds.

The output is shown automatically when nagios_exit is run, provided that the performance data were defined before the first nagios_exit call.

The Nagios::Plugin package also contains the module Nagios::Plugin ::Performance, which provides a parser for performance data in parse_perfstring(), which splits up a performance data string. If you are programming addons in Perl that process performance data, you can save yourself a lot of work with this function.

25.6   Configuration Files for Plugins

A simple plugin can always be configured entirely on the command line. But if you need to incorporate more complex defaults, or if parameters should not appear as arguments in the process list, a configuration file may be of use. The module Nagios::Plugin enables you to access configuration files in a simple manner—one reason certainly being to encourage plugin programmers to use a uniform format, since this would considerably simplify configuration work for the Nagios admin, who no longer has to get used to different formats for every plugin.

`Nagios::Plugin` provides an interface for the module `Config::Tiny`. The file format corresponds to that of the INI files:

```
rootproperty=10.0

[math]
pi=3.1415
euler=2.78
```

A section begins with an entry in square brackets, in this example `[math]`. Everything written before this (in the example here, the variable `rootproperty`) is referred to as *root property*. Instructions are given according to the pattern *parameter=value*. Lines beginning with # and ; are comments; spaces before and after the equals sign are allowed and are simply ignored. More information is provided by the man page man `Config::Tiny`.

Access to the configuration file is made through a `Config` object from the module `Nagios::Plugin::Config`, which is generated using the `read()` method:

```
$Config = Nagios::Plugin::Config->read('/etc/nagios/myplugin.ini');

my $rootproperty = $Config->{_}->{rootproperty};
my $pi    = $Config->{math}->{pi};
my $euler = $Config->{math}->{euler};
```

At the same time, `read()` reads in the configuration file specified. If you omit the path details and call `read()` without parameters, the module will search for various configuration files. The exact listing of the search paths is contained in the man page man `Nagios::Plugin::Config`.

Although it is conceivable that a single configuration file might be used for all plugins, for reasons of maintenance it is recommended that you set up a separate configuration file for each plugin, each containing an example.

Configuration parameters in the `[math]` section are now addressed via the construct

```
$Config->{math}->{pi};
```

and for the root properties, _ is used as a section delimiter:

```
$Config->{_}->{rootproperty};
```

26

Monitoring Oracle with the Instant Client

If a specific task requires you to manipulate the STDIN and read the STD-OUT of the external program at the same time, another tool is needed, in the form of the module `IPC::Open2`.

The following chapter will not introduce any finished plugins, but illustrate how you can build your own Oracle plugin, using an example that monitors Oracle. Some plugins do already exist for this DBMS, such as `check_oracle`, one of the standard Nagios plugins, or `check_oracle_writeaccess`[1] by Mathias Kettner. But both of them require the normal Oracle client, and most non-Oracle administrators will be out of their depth attempting to install it.

---

[1] `http://mathias-kettner.de/nagios_plugins.html`

Luckily there is an easier solution: For some time now, Oracle has been offering an *instant client*, which drastically reduces the installation work: unpack the zip files, set the variables, and the installation is finished—the command-line tool sqlplus can be used immediately. The latter can be used in a plugin—just like the Perl script introduced in this chapter does, which sends a request to the Oracle database using sqlplus and evaluates the response.

26.1 Installing the Oracle Instant Client

Even though the instant client has been available only since Oracle version 10g, it can be used just as well with older Oracle databases such as 8i or 9i. The software is available in the form of zip files at the Oracle homepage,[2] provided you have previously registered on the Web site of the company. When downloading, you are asked some additional questions on export conditions.

Although the software costs nothing, you must observe Oracle's license terms. If your Oracle database is licensed on a CPU basis, you do not need to worry about additional access by another user (Nagios).

For sqlplus you require two zip files,[3] instantclient-basic-linux32-10.1.0.3.zip and instantclient-sqlplus-linux32-10.1.0.3.zip.

The instantclient-basic package, some 31 MB in size, contains all the necessary libraries, and the instantclient-sqlplus included, only 320 KB in size, contains a short documentation (READFROM_IC.htm) as well as the client itself with a further library. It does not matter for the installation where the files are unpacked; in this case we will use /usr/local/oracle:

```
linux:~ # mkdir /usr/local/oracle
linux:~ # cd /usr/local/oracle
linux:local/oracle # unzip instantclient-basic-linux32-10.1.0.3.zip
Archive:  instantclient-basic-linux32-10.1.0.3.zip
  inflating: instantclient10_1/classes12.jar
  ...
linux:local/oracle # unzip instantclient-sqlplus-linux32-10.1.0.3.zip
Archive:  instantclient-sqlplus-linux32-10.1.0.3.zip
  inflating: instantclient10_1/READFROM_IC.htm
  inflating: instantclient10_1/glogin.sql
  inflating: instantclient10_1/libsqlplus.so
  inflating: instantclient10_1/sqlplus
```

---

[2] http://www.oracle.com/technology/software/tech/oci/instantclient/
[3] Apart from the Linux version introduced here on Intel x86-32 systems, the client is also available for Linux x86-64, Linux Itanium, MAC OS-X, HP-UX (32- and 64-bit, for both PA-RISC and Itanium), Solaris SPARC (32- and 64-bit), Solaris x86-32, AIX 5L (32- and 64-bit), and HP Tru64 UNIX.

This creates a subdirectory `instantclient10_1`, containing all the required files. After setting two environment variables, the instant client is ready for use:

```
LD_LIBRARY_PATH=/usr/local/oracle/instantclient10_1
SQLPATH=/usr/local/oracle/instantclient10_1
```

LD_LIBRARY_PATH ensures first that all shared libraries from the instant client directory are taken into account when programs are run, before the libraries installed system-wide are loaded. SQLPATH reveals to `sqlplus` where it needs to look for the file `glogin.sql`. This file makes a number of default settings for accessing the Oracle database, and no adjustments are necessary for our purposes.

26.2   Establishing a Connection to the Oracle Database

`sqlplus` requires the following details to make contact with the database:

```
sqlplus user/password@//host/database
```

The placeholder `user` is replaced by a user who exists in the database, and the password is followed by a forward slash. After the `@//` sign comes the host name or IP address, followed by the name of the database to which `sqlplus` should make a connection. In the following example we will use the database DEMO:

```
user@linux:~$ sqlplus wob/password@//192.168.1.9/DEMO

SQL*Plus: Release 10.1.0.3.0 - Production on Sat Aug 13 14:12:52 2005
...
SQL> quit
Disconnected from Oracle8i Release 8.1.7.0.0 - Production
JServer Release 8.1.7.0.0 - Production
```

On the connect you are shown the version of the instant client used (here: 10.1.0.3.0) as well as a note on the version of the Oracle database used, in this case 8.1.7.0.0. The `quit` command terminates the connection. If the password is wrong, or if the user does not exist, Oracle explicitly requests the user to enter both again.

26.3 A Wrapper Plugin for `sqlplus`

To query an Oracle database, `sqlplus` is given the appropriate SQL statement via standard input and receives a reply via the standard output:

```
user@linux:~$ echo "select trash from nothing" |\
    sqlplus -i wob/password@//192.168.1.9/DEMO
select trash from nothing
                   *
ERROR at line 1:
ORA-00942: table or view does not exist
```

The switch -s (*silent*) prevents the output of things like version and copyright, and restricts the reply to the really interesting part. If the query fails, as above, the text merely points out the error that has occurred. `sqlplus` itself only returns an error status as a return value if the error occurred when using the client itself, otherwise it just returns OK (command executed). This is why `sqlplus` cannot be used directly by Nagios. Instead, a *wrapper* must be written around the actual query which evaluates the reply of the database, which in the above example generates a CRITICAL return value appropriate for Nagios from the ERROR reply, and adds a short one-line reply.

`sqlplus` can in principle be run with any scripting language that enables the text response to be interpreted. Since this is one of the strengths of Perl, we shall use this language for the wrapper plugin—but it could also be written in a shell like Bash; the basic principle is always the same.

26.3.1 How the wrapper works

The wrapper plugin is constructed on the following lines:

```
sql-statement | sqplus arguments | output_processing
```

`sqlplus` receives an SQL statement on the standard input, and the plugin retrieves the result from the standard output. Wrappers can be built around (almost) any program which does not provide sensible return values, but "hides" the result in text.

Perl itself does not provide a direct way of checking standard input and output at the same time. But Perl would not be Perl if there were not a module created specifically for this purpose. `ICP::Open2`[4] fullfils exactly this purpose:

---

[4] The module is included in the standard package of Perl 5.8.

```
use IPC::Open2;

open2(*READFROM, *WRITETO, program, list_of_arguments);
print WRITETO "instruction_via_standard_input\n";

while (<READFROM>) {
   processed_standard_output;
}

close(READFROM);
close(WRITETO);
```

The routine `open2` requires two file handles. Their names, WRITETO and READFROM, describe the interaction from the point of view of the wrapper, and seen from `open2` its behavior is exactly the opposite: `open2` reads from its standard input (WRITETO) and writes to its output (READFROM), where no distinction is made between standard output and error output. The third argument is a program with its complete path, followed by any number of arguments for the program, each separated from the next by a comma.

With the WRITETO file handle, the desired commands are sent with `print`. Each line for `sqlplus` should end here with a correct end-of-line (Perl: '\n'). With the `while (<READFROM>)` construction, Perl reads line by line from the standard (or error) output until there are no more lines. Then `close()` closes the two file handles.

Using IPC::Open2 can cause problems, however: it is conceivable that the program used (in our case, `sqlplus`) gets blocked, because it continues processing a part of the input only after it has written something. If the plugin only processes the output once all the input is completed, you have the classic situation of a deadlock. For this reason you must make sure there are no blocks when reading and writing. Luckily the danger of this happening in our simple application is minimal.

26.3.2   The Perl plugin in detail

A good Perl script starts with the instructions use `strict` and use `warn-ings`. Then all variables must be declared, and in other ways Perl is very particular with syntax.[5]

```
#!/usr/bin/perl -w
use strict;
use warnings;
```

---

[5] Some programmers get very irritated, especially at the start, because Perl reacts very pettily with use `strict`. Without this instruction, variables do not need to be declared. One single typing error in a variable name is sometimes sufficient to keep you searching for hours to find out why the value at a certain position is always 0.

```
use IPC::Open2;

my $ipath = "/usr/local/oracle/instantclient10_1";
my $sqlplus = "$ipath/sqlplus";
my $connectstring =  "wob/password@//192.168.1.9/DEMO";
```

```
# -- Set environment variables
$ENV{'LD_LIBRARY_PATH'} = $ipath;
$ENV{'SQLPATH'} = $ipath;
```

$ipath contains the path to the directory in which the instant client is
located, and $sqlplus has the absolute path to the program sqlplus. The
connect string was already explained above. With the hash %ENV, the script
sets the two required environment variables. Hash entries are referenced
by Perl with $ENV{'variable name'}.

The database query statement is defined for this example in a variable:

```
# -- SQL-Statement
my $select = "SELECT table_name FROM all_tables ";
   $select .= " where table_name = 'VERSION';";
```

The instruction .= appends the following text to that already existing in
$select. The SQL statement therefore selects, from the Oracle system ta-
ble all_tables, which contains all the names of existing tables, the column table_name, in this case with an additional restriction to the table
name VERSION.

In the next step the plugin opens the standard input and output with the
routine open2:

```
# -- open2 with error processing
eval {
   open2(*READFROM, *WRITETO, $sqlplus, "-s", $connectstring);
};
if ($@) {
   die "Error in open2: $!\n$@\n";
}
```

The sqlplus switch -s prevents unnecessary connect output. For ade-
quate error processing, we embed the open2 command in an eval environment: since open2 aborts directly if there is an error, the programmer
would otherwise have no chance to display a sensible error message. If it is
needed, the error output is obtained in the eval environment through $@.
The die function outputs this and aborts the execution of the Perl script.

The only thing remaining now is to send the SQL statement, with print
WRITETO, to sqlplus (afterwards we close down the standard input WRITE-
TO, to be on the safe side) and evaluate the output:

```
# -- Write instruction
print WRITETO $select;
close(WRITETO);

# -- Process reply
while (<READFROM>) {
   print $_;
}
```

`while <READFROM>` reads the output line by line. The contents of the current line are contained in `$_`. With your first attempts, we recommend that you have the output of all lines displayed with `print $_;` so that you can determine whether everything is working.

If this is the case, the actual logic can be expanded: if the table name sought exists in the database, Oracle first displays the column header, then (separated by hyphens) the actual contents, that is, the name of the table being sought:

```
TABLE_NAME
------------------------------
VERSION
```

If such a table does not exist in the database, the response is:

```
no rows selected
```

If an error occurs in the query, perhaps because the column sought, `table_name`, is missing or the table `all_tables` does not exist, `sqlplus` returns a message containing the keyword ERROR, as in the initial example on page 578.

The `while` loop now looks like this:

```
# -- Process response
while (<READFROM>) {
   if ( /^VERSION/i ) {
      print "OK - Table VERSION found\n";
      exit 0;
   } elsif (/no rows selected/i) {
      print "WARNING - Table VERSION not found\n";
      exit 1;
   } elsif (/ERROR/i) {
      print "CRITICAL - SQL-Statement failed\n";
      exit 2;
   }
}
close(READFROM);
print "UNKNOWN - unknown response\n";
exit 3;
```

The search instruction /^VERSION/i contains two special features: the i at the end ensures that the comparison ignores upper or lower case. The ^ at the beginning ensures that the text VERSION must stand at the beginning of the line. If the SQL statement sent by Oracle was incorrect, the error message repeats this first—but then the text VERSION is *not* at the beginning of the line.

If the plugin finds the sought table name VERSION in the response sent, an OK text message is displayed and it terminates with the return value 0.

If the database issues no rows selected or even an ERROR, however, the script feeds Nagios a corresponding reply and terminates with exit and the corresponding return value. If none of the three search patterns match, a return value must also be accounted for; otherwise the script will end with the status 0, and Nagios will announce: "Everything in order." Here we take advantage of the UNKNOWN status, which is actually reserved for error processing for the plugin.

Armed with this background knowledge, it should not be too difficult to write your own Oracle plugin. Its use here is not restricted to read access: provided you have write permissions for the user in question, you can just as well formulate SQL statements with UPDATE, INSERT, or DELETE, and evaluate the answer.

Appendixes

An Overview of the Nagios Configuration Parameters

Nagios contains two independent main configuration files: `nagios.cfg` controls operation of the Nagios daemon, `cgi.cfg` configures the Web interface. Both files should be located in the Nagios configuration directory, which is normally /etc/nagios.

`nagios.cfg` specifies a series of further configuration database and log files, and their functions for the respective parameter will be briefly described in the following reference. The notation ⇒`parameter` refers to the description of the `parameter` in the configuration file currently being discussed.

Unless specified otherwise, parameters may have either the value 0 (disabled) or 1 (enabled). If a parameter has a default value, this is specified accordingly. For some path details, the standard value is defined by options during compiling. The values listed in this case correspond to the paths used in the book (see Table 1.1, page 40).

For some parameters there are no defaults. If these are missing from the configuration, Nagios does not provide the corresponding function (so, for example, without the `cfg_dir` parameter, Nagios ignores the object definitions stored in separate directories).

Depending on the version of Nagios you're using, not all parameters will always be available. (Nagios 2.x) denotes those limited to Nagios 2.x, while (Nagios 3.0) denotes those that have been added in Nagios 3.0.

A.1   The Main Configuration File `nagios.cfg`

`accept_passive_host_checks`
> Global switch for passive host checks; the value 0 suppresses them. Even though passive host checks are allowed according to `nagios.cfg`, this feature must be explicitly enabled when defining the host object. Default value:
>
> `accept_passive_host_checks=1`

`accept_passive_service_checks`
> Global switch for passive service checks. Even though the value 1 allows corresponding tests, this feature must be explicitly enabled when defining the service object. Default value:
>
> `accept_passive_service_checks=1`

`additional_freshness_latency` (Nagios 3.0)
> Adds the latency, specified in seconds, to the fixed freshness interval. An upcoming freshness check (see Section 13.4 from page 295) is delayed by this time before it is run. Example:
>
> `additional_freshness_latency=15`
>
> The default is 0 (no additional delay).

`admin_email`
> The e-mail address of the administrator responsible for the Nagios server, to which you have access through the macro $ADMINEMAIL$. If there is no explicit configuration of a contact object, Nagios will not send an e-mail to this address. Example (no default value):
>
> `admin_email=nagios`

admin_pager

> Pager number, SMS number, or e-mail address for a pager gateway/
> SMS gateway through which the administrator of the Nagios server
> can be reached. Accessible through the macro $ADMINPAGER$. Ex-
> ample (no default value):

> admin_pager=pagenagios

aggregate_status_updates

> Specifies whether Nagios writes status information from hosts, ser-
> vices, and its own programs for the time interval ⇒status_update_
> interval in a block to the ⇒status_file. The value 0 means Na-
> gios updates this file immediately after every event. Default value:

> aggregate_status_updates=1

> Nagios 3.0 works fundamentally according to the first method, which
> is why the parameter is omitted.

auto_reschedule_checks

> With this experimental feature, Nagios spreads tests equally over the
> time period, to avoid peaks. This can considerably reduce perfor-
> mance and in particular is of no use if Nagios is already struggling to
> keep on schedule because of poor performance. Normally this option
> should be switched off. Default value:

> auto_reschedule_checks=0

auto_rescheduling_interval

> In the intervals specified here, Nagios distributes tests which are to be
> executed in the next auto_rescheduling_window seconds, so that
> there is an equal load. Default value:

> auto_rescheduling_interval=30

auto_rescheduling_window

> All tests that are to take place in the next number of seconds specified
> here are rescheduled by Nagios so that they are spread equally over
> this time period. Checks specified for a future time that lie outside
> this interval are not (yet) taken into account. Experimental feature;
> use only in exceptional cases! Default value:

> auto_rescheduling_window=180

broker_module (Nagios 3.0)

> This parameter integrates the specified event broker module (see Sec-
> tion 17.1 from page 376) during the system start. Apart from the full
> path, you can also specify the module-specific arguments. The fol-
> lowing example integrates the NDO event broker module (see also
> Section 17.4.4, page 386):

```
broker_module=/usr/local/nagios/bin/ndomod-3x.o config_
file=/etc/ nagios/ndomod.cfg
```

The module-specific argument `config_file` provides the path for its configuration file. To integrate several modules, just specify the parameter `broker_module` for each module separately.

cached_host_check_horizon (Nagios 3.0)

Specifies the time in seconds in which Nagios recycles the result of a host check. Nagios does not repeat the test within this time frame but considers the cached result of the last check to still be up to date. This saves time and resources. Example:

```
cached_host_check_horizon=30
```

The value 0 switches off caching; the default is 15. How large this value should be depends on circumstances. Large values take considerable strain off Nagios, but then there is a danger that the values may become obsolete and will no longer be valid.

cached_service_check_horizon (Nagios 3.0)

Like ⇒cached_host_check_horizon, but Nagios uses cached service check results only for dependencies. This parameter therefore only has an effect on performance if there is a very large number of service dependency checks. Example:

```
cached_service_check_horizon=30
```

The value 0 switches off caching; the default is 15.

cfg_dir

The directory in which the configuration files containing object definitions are located. Nagios searches through it recursively for configuration files with the extension `.cfg`. Files with other names are ignored, so that you can place help files in this directory, such as a CSV file from which host definitions are generated automatically by a script. To integrate individual files ⇒cfg_file. The directive may be specified as often as you want (see also Section 2.1, page 55). Example (no default value set):

```
cfg_dir=/etc/nagios/servers
```

cfg_file

Integrates a single file with object definitions. More on this in Section 2.1, page 55. The directive can be specified as often as you want. Example (no default value set):

```
cfg_file=/etc/nagios/checkcommands.cfg
```

Nagios 3.0 allows relative paths to be set, starting from the directory in which the file `nagios.cfg` is located.

`check_external_commands`

Enables the interface for external commands. Necessary for passive checks or if commands are to be executed through the Web interface. More on this in Section 13.1, page 292. Default value:

`check_external_commands=0`

`check_for_orphaned_hosts` (Nagios 3.0)

Starting with Nagios 3.0, this parameter adds the host pendant to the ⇒`check_for_orphaned_services` that already existed in Nagios 2.x.

`check_for_orphaned_services`

If the results of a service check are not received after a certain time, this is referred to as an *orphaned service*. Since Nagios only reschedules service checks if a result exists, it could be the case that a service is never again tested. Normally this only happens if a running service check is terminated manually from outside.

If there is a suspicion that such orphaned services have occurred, you should set `check_for_orphaned_services` to 1 for debugging purposes. This is then confirmed if Nagios writes a corresponding error entry to the log file. Whether this is justified or not can easily be seen in the Web interface: you can have all services displayed independently of their status, and sorted by the last test time, in ascending order. Normally the execution of an active check should not be longer ago than specified in `normal_check_interval`. Default value:

`check_for_orphaned_services=0`

`check_host_freshness`

Allows a passive host check to be tested actively if no check result has arrived for a long time. If Nagios considers the test result to be too old, ⇒`host_freshness_check_interval` steps in. More on *freshness checking* in Section 13.4, page 295. Default value:

`check_host_freshness=1`

`check_result_path` (Nagios 3.0)

The path in which check results are cached in file form from Nagios 3.0. There should be no other files in this directory, since Nagios regularly empties it. Each Nagios instance requires a separate directory. Example:

`check_result_path=/var/nagios/checkresults`

`check_result_reaper_frequency` (Nagios 3.0)

Reaper processes gather in check results and process these for Nagios. `check_result_reaper_frequency` defines in seconds the interval at which these processes are started. A short interval increases the system load; a long interval could lead to delays in the Nagios scheduling. Example:

```
check_result_reaper_frequency=5
```

The parameter replaces ⇒service_reaper_frequency from Nagios 2.x.

check_service_freshness

The service equivalent to check_host_freshness. The time after which Nagios considers the test result to be too old is defined by the parameter ⇒service_freshness_check_interval. Default value:

```
check_service_freshness=1
```

child_process_fork_twice (Nagios 3.0)

Nagios normally starts two sub-processes when service or host checks are performed. This is not necessary but is intended to make the system more robust against plugin calls that crash. Default:

```
child_process_fork_twice=1
```

The parameter use_large_installation_tweaks (page 605) sets the value 0 (just one sub-process); child_process_fork_twice=1 activates this, despite the fact that use_large_installation_tweaks is set.

command_check_interval

Defines the time interval in which Nagios tests the External Command File (see Section 13.1, page 292) for new entries. For this to happen at all, ⇒check_external_commands must be enabled.

A simple number as the value refers to the time unit specified by ⇒interval_length (normally 60 seconds, so that 1 stands for one minute). The value -1 means that Nagios tests the interface as often as possible. If the number is supplemented (without a space) with the unit s, seconds can also be explicitly specified.

The interval dependent on passive checks may not be too large, since the operating system in the External Command File, a named pipe, can normally only save 4 KB. Default value:

```
command_check_interval=-1
```

command_file

The named pipe that serves as an External Command File. It should only be writable for the user nagios and the group nagcmd (see also Section 13.1, page 292). Default value:

```
command_file=/var/nagios/rw/nagios.cmd
```

comment_file (Nagios 2.x)

File in which Nagios stores the comments, which can be specified through the Web interface. Default value:

`comment_file=/var/nagios/comments.dat`

This parameter has been removed in Nagios 3.0; comments are now stored in the file `status.dat`.

`date_format`

> The date format that Nagios displays in the Web interface or uses in the date and time macro. Possible values are us (*mm*/*dd*/*yyyy hh*:*mm*:*ss*), euro (*dd*/*mm*/*yyyy hh*:*mm*:*ss*), iso8601 (*yyyy*-*mm*-*dd hh*:*mm*:*ss*), and `strict-iso8601` (*yyyy*-*mm*-*dd*T*hh*:*mm*:*ss*). Default value:

> `date_format=us`

`downtime_file` (Nagios 2.x)

> File in which the downtime details are saved, which can be specified through the Nagios Web interface for hosts and/or services (see Section 16.3, page 359). Default value:

> `downtime_file=/var/nagios/downtime.dat`

> This parameter has been removed in Nagios 3.0; comments are now stored in the file `status.dat`.

`debug_file` (Nagios 3.0)

> For Nagios 2.x, debugging still had to be activated when compiling (for instance, with `./configure --enable-DEBUGALL`; see `configure --help`). In Nagios 3.0 this can normally be configured in `nagios.cfg`. `debug_file` defines the file to which the debugging output is written. Example:

> `debug_file=/var/nagios/debug.log`

`debug_level` (Nagios 3.0)

> This defines what information is logged. The parameter has the following values, which can also be combined:

> -1 all information

> 0 switches off debugging

> 1 Start/end of function calls

> 2 Information on the configuration

> 4 Information on processes

> 8 Scheduling details

> 16 Host and service checks

> 32 Messages

> 64 Event broker

Example:

```
debug_level=-1
```

debug_verbosity (Nagios 3.0)

Defines the level of verbosity when debugging: The value 0 provides only basic information, while 1 information is slightly more detailed. The value 2 provides much more detailed information that is generally only of interest to developers. Default:

```
debug_verbosity=1
```

enable_embedded_perl (Nagios 3.0)

Switches on the Embedded Perl Interpreter (Appendix G from page 669), provided it has been built in. In Nagios 2.x a built-in Interpreter is always active, whereas Nagios 3.0 allows this to be set with this parameter. Example:

```
enable_embedded_perl=1
```

switches on the Interpreter, the value 0 switches it off. The default is 1 if the Interpreter has been built in, otherwise 0.

enable_environment_macros (Nagios 3.0)

Nagios standard macros, such as $HOSTADDRESS$ (see Section D.1.8, page 631) can (even in Nagios 2.x) be accessed as environment variables. In Nagios 3.0 the number of available macros has increased so drastically that to process them in large environments would lead to performance problems. Default:

```
enable_environment_macros=1
```

The value 0 switches off this mechanism.

enable_event_handlers

Globally switches the option on (or off) to work with event handlers for service and host checks. More on this in Appendix C, page 619. Default value:

```
enable_event_handlers=1
```

enable_flap_detection

Defines whether Nagios is generally able to detect continually changing states (*flap detection*, more on this in Appendix B, page 611). Default value:

```
enable_flap_detection=0
```

enable_notifications

Defines whether Nagios can send notifications. Switching off this feature normally only makes sense on the central hosts of a distributed installation, which themselves cannot generate notifications, and instead forward their test results to a central Nagios instance (see Chapter 15 from page 317). Default value:

```
enable_notifications=1
```

`enable_predictive_host_dependency_checks` (Nagios 3.0)

Nagios 3.x caches host check results if a corresponding time frame is given with ⇒`cached_host_check_horizon`. The parameter `enable _predictive_host_dependency_checks` uses caching not only to decide between DOWN and UNREACHABLE for unreachable hosts, but also for host dependency checks, provided some have been defined (see Section 12.6.2, page 289).

`enable_predictive_service_dependency_checks` (Nagios 3.0)

If this parameter is enabled (value 1), service checks will use cached results to resolve dependencies instead of peforming the checks again. There is more on service dependency checks in Section 12.6.1, page 285.

`event_broker_options`

The event broker as a new interface in Nagios 2.0 allows third parties to add some features to Nagios in the form of loadable modules, for example to save test results to a database instead of to a file. One application that uses the event broker interface is the NDOutils (Chapter 17 from page 375). Possible values are 0 (switched off) and -1 (accept all broker modules). Default value:

```
event_broker_options=0
```

`event_handler_timeout`

The time after which Nagios terminates the event handlers which have not yet finished. Default value:

```
event_handler_timeout=30
```

`execute_host_checks`

Enables/disables active host checks globally. This is only worth switching off in distributed environments with a central Nagios instance that only accepts passive results from other Nagios servers (see Chapter 15, page 317). Default value:

```
execute_host_checks=1
```

`execute_service_checks`

Like `execute_host_checks`, but for service checks. Default value:

```
execute_service_checks=1
```

`external_command_buffer_slots` (Nagios 3.0)

Specifies the maximum number of external commands that the external command file interface (Section 13.1 from page 292) can store temporarily. If the buffer is not large enough, some results might be lost. Default:

```
external_command_buffer_slots=4096
```

`free_child_process_memory` (Nagios 3.0)

Nagios normally clears up sub-processes from the memory, but the parameter `use_large_installation_tweaks=1` (see page 605) switches off this behavior by default. With

```
free_child_process_memory=1
```

you can reactivate the cleaning up process, despite `use_large_installation_tweaks=1` being set.

`global_host_event_handler`

Defines a global host event handler, in addition to the host-specific event handlers defined with `event_handler`. For this, both the global parameter ⇒`enable_event_handlers` as well as the parameter `event_handler_enabled` must be enabled in the host definition. Nagios executes the global event handler, a normal command object, before the host-specific one. Example (no default value set):

```
global_host_event_handler=name_of_the_command-object
```

`global_service_event_handler`

The service-specific equivalent to `global_host_event_handler`. Apart from ⇒`enable_event_handlers`, the parameter `event_handler_enabled` in the service definition must also be enabled. Example (no default value set):

```
global_service_event_handler=name_of_command_object
```

`high_host_flap_threshold`

Upper limit of flap detection for host checks. Details are given in Appendix B, page 611. Default value:

```
high_host_flap_threshold=30.0
```

`high_service_flap_threshold`

Upper limit of flap detection for service checks (see Appendix B). Default value:

```
high_service_flap_threshold=30.0
```

`host_check_timeout`

Time in seconds after which Nagios aborts a host check if this has not yet returned a result. Default value:

```
host_check_timeout=30
```

`host_freshness_check_interval`

Interval between two *freshness checks* in seconds. Default value:

```
host_freshness_check_interval=60
```

`host_inter_check_delay_method`

Controls how Nagios processes host checks after a restart. A sophisticated procedure aims to prevent Nagios in this situation from executing all tests simultaneously, and thus overloading the server. Possible values are: s (*smart*, intelligent, automatic distribution of the host checks), n (*no*, all checks start simultaneously), d (*dumb*, Nagios processes the tests at intervals of seconds), and an interval specified in seconds, in the format $x.xx$. Default value:

`host_inter_check_delay_method=s`

`host_perfdata_command`

A Nagios command object that should check the performance data after every host check. Requires the ⇒`process_performance_data` parameter to be set.

This parameter only makes sense in a few cases, since Nagios executes host checks only if necessary, and therefore at very irregular intervals. It is used if performance data are to be processed without a template (Section 19.1, page 404). Example (no default value set):

`host_perfdata_command=process-host-perfdata`

`host_perfdata_file`

Specifies a file or named pipe through which Nagios forwards performance data from host checks via a template mechanism to an external program (see Chapter 19, page 403). ⇒`process_performance_data` must be set. Example (no default value set):

`host_perfdata_file=/tmp/host-perfdata`

`host_perfdata_file_mode`

Defines how data is passed on to the file ⇒`host_perfdata_file`. Possible values are a (*append* to a normal file) or w (*write* to a new file), and for Nagios 3.0 also p (*non blocking write*), which is particularly useful for pipes. Example (no default value set):

`host_perfdata_file_mode=a`

`host_perfdata_file_processing_command`

Nagios command object that is called after host performance data is passed on to the ⇒`host_perfdata_file` interface. The parameter is only used with the template mechanism and is optional. Programs such as perf2rrd (Section 19.3, page 415) have their own daemon that permanently reads data from the interface. Example (no default value set):

`host_perfdata_file_processing_command=process-host-`
`perfdata-file`

host_perfdata_file_processing_interval
> If this interval—specified in seconds—is larger than 0, the command belonging to it (⇒host_perfdata_file_processing_command) is run periodically at these intervals. 0 ensures that it is not used. Example (no default value set):
>
> host_perfdata_file_processing_interval=0

host_perfdata_file_template
> Describes the output format of the performance data. The Nagios macros and format details in it, such as \t (tabulator) or \n (linefeed) are replaced in the output. More on the use of templates in Section 19.1, page 404. Example (no default value set):
>
> host_perfdata_file_template=$TIMET$\t$HOSTNAME$\t$HOST-EXECUTIONTIME$\t\$HOSTOUTPUT$\t$HOSTPERFDATA$

illegal_macro_output_chars
> Lists characters that are discarded when macros are substituted for notifications, to avoid problems such as interpretation by the shell. The parameter has no influence on the substitution of macros in host or service definitions. Example (no default value set):
>
> illegal_macro_output_chars=`~$&|´"<>

illegal_object_name_chars
> Specifies impermissible characters in the names of Nagios objects. It is recommended that at least the characters listed in the following example be specified (no default value set):
>
> illegal_object_name_chars=`~!$%^&*|´"<>?,()=

interval_length
> Defines the time unit in seconds to which time details in object definitions (such as with normal_check_interval or retry_check_interval) refer. If interval_length is 60 seconds, the time specification is 5 five minutes. You should only change the default of 60 seconds if there is good reason to do so. interval_length has no influence on time parameters in nagios.cfg, however. Default value:
>
> interval_length=60

lock_file
> Specifies a lock file for the Nagios daemon containing the process ID (PID) of the daemon running. Is required for start/stop purposes. Default value:
>
> lock_file=/var/nagios/nagios.lock

`log_archive_path`
> The archive directory for rotating Nagios log files. Evaluations are based on the archive files copied there. If one of the files is deleted, the information contained in it is lost. Nagios uses the directory only if log rotation is enabled with the ⇒`log_rotation_method` parameter. Default value:

> `log_archive_path=/var/nagios/archives`

`log_event_handlers`
> Should event handler actions appear in the log file? The parameter is used primarily to search for errors. Default value:

> `log_event_handlers=1`

`log_external_commands`
> Should Nagios log external commands (see Section 13.1, page 292) in the log file? Default value:

> `log_external_commands=1`

`log_file`
> The central log file. Apart from errors and problems, it also retains all events. All history evaluations use this file. For log rotation, Nagios provides a separate mechanism, with ⇒`log_rotation_method`, and you should not use external programs here. Default value:

> `log_file=/var/nagios/nagios.log`

`log_host_retries`
> Specifies whether Nagios should log host check repeats because of an error state. This is absolutely essential if event handlers (see Appendix C, page 619) are used which are to react to soft states. Default value:

> `log_host_retries=0`

`log_initial_states`
> Specifies whether the start state of services and hosts should appear in the log file when the Nagios system is started. Default value:

> `log_initial_states=0`

`log_notifications`
> Defines whether Nagios should also log notifications in the log file. Default value:

> `log_notifications=1`

`log_passive_checks`
> Specifies whether Nagios should log passive checks in the log file. Default value:

> `log_passive_checks=1`

log_rotation_method
>	Defines whether the log file ⇒log_file should be saved periodically to the archive ⇒log_archive_path. Log rotating should always be left to Nagios itself, rather than any external programs, or otherwise the software will have difficulties in evaluating history data. Possible values are n (*none*, no archiving), h (*hourly*, at the beginning of each hour), d (*daily*, each day at 00:00 hours), w (*weekly*, at midnight from Saturday to Sunday), and m (*monthly*, the first day of each month at 00:00 hours). Default:
>
>	log_rotation_method=n

log_service_retries
>	Should Nagios log the repeat of a service check because of a soft state error? This is useful for debugging when developing event handlers, but otherwise it is best to leave this out. Default value:
>
>	log_service_retries=0

low_host_flap_threshold
>	Lower limit for flap detection for hosts checks. Details are described in Appendix B, page 611. Default value:
>
>	low_host_flap_threshold=20.0

low_service_flap_threshold
>	Like low_host_flap_threshold, but for service checks. Default value:
>
>	low_service_flap_threshold=20.0

max_check_result_file_age (Nagios 3.0)
>	Defines the maximum age of a check result file in seconds, which the Reaper process from the directory check_result_path still processes. Older files are discarded. Example:
>
>	max_check_result_file_age=1800
>
>	Check results are only processed here if the accompanying file is not older than 30 minutes. A value of 0 ignores the age of the result files.

max_check_result_reaper_time (Nagios 3.0)
>	Restricts the runtime of an individual Reaper process to the time in seconds specified. Example:
>
>	max_check_result_reaper_time=10
>
>	Here the Reaper process is canceled after 10 seconds. Check results left over are processed by the next reaper process.

max_concurrent_checks
>	Specifies how many checks Nagios may execute simultaneously. The value 0 allows an unlimited number. A restriction through a value

larger than zero may, under unfavorable circumstances, lead to the test not being executed in time. Default value:

```
max_concurrent_checks=0
```

`max_debug_file_size` (Nagios 3.0)
Limits the size of the debugging file to the value specified in bytes. Example:

```
max_debug_file_size=2048000
```

If the size exceeds the given value, Nagios adds the ending `.old` to the file. If a file already exists with the same name, it will be deleted. You must therefore make provision for twice the size specified here, since there could be two files (with and without the suffix `.old`) with the maximum size at the same time.

`max_host_check_spread`
At what time interval (in minutes) should Nagios have started all host checks after a restart? Prevents all tests from being executed simultaneously, which would overload the Nagios server. Default value:

```
max_host_check_spread=30
```

`max_service_check_spread`
Like `max_host_check_spread`, but for service checks. Default value:

```
max_service_check_spread=30
```

`nagios_group`
The group with whose permissions the Nagios daemon runs. Default value (is defined during compilation):

```
nagios_group=nagios
```

`nagios_user`
The user with whose permissions the Nagios daemon runs. Default value (is defined during compilation):

```
nagios_user=nagios
```

`notification_timeout`
After how many seconds should Nagios abort the attempt to deliver a notification? Some actions, such as sending an SMS message, require a certain amount of time, since the system first waits for confirmation from the recipient. The value should therefore not be too low. Default value:

```
notification_timeout=30
```

`object_cache_file`
The file in which Nagios stores all objects after it starts. Since the Web interface uses this file, the normal configuration files with the object

definitions can be edited while Nagios is running, without jeopardizing the functionality of the Web interface. Default value:

```
object_cache_file=/var/nagios/objects.cache
```

obsess_over_hosts

Defines in general whether host check results are forwarded to a central Nagios instance. If the parameter is enabled, the command defined in ⇒ocsp_command is run. This is used in distributed environments; a description can be found in Chapter 15, page 317. Default value:

```
obsess_over_hosts=0
```

obsess_over_services

Defines in general whether service check results should be forwarded to a central Nagios instance. If the parameter is enabled, the command defined in ⇒ohcp_command is used. This feature is used in distributed environments (see Chapter 15, page 317). Default value:

```
obsess_over_services=0
```

ochp_command

Defines the *obsessive compulsive host processor*, a Nagios command object that forwards all host check results in a distributed environment to a central instance (see Chapter 15, page 317). Example (no default value set):

```
ochp_command=name_of_the_command_object
```

ochp_timeout

Defines the timeout for the ⇒ochp_command. After this time has expired, Nagios aborts the execution of the command. Default value:

```
ochp_timeout=15
```

ocsp_command

Specifies the command object that, as the *obsessive compulsive service processor*, should forward all service check results in a distributed environment to a central instance (see Chapter 15, page 317). Example (no default value set):

```
ocsp_command=name_of_the_command_object
```

ocsp_timeout

The timeout for the ⇒ocsp_command. After the time specified here has expired, Nagios aborts the execution of the command. Default value:

```
ocsp_timeout=15
```

`passive_host_checks_are_soft` (Nagios 3.0)

Normally, the results of passive host checks are always regarded as hard states. With

`passive_host_checks_are_soft=1`

the same behavior can be set for active host checks. Assigning soft or hard states can now be regulated by the parameter `max_check_attempts` from the host definition.

`perfdata_timeout`

Defines after how many seconds a performance command (⇒`host_perfdata_command`, ⇒`service_perfdata_command`, ⇒`host_perfdata_file_processing_command`, or ⇒`service_perfdata_file_processing_command`) should be aborted. Default value:

`perfdata_timeout=5`

`precached_object_file` (Nagios 3.0)

Starting with Nagios 3.0, it is possible to carry out reading and checking the configuration even before a Nagios restart and to cache the result in the file specified with `precached_object_file` (see Section H.8 from page 690). Example:

`precached_object_file=/var/nagios/objects.precache`

`process_performance_data`

Switches on processing of performance data. This parameter should be enabled only if performance data really is evaluated. Otherwise it only uses up resources on the Nagios server. Default value:

`process_performance_data=0`

`resource_file`

The configuration file containing the definitions of the (maximum of 32) $USERx$ macros. $USER1$ normally specifies the path to the Nagios plugins. Otherwise you could save passwords here, for example, which should not be readable in the normal Nagios configuration files. The file must then be protected from all external access, and only the user `nagios` should be able to read it. Example (no default value set):

`resource_file=/etc/nagios/resource.cfg`

`retain_state_information`

Determines whether Nagios will save current states to a file on shutdown (⇒`state_retention_file`) and read these again when it starts. Default value:

`retain_state_information=0`

`retention_update_interval`
>   Every how many minutes should Nagios store current state informa-
>   tion in the ⇒`state_retention_file`? With a value of 0, the sy-
>   stem only saves information if Nagios is shut down. The parameter
>   ⇒`retain_state_information` must be enabled for this. Default
>   value:
>
>   `retention_update_interval=60`

`service_check_timeout`
>   Number of seconds after which Nagios aborts a service check if this
>   has not returned a result by then. Default value:
>
>   `service_check_timeout=60`

`service_freshness_check_interval`
>   Interval between two freshness checks in seconds. Default value:
>
>   `service_freshness_check_interval=60`

`service_inter_check_delay_method`
>   Controls how Nagios processes service checks after a restart. An
>   "intelligent" procedure should prevent them from all starting at the
>   same time, to avoid putting an unnecessary load on the server. Pos-
>   sible values are s (*smart*, automatic distribution), n (*no*, start all tests
>   simultaneously!), d (*dumb*, one second interval between checks), as
>   well as an explicitly specified interval in seconds, in the form *x.xx*.
>   Default value:
>
>   `service_inter_check_delay_method=s`

`service_interleave_factor`
>   Prevents the checks accumulating for a specific host from being ex-
>   ecuted at the same time (⇒`max_concurrent_checks`, 598), through
>   Nagios distributing the planned checks for all hosts "intelligently"
>   over a period of time. Possible values are s (*smart*, automatic distri-
>   bution) or an integer larger than 0. With a value of 1, Nagios does not
>   carry out any distribution, with a value of 4, Nagios initially plans ev-
>   ery fourth service check (that is, from the amount of intended checks,
>   the 1st, 5th, 9th, etc.), then the following number (that is, the 2nd,
>   6th, 10th, etc.), and so on. The test sequence is shown by the `Service`
>   `Detail` item in the Web interface. In case of doubt, the default value
>   can be left as it is:
>
>   `service_interleave_factor=s`

`service_perfdata_command`
>   The Nagios command object that is run after each service check to
>   process performance data. A requirement for this is that ⇒`process_`
>   `performance_data` must be set.

The parameter is used if the performance data is to be processed without a template (Section 19.1, page 404). Example (no default value set):

```
service_perfdata_command=process-service-perfdata
```

`service_perfdata_file`
: Path to the file or named pipe through which Nagios forwards performance data from service checks via a template mechanism to an external program. This only works if ⇒`process_performance_data` is set. More on processing performance data in Chapter 19, page 403. Example (no default value set):

```
service_perfdata_file=/tmp/service-perfdata
```

`service_perfdata_file_mode`
: Defines the mode in which data is passed on to ⇒`service_perfdata_file`. Possible values are a (*append* to a normal file), w (*write* to a new file) and in Nagios 3.0 p as well (*non-blocking write*), which is useful for pipes. Example (no default value):

```
service_perfdata_file_mode=a
```

`service_perfdata_file_processing_command`
: A command object that is executed after Nagios has passed on service performance data to the ⇒`service_perfdata_file`. The parameter is optional and is only used together with the template mechanism. As long as programs that further process the data, such as perf2rrd (Section 19.3, page 415), include their own service that permanently reads out the `service_perfdata_file`, you can manage without defining a command for reading out. See also Chapter 19, page 403. Example (no default value set):

```
service_perfdata_file_processing_command=process-
service-perfdata-file
```

`service_perfdata_file_processing_interval`
: Interval in seconds in which the command defined in ⇒`service_perfdata_file_processing_command` is periodically run. Setting the value 0 ensures that it is never used. Example (no default value set):

```
service_perfdata_file_processing_interval=0
```

`service_perfdata_file_template`
: The output format for performance data; Nagios macros and format details such as \t (tabulator) or \n (linefeed) are substituted in the output. See also Section 19.1, page 404. Example (no default value set):

```
service_perfdata_file_template=$TIMET$\t$HOSTNAME$\t
$SERVICEDESC$\t$SERVICEEXECUTIONTIME$\t$SERVICELATENCY$
\t$SERVICEOUTPUT$\t$SERVICEPERFDATA$
```

service_reaper_frequency (Nagios 2.x)

Every how many seconds should Nagios process accumulated service test results? Default value:

```
service_reaper_frequency=10
```

In Nagios 3.0 the corresponding parameter is called ⇒check_result _reaper_frequency and influences not only service checks but also host checks.

sleep_time

Pause in seconds for which Nagios waits before searching again in the scheduling queue for checks to be performed. Default value:

```
sleep_time=0.5
```

state_retention_file

The file in which Nagios stores status information on shutdown, and from which the information is read in again when Nagios is started. This is used only if the ⇒retain_state_information parameter is set. Default value:

```
state_retention_file=/var/nagios/retention.dat
```

status_file

Path to the file in which Nagios saves all current status values and from which the Web interface retrieves them. Default value:

```
status_file=/var/nagios/status.dat
```

status_update_interval

At what interval should Nagios store status values in the file ⇒status _file? If ⇒aggregate_status_updates is not set, the system ignores this parameter and immediately writes the status values to this file (not recommended). Default value:

```
status_update_interval=60
```

temp_file

Path to a temporary file that Nagios uses if necessary, and deletes each time when it no longer requires it. Default value:

```
temp_file=/var/nagios/tempfile
```

temp_path (Nagios 3.0)

A directory in which Nagios may store temporary files. The directory should be emptied regularly. Example:

```
temp_path=/tmp
```

`translate_passive_host_checks` (Nagios 3.0)

Determines whether Nagios should translate the result of a passive host check from a topological perspective to DOWN or UNREACH-ABLE. The default is "no":

`translate_passive_host_checks=0`

Passive host checks are often used in distributed environments, and Nagios does not have all the information concerning the topological structure of these environments. In that case, the default makes sense. The value 1 switches the translation to DOWN or UNREACH-ABLE.

`use_aggressive_host_checking`

Nagios makes a number of assumptions in deciding whether unreachable hosts are DOWN or UNREACHABLE. If this parameter is set to the value 1, Nagios is very particular in the host check and in some circumstances may perform considerably more individual checks. Although the result will be more precise, this puts quite a strain on the system. This parameter should only be set if there are problems in detecting failed hosts. Default:

`use_aggressive_host_checking=0`

`use_embedded_perl_implicitly` (Nagios 3.0)

Automatically runs all Perl scripts in the Embedded Perl Interpreter, provided the script itself does not contain an explicit instruction to avoid the Interpreter. More on this in Section G.2, page 672.

`use_large_installation_tweaks` (Nagios 3.0)

This parameter covers a number of settings intended to improve the performance of Nagios in large environments. The following entry switches it on:

`use_large_installation_tweaks=1`

There is more on this in Section F.2.7, page 667.

`use_regexp_matching`

Defines whether the wildcards * (any character) and ? (a single character) are allowed in object definitions. If you want to work with regular expressions, ⇒`use_true_regexp_matching` must be used. Default value:

`use_regexp_matching=0`

`use_retained_program_state`

Should changes to the parameters ⇒`enable_notifications`, ⇒`enable_flap_detection`, ⇒`enable_event_handlers`, ⇒`execute_service_checks` and ⇒`accept_passive_service_checks` on the

Web interface survive a Nagios restart? Only works if ⇒`retain_sta-tus_information` is enabled. Default value:

`use_retained_program_state=1`

`use_retained_scheduling_info`
Should Nagios save current scheduling information on shutdown so it can read it in again when it restarts? You can temporarily disable the parameter if you are adding a large number of tests; otherwise it is sensible to keep it enabled. Default value:

`use_retained_scheduling_info=1`

`use_syslog`
Ensures logging of all Nagios activities in the syslog. Default value:

`use_syslog=1`

`use_timezone` (Nagios 3.0)
Explicitly sets a time zone for Nagios. Normally, Nagios uses the time zone of the system on which it is running. This parameter is only required if several instances for different time zones are being run on one host. Example:

`use_timezone=Europe/Berlin`

The relative path for the desired zone information file is specified, usually in `/usr/lib/zoneinfo` or `/usr/share/zoneinfo`.

`use_true_regexp_matching`
In contrast to ⇒`use_regexp_matching`, allows the use of real regular expressions in accordance with the POSIX standard.[1] Default value:

`use_true_regexp_matching=0`

A.2   CGI Configuration in `cgi.cfg`

A.2.1   Authentication parameters

Through the contact and the contact group, Nagios allocates responsibilities to users from which permissions for the Web interface can likewise be inferred: each contact may normally only see those hosts and services for which he is also responsible. This is why the name of the Web login must match the contact name.

The parameters listed below work around this concept to some extent. They are not intended to solve problems, however, caused by contact and Web user names not matching.

---

[1] See man 7 `regex`.

cmduse_authentication
>   Determines whether you normally need to log in to the Web interface. Like the user name, the contact name is always used; how you store passwords is described in Section 1.5, page 47.
>
>   In general you should never permit this authentication, but if you do, you should make sure that the interface for external commands (Section 13.1, page 292) is switched off completely. Default:
>
>    ```
>    use_authentication=1
>    ```

authorized_for_all_host_commands
>   Allows the users specified here to run commands through the Web interface for all hosts, without them belonging to the appropriate contact group. Example (no default value set):
>
>    ```
>    authorized_for_all_host_commands=nagiosadmin
>    ```

authorized_for_all_hosts
>   Allows the users specified here to look at all host information, irrespective of their actual responsibility. Example (no default value set):
>
>    ```
>    authorized_for_all_hosts=nagiosadmin,guest
>    ```

authorized_for_all_service_commands
>   Allows the users defined here to run commands for all services via the Web interface, independently of membership of contact groups. Example (no default value set):
>
>    ```
>    authorized_for_all_service_commands=nagiosadmin
>    ```

authorized_for_all_services
>   Allows the users specified to view all service information, irrespective of their own permissions. Example (no default value set):
>
>    ```
>    authorized_for_all_services=nagiosadmin,guest
>    ```

authorized_for_configuration_information
>   Enables the users specified to view all configuration data via the Web interface. This should be reserved for the Nagios administrators. Example (no default value set):
>
>    ```
>    authorized_for_configuration_information=nagiosadmin,
>    jdoe
>    ```

authorized_for_system_commands
>   Allows the specified users to shut down or restart Nagios via the Web interface. Normally, nobody has this authorization. Example (no default value set):
>
>    ```
>    authorized_for_system_commands=nagiosadmin
>    ```

`authorized_for_system_information`
>   Allows the specified users to view Nagios process information. Nor-
>   mally, nobody may do this. Example (no default value set):
>
>   `authorized_for_system_information=nagiosadmin,theboss,`
>   `jdoe`

A.2.2 Other Parameters

`action_url_target` (Nagios 3.0)
>   Sets the HTML tag `target` for an action URL (see page 366). The
>   default is `blank`, which opens a new window:
>
>   `action_url_target=blank`

`default_statusmap_layout`
>   Defines the layout for the status map. Possible values are 0 (coordi-
>   nates defined through a `hostextinfo` object), 1 (the user must move
>   by mouse click from one layer to the next one), 2 (compressed tree—
>   somewhat confusing, because branches cut across each other in the
>   picture), 3 (balanced tree, the branches are displayed so that there
>   are no crossovers in the graphic—clearer, but requires much space),
>   4 (circular representation, with Nagios at the center: hosts that can
>   be reached directly[2] are shown in the inner circle, while on other cir-
>   cles are located those hosts that can be reached from hosts already
>   entered in the graphic), 5 (circular, like 4; the area around the host
>   is marked in color—gray for OK, red for DOWN or UNREACHABLE;
>   Figure A.27 on page 346 shows an example), and 6 (circular; the hosts
>   are shown as balloons). The settings can also be changed in the Web
>   interface without the need to adjust the configuration file each time,
>   which makes it easier to try things out. Example:
>
>   `default_statusmap_layout=5`

`default_statuswrl_layout`
>   Determines the layout for the VRML representation of the status page
>   through `statuswrl.cgi`. Possible values are 0, 2, 3, and 4; the cor-
>   responding appearance is based on the values of the same name for
>   ⇒`default_statusmap_layout`. Example:
>
>   `default_statuswrl_layout=4`

`default_user_name`
>   Name of a guest user who may use the Web pages without authenti-
>   cation. You should only use this parameter if the Web server is pro-
>   tected from unauthorized access, and you should look closely at what

---

[2] That is, without the "diversion" via `parents`.

permissions this user is allocated through the contact groups. Example (no default value set):

`default_user_name=guest`

`enable_splunk_integration` (Nagios 3.0)
Activates integration of the Splunk tool, a search engine for log files.[3]

`escape_html_tags` (Nagios 3.0)
The value 1 disables HTML formatting in the plugin output:

`escape_html_tags=1` Corresponding formatting thus has no effect. The default is 0, which causes HTML formatting to be passed on.

`lock_author_name` (Nagios 3.0)
For various CGI actions, such as setting acknowledgements, an author name is specified. With the setting

`lock_author_names=1` this can no longer be changed (the default is the user logged in).

`main_config_file`
The Nagios main configuration file. Default value:

`main_config_file=/etc/nagios/nagios.cfg`

`notes_url_target` (Nagios 3.0)
Sets the HTML tag `target` for Notes URLs (see page 366). The default is `blank`, which opens a new window:

`notes_url_target=blank`

`physical_html_path`
Path in the file system that leads to the Nagios directory for documentation and images. See also ⇒`url_html_path`. Default value:

`physical_html_path=/usr/local/nagios/share`

`refresh_rate`
Specifies at what intervals the Web page is automatically updated. Default value:

`refresh_rate=60`

`splunk_url` (Nagios 3.0)
Defines the URL for the Splunk search engine. Example:

`splunk_url=http://127.0.0.1:8000/`

The parameter ⇒`enable_splunk_integration` (page 609) must also be enabled for this.

---

[3] `http://www.splunk.com/`

statusmap_background_image
>   The background image for the status map display. Example (no default value set):
>
>   statusmap_background_image=smbackground.gd2

statuswrl_include
>   A file with its own VRML objects used in the VRML representation. The path is specified relative to ⇒html_physical_path. Example (no default value set):
>
>   statuswrl_include=myworld.wrl

url_html_path
>   The logical path to the Nagios documents and images from the point of view of the browser, starting from the document root of the Web server. If you use this path in a URL, you will be taken to the Nagios start page. Default value:
>
>   url_html_path=/nagios

use_pending_states (Nagios 3.0)
>   How should hosts and services be displayed in the Web interface if no check has yet taken place for this?
>
>   use_pending_states=1 shows unchecked hosts and services with the state **PENDING**; the value 0 can be left as it is.

Rapidly Alternating States: Flapping

If the state of a host or service keeps on changing over and over, Nagios inundates the administrator with a flood of problem and recovery messages, which can not only be very irritating but also distract the administrator's attention from other, perhaps more urgent problems.

With a special mechanism, Nagios quickly recognizes alternating states and can inform the administrator of these selectively. The Nagios documentation refers to such alternating states as *state flapping* and to their detection as *flap detection*.

Whether these alternating states involve hosts or services has no influence on the detection mechanism itself. The differences are more to be found in the nature of host and service checks: Nagios carries out service checks periodically, and therefore regularly. In this way the system continuously receives new information on the current status. Regular host checks only make sense from Nagios 3.0 onward (see Section H.7 from page 689). In Nagios 2.x, host checks generally take place only if needed, so Nagios has to obtain the appropriate information in other ways.

B.1 Flap Detection with Services

To detect alternating states you need a complete list of all states that occurred during the last service checks. For this purpose Nagios stores the last 21 test results for each service and then overwrites the oldest value in each case in the memory. In these 21 states, a maximum of 20 changes can occur.

Figure B.1 shows an example. The x-axis numbers the possible alternating states in each case from 1 to 20, and the heads of the arrow indicate alternating states that have actually occurred.

Figure B.1:
Nagios saves the last
21 states to detect
frequently
alternating states.
This service changed
its state twelve times

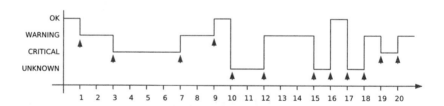

In the period specified, the state of the system shown changed 12 times out of a possible 20, which as a percentage is 60 percent. At 0 percent, not one alternation state has taken place, and 100% means that the service really was in a different state every time it was recorded.

When determining the percentage value, Nagios assigns less significance to older changes of state than to more recent ones. Accordingly it weights the oldest change in state at 1 in Figure B.1 with 0.8, and the most recent at 20 with 1.2. From left to right, the factor increases each time by approx. 0.02,[1] resulting in a linear progression.

This weighting does not have any major effects on the end result in this example: for Figure B.1, this results in 62.21 percent (instead of 60), a slight shift, since the state in the second half changed more often. If there was only a single change of state at 20, the weighting would have the most

---

[1] $(1.2-0.8)/19 = 0.0211$

effect: instead of 5% (that is, one change out of a possible 20) this would result in 5 * 1.2 = 6 percent.

Using threshold values which can be defined—two for services, two for hosts—Nagios defines whether a service or host is "flapping". Both the upper and lower limits are specified as percentages. If the detected change state exceeds the upper threshold, Nagios categorizes the service as *flapping*. This has consequences: Nagios logs the event in the log file, adds a nonpermanent comment,[2] and stops any notifications concerning this from being sent.

If the percentage value falls below the lower limit, the system undoes this step; that is, the comment disappears, notifications are sent again, and the result also appears in the log file.

B.1.1   Nagios configuration

Flap detection is configured at two locations: in the central configuration file and in the definition of the service object. In `nagios.cfg` the feature is switched on generally with the parameter `enable_flap_detection`, and global limit values are also defined here, which will always apply if nothing else is defined for the service in question:

```
# /etc/nagios/nagios.cfg
...
enable_flap_detection=1
low_service_flap_threshold=5.0
high_service_flap_threshold=20.0
...
```

The value 1 set here for `enable_flap_detection` enables flap detection, and 0 switches it off.

The lower limit `low_service_flap_threshold` lies at 5 percent in this case, the upper `high_service_flap_threshold` limit at 20. This means that Nagios categorizes a service as flapping if the history saved detects at least five changes in state (more than four out of a possible 20).[3] The lower five percent limit corresponds to one change in state. To drop below this, all 21 states must be identical.[4]

In the definition of a service object, you have another chance to decide whether flap detection is desired in this case. You also have an option to specify threshold values for this service that differ from the global settings:

---

[2] Nonpermanent comments disappear after the monitoring system is restarted, but permanent ones remain.

[3] If the changes in state took place recently, the weighting would ensure that four changes in state would already be enough to exceed the 20 percent limit.

[4] If a single change of state takes place in the first half, the weighting results in a value of less than 5 percent.

```
define service{
    host_name              linux01
    service_description    NTP
    ...
    flap_detection_enabled 1
    low_flap_threshold     5.0
    high_flap_threshold    20.0
    ...
}
```

The value 1 in `flap_detection_enabled` switches on the feature for this service, and 0 (the default) switches it off. The two limit values `low_flap_threshold` and `high_flap_threshold` define the limit values that override the globally defined values. If they are set to 0, or are omitted, the global thresholds will apply.

Starting with Nagios 3.0, the parameter `flap_detection_options` enables only specified states to be taken into account when detecting changes in states. Possible values are o (OK), w (WARNING), c (CRITICAL), and u (UNKNOWN). The default is

```
flap_detection_options u,w,c,u
```

If the values are restricted to `w,c`, only WARNING and CRITICAL play a role in detection; the other states are ignored. Nagios 3.0 also saves states when flap detection is switched off globally and introduces a corresponding new message type. More on this in Appendix H.4 from page 687.

B.1.2 The history memory and the chronological progression of the changes in state

Since the history only saves hard states and soft recovery, the sections on the x-axis cannot be allocated so easily on a chronological basis, because the intervals between possible changes of state are not equal. Assuming that the service object has the following definitions:

```
max_check_attempts     3
normal_check_interval  5
retry_check_interval   1
```

Nagios checks the service two more times after a change in state from OK to WARNING has taken place, before the service changes to the hard state WARNING (state 1 in Figure B.1 on page 612). Since the last check, which returned OK, a total of seven minutes[5] has elapsed, since the two soft states after five and six minutes are not included in the history.

[5] $5 + 2 * 1 = 7$

If the next service check, as in Figure B.1, again detects a WARNING (i.e., the state does not change this time), then only five minutes elapse this time between states 1 and 2. The x-axis therefore only illustrates time in a linear form in exceptional circumstances—if no change of state occurs, for example.

B.1.3   Representation in the Web interface

Services that Nagios categorizes as flapping are visible in the Web interface at three points: in the summaries generated by tac.cgi (Section 16.2.4, page 345) and status.cgi (Section 16.2.1, page 334), as well as on the information page created by extinfo.cgi (Section 16.2.2, page 339).

The quickest way to get there is through tac.cgi (Figure B.2): a link in the Monitoring Features section marked by x Services Flapping takes you to the status overview of services which continually change their state. The status overview shown in Figure B.3 can also be opened directly with status.cgi?host=all&style=detail&serviceprops=1024.

serviceprops=1024 describes all services that Nagios categorizes as flapping. style=detail provides a detailed view (in contrast to overview, as can be seen in Figure B.10 on page 334), and host=all includes all hosts.

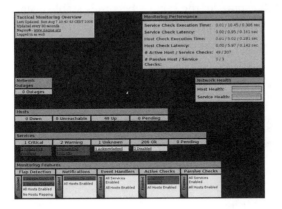

Figure B.2:
tac.cgi notes
changing states in
section Monitoring
Features

In the status view in Figure B.3, a white field with several horizontal gray bars moving to and fro reveal that a flapping service is involved. At the same time a white speech bubble denotes the existence of a comment on this (generated automatically by Nagios).

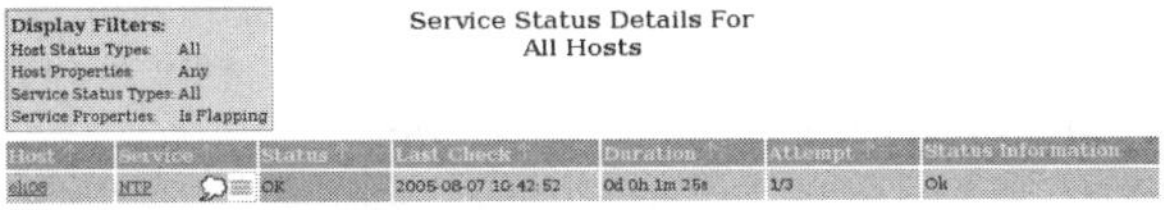

Figure B.3:
Animated horizontal
bars denote flapping
states

If you click in the status view on the flapping icon next to the service in question, `extinfo.cgi` generates additional information on the service (Figure B.4), showing the changes in state in percent next to the flapping category, depicted by a red bar labeled with **YES**.

Figure B.4:
Percent State
Change: reveals how
often the hard state
changed, as a
percentage

Service State Information	
Current Status:	**OK**
Status Information:	Ok
Performance Data:	
Current Attempt:	1/3
State Type:	HARD
Last Check Type:	PASSIVE
Last Check Time:	2005-08-07 10:42:52
Status Data Age:	0d 0h 0m 22s
Next Scheduled Active Check:	2005-08-07 10:45:24
Latency:	N/A
Check Duration:	0.000 seconds
Last State Change:	2005-08-07 10:42:52
Current State Duration:	0d 0h 0m 22s
Last Service Notification:	N/A
Current Notification Number:	0
Is This Service Flapping?	**YES**
Percent State Change:	24.08%
In Scheduled Downtime?	**NO**
Last Update:	2005-08-07 10:43:13

The page also contains the nonpermanent comment generated by Nagios (Figure B.5), which points out that the sending of messages has been stopped until the status of the service becomes stable again. It disappears, therefore, when Nagios is restarted.

Figure B.5:
With this comment,
Nagios categorizes a
service as flapping

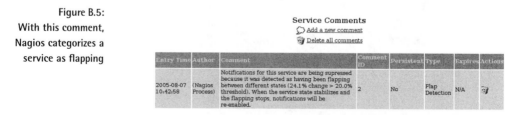

Service Comments
○ Add a new comment
🗑 Delete all comments

Entry Time	Author	Comment	Comment ID	Persistent	Type	Expires	Actions
2005-08-07 10:42:58	(Nagios Process)	Notifications for this service are being supressed because it was detected as having been flapping between different states (24.1% change > 20.0% threshold). When the service state stabilizes and the flapping stops, notifications will be re-enabled.	2	No	Flap Detection	N/A	🗑

B.2 Flap Detection for Hosts

Nagios tries to detect changing states of a host in two ways: in the host check itself (either in the context of the active check from Nagios 3.0 or in on-demand checks), and also if a service check for a host was performed, the last flap detection of which took place some time ago. When Nagios next performs a service check to detect a changing state is determined by the average value for all service check intervals.

Regular host checks are also not necessary from Nagios 3.0 onward, and recent versions of Nagios manage perfectly well without them. For reasons of performance, they really should be avoided in Nagios 2.x (Section 4.2, page 95). By making use of a trick to perform service checks only when required, Nagios compensates for the fact that regular host check results are missing. If at least one service check returns an OK, Nagios concludes from this that the host is also reachable and is in an OK state. The results of flap detection are stored by Nagios in the history.

The same flap detection mechanism is used for hosts as for services. So the difference is only in how Nagios determines the corresponding data basis.

Whether flap detection is desired for hosts is revealed by the central configuration file nagios.cfg and the definition of the host objects. The global parameter enable_flap_detection, which applies equally to hosts and services, must be set to 1:

```
# /etc/nagios/nagios.cfg
enable_flap_detection=1
low_host_flap_threshold=5.0
high_host_flap_threshold=20.0
```

The threshold parameters for hosts include host in their names, but they have the same effect as their service equivalents.[6]

For the host object itself, detection is switched on with flap_detection_enabled 1 and off with 0:

```
define host{
    host_name              linux01
    ...
    flap_detection_enabled 1
    low_flap_threshold     5.0
    high_flap_threshold    20.0
}
```

The optional parameters low_flap_threshold and high_flap_threshold allow for host-specific thresholds. If these are omitted, the global threshold values are used.

As for service checks, Nagios from 3.0 onward also has the additional flap_detection_options parameter here. Possible values in the host definition are o (OK), d (DOWN), and u (UNREACHABLE). Only the states specified for the parameter are used in flap detection, and if this parameter is not given, then all possible states are used.

---

[6] See page 613.

Event Handlers

If the state of a host or service alternates between OK and error states, you can use an *event handler* to run any programs you want. You can make use of this if a service fails, for example, and you want Nagios to try and restart it. This provides an opportunity to solve minor problems without the administrator needing to intervene.

Use of the *event handlers* is not just restricted to self-healing, however: with an appropriate script you can just as easily log current values or the event itself in a database. But there are more suitable methods for doing this, described in Section 19.1, page 404. A failed printer service serves as an example here of using an event handler for self-healing. In this example the printer service lpd is used, but this method can be applied in general to any service for which a start-stop script is available.

C.1 Execution Times for the Event Handler

The following parameters in the service definition ensure that Nagios tests the service under normal circumstances every five minutes, but in cases of error, every two minutes:

```
normal_check_interval  5
retry_check_interval   2
max_check_attempts     4
```

An error state becomes hard after four tests leading to the same result.

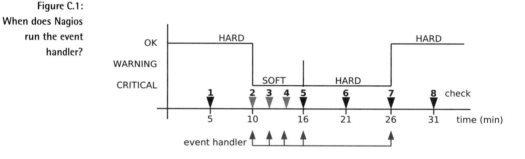

Figure C.1 shows an example of the change of the lpd service from an OK state to CRITICAL, and back again. After 10 minutes test No. 2 detects that the service is no longer available. The soft state that results causes Nagios to examine lpd more closely at two-minute intervals (checks No. 3, 4, and 5). Test No. 5 returns a CRITICAL for the fourth time, causing Nagios to categorize this as a hard state and to go back to the normal, five-minute test interval. In check No. 7 the service is functioning again, and the state changes from CRITICAL to OK (for hard state, see Section 4.3, page 96.).

Event handlers are carried out by Nagios for soft error states (in checks No. 2, 3, 4), the first time a hard error state occurs (in check No. 5), and in the resetting of the OK state after an error (irrespective of whether this is a hard or soft recovery).

Since hard error states lead to the administrator being notified, it is recommended that the repair attempt is moved to the time of the soft error states. If it succeeds at this point in time, the administrator is spared these minor details. Ideally the service will be running again before a user even notices that it has failed.

The fact that Nagios only executes the event handler when a hard error state first occurs prevents periodic attempts at repair that do not lead to the desired result after all (if the attempt had succeeded, no further hard error states would have occurred).

C.2 Defining the Event Handler in the Service Definition

Although Nagios executes the event handler for every event, it does not have to carry out an action each time. In our example the handler should attempt to reset the printer service on the third soft error state (check No. 4) and on the first hard error state (check No. 5), and do nothing at all the other execution times.

For this purpose, the service definition is modified as follows:

```
define service{
    host_name              printserver
    service_description    LPD
    ...
    event_handler          restart-lpd
    ...
}
```

The `event_handler` parameter expects a Nagios command object that will run the handler script:

```
define command{
    command_name  restart-lpd
    command_line  $USER1$/eventhandler/restart-lpd.sh $SERVICESTATE$ $SER
VICESTATETYPE$ $SERVICEATTEMPT$

}
```

In this example it is called `restart-lpd.sh` and is not located directly in the Nagios plugin directory `/usr/local/nagios/libexec`, but in a subdirectory called `/usr/local/nagios/libexec/eventhandler`, as suggested in the Nagios documentation. The script receives three macros as parameters: the current state $SERVICESTATE$ (OK, WARNING, CRITICAL, or UNKNOWN), the state type $SERVICESTATETYPE$ (SOFT, or HARD), and the number of the current (possibly repeated) attempt $SERVICEATTEMPT$ (e.g., 3 if the test is being performed for the third time). If the event handler is to be used for host checks, then the macros $HOSTSTATE$, $HOSTSTATE-TYPE$, and $HOSTATTEMPT$ are used instead.

C.3   The Handler Script

The actual treatment of the error—depending on the current event—is dealt with by the script defined in the command definition. So that we can concentrate on the essential aspects in this context, we shall assume that lpd is installed on the Nagios server itself. This enables the service to be restarted locally, without the need for a remote shell such as the Secure Shell.

The script restart-lpd.sh checks to see exactly what event is involved, using the macros passed on to it, and either does nothing at all or tries to restart lpd:

```bash
#!/bin/bash
# /usr/local/nagios/libexec/eventhandlers/restart-lpd.sh
# $1 = Status, $2 = status type, $3 = attempt

case $1 in
   OK)
      ;;
   WARNING)
      ;;
   CRITICAL)
      if [ $2 == "HARD" ] || [[ $2 == "SOFT"  && $3 -eq 3 ]]; then
         echo "Restarting lpd service"
         /usr/bin/sudo /etc/init.d/lpd restart
      fi
      ;;
   UNKNOWN)
      ;;
esac
exit 0
```

The case statement first checks to see what state exists. Only if it is CRITICAL will the script do anything; it does not carry out any action for other states. If the service is in a critical state, either the state type must be HARD or (||) a corresponding soft state must occur for the third time in succession, so that restart-lpd.sh can execute the lpd init script with the argument restart.[1]

The script is executed with the permissions of the user nagios, who may neither stop nor restart system services. This is why sudo is used, which provides temporary root permissions exclusively for the start-up script /etc/init.d/lpd, just for this user. The corresponding configuration can be found in the file /etc/sudoers, but if it is edited then you must use the program visudo rather than a standard editor (this checks the configuration file for syntax errors when it is saved):

---

[1]   If you want to get to know Bash programming more closely, we can recommend the excellent *Advanced Bash-Scripting Guide* (http://www.tldp.org/LDP/abs/html) by Mendel Cooper.

```
linux:~ # visudo
```

Then you add the following line to the configuration file:

```
nagios  nagsrv=(root) NOPASSWD: /etc/init.d/lpd
```

In plain language this means: the user `nagios` may run the command `/etc/init.d/lpd` on the host `nagsrv`. The command is run as the user `root`, but no password is required for this.

C.4 Things to Note When Using Event Handlers

If you restart a service that is already in a soft error state as described here, the administrator will not receive any notification as long as the action was successful. Although the log file records the restart, it will scarcely be noticed unless you search the log file explicitly for such events. This means that the administrator will seldom investigate the cause of the service failure.

You should therefore bear in mind that eliminating the problem is the best solution, and that a restart is only second best. Like air bags in automobiles, the event handler should just be regarded as an additional security measure, and should certainly not represent the primary method of handling errors. If you carry out the restart only when a hard error state occurs, the administrator is confronted with the problem through the notification mechanism.

In addition, not every service is suitable for an automatic restart. With OpenLDAP in versions before 2.1.17, a problem occurred sporadically in the replication through `slurpd`, which left behind a corrupted replication file. Although the replication service could be restarted, it died again after a short time. To really get the replication up and running again, you would have to repair the replication file manually.

You should always remember this example and never have complete faith in self-healing. In the worst case, restarting a service repeatedly and without thought could lead to loss of data, which might be rectified only by retrieving data from the backups.

Macros

Macros are the salt in the Nagios soup, for without them each service would have to be defined individually for each host and each command defined separately for each host and each service. They are identified by the dollar signs surrounding them: $macro$. We will look at the definition of a command with the plugin check_http (see Section 6.4.2, page 119):

```
define command{
    command_name check_http
    command_line $USER1$/check_http -H $HOSTADDRESS$ $ARG1$
}
```

The definition contains three different macros: the user macro $USER1$, defined in the file resource.cfg (see Section 2.14, page 79), as well as $HOSTADDRESS$ and $ARG1$. The 32 possible user macros $USER1$ to

$USER32$ are like constants that you use to record information, such as the path to the plugin directory (normally in $USER1$) or even passwords that should not appear in the normal configuration. The file resource.cfg may then be readable only for the user nagios.

The second macro, $HOSTADDRESS$, is a so-called *standard macro*, which is replaced by the host address of the host definition before the command is run:

```
define host{
    host_name   linux01
    address     192.0.2.1
    ...
}

define service{
    host_name           linux01
    service_description HTTP
    check_command       check_http!-u test.html
    ...
}
```

If the service linux01;HTTP calls the command check_http, the command will obtain the host address from the parameter address. However, standard macros can provide not only the contents of a parameter from an object definition, as in this case, but also dynamic values that can change. Examples include the state of a host (e.g., $HOSTSTATE$), the output of a plugin (e.g., $SERVICEOUTPUT$), and system information, such as the start time of Nagios or the current time, or information on the configuration or static values.

The $ARGx$ macros contain the command line arguments in sequence. These appear in the service definition after the exclamation mark following the command check_http. The exclamation mark is also used as a separator between the individual arguments. In this way, spaces can be used within an argument, as in the example here (-u test.html), without any problem whatsoever.

Nagios can handle two other groups of macros: on-demand and custom macros. *On-demand macros* (see Section D.2 on page 632) are extended standard macros that are used to access values belonging to an external object: for example, $HOSTADDRESS:linux02$ returns the IP address of linux02, irrespective of whether we are in the host or service definition of linux01 or linux04.

Custom macros, also referred to as *user-defined variables*, were only introduced in Nagios 3.0. The definition of host, service, and contact objects is now supplemented with definitions you can make yourself, in whatever manner you like. Section D.3 from page 633 deals with these custom macros in more detail.

D.1   Standard Macros

It would go beyond the scope of this book to describe all the available macros. The description below concentrates on the most important ones. A complete list is given in a tabular overview in the online documentation.[1]

Not all macros can be used everywhere. For this reason the tables provide information on the contexts in which each one is applicable. Normally this can be deduced with a bit of common sense. A service macro does not belong in a host check or a host notification, and likewise, a notification macro has no place in a host or service check. A value (such as a host state) which first has to be found is of course not yet available while it is being identified (that is, during the host check).

Macros can basically be used in the following actions: for host and service checks, for host and service notifications, when running event handlers (Appendix C, page 619) or the OCSP/OHCP commands (Chapter 15, page 317), and also when processing performance data with the accompanying commands (Section 19.1.1, page 405 and Section 19.1.2, page 407).

D.1.1   Host macros

Macro	Description
$HOSTNAME$	Host name from the host_name parameter for the host definition
$HOSTALIAS$	Alias from the alias parameter for the host definition
$HOSTADDRESS$	IP address or FQDN from the host definition parameter
$HOSTSTATE$	State as text: UP, DOWN, UNREACHABLE
$HOSTSTATEID$	State in numerical form: 0 (UP), 1 (DOWN), 2 (UNREACHABLE)
$HOSTSTATETYPE$	HARD, SOFT
$HOSTOUTPUT$	The first line of the text output of the host check
$HOSTLONGOUTPUT$ (Nagios 3.0)	Long text of the host check, if this provides multiple-line information
$HOSTPERFDATA$	Performance data from the host check

Table D.1: Selected host macros

[1] Nagios 2.x: http://nagios.sourceforge.net/docs/2_0/macros.html; Nagios 3.0: http://nagios.sourceforge.net/docs/3_0/macrolist.html

Table D.1 documents the most important macros in connection with hosts. The macros $HOSTNAME$, $HOSTALIAS$, and $HOSTADDRESS$ provide information from the host definition itself, so they are static. $HOSTSTATEID$ and $HOSTSTATE$ do *not* give the return value of the plugin—1 (OK) or 2 (CRITICAL)—but the result after the topological evaluation by Nagios. $HOSTSTATETYPE$ defines whether Nagios really has completed the check (hard state) or whether the check is to be repeated (soft state).

D.1.2 Service macros

Table D.2 presents selected service macros.

Macro	Description
$SERVICEDESC$	Name of the service, taken from the parameter service_description from the service definition
$SERVICESTATE$	The state in text form: OK, WARNING, CRITICAL, UNKNOWN
$SERVICESTATEID$	The state numerically: 0 (OK), 1 (WARNING), 2 (CRITICAL), 3 (UNKNOWN)
$SERVICESTATETYPE$	HARD, SOFT
$SERVICEOUTPUT$	The first line of the text output of the plugin during the service check
$SERVICELONGOUTPUT$ (Nagios 3.0)	The long text of the service check, if this provides multiple-line output
$SERVICEPERFDATA$	Performance data of the service check

D.1.3 Group macros

The host group macros described in Table D.3 are provided by Nagios for service and contact groups as well. The string HOST in the macro name is replaced accordingly by SERVICE or CONTACT.

The macros $HOSTGROUPNAME$ and $HOSTGROUPNAMES$ are always connected to the host. The same applies for the equivalent SERVICEGROUP (connected to a service) and CONTACTGROUP macros (connected to a contact). Whereas $HOSTGROUPNAME$ always returns the first host group of the associated host, $HOSTGROUPNAMES$ displays a complete, comma-separated list of all host groups of which the host is a member.

Macro	Description
$HOSTGROUPNAME$	Name of the first host group
$HOSTGROUPNAMES$	Comma-separated list of all host groups to which the associated host belongs
$HOSTGROUPALIAS$	Alias of the host group
$HOSTGROUPMEMBERS$	Members of the host group

Table D.3: Selected group macros

In contrast, the macros $HOSTGROUPALIAS$ and $HOSTGROUPMEMBERS$ refer to a host group. However, now there are no activities using a host group as a reference point.[2] So what is the purpose of these macros? They can be implemented as on-demand macros (see Section D.2 from page 632). For example, $HOSTGROUPMEMBERS:Linux$ displays a list of all members of the Linux host group.

On the other hand, if the macro is run in a "normal" context, Nagios identifies the first host group specified in the host definition and assesses the accompanying value. The same applies for service and contact groups.

D.1.4 Contact macros

The macros listed in Table D.4 reference all the parameters in the respective contact definition.

Macro	Parameter to be read out
$CONTACTNAME$	contact_name
$CONTACTALIAS$	alias
$CONTACTEMAIL$	email
$CONTACTPAGER$	Parameter pager of the contact
$CONTACTADDRESS$n$	One of six possible contact addresses, where n is a digit between 1 and 6[3]

Table D.4: Selected contact macros

---

[2] It is possible to run commands for a host group from the Web interface, but Nagios always resolves these into single actions for each host.

[3] The exact contents of $CONTACTADDRESS$n$ are specified by the Nagios administrator. Anything goes: other telephone numbers, e-mail addresses, or even Granny's phone number.

D.1.5 Notification macros

Table D.5 shows a selection of macros for notifications.

Macro	Description
$NOTIFICATIONTYPE$	Notification type (for values, see text)
$NOTIFICATIONRECIPIENTS$ (Nagios 3.0)	Comma-separated list of all recipients
$HOSTNOTIFICATIONNUMBER$ (Nagios 3.0)	Notification counter
$SERVICENOTIFICATIONNUMBER$ (Nagios 3.0)	Notification counter

$NOTIFICATIONTYPE$ describes the type of notification. For Nagios 2.x the notification types are PROBLEM, RECOVERY, ACKNOWLEDGEMENT, FLAPPING-START, and FLAPPINGSTOP. Nagios 3.0 also has FLAPPINGDISABLED, as well as DOWNTIMESTART, DOWNTIMEEND, and DOWNTIMECANCELLED.

The macro $NOTIFICATIONRECIPIENTS$ is only available from Nagios 3.0; it contains a comma-separated list of all recipients of the notification that has just been sent. Also new in this version are the two macros $HOSTNOTI-FICATIONNUMBER$ and $SERVICENOTIFICATIONNUMBER$. These contain the incremented number of the last sent message, which is important for escalation management. Acknowledge messages are ignored in this case, as are flapping messages or messages on planned maintenance periods. As soon as the state of the host or service is again OK, this counter is reset to 0, and in the event of an error, counting starts again from the beginning.

D.1.6 Macros to specify time and date

The output of the date macro from Table D.6 depends on the date form specified in the parameter date_format (page 591).

Macro	Example
$LONGDATETIME$	Sa 29 Dec 17:23:22 CET 2007
$SHORTDATETIME$	2007-12-29 17:23:22
$DATE$	2007-12-29
$TIME$	17:23:22
$TIMET$	1198945589

$LONGDATETIME$ outputs a format also provided by the date program without any parameters. The examples for $SHORTDATETIME$ and $DATE$ correspond to the date_format=iso8601 setting. With the value date_format=us, the date would be written here as 12/29/2007. $TIME$ contains only the time, whereas $TIMET$ shows the epoch time (seconds elapsed since 01.01.1970).

D.1.7 Statistics macros

If you use the macros shown in Table D.7 in notifications, the macro in each case will show the number of hosts or services for which the contact to whom the notification is sent is responsible. This means that different recipients may receive different figures for the same notification.

Macro	Description
$TOTALHOSTSUP$	Number of hosts in UP state
$TOTALHOSTSDOWN$	Number of hosts in DOWN state
$TOTALHOSTSUNREACHABLE$	Number of hosts in UNREACHABLE state
$TOTALSERVICESOK$	Number of services in OK state
$TOTALSERVICESCRITICAL$	Number of services in CRITICAL state
$TOTALSERVICESWARNING$	Number of services in WARNING state
$TOTALSERVICESUNKNOWN$	Number of services in UNKNOWN state
$TOTALSERVICEPROBLEMS$	Total number of services with problems

Table D.7:
Selected macros for
statistical purposes

D.1.8 Using standard macros about the environment

All standard macros can be provided by Nagios as environment variables, if required. The variable name here is derived from the name of the macro without the dollar sign, to which the prefix NAGIOS_ is added. The macro $HOSTADDRESS$ thus converts to the environment variable NAGIOS_HOST-ADDRESS. Among the on-demand macros (see next section), the host and service macros are not available as environment variables for reasons of security, and the same goes for the $USERx$ macros, since these could contain sensitive information such as passwords.

Providing these environment variables takes a great deal of time. You should therefore consider whether you can do without them altogether in Nagios 3.0 (see the parameters use_large_installation_tweaks, page 605, and enable_environment_macros, page 592). In Nagios 2.x the environment variable cannot be switched off.

Instead of accessing the Nagios environment variable directly from an external script, as in the following example,

```
#!/bin/bash
# badscript

HOST=$NAGIOS_HOSTADDRESS
...
```

which is called as follows,

```
define command{
command_line $USER1$/badscript
...
}
```

as an alternative, you could pass on the contents of the macro to the script explicitly as an argument:

```
define command{
    command_line $USER1$/goodscript $HOSTADDRESS$
...
}
```

Then you can manage without the Nagios environment variable in the script itself:

```
#!/bin/bash
# goodscript

HOST=$1
...
```

goodscript retrieves the relevant value from the command line, with $1.

D.2 On-Demand Macros

On-demand macros—which have existed since Nagios 2.0—reference the same contents as standard macros do. The subtle difference between them lies in the context of what they reference. Whereas standard macros refer exclusively to the host, service, or contact object currently being used, on-demand macros enable access to values from any external objects you please:

```
$HOSTADDRESS:linux01$
$HOSTSTATE:switch05$
```

The macros are the same as standard macros, but their names include the name of the host to which the reference is made. The colon is used as a separator. For services, the service name also needs to be specified, again separated with another colon:

```
$SERVICESTATE:switch05:PING$
$SERVICESTATE::NRPE$
```

If the host field is left empty, the macro refers to the host in whose context the macro is called. If, for instance, you are checking the disk usage via NRPE on the host linux01 with the service Disks NRPE, then the standard macro $SERVICESTATE$ will return the state of the service linux01;Disks, whereas the on-demand macro $SERVICESTATE::NRPE$ will display the state of the service linux01;NRPE. An appropriate script can take into account the dependency here between the service NRPE and an NRPE-based check such as Disks.

For contact objects, the external reference point is a contact in each case:

```
$CONTACTNAME:gregor$
$CONTACTEMAIL:smith$
```

In addition to this, there are also on-demand macros for host, service, and contact groups, and in each case the reference point is the group concerned.

D.3 Macros for User-defined Variables

Starting from Nagios 3.0, you can specify your own macros in host, service, and contact definitions. These macros, called *custom macros* in Nagios jargon, are treated like normal standard macros, and their names begin with an underscore to make them more easily identifiable:

```
define host {
   host_name       linux01
   ...
   _NSCLIENT_PORT 12489
   _ASSETID        734287
}
define service {
   host_name          linux01
   service_description HTTP
   ...
   _HTTP_PORT         8080
}
define contact {
```

```
    contact_name  wob
    ...
    _DEPARTMENT   41ZBV
}
```

They are addressed with a prefixed object type:

```
$_HOSTNSCLIENT_PORT$
$_HOSTASSETID$
$_SERVICEHTTP_PORT$
$_CONTACTDEPARTMENT$
```

The macro again starts with an underscore, but the underscore supplied in the definition is omitted. This is difficult to read. If you want to use the underscore as a separator, for instance between HOST and NSCLIENT_PORT, the custom macro must begin with a double underscore. Thus,

```
define host {
    host_name      linux01
    ...
    __NSCLIENT_PORT 12489
    __ASSETID       734287
}
```

turns into

```
$_HOST_NSCLIENT_PORT$
$_HOST_ASSETID$
```

In the definition of a custom macro, upper and lower case are not distinguished, but when the macro is called it is always written in capitals. Besides providing abbreviations for content used mainly for documentation purposes, such as ASSETID or DEPARTMENT, such user-defined macros can also be used to neatly define commands.

For example, if you are monitoring a Windows environment with the NS-Client mechanism, a service is installed on the host being monitored that listens to a specific port (Section 20.2.1, page 464). Under certain circumstances you will be forced to change the standard port. If you now have several servers with different ports, you must tell the plugin on which port it is to run the query.

One method would be to also include the port as an argument for each service definition, or to define a second command with a permanently stored, alternative port. However, if the port on the target system is now changed, the entire service definition of the target system must be modified.

A more elegant solution is to store the port, as above, as a custom macro in the host definition and to evaluate the custom macro in the command.

This solution, which unfortunately works only in Nagios 3.0, is described for the NSClient service in Section 20.2.5 from page 471, and an equivalent example for NRPE can be found in Section H.2 from page 685.

D.4 Macro Contents: Not Everything Is Allowed

A number of macros contain values that were not defined within the Nagios configuration or defined by Nagios itself, but which originate from external programs. These include macros that record the plugin output ($HOSTOUTPUT$, $LONGHOSTOUTPUT$, $HOSTPERFDATA$), and the corresponding macros for services. Via the Web interface, the administrator can pass on values to Nagios through acknowledgments, which can be read out from the macros $HOSTACKAUTHOR$, $HOSTACKCOMMENT$, and the equivalent service macros.

To guard against the possibility that these macros might contain damaging code, which might trigger a buffer overflow or enable other mischievous things, Nagios removes "dangerous" lines. What these are is defined by the parameter illegal_object_name_chars (page 596):

```
illegal_object_name_chars='~$^&'<>
```

The Nagios administrator can change these, but he must be aware that fewer characters means a higher potential of risk.

Single Sign-On for the Nagios Web Interface

For the login to the Web interface, Nagios takes the user who has authenticated himself to the Web server, usually Apache. In principle it makes no difference how this authentication comes about, but the name of the contact must match the user name passed on to the CGI programs from the Web server. Nagios is quite tolerant in terms of its name conventions here. Even user names such as wob@EXAMPLE.NET or EXAMPLE/wob are possible. This is enabled by *single sign-on (SSO)*, which means that users only need to log on a single time. Ideally, all applications should accept the authentication that has already been performed, and the user will not be asked for a password every time.

Security experts have been busy discussing the pros and cons[1] of single sign-on, but it is very popular with users. We will therefore not go into the disscussion on security.

Single sign-on, in combination with the Nagios Web interface, means that the user is automatically authenticated from the browser when the Nagios CGI programs are called, and a password is no longer required. Of course, what is described here can also be used for other Web pages—this could be the NagVis, PNP, or a Wiki. There are hardly any limits to the opportunities for using single sign-on.

This chapter describes the use of two alternative Apache modules for Apache 2 that enable a single sign-on scenario. As the authentication server, a running Active Directory in Windows 2003 is required.[2] On the client side, the browser used must support the selected HTTP authentication procedure. Microsoft Internet Explorer and Firefox are both suitable for this.

The Apache module `mod_auth_kerb` uses Kerberos directly, and could therefore be used in an exclusively Linux environment (without Active Directory). Since the author himself does not have a production Kerberos environment with Linux clients available, we will not deal with this topic here. If you are running a fully functional Kerberos environment in Linux/Unix, you should find it easy to modify the `mod_auth_kerb` section to your environment.

The Apache module `mod_auth_ntlm_winbind` makes use of `ntlm_auth`, a program that is a component of Samba 3.0. It therefore requires a complete Samba installation, and the server must be a member of an Active Directory domain.

E.1   HTTP Authentication for Single Sign-On

Microsoft has supported single sign-on via Web browser for some time now. The original procedure was based on (*NT LAN Manager (NTLM)*, a protocol that is also used in networks, for example when logging in to a domain or when accessing network drives. Here the client sends a so-called *type 1 message* containing the host and domain names of the client. The server replies with an NTLM challenge (an NTLM *type 2 message*), and the client completes authentication with a *type 3 message*, which in turn sends back to the server not only the client name and domain, but also the challenge, which has been encrypted with the client's password. The procedure is Microsoft-specific and was never published as a standard. Nevertheless,

---

[1] `http://en.wikipedia.org/wiki/Single_sign_on`

[2] The scenario described may also work with Windows 2000, but the author was not able to test this. Nevertheless, there are certainly differences in the Kerberos implementation between Windows 2000 and Windows 2003, which probably require adjustments to the procedure descrbed here.

Firefox is able to use it. The HTTP authentication–related descriptions of the NTLM protocol can also be found on the Internet.[3]

Microsoft will soon replace the NTLM-based authentication with a newer, Kerberos-based authentication. With Windows Server 2008, NTLM will no longer be available for HTTP authentication, at least on the server side.

The successor to this has already been in practical use for some time. It uses a generic interface called *Generic Security Services Application Program Interface (GSSAPI)*. For HTTP authentication, as well as GSSAPI, a mechanism called *SPNEGO* (*Simple and Protected Negotiate*) is used, through which concrete authentication is negotiated. Microsoft describes the HTTP authentication in an informal Request for Comment, RFC 4559.[4] This also discusses the NTLM procedure. The SPNEGO, used for the newer variation, is described in RFC 4178.[5]

The SPNEGO procedure is somewhat shorter than the NTLM authentication and is closer to the HTTP authentication methods `Basic` and `Digest`. First, the client requests a protected page with the command GET. The server replies with the status code 401 (Unauthorized) and includes the possible authentication procedures:

```
HTTP/1.1 401 Authorization Required
...
WWW-Authenticate: Negotiate
WWW-Authenticate: NTLM
WWW-Authenticate: Basic realm="Nagios Monitoring"
...
```

The server in this example provides a choice of three procedures: `Negotiate` stands for the Kerberos-based SPNEGO procedure, `NTLM` stands for the older NTLM authentication, and `Basic` refers to the classic user password method in which the authentication data are transmitted in plain text. It is now up to the client to decide on one of the three procedures. The client—here an instance of Microsoft Internet Explorer 6.0—selects the secure Kerberos-based procedure:

```
GET /nagios/index.html HTTP/1.1
...
Authorization: Negotiate YIIIlwYGKwYBBQUCoIIIizCCCIegJDA...
```

After the HTTP header field `Authorization` comes the keyword `Negotiate`, followed by the Base64-encoded authentication data. If this is success-

---

[3] http://www.innovation.ch/personal/ronald/ntlm.html, in more detail at http://davenport.sourceforge.net/ntlm.html
[4] http://rfc.sunsite.dk/rfc/rfc4559.html
[5] http://rfc.sunsite.dk/rfc/rfc4178.html

ful, the server replies in turn with the HTTP code 200 (OK), and the HTTP header also contains authentication data,[6] which the client processes:

```
HTTP/1.1 200 OK
...
WWW-Authenticate: Negotiate oYGeMIGbo...
```

If successful, the browser will display the HTTP page it has received. The negotiate procedure is shown in a somewhat simplified form here, and it is possible that the server sends back a 401 code (Unauthorized) with the WWW-Authenticate field after it receives the Authorization packet of the client, because further authentication data is required. The client then sends another Authorization header entry, as requested. This is repeated until the server answers with 200 OK.

E.2 Kerberos Authentication with mod_auth_kerb

The module mod_auth_kerb integrates Apache into an existing Kerberos environment and allows authentication through two procedures: simple authentication with the Basic method or the negotiation procedure SP-NEGO, described in RFC 4559.

Both procedures are shown in Figure E.1. For an authentication via negotiate (only Kerberos v5), the client fetches a ticket from the Kerberos server (1), which it forwards to the Web server (2). The Web server in turn sends the ticket via the Kerberos protocol to the Kerberos server for inspection (3). What is not shown is the response of the Web server to the client if authentication is successful (or if it fails).

Figure E.1:
mod_auth_kerb
allows full authentication via Kerberos,
via SPNEGO. With
the Basic procedure,
communication
between Web server
and Kerberos server
also runs via the
Kerberos protocol.

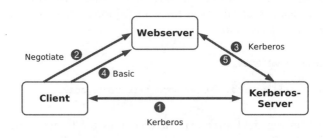

---

[6] In general, Kerberos provides authentication on both sides, so the server must also authenticate itself with the client.

With the `Basic` authentication the client sends a user/password pair in plain text to the Web server (4). The server for its part, however, transmits the authentication data via the Kerberos protocol to the Kerberos server (5)—which doesn't alter the fact that the authentication between the Web server and client takes place without protection. It is essential that SSL encryption is used here. The Web server itself has a permanent ticket for the HTTP service so that it can communicate with the Kerberos server in the first place.

E.2.1 Installation

The module is available at SourceForge,[7] where you can also find some notes on the installation and a little documentation. Modern distributions include the module as a package, which has the advantage that you don't need to worry about the dependencies of other packages—the installer automatically installs the required software. In Debian "Etch" the module is called `libapache2-mod-auth-kerb`. You should have at least version 5.3, since earlier versions have some minor bugs, especially when working with Microsoft Internet Explorer 6.0.[8]

To carry out the configuration, the programs `klist` and `kinit` are also required, and in Debian "Etch" these can be found in the package `krb5-user` (and not in `krb5-clients`!). One more note on Kerberos itself: The description in this book is based on the Kerberos implementation of the Massachusetts Institute of Technology (MIT), which is also used in Microsoft Windows.

E.2.2 Creating a service ticket for Apache

To participate in the Kerberos procedure, Apache requires a service ticket with a quite specific realm:

`HTTP/fqdn@EXAMPLE.NET`

This consists of the protocol, in this case HTTP, the fully qualified domain name (FQDN), and the realm of the domain. The protocol and the domain realm must be written in capitals, and the FQDN must exactly match the name with which the Web server is addressed later on. Otherwise, the client will refuse to work during the negotiate procedure. Below, `nagios.example.net` will be used as the FQDN, and the domain controller has the name `dc01.example.net`.

---

[7] `http://modauthkerb.sourceforge.net/`

[8] Even if the negotiation procedure was being used at browser startup, a password window pops up after a while and the IE switches back to `Basic` authentication.

The Kerberos implementation in Windows 2003 requires that the service ticket is bound to one user. To do this, a user is set up (in the example, webnagios) who does not need to have any special permissions. To create a ticket manually, you need the support tools in an Active Directory environment, which are best installed on a domain controller. After the installation, you change to the directory where the support tools are located and create the service ticket with the program `ktpass`:

```
C:\> cd \Programs\Support Tools
C:\Programs\Support Tools> ktpass -princ HTTP/nagios.example.net@EXAMP
LE.NET -mapuser webnagios@example.net -pass ***** -out c:\temp\webnagios
http.keytab

Targeting domain controller: dc01.example.net
Successfully mapped HTTP/nagios.example.net
to webnagios. Key created. Output keytab to
c:\temp\webnagioshttp.keytab: Keytab version:
0x502 keysize 81 HTTP/nagios.example.net@EXAMPLE.NET
ptype 1 (KRB5_NT_PRINCIPAL) vno 3 etype 0x3 (DES-CBC-MD5)
keylength 8 (0x7fc42302a7342952) Account webnagios has
been set for DES-only encryption.
```

The ticket is then copied to a directory, preferably in the Apache installation, for example to /etc/apache2/keytabs.

E.2.3 Kerberos configuration

/etc/krb5.conf is used as the configuration file for Kerberos:

```
# /etc/krb5.conf
[libdefaults]
   default_realm = EXAMPLE.NET

[realms]
   EXAMPLE.NET = {
       kdc = dc01.example.net:88
       kdc = dc02.example.net:88
       admin_server = dc01.example.net
   }
```

The [libdefaults] section basically defines the defaults. It is important here that the domain realm is written in upper case. In the [realms] section, the individual realms are defined with their respective servers. The parameter kdc describes Kerberos servers that act as a key service (all domain controllers in the Active Directory), and admin_server is the Kerberos master (normally the first domain controller in the Active Directory). It must be possible to resolve the name specified here into an IP address, which can be tested with a ping to the FQDN given here.

To see if Kerberos is working, it is best to use the program `kinit`, which—if successful—will obtain a valid ticket from the Kerberos server:

```
linux:~ # kinit administrator@EXAMPLE.NET
Password for administrator@EXAMPLE.NET: ******
```

`kinit` requires a valid account as an argument, and it is important that the domain after the user name is written in upper case. If the password is correct and everything works, `kinit` will have no output. The ticket obtained can now be shown, with `klist`:

```
linux:~ # klist
Ticket cache: FILE:/tmp/krb5cc_0
Default principal: administrator@EXAMPLE.NET

Valid starting     Expires            Service principal
08/26/07 14:31:47  08/27/07 00:31:49 krbtgt/EXAMPLE.NET@EXAMPLE.NET
       renew until 08/27/07 14:31:47

Kerberos 4 ticket cache: /tmp/tkt0
klist: You have no tickets cached
```

E.2.4 Apache configuration

You must make sure that Apache really does load the module `mod_auth_kerb` when it starts. When installing through a distribution, the module is already preconfigured. In Debian "Etch" the accompanying LoadModule directive can be found in the file `/etc/apache2/mods-available/auth_kerb.load`:

```
LoadModule auth_kerb_module /usr/lib/apache2/modules/mod_auth_kerb.so
```

For activation, Debian uses the command a2enmod, which basically does nothing more than place a symlink in the directory `/etc/apache2/mods-enabled/`, pointing to the configuration file:

```
linux:~ # a2enmod auth_kerb
Module auth_kerb installed; run /etc/init.d/apache2 force-reload to
enable.
```

To be able to use Kerberos for authentication, you need to modify the Apache configuration file `/etc/apache2/conf.d/nagios.conf`, which was described in Section 1.5.3 (page 49):

```
<Directory "/usr/local/nagios">
   AllowOverride None
   Order allow,deny
   Allow from all

   # -- Authentification
   AuthType Kerberos
   AuthName "Nagios Monitoring"
   KrbAuthRealms EXAMPLE.NET
   Krb5Keytab /etc/apache2/keytabs/webnagioshttp.keytab
   KrbMethodK5Passwd on
   KrbMethodNegotiate on
   KrbSaveCredentials off

   require valid-user
</Directory>
```

AuthType specifies that Kerberos should be used. With AuthName the authentication is given a name, which is displayed in the Basic authentication. KrbAuthRealms describes one or more domain realms, and if there are several, they are separated by spaces.

The service ticket generated on the domain controller is specified under Krb5Keytab. KrbMethodK5Passwd on, apart from the negotiate procedure, allows simple authentication using a password, in which the browser sends the password via Basic authentication to the Web server. With KrbMethodNegotiate on the negotiate procedure is switched on, and a completely closed Kerberos circuit is established. Then KrbSaveCredentials determines whether received authentication data are to be cached, in case other CGI applications should use these automatically. This is not necessary for our purposes, which is why we switch it off with the off option. Finally, require valid-user ensures that only valid users can gain access. A more detailed configuration, such as specifying a group or individual users, is not necessary, because Nagios manages its users itself and needs only the name of the authenticated user.

E.2.5 Definition of a Nagios contact

To be able to use single sign-on in Nagios, you now just need to adapt the name of the contact to the new, authenticated Web user *user@REALM*:

```
define contact{
        use             template-contact-webuser
        contact_name    wob@EXAMPLE.NET
        alias           wob@EXAMPLE
        contactgroups   admins
        email           w.barth@example.net
}
```

The contact definition (see Section 2.7 on page 70) assumes that a template (see Section 2.11 on page 75) exists with the name `template-contact-webuser`.

When modifying the authentication and the name change connected with this, you must also modify the CGI configuration file `cgi.cfg` (see Appendix A.2 from page 606), if this is to explicitly contain entered users in the `authorized_*` parameters.

E.3 Single Sign-On with `mod_auth_ntlm_winbind`

The Apache module `mod_auth_ntlm_winbind` uses the program originally developed for Squid, `ntlm_auth`, for authentication, and so one of its requirements is a Samba server installation in which the server itself is a member of an Active Directory domain. `ntlm_auth` uses `winbind` and therefore offers smooth integration into an existing Active Directory.

The module has three methods available for authentication: NTLM, Negotiate (SPNEGO), and the `Basic` authentication. In Summer 2007 there were still problems with Negotiate. Developed originally for a proxy, the method did not quite fit the needs of a Web server and therefore was not used. At the time of writing, NTLM and `Basic` authentication remain, but this may change after this book is published. NTLM works very well, whereby `ntlm_auth` also allows the selection of a specific group. But you should also bear in mind that Microsoft is discontinuing NTLM for HTTP authentication with Windows Server 2008.

E.3.1 Installation

The module is still very new. It has the version number 0.0.0 and can only be obtained in the source code from Subversion[9] or from corresponding unpacked directories.[10] Some documentation, in addition to the included README, can be found at SourceForge.[11]

For the installation you change to the directory where the source code has been unpacked:

```
linux:~ # cd /usr/local/src/mod_auth_ntlm_winbind
linux:src/mod_auth_ntlm_winbind # autoconf
...
linux:src/mod_auth_ntlm_winbind # ./configure
```

[9] svn co svn://svnanon.samba.org/lorikeet/trunk/mod_auth_ntlm_winbind
mod_auth_ntlm_winbind
[10] http://samba.org/ftp/unpacked/lorikeet/mod_auth_ntlm_winbind/
[11] http://adldap.sourceforge.net/mod_auth_ntlm_winbind.php

```
...
linux:src/mod_auth_ntlm_winbind # apxs2 -DAPACHE2 -c -i mod_auth_ntlm_ \
winbind.c
...
```

autoconf generates a configure file, which is then run to query the specific system parameters. The classic make ; make install usually doesn't work; luckily, there is no more work involved in running the Apache extension tool apxs2 directly, which knows the precise settings of the installed Apache environment. The option -c compiles the C file specified, and -i installs the result to the directory where the other dynamically loadable modules are located.

For Debian there is an Apache configuration file in the form of the file auth_ntlm_winbind.load in the subdirectory debian, which automatically loads the module when Apache is started:

```
LoadModule auth_ntlm_winbind_module /usr/lib/apache2/modules/mod_auth_nt
lm_winbind.so
```

This file is copied to the directory /etc/apache2/mods-available, and it is activated with a2enmod auth_ntlm_winbind.

For other distributions the entry shown is entered in the file in which the dynamic modules are loaded, and the path to the module directory is adjusted accordingly. Then Apache is started again:

```
linux: # /etc/init.d/apache2 stop; /etc/init.d/apache2 start
```

A simple restart will not be sufficient in most cases.

E.3.2 Preparing Samba

So that mod_auth_ntlm_winbind can perform its services, the server on which Apache is running must be included in the Active Directory domain as the Samba server. To do this, you need a current Samba-3 server package. The installation is best performed using the on-board resources of the distribution.

For the domain membership, Kerberos (as described in Section E.2.3 from page 642) must be completely configured, and in addition you need a valid administrator ticket for access to the domain, obtained using kinit. If Samba is used only for the Apache module, a very simple Samba configuration is sufficient:

```
# /etc/samba/smb.conf (Minimalkonfiguration)
[global]
```

```
workgroup                = EXAMPLE
realm                    = EXAMPLE.NET
security                 = ads
password server          = dc01.example.net dc02.example.net
encrypt passwords        = yes
idmap uid                = 10000-20000
idmap gid                = 10000-20000
winbind enum users       = yes
winbind enum groups      = yes
winbind separator        = /
# winbind use default domain = yes
hosts allow              = 127.0.0.1
```

`workgroup` and `realm` correspond to the NetBIOS domain names and the fully written-out domain name of the Active Directory domain. For `realm`, it is again important that you write the name in capitals. `security=ads` describes the membership in an Active Directory domain. For the password server you must give at least one, and preferably two, domain controllers; `encrypt passwords = yes` is mandatory.

The parameters `idmap*` and `winbind enum*` map Windows users and groups to Unix users and groups. For the `winbind separator` you should select a Unix-compatible character, normally /, to separate the domain from the user name, as in EXAMPLE/wob. If this results in problems with applications, however, you can replace this character with another one, provided that Nagios can handle it. Here `hosts allow` allows access only from the local host.

The parameter `winbind use default domain` defines whether a missing domain should be replaced automatically by the default domain from `workgroup`. Then the domain can be omitted in the `Basic` authentication. At the same time, `mod_auth_ntlm_winbind` removes the domain name in the HTTP user. Users are treated differently, depending on the domain membership: Users from external domains are assigned to the HTTP user FOREIGN/*user*, whereas users from the same domain are assigned only to *user* (without a domain in front). If you are just using a single domain, you can set the parameter to `yes`, and you will no longer need to worry about a possible prefixed domain.

Access to the domain is achieved with the Samba command `net ads join`:

```
linux:~ # net ads join -U administrator@EXAMPLE.NET
administrator's password: ******
Using short domain name -- EXAMPLE
Joined 'NAGIOS' to realm 'EXAMPLE.NET'
```

After successfully joining, it is essential that you restart both Samba and Winbind:

```
linux:~ # /etc/init.d/samba restart
linux:~ # /etc/init.d/winbind restart
```

You can test whether everything is working properly with `wbinfo -t`. The command runs an encrypted RPC call, which is only possible if the server really is a member in the domain:

```
linux:~ # wbinfo -t
checking the trust secret via RPC calls succeeded
```

If you still want to play around a bit with Winbind, you can display all users displayed with `wbinfo -u` and all groups with `wbinfo -g`. When run for the first time after being started, it will take a while until the two programs display anything.

For authentication, Apache calls the program `ntlm_auth` with the permissions under which the Web server is running. In Debian this is the user `www-data` from the group `www-data`. With his permissions, `ntlm_auth` tries to access the directory `/var/lib/samba/winbindd_privileged/`. This must belong to the user `root` and be readable for the user under which Apache is running, and otherwise nobody else may access the directory:

```
user@linux:~$ chgrp www-data /var/lib/samba/winbindd_privileged
user@linux:~$ chmod 750 /var/lib/samba/winbindd_privileged
user@linux:~$ ls -ld /var/lib/samba/winbindd_privileged
drwxr-x--- 2 root www-data 4096 Aug 26 17:51 /var/lib/samba/winbindd_pri
vileged/
```

If the access permissions are incorrectly set, `ntlm_auth` will refuse its services.

E.3.3 Apache configuration

The module `mod_auth_ntlm_winbind` requires only a few entries in the Apache configuration file `/etc/apache2/conf.d/nagios.conf`, since the overwhelming part of the configuration takes place in Kerberos and Samba. The file `nagios.conf`, described in Section 1.5.3 (page 49), is changed as follows:

```
<Directory "/usr/local/nagios">
  AllowOverride None
  Order allow,deny
  Allow from all

  AuthName "Nagios Monitoring"
```

```
# -- NTLM
AuthType NTLM
NTLMAuth on
NTLMAuthHelper "/usr/bin/ntlm_auth --helper-protocol=squid-2.5-ntlmssp"

# -- Basic
NTLMBasicAuth on
NTLMBasicAuthoritative on
PlaintextAuthHelper "/usr/bin/ntlm_auth --helper-protocol=squid-2.5-bas
ic"
NTLMBasicRealm "Nagios Monitoring (Basic)"

# -- Negotiate
# AuthType Negotiate
# NegotiateAuth on
# NegotiateAuthHelper "/usr/bin/ntlm_auth --helper-protocol=gss-spnego"

  require valid-user
</Directory>
```

Only three parameters are needed for NTLM authentication: `AuthType` selects the authentication module, `NTLMAuth` on activates the NTLM procedure, and `NTLMAuthHelper` defines the specific call of `ntlm_auth`. Here the protocol `squid-2.5-ntlmssp` is used, which was originally intended for Squid.

The `Basic` authentication, in which the browser sends user and password in plain text to the Web server, also requires a *Basic Realm* to be specified in the form of the parameter `NTLMBasicRealm`. The value of the parameter `NTLMBasicAuthoritative` controls whether a failed attempt (User not found) can then be answered (`on`) or whether further authentication modules—if they exist—should be queried (`off`).

If it does not really functon properly, the negotiation procedure should not be configured under any circumstances. If the Web server offers negotiation along with the other procedures, the browser will always choose to negotiate. The authentication is then bound to fail.

By the way, with the `ntlm_auth` parameter `--require-membership-of`, membership in a particular group can be forced. `/usr/bin/ntlm_auth --require-membership-of=EXAMPLE/admins` returns OK only if the user who is authenticating himself is a member of the group `admins`. The separator / corresponds to the value of `winbind separator` given in `smb.conf`.

E.3.4 Defining a Nagios contact

In the definition of the contact, the setting `winbind use default domain` in the Samba configuration file `smb.conf` must be taken into account. If the value `no` is given there (or if the parameter is not given at all), the contact name will always consist of the domain, written in capitals, the `winbind separator`, and the user name:

```
define contact{
        use             template-contact-webuser
        contact_name    EXAMPLE/wob
        ...
}
```

On the other hand, if `winbind use default domain` is set to yes, the domain is omitted for users in the domain to which the Nagios server belongs. For users in external domains, the naming convention with the prefixed domain is retained.

E.4   Mozilla Firefox as a Web Client

Configuring the Mozilla Web browser in Windows XP is very simple, provided that the workstation is a member in the Active Directory domain. With the address `about:config` you can call up the current configuration in Firefox and enter `negotiate` as the filter (see Figure E.2). In the `network.negotiate-auth.trusted-uris` parameter you enter all hosts or domains for which an automatic login should take place. Multiple entries are separated by spaces or commas. If a target host or its domain is not in the list, Firefox will certainly ask for the user name and password. These are transmitted in plain text, however, which is why you should prefer automatic login in all cases.

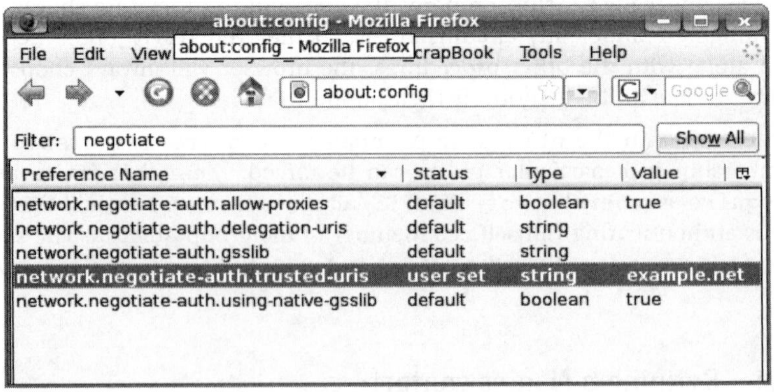

Figure E.2:
Single sign-on via
SPNEGO/Kerberos is
enabled in the
Firefox settings
under
`network.negotiate`

In Linux you can also authenticate yourself with Firefox automatically via the negotiation procedure. You need only a valid user ticket to do this.

As long as the Linux workstation logins are not already actively processed via Kerberos, it is enough just to obtain the ticket manually with `kinit`. In addition the file `/etc/krb5.conf` must be configured as described in Section E.2.3 from page 642. As a normal user, you fetch the ticket with the realm of the corresponding Windows user:

```
user@linux:~$ kinit myuser@EXAMPLE.NET
Password for myuser@EXAMPLE.NET: ******
```

Afterward, you can check with `klist` to see whether you really have received a ticket. This is usually only valid for eight hours. After the time has expired, you must fetch a new ticket, because without a valid ticket Firefox will announce itself again with the user/password query.

E.4.1 Firefox and NTLM

Along with the SPNEGO/Kerberos procedure, Firefox is also capable of performing authentication via NTLM. To do this, you enter the desired domains or hosts in the parameter `network.automatic-ntlm-auth.trusted-uris`. In Windows XP, everything else runs automatically.

In Linux, NTLM authentication is normally not available, since a Linux client cannot authenticate itself via NTLM to a Windows domain in the Active Directory. But there is also a solution here: the *NTLM Authorization Proxy Server* `ntlmaps`[12] allows even Linux clients to take part in an NTLM-based Web authentication. A description of this would go beyond the scope of this book, however.

E.5 Microsoft Internet Explorer as a Web Client

Microsoft Internet Explorer can handle both the SPNEGO/Kerberos and the NTLM authentication procedures. For reasons of security, however, Internet Explorer does not always immediately provide information on account data. You should therefore enter the Nagios host in the security settings under **Trusted Sites**, using exactly the same URL that it will be called with later on.

In addition you should check, in **Custom Level**, whether the user name and password really need to be transmitted for the level selected. After the changes, it does not do any harm to restart Internet Explorer.

---

[12] http://ntlmaps.sourceforge.net/

Tips on Optimizing Performance

It is very difficult to describe, in general terms, a Nagios installation that performs well. Nagios should perform checks immediately, that is, it should have a small *latency time* for host and service checks. This is the difference between the planned and actual execution times of the check. If this is an hour or more, you can certainly talk about disastrous performance. On the other hand, latency of less than a second represents very good performance. In between these extremes, the borders between acceptable and unacceptable are somewhat hazy.

The latency time of host and service checks can be measured objectively. Other, more subjective impressions are more difficult to evaluate. Doggedly working on the command line of the host, a really high system load, or a long time lag for a page to be displayed when the Nagios Web interface is called: whether such things are regarded as performance problems or can be tolerated, depends on what your specific requirements are. If the Web interface always needs more than ten seconds to display even just a few services, this is certainly not acceptable for interactive use. A load of 40 on a powerful 4-CPU machine may not be a problem, while a load of 10 on a less powerful system may already be catastrophic.

Of course, the capacity of the host system on which Nagios is installed also heavily influences the overall performance. A very slow RAID system, for instance, could slow down Nagios considerably if Nagios wants to write a large number of check results to the RAID within a short period of time, and the NDOUtils simultaneously want to save all events to a database. If the latency values of Nagios are within tolerance, there is no reason from the perspective of Nagios to change the configuration of the RAID system.

So that we can better distinguish between individual qualities, we will introduce two concepts here. A *performance indicator* is a measure of the objective performance of Nagios. The latency time of service and host checks is by far the best choice for a performance indicator. As soon as anything at all starts creating problems for Nagios, this nearly always manifests itself directly in the latency.

Problem indicators, on the other hand, are parameters which may point to a possible problem, but whose absolute values alone does not allow a judgment to be made about the actual performance. These may be system measurements, such as a high CPU load or permanent swapping of the host on which Nagios is running, or they may be internal Nagios measurements, such as a permanently full queue for the results of external commands (see Section F.2.6 on page 666).

F.1 Internal Statistics of Nagios

Nagios displays a short version of the performance indicators in the so-called tactical overview of the Web interface, at the top right, (see Figure on page 346), and a slightly more detailed version via extinfo.cgi (see Figure on page 341). In addition, the command-line program nagiostats shows individual performance values or a summary of all data.

F.1.1 The command-line tool nagiostats

nagiostats is installed automatically during the Nagios installation and is located in the same directory as the main nagios program itself (in our case: /usr/local/nagios/bin). It requires, as a parameter, the main configuration file nagios.cfg, along with the path to it, in order to display all values in Nagios 2.x. (For Nagios 3.0 this is not necessary.)

```
user@linux:~$ /usr/local/nagios/bin/nagiostats -c /etc/nagios/nagios.cfg
Nagios Stats 3.0b3
```

```
Copyright (c) 2003-2007 Ethan Galstad (www.nagios.org)
Last Modified: 08-30-2007
License: GPL


CURRENT STATUS DATA
-----------------------------------------------------
Status File:                        /var/nagios/status.dat
Status File Age:                    0d 0h 0m 5s
Status File Version:                3.0b3

Program Running Time:               1d 23h 26m 57s
Nagios PID:                         8184
Used/High/Total Command Buffers:    0 / 1 / 4096

Total Services:                     1997
Services Checked:                   1997
Services Scheduled:                 1995
Services Actively Checked:          1995
Services Passively Checked:         2
Total Service State Change:         0.000 / 30.260 / 0.040 %
Active Service Latency:             0.000 / 2.233 / 0.361 sec
Active Service Execution Time:      0.063 / 20.081 / 0.518 sec
Active Service State Change:        0.000 / 7.630 / 0.011 %
Active Services Last 1/5/15/60 min: 308 / 1417 / 1922 / 1944
Passive Service State Change:       26.250 / 30.260 / 28.255 %
Passive Services Last 1/5/15/60 min: 0 / 0 / 0 / 0
Services Ok/Warn/Unk/Crit:          1904 / 61 / 5 / 27
Services Flapping:                  2
Services In Downtime:               0

Total Hosts:                        166
Hosts Checked:                      166
Hosts Scheduled:                    166
Hosts Actively Checked:             166
Host Passively Checked:             0
Total Host State Change:            0.000 / 0.000 / 0.000 %
Active Host Latency:                0.000 / 1.527 / 0.638 sec
Active Host Execution Time:         0.066 / 0.537 / 0.155 sec
Active Host State Change:           0.000 / 0.000 / 0.000 %
Active Hosts Last 1/5/15/60 min:    52 / 148 / 166 / 166
Passive Host State Change:          0.000 / 0.000 / 0.000 %
Passive Hosts Last 1/5/15/60 min:   0 / 0 / 0 / 0
Hosts Up/Down/Unreach:              166 / 0 / 0
Hosts Flapping:                     0
Hosts In Downtime:                  0

Active Host Checks Last 1/5/15 min: 59 / 209 / 622
   Scheduled:                       54 / 154 / 475
   On-demand:                       5 / 43 / 108
   Parallel:                        59 / 198 / 584
   Serial:                          0 / 0 / 0
   Cached:                          0 / 12 / 39
```

```
Passive Host Checks Last 1/5/15 min:    0 / 0 / 0
Active Service Checks Last 1/5/15 min:  345 / 2148 / 6342
    Scheduled:                          345 / 2148 / 6342
    On-demand:                          0 / 0 / 0
    Cached:                             0 / 0 / 0
Passive Service Checks Last 1/5/15 min: 0 / 0 / 0

External Commands Last 1/5/15 min:      0 / 0 / 0
```

The program first provides information on the evaluated status file and the Nagios version. The details of the Command Buffers in the second paragraph are of more interest. If the command buffer becomes full, Nagios will have problems processing commands via the interface for external commands. All passive checks will suffer from this (see Section F.2.6).

The next two blocks provide values on host and service checks. Many of them are of a purely informative nature. If the right column contains several values, as for the two performance indicators Active Service Latency and Active Host Latency (shown here in bold type), without the page on left offering any explanation of this, then these are the minimum and maximum values and a mean value.

You should keep an eye on the two problem indicators Active Host Execution Time and Active Service Execution Time. Long execution times for host checks due to failed hosts certainly have a negative influence on Nagios's performance. With a standard timeout of 10 seconds for plugins, average values of more than 30 seconds are rather ominous, assuming that long timeouts were not configured explicitly. Although long execution times for service checks usually have no significant effect on performance, they nevertheless reveal that something is not right.

The details for Active/Passive Host/Service Checks Last 1/5/ 15 min in the final information block provide statistics that describe how the current check results were determined. The details under Scheduled deal with the checks planned regularly by Nagios, and the On-demand lines deal with tests executed while taking account of current circumstances. For hosts, these include checks made due to failed hosts, and, for services, tests triggered by dependencies. If a test can be avoided because of an already existing and relatively up-to-date value, this is listed in the Cached line.

For host checks, the statistic in the line Serial also reveals how many tests were executed in series in accordance with the inefficient old host check logic. The line Parallel deals with host checks executed in parallel and also shows the values for regularly planned and executed host checks. Active host checks can contribute in Nagios 3.0 to an improvement in performance. In Nagios 2.x you should leave them out if possible. The improvements in the host check logic are described in Section H.7 on page 689.

The 5-minute average resource of `Active Service Checks Last` gives information on the activities of Nagios rather than on the absolute number of service checks: 10,000 service checks with a check interval of 20 minutes result in just 2,500 checks in the 5-minute average, but 1,000 checks with a check interval of just 1 minute lead to 5,000 in the 5-minute average.

The absolute number of all checks therefore does not mean a lot. The crucial issue is how many checks Nagios carries out per time unit: 2,500 service checks in 5 minutes results in an average of 8.33 checks per second. This means that Nagios starts 8.33 checks every second and at the same time has to gather and process the results of 8.33 other checks, forward any performance data to an external program, and then it might even have to wait for each check to be handed over. If the NDOUtils are used in addition (see Chapter 17, page 375), the system also passes on results to the event broker.

Determining single values

nagiostats also displays selected values, with the options `--mrtg` and `--data=variables`. What values are available here can be seen by running `nagiostats -h`:

```
user@linux:~$ /usr/local/nagios/bin/nagiostats -h
 ...
 NUMACTSVCCHECKSxM      number of total active service checks
                        occuring in last 1/5/15 minute
 ...
 xxxACTSVCLAT       MIN/MAX/AVG active service check latency (ms).
 ...
```

Here, the x in NUMACTSVCCHECKSxM is replaced with the desired time period in minutes: 1, 5, 15, or 60:

```
user@linux:~$ /usr/local/nagios/bin/nagiostats -c /etc/nagios/nagios.cfg\
    --mrtg --data=NUMACTSVCCHECKS5M
2195
```

With xxxACTSVCLAT, nagiostats behaves in a similar manner; now xxx is replaced by MIN (Minimum), MAX (Maximum), or AVG (mean value). Multiple target values are separated by commas:

```
user@linux:~$ /usr/local/nagios/bin/nagiostats -c /etc/nagios/nagios.cfg\
    --mrtg --data=MINACTSVCLAT,MAXACTSVCLAT,AVGCTSVCLAT
0
934
203
```

The output here is given in milliseconds, and each value has its own line. The average latency time for service checks is therefore 0.203 seconds, and the maximum, 0.934 seconds. The switch --mrtg indicates that this output is intended primarily for processing by MRTG, as will be seen in the next section. Individual output of performance indicators is also very useful when you are writing your own plugins. We will look at this in Section F.1.3 from page 660.

F.1.2   Showing Nagios performance graphically

The *Multi Router Traffic Grapher (MRTG)*[1] was originally developed to represent the bandwidth of active network components in graphical form. MRTG always displays two measured values in a graphic, one as a green area, the other as a blue line. When representing network bandwidths, these are normally for incoming and outgoing traffic. Nagios uses MRTG to display the values delivered by nagiostats.

Usually the best way to install MRTG is from the package of the same name provided by the distribution you are using. The sources can be found on the homepage.[2]

MRTG is run by cron every five minutes. Debian includes the ready-made cron table /etc/cron.d/mrtg; the tool expects its configuration to be in /etc/mrtg.cfg. The file provided by Debian contains just two global settings:

```
# Global configuration
WorkDir: /var/www/mrtg
WriteExpires: Yes
```

WorkDir specifies the directory in which MRTG should save the current graphics, and WriteExpires creates additional Expire files for Apache. This parameter can be omitted, however.

To these two lines you simply append the configuration file mrtg.cfg included by Nagios in the ./sample-config directory of the source code.

Finally, you use the program indexmaker, which is also part of the MRTG package, to generate the overview page shown in Figure F.1:

```
linux:~ # indexmaker /etc/mrtg.cfg > /var/www/mrtg/index.html
```

[1] http://www.mrtg.org/
[2] http://www.mrtg.org/

MRTG Index Page

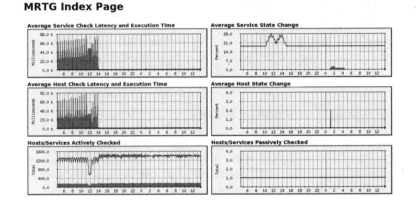

Figure F.1:
MRTG overview page
for the Nagios
performance
indicators

If you click on one of the graphics on this page, a detailed view will appear that displays the graphs in different time resolutions, as shown in Figure F.2 (daily, weekly, monthly, and annually).

Average Service Check Latency and Execution Time

Figure F.2:
Detail view for the
latency time for
service checks

The statistics were last updated **Sunday, 9 September 2007 at 14:15**,
at which time **'Nagios 3.0b3 (pid=22167)'** had been up for **1d 0h 28m 48s**.

`Daily' Graph (5 Minute Average)

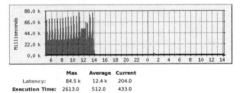

	Max	Average	Current
Latency:	84.5 k	12.4 k	204.0
Execution Time:	2613.0	512.0	433.0

`Weekly' Graph (30 Minute Average)

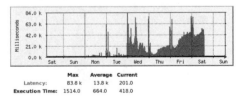

	Max	Average	Current
Latency:	83.8 k	13.8 k	201.0
Execution Time:	1514.0	664.0	418.0

The graphical display of the check latencies over the course of time allows you to see at a glance whether a high latency is a isolated event, part of a trend, or a permanent problem. The view in Figure F.2 clearly shows that the measures taken on Saturday afternoon[3] have had a positive effect (see weekly graphic). Instead of 20–80 seconds, the service check latency now lies at values below one second.

The accompanying online documentation[4] contains more detailed links for each individual graphic, with links to the documentation of various parameters that can be used to influence the indicators shown in each graphic.

F.1.3 A plugin to monitor latency

What could be more appropriate than to have Nagios monitor its own performance and, if necessary, use the notification system? To do this, you can query the latency values with `nagiostats` or use the plugin `check_mrtg` to query the performance data already collected through MRTG.

We will choose the first method here and provide the latency time for service checks as a passive check result for Nagios. The shell script intended for this purpose is run via cron independently of the Nagios scheduling. A plugin actively run by Nagios may in some circumstances return no results, or only irregular ones, if the Nagios schedule has become totally messed up because of performance problems. The script looks like this:

```
#!/bin/bash
# Attention: thresholds in milliseconds
WARN=20000
CRIT=60000
TIMESTAMP=`date +%s`
CMDFILE='/var/nagios/rw/nagios.cmd'

LATENCY=`/usr/local/nagios/bin/nagiostats \
         --config=/etc/nagios/nagios.cfg \
         --mrtg --data=AVGACTSVCLAT`

if [ $LATENCY < $WARN ]; then
   STATUS=0; INFO="OK"
elif [ $LATENCY < $CRIT ]; then
   STATUS=1; INFO="WARNING"
else
   STATUS=2; INFO="CRITICAL"
fi

CMD="PROCESS_SERVICE_CHECK_RESULT"
OUTCMD="[%lu] $CMD;nagios-server;Service Latency;$STATUS;"
OUTINFO="$INFO Service Latency = ${LATENCY}ms "
```

---

[3] Namely, enlarging the free memory that Linux uses for file system caching, in order to improve I/O performance for the MySQL database used by the NDOUtils and the overall file system accesses.

[4] http://nagios.sourceforge.net/docs/3_0/mrtggraphs.html

```
OUTPERF="svclat=$LATENCY;$WARN;$CRIT;\n"

printf "${OUTCMD}${OUTINFO}|${OUTPERF}" $TIMESTAMP > $CMDFILE
```

First `nagiostats` determines the current value for average service latencies (AVGACTSVCLAT). The script saves the result in the variable LATENCY and decides, using the thresholds in WARN and CRIT, whether it should return OK, WARNING, or CRITICAL.

`OUTCMD`, `OUTINFO`, and `OUTPERF` compose the command that is passed on to the interface for external commands (see also Section 13.1, page 292). It begins with the timestamp in square brackets. The command PROCESS_SER-VICE_CHECK_RESULT is followed by the host name and the service name Service Latency, the status, and the actual output, including performance data. In Nagios 3.0 it is better to omit the detail of the configuration file, with `--config`, because `nagiostats` will otherwise begin its output with an additional info line that only interferes with the script:

```
NEW VALUE: /etc/nagios/nagios.cfg
```

In Nagios 2.x, however, you need to specify the configuration file. So that the cron daemon runs the script at regular intervals, a `nagios` file is created in the directory `/etc/cron.d` containing the following line:

```
*/3 * * * * nagios /usr/local/nagios/libexec/passive/check_svc_latency.sh
> /dev/null
```

All that is missing now is an appropriately defined service:

```
# -- service latency check
define service{
    host_name               nagios-server
    service_description     Service-Latenz
    active_checks_enabled   0
    passive_checks_enabled  1
    check_freshness         0
    check_command           check_dummy!3!active check, should not happen!
    max_check_attempts      3
    flap_detection_enabled  0

    use                     template-service
}
```

`host_name` and `service_description` must match the corresponding details in the script. Active checks are switched off, passive ones enabled. So that Nagios doesn't perform a check itself at some point, `check_freshness` must be set to 0 (see also Section 13.4, page 295). The definition here uses a service template defined somewhere else (see also Section 2.11, page 75).

After a reload, Nagios accepts the information from the script and processes it. If you use PNP to process the performance data (Section 19.6, page 446), you should make sure that Nagios includes the name of the check command (in this case, check_dummy). If you want to use a different name, you need to specify the performance label svclat in the script:

```
OUTPERF="check_svc_latency::check_svc_latency::svclat=$LATENCY;$WARN;
$CRIT;"
```

PNP accepts labels in the form *wrapper::check_command::label*, from which the tool extracts the name between the double colons (in this case, check_svc_latency), so that it can use it as the plugin name. This trick normally works for all passive checks.

F.2 Measures for Improving Performance

If performance is subjectively poor and the latency of the service check lies permanently in the red zone, then you need to act. But where do you start? Trying things out is preferable to studying the problem, and there are no patent recipes. Normally you will lose sight of the overall picture very quickly if you try making small adjustments here and there. You should therefore always change just one parameter at a time and give Nagios time to adjust to the new state of affairs. Depending on the system, the number of checks to be performed in the five-minute average, and other indicators, sometimes a few minutes is enough to notice changes using nagiostats or MRTG, but at other times even half an hour may not be long enough if the latency has built up over a longer period of time.

The following sections deal with various problem zones in Nagios that could be the cause of poor performance.

F.2.1 Service checks: as often as necessary, as few as possible

Would you use a cannon to shoot at sparrows? Surely not. Apart from the fact that you would ordinarily never shoot at sparrows, even if you had to; you would never use such an oversized weapon as a cannon. Likewise, what is the proper choice for the intervals for your service checks? Why check the usage of a hard drive every 60 seconds, unless you or a colleague will react within a few minutes to a warning threshold being overstepped? Maybe an interval of five to ten minutes will do the job just as well. And if the typical growth rate of the data stored in the file system lies at five percent per week, then a check interval of 15 minutes is certainly enough.

If you install security patches only once per day and non-critical security updates just once per week, it is of little use to check the relevant version status every five minutes. And why check virus signatures every fifteen minutes if you only download them every two hours? Do you react immediately after the first alarm, or only if no update has been performed for several hours?

These are not just academic questions—they are intended to make you think. There are certainly situations in which a service needs to be checked once per minute, for instance when compliance with Service Level Agreements is concerned, and the contract penalties for outages are calculated on a per-minute basis. But this is no reason to test other services every minute if a fifteen-minute check would be sufficient. The bottom line is *check as often as necessary, but as little as possible.*

Start with an average check interval of 5 minutes. For less critical or static services, you can extend the interval to 10, 15, 30, or 60 minutes, or perhaps even more. Only if it is absolutely essential should you lower the interval below the 5-minute limit—and do it selectively for individual checks. 2,000 service checks, performed on average every two minutes, generate about the same load as 5,000 service checks with an average interval of 5 minutes. This small difference of 3 minutes can be a real problem for Nagios.

F.2.2 Processing performance data intelligently

Processing performance data can, under unfavorable conditions, be a real performance killer.

For the template mechanism, in which Nagios first has to format performance data and then write them to a file, and have these files processed at regular intervals by an external command (Section 19.1.1, page 405), the internal Nagios logic stops when the command is called. Nagios expects a confirmation when the program called has finished its work. If the external program requires some time to do its task, it is easy to work out that calling an external command directly for each individual check result (Section 19.1.2, page 407) can put a considerable strain on Nagios. The template mechanism can provide relief here. If 400 check results are waiting each minute (2,000 checks in the 5-minute average) and Nagios calls the external command for the template mechanism every 30 seconds, this will process some 200 results in one go. Although this will take somewhat longer than an external program that processes just one single result, 199 program starts are no longer needed.

With a large number of check results, this may still not be enough, because Nagios also waits here every 30 seconds for the external program and waits until it has terminated.

To keep this pause as brief as possible, you can make use of the bulk mode in PNP (Section 19.6, page 446): then Nagios just moves the file with the cached results to a special directory every 30 seconds. This happens without any time loss. Full responsibility for processing the external data is given to a daemon that Nagios does not have to control. Details of this are described in Section 19.6.4 from page 452.

Another aspect of intelligent processing is to record performance data only where they are evaluated and required. An example of the opposite would be to send performance data for all checks to a tool such as NagiosGrapher (Section 19.5, page 426) and then discard the data not required on the side of the collector daemon `collect2.pl`. Processing performance data for required services is switched on with `process_perf_data=1` in the service definition.

F.2.3 Avoiding plugins in interpreted languages

The standard plugins for Nagios were written predominantly in C and C++, and there are good reasons for this. Admittedly, it is usually easier to write a plugin in a script language; however, a plugin in an interpreted language is checked for correct syntax each time it is run, then interpreted at runtime, and finally executed.

Not only that, every time such a plugin is called, the relevant interpreter is started. With a compiled plugin, one does not have to put up with all of this. Syntax checking and the compiling process only take place once, and the result can be executed directly, without the additional support of another program, such as an interpreter, which is not exactly small. Considering the many hundreds of thousands of calls that are made during the lifetime of an interpreted plugin, you are looking at resource commitments that could really be used for more sensible purposes.

This is not to fundamentally question the use of interpreted languages in general. For certain purposes, it is simply easier to implement a plugin into a script language. But you should not be surprised at the resources that will be needed if you perform 5,000 service checks in the 5-minute average exclusively with interpreted plugins. Then simple PC hardware will certainly not suffice for the Nagios server.

There is an almost perfect solution if you want to use Perl plugins: Nagios's built-in Perl interpreter (see Appendix G from page 669). Although not all Perl plugins will run under this, the majority do, which considerably reduces strain on the Nagios server.

F.2.4 Optimizing host checks

One performance factor that should not be underestimated is the way in which Nagios executes a host check. Sometimes considerable time can be lost here, regardless of the Nagios version.

For host checks, a check_ping or check_icmp is normally used (see page 111). Older check_ping versions wait for an ICMP echo reply or wait for the timeout. It does not evaluate "ICMP Host Unreachable" messages, so that time is lost unnecessarily. check_icmp uses a special host detection mode if it is run under the name check_host (see page 111). This causes the check to be interrupted immediately if an ICMP Host Unreachable message arrives.

Newer versions of check_icmp and check_ping take the ICMP error message into account, even without a special prompt. Version 1.4.11 of the Nagios plugins does have a faulty check_icmp, however. If you run it as check_host, it will not detect the ICMP error message immediately and requires more time than necessary. Nagios 2.x calls all host checks in series, or one after the other. If a central network node should fail, it checks several hundred hosts in many setups. If the host check for unreachable hosts is only interrupted after ten seconds, it will take a huge amount of time until Nagios has checked all hosts. The length of a host check in case of error is of considerable significance here. You could, if need be, use a shorter timeout, but then you run the risk of false alarms, if a network connection with narrow bandwidth is overloaded at that moment, for instance, and the response times are longer than the reduced timeout. The evaluation of ICMP error messages is much safer here. The catastrophic performance, with hundreds of failed hosts due to the serial checks, will still remain, however—an important reason to change to Nagios 3.0 in large environments.

Whereas it is usually better in Nagios 2.x to do without active host checks, in Nagios 3.0 these may help in certain circumstances to improve performance, if you can have the check results cached with the parameters cached_host_check_horizon and cached_service_check_horizon (see page 588) for the interval specified. If an on-demand check occurs, this will not even be run if the existing result is sufficiently up to date.

Whether active host checks really do improve performance must be tested in individual cases by means of nagiostats. If the number of cached host checks is relatively small in comparison to the number of on-demand checks, caching will not be of much use. You could increase the cached_host_check_horizon—the interval for caching—but then you run the risk of using old results that are no longer relevant. It is best to try out different time horizons and observe the latency. As a comparison, you should try turning off caching altogether, with cached_host_check_horizon=0.

In connection with host checks, Nagios 3.0 also has the parameter aggressive_host_checks. If this is set to the value 1 (and therefore active), Nagios will be very exact in its checking, but it needs time to do this. In normal operation you should therefore always make sure that the system makes more sensible assumptions for host checks with aggressive_host_checks=0 and so does not test hosts with scrupulous precision.

F.2.5 The matter of the Reaper

Nagios 3.0 stores the check results in a directory intended for just this purpose, specified by the parameter `check_result_path` (see page 589). The *Reaper* (this is the "harvesting machine" of the Nagios core) retrieves these regularly.

Two parameters control the procedure: `check_result_reaper_frequen-cy`[5] specifies the interval, in seconds, at which the Reaper searches the directory for new results (see page 589). If the interval is increased, it is possible that latency times may also increase. You should only change the default of 5 seconds to a lower value, and only do this if a large number of checks are waiting and Nagios never really empties the directory for the check results.

The second parameter, `max_check_result_reaper_time`, interrupts activities after the time specified, so that Nagios is not held up for ages by the Reaper. The default here is 30 seconds (see page 598).

In Nagios 2.x only the parameter `service_reaper_frequency` (page 604) is available, and moreover Nagios does not store check results in file form, but in a message queue.

At this point we ought to mention that the Reaper has only a limited influence on performance. Provided that you keep the defaults of the two parameters unchanged, changing the parameter `check_result_reaper_frequency` will not solve any problems that have arisen elsewhere. Nevertheless, if you are running out of ideas as to what else you can try, it is certainly worthwhile to change this setting. In any case, you should monitor the check latency times graphically. If there are no changes, you should go back to the defaults.

F.2.6 Preferring passive checks

Instead of getting Nagios to actively start each check individually, you can also use external applications and forward check results as passive checks to Nagios. The external application—even if this is just a cron job—relieves strain on Nagios in several areas, including scheduling. Nagios needs only to accept the result and sort it accordingly.

In a number of cases you can even go a step further and do without a regular check, for instance if a UPS sends an SNMP trap when there is a power failure, which Nagios processes as a passive check (see Section 14.6, page 312).

Passive check results are cached by Nagios. By default there are 4096 so-called *Command Buffer Slots* available for this. Each buffer slot accepts just

---

[5] In Nagios 2.x the parameter is called `service_reaper_frequency`, see page 604.

one external command. If this maximum has almost been reached, you should certainly enlarge the value with the parameter `external_command_buffer_slots` (see page 593), whether or not you have concrete performance problems. One report on the buffer slots used is provided by `nagiostats`; its values are best displayed by MRTG on the time axis (see Section F.1.2). Too few buffer slots will certainly lead to a loss in performance.

F.2.7 Optimizing large Nagios environments

For very large environments, Nagios has available the parameter `use_large_installation_tweaks` (page 605). If this is set to 1, Nagios optimizes a number of processes that can be very time-intensive, especially in large environments. Thus the system does without explicit memory release for child processes. leaving this task entirely to the operating system.

Normally Nagios starts checks via a two-pronged fork so that it can defend itself against crashes and other abnormalities when the plugin is run. Checks are then performed not as child processes, but as grandchild processes. The two-pronged fork leaves cleaning up after grandchild processes to the operating system. If, instead of this, Nagios is happy with a simple fork (with `use_large_installation_tweaks=1`), it will have to look after all the cleaning up work for all check processes, because these are now running directly as child processes. But in return the system load is reduced, because only half as many processes need to be started. This generally improves performance.

As a third measure, Nagios switches off the environment variables for *summary macros* (Section D.1.7, page 631). It takes up a great deal of time to make these available.

The parameter `enable_environment_macros` (page 592) goes even further —with the value 0, Nagios in general no longer makes available the content of macros as environment variables (see Section D.1.8 from page 631).

The macros can be used as normal within the Nagios configuration, but now external scripts can no longer access them implicitly. Switching this off saves considerable resources, especially in large environments, and in many cases the environment variables are not needed at all.

F.2.8 Optimizing the NDOUtils database

The NDOUtils take advantage of the possibility of writing all information which is at the disposal of Nagios to an external database, via the event broker (Chapter 17 from page 375). The parameter `event_broker_options` controls which data Nagios passes on here. The default is `-1`, which means that any information available is passed on.

From a performance point of view, this is quite a bad choice. If you just require selected data—such as the results of host and service checks—you should pass on only this information. Everything else consumes unnecessary resources and influences performance without providing any benefits in return. Further information, including possible values for the parameter `event_broker_options`, is given in Section 17.1 from page 376.

G

The Embedded Perl Interpreter

Perl is an interpreted scripting language. When a Perl script is started, it is read by the Perl interpreter, checked for errors, transformed into executable code only at runtime, and finally executed. Programs in languages such as C or C++ are checked for errors, compiled only once, and saved as binary code that can be run directly. Here the checking and compilation process takes place just once—before the program is run for the first time—whereas a Perl script is checked and compiled each time it is run. This takes place at an astounding speed, but it still takes time.

But things get worse—for each script, no matter how small it is, the heavyweight Perl interpreter is loaded every time. It's as if, in order to add two numbers together, you needed to switch on your PC, wait until you can log in, then run a spreadsheet program in which you can finally enter the two numbers.

What if you want to continue using the spreadsheet? Well, then the computer must be turned on and the spreadsheet program must be installed and running so you can enter your numbers. Transferring the analogy to Nagios scripts, this means that an instance of the Perl interpreter must already be running on the Nagios server—and preferably this instance should be used for all plugins, so that each plugin can be executed immediately when it is called. This is precisely what the Embedded Perl interpreter, which is embedded into Nagios, does. The technique is not new; the Apache module `mod_perl` works in the same way.

However, the Embedded Perl interpreter does have one slight drawback: It makes more demands of a Perl script than the normal Perl interpreter does. Not every plugin that runs on the command line without problems will work under the embedded interpreter. It is often a matter of small details. Debugging is very difficult with this interpreter, and even with simple errors, it is not easy to localize them and adjust the plugin accordingly. But you should not be put off by this, because in Nagios 3.x the interpreter can be selectively switched off, and in Nagios 2.x a trick can be used to bypass it.

A quick note on terminology: In the official Nagios documentation, ePN stands for *Embedded Perl Nagios*, that is, Nagios with a Perl interpreter compiled into it. In general usage, the term means the integrated Perl interpreter itself. This is how we use the term in this book as well. Either way, Nagios is needed in order to use it.

G.1 Requirements of an ePN–capable Plugin

Many primitive errors can be avoided from the beginning if you use the pragmas use `strict` and use `warnings`:

```
#!/usr/bin/perl
use strict;
use warnings;
...
```

use `strict` treats the code very precisely and forces the predefinition of all variables (e. g., my `$var;`). use `warnings` displays extended error information, which greatly simplifies the search for the line or statement causing the error. For Perl versions prior to 5.6, use `warnings` does not exist, and you must use the -w switch, for example in the first line of the script:

```
#!/usr/bin/perl -w
...
```

Detailed information on pragmas can be found in man 3perl strict and man 3perl warnings, as well as the corresponding Perldoc pages on the Internet.[1]

To obtain a better understanding of the following notes, you must be aware of two things. On one hand, the plugin is loaded just once into the interpreter, so initialization sequences are performed explicitly only the very fist time it is run. On the other hand, the interpreter embeds the Perl code into other Perl code. Thus the end of the plugin code itself is not the end of the complete Perl code executed for this plugin. Actions that refer implicitly to the end of the respective script therefore sometimes generate undesired side effects, and you should take notice of the following tips:

If possible, make do without BEGIN!

In a BEGIN statement you normally include statements that initialize values or should, for one reason or another, be executed before the rest of the code. ePN runs this section only the very first time the plugin is executed. Statements that must be executed every time a plugin is called will come to nothing. It is therefore better to leave out the BEGIN section altogether.

Define an explicit exit code!

A normal Perl script always ends (provided you do not explicitly specify an exit code) with the exit code 0. This does not work with the ePN, since other code is run after the script code. Although such plugins return an OK when run on the command line (without ePN), they return UNKNOWN under ePN.

Make do without __DATA__ or __END__ sections!

Both instructions explicitly terminate the execution of the Perl code. In ePN this is not the case, however. For this reason you must leave out such instructions. For example, instead of the __DATA__, section you could use a Here instruction:

```
my $data = <<DATA;
a 1 30
b 2 40
c 7 80
...
DATA
```

Do not misuse lexical variables as global variables!

Lexical variables such as my $value define values required locally. You should therefore not access these directly from subroutines. Store the corresponding values as global values instead:

---

[1] http://perldoc.perl.org/strict.html and
http://perldoc.perl.org/warnings.html

```
use vars qw($value);
```

It is better still to pass on the variable as a reference:

```
$result = &mysub( \$value );
```

Terminate all actions and functions!

The Embedded Perl Interpreter also stumbles over small details. To cite an example, consider POD documentation integrated into the script (see Section 25.2, page 566): Normally the documentation section is completed with =cut. At the end of the Perl script, Perl ensures an implicit end, so that a documentation section not finished with =cut at the end of the script will not cause a problem on the command line. But ePN appends Perl code to this, so that omitting =cut always leads to an error.

This error pattern also recurs in other contexts, so that you should make a habit of always explicitly cleaning up. If the plugin opens a file, it must also explicitly close it.

More information is provided by the Nagios online documentation[2] and the mod_perl Users Guide.[3] For errors that occur exclusively with the ePN, the included mini-version is of help, and is described in Section G.3 on page 674.

G.2 Using ePN

In order to use the Embedded Perl interpreter, this feature must be compiled into Nagios. This suffices for Nagios 2.x, but for Nagios 3.0 you must also set parameters in the main configuration file nagios.cfg. In addition, Nagios 3.0 allows each individual Perl plugin to activate or to switch off the Embedded Perl interpreter.

G.2.1 Compiling ePN

The interpreter is integrated during the configure call, with the switch --enable-embedded-perl. In Nagios 2.x you should also use the option --with-perlcache, which ensures that the interpreter caches scripts that have already been loaded, thus speeding them up if they are run again. Nagios 3.0 sets this implicitly if --enable-embedded-perl is specified.

Caching in Nagios 2.x has one drawback: In some circumstances Nagios will not recognize changes made later on to a Perl script. The only remedy

---

[2] http://nagios.sourceforge.net/docs/3_0/epnplugins.html
[3] ttp://perl.apache.org/docs/1.0/guide/

here is a reload or a restart of Nagios. On a development system, which is only used to develop or test plugins, it certainly makes sense to do without caching. On production Nagios systems, however, the benefits of caching cannot be overlooked. In Nagios 3.0, the Perl interpreter takes account of changes to the script and reloads these if required.

G.2.2 Interpreter-specific parameters in `nagios.cfg`

Starting from Nagios 3.0, parameters in the main configuration file `nagios.cfg` determine whether the Embedded Perl interpreter is used or not:

```
# /etc/nagios.cfg
...
enable_embedded_perl=1
use_embedded_perl_implicitly=1
...
```

`enable_embedded_perl=1` enables the general use of the interpreter, and the value 0 switches it off. The second parameter is used for fine-tuning. `use_embedded_perl_implicitly=1` automatically switches on the interpreter for each plugin, provided the plugin itself does not contain any further instructions (see next section). The value 0 switches ePN off for the time being, and then each plugin must decide for itself whether to use it or not.

G.2.3 Disabling ePN on a per-plugin basis

In Nagios 3.0, the parameter `use_embedded_perl_implicitly` is supplemented with an instruction that can be set within every plugin:

```
#!/usr/bin/perl -w
# nagios: -epn
...
```

The text `# nagios:   +epn` or `-epn` must appear within the first ten lines. With +epn the plugin is executed in the ePN environment, and with -epn it is not. This explicit detail in the plugin has the highest priority. Only if the instruction is missing does Nagios 3.0 use the parameter `use_embedded_perl_implicitly`.

In many cases, existing Perl plugins will work in ePN. We therefore recommend that you use the setting `use_embedded_perl_implicitly=1`. For plugins that cause problems, you can explicitly switch off the use of the interpreter with -epn.

In Nagios 2.x there is no option to switch the Embedded Interpreter on or off at runtime or in the plugin. Once it has been compiled into Nagios, it is always active. But there is a workaround that you can use when defining a command, by prefixing /usr/bin/perl to the actual command line:

```
define command{
    command_name    check_disk
    command_line    /usr/bin/perl $USER1$/check_disk.pl $ARG1$
}
```

Thus, for the plugin check_disk.pl, the normal Perl interpreter is started each time the plugin is run, and ePN is sidestepped.

G.3   The Testing Tool new_mini_epn

In its source code, Nagios includes two utilities that simulate an ePN environment, which considerably simplifies searching for errors: mini_epn and the more recent new_mini_epn. They are not absolutely identical in behavior to ePN, but this involves only a small number of exotic scenarios. In general the following applies: If a Nagios plugin does not run in the mini-interpreter, it won't run in the ePN either.

The two programs are located in the subdirectory ./contrib of the source code and are not installed automatically. If you want to use them, run

```
linux:nagios/contrib # make mini_epn
...
linux:nagios/contrib # make new_mini_epn
...
```

but *under no circumstances* should you run make install! The Makefile in this directory does not take into account the defaults for paths and may change the access permissions for directories such as /bin and /var. The programs must be executed in the directory in which the file p1.pl is located. During the basic installation of Nagios, this is copied to /usr/local/nagios/bin, and so these two programs are also copied there:

```
linux:nagios/contrib # cp mini_epn new_mini_epn /usr/local/nagios/bin/.
```

In the ./contrib directory itself there is an obsolete p1.pl, which should not be used. The up-to-date p1.pl installed by Nagios is located in the main directory of the source code.

In order to run the mini-interpreter, you change, as the user nagios, to the directory /usr/local/nagios/bin and run the program without parameters:

```
user@linux:nagios$ ~cd /usr/local/nagios/bin
user@linux:nagios$ nagios/bin./new_mini_epn
plugin command line:
```

You are taken to a simple comand line from which you can run plugins. You should always include the full path to the plugin:

```
plugin command line: /usr/local/nagios/libexec/check_file_age -f /etc/ho
sts
embedded perl plugin return code and output was: 2 & FILE_AGE CRITICAL:
/etc/hosts is 3718127 seconds old and 2671 bytes
```

The mini-interpreter displays the return code, along with the actual output of the plugin after the & character.

If one mini-interpreter does not find an error, you should try the other one out, as it is possible that it may react differently in this special case. In addition, you should always run the interpreter with the permissions of the user under which Nagios is running (in this book, this is `nagios`), to rule out problems with access permissions from the start.

The mini-interpreter caches the executed plugin just like its big brother does and is not aware at runtime of any changes made to the plugin. If you have made changes to the plugin, you should restart the mini-interpreter, otherwise you may be searching in vain for an error at the wrong spot.

What's New in Nagios 3.0?

Nagios 3.0 presents a series of improvements and innovations compared to the 2.x versions.[1] Much of this is not noticeable from the outside, and the configuration is also nearly identical; normally Nagios 3.0 will also start with a functioning Nagios-2.x configuration. None of the new configuration parameters are absolutely essential.

Some parameters were renamed, and Nagios 3.0 complains on startup that a parameter contained in the configuration has been removed, then sets the new variable to a sensible value. The objects `hostextinfo` and `service-extinfo` are considered to be obsolete, but can still be used, at least in version 3.0.

---

[1] See also `http://nagios.sourceforge.net/docs/3_0/whatsnew.html`.

Apart from the configuration, the internal logic has been improved in many places. For instance the changed way of running host checks has led to significantly higher performance, especially for very large installations.

H.1 Changes in Object Definitions

Nagios 3.0 now allows floating point decimals when specifying check and notification intervals. The new parameter `check_interval = 2.5`, which replaces the `normal_check_interval`, determines that Nagios will perform a check every two-and-a-half time units. The time unit itself is defined by `interval_length` in the main configuration file `nagios.cfg` (see page 596). With the default of 60 seconds, a `check_interval` of `2.5` corresponds to 150 seconds.

H.1.1 The `host` object

Aliases are no longer absolutely essential in Nagios 3.0. If this detail is missing in the host definition, the host name is used automatically. `host` objects can make use of the following options from version 3.0:

```
define host {
    ...
    display_name             display_name
    contacts                 contacts
    first_notification_delay number
    flap_detection_options   o,d,u
    notification_options     d,u,r,f,s
    initial_state            o,d,u
    retry_interval           number
    ...
}
```

`display_name`

> Defines an alternative name that should appear later in the Web interface and other future user interfaces. The CGI programs of Nagios 3.0 do not yet use this parameter. The default is `host_name`.

`contacts`

> Nagios 3.0 now allows individual contacts to be specified directly in the host definition. Until now you could only enter contact groups here, so you always had to first define a specific contact group for each individual contact. You can still use contact groups and specify them together with individual contacts.

`first_notification_delay`
> Delay the sending of the first notification (in Nagios time units, defined by the new parameter `interval_length`; see page 596). Normally Nagios sends a notification immediately after a error turns into a hard state. In order for the first notification to be sent only after a certain time has elapsed, you previously had to use the escalation mechanism (see Section 12.5, page 282). With the parameter `first_notification_delay` this can now be done more easily.

`flap_detection_options`
> With `flap_detection_options`, certain states of flap detection (Section B, page 611) can be ruled out.
>
> Possible values are o (OK), u (UNREACHABLE), and d (DOWN). If you exclude the OK states with `flap_detection_options o`, Nagios will only take into account the change between UNREACHABLE and DOWN.

`notification_options`
> If the new value s is specified, Nagios will send a notification if a maintenance interval (see Section 16.3 from page 359) is started, finished, or canceled.

`initial_state`
> Sets the initial state of the host. Normally Nagios assumes that this is UP (`initial_state o`). d sets the initial state to DOWN, u to UNREACHABLE.

`retry_interval`
> After how many time units will an active host check be repeated if `max_check_attempts` is larger than 1? There is more on the new features for host checks in Section H.7.

Extended host information

The objects `hostextinfo` and `serviceextinfo` are considered obsolete, but are still evaluated by Nagios 3.0. When checking the configuration, as well as on restarting, Nagios issues a corresponding warning. Later Nagios versions will no longer support this object type.

Additional information for the Web interfaces (see Section 16.4.1 from page 363) are now defined directly in the host (or service):

```
define host {
   ...
   # -- extended host information
   notes           free text
   notes_url       url
```

```
    action_url           url
    icon_image           image file
    icon_image_alt       free text
    vrml_image           image file
    statusmap_image      image file
    2d_coords            x,y
    3d_coords            x,y,z
}
```

H.1.2 The `service` object

The innovations for the service object are essentially the same as those for the host object. The parameters `flap_detection_options`, `notification_options`, and `initial_state` are now assigned the values w (WARNING) and c (CRITICAL) instead of the host states DOWN and UNREACHABLE:

```
define service {
    ...
    display_name              display_name
    contacts                  contacts
    first_notification_delay  number
    flap_detection_options    o,c,w,u
    notification_options      w,u,c,r,f,s
    initial_state             o,d,u
    check_interval            number
    retry_interval            number
    ...
    # -- extended service information
    notes                 free text
    notes_url             url
    action_url            url
    icon_image            image file
    icon_image_alt        free text
    vrml_image            image file
    statusmap_image       image file
    2d_coords             x,y
    3d_coords             x,y,z
}
```

The three parameters `contact_groups`, `notification_interval`, and `notification_period` are no longer mandatory in Nagios 3.0. If they are omitted, they are taken from the `host` object. The parameter `alias` is also optional, and if it is not set, the name is taken from `service_description`.

The parameter `parallelize_check`, which in Nagios 2.0 is set by default to 1 and can be altered to prevent parallel service checks, is dropped entirely in Nagios 3.0; service checks here are always performed in parallel.

The parameters `normal_check_interval` and `retry_check_interval` were renamed to `check_interval` and `retry_interval`, in order to use the same identifier as for the host definition. The old name remains valid so that Nagios does not show an error message.

H.1.3 Group objects

With the parameters `hostgroup_members`, `servicegroup_members`, and `contactgroup_members` you can now also define groups of the same type as members of a group, and thus form hierarchies:

```
define hostgroup {
   hostgroup_members host groups
   ...
   notes             free text
   notes_url         url
   action_url        url
}
define servicegroup {
   servicegroup_members service groups
   ...
   notes             free text
   notes_url         url
   action_url        url
}
define contactgroup {
   contactgroup_members contact groups
   ...
}
```

Extended group information for the group types `hostgroup` and `servicegroup` allows additional information to be stored, in a similar way as for host and service definitions. `notes` here is a simple text which is displayed on the page with the extended status information (see Section 16.2.2 on page 339). The two URLs point to external Web pages, for instance so that a Wiki can be integrated for the purpose of online documentation.

H.1.4 The `contact` object

The value n (none) for the parameters `host_notifications_options` and `service_notifications_options` switches off notifications completely. This can also be achieved with a separate on/off function via the interface for external commands (Section 13.1, page 292), which requires the new parameters `host_notifications_enabled` and `service_notifications_enabled`:

```
define contact {
    host_notifications_enabled     value
    service_notifications_enabled  value
    can_submit_commands            value
    ...
}
```

They can be set to 1 (on) or 0 (off). `can_submit_commands` controls whether a contact may only view his hosts and services, or whether he can run commands for them via the Web interface. In Nagios 2.0 every user who has access to hosts and services may do this. The default is 1 (commands are allowed), 0 allows only viewing.

H.1.5   Time definitions

Periods of time can be defined much more flexibly in Nagios 3.0 than was previously the case:

```
define timeperiod {
    timeperiod_name veryspecial
    2007-12-23        00:00-24:00
    april 1           00:00-24:00
    day 1             00:00-24:00
    monday 2 may      00:00-24:00
    monday 3          00:00-24:00
    monday            00:00-24:00
    2007-12-01 - 2009-04-01 / 3   00:00-24:00
    ...
    exclude timeperiod_name1,timeperiod_name2,...
}
```

Whereas Nagios 2.x allows only single weekdays to be defined, you can now also specify an ISO date (2007-12-23), the first day of a specific month (april 1), the first day of each month (day 1), the second Monday in May (monday 2 may), or every third Monday in the month (monday 3). Intervals are also allowed here, consisting of two time specifications separated by a - sign. In addition, time periods independent of the month or day of the week are possible: 2007-12-01 - 2009-04-01 / 3 describes evey third day from 01. 12. 2007 to 01. 04. 2009.

The parameter exclude rules out the time periods that follow (themselves also timeperiod objects).

More information on defining times can be found in Section 2.10 from page 74.

H.1.6 Dependency descriptions

There is a new parameter for the objects `hostdependency` and `servicedependency` called `dependency_period`, which defines how long dependencies are valid. An object of the type `timeperiod` is specified as the value. If this parameter is missing, dependencies are unrestricted in time:

```
define hostdependency {
   dependency_period   timeperiod_name
   ...
}

define servicedependency {
   dependency_period   timeperiod_name
   ...
}
```

So-called *Same-Host Dependencies* are also new; these are `servicedependencies` that refer to the same host. In this case the parameter `dependend_host_name` is simply omitted:

```
define servicedependency {
   host_name                          linux
   service_description                Disk_Usage
   dependent_service_description NRPE
   ...
}
```

The `Disk_Usage` service therefore depends on the `NRPE` service on the same host.

If the parameter `host_name` is replaced with `hostgroup_name`, the same dependency can be defined for an entire host group. In Nagios 2.x this is not possible. If you defined `dependent_hostgroup_name`, the `Disk_Usage` services for all hosts of the group would be dependent on all the `NRPE` services for these hosts, which would be counterproductive in many cases.

H.1.7 Escalation objects

As with the host and service definition, it is also possible starting with Nagios 3.0 to specify individual contacts instead of a whole contact group for host and service escalations, by means of `contacts`:

```
define hostescalation {
   contacts   contact
   ...
}
```

```
define serviceescalation {
  contacts  contact
  ...
}
```

H.1.8 Inheritance

It was already possible in Nagios 2.x to define templates for objects and
for the actual object to inherit the properties of the template. Multiple
inheritance is now possible in Nagios 3.0, and an inheritance can also
be selectively suppressed. In the following example, the two templates
host_generic_t and host_site_t are inherited by the host linux01:

```
define host {
  name host_generic_t
  register 0
  #
  check_period      24x7
  max_check_attempts 3
  check_interval    10
  retry_interval    2
  ...
  hostgroups        ALL_HOSTS
}
define host {
  name host_site_t
  register 0
  #
  check_interval  5
  retry_interval  1
  ...
  parents         switch01
  hostgroups      HAMBURG
}
define host {
  host_name linux01
  use       host_site_t,host_generic_t
  ...
  parents   null
  hostgroups +LINUX
}
```

The parameters check_interval and retry_interval are defined in both
templates. In this case the first template to be defined (host_site_t) is
used, and the result appears as follows:

```
define host {
  host_name         linux01
```

```
check_period        24x7
max_check_attempts  3
check_interval      5
retry_interval      1
...
hostgroups          HAMBURG,LINUX
}
```

Both check intervals originate from the template `host_site_t`. The value zero for `parents` suppresses the inheritance; a value defined in the templates is not carried over, and the parameter is not set.

Equally new is the option of combining a specified value with the value from the template. The plus sign in `hostgroups` carries over the value from the template and adds the specified value to this. Until now, inherited values were completely overwritten by an object. The defaults from the templates, however, can only be combined with the values specified in the object for standard parameters containing a list in text form (for example, `hostgroups`, `servicegroups`, `contact_groups`).

For `contact_groups` within escalations, there is an additional variation of the plus sign. If the enclosing escalation object does not define a contact group whose properties can be inherited, the accompanying host (for host escalations) or service definition (for service escalations) is used. The three parameters `contact_groups`, `notification_interval`, and `notification_period` are inherited from the host object automatically by the service object, so that their definition there is no longer mandatory.

The online documentation included in Nagios uses a more complex example to describe multiple inheritance.[2]

H.2 Variable and Macros

You can define your own variables in the objects `host`, `service`, and `contact`. The names of these always begin with an underscore and are inherited like normal variables:

```
define host {
   host_name   linux01
   use         host_site_t,host_generic_t
   ...
   _NRPE_PORT 5666
}
```

The variable `_NRPE_PORT` is accessed with `$_HOSTNRPE_PORT$`, which means that the object type (HOST, SERVICE, or CONTACT) is added *after* the

---

[2] http://localhost/nagios/docs/objectinheritance.html

underscore. This is slightly unfortunate, as it is more difficult to read. The macro created can be used elsewhere, for example in the definition of a command:

```
define command {
   command_name check_nrpe
   command_line $USER1$/check_nrpe -H $HOSTADDRESS$ -p $_HOSTNRPE_PORT$
-c $ARG1$
}
```

Macros allow access to configuration data, states, and check results. In Nagios 3.0 the macro $NOTIFICATIONNUMBER$, which contains the number of notifications sent for the current state, has been removed. It has been replaced by the host- and service-specific macros $HOSTNOTIFICATIONNUM-BER$ and $SERVICENOTIFICATIONNUMBER$.

The list of available macros has grown considerably. Some new ones are $LONGHOSTOUTPUT$ and $LONGSERVICEOUTPUT$, for example, which contain the extended plugin output of multiple-line plugin results (see Section H.10 and Section 8.5.1, page 193).

The macros $HOSTNOTIFICATIONID$, $SERVICENOTIFICATIONID$, $HOST-EVENTID$, $SERVICEEVENTID$, $LASTHOSTEVENTID$, and $LASTSERVICE-EVENTID$ assign to each event a unique identification number that has been added in Nagios 3.0.

$HOSTDISPLAYNAME$ and $SERVICEDISPLAYNAME$ return the display_ name set in the host and service definition.

Also of interest are the new macros that enable the last state to be accessed: $LASTHOSTSTATE$ and $LASTHOSTSTATEID$ give the previous host state, and $LASTSERVICESTATE$ and $LASTSERVICESTATEID$ are used for the previous service state. The *ID macros provide the numerical value (e. g., 2 for the critical state of services), and the other two provide the corresponding text (e. g., WARNING for services and DOWN for hosts).

Macros can usually also be read out via the environment, but the increased number of macros has an effect on performance. If you don't access Nagios macros through environment variables, it is therefore better to switch this feature off entirely in Nagios 3.0:

```
enable_environment_macros=0
```

How you can use macros is described in Appendix D on page 625. The complete list of all macros can be found in the online documentation.[3] The change log for Nagios 3.0[4] will tell you which of these are new.

---

[3] http://nagios.sourceforge.net/docs/3_0/macrolist.html
[4] http://nagios.sourceforge.net/docs/3_0/whatsnew.html

H.3   Downtime, Comments, and Acknowledgments

Comments and maintenance intervals are now saved together with other information in the status and retention file. These special files and the accompanying parameters `downtime_file` and `comment_file` have been removed from Nagios 3.0. With an upgrade from Nagios 2.x to this version you can keep any existing comments and maintenance intervals—how to do this is described in Section H.13.

A further change involves the commenting of acknowledgments. Until now, non-persistent acknowledgments were deleted with every restart. In Nagios 3.0 they now survive; the system deletes the comment for an acknowledgment only when the problem has been rectified, so that the service or host status is OK.

H.4   Rapidly Changing States

Nagios 3.0 now records the state history even when flap detection is switched off. If you switch this on globally, with `enable_flap_detection` (see page 592), Nagios will test all hosts and services immediately for flapping.

For globally switched off flap detection, Nagios logs flapping states to the log file and sends messages of the notification type FLAPPINGDISABLED, if you have specified f (flapping) in the `notification_options` in the host or service definition.

Whereas Nagios 2.x still recorded every change in state, in Nagios 3.0 the parameter `flap_detection_options` (see Section H.1.1, page 679) allows this to be restricted to certain states. Only the states specified are then included in the calculation of the change in state.

H.5   External Commands

The list of external commands has grown larger in Nagios 3.0, so that considerably more things can be set through the relevant interface (see Section 13.1, page 292.).

Of special interest here is the command `PROCESS_FILE`, which is passed a file that itself contains external commands. This allows for the bulk processing of passive checks:

```
PROCESS_FILE;path/to/file;number
```

PROCESS_FILE requires the full path to the file that is to be processed. The second argument determines whether the file is kept after processing (0) or deleted (a value not equal to 0).

Two other new commands allow you to make your own notifications. Notifications actually have a fixed type (PROBLEM, RECOVERY, ACKNOWLEDGE, etc.; see Table 12.1 on page 277), which is queried via the macro $NOTIFICATIONTYPE$. The so-called *Custom Notifications*, in contrast, are of the type CUSTOM and allow notifications outside the otherwise strict rules. This means that broadcasts—messages to all—are also possible:

```
SEND_CUSTOM_SVC_NOTIFICATION;host;service;options;author;comment
SEND_CUSTOM_HOST_NOTIFICATION;host;options;author;comment
```

Instead of the *options* placeholder, you specify a bitmask, which controls the behavior of the two commands. The value 0 means "no option set." 1 ensures a broadcast message to all normal contacts and to those who are added during an escalation. 2 forces the message to be sent, regardless of whether notifications are switched on or off for the host, service, or contact, and ignores any time window that may be set. Finally, the value 4 increments the notification counter, and the message is then counted in the escalation procedure. Normally a Custom Notification is not counted.

A complete description of all external commands is provided on the developer pages of the Nagios homepage.[5] The Web interface there enables a selective search to be made for commands that are allowed in a specific Nagios version or deal with a certain topic (for example, **services**, **hosts**, **scheduled downtime** (maintenance window), **notifications**).

H.6   Embedded Perl

Handling the Embedded Perl Interpreter (see Appendix G from page 669) is also easier in Nagios 3.0. It can be switched on or off with the parameter enable_embedded_perl in the main configuration file nagios.cfg. The parameter use_embedded_perl_implicitly controls whether a plugin should implicitly use the activated interpreter if there are no instructions to the contrary (see also Section G.2 from page 672). In Nagios 2.x there was only the option of switching the interpreter on or off when compiling the Nagios system.

If the switch --with-embedded-perl is enabled, the configure script of Nagios 3.0 automatically uses the switch --with-perlcache as well. If Nagios detects that something has changed in the script to be executed, it will reload the script. In version 2.x you had to restart Nagios with the Perl cache switched on.

---

[5] http://www.nagios.org/developerinfo/externalcommands/commandlist.php

H.7 A New Logic for Host Checks

Nagios 2.x performs host checks serially, so it waits for the results of the individual check before checking other hosts in the direct vicinity to find out if the first host is DOWN or UNREACHABLE (see the figure on page 94). In contrast, Nagios 3.0 works in parallel here, provided that the parameter `max_check_attempts` for the host to be checked is larger than 1. For `max_check_attempts=1` the system behaves as in version 2.x.

In some cases this strongly influence performance, so you should always set a value larger than 1 in Nagios 3.0. Running host checks in parallel also means that a check result will sometimes get lost, since Nagios no longer waits until the result for every single check is available. The parameter `check_for_orphaned_hosts` now ensures that Nagios will deal with orphaned checks.

Active host checks can even improve performance in certain environments, if the equally new feature of *check caching* is used. Here Nagios accesses the result of a recently performed check, provided that this can be considered to be up to date. This means that the system saves a considerable amount of time in host checks for failed services, in resolving the topology for failed hosts, and for forward-looking dependency checks (see last section). For service checks, caching only plays a role for service dependencies.

How large the time horizon for caching should be is defined for host checks by the parameter `cached_host_check_horizon` (see also page 588) and for service checks by the parameter `cached_service_check_horizon` (page 588). The default is 15 seconds in each case, and the value 0 switches caching off entirely.

The larger the time interval in which Nagios caches results, the more often Nagios accesses the cache without actually performing the check itself. However, this does have a crucial disadvantage: The cached result may be obsolete. Therefore, you always need to compromise between obsolete results and taking the strain off Nagios. You will have to decide for yourself how large the time interval for caching should be. Again, the preferred method is to measure the latency times of service checks, which are a good indication of the performance of Nagios. If there is no visible difference over a long period of time between a caching time of 30 seconds and one of 60 seconds, it is better to select the shorter period, since you will be working with more up-to-date results in this case. How you measure the latency times of checks is described in Section F.1.3 from page 660.

Whether or not active host checks in combination with check caching lead to an improvement in performance can also be tested with `nagiostats` (Section F.1.1, page 654). The program displays the number of cached host checks whose results have been reused by Nagios in the last minute, in the last five minutes, and in the last fifteen minutes.

In distributed environments, or for redundant Nagios installations, the perspective is sometimes altered: Nagios server A has a different topological view of the network than Nagios server B. The result of a host check that server A sends to server B as a passive check result may in some cases no longer match. What is categorized by server A as UNREACHABLE may be a failed host in the DOWN state from the perspective of server B. The parameter `translate_passive_host_checks` (page 604) enables Nagios to reclassify passive host checks that it has been sent.

To achieve greater fine-tuning, passive host checks may now also accept a soft state if you set the parameter `max_check_attempts` in the host definition to a value larger than 1 and enable the parameter `passive_host_checks_are_soft` (page 600) in the main configuration file. Until now, passive host checks were always "hard."

H.8 Restart

When you start Nagios, it rechecks the configuration each time for errors and dependencies. Depending on the specific environment, this can be very quick, or it may last a long time, during which Nagios will not operate. In Nagios 3.0 there is an option to disconnect this test from the restart and instead save the result in a separate temporary file. When Nagios starts, it will read this file, and the otherwise usual processing of objects is left out at this point. Whether this is worthwhile or not is revealed by `nagios -s`:

```
nagios@linux:~$ /usr/local/nagios/bin/nagios -s /etc/nagios/nagios.cfg
OBJECT CONFIG PROCESSING TIMES
(* = Potential for precache savings with -u option)
----------------------------------
Read:                 0.019277 sec
Resolve:              0.001001 sec  *
Recomb Contactgroups: 0.000737 sec  *
Recomb Hostgroups:    0.003890 sec  *
Dup Services:         0.005938 sec  *
Recomb Servicegroups: 0.048659 sec  *
Duplicate:            0.001527 sec  *
Inherit:              0.005602 sec  *
Recomb Contacts:      0.000001 sec  *
Sort:                 0.030277 sec  *
Register:             0.010132 sec
Free:                 0.001831 sec
                      ============
TOTAL:                0.128874 sec  * = 0.097634 sec (75.76%)
                                        estimated savings

CONFIG VERIFICATION TIMES
(* = Potential for speedup with -x option)
```

```
----------------------------------
Object Relationships: 0.013131 sec
Circular Paths:       0.002341 sec  *
Misc:                 0.001032 sec
                      ============
TOTAL:                0.016504 sec  * = 0.002341 sec (14.2%)
                                        estimated savings
```

The times marked with * are saved with this *precaching* procedure. In this example, 75 percent of the startup time is occupied with processing the defined objects, but in absolute terms, this is just a tenth of a second and so is hardly worth mentioning.

If there is real potential for savings, precaching is turned on with the following steps:

```
nagios@linux:~$ /usr/local/nagios/bin/nagios -vp /etc/nagios/nagios.cfg
nagios@linux:~$ /etc/init.d/nagios stop
nagios@linux:~$ /usr/local/nagios/bin/nagios -udx /etc/nagios/nagios.cfg
```

The first call uses the options -v to check the configuration and -p to cache the processed objects in a separate file. The file is defined in nagios.cfg with the parameter precached_object_file (page 601). Then Nagios is stopped in the second step.

The third step is to start the system with the options -udx. The option -u reads the contents of the precaching file, and -d starts Nagios as a daemon, as normal. -x prevents the test for circular dependencies, but assumes that this call is always based on a tested configuration, like the one generated in step 1. Whether the option -x really saves time or not can be seen in the example above from the line Circular Paths in the CONFIG VERIFICATION TIMES section.

H.9   Performance Optimization

Besides performance optimizations that are not externally visible, Nagios 3.0 includes a number of parameters intended to improve performance in large installations. The most important of these is large_installation_tweaks (page 667).

The improvement of performance in an existing environment is dealt with in Appendix F from page 653.

H.10   Extended Plugin Output

Nagios 3.0 is finally capable of processing multi-line plugin output. The total length of the output must not exceed 8 KB—but you must also make sure that all the transmission paths are compatible for such an amount of data. NRPE currently still needs to be adjusted in the source code (page 194); the plugin check_by_ssh from the standard plugins in version 1.4.10 (page 206) can deal with the 8 KB.

The format of the extended and muti-line outputs are described in Section 8.5.1 (page 193), and an example of the use of the extended format is provided by the plugin check_multi (Section 8.5 from page 191).

H.11   CGI

The Nagios Web interface has also undergone some interesting changes. Some new parameters have been added to the configuration file cgi.cfg (Section A.2, page 606). lock_author_names prevents the user name, which is included if you set an acknowledgement or a comment on a host or service, from being changed. Instead the user name specified by the user when authenticating himself to the Web server is used. Each registered user is thus an authenticated user.

escape_html_tags determines whether HTML formatting in the plugin output is used (value 0) or whether Nagios removes it (value 1). In order to link it with action_url (page 366) and notes_url (page 366), there is now an additional option to specify a target window, with action_url_target and notes_url_target.

With the CGI program status.cgi (Section 16.2.1, page 334) you can now select hard and soft states via hostprops and serviceprops as well. This is particularly useful when using NagVis (Section 18, page 389), since NagVis by default only displays hard error states.

H.12   Miscellaneous

One of the improvements that does not fit into any of the above sections is the parameter use_timezone (page 606), with which you can set the time zone independently of the time zone set on the Nagios server. This is only necessary if several Nagios instances are running on a single machine.

The parameter additional_freshness_latency (see page 586) delays freshness checks (see Section 13.4, page 295), normally using a time period specified in seconds, in case Nagios has to wait too long for a result for passive checks.

The directives `cfg_file` and `cfg_dir` (page 588) can now also handle relative paths. The base directory is the directory containing the file na-gios.cfg.

The parameter `temp_path` allows a temporary directory to be specified explicitly (in Nagios 2.x the temporary space consists of only a single file, defined in the parameter `temp_file`).

Nagios 3.0 now allows multiple-line instructions in all configuration files. An instruction that is continued on the following line must end with a backslash \.

H.13   Upgrade from Nagios 2.x to 3.0

If you already have a running Nagios-2.x environment, you can change over to Nagios 3.0 with little effort. The existing configuration will usually run unchanged.

Nagios 3.0 is very particular when testing, however. It is quite possible that a so far undiscovered error—one tolerated or ignored by Nagios 2.0—will prevent Nagios 3.0 from starting. It is therefore a good idea to test your configuration before upgrading. To do this, you run the installation as described in Section 1.2 on page 39 with `configure` and `make all`, but without running `make install`. You will obtain an executable Nagios-3.0 binary in the `base` subdirectory, which you can use to test the existing configuration from the source code directory:

```
linux:src/nagios-3.0 # ./base/nagios -v /etc/nagios/nagios.cfg
...
```

If Nagios finds an error here, this error will prevent the start of the new Nagios version if it is not eliminated. At some points Nagios 3.0 will give warnings and information about the new features, but these do not stand in the way of a restart.

Nevertheless, there are a few small details that you should attend to before Nagios 3.0 goes into operation. The parameter `service_reaper_frequency` is now called `check_result_reaper_frequency` (page 589); it is simply renamed in `nagios.cfg`. `aggregate_status_updates` is removed altogether, so it is commented out in `nagios.cfg`.

The macro `$NOTIFICATIONNUMBER$` was sensibly split up into a host- and a service-specific macro (`$HOSTNOTIFICATIONNUMBER$` and `$SERVICENOTIFICATIONNUMBER$`). Commands and scripts that use the macro must be adjusted to ensure that they work correctly.

In order to retain the maintenance intervals and comments from the no longer used files specified in `downtime_file` and `comment_file` (in this book, `comments.dat` and `downtime.dat`), you must stop Nagios, save them, and then remove the Info block at the beginning from them, since this may occur only once in the new file, specified in `retention_file`:

```
info {
    created=1144429286
    version=2.0
}
```

Then the contents of the two files are copied to the end of the retention file, which here in this book is the file `/var/nagios/retention.dat`:

```
linux:~ # /etc/init.d/nagios stop
linux:~ # cd /var/nagios
linux:var/nagios # cat comments.dat downtime.dat >> retention.dat
```

Now the three remaining installation steps are performed (see page 42):

```
linux:src/nagios-3.0 # make install
...
linux:src/nagios-3.0 # make install-init
...
linux:src/nagios-3.0 # make install-commandmode
...
```

Index